List of Inscriptions
on
Christian Tombs and Tablets of Historical Interest

List of Inscriptions

on

Christian Tombs and Tablets of Historical Interest

in the

United Provinces of Agra and oudh

BY

E. A. H. BLUNT, I.C.S.

GYAN

Published by

GYAN

Gyan Publishing House
5, Ansari Road
Daryaganj, New Delhi-110002
Phone: 011-47034999, 9811692060
E-mail: books@gyanbooks.com

Distribution Network
gyanbooks.com
India, USA, Canada, UK, Australia, France

ISBN: 978-81-212-8564-3 (PB)
First Published, 1911

2nd Impression 2023

Printed at: Gyan Press, Delhi.

LIST OF INSCRIPTIONS ON CHRISTIAN TOMBS AND TABLETS OF HISTORICAL INTEREST
Author: E. A. H. Blunt

The oldest British tomb in the Province.
(JOHN MILDENHALL, 1614).

List of Inscriptions

on

Christian Tombs and Tablets of Historical Interest

in the

United Provinces of Agra and Oudh

by

E. A. H. BLUNT, I.C.S.

"*Qui procul hinc*"—the legend's writ—
The frontier grave is far away—
"*Qui ante diem periit,*
Sed miles, sed pro patria."

(NEWBOLT.)

ALLAHABAD:

PRINTED BY W. C. ABEL, OFFG. SUPDT., GOVT. PRESS, UNITED PROVINCES.

1911.

Addenda.

No. 66.—I have lately been shown a photograph of this inscription by Mr. G. Sanderson, Superintendent of British and Muhammadan Monuments, Northern Circle. The inscription as given in the text is wrong (it was reproduced from Führer.) It reads

مرقد کپتان طامس رس صاحب

and the rest as in the text, save that after the date 1816, should be read

تمیعر ثعصت و پنج سال

The name therefore is Thomas Ross, not Smith.

List of Errata.

Page 32, 28th line.—*For* " Christian " *read* " Christison."

Pages 38-39, last word of page 38 and first word of page 39.—*For* " Germensis " *read* " Germanus."

Page 40, 4th line from the bottom.—*For* " Results " *read* " Jesuits."

Page 46, no. 140, 2nd line of note.—*For* " Melld " *read* " Mdlle."

Page 49, no. 162, first line of note.—*For* " and the next two " *read* " with nos. 163 and 165."

26th line of note.—*For* " no. 155 " *read* " no. 165."

Page 54, no. 186, 9th line of *inscription*.—*For* " Speci osi " *read* " speciosi."

Page 68, no. 257, 3rd line of note.—*For* " had " *read* " has."

Page 103, no. 407, 6th line of note.—*For* " eror " *read* " error."

Page 110, no. " 392." 1st line.—*For* " 392 " *read* " 414."

Page 111, no. " 392," 2nd line of note.—*For* " 313 " *read* " 813."

Page 115, no. 418, 20th line of note.—Omit word " other."

Page 169, no. 614, 12th line of note.—*For* " remarkable " *read* " remarkably."

Page 174, no. 639, 8th line of note.—*For* " 1349 51 " *read* " 1349-51."

Page 204, no. 811, 1st line of note.—*For* " inscriptoin " *read* " inscription."

Introduction.

The present list is an attempt to revise and enlarge the former list of Christian Tombs and Monuments, published by Dr. Führer in 1895. The revision consists in a simpler arrangement, in the verification of all epitaphs by district officers or myself, in the compilation of a bibliography, and the addition of historical and biographical notes. The enlargement is considerable ; there are now 989 entries as against 599. Part of this increase is due to rearrangement, but chiefly it is due to fresh entries.

Before 1895, the only attempt to deal with the epitaphs of the U. P. was the " Bengal Obituary," published in 1848. It contained but the merest selection of tombs from this province ; but the book is now rare, and I have thought it would prove of interest to distinguish the inscriptions in this list which also appeared in the old obituary. This is done by the letters " B. O." after the inscription.

I have kept in the list the inscriptions of a certain number of monuments which cannot now be traced, but were in the two former lists. It is possible that they may some day be of interest, even of use, to some pious descendant desirous of keeping green the memory of an ancestor by a new tablet in church or cemetery.

The period covered is 1611 to 1908. The epitaphs refer to many events of great importance, from the old English and Dutch factories and the Jesuit Mission at Agra, down to the Naini Tal landslip of 1880 and the Manipur rebellion. Of the whole *posse* of Anglo-Indian worthies, forgotten, half forgotten and unforgettable, the Province can claim its full share,—from John Mildenhall, the self-styled " ambassador " of Elizabeth, whose tomb is said by competent authority to be probably the oldest English tomb in India, down to Quinton and Capper and Sir John Strachey. A complete list of the great men who died in the U. P. would commence with an English Marquess who fought in three continents and ruled in two : it would end, perhaps, with a gallant French circus-master who went out to fight with Anglo-Indian Volunteers at Agra " *pour l'honneur de l'alliance.* " Soldier, statesman, civilian, doctor, missionary, factor, man of learning, heroes of Lake's wars, of Gurkha and Pindari and Afghan and Sikh and Central Indian and Mutiny campaigns, Viceroys and Lieutenant Governors and Political Agents and Judges and Collectors,—such is the medley of famous men which this list commemorates.

Rudyard Kipling in one of his famous stories has laid stress on the way in which certain families have served, and are still serving, India from father to son. Of this fact this list affords ample proof. It would be interesting to calculate how many of the persons buried in this province were born as well as died in India; the figure would be high indeed. The families of LaTouche and Thornhill are two conspicuous instances. There are no less than five of the former race buried in this province alone; no less than seven of the latter family were serving in this province at one and the same time. Cherry, Hogg, Currie, Muir, Boileau, Lawrence, Strachey, Lushington, Havelock, Lindsay, Hope—all these families can boast a similar succession of Anglo-Indian officers.

No list of epitaphs can be without its instances of unconscious humour. I found an epitaph to a man who died "craving a large widow and family to mourn his loss"; an exquisite instance of a "nice derangement of epitaphs." There are many curious verses such as the somewhat prosaic lines beginning—

> "Good attendance was applied,
> Physicians were in vain;"

and, above all, the little poem entitled "To-day and tomorrow."

Nor is the list without its puzzles. How came a Major "of the Brazilian service" to be buried in Chunar? Who was Elizabeth R————, "of His Majesty's —th Foot?" Was she one of those Amazons of whom one occasionally reads, who joined a regiment in male attire and fought with it for years? The Indian sculptor, "Ramjohn Mistry" of the Chunar inscription and his kind, is responsible for many curiosities. His weird genius turns "Cathcart" into "Cat. H. Cart", "R. E. Parry" into "Reparry", "Cha. Wil. Burton" into "Chawil Barton." In Führer's list was to be found an exact replica of the inscription on the monument to the officers killed at Bhitaura in 1794, which was described as in a Chunar cemetery. The explanation is this. Many of these funeral monuments were of Chunar stone. The duplicate at Chunar was on a flawed stone, which had been rejected, and left lying about at Chunar. A collector, *vir pius*, found it and put it up in the cemetery, to cause (as I myself know) much searching of heart and history to various gentlemen who wondered how on earth we came to be embroiled with the Rohillas so far east as Mirzapur!

A few words about some of the less well-known authorities in the bibliography may be of value:—

(1) *The calendar and directory of the Agra archdiocese* (No. 15) is much more than its name implies. It contains very valuable notes on many old tombs at Agra compiled from the old mission archives by Father Felix, O. C.

(2) *Dyce Sombre* versus *Solaroli, &c.* (No. 16), is a book containing the depositions in the famous will suit of 1852 (*vide* note on Dyce Sombre).

(3) *The sketch of the rise and progress of the Benares Patshalla* (No. 36) is a history, existing in manuscript in the Benares College Library, of Jonathan Duncan's Sanskrit College from the foundation up to 1848, written by a Professor at the College, and printed in 1907.

(4) *Dodwell and Miles' Lists* (No. 117-9), and Prinsep's General register" (No. 120) are similar to the present "History of services of Gazetted officers", but much less complete. For soldiers and medical men, the dates of commissions and death or retirement are given: for Civilians, the various posts held.

(5) *The E. I. register* (No. 121) is the forerunner of the present Civil Lists and India Army Lists, combined in one volume. But it also contains (up to 1835 or so) lists of non-official residents, with births, marriages and deaths.

(6) *The Services Bengal Army List* (No. 125) is a series of manuscript volumes containing details about many officers, obviously extracts from letters written home to the Court of Directors. There is much curious information in this book; for instance I found one field officer who was tried by court martial on 23 charges, one of which was swearing at the standing orders! He was reprimanded.

(7) *The Writer's Petitions, Cadet's Papers, and Assistant Surgeon's Petitions* (Nos. 126-9) are the original papers referring to the nominations of the civil, military and medical officers of the Company. They begin with little more than a birth certificate; later, they contain also information of all kinds, notably about the father's profession, and the schools at which the officer concerned was educated.

One other point I may be permitted to mention. It may be noticed that I have been silent on the controversies which have raged and are still raging round the names of certain great men. My reason is simply that if pigmies must squabble about a dead giant, they should at least have the decency not to do so over the giant's tomb. And further *cui bono?* we may surely say of their memories, as of their souls, "*Requiescat in pace.*"

My thanks are due to the gentlemen mentioned at the end of the bibliography for the courtesy with which they have always answered my requests for information. I am also indebted to Mr. R. Burn, C. S., for many useful hints which led me to sources of information; to Mr. A. G. Ellis of the India Office for assistance with the Armenian inscriptions; and to Miss Milford for the excellent photograph of John Mildenhall's tomb which is reproduced as a frontispiece. Other civilians who took much trouble in collecting inscriptions for me are

Messrs. J. V. S. Wilkinson, J. C. Moore and H. G. Smith. But most of all am I indebted to four gentlemen—Mr. W. Irvine for the loan of various authorities otherwise inaccessible; Captain E. Milford, who collected for me all the information given about the Indian and other services of British Regiments; the Reverend Father H. Hosten, S. J., who not only furnished me with a mass of material and hints on that difficult subject, the Jesuits in Agra, but was good enough to look through and criticize my account of them; it is to be hoped that he will some day take this subject in hand and deal with it as it deserves; and lastly Mr. W. Foster of the India Office, not only for many valuable suggestions and the readiness with which he put both private and official sources of information at my disposal, but for the sympathy with which he viewed my attempt to deal adequately with the deeds of "famous men, and our fathers who begat us."

NAINI TAL:
The 22nd June 1911.

E. A. H. BLUNT.

BIBLIOGRAPHY.

	Name of book.	*Quoted as*
1.	Description Historique et Geographique de l' Inde by J. Tieffentaller (Bernoulli's edition 1786).	Tieffentaller.
2.	A voyage to East India, by Edward Terry (1655)	Terry.
3.	Letters received by the E. I. C. from its servants in the East; Edited by W. Foster (1902 599).	Foster, Letters.
4.	The English Factories in India, 1618—1629, by W. Foster.	Foster, Factories.
5.	History of the Armenians in India, by M. J. Seth, 1895.	Seth.
6.	History of British India, by Sir W. W. Hunter, 1900.	Hunter.
7.	Sketch of the History of Hindustan, by H. G. Keene.	Keene.
8.	Purchas, his Pilgrims and Pilgrimage, by S. Purchas, 1624-6.	Purchas.
9.	Embassy of Sir T. Roe, by W. Foster 1899 (Hakluyt Society).	Roe.
10.	Travels in India, by J. B. Tavernier, edited by V. Ball, 1889.	Tavernier.
11.	Tale of the Tulsi Plant, by C. A. Kincaid ..	Tale of the Tulsi Plant.
12.	Storia do Mogor, by N. Manucci, edited by W. Irvine, 1908.	Manucci.
13.	Relations de divers voyages curieux, by M. Thevenot, 1696.	Thevenot.
14.	Travels in the Mogul Empire, by F. Bernier, edited by A. Constable, 1891.	Bernier.
15.	Calendar and Directory of the Agra Archdiocese, 1907.	Calendar Agra Archdiocese, 1907.
16.	Dyce Sombre *versus* Troup, Solaroli and Prinsep and the H. E. I. C., Depositions of Witnesses, 1852.	Dyce Sombre Depositions.
17.	Statistical Report of the District of Cawnpore, by R. Montgomery, C. S., 1848.	Statistical Report, Cawnpore.
18.	Banda settlement Report, by A. Cadell, C. S., 1884.	Cadell.
19.	Selections from State Papers preserved in the Foreign Department of the Government of India, 1772-1785, by G. W. Forrest, 1890.	Forrest, 1772-85.
20.	Narrative of a journey through the Upper Provinces of India, by Bishop Heber, 1858.	Heber.
21.	A History of the Boondelas, by Captain W. R. Pogson, 1828.	Pogson.
22.	Das Furstentüm Sardhana, by S. Noti, S. J., 1906	Noti, Sardhana.
23.	Wanderings of a Pilgrim in Search of the Picturesque, by Fanny Parkes, 1850.	Wanderings of a Pilgrim.
24.	Journey through the Kingdom of Oude, by Sir W. H. Sleeman, 1858.	Sleeman.
25.	Selections from the despatches of the Marquess Wellesley, edited by S. J. Owen, 1877.	Wellesley's Despatches.
26.	Memoirs of Muhammad Amir Khan, translated by H. T. Prinsep, 1832.	Amir Khan.
27.	History of the Political and Military transactions in India, 1813-23, by H. T. Prinsep, 1825.	Prinsep.
28.	A History of the Sikhs, by J. D. Cunningham, 1853.	Cunningham.
29.	History of the Marathas, by C. Grant Duff ..	Grant Duff.
30.	Hastings and the Rohilla war, by Sir J. Strachey, 1892.	Strachey.

	Name of book.	*Quoted as*
31.	Vizier Ali Khan, or the Massacre at Benares, by J. F. Davis, 1844.	Davis.
32.	Historical and Statistical memoir of Dehra Dun, by G. R. C. Williams, B. C. S., 1874.	Williams.
33.	Narrative of the insurrection in the zamindary of Benares, by Warren Hastings, 1781.	Hastings.
34.	Archæological Survey of India Reports, Volume I, by A. Cunningham, 1871.	A. S. Reports.
35.	Memoir of the War in India conducted by Lord Lake, by Major W. Thorn, 1818.	Thorn.
36.	Sketch of the Rise and Progress of the Benares Patshalla, by G. Nichols, 1848.	Nichols.
37.	Centenary Review of the Researches of the A. S. B., 1885.	A. S. B. Cent. Rev.
38.	Account of the European Military Adventurers of Hindustan, by H. Compton, 1892.	Compton.
39.	Notes on Indian Affairs, by F. J. Shore, 1837 ..	Shore.
40.	Handbook to Agra, by H. G. Keene, 1874 ..	Keene's Agra.
41.	Treaties and Sanads, by C. V. Aitchison ..	Aitchison.
42.	History of the Organization, Equipment and War Services of the Regiment of Bengal Artillery, by Major F. W. Stubbs, 1874 (with a list quoted as B. A. List).	Stubbs.
43.	The E. I. Military Calendar, containing the services of General Field Officers, 1828.	E. I. M. Calendar.
44.	Addiscombe, its heroes and men of note, by Colonel H. M. Vibart, 1894.	Vibart.
45.	History of the Rise and Progress of the Bengal Army, Volume I. by Captain A. Broome, 1850.	Broome.
46.	Sketch of the Services of the Bengal Native Army to the year 1895, compiled by Lieutenant F. G. Cardew, 1903.	Cardew.
47.	The History of the Bengal European Regiment, by Lieutenant-Colonel P. R. Innes, 1885.	P. R. Innes.
48.	Selections from the letters, despatches, and other state papers preserved in the Military department of the Government of India, 1857-8, by G. W. Forrest, 1893.	Forrest.
49.	Mutiny Narratives of N.-W. P., 1857-8 ..	M. N.
50.	History of the Indian Mutiny, by T. Rice Holmes, 1904.	Rice Holmes.
51.	Memoirs of my Indian Career, by Sir G. Campbell, 1893.	Campbell.
52.	The Story of Cawnpore, by Captain Mowbray-Thomson, 1859.	Mowbray-Thomson.
53.	Lucknow and Oudh in the Mutiny, by Lieut.-General J. J. M. Innes, V. C., 1895.	Macleod Innes.
54.	A History of the Sepoy War, by J. W. Kaye, 1876.	Kaye.
55.	Notes on the Revolt in the N. W. P., by C. Raikes, 1858.	Raikes.
56.	Personal Narrative of the Siege of Lucknow, by L. E. R. Rees, 1858.	Rees.
57.	Reminiscences of the Great Mutiny, by W. Forbes-Mitchell, 1894.	Forbes-Mitchell.
58.	Narrative of the Mutinies in Oudh, by Captain G. Hutchinson, 1859.	Hutchinson.
59.	Personal adventures during the Indian Rebellion, by W. Edwards.	Edwards.
60.	Forty-one years in India, by F. M. Earl Roberts, 1898.	Roberts.
61.	A lady's diary of the siege of Lucknow (by Mrs. Harris), 1858.	Harris.

	Name of book,	*Quoted as*
62.	Account of the Mutinies in Oudh and of the siege of the Lucknow Residency, by M. R. Gubbins, 1858.	Gubbins.
63.	A Lady's Escape from Gwalior and life in the Fort at Agra during the Mutinies of 1857, by Mrs. R. M. Coopland, 1859.	Coopland.
64.	The life of Hodson, by L. J. Trotter.	Trotter.
65.	"For Valour," by J. E. Muddock	Muddock.
66.	"On Service," by Captain P. Groves	Groves.
67.	The story of the Delhi Mission (S. P. G.) ..	Delhi Mission.
68.	The story of the Cawnpore Mission (S. P. G.) ..	Cawnpore Mission.
69.	History of India from the earliest ages, by J. P. Wheeler, 1869.	Wheeler.
70.	Memoirs of old Haileybury, by Sir M. Monier Williams, etc.	Haileybury.
	The following volumes of the "Rulers of India" series :—	
71.	Marquess of Hastings, by Major Ross of Bladensburg, 1900.	Hastings (R. of I.)
72.	Marquess Cornwallis, by W. S. Seton-Karr, 1898..	Cornwallis (R. of I.)
73.	Lord Amherst, by A. T. Ritchie and R. Evans, 1894.	Amherst (R. of I.)
74.	Viscount Hardinge, by Viscount Hardinge, 1300..	Hardinge (R. of I.)
75.	Sir Henry Lawrence, by Lieutenant-General J. J. M. Innes, 1898.	Lawrence (R. of I.)
76.	John Russell Colvin, by Sir Auckland Colvin, 1895.	Colvin (R. of I.)
77.	James Thomason, by Sir W. Muir, 1897 ..	Thomason.
78.	The Hearseys, by H. Pearse, 1905	Pearse.
79.	Almoriana, by "V."	Almoriana.
80.	Peerage, Baronetage and Knightage, by Sir B. Burke, 1908.	Burke, P.
81.	Landed Gentry of Great Britain, by Sir B. Burke, 1908.	Burke. L. G.
82.	Landed Gentry of Ireland, by Sir B. Burke, 1904.	Burke, L. G. I.
83.	Foster's Baronetage, 1884	Foster, B.
84.	Dictionary of Indian Biography, by C. E Buckland.	Buckland.
85.	The Bengal Obituary, published by Holmes and Co., 1848.	B. O.
86.	List of tombs, &c., in the N.-W. P. & O., by A. Führer.	Führer.
87.	List of Tombs, &c., in Madras, by J. J. Cotton...	Cotton.
88.	Marlborough College Register.	M. C. Register.
	Articles in various periodicals.	
89.	J. A. S. B. Vol. LXV—" Jesuit Missions to the Emperor Akbar," by E. D. Maclagan; 1896. ..	J. A. S. B. Vol. LXV.
90.	Asiatic Quarterly Review, 1887—" The Indian Bourbons," by W. Kincaid.	As Quarterly, 1887.
91.	J. R. A. S. 1910 ; " Austin of Bordeaux," by W. Foster.	J. R. A. S., 1910.
92.	Gentleman's Magazine, 1906—"An Englishman at the Court of Akbar."	Gent. Mag., 1906.
93.	" Nineteenth century and after, 1903"–The Taj and its designers, by E. B. Havell.	Havell.
94.	Agra Archæological Society Transactions, 1874-8..	Agra Arch. Soc. Trans.
95.	J. R. A. S., 1910; " The tomb of John Mildenhall " by E. A. H. Blunt.	J. R. A. S. 1910.
96.	East and West, 1906, " Joseph Tieffentaller S. J." by S. Noti, S. J.	Noti, East and West.
97.	Jesuit Missionaries in Northern India, by Revd. H. Hosten, S. J., 1906.	Hosten.

	Name of book.	*Quoted as*
98.	"Bengal, Past and Present, 1910, some 17th century tombs at Agra, by W. Foster."	Bengal Past and Present.
100.	Selections from the revenue records of the N.-W. P., 1818-23.	Rev. record.
101-120.	Gazetteers (old or new editions, or both) of following districts :— Naini Tal, Almora, Gorakhpur, Basti, Azamgarh, Agra, Budaun, Muttra, Moradabad, Aligarh, Fatehgarh, Bundelkhand, Fatehpur, Allahabad, Lucknow, Hardoi, Sitapur, Kheri, Bahraich, Fyzabad.	Gazetteer.
	Official lists :— *Dodwell and Miles lists :—*	
121.	Alphabetical list of officers of the Indian Army, 1760-1837.	D. and M.
122.	.. .. .. H. E. I. C. Bengal Civil Servants, 1773-1838.	D. and M.
123.	.. .. ..Medical officers of the H. E. I. C., 1764-1837.	D. and M.
124.	General Register of the H. E. I. C. Bengal Civil Servants, 1790-1842, compiled under H. T. Prinsep's directions, 1844.	Prinsep C. L.
125.	The East India Register and Army list (various years).	E. I. R.
126.	Quarterly Civil list, N.-W. P., 1879.	N.-W P. C. L., 1879.
127.	Indian army list (last edition) ..	Not quoted.
128.	Hart's army list	Not quoted.
129.	Services, Bengal army list (India Office records.)	Services B. A. List.
130.	Writer's Petitions (India Office Records) ..	W. P.
131.	Cadet's Papers (India Office Records) ..	C. P.
132.	Assistant Surgeon's Petitions and certificates (India Office Records).	S. P.
133.	"Agra" by S. Muhammad Latif	Latif.
134.	Communications from the following gentlemen :— Right Revd. Bishop of Lucknow (both the late, Bishop Clifford, and the present, Bishop Westcott); Sir J. J. D La Touche, K.C.S.I.; Messrs. W. Irvine, C. S. (retired), L. G. Evans, C. S.; R. L. H. Clarke, C. S.; W. B. Cotton, C. S.; G. B. F. Muir, C. S.; A. H. Bensley; and W. Foster of the India Office; the Revd. J. R. Hill, S. P. G., the Revd. W. Hutton L. M. S.; the Revd. R. M. Kirwan, the Revd. Father Hosten, S. J.; and through him the Revd. Father S. Noti, S. J., the Revd. Father Hyacinth, O. C., and Mr. Ismael Garcias of Goa; Messrs. J. F. Fanthome and E. C. Le Maistre, Major C. C. Jackson and Captain E. Milford; also private papers and personal inquiries.—	Communicated.

MEERUT DIVISION.

Dehra Dun District.

LANDOUR CEMETERY.

1.—**1828**—BOLTON, G., Captain. *Inscription :*—Sacred to the memory of Captain George Bolton, H. C.'s 2nd European Regiment, who after some months of painful suffering departed this life on the 13th of June in the year of the Lord 1828, aged 40. His virtuous and amiable disposition rendered him generally beloved in life and lamented in death. This memorial is erected by his afflicted widow as the last earthly tribute of affection and respect to an indulgent and affectionate husband.

[Appointed cadet 1803, lieutenant 1804, captain 1818. He was born at Dinapore in 1788 and served in Java.]

(References : *D. and M.; C. P.; P. R. Innes.*)

2.—**1830**—GRAHAM, J. R., Captain. *Inscription :*—Sacred to the memory of John Richard Graham, Esq., late a Captain of the 5th Regiment of Bengal Light Cavalry. This monument is erected by his brother officers as a mark of their esteem and regard for the character of one universally beloved for his many good and amiable qualities. He died on the 30th day of May A. D. 1830, aged 29 years.

[He was appointed cadet in 1817, lieutenant in 1819, captain in 1829. He was the son of J. Graham of Barrock Lodge, born 1800, and a relative of Sir J. Graham, Bart.]

(References : *D. and M.; C. P.*)

3.—**1834**—BLUNDELL, W., Major. *Inscription :*—Sacred to the memory of Major William Blundell, XI Dragoons, who was killed by falling with his horse on the south side of the Landour Hill, on the 12th November 1834, aged 54 years.

"*It is a faithful saying and worthy of all acceptation that Jesus Christ came into the world to save sinners.*"—In Him alone is our hope of salvation for this our dear brother, whose kind and affectionate heart endeared him as a son and as a brother, and whose departure hence is severely felt, and deeply mourned by his family and by many friends. (B. O.)

[".... A house called Newlands, which has been struck and burnt three times by fire. The hill is said to contain a quantity of iron which attracts the electric fluid....A short time ago as Major Blundell was going to that very house, Newlands, by some accident, his *gūnth* (hill-pony) fell over the precipice, and they were both dashed to pieces." This tomb is not now traceable and is reproduced from Führer's List. In the B. O. it reads "falling with his *Ghoont.*" The 11th Dragoons are the present 11th (Prince Albert's Own) Hussars, who were in India from 1819 to 1838.]

(Reference : *Wanderings of a Pilgrim.*)

4.—**1835**—RAIKES, S. M., Mrs. *Inscription :*—Sacred to the memory of Sophia Mary Raikes, the fondly beloved wife of Charles Raikes of the Bengal Civil Service. She departed this life on the 16th April 1835, in the 19th year of her age.

Those who in agony, but in humility deplore her loss deem not her death premature, for through the mercies of that Saviour in whom she trusted she was already meet for immortality; her rare personal and mental endowments were but the blossoms of the tree whose fruits were Christian purity and holiness. May those who now mourn her on earth be made partakers with her in the resurrection of the Blessed! (B. O.)

[This tomb is stated by B. O. to be at Meerut. Mrs. Raikes was the daughter of Colonel Matthews, and the first wife of Charles Raikes, B.C.S., C.S.I., Commissioner of Lahore; he was at Agra during the Mutiny and wrote "Notes on the Revolt in the North-Western Provinces." Her daughter Sophia married George Christian, B.C.S., Commissioner of Sitapur, where both she and her husband were murdered. The family is that of Raikes of Treberfydd, cf. No. 416.]

(Reference: *Burke, L. G.*)

5. —**1841**—MADDOCK, T., Colonel. *Inscription :*—Erected by the Officers of the 10th Regiment N. I. to the memory of their esteemed and much valued friend and Commandant, the late Lieutenant-Colonel T. Maddock, who departed this life on the 14th day of October 1841, *æt.* 58. During a command of 12 years, his undeviating kindness and the warm interest ever displayed towards all under him, secured to Colonel Maddock the love and respect of his Regiment by the officers and men of which his worth was justly appreciated and his death keenly deplored. *Requiescat in pace!*

[Colonel Maddock was appointed cadet in 1803, lieutenant 1804, captain 1819, major 1828 and Lieutenant-Colonel 1833. He was the son of E. Maddock, born 1788 and served mostly in the Military Secretary's department.]

(References: *D. and M.; Services B.A. List.*)

DEHRA CEMETERY.

6.—**1847**—EVANS, M., Mrs. *Inscription :*—Sacred to the memory of Mary Evans, the affectionate wife of Major F. R. Evans, Commanding Sirmoor Battalion, aged 26 years, 1 month and 16 days, beloved and respected by all who knew her. Dehra Dun, February 22nd, 1847.

While sorrow weeps o'er virtue's sacred dust,
Our tears become us, and our grief is just.
Such were the tears he shed, who grateful pays
This last sad tribute of his love and praise;
Who mourns the best of wives and friends combined,
Where female sweetness met the accomplished mind:
Mourns, but not murmurs, sighs but not despairs,
Feels as a man, but as a Christian bears. (B. O.)

[Mary, daughter of William Eccles, of Eccles Street, Dublin, married Francis Robert Evans, eldest son of Major-General R. Evans, R. A., of a Limerick family. The family seat is now Carker House, Co. Cork. The Sirmoor Battalion is the present 2nd King Edward's Own Gurkha Rifles (the Sirmoor Rifles).]

(Reference: *Burke, L. G. I.*)

RAJPUR-MUSSOORIE-LANDOUR ROAD.

7.—**1828**—FARRINGTON, C. H., Sir, Bart. *Inscription :*—Sacred to the memory of Charles Henry Farrington, Bart., late Captain, His Majesty's 31st Regiment, who departed this life 26th day of March 1828 in the 35th year of his age.

[This tomb is near the 3rd mile-stone and the Jharipani Bazar. It has lately been reported destroyed by a slip.

Sir Charles Henry Farrington, 2nd Baronet, was born in 1794. He was the son of Capt. C. C. Farrington and grandson of Sir Anthony Farrington, 1st Baronet, a General of Artillery. Sir Charles served in the Peninsular War, at Talavera, and later at Waterloo. He came out to India in the *Kent* East Indiaman and was wrecked. He was one of the first officers sent up to Landour with troops and was accompanied by a Captain Skinner [later Col. Thomas Skinner, C.B., of the 31st (East Surreys) and author of "Excursions in India"] who mentions the fact. The family is connected with the family of Evans (H. F. Evans and L. G. Evans, both members of the C. S. in these provinces); a daughter of Sir H. M. Farrington, 3rd Baronet (uncle of Sir C. H. Farrington) married the Rev. G. H. Evans. The present (6th) baronet Sir H. A. Farrington is in the Forest Department in Bengal.]

(References: *Communicated; Burke, P.*)

KALANGA MONUMENTS, NEAR MEERUT-RURKI-LANDOUR ROAD.

8.—1814—OFFICERS AND MEN KILLED AT KALANGA.

Inscription:—

On the west side.—To the memory of Major-General Sir Robt. Rollo Gillespie, K.C.B., Lieutenant O'Hara, 6th N. I, Lieutenant Gosling, Lt. Battalion, Ensign Fothergill, 17th N I., Ensign Ellis, Pioneers, killed on the 31st October 1814; Captain Campbell, 6th N. I., Lieutenant Luxford, Horse Arty., Lieutenant Harington, His Majesty's 53rd Regiment, Lieutenant Cunningsam *(sic)*, 13th N. I., killed on the 27th November, and of the Non-Commissioned Officers and men who fell at the assaults.

On the east side.—Troops engaged: detachments Horse and Foot Arty., 100 men of the 8th Royal Irish Lt. Dragoons, who were dismtd. and led to the assault by Sir R. R. Gillespie, His Majesty's 53rd Regiment; 5 Light Companies from Corps in Meerut; 1st Battalion, 6th N. I.; 1st Battalion, 7th N. I.; 1st Battalion, 13th N. I.; 1st Battalion, 17th N. I.; 7th Native Cavalry; 1 Risalah of Skinner's Horse.

9.—1814—GURKHAS KILLED AT KALANGA. *Inscription:—*

On the west side.—On the highest point of the hill above this tomb stood the fort of Kalanga. After two assaults on the 31st October and 27th November, it was captured by the British troops on the 30th of November 1814 and completely razed to the ground.

On the east side.—This is inscribed as a tribute of respect for our gallant adversary Bulbudder, Commander of the Fort, and his brave Goorkhas, who were afterwards, while in the service of Ranjit Singh, shot down in their ranks to the last man by the Afghan Artillery.

[The exact position is on a low hill 3½ miles N.-E. of Dehra, opposite the 6th furlong of mile 110 on the road mentioned in the title, and half a mile distant on the right hand side of the road.

Kalanga is also called Nalapani. In 1814 Lord Hastings declared war on Nepal and invaded it with 4 columns, of which one, under General Gillespie, was to penetrate the Siwaliks and occupy the Dun. The Kalanga fort was held in force. Contrary to direct orders against rash attacks on strong places, Gillespie decided to storm it. He arranged a signal for the attack: but gave it an hour too soon, and only two out of four columns obeyed it. Ensign Ellis led his Pioneers up to the wall but was killed almost immediately, and the columns were repulsed. Gillespie seeing this led a second assault himself but was not too readily followed except by about 100 men of the 8th Dragoons, which he had once commanded. He was shot close under the wall, and his A. D. C., Lieut. O'Hara, was also killed by his side. Col. Mawbey waited for a siege train, and when it arrived bombarded the place for two days. On the 27th November another assault was made. The troops hung back: Lieut. Harrington of the 53rd mounted the breach alone, to show how easily it could be ascended: but being unsupported "fell a victim to his gallantry and zeal." Lieut. Luxford then took up a light gun as close as he could to fire it into the breach; he too was killed in so doing. The men would not attack again and the retreat was sounded. Nine officers and 62 men were killed, 20 officers and 649 men were wounded in the two assaults. The place was then regularly shelled and evacuated on the 30th. It was a disastrous affair, wasting many lives, and what was almost as important, two cold weather months. Balbhaddar Singh was nephew of General Amr Singh, regent for Raja Bir Bikram Sah. He had only 200 men to defend Kalanga with.

The 8th R. I. L. D., are now the 8th (King's Royal Irish) Hussars. Their Indian honours are Laswaree, Hindostan, Central India and Afghanistan 1879-80. They also fought in the Crimea and Boer war; we shall find them again at Kalinjar. The 53rd are now the 1st Battalion, the King's (Shropshire Light Infantry). They were raised in 1755 and were in India from 1805 to 1823, 1844 to 1860, and 1894 to 1903. Their Indian honours are Aliwal, Sobraon, Punjab, Gujarat and Lucknow. They have also fought at Nieuport and Tournay, in the West Indies, Egypt and the Soudan: and a 2nd battalion, in existence from 1803 to 1817, fought through the Peninsular war.

The "1 Risalah of Skinner's Horse" is now represented by the 1st Duke of York's Own Lancers (Skinner's Horse), for the 2nd Risalah of Skinner's Horse (now 3rd Lancers), was not raised till December of this year. This famous regiment was raised by Colonel J. Skinner from a body of Perron's Horse, who came over after Lake's victory at Delhi: their honours are Bhurtpore, Candahar 1842, Afghanistan 1879-80 and Pekin 1900. It is to be noted that "Risalah" at this time meant not a regiment but a body of 114 rank and file, exclusive of English officers. There were up to 1814-15 eight "Risalahs" of Skinner's Horse: it was then increased to three regiments of 1,304 rank and file each, including galloper guns. The 3rd Lancers was the 2nd of these corps.

For Gillespie vide No. 10. Brabazon R. O'Hara joined the service in 1805, Francis Fothergill in 1812, J. Campbell in 1807, J. Cunninghame in 1804, R. H. Gosling in 1810 (he belonged to the 27th N. I.), and R. Ellis in 1807 (he belonged to the 2nd N. I.). For Luxford cf. No. 11.]

(References: *Prinsep; Williams; Hastings (R. of I); D. and M; Cardew.*)

Meerut District.

ST. JOHN'S CHURCHYARD.

10.—**1814**—GILLESPIE, R. R., Sir. *Inscription:*—Vellore—Cornellis—Palimbang. Sir R. R. Gillespie, K. C. B., Djoejocarta, 31st October 1814. Kalanga.

Repaired in 1862 by his old corps, the 8th King's Royal Irish Hussars.

[This monument is a large column 50 feet high on a square masonry base. The first three words are on a scroll, the rest on a funeral urn, both in bas relief on the same slab. Though the prefix of three of Gillespie's famous battles and the affix of his last are intelligible, the interposition of "Djoejocarta"—an affair in the Java expedition—is curious.

Robert Rollo Gillespie (1766—1814), joined the 3rd Irish Horse in 1783. He fought first in the W. Indies, notably at Saint Domingo (1792-6). He came to India in 1804. When at Arcot, in 1806, he rescued the survivors of the 69th Foot from the mutineers at Vellore with a regiment of Dragoons, a squadron of native cavalry and some galloper guns. He commanded the cavalry in the expedition against Ranjit Singh in 1809, the Mysore division, and the advance of Sir S. Auchmuty's expedition to Java (1807—13). He fought at Cornellis and Djoejocarta. He left Java in 1812 and went as Major-General to Meerut. He was made K. C. B. on the 1st January 1815, after his death. There is a monument to him in St. Paul's Cathedral. Cf No. 8 for his death.]

(References: *Prinsep; Cunningham; Williams; Rice-Holmes; Buckland.*)

11.—**1814**—LUXFORD, J. B. B., Lieutenant. *Inscription:*—Sacred to the memory of Lieut. John B. B. Luxford of the Bengal Horse Artillery, who fell mortally wounded in the attack of Fort Kalanga on the 27th, and died on the 30th November 1814, aged 22 years. This conotaph is erected by his brother officers in testimony of their affection and esteem.

[Cf. No. 8 above. The Luxford family is an old Sussex family, dating at least as far back as the Armada, against which two Luxfords, belonging to different branches, fought. John Bellamy Bowes Luxford was appointed cadet in 1807 and Lieutenant Fireworker in 1809. He was the son of John Luxford, born at Ewell in 1791.]

(References : *Burke, L. G. ; D. and M. ; C. P.*)

12.—**1816**—LUMSDEN, Major. *Inscription :*—Sacred to the memory of Major Lumsden, late Deputy Commissary-General to the Bengal Forces, who died 30th September 1816, in the 32nd year of his age. This monument is erected by his afflicted widow, who though she mourned her early separation from one in every way calculated to inspire her with the most lasting affection, and thus to form the greatest earthly happiness, humbly hopes through the merits of that "Great Redeemer" in whom he trusted, to meet again in the realms of peace and joy.

Where God shall wipe away all tears from their eyes, and where shall be no more deaths, neither sorrow nor crying.

Rev. XXI—4.

[The monument is a large brick masonry cenotaph with a stone altar inside. The inscription is on a marble slab fixed in the masonry floor in front of the altar. This is probably James Lumsden, appointed cadet in 1800, cornet in 1802 and lieutenant in 1805. He is recorded by Dodwell and Miles as dying at Meerut on the 14th September 1816 : but there is no other Lumsden to whom the inscription could possibly be referred, and Dodwell and Miles' dates of death are frequently inaccurate, as were indeed their authorities—the "Services Army List," and presumably the letters on which these were founded. James Lumsden was the son of William Lumsden, writer to the signet, born at Edinburgh in 1785.]

(References : *D. and M. ; C. P. ; Services B. A. List.*)

13.—**1817**—HUNTER, J , Captain. *Inscription :*— Sacred to the memory of Captain James Hunter, of the 26th N. I., who departed this life, 8th December 1817, aged 39 years.

[He was appointed cadet in 1798, ensign and lieutenant in 1800, captain in 1811, and was the son of J. Hunter, an Edinburgh merchant (born 1777)].

(References : *D. and M. ; C. P.*)

14.—**1821**—HARDYMAN, B., Major-General *Inscription :*—In this spot are deposited the remains of Major-General B. Hardyman, C.B., late in command of the 2nd Division in Lord Lake's Field Force (late of 17th Foot), 1816.

He departed this life on 28th November 1821, in the 55th year of his age ; greatly and deservedly regretted by all who knew him, but by none more than the Officers of His Majesty's 17th Foot, who raised this monument as a small but sincere token of the high esteem and regard in which his memory is held by a Corps, which he so long and so happily commanded.

[A large cenotaph of masonry with a marble tablet. Major-General Hardyman commanded a force in the Pindari War and also fought in the Nepalese War and at Kamona. The 17th Foot are now the Leicestershire Regiment, in India 1804-23. The initial B. is wrong : the name was Frederick.]

(Reference : *Stubbs : Prinsep : Cardew.*)

15.—**1825**.—(1) BLACKNEY, M. M., Mrs. (2) BLACKNEY, JOHN. *Inscription :*—Sacred to the memory of Mrs. M. M. Blackney, wife of Lieutenant-Colonel Blackney, who departed this life, 11th January 1825, aged 24 years. This monument is erected in testimony of her worth and of his unfeigned grief by her affectionate husband.

Here also resteth John, son of Colonel Blackney, deceased on 20th July 1825, 7 months. (B. O.)

[The relatives of Colonel James W. Blackney, 35th N. I., appointed cadet in 1798, Lieutenant-Colonel in 1824, and retired in 1829.]

(References : *D. and M. ; J. R.*)

16.—**1825**—OCHTERLONY, D., Sir. *Inscription :*—Major-General Sir David Ochterlony, Baronet, G.C.B., born February 12th, 1758, died July 14th, 1825.

[The tomb is a large cenotaph of ornamental brickwork: the inscription is on a marble slab on the north side. Sir David Ochterlony, Bart., G.C.B. (1758—1825), son of David Ochterlony, was born at Boston, New England. He joined the H. E. I. C's Bengal Army in 1777, served under Sir E. Coote (1781-3.) and was taken prisoner at Cuddalore (1783) and released in 1784. He fought under Lake in 1803 in the Doab. After the battle of Delhi he was appointed resident at the Emperor's court. He commanded at Allahabad in 1806, and on the Sutlej against Ranjit Singh in 1808. In 1814-15, he commanded one of the four columns sent against the Gurkhas—the westernmost which operated near the Sutlej and the only one successful. He took Fort Malagarh and defeated Amr Singh at Malaun (cf. No. 7 note). He was made a Baronet and K. C. B. for his services ; in 1816 he took command of the main army operating against Khatmandu, defeated the Gurkhas at Magwampar and ended the war. He became a G. C. B. in 1816. In the Pindari-Mahratta War (1817-18) he commanded the reserve column at Rewari. His advance south of Jaipur forced the Pindari Amir Khan to accept a treaty without striking a blow and further clever strategy compelled the surrender of the Pathan forces. In 1818 he became Resident in Rajputana, which he pacified. In 1825 he prepared to support with arms Balwant Singh, the six-year old Raja of Bhartpur, against an usurper, on the ground that he, as Resident, by the presentation of a "*Khilat*" had pledged the Government to recognize the succession : but Lord Amherst refused to put this construction on his action, or to intervene ; and his death is ascribed to chagrin at the insult to his honour. A column has been erected to him at Calcutta. He obtained a second patent in 1823 recreating him a baronet with remainder to Charles Metcalfe Ochterlony, son of Roderick Peregrine Ochterlony. The present baronet is Sir David Ferguson Ochterlony, of Ochterlony, Forfarshire. The family formerly belonged to Pitforthy, of which Sir David's grandfather was laird : but in the direct line, at all events, it is extinct.]

[References : *"Hastings" and "Amherst" (R. of I.) : Wellesley's Despatches ; Buckland ; Amir Khan ; Thorn ; Burke, P.)*]

17.—**1825-6**—N.-C. O.'S AND MEN, 14TH FOOT. *Inscription :*—Sacred to the memory of those gallant soldiers, Non-Commissioned Officers and Privates of His Majesty's 14th Regiment of Foot, who fell or who subsequently died of wounds received during the siege and at the storming of the fortified town and fortress of Bhartpur, under the personal command of His Excellency the Right Hon'ble Stapleton Lord Combermere, G.C.B., Commander-in-Chief of British India, in the latter end of December 1825 and on the memorable 18th January 1826.

SERGEANTS.

W. Livingstone.
B. Lewis.
R. Chields.
J. Gray serving as Quarter Master Sergeant.
D. Craw.
W. Weston, 11th Native Infantry.
W. Reynolds.
J. Dyson.
J. Belcher.
T. Sagg.
T. Fryer.
J. Haugh.
T. Smith.
F. Gibbs.
L. Woods.
W. Thomas.
W. Handcock.
J. Abbots.

SERGEANTS.

T. Watsons.	P. Dalton.
E. Jermyer.	R. Wood.

CORPORALS.

J. Rowner.	J. Cartby.
W. Endicote.	J Hammerton.
J. Evans.	T. Springham.
P. Symes.	J. Hores.

PRIVATES.

R. Byran.	T. Turner.
J. Waitt.	W. Irons.
B. Jiffs.	A. Bennett.
J. Mauldn.	H. Wells.
J. Pulpit.	G. Kerr.
J. Dickens.	J. King.

While darkness veiled the vaulted sky,
In solemn silent march they trod,
Eager to shout their battle cry,
And prompt to war for Britain and for God.
And when the earthquake signal shock,
Gave angry summons to advance,
And firm and stern as planted rock,
Each hero braved the hostile lance:
Remember, soldiers, nothing could uphold
The warrior spirit like the hope of Heaven;
And woulds't thou bear thyself with front as bold,
Believe in Him in whom thy sins forgiven.
He shall support them more awful seems, *(sic)*.
When louder trumpets' clang shall rouse their ear,
When nature's universal wreck is seen,
And saints victorious shout, and sinners sink with fear.

This tablet here inscribed with the sanction of Major-General Sir Thomas Reynell, K C.B, (in whose division and under whose immediate charge, His Majesty's 14th Regiment had the honour to do their duty) is placed as a mark of esteem and of faithful remembrance by their surviving comrades.

[Bharatpur was a virgin fortress which had repulsed Lake in 1805. At this time it had been seized by an usurper, who had imprisoned the boy heir. Sir D. Ochterlony assembled a force to assault it: and though Lord Amherst put off the evil day, a few months later it was found imperative to send a force against it. Lord Combermere commanded the army of 21,000 men. Lieutenant-Colonel Edwards was in charge of a brigade of three regiments. There was a good deal of desultory fighting at the end of December and there was an ineffective bombardment on the 24th December. Lord Combermere then decided to mine the walls of the town. Gokulgarh, which was nearest the citadel. By the 18th two breaches had been made and that day an assault by four columns was carried out. The garrison was driven back in spite of a gallant defence; Brigadier Edwards (No. 18 below) was wounded severely, and died of his wounds.

The 14th Foot had two battalions. This was the 1st battalion, raised in 1685. It was in India from 1810 to 1831 and 1867 to 1879. Its Indian honours are "Java," "Bhartpore" and "India" (with Royal Tiger). It was formerly the 14th (Buckinghamshire, the Prince of Wales' Own) Regiment, and is now the Prince of Wales' Own (West Yorkshire) Regiment. It also fought at Tournay, Corunna, Waterloo and Sevastopol, as well as at the siege of Gibraltar, Falkirk, Culloden and Walcheren. Sir T. Reynell commanded the 1st Infantry Division; Brigadier Edwards (No. 18) was Colonel of the 14th and commanded the 2nd Brigade, 2nd Division, under Sir Jasper Nicolls.]

(References: *Amherst*: *(R. of J.)*: *Pearse*: *Stubbs.*)

18.—1826—(1) EDWARDS, W. I., Brig.-General. (2) ARMSTRONG, H. B., Captain. *Inscription* :—Sacred to the memory of Brigadier-General W. I. Edwards, His Majesty's 14th Regiment, and Captain H. B. Armstrong of the same corps, who in the successful assault of the fortress of Bharatpur on the morning of the 8th July 1826, fell on the ramparts in the gallant discharge of his duty, General Edwards leading the left column of attack. This tablet is erected by their brother officers.

(*Cf.* No. 17 above.)

19.—1827—MAXWELL, R., Lieutenant. *Inscription* :—Sacred to the memory of Robert Maxwell, Esquire, Lieutenant H. M.'s. XI Light Dragoons, who died on 27th August 1827, aged 27 years and 10 months. This tablet is erected as a tribute of the esteem in which he was held while living, and sorrow for his premature fate, by some of his brother officers, who intimately knew and deeply appreciated the many excellences of his head and heart. Alas !! Poor Maxwell !!! (B O.)

[The 11th L. Dragoons are now the 11th (Prince Albert's Own) Hussars. They were in India from 1819 to 1838 and fought at Bhartpore.]

20.—1836—NEVILLE, W. F. *Inscription* :—Sacred to the memory of W. F. Neville, Paymaster, H. M.'s 11th Regiment of Light Dragoons, who departed this life on 3rd February 1836. This tablet is erected by his brother officers as a tribute of esteem for his sterling worth and uniform kindness of heart, and a memento of grief for his departure. (B. O.)

21.—1839—WARLOW, T., Captain. *Inscription* :—Sacred to the memory of Captain Thomas Warlow, Bengal Engineers, who departed this life on the 2nd February 1839, aged 41 years. He lived beloved and died lamented. (B. O.)

[He was appointed cadet in 1815. As an ensign he fought at the siege of Asirgarh and became lieutenant in the same year (1819). He was promoted captain in 1827. He was at Addiscombe 1812-4. He was mentioned in despatches af er Mundela, Hathras and Asirgarh ; and was much in civil employ. He was Superintending Engineer in the North-Western Provinces in 1835, in the Central Provinces in 1837, and in charge of canals in the Western Provinces (whatever that name in the Services List precisely means) in 1839. The son of J. Warlow, he was born in 1797 and died at Delhi.]

(References : *Stubbs : Vibart : D. and M. ; Services B. A. List.*)

22.—1839—(1) ARNOLD, R., Lieut.-Colonel. (2) HILTON, W., Captain. (3) JEWERARITY, D., Lieutenant. *Inscription* :—Sacred to the memory of Lieutenant-Colonel Robert Arnold, 16th Lancers, Brigadier, commanding the Bengal Cavalry of the Army of the 'Indus,' who died at Kabul, 20th August 1839 ; also of Captain William Hilton, drowned in crossing the river Jhelum on the 11th December 1839 ; and of Lieutenant David Jewerarity, barbarously murdered at Kandahar, 18th May 1839. This tablet is erected by the Regimental Officers and men as a record of their affection and esteem for their commanding officer, and respect for the memory of their deeply lamented comrades.

[Col. Arnold died at Kabul. He "had long remained in a hopeless state : .. I do not think he ever recovered the attack he had at Meerut." At Meerut, nearly a year before, Col. Arnold had burst a blood vessel in his lungs. At Waterloo he had been shot through the lungs and recovered. The 16th Lancers, now the 16th (the Queen's) Lancers, were raised in 1759 and in India from 1822 to 1846. They were at Bhartpore, Ghazni, Maharajpore, Aliwal, Sobraon, and

Afghanistan—all of which honours they bear—and also fought in the Peninsular War at Waterloo and the last Boer war.]

(References: *Communicated; Wanderings of a Pilgrim*).

23.—**1845**—(1) GWITT, B., Lieutenant.—1846—(2) BEALE, W. Y., Lieutenant. *Inscription*:—Sacred to the memory of Lt. Richard Brandram Gwitt of Her Majesty's 10th Regiment of Foot, who died at Meerut on the 3rd June 1845; also to the memory of Lieut. Walter Young Beale, Her Majesty's 10th Regiment of Foot, who fell in action gallantly leading on his company to the attack of the trenches at 'Sobraon' on the 10th February 1846. This tablet is erected by their brother officers as a token of the regard they felt for them and regret at their loss.

[Sobraon was a strongly intrenched position on the Sutlej. There were 67 guns in position and some 35,000 men in the trenches; but the latter were not all trained and the former not of uniform design. The action commenced with a tremendous cannonade. Sir R. Dick's leading brigade on the right carried the entrenchments; the second line was checked, but re-formed and again advanced. Gilbert's division was checked but also rallied, and Sir H. Smith's division was successful. Even the cavalry rode through an opening in the entrenchments and charged. The trenches were carried with the bayonet. The enemy broke and were cut to pieces on the bridge which gave way under them. The battle of Sobraon was decisive and ended the First Sikh War. The 10th Foot present at Sobraon was the present 1st Battalion, the Lincolnshire Regiment.]

[Reference: *Cunningham; Hardinge (R. of I.); Pearse*].

24.—**1846**—SWETENHAM, H. D., Lieutenant. *Inscription*:—Sacred to the memory of Henry D. Swetenham, Esq., Lieutenant in Her Majesty's 16th Lancers, who fell at the battle of Aliwal, 28th January 1846, in the hour of victory, whilst charging the enemy's batteries, *anno ætatis* 27. This tablet is erected by his brother officers, as a token of esteem and affection.

[This battle was won by Sir Harry Smith against Ranjit Singh. They came into collision at Aliwal: the Sikh line inclined towards and extended beyond the British right, whilst the other flank was more distant. The Sikh line rested on Aliwal on the left, and this Sir Harry attacked with success: for his opponents at this point were not the trained army, but levies: they broke and left the Sikh gunners to be cut down. The cavalry made a successful charge and rolled up half the Sikh army. On the left, however, the trained Sikhs stood, until charged by the 16th Lancers, who rode thrice through them. It is not clear whether this young officer was killed in capturing the guns on the Sikhs' left, or in the charge on the infantry, or in capturing the guns subsequently. It may have been any of the three—most probably from the wording of the epitaph the third.]

[References: *Cunningham: Pearse; Hardinge (R. of I.)*].

25.—**1850**—(1) PARKER, G., Lady.—1857—(2) PARKER, G., Captain, Sir Bart. *Inscription*:—1st Tablet.—Sacred to the memory of Gertrude, Lady Parker, wife of Captain Sir George Parker, Bart, 74th Regiment Native Infantry, who departed this life on 12th May 1850, aged 26 years. Deeply and sincerely regretted by all who knew her. 2nd Tablet.—Sacred to the memory of Sir George Parker, Bart., Captain, 74th Native Infantry, who died of sunstroke in the trenches at Cawnpore in the month of July 1857.

"They shall hunger no more neither thirst any more, neither shall the sun light on them, nor any heat."

John VI—47.

[Sir George Parker, 2nd son of Vice-Admiral Sir William George Parker, 2nd Baronet, and Vice-Admiral of the White was educated at Addiscombe. He went out to India in 1833 and succeeded to the title in 1848. He was Cantonment Joint Magistrate at Cawnpore in 1856-7. He belonged to the now extinct family of Parker of Harburn, The 1st and 2nd Baronets were both Vice-Admirals; Sir George was the 3rd. Lady Gertrude Parker was daughter of Lieut.-Col. Elderton, and his second wife. Sir George had a son and two daughters, one of the latter by Lady Gertrude. He was succeeded by his son (lieutenant in the Gurkhas) who died in 1866. The last two baronets were brothers of Sir George and both died without male issue. The reference of the text is wrong. It should be Revelation vii, 47.]

(References: *Mowbray-Thomson: Forrest: M.N.: Buckland: Burke, P.*)

26.—**1857**—COXEN, E., Captain. *Inscription*:—Sacred to the memory of Captain Edward Coxen, for 31 years Paymaster to the 1st Battalion, 60th-Royal Rifles, who died at Meerut on the 14th February 1857, aged 77 years. He served at Flushing, throughout the Peninsular War, at Waterloo, and in the campaign of 1848-49 and received three medals and 12 clasps. Erected by the officers of the 1st Battalion, 60th Royal Rifles.

[For the 60th, *cf.* No. 55.]

27.—**1857**—(1) PHILLIPS, J, Vet.-Surgeon. (2) DAWSON, C. J., Vet-Surgeon. (3) DAWSON, E., Mrs. *Inscription*:—Sacred to the memory of John Phillips, Veterinary Surgeon, 3rd Bengal Cavalry, murdered during the Mutiny at Meerut on 10th May 1857. This tomb is erected by George Carmichael Smyth, Colonel of the Regiment, in token of affection and regard.

Oh! tell me, hope and faith,
Is there no resting-place,
From sorrow, sin and death:
Is there no happy spot,
Where mortals may be blest,
Where grief may find a balm,
And weariness a rest?
Faith, hope and love,
Best boons to mortals given,
Waved their bright wings,
And whispered, 'yes, in Heaven.'

This tablet was erected by Colonel G. Carmichael Smyth, 3rd Bengal Cavalry, to the memory of his friend Charles John Dawson, Veterinary Surgeon, Bengal Cavalry, and Eliza, his wife, both murdered at Meerut on 10th May 1857.

[The 3rd B. C. was the regiment whose men refused to take the cartridge at Meerut. Eighty of them where sentenced to 10 and five to 5 years' hard labour, and ironed on the parade-ground in front of their comrades—"inconceivable folly" in Lord Canning's words, which irritated troops already disaffected, and drove the regiment to attempt their comrades' rescue. In doing this, they also liberated the other prisoners and then, joined by the population of the bazar and city, fired many Europeans' bungalows and murdered every European they met, amongst them Mr. and Mrs. Dawson and Mr. Phillips. The latter was murdered on the road with a sword-cut on the head, and found by Lt. Furnell.]

(References: *Forrest: M. N.: Kaye: Rice-Holmes.*)

28.—**1857**—FINNIS, J., Colonel. *Inscription*:—To the memory of John Finnis, Colonel, 11th Regiment, Native Infantry, 10th May 1857, aged 33 years.

[Whilst the 3rd B. C. were liberating the prisoners (cf. No. 27 above) the 11th and 20th N. I. began to show symptoms of mutiny. Colonel Finnis was shot dead by the 20th whilst imploring them to remain faithful, and assuring them they had nothing to fear from the cartridge.]

(References: *Forrest: M. N.*)

29.—**1857**—(1) MACDONALD, D., Captain. (2) MACDONALD, L. S., Mrs. *Inscription*:—Sacred to the memory of Donald Macdonald, Captain, 20th Regiment, Native Infantry, who was killed by his own men on the 10th May 1857, aged 35 years; and Louisa Sophia, his wife, aged 30 years, who was barbarously murdered the same night, while trying to make her escape with her three infants from her burning house to the European Lines.

Awake and stand up to judge my quarrel: avenge Thou my cause, my God and Lord.

Psalm XXXV—33.

I am the Resurrection and the Life. He that believeth in Me, though he were dead, yet shall he live.

John XI—25.

[Captain MacDonald, son of Lieutenant MacDonald, R. N., was born in 1823. He was shot by his own men whilst trying to pacify them at their magazine.

Mrs. MacDonald was in her bungalow at the time of the outbreak. Dressed in native clothes, she went with three faithful servants, Nasiban, nurse, Bakhtawar *chaukidar*, and Sukha, *dhobi*, to a house of the second in the city: her three children were with them. They were met by a crowd who killed Mrs. MacDonald with swords. The three infants were saved by the servants.]

(References: *Forrest: C. P.: M. N.*)

30.—**1857**—(1) TREGEAR, V.—1880.—(2) TREGEAR, E. H., Mrs. *Inscription:*—Sacred to the memory of Vincent Tregear of the Department of Public Instruction, who was killed by the mutineers at Meerut on 10th May 1857, aged 48 years; also Eliza Hannah, his widow, who died at Meerut on the 3rd June 1880, aged 60 years.

Lord, all pitying Jesus blest,
Grant them their eternal rest.

[Mr. Tregear had gone to the lines by accident and was shot there with Col. Finnis and Captain MacDonald. His son is Major-General Vincent W. Tregear, C. B., formerly in the Bengal Army, who commanded the Lushai Expedition of 1889 and the Chittagong column of the Chin-Lushai Expedition 1889-90.]

(References: *M. N.: Burke, P.*)

31.—**1857**—CHAMBERS, C., Mrs. *Inscription:*—Sacred to the memory of Charlotte, the beloved and deeply lamented wife of R. W. Chambers, Captain, 11th N. I., who died on the 10th May 1857, an innocent victim of the murderous insurrection of 1857.

Jesus said unto her, "I am the Resurrection and the Life. He that believeth in me, though he were dead, yet shall he live."

John X—25.

[Wife of the Adjutant of the 11th N. I., the son of E. E. Chambers, born 1823. She was murdered in her own compound, where her body was found by Captain Earle. The reference of the text is John XI, not X.]

(References: *C. P.: M. N.*)

32.—**1857**—PATTLE, W., Lieutenant. *Inscription:*—William Pattle, Lieutenant, 20th Regiment, Native Infantry, born 21st June 1832, was killed in the Mutiny at Meerut on 10th May 1857.

[This officer's death is mentioned, but no circumstances are given. He was the son of Colonel W. Pattle, born at Meerut in 1834 and educated at Brighton.]

(References: *C. P.: Forrest.*)

33.—**1857**—HENDERSON, D. H., Lieutenant. *Inscription:*—Sacred to the memory of David Henry Henderson, Lieutenant, Bengal Native Infantry, who was killed during the Mutiny at Meerut on the 10th May 1857, aged 31 years.

The Lord gave and the Lord hath taken away, Blessed be the name of the Lord.

[Lt. Henderson was the son of Lieutenant D. Henderson, R. N., and born at Winkfield, in Berks, in 1824. He was shot at and wounded at the same time as

Col. Finnis. He was taken into the hospital by Havildar Pancham Singh, of his own regiment, who succeeded in concealing him for a while.]

(References: *Forrest; C. P.; M. N.*)

34.—**1857**—MOORE, S., *Inscription:*—Sacred to the momory of Stewart Moore, Esq., Assistant Surgeon, H. M.'s 6th Dragoon Guards (Carbineers), who died at Meerut on the 2nd June 1857, of wounds received in action with the mutineers at Ghazi-ud-din Nagar, on the 31st May 1857, aged 26 years. This tomb was erected by his brother officers as a token of their sincere regard.

[Brigadier Archdale Wilson, on his march with the Meerut Brigade to join General Barnard's force in the attack on Delhi, was attacked near Ghazi-ud-din Nagar on the Hindun on the 30th and again on the 31st May 1857. In both actions the rebels were severely defeated. Assistant Surgeon Moore was wounded in the head by a grape shot on the second day. Cf. No. 55, below.]

(Reference: *Forrest.*)

35.—**1857**—GERRARD, J. G., Lieut.-Colonel. *Inscription:*—Sacred to the memory of Lieut.-Colonel John Grant Gerrard, 1st Bengal Fusiliers, who was killed in action whilst gallantly leading on to victory the movable column which he commanded against the Jodhpur Legion, at Narnaul, near Delhi, November 17th, 1857, aged 48 years.

[The Jodhpur Legion, quartered at Erinpura, mutinied in August 1857, and marched to Delhi. Col. Gerrard was the son of Major Gerrard, H. C. S., born in India 1808 and joined the service in 1825. He served with distinction at Ghazni, Jellalabad (severely wounded) and Pegu. He marched on the 10th November to cut off the Jodhpur mutineers. He met them near Narnaul and completely defeated them. In the pursuit "as he was sitting conspicuous on his white arab, his red coat covered with decorations, a rebel aimed deliberately at him, and wounded him mortally." He was greatly beloved of his regiment, with whom he had served almost all his time.]

(References: *P. R Innes: C. P., Rice-Holmes.*)

36.—**1858**—PENNY, N, Maj.-General. *Inscription:*—Sacred to the memory of Major-General N. Penny, C.B., Commanding the Meerut Division. Born at Weymouth, Dorsetshire, on the 12th March 1790; killed at the head of his column in a skirmish with the enemy, near the village of Kakirowlee in Rohilcund, on the morning of the 30th April 1858, after a service of 51 years. His precious remains were brought into Meerut through the kind exertions of Captain E. J. Simpson, Assistant Commissary-General.

Say yet to the righteous that it shall be well with him.

Thes. 3rd chapter, part of 10th verse.

Them also which sleep in Jesus will God bring with him.

Thes. 4th chapter, part of 11th verse.

[General Penny succeeded General Hewitt in the Meerut command in July 1857. In March 1858 he was engaged by Sir Colin Campbell's order in guarding the Ganges from Hardwar to Kadirganj against the rebels on the far side. The distance was 500 miles, his force was 2,500 strong and there were 50,000 rebels. Even in that war of miraculous achievements this was beyond human power to effect: and shortly after he was sent in command of a movable column into Aligarh and Rohilkhand. In April he was ordered to meet Sir C. Campbell at Miranpur Katra and it was during his march thither from Patiali that the affair of Kakrala (Kakirowlee of the inscription) occurred. The best account of this is to be found in Cracroft Wilson's narrative published as the Moradabad Mutiny narrative. The column marched at 9 p.m. Even in an enemy's country nothing would induce General Penny to expose "his Europeans" to the sun. Wilson was with the advanced guard of Carabineers. The march was leisurely, and the infantry were left in the rear. At dawn the staff had joined the advanced guard when suddenly they came on some horsemen, who opened out, and four guns loaded with grape were fired at them. By a miracle no one was hit; the British Artillery unlimbered, but not till four rounds had been fired by the enemy. As soon as our guns opened a body of Ghazis charged, but they were cut up by the Carabineers. The enemy then retreated. It was now discovered that General Penny was missing. His corpse was found 300 yards beyond the spot where the Carabineers had charged the Ghazis. His left arm had been broken by a bullet, his reins had dropped and his pony had galloped to the front, into the midst of the rebels: then he fell off and was despatched by two sword-cuts. General Penny fell a victim to his care for his European soldiers. The story is told of him that at Patiali he threatened to prohibit altogether some sports that were got up for the soldiers if they were not on the ground at dawn. A stern disciplinarian he was none the less beloved by his men. "The good old General," as Wilson affectionately calls him, was buried under a mango tree: his body was subsequently removed and re-interred in Meerut.

Nicholas Penny (1790—1858) entered the Bengal N. I. in 1807. He was present at the siege of Bhartpur in 1825-6 and commanded a brigade at Aliwal, Sobraon (1st Sikh War) and at Chilianwala and Gujrat (2nd Sikh War). He commanded the Sirhind Division in 1852, the Cawnpore Division in 1855 and the Meerut Division in 1857; Major-General 1854. The first text is from Isaiah iii, 10: the second from I Thessalonians.]

(References: *Rice-Holmes: Forrest: Gazetter: M. N.: Buckland.*)

OLD CEMETERY NEAR RACE-COURSE.

37.—**1808**—MERRYCK, J., Lieutenant. *Inscription:*—James Merryck, Lt., 22nd Native Infantry, died 10th September 1808.

[The 22nd N. I. of this date are now the 6th Jats. "James Merryck" is spelt by Dodwell and Miles and the Cadet Papers "James Meyrick," and they give the date of his death as the 19th September. He was appointed cadet in 1801 and lieutenant in 1804, and was the son of E. Meyrick, born at Hungerford, in Berks, in 1782.]

(References: *D. and M.: C. P.*)

38.—**1810**—REID, J. *Inscription:*—J. Reid, Residency Surgeon of Delhi, died 10th March 1810.

[This is probably John Reid, appointed assistant surgeon in 1772 and surgeon in 1781. "Gave up promotion and died April 1810, at Delhi," say Dodwell and Miles, the "at Delhi" probably being a deduction from the fact that his last post was there.)

(Reference: *D. and M.*)

39.—**1811**—MACARTNEY, T., Lieutenant. *Inscription:*—John Macartney, Lt., 5th Native Cavalry, died 29th April 1811.

[He was appointed cadet in 1798, cornet in 1801, and lieutenant in 1805. He was the son of the Revd. G. Macartney, Vicar of Antrim, born 1781.]

(References: *D. and M.: C. P.*)

PATPERGANJ, S.-E. OF SHAHDARA.

40.—**1803**—OFFICERS KILLED AT THE BATTLE OF DELHI. *Inscription:*—To the memory of the undermentioned gallant officers:—Major Middleton, 3rd Regt., Native Cavalry; Capt. McGregor, Persian interpreter; Lieut. Hill, 2nd battalion, 12th Native Infantry; Lieut. Preston, 2nd battalion, 13th Native Infantry; Cornet Sanguine, 27th Dragoons; Quarter master Richardson, 27th Dragoons. The following extract from the order of the Govt. of India refers to the action in which they fell: "The Governor General in Council sincerely laments the loss of Major Middleton, Captain McGreggor, Lieut. Hill, Lieut. Preston, Cornet Sanguine, Quarter master Richardson and of the brave soldiers who fell in the exemplary exertions of deliberated valour and disciplino spirit at the battle of Delhi. The names of these brave men will be communicated with the glorious events of the day on which they fell, and will be honoured and revered while the fame of that signal victory shall endure." This monument was repaired and the tablet which had disappeared was replaced by order of the Lieut.-Govr. of N.-W. P., 1898. The battle was fought on the 11th September 1800.

[There are several errors in the above, especially in the extract quoted. The whole order is given by Thorn. The errors are as follows:—

Lieutenant William Preston (joined service in 1798), belonged to the 2nd battalion, *15th* N.I.

"Captain McGreggor" should be "Captain McGregor."

"Exemplary . . . . spirit" should read "Exemplary *exertion* of *deliberate* valour and *disciplined* spirit."

"Communicated" should be "commemorated."

The troops of the enemy at Delhi consisted of 18 battalions of Perron's regulars, mostly belonging to the 2nd and 3rd brigades. They were commanded by Louis Bourquien, Perron's bosom friend, who had treacherously deserted him, won over both brigades (he had formerly only commanded the 3rd) and forced the poor old Emperor, Shah Alam, to invest him with the supreme authority. Shah Alam "deputed more authority from a prison than many a sovereign has done from a throne," but his keeper, Captain Drugeon, stood by Perron and had to be forced to submission by Bourquien. Meantime, Perron had been defeated and surrendered to the British; and this gave colour to Bourquien's assertions that Perron was a traitor. The remnants that remained after Aligarh and Shikohabad flocked to him and he found himself in command of 15,000 men and 70 guns. Lake marched against him from Aligarh, and on the 11th September was fought the battle of Delhi. He had only 4,500 men; the enemy were in a very strong position with a swamp on each side, so that according to Thorn a frontal attack alone was possible. Then followed Lake's famous ruse. He feigned retreat with his cavalry; which simple manœuvre drew the enemy out of their position in pursuit, to be met by the infantry in line. Lake could rely on the "personal equation" of Bourquien—"cook, pyrotechnist and poltroon," as one author calls him,—to make his ruse successful. The British infantry, led by Lake in person, marched through a storm of grape, fired one volley and charged. The enemy, for the first time in the history of DeBoigne's brigades, broke without showing fight: and then the infantry formed into columns of companies and let the cavalry through in pursuit. The defeat became a rout: they lost 3,000 men and 68 guns: Lake lost 477, of whom 131 belonged to the one English regiment, the 76th.

For the 76th *cf.* No. 64. The 2nd battalion, 15th N. I., are the present 2nd Queen's Own Rajputs. They were raised in 1798. They carry a third colour inscribed "Lake and Victory" for their valour at Delhi and Laswari: other honours are Deig, Bhurtpore, Afghanistan, Kelat, Maharajpore, Punjab, Chilianwala, Goojerat, Central India, Afghanistan 1879-80, Burma 1885—8, and China 1900.

Major Charles Middleton, who entered the service in 1778, died of sunstroke. Robert McGregor entered the service in 1779, and Thomas Hill in 1799.

Patperganj is a village on the battle-field.

[References: *Thorn.*: *Compton*: *D. and M.*]

ROMAN CATHOLIC CATHEDRAL, SARDHANA.

41.—1795—LE VASSOULT, COLONEL. *Inscription*:—(Illegible, save the words "priez Dieu pour son âme; requiescat in pace;" and the date, 18th October 1795.)

[This tomb is mentioned by Keene, writing in 1880. The name was then legible, and it is this which permits of this identification of it with the last resting place of the brave Frenchman, Le Vassoult. Father Noti, however, quotes another inscription in the grave-yard as follows: "Ci-gît N. Le Vassoult, âgé de 42 ans. Priez Dieu pour son âme." He describes the tomb as a low "platform in the middle of the graveyard." Very little is known of him before his marriage to the Begam Samru, which occurred either in 1792 or 1795. Before his marriage he commanded the Begam's Artillery, and now rose to the chief command. A man of birth and breeding, he despised his subordinate officers and showed the contempt which they certainly deserved. His marriage with the

Begam,—a lovematch on both sides, it is said—in all probability exasperated them: and unfortunately, as there were only two witnesses to it (M. Bernier and Colonel Saleur) the troops were able with some show of reason to denounce their relations as a mere vulgar intrigue. The troops were ripe for revolt, and a pretender was at hand. They entered into negotiations with Aloysius, or Louis, Balthazar Reynaud, Sombre's son by his first wife, to whom they swore fidelity. Le Vassoult had obtained Sir John Shore's permission to take the Begam to Anupshahr, where an English brigade was stationed, on his way to a French settlement. In October he and the Begam left Sardhana—he on a charger: she in a palanquin. They had agreed that either of them, on learning the news of the other's decease, would die by his or her own hand. The troops pursued and caught them. The Begam stabbed herself, but the wound was not mortal. Le Vassoult, thinking she was dead, at once blew out his brains though he could easily have escaped. We know little of the life of this chivalrous French gentleman, but we may well doubt if anything in his life became him like the leaving it.]

[References: *Noti, Sardhana*; *Compton*: *Calc. Rev.* 1880.]

42.—**1808**—CARDOZO, M. *Inscription*:—Sacred to the memory of Manual Cardozo, who departed this life, Thursday, September 15, 1808, aged 105 years.

[A. Frederick Cardozo is mentioned as a servant and then a pensioner of the Begam Samru, doubtless a relation of this centenarian.]

(Reference: *Dyce-Sombre Depositions*.)

43.—**1812**—SALEUR, J. R., Colonel. *Inscription*:—Sacred to the memory of Jean Remy Saleur, Colonel Commandant of Her Highness the Begum's troops, born at Nanci of Lorrain in France, who departed this life Sunday, July 12, 1812, aged 87. He was beloved and respected in life, and died as he had lived, a soldier without fear or reproach.

[Already mentioned as one of the witnesses of the Begam's marriage with Le Vassoult, whom he succeeded in the chief command. He took no part in the revolt, and indeed it was he who induced George Thomas to restore the Begam to her dominions and drive out the usurper, Reynaud. He increased the strength of her troops to six battalions, with 40 guns and 200 cavalry. In 1802, he assisted Sindhia after his defeat at Ujjain with five very mutinous battalions. One of his battalions was destroyed at Assaye, but the others escaped.]

[References: *Compton*: *Keene*: *Cal. Rev.*, 1880.]

44.—**1815**—JULIA ANNE, H. H. *Bahu Begam*. *Inscription*:—Sacred to the memory of Her Highness Bahu Begam Julia Anne, relict of the late Nawab Muzaffar-ud-daulah Louis Balthazar Reynaud, and daughter of the late Captain Louis Anthony Lefevre and Anne, who departed this life Wednesday, a.m., XVIII October A.D., MDCCCXV. Aged 45 years. This tomb is dedicated by her afflicted daughter and son-in-law.

[Nothing is known of this lady, save what is stated in the inscription. For Louis Balthazar Reynaud, *vide* no. 41. He died a prisoner at Delhi in 1803, and is buried at Agra. He had a daughter, Julia Anne, who married Col. Dyce, *vide* no. 45.]

(Reference: *Compton*.)

45.—**1820**—DYCE, J. A., Mrs. *Inscription*:—Sacred to the memory of Julia Anne (Begam Sahiba), the wife of Colonel G. A. D. Dyce, and daughter of the late Nawab Muzaffar-ud-daulah and Julia Anne, who departed this life Tuesday, a. m., June XIII, A.D., MDCCCXX at Delhi. Aged XXXI years and V months. She was a tender mother, a sincere friend, and an affectionate spouse; to the distressed and unfortunate, a kind and liberal benefactress; her heart the seat of patience and sympathy; loved and respected by all who knew her, and in death deeply regretted.

But now she is dead, can I bring her back again? I shall go to her; but she will not return to me!

2nd Sam. Ch. 12, V. 23rd.

This stone is inscribed by her disconsolate husband.

[Nothing is known of this lady save what is stated in the inscription. She had six children of whom three survived: Georgiana, who married Signor, afterwards Baron Solaroli, Anna Maria, who married Colonel J. R. Troup, both on the same day in 1831, and David Dyce-Sombre.]

(Reference: *Dyce-Sombre Depositions.*)

46.—1836—JOANNA ZEB-UN-NISSA, H. H. *Begam. Samru.* *Inscription:*—Sacred to the memory of Her Highness Joanna Zeb-un-nissa, styled "the distinguished of Nobles and beloved daughter of the State," who quitted a transitory court for an eternal world, revered and lamented by thousands of her devoted subjects at her Palace of Sirdhana on the 27th of January 1836, aged nearly ninety years, Her remains are deposited underneath in this Cathedral built by herself.

To her powerful mind, her remarkable talent, and the wisdom, justice, and moderation with which she governed for a period exceeding half a century, he to whom she was more than a mother is not the person to award the praise; but in grateful respect to her beloved memory is this monument erected by him who humbly trusts she will receive a crown of glory that fadeth not away.

DAVID OCHTERLONY DYCE-SOMBRE.

(Besides this, there are Urdu and Latin epitaphs to the same effect.)

[The real name and origin of this famous lady is uncertain. She is described variously as a Hindu dancing-girl, the daughter of a decayed Muhammadan nobleman of Kotana on the Jumna, and a Syudani, or descendant of the Prophet. "Zeb-un-nissa" is a title: Joanna Nobilis, her name after baptism. In the deed of gift of her property to Dyce-Sombre she is described as "Joanna Sombre, entitled Oomdur ool Arakeen Ferdenze Azizan Zebool Nissa Begam." This however is merely a trophy of titles. This lady was married to Sombre (vide No. 123) at Sardhana by Muhammadan rites, and possessed very great influence over her husband. At his death his property passed to her. She was beautful, clever and of a masculine spirit. She kept many foreign officers in her service: it was doubtless due to their persuasion that she was baptized into the R. C. Church in 1781. Among them were Pauly, George Thomas, Evans, Dudrenec, Le Vassoult, Saleur, Col. Dyce. and Signor Solaroli. George Thomas gained for her almost the only military fame her troops ever obtained, when he rescued the Emperor in 1788 beneath the walls of Gokulgarh, and won for his mistress the title of "Zeb-un-nissa" (Glory of the Sex). But her troops were mutinous, as they were in her husband's time: and her more respectable officers, Thomas, Evans, Dudrenec, left her one after the other. They were succeeded by Le Vassoult, a gentleman and a soldier, whom she married. It was apparently a match with love on both sides. But Le Vassoult was a strict disciplinarian, and his strictness drove the troops to mutiny in 1795. They swore to replace her by Sombre's son. Louis Balthazar Reinhardt (cf. No. 44). The Begam and Le Vassoult escaped. They had agreed to commit suicide in the event of capture: they were pursued and Le Vassoult blew his brains out: but the Begam's courage failed her, she only inflicted a slight wound on herself and was captured. Louis, her stepson, was installed as her successor: but George Thomas, forgetting the slights she had put on him, restored her to power by force. She joined the Marathas against the British, but her troops were defeated with great slaughter at Assaye. After the fall of Aligarh Robert Skinner induced her to submit to Lord Lake. When she arrived at the British camp, Lake rose from the dinner table to meet her: and in a moment of "enthusiasm," gave her a hearty kiss. Her attendants were startled: but the Begam, with considerable tact, described it to them as "the kiss of a Padre to his repentant child." It is easy to believe that "the red face and coat of this member of the church militant" struck these followers with a sense of incongruity: but Lake's boldness and the Begam's quick wit made the matter a complete success. She was confirmed in her estates, and maintained almost regal state at Sardhana, living on very friendly terms with the English. Amongst her visitors were such famous men as Bishop Heber, Lord Combermere and General Ventura. Her chaplain was Monsignor Scotti equally well known as "Father Julius Cæsar;" her chief military officer was Major Reghelini: her minister of state was Col. Dyce: her Chief Magistrate, Signor Solaroli.

In 1834 the Begam, who was childless, adopted David Dyce Sombre, son of Col. Dyce, by a daughter of Louis Balthazar. She divested herself of her property by deed of gift in his favour. She sent a sum of £18,700 to the Pope, and asked him to elevate Scotti to the see of Sardhana, give her grandson a decoration and herself a relic. She had built a church to the Holy Virgin Mary: she had bequeathed a lakh of rupees to support a college at Sardhana "for making priests of the natives," and a similar sum for the support of the see. She had also bequeathed a lakh to the residency churches, Rs. 30,000 to the church of Agra, half a lakh in trust for the poor of Calcutta, another half lakh for the poor of Sardhana, and a third for charitable purposes in England. The Pope (Gregory XVI) granted her wishes, making Dyce-Sombre a Chevalier of the Order of Christ, and Scotti Bishop of Amathunda and Vicar Apostolic of Sardhana. This wonderful old lady died, at an age it is said of over 80, on the 27th January 1836, leaving about £700,000, partly in charities and the residue to Dyce-Sombre.]

(References: - *Compton*: *Buckland*: *Heber*; *Calc. Rev.* 1880.)

47.—1839—MUTTI, C. *Inscription*:—Carolus Mutti Venetus, natus Sardhanæ, mortuus est ætatis suæ anno 34, die 15 Decembris 1839.

48.—1851—DYCE-SOMBRE, D. O. *Inscription*:—Sacred to the memory of David Ochterlony Dyce-Sombre of Sirdhana, who departed this life in London, 1st July 1851. His remains were conveyed to his Native country, (in conformity with his wishes) in the year 1867, and are deposited in the vault beneath, near those of his beloved and revered benefactress, Her Highness the Begam Sombre. He was born at Sirdhana, 18th December 1808, and married 26th September 1840, the Honorable Mary Anne Jervis, daughter of Edward Jervis-Jervis, Viscount St. Vincent of Meaford in the county of Stafford.

[David Ochterlony Dyce-Sombre, was born in 1808, and of course named after Sir David Ochterlony, who, as the Dyce-Sombre law suit depositions show, was a close friend of the family. His father was Col. George Alexander David Dyce, who was the son of an English officer, a friend of Ochterlony's. G. A. D. Dyce was educated in the Military Orphanage at Calcutta, and was sent up by Ochterlony to be married to the daughter of Louis Balthazar Sombre, at the desire of the Begam. He of course found a post in her service, in which he remained till his overbearing temper caused his dismissal in 1828. His mother was the grand-daughter of General Sombre, but not by the Begam, who was no relation of his. David Dyce, as he was then, was brought up in the zenana, though he was also taught for a while by the English Chaplain at Meerut, Mr. Fisher. There is abundant evidence that in India he associated with English people and English officers at their messes and houses: but that his habits and his disposition were rather Oriental than European. In 1834, as already stated (No. 45), he was adopted by the Begam Samru as her heir. He was made a Chevalier of the Order of Christ by Pope Gregory XVI at her request. In 1838, two years after her death, he came to England; Robert Skinner wisely advised him not to do so; Lord Combermere advised him to the contrary. He was singularly ill-fitted for European life and European society, for he had Oriental ideas of society and the position of women, and was wilful to a degree that amounted to eccentricity. He fell in love with the Hon. Mary Jervis, a daughter of Lord St. Vincent, and married her in September 1840: it is said that his horror at the ordinary attentions paid to her by other men drove him to give up the intention for a time. He stood for Sudbury, and was returned in 1841-2: but he was unseated on a petition for bribery and corruption. Shortly after a commission declared him to be of unsound mind and put him under restraint. It is unnecessary to go at any length into the question whether he was or was not insane. There were found at least as many medical men to deny it as to affirm it. At the same time, though his extraordinary conduct was possibly explicable by his ignorance of European customs on the one side, and by his Oriental habits and character, especially his Oriental jealousy, on the other, it can hardly be considered surprising that a commission of English gentlemen, knowing nothing of India and its customs, declared him insane on the evidence before them. An instance of his ignorance of European customs was his curious ideas about duelling. He challenged a Director of the East India Company over a law suit, and he wanted his wife to challenge another lady. When asked whether, if the matter had come to a meeting, he would have expected his wife to fight, he naively explained that "he would have taken that on himself." In 1843 he escaped from his keeper and went to Paris, Rome and other parts of the Continent. In 1849 he wrote and published in Paris a "Refutation of the Charge of Lunacy" and in 1850 prepared a petition to the Houses of Parliament. He died in London in 1851. He made a will the items of which need not be dealt with, for though he made the Chairman and Deputy Chairman of the Court of Directors his executors, and these gentlemen fought the case in every court up to the Queen in Council, the will was negatived, and the property passed to his widow who subsequently married Lord Forester.

Dyce Sombre had two sisters, Georgiana, wife of Baron Solaroli, and Anna Maria or Ann May, wife of Col. J. R. Troup. He had no legitimate children. The landed estates were resumed by Government when the Begam died: but all the house, personal and funded property now belongs to Lady Forester or her heirs.]

(References: *Buckland: Calc. Rev.* 1880: *Dyce Sombre Depositions.*]

49.—**1815**—OBALLO, M. P., Captain. *Inscription:*—Sacred to the memory of Captain Manuel Pereira Oballo, Begam Sombre's service, who departed this life the 25th December 1815, aged 80 years.

50.—**1816**—ROMMEL, Captain. *Inscription:*—

مزار متبرک یادگاری کپتان رومال صاحب آنکه ازین جهان فانی به
ملک جاودانی بتاریخ بست سوم محرم سنه ۱۲۳۱ هجری وصال نمود

[This tomb is not now discoverable.]

51.—**1818**—LEFEVRE, A., Mrs. *Inscription:*—To the memory of Anne, relict of the late Captain Louis Lefevre, who departed this life, Saturday, a.m., January III, A. D., MDCCCXVIII. Age 76 years.

[Capt. Lefevre commanded a regiment of the Begam's horse which murdered him. This lady was the mother of Bahu Begam, Julia Anne (No. 44).]

(Reference: *Dyce-Sombre Depositions.*)

52.—**1819**—PAETHOD, L. C., Colonel. *Inscription:*—Sacred to the memory of Colonel Louis Claude Paethod, Commandant of Her Highness Begam Sombre's Brigade, who departed this life, Wednesday, a.m., 13th January 1819, aged 78 years.

[His widow was one of the Begam's pensioners. That is all that is known of him, besides what is given in the inscription.]

(Reference: *Dyce-Sombre Depositions*)

53.—**1821**—KOINE, G., Major. *Inscription:*—Sacred to the memory of Major Gotlieb Koine, Native of Poland, born Sunday, 25th December A. D. MDCCXLV., died Sunday, p.m., 11 September, MDCCCXXI, who was in the service of Her Highness Begam Sombre for 50 years, the last 32 of which as Collector of Bhudhana. He lived and died with the reputation of an honest man and a pious Christian.

The memory of the just is blessed.
The righteous shall be had in everlasting remembrance.

[A Francois Koine was a servant of the Begam's and then a pensioner of Dyce-Sombre. Presumably a relation of the above.]

(Reference; *Dyce-Sombre Depositions.*)

54.—1820—DYCE, J. A., Mrs. *Inscription :—*

بیت

بجز گیاہ نہ پوسد کسی مزار مرا

کہ قبر پوس غریبان همین گیاہ بسست

این مرقد مطہر آرامگاہ عصمت قباب تقدس احتجاب صاحب بیگم
نبیرہ شمرو صاحب بہادر زوجہ ظفرالدولہ جارج الکسانڈر داوڈ ڈیس بہادر
مظفرجنگ بنت نواب ظفریابخان بہادر از بطن جلیانا عرف بہو بیگم کہ
بتاریخ دوم شہر ربیع الاول سنہ ۱۲۰۳ هجري ولادت یافتہ و غرہ رمضان
سنہ ۱۲۳۵ هجري مطابق سنہ ۱۸۲۰ ع شب سہ شنبہ ازین دار فنا بدارالبقا
شتافتہ – عیسی علیہ السلام فرمودند کہ تا روز قیامت هر کسی بر من ایمان
آرد اگر میرد زندہ باشد

Sacred to the memory of Julia Anne (Begam Sahiba) the wife of Colonel G A. D. Dyce, and daughter of the late Nawab Muzaffar-ud-daulah and Julia Anne, who departed this life Tuesday a.m., June XIII, A. D. MDCCCXX at Delhi. Aged XXXI years and V months. She was a tender mother, a sincere friend, and an affectionate spouse; to the distressed and unfortunate, a kind and liberal benefactress; her heart the seat of patience and sympathy, loved and respected by all who knew her and in death deeply regretted.

But now she is dead, can I bring her back again? I shall go to her; but she will not return to me!

2nd Sam., Ch. V., 23rd.

This stone is inscribed by her disconsolate husband.

"Alas! in this neglected spot is laid
A heart once full with the celestial fire;
Hands that the rod of Empire might have swayed
Or waked to ecstasy the living lyre.'

[Cf. No. 45.]

AT BEONJA KHASRA, ON GHAZIABAD-DELHI ROAD.

55.—1857—OFFICERS AND MEN, 60TH RIFLES. *Inscription :—Celer et audax.* Erected by the 60th Rifles in memory of—

Captain F. Andrews; Sergeant W. McPherson; Corporal T. O'Meaghe; Private J. Daring *(a)*; Private S. J. Gainty; Private D. Tommisson; Private H. Armitage; Private J. Scriven; Private P. Quirk; Private A. Edmond; Private J Casey; who were killed near this spot in action with the mutineers of the Bengal Army, on the 30th and 31st May 1857 *(b)*; And of Sergeant R. Hackett; Corporal J. Sherry; Corporal J Moore; Private J. Lehane; who died of sunstroke during the fight. They all belonged to the 1st Battalion, 60th Rifles, and were buried here. *(c)* And also of Ensign W. H. Napier, who was wounded on the 31st May and died at Meerut on the 4th June 1857 *(d)*.

[This is a monument of Agra sandstone, fenced in by four iron standposts and a chain. The inscription is on all four faces, ending as at *(a)*, *(b)*, *(c)* and *(d)* respectively, in the order west, south, east, north. The Meerut Brigade under Brigadier Archdale Wilson, marched to join the Delhi force on the 27th May. It consisted of: Carabineers—two squadrons; 60th Rifles—a wing;

Scott's light field and Tombs's horse batteries; two 18 pounders; some native sappers and irregular horse. On the 30th they met the enemy at Ghaziuddinnagar (now Ghaziabad) on the Hindun, which was here crossed by an iron bridge. There was a brisk cannonade, but Tombs crossed the river and took them in flank. The Rifles drove the enemy from the guns: but Captain Andrews and four men were blown up by an ammunition waggon. The enemy were repulsed but next day returned. On this second occasion it was chiefly an artillery duel; and the enemy were finally driven back on Delhi by the Rifles. Ensign Napier was wounded in the leg, which had to be amputated. "During the operation no sign betrayed a sensation of pain. When it was finished, there came from him the bitter cry; 'I shall never lead the Rifles again.'" He died a few days later. The Rifles lost on the two days, besides these two officers, two non-commissioned officers killed and one wounded, ten rank and file killed and nine wounded, including three men sun-struck. This official return does not agree with the list on the tomb.

The 60th are of course the present King's Royal Rifle Corps. They were raised as a regiment of four battalions in 1755. By 1815 it had eight battalions, reduced by 1819 to two. Two more were raised in 1855 and 1857 respectively. The Indian honours of the corps are Punjab 1848 and 1849, Mooltan, Goojerat, Delhi, Ahmad Khel, Kandahar 1880, Afghanistan 1878—80, Chitral. The battalion at the Hindun and Delhi was the first. It also fought in Canada, winning the motto "*Celer et Audax*" at Quebec: in the W. Indies, the American War, all the Peninsula operations (sixteen battles and three sieges), the Kaffir War, the China War, the Red River expedition, the Afghan War of 1879-80, the Zulu and both Boer Wars, and the Egyptian and Soudan campaigns of 1882 and 1884.]

(References: ***Roberts*** : ***Forrest*** ; ***Kaye*** : ***Rice-Holmes.***)

56.—**1857**—OFFICERS AND MEN, 2ND TROOP, 1ST BRIGADE, B. H. A. *Inscription* :—In memory of 1st Lieutenant Henry George Perkins, Bombardier Bernard Horan, Rough Rider Patrick O'Neil, Gunner John Riley of the 2nd Troop, 1st Brigade, Bengal Horse Artillery, who fell in action with the mutineers at the Hindan river on the 31st May 1857, nobly doing their duty. This monument is erected by their Commanding Officer, Colonel H. Tombs, in token of esteem and regret.

[For a description of the battle, vide No. 55 above.

Lt. Perkins was the son of C. Perkins, born at Greenwich in 1840, and educated at Lewisham and Addiscombe; he belonged to Tombs's famous troop of Bengal Horse Artillery. General Wilson says in his despatch: "I have to regret the loss of Lieutenant Perkins, ... an invaluable officer and a great loss to me." "I cannot cease talking of the splendid behaviour of Tombs's troop," writes Greathed; "the gun carriages are pitted with grape and shot marks, ... he has lost, killed and wounded, thirteen men out of 50, but the action of the troop never ceased for a moment."]

(References: ***Roberts*** : ***Vibart*** : ***C. P.*** ; ***Forrest.***)

Bulandshahr District.

CEMETERY.

57.—**1857**—HOME, D. C., Lieutenant. *Inscription* :—In memory of Lieutenant Duncan Charles Home, Bengal Engineers, aged 29 years, who was killed by the explosion of a mine when engaged in destroying the Fort of Malagarh, on the 1st October 1857. As leader of the Forlorn Hope which on the 21st September 1857, successfully attacked the Cashmere Gate, Delhi, he was awarded the first Victoria Cross given in India.

[Son of Maj-General Home, of the Bengal Army, born 1828, educated at Elizabeth College, Guernsey, and Addiscombe: went to Bengal (1848), was at Umedan and in Gujerat, and subsequently on irrigation works. He is most famous for the blowing up of the Cashmere Gate. He was one of the four Engineers attached to the 3rd column in the attack on Delhi. Home and his Sappers laid the train which was fired by Corporal Burgess under a murderous rain of bullets—"a devoted and glorious deed" that earned Home the first V. C. won in India. He was killed by a premature explosion when blowing up the Malagarh Fort, near Aligarh, which had been held by a rebel named Walidad Khan.]

(References: *Forrest : Rice-Holmes : M. N.*)

Aligarh District.

FORT CEMETERY.

58.—**1803**—THURTON, J., Lieutenant. *Inscription* :—To the memory of Lieutenant John Thurton, 1st Battalion, 4th Native Infantry, who was killed at the assault of Aligarh, on the 4th September 1803, *ætatis suæ* 25. This monument, the tribute of affection, was erected by a friend. (B. O.)

[Vide No. 64. The name as spelt by Thorn and Dodwell and Miles is "Turton." He was appointed cadet in 1798, ensign in 1799, and lieutenant in 1800, and was the son of J. J. Turton, of Great Sugnall, Suffolk, where he was born in 1781. He was educated at Charterhouse.]

(References: *D. and M.: C. P.*)

59.—**1807**—YOUNG, J. H., Lieutenant *Inscription* :—Lieutenant J. H. Young, who fell before Comonah, 14th November 1807, aged 25 years. (B. O.)

[When Holkar invaded this portion of the country in 1804, he found the district in a ferment, consequent on its transfer to the British, and he was at once joined by many of the zamindars. Dundi Khan of Pitampur, was one of these. He was crushed in 1805, bu pardoned; his estates were given to his son, Ranmast Khan. This man gave fresh signs of disaffection, and was ultimately expelled in 180 . In 1807, the father and son mounted cannon in their forts of Kamona and Gunnaura and prepared to resist any attack made on them. After the necessary legal procedure had been tried and failed, Major-General Dickens invested Kamona on the 12th October and endeavoured to storm it on the 19th November, but was driven back with great loss. The fort, however, was evacuated five days later and Dundi Khan took refuge in Gunnaura, where he held out for three weeks, and then escaped. His estates were confiscated.]

(References: *Stubbs : Gazetteer.*)

60.—**1830**—CLEMENT, F. W., Lieutenant. *Inscription* :—Sacred to the memory of Lieutenant Francis William Clement of the Bengal Engineers, who departed this life on the 4th June 1830, aged 21 years. As a mark of esteem and regret, this tomb has been erected by his sincere friends, Henry and Jane DeBude. (B O.)

[Major DeBude was a fellow officer of the Bengal Engineers. F. W. Clement was at Addiscombe 1825-6 and was appointed lieutenant in 1827. He was the son of Major J. A. Clement, R. A., born at Montreal in 1808.]

(References: *B O ; Vibart ; C. and M. ; C. P.*)

61.—**1830**—LOW, S., Sergeant. *Inscription* :—In memory of Sergeant Samuel Low of the Engineer Department, who died on the 12th June 1830, from the immediate effects of exposure to the sun, in the zealous performance of his duty. This tomb has been erected by his commanding officer. (B. O.)

62—**1830**—BENNET, F. E. B, Lieutenant. *Inscription* :—Sacred to the memory of Francis Edward Burton Bennet Lieutenant, Bengal Engineers, who died at Aligarh, 17th August 1830, aged 21 years. (B. O.)

[F. E. Burlton Bennett (so all lists) was at Addiscombe 1826-7 and was appointed ensign in 1827. He was the son of W. R. B. Bennett, B. C. S., and was born at Fort William in 1809.]

(References: *Vibart; D. and M.; C. P.*)

63.—'838—APPERLEY, H., Lieutenant. *Inscription:*—To the memory of Herbert Apperley, Esq., Lieutenant, 6th Regiment, Bengal Native Infantry, who died at Aligarh on the 7th November 1838, deeply and sincerely regretted, aged 32 years and 5 months. This tomb was erected by the officers of his regiment as a testimony of their regard and esteem. (B O.)

[He was appointed cadet in 1825 and lieutenant in 1828. He was the son of the Revd. T. Apperley, of Bromgard, Hereford, and born in 1806. He died at Cuttack according to Dodwell and Miles.]

(References: *D. and M.; Services B. A. List.*)

ALIGARH, NEAR EAST INDIAN RAILWAY CROSSING.

64.—1803—OFFICERS AND MEN, 76TH FOOT. *Inscription:*— To the memory of the undermentioned gallant Officers, H. M.'s 76th Regiment of Foot: Captain Ronald Cameron, Lieutenant Michael Bayling Fleming, Lieutenant John Brown, Lieutenant and Adjt. Frederic Wm. St. Aubin, Lieutenant Arthur Cuthbert Campbell, who were killed during the assault in which the strong fortress of Aligarh, defended by a numerous and well appointed Garrison, fell to the superior energy of British valour and British spirit on the 4th September A. D. 1803. Also of Lieutenant and Adjutant William Meulh, Lieutenant John Henry Hurd of H. M.'s 76th Regiment of Foot, who lost their lives nobly fighting in their country's cause, during the memorable victory afterwards gained over the army of Dowlut Rao Scindia near Laswarry in Hindustan by the British forces under the command of General Lake on the 1st November A. D. 1803. This monument was erected by their brother officers.

[The monument stands here: there were formerly two inscriptions, one in English, Urdu and Hindi, the other in English. The latter was renewed in 1892, and put up in the Fort. Aligarh had been very strongly fortified by Perron: as Lord Lake wrote, "a 74 might sail in the ditch." But Perron was no longer the man he had been, and was vacillating between Scindia and desertion. On the approach of the English he left his troops to a compatriot Pedron, whom he adjured to hold out in a characteristically vainglorious letter, and fled. Pedron was no more inclined to fight than Perron and was deposed by his troops for a Rajput, Baji Rao. The fort was stormed by four companies of the 76th, two battalions of the 4th N. I. and four companies of the 17th N. I. A party from the 76th seeing some of the enemy smoking near the gate, attacked them in the hope of being able to enter with them; this failed, but the party of the enemy were slain. At the firing of the morning gun, the stormers pushed up to the gate, covered by the fire of two batteries. In spite of a hail of grape shot, ladders were applied, though without success. A 12-pounder was brought up and for twenty minutes there was some brisk fighting as the enemy came down by our own scaling ladders to attack us. Col. Monson was wounded, four Grenadier officers and the Adjutant, all of the 76th, and Lieut. Turton of the 4th N. I. were killed. The 12-pounder battered down the gate and the troops poured into the fort, up a narrow circular lane under heavy fire to the second gate which was easily forced and so to a third, where the British got through before it could be closed. They were checked at a fourth gate; but on getting through this resistance ceased. 223 men were killed or wounded. All the five Officers were killed outside the first gate: also Turton (vide No. 58). "Their country, their friends and their King will receive consolation for their loss in reflecting upon the glory of their achievements, and upon the public advantage of their illustrious example," were the words of Wellesley's general order. The battle of Laswari completely broke Perron's power. It was fought against some seventeen of his battalions, with 72 guns and some four or five thousand cavalry. Lake came up with them after a forced night march of twenty- five miles and attacked them with the cavalry at once, without waiting for his infantry. Awful carnage on both sides was the result, without any definite result. At noon the infantry arrived and after some delay charged, with Lake at their head, and seized the guns. "The enemy fought like devils or rather like heroes" wrote Lord Lake. The 76th headed the attack. "It would be a violation of my feelings," runs Lake's despatch, "were I to close my despatch without bearing testimony to the gallant conduct of Major Macleod . . . . of H. M.'s 76th Regiment, and of every officer and soldier of that inestimable corps." The 76th were with Lake at Aligarh, Delhi, Agra, Laswari, Dig, and Bhartpore. They are now the 2nd Battalion The Duke of Wellington's (West Riding Regiment). They were raised in 1787 and were in India from 1788 to 1803, 1836 to 1876 and 1897 to 1905. Their Indian honours are Hindostan, Seringapatam, Allyghur, Delhi 1803, Laswari and Deig.]

(For a skit on the siege of Aligarh, and the battle of Laswari, *vide* Thackeray's "Adventures of Major Gahagan.")

(References ; *Thorn* ; *Keene* : *Compton* ; *Grant Duff* ; *Wellesley's Despatches* ; *Gazetteer.*)

RATHBANPUR, TAHSIL SIKANDRA RAO.

65.—**1803**—NAIRN, R., Major. *Inscription:*—Here lieth the remains of Major Robert Nairn who in command of the 6th Regiment, Bengal Native Cavalry, fell at the siege of Kachora on 12th March 1803. Reader, of him might in justice stand up and say all the world "This was a man."

["The Kutchowra which stopped and fought Lord Lake and killed the famous Major Nairn of tiger-killing memory." It was the fort of Adhikarin, a rebel zamindar, who, encouraged by the weakness of the Oudh Government, erected fortresses, trained soldiers and plundered the countryside—very much as the barons did in England in the reign of Stephen. These forts as a rule, though attacked by Lake in person "were not carried without the loss of many lives among whom was the gallant Major Nairn, who fell before the fort of Kachoura." It was one of many similar fight in what was known as the "mud war," from the mud forts attacked. Fanny Parkes' epithet "of tiger-killing memory" is explained by an anecdote told by Thorn. The incident occurred in 1802 at Kanauj. He describes how wolves, jackals and tigers secluded themselves in the ruins of splendid edifices "which formerly resounded with the voice of gladness." He then adds "On one of these hunting excursions a tiger of large size was shot with a *pistol* by General Lake, just as the ferocious animal was in the act of springing upon Major Nairn by whom it had been previously *speared.*" There were giants in the land in those days.]

(References : *Stubbs* ; *Wanderings of a Pilgrim* ; *Thorn.*)

TAPPAL FORT TAHSIL KHAIR.

66.—**1818**—SMITH, T. Captain. *Inscription* :—

مرقد طامس إسمتهه صاحب كه بتاريخ بست و دوم ذي الحجه سنه
١٢٣١ هجري نبوي مطابق سيزدهم نومبر سنه ١٨١٦ع تعمير بست وپنج
دولت حيات سپرد

[At Tappal are three tombs, of which only two have inscriptions. One is the above: Thomas Smith is said to have been a Captain, commanding the Begam Samru's troops at Tappal. The Dyce-Sombre papers show that she only kept a few hundred troops after her submission fo the British : it is more likely that he had some civil post, with possibly a few soldiers to back him. The other tomb has an inscription now undecipherable : it appears to be in French or Portuguese or both : and there is an Urdu date

بتاريخ ٩ ربيع الثاني سنه ١١١٥ هجري

or the 9th Rabi-Us Sani 1115 A. D. equivalent to 24th July 1713,—a date which makes it possible that the tomb is not European at all.]

ALIGARH-DELHI ROAD, 3RD MILE.

67.—**1857**—OFFICERS AND MEN, MAJOR MONTGOMERY'S COLUMN. *Inscription:*—N ar this spot fell the undermentioned gallant officers and men, on 24th August 1857, fighting in the defence of their Government against a large body of rebels who had come from the town of Koel, and were repulsed by a small force under Major Montgomery, 15th Bengal Native Infantry:

Ensign Henry Lewin Marsh, 16th Bengal Native Infantry, Mr. John O'Brien Tandy, Merchant Volunteer, and Robert Lockhart, 2nd Company, 5th Battalion, Bengal Artillery.

Corporal William Armstrong, Private Nicholas Fitzgerald, Patrick Lev'ng } 3rd Bengal European Infantry.

Their mortal remains lie buried at Hatras.

[During the early days of the Mutiny a Aligarh, the only force was a few Volunteers All but ten went or were recalled to Agra; these ten with Mr. Watson, the Magistrate, held out at Mandrak for about a month, and left for Agra early in July after defeating, with a single charge, a large number of rebels. In August they returned with a small force under Major Montgomery and defeated the rebels under Ghaus Khan and others near Koil. Mr. Tandy, a manager of the Agra Bank, was one of the Volunteers who was at Mandrak. Ensign H. L. Marsh was the son of Major H. Marsh, H. C. S., and was born at Calcutta in 1838. The officers and men are buried at Hathras in a tomb without an inscription.]

(References: *Coopland: C. P.; M. N.*)

SASNI, TAHSIL HATHRAS.

68.—**1857**—NICHTERLEIN. S *Inscription:*—Sacred to the memory of Samuel Anderson Nichterlein, much lamented, and the only son of John Nichterlein of Mudrock Factory, who was massacred by a band of rebellious villagers at Savamaeo village, during the Mutinies of 1857-58, on the 21st May A. D. 1857, aged 33 years.

[Close to the police station. Mr. Nichterlein was the son of an indigo planter, who was murdered at Sawamai by a party of "Mewathies and others," when hurrying to Agra. He was the only man murdered in Aligarh during the Mutiny.]

(Reference: *M. N.*)

MENDU, TAHSIL HATHRAS.

69.—**1827**—WESTROYS, C. S. L., Mrs. *Inscription:*—Sacred to the memory of Clarissa Sophia Louisa, the wife of George Westroys, who departed this life at Mendoo, on Monday, the 21st May, A.D. 1827, aged 27 years.

70.—**1827**—WESTROYS, ELIZA. *Inscription:*—Sacred to the memory of Eliza, the infant daughter of Clarissa Sophia Louisa and George Westroys, who departed this life at Mendoo on Thursday, the 7th of June, A.D 1827, aged one month.

GANGIRI, TAHSIL ATRAULI.

71.—**185**7—OFFICERS AND MEN, 6TH DRAGOON GUARDS AND 9TH LANCERS. *Inscription:*—In memory of the brave men who fell in the hour of victory at Gangiri on 14th December 1857, and whose mortal remains rest here upon the field of battle; George Wardlow, Captain; John Hudson, Lieutenant; Sydney Vyse

Lieutenant; Joseph Barnett, Private; Robert Chapman, Private; Walter Cosser, Private; Allen Eastwood, Private: all of H. M.'s 6th Dragoon Guards (Carabineers), and John Dyson, Private; Henry Trampton, Private, of H. M.'s 9th (Queen's) Lancers.

(At Kanohi-Gangiri, in tahsil Atrauli, is a monument erected to the officers and men who were killed, fighting against the rebels in 1857. The monument is situated in the ravines, on the left bank of the Nim Nadi.

Cracroft Wilson's account of this affair is as follows:—Col. Farquhar with some 600 men and two guns was operating in and from Bulandshahr. There were five or six thousand rebels belonging to Fatehgarh at Sohawar, Patiali, Qadirganj and Mohanpur. Kasganj was seized by them: and partly on Wilson's representaions a column marched from Delhi to Aligarh under Col. Seaton. The two columns then effected a junction at Gangiri, Colonel Farquhar arriving first, and encamped in a strong position. Gangiri is on the right bank of the Nim River, which is here crossed by an iron suspension bridge; and he encamped on the right bank, with his front protected by ravines and his rear resting on the village. The rebels at Kasganj decided to attack him next morning (the 14th.) But Col. Seaton meantime arrived and encamped on the left bank. In other words the river and ravines were between the two camps and Col. Seaton was nearer to Kasganj. The rebels arrived about 11 a.m., obviously unaware of Seaton's arrival: there was a brisk cannonade, and then the enemy's cavalry showed themselves in large numbers. Capt. Wardlow with his squadron was ordered up in support, with two more guns. The squadron charged, took three guns and routed the enemy. Capt. Wardlow then saw some rebels creeping away: he charged them and was shot through the head. Lieutenant Vyse was killed in charging the guns. Lieutenant (Wilson calls him Captain) Hodson was shot by some rebels he was pursuing through *arhar*. It appears probable that the charge was without orders. Wilson says that before leaving camp, some Dragoon officers were heard to mutter, "We will see who take the guns to-day,"—a reference to an incident at Narnaul. The charge would appear to have been a grave mistake. The rebels naturally thought they were opposed to Col. Farquhar who had no European cavalry, and by waiting, they might have been taken unawares and far more damage inflicted. The infantry never came into action at all. Three officers and six men were killed. "One noble looking Dragoon, stooping over the bed on which Lieutenant Vyse was lying, raised the corpse towards him and pressing it to him, said 'see Sir, he is but a boy,' while the tears trickled down his sunburnt face." (Wilson). A similar incident of course occurred at Lucknow, when Sir Henry Lawrence died. The 6th D. G.'s were raised at Monmouth's Rebellion in 1655. They fought in Marlborough's campaigns, at Sebastopol, Delhi, and in the Afghan and the last Boer war. The 9th (Queen's Royal) Lancers were raised in 1715. They fought in the Peninsula and last Boer War; otherwise their active service has been entirely in India. Their Indian honours are Punniar, Sobraon, Punjab, Chillianwalah, Goojerat, Delhi, Lucknow, Charasiah, Kabul 1879, Kandahar 1880, and Afghanistan 1878 to 1880.]

(Reference: *M. N.*)

BARLAH, TAHSIL ATRAULI.

72.—**1828**—BORROWES, MARY. *Inscription:*—Sacred to the memory of Mary Ann, daughter of Charles and Mary Borrowes. Born 2nd August 1827, died 8th July 1828.

The lovely babe beneath this tomb was cut off in the bud,
But she in Paradise will bloom and ever live with God.

[No longer traceable.]

ALIGARH, DISPENSARY COMPOUND.

73.—**1180**—HAMULIN, J. *Inscription:*—Monsieur Julien Hamulin, 1801.

[At Aligarh, in the compound of the dispensary, are eight tombs, but only one had an inscription. Nothing is known about them beyond what this inscription, which is now illegible and reproduced from Führer, gives.]

AGRA DIVISION.

Agra District.

Agra had no history of importance before the time of Akbar. But in the three centuries that have since elapsed, it has been the scene of more history than many of its older rivals have been in all their lives. The *European* history--and it dates nearly as far back as its Muhammadan history—is as romantic as that of any city in the world. The adventures of the Armenians, a nation that traces its descent to Haik, the grandson of Japheth, an "European" nation which somehow got left behind in Asia, and "European" in every but the purely geographical sense; the history of John Philip Bourbon, a relative of Henry IV of France; the Jesuit missions to Akbar, and the dallyings of that prince and his successors with Christianity: the trade missions and trade rivalries of English and Dutch: the tales of the military adventurers—such are the byepaths of history that Agra offers for exploration.

Agra naturally needs more detailed treatment than most districts. For this reason, I have given preliminary notes dealing with some of the main historical facts of which Agra's monuments are proof, and left only personal details to the notes on the tombs themselves.

ROMAN CATHOLIC CEMETERY, LASHKARPUR.

A.—*The Armenians.*—The Armenians, it is said, had traded in India as early as 780 A. D. Be that as it may, we find them already established in Agra in the palmy days of the Mogul Empire. It is said, for instance, that Akbar adopted the son of an Armenian merchant, Jacob by name; and attributed the birth of Jahangir in 1570 to their having erected a Christian church. Terry (1615), a shrewd observer, but distinctly biassed against everything that was not Anglican, said that "there are many Armenians...amongst them......the greatest part of whose Christianity lies in their name. They made and sold wine, tasted too much......by those too that make it." In 1609 William Hawkins arrived at Agra with letters to Jahangir from the King of England. Jahangir, says Hawkins, offered him a wife. "The king was very earnest with me to take a white maiden out of his palace ......and he would promise me she would turn Christian. In regard she was a Moore, I refused, but if so bee there could bee a Christian found, I would accept it, at which my speech, I little thought a Christian's daughter could be found." But Jahangir produced an Armenian maiden, daughter of one Mubarak Shah; "and I, havinge passed my word to the king, could not withstand my fortunes," and so he married her. (At a later date she married Captain Towerson who was put to death at Amboyna in 1623 by the Dutch; and she and her husband returned to India in 1617, either to push her husband's fortunes in India, or to recover her father's estate. He returned to England in 1619, but she remained with her relatives.) Jerome Xavier, again, writing in 1598 from Lahore, mentions an Armenian who wanted to marry his deceased wife's sister (or his niece—*neptem*—both versions are given); but in spite of an appeal by the Armenian to Akbar Xavier managed to prevent the marriage. About 1604, some Armenians conspired with an English heretic (John Midnall) and some Portuguese malcontents against the Jesuits and gave them a good deal of trouble. References to Armenians in the letters of the English factors are frequent, *e.g.*, in 1619 Kerridge writes of a quarrel in which some Armenian merchants were concerned, and asserted "that the custom of Turkee ingagethe the consule or cheife to answer the defects of all other men of their nation."

That the Armenians were not all the mock Christian wine bibbers Terry calls them, some of these references, as well as several epitaphs show clearly. The Armenian community was undoubtedly numerous and wealthy.

(References: *Seth ; Purchas ; Foster, "Letters" and "Factories" ; J.A.S.B., Vol. LXV ; Terry : Roe*).

B.—*The Jesuit Mission.*—Christianity found its way to Agra at a very early date. There are, or were, Persian documents in the Agra Mission archives, to show that a Father Joseph bought 12 (or 72) bighas of land in Lashkarpur for the use of a cemetery to be held free of rent. This father was probably Joseph da Castro (see further on *passim*). A lady named Mariam Pyari also granted two groves for the same purpose. The present cemetery is on these 12 bighas. As early as 1576, Akbar's attention was drawn to Christianity: and missions were sent to Agra from Goa at his request both in 1580 and 1590. The third and most important left Goa in 1595, under Fathers Jerome Xavier and Pinheiro, and Brother Benedict Goes. Akbar received them kindly: they were allowed to build a church at Lahore in 1597. Akbar allowed conversion, but would not himself be converted—"*venerunt filii usque ad partum, sed virtus non est pariendi*"—as the Fathers wrote. Still the Jesuits had several converts of high rank. In 1605 Akbar died, still unconverted. Jehangir was even more liberal to the Jesuits than his father; he allowed them to build church and college at Agra, with free liberty to preach or convert as they pleased. Withington, an Englishman, writing in 1614 (he was a factor of the E. I. Co.), says, "The Jesuits have a very faire church, built by the king, and a house. The king allows the chiefe 7 Rupias a day, and the rest 3, with license to convert as many as they can, which they doe, but alas! it is for money's sake." Terry says much the same; and also tells the history, how two of Akbar's brother's sons were baptized and then expressed a desire for Christian wives. The fathers would not grant them their request: whereupon "they delivered up their crucifixes into their hands and so left them." But Terry is in error; it was not Akbar, but Jahangir who had allowed the conversion of his nephews, the sons of his brother Danyal. Roe and Hawkins are divided as to whether this was an act of policy—to discredit possible heirs to the throne with the populace,—or due to a desire to have Portuguese ladies, the converts' wives, to grace his own seraglio. Finch describes how the three (not two) princes were conducted to the church to be christened, "by all the Christians of the citie, some sixtie horse, Captaine Hawkins in the head of them, with St. George's colours carried before him."

About 1621 was built the Jesuit college at Agra, founded and liberally provided with funds by a rich Armenian, Mirza Zu'l Qarnin, governor of Sambhar. He gave them lands at Bandra in Salsette and at Parel in the Island of Bombay; the rents were applied to the college.

These places were chosen as in Portuguese territory and safe from arbitrary exactions on the part of the Emperor.

Shah Jahan, a strict Muhammadan, treated the Christians with considerable severity. It is however doubtful whether his cruelties were not prompted as much by political as religious considerations. For this point, vide No. 77.

The Jesuits' influence lasted till 1759, when king Joseph of Portugal expelled them from his dominions; and those that were caught were taken to Lisbon and thrown into prison. With Tieffentaller and F. X. Wendel, the Order died out in Upper India. The results of their mission have been belittled by many. Terry writes that their conversions were mock-conversions: they worked "upon the necessity of some poor men who for want of means are content to wear crucifixes." Withington says much the same, adding that the converts "brought them their beads again saying they had been so long without their pay and would be Christians no longer." But we also find them blamed for devoting their attention too much to the court. But these criticisms must be largely discounted. Terry and Withington wrote as men born under Elizabeth naturally would write: they are biassed critics. Jesuits, always and everywhere, have made the best of missionaries. Picked men of more than ordinary ability, education and self devotion as they were, they could not have preached the gospel for two hundred years without achieving better results than a little mock Christianity induced by gain and if they devoted themselves rather to the upper than the lower classes, they had no small measure of success, though they never realized their dream—a Moghul Emperor who should be a Christian. The imperial grants to them, the presence of Christians in the court and seraglio, the very numbers of the Jesuits themselves, show that they were regarded without disapproval, if not with actual favour. So after two hundred years of vigorous and fruitful life passed away the old Agra Jesuit mission, founded by a heathen Emperor, and exterminated by a Christian king.

But though orders change, the church remains. As early as 1703, the prefecture of Tibet and the "adjoining countries" was erected, and entrusted to the Capuchin Fathers of the Marca D'Ancona province. In 1823, the Tibet-Hindustan mission was born: the first Vicar Apostolic was the Right Reverend Z. Benucci, O. C. In 1886 Pope Leo XIII made the Vicariate-Apostolic a metropolitan see, of which the M. Reverend M. A. Jacopi was the first archbishop.

(References: *J. A. S. B., Vol. LXV; Bernier; Roe; Terry; Purchas; Keene; Wheeler; Calendar, Agra Archdiocese, 1907; Hosten.*)

C.—*Other Europeans in Agra.*—The inscriptions that follow show that Agra from 1611 to 1800 was a cosmopolitan rendezvous. We find there Europeans of all nations, English, Dutch, French, Portuguese, Italian, German, Flemish, even Swiss. Who were these people and how did they get here? The Jesuits, of course, account for a considerable number of the inscriptions. Indian converts to Christianity who took European names, (of whom many are mentioned by Manucci—*cf.* for instance, no. 108 and the note to no. 114,—and the offspring of mixed marriages account for others. And after 1760, the influx of European military adventurers and the European flotsam and jetsam that they collected as subordinate officers explain most cases. But between 1611 and 1760, there are still many cases unexplained.

It is important to notice that the East about this time was overrun by Europeans of all sorts. There were settlements of all nations, especially English, French, Dutch and Portuguese, not only at Surat and Goa, not only in India and the Spice islands, but in Persia, Arabia, China and even Japan. We read of a diplomat accredited by Charles II in exile to the Shah of Persia: he found traders of all nations there. Jesuit priests are mentioned as reaching Agra from Tibet. There are letters extant from English traders in Japan and China; and the quarrels of English and Dutch in the Spice islands are history, and had far-reaching consequences at home, as well as in the East.

These settlements were primarily trade settlements: but they served as magnets for all sorts of persons interested in the East. Servants, artizans, tradesmen, sailors, soldiers, physicians, priests, explorers and diplomatists all congregated there on their way up country, and in going up country naturally gravitated to Agra. For Agra was one of the imperial towns in the Moghul dominions: if it was not the oriental London, it was at all events the oriental Windsor. And so we hear that Dara at the battle of Samugarh in 1658 had 200 European artillerymen; Mir Jumlah and Aurangzeb also employed such men as artizans; Veroneo the reputed designer of the Taj, Austin of Bordeaux, who is responsible for some of the Agra Fort decorations, and Bronzoni (no. 112), are instances. Of tradesmen there were many; for instance, Bravet the Frenchman, who got 60,000 rupees from Jahangir for some worthless French bric à brac. Of physicians, Manucci himself, of more or less bonâ fide travellers, Tavernier, Bernier, Marucci the Jesuit, Manrique, and Tieffentaller are examples; of scientists one may mention Roa, Strobl and Gabelsperger. Among English diplomatists alone there were Hawkins, Sir T. Roe, Lord Bellomont (sent by Charles II to the Shah of Persia and the Moghul Emperor to enlist their aid in his restoration) and Sir W. Norris. Earliest visitor of all perhaps, and by no means the least notable, is Jean Philippe Bourbon de Navarre, a scion of the French royal house. It is not therefore strange, what with Jesuits, factors, soldiers and all this polyglot assemlage of visitors of all kinds, that the old Roman Catholic cemetery is well-filled.

(References: *Manucci; Foster; Hunter.*)

D.—*The Padre Santos chapel.*—This building dates back at least to 1611. Tieffentaller writes of it as follows. "To its south (i.e of the cemetery) is a high and spacious vaulted building with pointed floral decorations inside; a sort of chapel where lie the sacred bones of the fathers, which are venerated not only among Christians, but Mahomedans and Gentiles, especially those of the venerable father Marc Antoine Santucci, an Italian, whose tomb they adorn with their offerings and accomplish their vows *(vota facta exsolvunt)* because of the renown of his pure and holy life." The name by which it is known "Padre Santos" is possibly a corruption of Padre Santucci though Father Symphorien (Agra Archaeological Society's Transactions, 1876, page x) explains it as "Padre Santo" or holy father, and says it is so called from the martyrs D' Anhaya and Garcia. The other explanation, backed as it is by Tieffentaller, certainly seems more probable. Originally it was probably the tomb of Mortenepus—whoever he was—for his tomb is the oldest and most conspicuous tomb in the place. The other epitaphs, save Santucci's, are on the flags of the pavement. I give the complete list of inscriptions found in the Archdiocesan calendar, placing in brackets those parts I could not decipher myself.

(References: *Tieffentaller; Calendar, Agra Archdiocese, 1907; Agra Arch.: So. Transactions.*)

E.—*Other Roman Catholic cemeteries in Agra.*—Father Hosten, S. J., on the authority of F. Felix, O.C., mentions three cemeteries at Agra; Lashkarpur cemetery, the graveyard of the old R. C. Cathedral in Padre Tola, and a cemetery about a mile north of Lashkarpur. Mr. Irvine in a note in his edition of Manucci, quoting the Agra Archaeological Society's Transactions, says the same thing. I was not able to discover any statement to that effect in the Transactions (which will not surprise any body who has seen them); but they mention the discovery of some Portuguese inscriptions "on a low mound under a tree 60 paces from the north wall of the enclosure of the tomb of Abul Ala and about ¼ of a mile from no. 4 milestone on the Poya Ghat Road". This site appears to correspond to the site mentioned by Father Hosten. The discovery was made by "A. C." (whom I suppose to be Dr. Christison) in 1870 though the discovery was reported only in 1876.

The Lashkarpur cemetery is not more than half full even now and is still in use. There seems no obvious reason why this other cemetery should have been required. From such dates as we have, the period when the third cemetery was in use appears to be roughly 1730 to 1770. And we find a distinct gap in the series of inscriptions of the Lashkarpur cemetery proper between 1728 and 1771. I cannot of course assert that there are no tombs of that period, for though I looked at every tomb and took down every inscription which was at all legible up to 1800, there are both illegible inscriptions and tombs with no inscriptions. Still this considerable gap is significant. Further, we know that Father F. X. Wendel petitioned Shah Alam in 1775 that the cemetery might be restored to the Jesuits; which shows that by order or force, it had previously been taken of them. The possible cause is said by local Agra authorities to be the "absence of the Jesuits." (They always had their headquarters there and there was always a Jesuit Rector of the college; but after the suppression of the Order, there were very few, who had to travel far afield. There might well have been times when there were no Jesuits in Agra; and it would be during such an absence that the cemetery was resumed.)

It is significant that in the Padre Santos' chapel, we find only six inscriptions between 1706 (the year before Aurangzeb's death) and 1767. Of these five are Jesuits and one a Carmelite. Further, of these six five died elsewhere, as their inscriptions record—at Delhi, Narwar, Janegar (Jainagar), Troyabad (which may be Faizabad); and the sixth, (Strobl) died at either Jaipur or Jainagar. From 1633 to 1706 twenty Jesuits died; from 1706 to 1767 only six. It is obvious that the Jesuit mission began to decline with the death of Aurangzeb. There is evidence of this in the history of Tieffentaller's life; but apart from that, it is only what might be expected. Agra, after Aurangzeb, was no longer the Moghul capital; the Jesuits followed the court. It was, moreover, between 1722 and 1773 a bone of contention to be fought for by Moghul, Maratha and Jat. From 1722 to 1738 Jai Singh of Jaipur held it for the Moghul; from 1758 to 1773 Maratha and Jat held it against him. In such troublous times it is not surprising that the Jesuits left Agra. It is quite possible that some of these inscriptions are merely commemorative and cover no grave though Father Hosten has expressed to me an opposite opinion. Nothing is known of the persons commemorated save Gabelsperger and Strobl. Further, in 1759 the Jesuits were expelled from the Portuguese dominions, in 1764 from France, and in 1773 the Order was abolished altogether by Clement XIV; and so all recruitment from Goa was stopped.

From 1773 however we find the Moghul once more in possession of Agra; which doubtless explains Wendel's petition in 1775. And it is to be noticed that between 1707 and 1775 we find only three inscriptions in the cemetery. Two are Armenians, and one of them a "Captain" doubtless a military adventurer, the other is Madec's child who died in 1771, when her father was in the Jat service and the Jats still held Agra. It is not difficult to suppose that they allowed him to bury his child where he pleased. From 1775 the series commences again.

It is not unlikely therefore that the cemetery was resumed by some definite order of some governor of Agra, and if so, probably by Jai Singh. But even if it was not, it is highly likely that it was not particularly safe in the absence of the tolerant Moghuls, and the presence of Maratha and Jat ruffians, for the deceased's relatives to confess Christianity by burial in so obviously Christian a spot. And this may account for the graves in the immediate vicinity of a Muhammadan cemetery, certainly the tomb of a famous Muhammadan saintly personage like Abul Ala. It is quite possible that this spot was never consecrated at all; though in all probability its site had belonged to the Jesuits who owned a good deal of land in and round Lashkarpur, for we find it resumed by the British government in 1824. And though their "cemetery" was probably disused before this date, it doubtless fell into neglect then, until at last the tombs disappeared altogether, to be restored to the light of day by Dr. Christian.

[References: *Gazetteer; Calendar, Agra Archdiocese, 1907; Agra Arch: Soc. Trans.; Latif; Hosten.*]

PADRE SANTOS' CHAPEL.

74.—**1611**—MORTENEPUS. *Inscription*:—Here lies the Holy Khoja Mortenepus who was a professed disciple of Jesus Christ and who was a righteous man. Whatever he had he gave in charity to the poor, in token of fidelity to his Divine Master in the year 1611 from the birth of Christ. (Translation from Armenian and Persian, now scarcely legible.)

[Nothing is known of Mortenepus. I am informed by Mr. Ellis of the India office that the name itself is no Armenian name; and that possibly "Martin epos," (abbreviation for episcopus or bishop) is correct, though if "Martin" was a bishop, Khoja (which is a title of respect for merchants = Khwaja) must be wrong. As every other inscription in the chapel is that of a cleric, the probability that this man was a priest is considerable. The translation, which is from the Persian, first appeared in the transactions of the Agra Archaeological Society for 1874. With the help of the District Engineer of Agra I have succeeded in getting a reading of the Persian inscription. It is as follows:—

این جا مدفونست خواجه مرتینپس ارمني مقدسي که خودرا غلام
کریستپس میگفت چون صاحب خیر بود هرچه باخود داشت بنذر
آنحضرت بفقرا ایثار کرد در سنه یک هزار و ششصد و یازده از تولد
حضرت عیسی

"Here lies Khwaja Mortenepus the holy Armenian who used to call (or "boasted himself") a servant of Christ (Chrisiptus). In his charity (or "virtue") he gave away whatever he had to the needy as a gift to Christ. In the year 1611 from the birth of Christ."

75.—1615—ZAKHAR, Father. *Inscription:*—Father Zakhar Bishop. I am from Tabrez, 1615. (Translation from Armenian).

[Said to be at top of a cross in a niche to the right of the dome. I could not find it.]

[76.—1633—DE PEYRA, M., Padre. *Inscription :*—Aqui iazo P. Matthaeos de Peyra, faleceo aos 2 de Novembro de 1633.]

77.—1633—D'ANHAYA, M., Padre. *Inscription :*—Aqui iazo P. Mel D'Anhaya, clerigo morto pela fee na prisão a 2 d'Agosto 1633.

[In 1631-2, Shah Jahan besieged and took the Portuguese settlement at Hugli, and sent some four thousand captives to Agra, where they were sold as slaves. There is a story that four priests were torn in pieces by wild elephants. It is related in the Bengal Catholic Herald for 1842, but there seems no authority for it whatever. There is a further story to the effect that Father John da Cruz was brought into the arena to undergo a similar fate, but the elephant refused to attack him and on the contrary fawned on him: and that Shah Jahan, much impressed, released the captives and sent them back to Bengal where they built a town, Bandal, in 1633.

Everything goes to disprove this story. If the captives were sent back in 1633, how came Garcia and D'Anhaya to be in prison in 1633 and 1634? Further, as late as 1640, we find Manrique, S. J. with the assistance of Da Castro, obtaining the liberation of Antonios da Cristo, prior of Hugli, from Asaf Khan in Lahore; so that a Hugli priest was in prison no less than 8 years after these events. The fact is simply that Shah Jahan, though a strict Muhammadan and no lover of Christianity, was moved to wrath rather by the aggressions of the Portuguese than by the religion of the Jesuits or Augustinians who were proselytizing in Bengal; and they suffered quite as much because they were Portuguese as because they were Christians. Bernier indeed says that all through these troubles the Jesuits at Agra were left unmolested in their Colleges. Bernier, however, is probably exaggerating: one Jesuit (Fialho) was killed in 1633 "with scimitars, in the Moghul Empire;" and Da Castro is said to have been scourged, bastinadoed, and otherwise maltreated At all events, Shah Jahan's wrath cannot have lasted long—even if these cruelties to Fialho and Da Castro are to be laid to his charge at all,—for obviously, a sycophant in power might well imagine that he would please the king by such rigours. For we find Manrique honourably received in 1640; we find the Jesuits as numerous and as influential as ever after 1634. Soon after that date, too, we find them with all their old privileges. The story of the soft hearted elephant is said to rest on certain manuscripts; but one may take leave to doubt those manuscripts as Father Hosten does.]

(References: ***Keene ; Calendar, Agra Archdiocese, 1907 ; Hosten.***)

78.—1634—GARCIA, M., Padre. *Inscription :*—Aqui iazo P. Mel Garcia clerigo morto no carcere pela fe a 23 de Marco d' 1634.

[*Cf.* above, no. 77. Father Hosten draws attention to the numerous tombs in 1633 and 1634, and conjectures that all these—76 to 80—are the tombs of priests who died in the persecution subsequent on the Hugli massacre, and that they are not Jesuits, but Augustinians.]

(Reference: ***Hosten.***)

79.—1634—LANFRANKI, F., Padre. *Inscription :*—Aqui iazo Pe Frco. Lanfranki, faleceo ao I de Julho de 1634.

[He left Lisbon in 1632.]

(Reference: ***Hosten.***)

80.—1634—DA FONSECA, A., Padre. *Inscription :*—Aqui iaz[o Pe] Anto da Fonseca, faleceo [a 7] D'Agosto 1634.

81.—1635—CORSI, F., Padre. *Inscription :*—Aqui iazo Pe Franco Corsi, faleceo ao lo d'Agosto d' 1635.

[Corsi was a Florentine born in 1575. He entered the Order in 1593 and in 1599 was sent from Portugal to India, where he lived ordinarily in the house of the Great Moghul. He learnt to speak Persian, Urdu and Arabic, all well, so Jerome Xavier tells us. The relations between Roe and Corsi were very amicable. Terry describes him as a man of a severe life, yet of a fair and an affable disposition: "he lived at that Court as an Agent for the Portuguese." Corsi suggested to Roe that they should disguise their religious differences, lest it should be "a very main obstacle . . . unto his great design . . . to convert people to Christianity." Roe states that he instructed Jahangir's brother's sons, and goes on to tell the story about the Portuguese wives. He also tells a story of how Corsi's house and church was burned and nothing but the crucifix saved—"which underhand was given out for a miracle." Corsi however told Roe privately it was no miracle, "insinuating that the Moores had caught up this opinion of miracle without his consent." Jahangir however challenged Corsi to throw the crucifix into the fire. Corsi refused, saying that "God was not tyed to the call of men . . . but offered to enter the fire himself for proofe of his faith," which the king refused. He is mentioned on more than one occasion as mediating between the English and the Portuguese It is clear that Roe had a great liking for him, and used him as a friend: he constantly mentions services Corsi rendered him, and Terry tells us Corsi used to visit him about once a week. Curiously enough, so far as I have been able to discover, Roe only mentions his name once—in a letter to the Lord Bishop of Canterbury; everywhere else he refers to him as "the Jesuite."]

(References: *Roe; Terry; Hosten; J.A.S.B., LXV.*)

82.—**1636**—MACHADO, A., Padre. *Inscription:*—Aqui iazo Pe Antonio Machado faleceo aos 4 de Abril do 1636.

[Nothing is known of this father save that he reached Agra in 1602. One Jesuit authority says he became superior of the Moghul Mission and died at Angola in 1627. But this is clearly wrong. There is an unpublished letter of his in the British Museum.]

(Reference: *Hosten.*)

83.—**1646**—DA CASTRO, J., Padre. *Inscription:*—Aqui iazo P. Ioseph da Castro, faleceo aos 15 de Dezbro d' 1646.

[About this father the following facts are known:—

(1) There is a letter from him to Father Claude Aquaviva (dated Agra 1615) in the British Museum.

(2) In 1617 he went to arrange for the purchase of the Salsette and Parel lands, for which Mirza Zu'l Qarnin found the funds (cf. note B.)

(3) In 1633, he was tortured, as a result of the Hugli persecutions (cf. No. 77.)

(4) In 1637, he was at Agra and reported Drake's death to the English factors at Surat (No 173.)

(5) In 1640, he was in Lahore and assisted Manrique, S. J., to obtain the liberation of the Prior of Hugli (cf. No. 77.)

(6) Father Hosten asserts that he was the Father Yusuf, or Joseph mentioned by Fanthome as obtaining a firman from Akbar. (Query. Was this the firman referring to the cemetery, mentioned in Note B. *ad init?* See note on page 39.)

(7) Mr. Irvine identifies him with Manucci's "Padre Atash."

The "Padre Atash" tale is one of several variations of a story referring to a suggested ordeal by fire to test the comparative value of Christianity and Muhammadanism. Manucci's story is that a certain father offered a Qazi the ordeal: both were to sit on a fire of straw with Bible and Quran respectively in their hands. The Qazi refused, and Jahangir at once dubbed the priest "Padre Atash." Bernier has another version, in which the Padre is already known as "Padre Atash" from his fiery temper, and Jahangir suggests the ordeal. Budaoni and Abul Fazl tell a similar tale of Aquaviva (in which Jesuit and Qazi change roles): and Roe has a similar story to tell of Corsi, already related (No. 81.)

The claimants to the name are:—

(1) Manucci's Joseph da Costa, a Portuguese.

(2) Corsi (Roe).

(3) A Florentine, (Bernier) and
(4) da Castro, (Irvine.)

Mr. Irvine quotes Marucci, S. J., who mentions a "J. da C. (so written in Mr. Irvine's note), a Piedmontese, who died *last year* aged 70 years, of which 35 were spent in the Indian Mission. His services were especially valuable after the siege of Hugli." This book of Marucci's was written in 1651, so that "last year" means (in default of more definite evidence) a year preceding 1651. Mr. Irvine identifies "J. da C." with Da Castro. His note is a little confused, as in one place, quoting Keene, Mr. Irvine, says *Da Castro* died in Agra in 1646; and in another, quoting this inscription, says *Da Costa* died in Lahore in 1646. There can be no doubt of the identification: we know Da Castro was in Agra in 1615, so that no less that 31 years out of Marucci's 35 are accounted for; and there is no question that Da Castro *did* render valuable services after the sack of Hugli. But the further identification of Da Castro with Manucci's Da Costa is less plausible; at all events there appears to be nothing whatever to support it.

Bernier says Padre Atash was a Florentine and this remark probably points to the truth. Manucci and Bernier, it must be remembered, were both reporting the story as told them some thirty odd years after the events, and the evidence of both is equally valuable or valueless. But when we find a very similar story told by an eye-witness, namely Roe, of Corsi, who *was* a Florentine, it seems very probable that Manucci and Bernier are relating somewhat garbled versions of the events related by the English ambassador, but Bernier has got the right man. It may be objected that Roe says nothing of the name "Padre Atash," which to some extent is the point of the story as related by Manucci. But if Padre Atash was, as Bernier says, an already existing nickname, one can quite understand that Roe would not think it worth while mentioning. If, as Manucci says, it arose out of these events, then Roe, who was no Persian scholar, may not have understood the imperial jest; or if he did may not have thought it becoming to mention it in a letter addressed to the Archbishop of Canterbury. At all events it seems more likely that we have here three versions of the same story than three (or even two) different stories. One can hardly suppose that offering ordeals by fire to persons who never by any chance accepted the offer had grown into a positive habit at Jahangir's court.

The Joseph da Costa (no. 92) who died in 1685 is clearly barred by dates. He must have been a raw lad at the most in the reign of Jahangir (1605-1627.)]

(References: *Roe; Manucci; Bernier; J. A. S. B., Vol. LXV; Hosten.*)

84.—1656—CESQUES, A., Padre. *Inscription*:—Aqui iazo P. Antonio Cesques faleceo aos 28 d' Junho d' 1656.

[Antonio Cesques, or Ceschi di Santa Croce, called Father Chesco by Manucci, was born at Borgo (Val Sugana) in 1618, entered the novitiate at Rome in 1633 and came to Goa in 1645. In 1648 he went to Lahore as confessor to a Christian Governor called Mirza (query—Mirza Zul Qarnin? cf. no. 82) and came to Agra in 1651. He is mentioned by one authority (Fr. A. de Rhodes, "Voyages and Missions" 1854) who met him in Surat on their way from Goa: "The two others were Fr. Anthony Ceski *(sic)* a German, and Fr. Henry Busce, a Fleming, both of them young men already in priest's orders, with aptitudes for learning the languages of the country. The letters I received lately in Rome (1651-2?) tell us of the great fruits which accompany the labours of these . . . fathers." This would be in 1648; and as we shall see later (No. 88) Busce also went to Agra in 1648. It is also mentioned that Fr. Roth composed at Trent an eulogy of "Fr. Anthony Ceski, *(sic)* died 1656, whom he had known in the Missions."]

(References: *Manucci; Hosten.*)

85.—1657—D'SOUZA, F., Padre. *Inscription*:—Aqui iazo Pe Francesco d'Souza, faleceo aos 4 d' Novēbro 1657.

86.—1662—DERVILLE, A., Padre. *Inscription*:—Aqui iazo Pe Alberto Derville faleceo aos 8 d' Abril 1662.

[Padre D'Orville (or Derville) was a Belgian born at Brussels. He went as a missionary to China in 1657 and laboured in Shansi. He was an associate of Fr. Martin Martini, editor of the *Novus Atlas Sinensis*. In 1661 he returned with a certain Father Grueber by way of Lhassa and Tibet. They also preached in Nepal. Thevenot amongst his collection of travels has the "Voyage a la Chine, des P. P. J. Grueber et D'Orville." There is also a letter by Grueber himself in which he thus describes D'Orville's death: "Hinc Battanam (Patna?) Bengalae ad Gangem sitam urbem, et Benares urbem academia Brachmanum celebrem, ac tandem Agram Mogori regiam attulerunt: ubi P. Albertus D'Orville, itinerum fractus laboribus, intra paucos dies, meritorum cumulo plenus, relicta terrestri in coelestem patriam, uti pie credimus, abiit, media Europam inter et Chinam via." This return journey commenced in 1661.]

(References:—*Calendar, Agra Archdiocese, 1907; Thevenot.*)

87.—**1664**—DE MATTOS, P., Padre *Inscription*:—Aqui iazo P. Po. de Mattos faleceo ao 12 de 7bro de 1664.

88.—**1667**—BUSES, H., Padre. *Inscription*:—[Aqui iazo P. Henrique Buses faleceo em Delhy aos] 6 [de April 166]7. Coloniensis Germanus.

Of this inscription only the figures "6" and "7" remain. Busi or Buis was born at Nimeguen in 1613, entered the Society at Mechlin in 1632, taught mathematics at Lisbon for four years and then went to India in 1647. (Mr. Irvine confuses him with a kinsman Hendrik Uwens, following Hazart: but Uwens went to China. The above facts are stated by F. Hosten.)

He was a mathematician and taught the subject in Lisbon, which may partly account for his selection as instructor to Dara. Dara was very fond of him: "he hearkened of late very willingly" to him and began "very well to relish" what he suggested. When about to be executed by Aurangzeb, Dara wished, but was not allowed, to see Buses, and died with the words on his lips "*Muhammad mara mi-kushad, Ibn Ullah mara jan mi-bakshad.*" Buses is described as a man of judgment and learning, hale and hearty, of a fine presence and very polished. He was well known to Bernier and was one of his sources of information. We are told that he once gave expression to the somewhat unchristian opinion that the only way to preach in India was with a well sharpened sword. His death was the result of an extraordinary action on his part. The relapse of a convert made him very ill. His age and feeble condition forbade bleeding him and he himself opened his bowels and removed a part of his colon. It does not sound like Buses and is quite possibly untrue.]

(References: *Manucci; Keene; Calendar, Agra Archdiocese*, 1907; *Hosten.*)

89.—**1668**—ROA, H., Padre. *Inscription*:—Aqui iazo Pe Henrique Roa faleceo aos 20 de Junho de 1668.

Heinrich Roa or Roth (born 1620) was a native of Dillingen (Hosten), Dillingen or Augsburg (Irvine.) He came to the East *via* Smyrna and Ispahan, whence he wrote a letter, dated 1651. He was first sent to Salsette, and thence as rector to the college at Agra. Bernier knew him there, and obtained much information concerning religious and philosophic beliefs of India from him. He is said to have been a Sanskrit scholar and have written a work on Sanskrit grammar—"*Exactissimum opus totius grammaticae Brahmanicae cujus et rudimenta is primus Europae communicavit.*" He also wrote an account of the Christian community at Kabul, which be visited on an overland journey to Europe in 1662 to ask for a new batch of missionaries at Rome. We have already found him pronouncing an eulogy on F. Cesques in 1664. He returned to Agra in that year. Mr. Irvine tells me that Roth's *Relatio* is in the Bibliotheque Nationale at Paris: whilst in the British Museum, in Kircher's "*China Illustrata*," there is a map showing Roth's route from "India" into "Mogor"—*viz* Goa, via "*Visiapoor*," Ratipoor, Delhi, to Agra, and another showing the route of fathers Grueber and Roth from Agra to Europe.]

(References: *Manucci; Hosten.*)

90.—**1682**—JOHANNES, Father. *Inscription*:—Father Johannes, son of Jakob of Linhouse (?) 1682.—(Translation from Armenian.)

91.—**1683**—PETROS, Father. *Inscription*:—Father Petros of Karabagh, 1683.—(Translation from Armenian).

92.—**1685**—DA COSTA, J., Padri. *Inscription* :—[Aqui] iaso Padre [Josep]h DaCosta [da co]mpa de Iesu [morr]eo em Deli [aos 21] Mar[co] de 1685.

93.—**1689**—SANTUCCI, M. A., Padre. *Inscription* :—[Aqui iaz]o Mar[co Antonio S]atucci, [faleceo aos 1 . . . .] de Agosto de 1689.

[Vide note D. above. Nothing else is known of him.]

[94.—**1689**—BALTASAR. Father. *Inscription* :—Baltasar 1689 (Translation from Armenian)].

[The Agra Archdiocesan calendar identifies this father with a Padre Balthazar Loyola, S. J., son of the king of Fez, who was captured by the Maltese, baptized in Sicily and became a Jesuit. It is of course an error. This is the tomb of an Armenian priest ; Father Balthazar Loyola Mendez, S. J., did intend to come to Agra but died in Spain in 1667 on his way thither.]

(Reference : *Hosten*.)

95.—**1702**—DE MAGALHAENS, A., Padre. *Inscription* :—Aqui iazo Pe Anto de Mages que morreo em Dilly aos 17 d' 8bro de 1702.

[F. Hosten thinks that this may possibly be a Fr. Magallens or de Magalhaens. He is said to have been sent for to Kabul by Selim *circa* 1701 ; de Mages would be a contraction for the full name.]

(Reference : *Hosten*.)

96.—**1706**—DE PAIVA, J., Padre. *Inscription* :—Aqui iazo Pe Iozeph de Paiva faleceo em Pexaor aos 7 de Ianro de 1706 e foi sepultado aos 19 de Fevro da mesma hera.

[This inscription is very much corrupted in the Agra calendar : yet it is quite simple : " Here lies father J. De Paiva died in Pexaor on the 7th January 1706 and buried on the 19th February of the same year (mesma, *cf.* French même, or in its old spelling mesme.) Nothing is known of this father. Pexaor may be Peshawar or Buxar.]

[97.—**1706**—MONTEY, M., Padre. *Inscription* :—Aqui Jazo Pe. Manuel Montey, faleceo em Agra aos 25th Octobre de 1706.]

98.—**1710**—LA CONCEYCAO, P., Padre. *Inscription* :—Aqui iazo Pe. Philippe la Conceycao discalco Carmelita faleceo em Dely aos 10 de Octobre de 1710.

[A Carmelite monk.]

99.—**1741**—GABELSPERGER, A., Padre. *Inscription* :—Aqui iaso Pdre Antam Gabelsperger, faleceo em Janegar aos 9 de Marco de 1741.

[Jai Singh, the famous Indian astronomer, who built observatories at Jaipur, Delhi, Benares, Muttra and Ujjain, had been using European assistance as early as 1728. In 1736 he secured the help of two Bavarian Jesuits, Gabelsperger and Strobl (no. 102) who came out at his expense.]

100.—**1742**—DA CRUZ, F., Padre. *Inscription* :—Aqui iaso Pdre Francisco da Cruz faleceo em Delly aos 22 de Mayo de 1742.

101.—**1748**—RODRIQUES, M., Padre. *Inscription* :—P. Mattii Rodriques *obiit* Navare 6to Oct 1748.

102.—**1758**—STROBL, A., Padre. *Inscription* :—[Aqui jazo P. Andre Strobl nascido em Schvandorf no Palatinato Superior, faleceo] aos 30 de Ma de 1758.

[*Cf.* no. 99. Four letters of Strobl's written from Jaipur between 1742 and 1744 are in existence. When Jai Singh died in 1743 the observatory went to ruin, and in 1746 we find Strobl at Delhi, probably in charge of the observatory there. In 1749 he went to Narwar. He was frequently visited by Tieffentaller from Narwar.]

(References : *Hosten* : *Tieffentaller*.)

103.—**1767**—XAVIER, F., Padre. *Inscription:*—Aqui jazo P. F. Xavier faleceo em Toyubad (?) Ano (?) 1767.

104.—[**1776**—HAROOTHIUN, Father. *Inscription:*—Father Haroothiun (Arratoon) 13th July 1776] (translation from Armenian.)

[The name Haroothiun is commonly pronounced Aratoun, Aroutin or Artin. It is equivalent to the English "Paschal."]

I.—*Further note on the Inscriptions in the Padre Santos Chapel.*—I endeavoured to decipher these on three occasions—in March 1909, in March 1910 and July 1910. On the last occasion I had the advantages of three previous readings of varying dates—one by Colonel A. S. Allan (published in the Bengal Catholic Herald of September 1849), one by A. C. (Dr Christison,—published in the Transactions of the Agra Archæological Society of 1876), and a third by Father Felix, O. C. (published in the Archdiocesan Calendar, 1907.) For these I am indebted to the kindness of Fr. Hosten, S. J., St. Xavier's College, Calcutta. The readings given above are my own and except in minor points correspond with those of A. C. (Such minor points are that I read *e.g.* clerigo where he read clerico.) Blanks now illegible I have filled up from these earlier readings.

F. Felix's list was, I understand, compared with an old manuscript in the archives of the mission. The result is many glosses of some commentator, which though of value in themselves should not be and never could have been, in the inscriptions—for the sufficient reason that there is no room for them. Several inscriptions (placed in square brackets) are put in the list on the authority of F. Felix: they have now disappeared altogether, whilst one at all events was never in the place to which his plan assigns it because there is no room—though it may have been somewhere else. This is no. 98; that of the Carmelite monk. All the Armenian inscriptions (save that of Khwaja Mortenepus) were on the walls and are now hidden behind a veil of whitewash from which I hope that some day they will be rescued.

I give below a few notes which may serve to show where I have ventured to diverge from former readings in important points. I do not give small details of spelling.

Da Fonseca (no. 80*)*.—Allan reads "Fonsea," Felix "Foseca", A. C. "Fonseqa." The 6th letter of Fonseca might be anything, but "c" seems most probable.

Santucci (no. 93*)*.—All I can get is—

.... O. MAR.
.... ATUCCI.
.... DE.
1689.

Allan read the last line de Agosto de 1689; A. C. notes that it is illegible. The proposed restoration in the note on the tomb is from Felix, omitting the gloss "*Italus.*" He gives the date variously as "1" and "10".

Strobl (no. 101).—All I could read was—

....
.... AOS 30 DE.
.... MA DE 1758.

A. C. records it as illegible, Allan read it as "Aqui iazo P. Andre Strobl faleceo aos 30 de Marco 1758. "MA DE" is very much effaced and might be "Marco." Felix reads (with two glosses) "Aqui iazo P. Andre [*aliter* "Padre"] Strobl [nascedo (*aliter* "nacido") em Schvandorf (*aliter* Schrandor) no Palatinato (*aliter* "Calatinato") Superior faleceo em Agra aos 30 de Marco de 1758".

Xavier (no. 103).—The place of death is in italics and very difficult to read. It looks more like "Toyubad" than anything else. Allan omits it, A. C. reads it "Toyebed." Felix "Foyabad."

Derville (no. 86).—Allan and A. C. read Derville as I do. But the name was really Dorville or D'orville, which Felix reads.

Buses (no. 88).—Allan read "Aqui iazo Pe .... ueeo faleceo aos 6 d'Abril de 1667" A. C. calls the inscription illegible. F. Hosten conjectures, from Allan, "Pe Henrique Buseo", Felix reads (with two glosses) "Aqui iazo P. Henrique Buses faleceo [em Delly] aos 6 de Abril 1667 [coloniensis Germensis]." I have adopted F. Hosten's reading; all that is now left is the 6 and the 7.

Da Costa (*no.* 92).—Allan read "Aqui iazo Padre Joseph da Costa da Compa de Jesu, Morto em Deli aos 21 de Marco de 1685."

A. C. read "—ui iaso Padre .... fh da Costa .... mpa de Iesu ...... reo em Deli .... 21 de Mar .... de 1685."

Felix reads as Allan, with the exception "faleceo em Delly" for "morto em Deli."

Putting all these together, I think there can be no doubt that the true reading is "(Aqui) iaso Padre (Josep)h da Costa (da co)mpa. de Jesu (morr)eo em Deli (aos 21) de Mar(co) de 1685."

22. *De Paiva* (*no.* 96).—A mess has been made of this inscription though it is absolutely clear.

Allan's reading was right save that he made "Pexaop" instead of "Pexaor."

A. C. read as Allan, down to "1706"; when he goes on "Efoise Puefado aos 10 de Fevro da mesma hera." He, Father Symphorien, and Führer following them, both make a fresh person of "Efoise Puefado" or "Puefada"; an error even F. Felix follows. The inscription means merely 'F. Joseph da Costa died in Pexaor on 7th January 1706, *and was buried* on 10th February *of the same year*." F. Felix inserts a gloss after "Fevro" which betrays the hand of the scholiast, and shows that this view is correct. It reads "mores a anno dé 1706" (mores=moreo or morreo)—"died in the year 1706."

De Magalhaes (*no.* 95).—De Mages is on F. Hosten's authority an abbreviation for "De Magalhaes;" "que morreo" is simply "who died." A. C. gets the inscription correctly, but Allan turns the name into De Magesque and Felix into "de Magathenesque;" or into "De Magathenes," in another place.

Besides these readings there are lists of the names, only more or less correct and complete, given by Felix (1906), Symphorien (Agra Arch. Soc. Trans.) and Fanthome.

II.—*The alleged firman of Akbar* (*page* 34).—Father Hosten's kindness has put at my disposal the following extract from an unpublished letter of Da Castro's dated 1637 to the General of the Society at Rome. After detailing how the Jesuits had been expelled from their college and church he says "on the day of the Immaculate Conception (8 December 1636 (?)) I, having made many requests through the King's father-in-law (Asaf Khan), our ancient friend and the ancient protector of all the Christians, we were on the above-said day granted by the King not only the favour of returning to our college but also the permission of asking whatever requests we might make, to wit, leave to administer freely the Sacraments, to bury our dead after our own manner in the cemetery given us by his father and confirmed to us by him." He also mentions the destruction of the Churches at Lahore and Agra.

This seems to point to a necessary reconstruction of the history of this cemetery.

It dates back certainly to 1611, the year in which Mortenepus died; but it is improbable that it is much older. The firman alleged to be Akbar's states that one Padre Joseph was to possess certain lands he had bought, free of rent, and to use it for a cemetery. It cannot be Akbar's as it is dated 1035 A. H. or 1624 A. D., in Jahangir's reign. Yet we know Jesuits owned the cemetery as early as 1614 for they buried Mildenhall there in that year. Doubtless the land was bought between 1605 and 1611 by Padre Joseph, and made rent free by Jahangir in 1624, which explains both gift and confirmation mentioned in the letter quoted. That Padre Joseph is Da Castro is almost certain, for no other "Joseph" was in Upper India in the first decade of the 17th century.

CEMETERY PROPER.

105.—**1614**—DE MENDENAL, J. (MILDENHALL, J.) *Inscription*:—Joa de Mendenal, Ingles, morreo aos 1(...) de Junho de 1614.

[It is known that John Mildenhall (*aliter* Midnall) died in Ajmer 1614. It is further known that he was a Roman Catholic, and that he was buried in Agra. There is no other Englishman of a name which could possibly become "de Mendenal" in a Portuguese inscription who is known to have been in India at the time. Furthermore, there was at the time no other place of sepulchre in Agra save this cemetery. It seems therefore certain that this tomb is the resting place of John Mildenhall: this is the opinion of Mr. Foster, of the India office, a well-known authority on this period. The tomb therefore is an important and interesting tomb, as it is the oldest English tomb in the province, or in all probability in India.

John Midnall (to spell his name in the way Mr. Foster considers most probably correct) has no small fame of his own: but he has, in addition, gained an entirely spurious fame as Queen Elizabeth's "ambassador" to the Great Moghul. The story has passed unquestioned through the pages of various historians, till it culminated in a certain well-known London periodical, which not only dubbed him "ambassador," but gave him a knighthood, and published a fancy picture of "Sir John Mildenhall" being received, with a large suite, by the Emperor (who, as an article in the "Gentleman's Magazine" points out, is represented some twenty years too old and several shades too dark.) As a matter of fact, Midnall was an ordinary, in some respects a very ordinary, London merchant: the famous "letter" sent by Elizabeth through him, was nothing more nor less than a "letter commendatory," such as any traveller could obtain, a mere passport, such as at a later date are mentioned as sent out by the company in batches to their servants, with blanks for the names. It is true that Midnall chose to represent himself as an ambassador, and to play the game for all it was worth: but that was merely the man's characteristic impudence.

Our knowledge of Midnall is derived chiefly from two letters of his own which are printed in "Purchas's Pilgrimes," and scattered references in Purchas' works and the letters of the servants of the East Indian Company. Of his early years we know little. On the 12th February 1599, he started on his famous voyage to the East Indies. He arrived in Constantinople in October and stayed "about his merchandize" till May 1600. This long stay is an incidental proof that he was no ambassador, or he would have gone direct to Agra. Thence he travelled via Aleppo, Julfa, Tabriz, Kazvin, through Yezd and Seistan to Kandahar, and finally reached Lahore in 1603. He requested permission from Akbar to present himself at court and "treat of such business as I have to do with him, from my Prince." Admitted to Akbar's presence, he demanded, in Elizabeth's name, permission to trade, and also to attack the ships and settlements of the Portuguese, as being enemies of England, and to keep them if taken. Akbar consulted the Jesuit fathers present at the time, one of whom was probably Jerome Xavier. They naturally opposed him, and told Akbar the English were thieves and Midnall a spy, who meditated designs on the Emperor's ports. The Jesuits were in high repute, and Midnall's requests were politely ignored, but in the end he obtained, or at all events says he obtained, "*farmans*" for all his demands save that of permission to attack the Portuguese. Playing his part of ambassador to the last, he insisted even on this, and at last was given the perfectly useless concession; and so he returned home, to try and sell his concessions and his own services to the East India Company for "£1,500 in hand." They refused to buy: and in 1609 he petitioned James I for permission to use his privileges and trade on his own account. The company, dismayed by this action, had thoughts for a while of employing him, but ultimately decided not to do so.

Midnall disappears till 1614, and we then find him on a second and much more discreditable voyage to the East, which commenced, it would seem, in 1611. He absconded to Persia with goods which had been entrusted to him to sell in the Levant. Two English merchants, Newman and Steel, pursued him and compelled him to restore the value of the goods; then he and Steel came on to India, and Midnall fell ill at Lahore. Purchas hints that he had intended to poison three fellow-adventurers so as to obtain possession of the whole of their joint property and drank of the poison himself by mistake, but the story has no confirmation. There were many natural ways of death available to one who had ventured across Persia to India thrice. He got as far as Ajmer and there died; he was, as a Papist, buried in Agra by the Jesuits. He left his property to two natural children of his in Persia, and made a Frenchman, Augustine by name, (whom Mr. Foster is inclined to identify with the famous Austin of Bordeaux) their executor. Kerridge attempted to get possession of his property on behalf of the company, and ultimately succeeded in obtaining £500 which he sent home, in spite of the opposition of the results. It is from Kerridge that we obtain definite confirmation of the fact that Midnall was buried in Agra. He writes (Factory Records, Surat volume 84, part I, page 131) that out of his estate rupees 250 were given to servants and for the "carrying of Midnall's corpse and interring at Agra."

Midnall was not an estimable character : but, with the exception of the three refugees from Goa (Needes, Fitch and Newbery), he was the first Englishman who visited Agra and spoke face to face with Akbar. It is the intention of Government to put a tablet with an English inscription on his tomb.]

(References : *Purchas ; Foster, Letters ; gentlemen's Mag. 1906 ; J. R. A. S. 1910.*)

106.—1614—DE GENEVA, G. *Inscription :*—Gulhelhme de Geneva, morreo aos 30 de Maio 1614.

[This means clearly no more than "William of Geneva." Very possibly a servant.]

107.—1619—ALEMAN, J. *Inscription :*—Joa Aleman, morreo 1619.

[This too may mean simply "John the German. Father Hosten has shown me a letter of Father Not , S. J., to him which states that Zu'l Qarnin's wife was an "Allemana"—"*femina illustrissima,*" who bore him three sons. He says she must have been the daughter of this Aleman. I do not know the authority for F. Noti's statement ; but might not "an Allemana" mean simply "a German lady ?" She might still be this Aleman's daughter, or other relation, of course.]

108.—1624 ? 1654 ?—BORGES, F. *Inscription :*—Francisca Borges morreo aos 16 de Marco de 1624 (1654 ?)

[*Cf.* note on No. 114.]

109.—1628—MAFEI, B. *Inscription :*—Aqui giaze ilgon dam Bernardino...Mafei......Veneziano......Sirurgioo d'l grã Rei Mogol qual......da la corte foi multo......estimado por sua cure fate morreo aos 11 d'Agosto no anno 1628.

110.—1640—VERONEO, F. *Inscription :*—Aqui jaz Ieronimo (or Jeronimo) Veroneo faleceo em Lahor 2 d'Agosto de 1640.

[Considering that the tomb of this famous old worthy is close to Hessing's tomb right in the pathway of people going to the Padre Santos chapel, and that archaeologists have been at work on that chapel off and on ever since 1875, it is more than a little surprising that, so far as I can discover, no previous mention of the grave has been made. It is possible that such an announcement lurks in the back numbers of some learned society's journal ; but certainly it does not appear to be generally known. Mr. Havell, for instance, in his criticism of the Taj and its designers in the June number of the "Nineteenth century" for 1903, makes no mention of it. (I have since learnt that this tomb was first discovered in 1905 by Mr. F. O. Oertel and Mr. A. G. P. Pullan, C.S.)

There is little that is known about Veroneo, though he has acquired a possibly spurious fame as the Taj's designer. I summarize below what is known of him. There is first, Manrique's famous statement, a bone of contention among antiquarians, that connects him with that famous building. "El architecto destas fabricas," he writes, "fue un Veneciano por nombre Geronimo Veroneo que passo a aquellas partes en las naves de Portugal y murio en la ciudad de Laor poco tiemps antes de ma llegada." "(The architect [or designer] of these buildings [i. e., the Taj] was a Venetian, by name Geronimo Veroneo, who came to these parts in the Portuguese ships and died in the city of Lahore a short time before my arrival.") Manrique reached Agra on December 14-24, 1640. In 1637 we find him reporting Drake's death (no. 191) to the Surat factors ; he is there described as a Venetian jeweller and Manucci states that some of the Portuguese captured at Hugli (1632) were released "through the money paid by a Venetian my compatriot, called Hieronomo Veroneo, a man ransomed by the Portuguese." (What the last few words mean is very dubious.) And save the other details given by Manrique about his connection with the Taj—how the Padshah told him to build a grandiose monument to his dead consort, and how he produced various designs which were rejected as costing too little, and he was told to spend three krores—this is absolutely all that is known of him though we also know that the ubiquitous Father Da Castro was his executor, and told this story to Manrique (*cf.* no. 83). This is not the place to discuss the much debated question of the origin of the Taj. The curious can see the one side presented by Havell in the "19th Century" of June 1903, and the other by F. Hosten in J. A. S. B. Vol. VI, 1910.

Veroneo, in one way, is in a similar case to Mildenhall. Both have won fame for actions which it is dubious whether they ever really did. But the old English rascal was himself the cause of his ill founded celebrity, the worthy Venetian owes it to a writer whom he never even saw. On one point, I may however venture on a protest. Mr. Havell says, "He (Veroneo) returned to Lahore and poured the garbled account of his doings (with Shah Jahan) into the too credulous ears of Father Da Castro, who retailed it as history to his fellow priest." I venture to suggest that this statement is a trifle hard on Veroneo and Da Castro. Between 1631 (when the Taj was apparently commenced), and 1641 when Manrique came to Lahore, Da Castro would certainly have found out that Veroneo had nothing to do with the Taj, if indeed this was so. It would have been a futile and ineffective lie of Veroneo's which could not escape being found out. And a very strong point in favour of Veroneo's having designed the Taj is that the ultimate authority for the statement is Da Castro—one of the noblest missionaries even the Jesuits have ever produced. He was not the man to back a lie, which would have in any case no point save being "*ad majorem gloriam*" of Europeans; for Manrique came through Agra and must have known the truth himself.

(References: *Havell: Manucci; Foster, Factories; Hosten, Taj; Gazetteer.*)

111.—**1640**—FABANO, Z. *Inscription*:—I. H. S. Zeri Fabano morrie aos 25 de Septembre ano 1640.

112.—**1645**—OHANJAN. *Inscription*:—Ohanjan, son of Polos of Ispahan 1645. (Translation from Armenian.)

[Ohan pronounced Wohan or Yohan, is vulgar for Yohannes. Polos or Poghos is equivalent to Paulos.]

113.—**1672**—CORDEIRO, J. *Inscription*:—Aqui jazo Jeronimo Cordeiro faleceo aos 27 Dec......1672.

114.—**1377**—BRONZONI, H. *Inscription*:—Aqui esta sepultado Hortenzio Bronzoni Veneciano faleceo aos 11 de Agosto do anno 1677.

[Hortenzio Bronzoni, a Venetian lapidary, is first mentioned as sent to cut a large diamond presented by Mir Jumlah to Shah Jahan, which stone is held by Ball to be the Koh-i-nur. Tavernier calls him Hortensio Borgio, and in telling this story adds that he cut the stone very badly. He is again mentioned as making a model ship of war for Aurangzeb who had been annoyed by the depredations of some Portuguese pirates, and was anxious to create a navy. It was set afloat in a tank and manoeuvred by some European artillerymen; and the sight convinced the Emperor that a navy was beyond his powers. Bronzoni's wife was a Hindu (or negro) slave, doubtless a convert, named Suzana Borges. She was a widow, with a son Nicolao Borges, who married the daughter of one Francisco da Souza. Manucci tells a curious story of her use of magic to discover how long this girl had to live. It is possible that Francisca Borges (no. 108) is this girl, or a relative. The date of no. 108 is uncertain; I made 1624 of it, but another officer read it 1654. The latter date would agree with this supposition. Manucci does not actually say so, but it is not probable that the girl lived particularly long in the circumstances.]

(References: *Manucci; Tavernier.*)

115.—**1379**—TAVARES, M. *Inscription*:—Aqui jaz Monica Tavares faleceo aos 20 de Janeiro 1679.

116.—**1702**—MAROUTH. *Inscription*:—Marouth, son of Hopsep, and grandson of Martin of Ispahan, 41 years of age, 1702. (Translation from Armenian.)

[Hopsep is the same as Yoseph; initial Y is often pronounced as H.]

117.—**1707**—BORGES, F. *Inscription*:—Aqui jazo Francisco Borges faleceo em Ambala, e foi sepultado aos 12 de Maio de 1707.

118.—**1723**—MEKERTICH. *Inscription :*—Mekertich, bearing the title of Shah Mirza Khan, son of Shah Nazir, died at Gwalior, buried here 1723, December 25th (Translation from Armenian.)

[Mekertich means Baptist.]

119.—**1728**—SIMEON, Captain. *Inscription :*—Captain Sahib Simeon, of Hamadan, died at Gwalior; buried here 1728, May 27th (Translation from Armenian.)

[Simeon is some times spelt "Sh'mawon."]

120.—**1771**—MADEC, M. *Inscription :*—I. H. S. Ici repose le corps de Marye fille de René Madec dcédé (*sic*) a Bartepour le 21 de Mai 1771.

[René Madec had a most adventurous career. Born at the old Brittany town of Quimper in 1736, he started life as a sailor. In 1748 he became a soldier in the service of the French E. I. Co., but deserted. He was taken prisoner by the British, and served in their army, but deserted from that too and raised a body of troops, both French and sepoys; and from 1765 to 1777 he lived as "a guerilla leader,"—which in the circumstances could only have been a polite term for a highway robber. He served also under various princes, but always under the French flag: amongst these were the Nawab of Oudh, Shuja-ud-daula, till his defeat at Buxar: and then the Jats. He left their service in 1772 and it was doubtless during his service with them that this child of his died. In 1772 he joined the Moghul Emperor, and after many valuable services was made a Nawab. After his defeat by the Jats and Marathas he went back to Pondicherry and helped his countrymen against the English. In 1778 he returned to France where he died in 1784. He is confused both by Compton and Malleson with Madoc or Medoc, another adventurer of a much lower type.]

(References: *Compton* ; *Buckland.*)

121.—**1775**—DUXAMEL, J. *Inscription :*—Jean Duxamel fils de ......Duxamel...... 1775.

122.—**1776**—BRUGEON, F. *Inscription :*—D. O. M. Ci gît François Brugeon fils de Louis Brugeon et de Johanna Martin décédé à Agra le 11 Mai MDCCLXXVI.

(D. O. M.=Deo optimo maximo.)

123.—**1776**—MONTMIREL, R. M. *Inscription :*—Ici repose le corps de René Murgé Montmirel décédé le 4 Juin l'an 1776, âgé de 4 mois 13 jours.

124.—**1776**—ZAPRABEG. *Inscription :*—Zaprabeg, son of Gorgin Khan of Tiflis, 1776, September, 8th (Translation from Armenian.)

[The name is most probably Sarfaraz Beg. The most famous Gorgin Khan, is Gregory, Mir Kasim's general; but he was of Ispahan. There was another Gorgin Khan, the renegade Governor of Kandahar, assassinated in 1702.]

(Reference: *Manucci.*)

125.—**1777**—BRUGEON, P. *Inscription :* D. O. M. Ci gît Pierre Brugeon natif de Barpour, décédé à Gohud le XVME Mars MDCC-LXXVII, âgé de V ans et demi.

126.—**1777**—MARIAM KHANUM. *Inscription :*—Mariam Khanum, daughter of Lazarus 1777, January 18th. (Translation from Armenian.)

127.—**1778**—BORGESCANA, J. *Inscription :*—Aqui jazo Dom Joseph Borgescana.........1778.

128.—**1778**—REINHARDT, W. (General Sombre). *Inscription :*—Aqui jazo Walter Reinhard morreo aos 4 de Mayo no anno de 1778. (With an only partially legible Persian inscription which contains a chronogram of the date of death, and which is, according to most authorities, wrong.)

[" So much only is certain, that he was a German." So says Father Noti in his book "*Das Furstentum Sardhana.*" The generally accepted version of Walter Reinhardt's parentage is that he was "a sort of German," as Keene puts it, the son of a Saltsburg or Strasburg butcher. Polier (quoted by Noti from the *Asiatic Annual Register* of 1800), who knew Reinhardt, says he was a carpenter born in Strasburg and that his name was Balthasar. Others (Colonel Skinner for instance) say he was born in 1720 in Luxembourg. The Calendar and Directory of the Agra Archdiocese has two other, in some respects, contradictory accounts. From the burial register that is, or used to be, in the archives, it appears, on the strength of a birth certificate, that his name was Joseph Joachim Reinhardt, born at Piel in Tyrol on the 19th March 1732. And in the same archives, there used to be a curious old MS., undated and unsigned, which stated that his name was Joannes Reiner, born at La Rochelle in Luxembourg in August 1707, the eldest son of Martin Buzerin Reiner and his wife Catherine Rosport, who were immigrants from Tyrol. I understand from Mr. Irvine that Father Noti is now of opinion that Reinhardt's father came from Tyrol to Luxembourg, that the name was originally Reiner, and that descendants of his relations still live in a village near La Rochelle or Fels, and that one of them is constantly hoping to receive millions from the Indian Government. This MS. looks like very interesting confirmation of Father Noti's view. None the less, in itself, it is so full of extraordinary statements, some improbable, some practically impossible, that it can hardly be held to prove it. It asserts for instance that Reinhardt went to India in 1744; that a nephew of his (born in 1752) came out to him in 1772, could not find him, and was never heard of again till 1857, when the family of General Sombre found him by advertisement. He was then in flourishing circumstances. Lastly, in May 1840, Dyce Sombre is said to have been hunting for his ancestor's relatives in Treves. Now in 1772 Sombre's name was a byeword in India, and it is indeed curious that his nephew could not find him. In 1857 this man was 105; he had been lost for 85 years: and he suddenly emerges from the mists, a centenarian in flourishing circumstances—"enjoying success", as the MS. puts it, at an age when he might have been expected to be past enjoying anything. Further, in 1857 General Sombre's family consisted of two ladies, Baroness Solaroli and Mrs. Troup, both of whom appear to have been in Europe, and who had probably never heard of their long-lost relative. As for Dyce Sombre, he was undoubtedly in Brussels in October 1840 but on his wedding tour (he was married in the previous September). But this only makes it the more unlikely that he was in Treves in the preceding May. This MS. may be of value, taken with other evidence, to assist in the proof of Reinhardt's Tyrolese origin: but by itself, it looks only like a rather crude attempt to trace a connection with the extremely wealthy Sombre family.

To pass on to less disputed facts, Reinhardt came out to India in the French service, either as a sailor, or as a soldier in a French regiment. The date of this is uncertain, it may have been as early as 1746, or as late as 1750. Whether he was or was not a soldier in the first place, he soon became one—probably under Labourdonnais and Dupleix. Subsequently he deserted to the British, and became a soldier in a corps of Swiss mercenaries in the employ of the Company. The date of this is also uncertain: but it may well have been, as Keene says, after the defeat of the French, which led up to the peace of 1754. He served with them for a time—probably not a long time, though different tales put it as low as 18 days (Compton) and as high as 2 years (Keene). He then deserted to Law at Chandarnagore, rose to be a sergeant, and in 1757 when Chandarnagore was taken wandered about Bengal, taking service first with Suraj-ud-daula, then with a rebel *faujdar* at Purnea, and lastly with Kasim Ali Khan's Armenian General, Gregory. Here he rose to command a battalion. In 1763 he stamped his name with infamy by the murder of the British residents of Patna whom Kasim Ali had taken prisoner. When the British advanced he fled to the Nawab Wazir of Oudh, Shuja-ud-daula. He was given a strong force—4 battalions of infantry one of cavalry and a force of artillery. After the battle of Buxar, his surrender was demanded by the British as a condition of peace. The Nawab replied that arresting a general at the head of his troops was easier said than done; but he offered to assassinate him in the presence of duly accredited representatives! The offer was declined and Reinhardt clinched the matter by robbing the Nawabs' Begams, and his late master, Kasim Ali, and marching to Rohilkhand. There he took service with Hafiz Rahmat Khan, and later with the Jat Raja of Bharatpur. Him he deserted in 1775, when Mirza Najaf Khan, Wazir of Shah Alam, defeated him in battle, and passed over to the victor, who gave him a rich estate round Sardhana, and Rs. 65,000 per mensem for his services. This estate he retained till his death in 1778.

Many hard things have been written of Sombre. He was illiterate, cruel, avaricious and unscrupulous: he had little personal courage and no military skill. He had some low cunning: almost his only virtue was that he despised ostentation. His troops, seldom paid, were generally in a state of mutiny, and adopted, if the stories told are true, somewhat high handed measures to obtain their money, *e.g.*, sitting Reinhardt astride a gun that was burning hot in the sun. His officers were the dregs of European society. His troops never lost a gun, or gained one: but were "remarkable for judicious retreats." It is not certain how he got the name of "Sombre." One statement is that it was due to his complexion; another that he enlisted in the British service as "Summers" or "Somers" or "Sommer" which was first softened by Indian tongues into "Samru" and then dignified into Sombre. Whatever its origin, no nickname was ever more happily given.

He married a Muhammadan woman, name apparently unknown, by whom he had a son Louis, or Aloysius, Balthazar Reynaud or Reinhardt (vide no. 41). At Sardhana he married the famous Begam Samru (vide no. 46).

(References: *Buckland; Compton; Calcutta Review*, 1880; *Calendar, Agra Archdiocese*, 1907; *Dyce Sombre Depositions; Noti, Sardhana.*)

129.—**1779**—ABINA KHANUM. *Inscription:*—Abina Khanum, daughter of Daud Khan, of Arghood, 1779, September 6th. (Translation from Armenian.)

[Abina, query Amina? Arghoud, says Mr. Ellis, suggests the well known Armenian family "Arghoutinski"].

130.—**1779**—JEBRIL. *Inscription:*—Jebril, son of Moses, of Tiflis 1779 January 12th. (Translation from Armenian.)

[Jebril is an Arabicized form of Gabriel.]

131.—**1783**—SIMEON KHAN, Commander. *Inscription:*—Commander Simeon Khan, son of Harootbiun, killed in battle, buried here from Salian, 1783, January 31st. (Translation from Armenian.)

132.—**1786**—LAZARUS. *Inscription:*—Lazarus, son of Harootbiun of Ghors, village Dilanukh, entitled here Hakh Verdi Khan, 1786, September 22nd. (Translation from Armenian.)

133.—**1789**—THOMAS. *Inscription:*—Thomas, son of Khoja Malli of Ispahan. I was a servant of the Council of Chinsurah, 1789, January 22nd. (Translation from Armenian.)

134.—**1790**—FERNANDEZ, L. *Inscription:*—Ca giaz Luzia Fernandez morreo aos 7 de Novembro 1790.

135.—**1792**—FREDERIC, P. *Inscription:*—Ici repose le corps de Paulo Frederic, tué au siége de Kama, le 3 Octobre 1792. *Memento mori.*

[This tomb is inside the mausoleum of Reinhardt, no. 128. Who he was does not appear, nor when Kama was besieged.]

136.—**1793**—PERRON, four children. *Inscription:*—Here lies interred the 4 children of Genrl Perron, commanding 3 brigds in the service of Maharaja of Sindiah, A.D. 1793.

(Same inscription in French, Urdu and Hindi. Curiously, the grammatical mistake "here *lies*" reappears in the French "Ici *reste* les corps.")

[General Perron, born Pierre Cuillier (1755-1834) was a famous military adventurer. He went out to India in 1780, deserted—the preliminary step of most French adventurers,—and entered the service of the Rana of Gohud about 1781. In 1790 he joined De Boigne. He fought at Patan and Merta, won the battle of Kurdla against the Nizam and lost a hand at the siege of Kanaund. In 1796 he succeeded De Boigne and subdued Rajputana and George Thomas. He was looked on, rightly or wrongly, as an instigator of Bonaparte's designs on India, and the war of 1803 was as much directed to crushing his very great military power as to crushing Sindhia. After the capture of Aligarh, he was superseded and surrendered to Lake. He retired to France in 1805. Perron's first wife was a Mlle. Derridon, and these are probably her children though it is quite as likely that they were the offspring of a less reputable union. When he returned to Europe he had two children by an Indian mother with him, who spoke no French. One of them, a girl, married M. Alfred de Montesquiou. Perron settled down near Vendome and married a Mlle. du Trochet, by whom he had a large family. For the Derridons see no. 250.]

(References : *Compton ; Buckland : Thorn ; Wellesley's Despatches.*)

137.—**1793**—BORGION, L. *Inscription* :—Ca giaz o corpo de Luiz Borgion morreo . . . aos 12 de Gigulis de 1793.

[Probably the Louis Borgion of no. 122. It can be no relation of the adventurer Louis Bourquien as he did not come to Upper India till 1794.]

138.—**1796**—ANNA KHANUM. *Inscrption* :—Anna Khanum, wife of Mikhayel of Ispahan 1796, March 10th. (Translation from Armenian.)

139.—**1800**—LANGRENEC, E., Captain. *Inscription* :—Ici repose le corps de M. le Captne E. Langrenci (Langrenec ?) décédé le 28th December 1800, âgé de............ans.........

140.—**1801**—DORIDON, E. *Inscription* :—Ca giaz o corpo de Esperanza Doridon morreo aos 7 de Maio 1801.

[This tomb is next to the tomb of Perron's children, no. 136 above. His first wife was a Melld. Derridon and there may be something in this juxtaposition.]

141.—**1801**—HRIPHSIME. *Inscription* :—Hriphsime, wife of Gorgeen Beg of Viratze 1801, August 8th. (Translation from Armenian.)

142.—**1802**—MAROUTHA YOSEPH. *Inscription* :—Here lies the body of Maroutha Yoseph who died 3 Janry. 1802, aged 43 years.

143.—**1803**—MCKENZIE, R. Captain. *Inscription* :—Robert McKenzie, Capt. Lieutt. in Scindiah's army, died 25th December 1803, aged 24 years.

[Lieutenant McKenzie was an officer commanding a battalion in Perron's third brigade under Bourquien. He took part in the campaign against Thomas and behaved with gallantry at the final assult on Hansi, where he was wounded.]

144.—**1803**—AIVYBEG KHAN. *Inscription* :—Aivybeg Khan, commandant of Shaighol, aged 32 years, 1803, September 11th. (Translation from Armenian.)

145.—**1803**—HESSING, J. W. Colonel.—*Inscription* :—John William Hessing, late a Colonel in the service of Maharaja Daulat Rao Sindhia, who, after sustaining a lingering and very painful illness for many years with true Christian fortitude and resignation, departed this life, 21st July 1803, aged 63 years, 11th months, and 5 days. As tribute of their affection and regard this monument is erected to his beloved memory by his disconsolate widow, Anne Hessing, and afflicted sons and daughters, George William Hessing, Thomas William Hessing and Magdalene Sutherland. He was a native of Utrecht in Holland and came out to Ceylon in the

Military service of the Dutch E. I. Company in the year 1752, and was present at the taking of Candia by their troops. Five years afterwards he returned to Holland and came out again to India in the year 1733, and served under the Nizam of the Deccan. In the year 1784, he entered into the service of Madho Rao Sindhia and was engaged in the several battles that led to the aggrandizement of that Chief and wherein he signalized himself so by his bravery as to gain the esteem and approbation of his employer, more particularly at the battle of Bhondagaon near Agra in the year 1787, which took place between this Chief and Nawab Ismael Beg, when he then became a Captain, and was severely wounded. On the death of Madho Rao Sindhia in 1793, he continued under his successor, Daulat Rao Sindhia, and in 1798 he attained to the rank of Colonel and immediately after to the command of the Fort and City of Agra, which he held to his death.

[There is little to be added to the history given in the epitaph. He was born in 1740. There is no record of his adventures between 1763 and 1784. He served in De Boigne's brigades of regular troops. The "several battles" are Lalsot, Chaksana and Patan. After Patan, he quarrelled with De Boigne and left him but Madhoji Scindia employed him to raise a bodyguard for him, which grew to 4 battalions. In 1800 he was compelled to resign his command by ill-health and retired as commandant of Agra to that city. He is described as a "good, benevolent man and a brave soldier." His tomb is a miniature of the Taj in red Agra sandstone.]

(References: *Thorn; Compton; Buckland.*)

146.—**1804**—ARMSTRONG, ANNE. *Inscription*:—Anne Armstrong died 20th of January 1804, aged 3 years 4 months.

[Possibly the child of a Major Armstrong, in command of Holkar's 2nd Brigade in 1802. He left him when war broke out with the English, but had great difficulty in escaping; he obtained a pension of Rs. 1,200 per mensem from the British Government.]

(Reference: *Compton.*)

147.—**1804**—DERRIDON, THOMAS. *Inscription*:—Here lies the body of Thomas Derridon, son of Major L. Derridon, who died 29th January 1804, *et.* 10m. 15d.

[For Derridons *v.* no. 250. Major L. Derridon is the original Derridon, the adventurer.]

148.—**1805**—YAKOB. *Inscription*:—Yakob, son of Khoja Mourat 1805 (Translation from Armenian.)

149.—**1805**—STEPHANNOS. *Inscription*:—Stephannos, son of Petros of Illavan 1805. (Translation from Armenian.)

[Illavan possibly=Erivan.]

150.—**1808**—KHOJA MOURAT. *Inscription*:—Khoja Mourat, who died in 1808. (Translation from Armenian.)

151.—**1809**—DERRIDON, ANN. *Inscription*:—Sacred to the memory of Miss Ann Derridon, daughter of Major Lewis Derridon, died 28th July 1809 aged 9 months 9 days, 7th ch.

[7th ch.=7th child. *Cf.* no. 250.]

152.—**1809**—KIRAKOS. *Inscription*:—Kirakos, son of Haroothiun, entitled Nourouz Beg, of Ghors in village Dilanukh 1809, September 22nd. (Translation from Armenian).

[Kirakos=Cyriacus.]

153.—**1812**—BURGOIN, J. B. *Inscription* :—Here lies the body of John Baptist Burgoin who departed this life on the 17th of May 1812, aged 60 years.

[There is also a Persian inscription.]

154.—**1813**—DERRIDON, MARY A. *Inscription* :—Sacred to the memory of Miss Mary Ann Derridon, daughter of Major L. Derridon, died 17th October 1813, aged 4 days, 11th chd.

[11th ch.=11th child ; *cf.* no. 250.]

155. —**1817**—DERRIDON, JOHN. *Inscription* :—Sacred to the memory of Master John Derridon, son of Major L. Derridon, died 17th July 1817, aged 1 year 6 months.

[*cf.* no. 250.]

156.—**1817**—BURGOIN, E. *Inscription* :—Sacred to the memory of Enaetmussy Burgoin who departed this life on 23rd November in the year of our Lord 1817, aged 65 years.

[Enaetmussy, i. e., Inayat Masih. There is a Persian inscription also.]

157.—**1818**—PEDRON, C., Mrs. **1834**.—PEDRON, L.—*Inscription* :—In memory of Lewis Pedron, 9th and youngest son of the late Colonel Pedron of Scindia's service who died 16th February 1834, aged 27 years. This tomb was erected by his sister Mrs. M. A. Ross as the last tribute of her affectionate regard. In the next tomb at the foot of this is interred his mother, Catherine, who died 14th August 1818, aged 33 years.

[Colonel Pedron was a native of Hennebon near L'Orient. He served first under Law but left him for the Nawab Wazir of Oudh's service, and subsequently for that of the Raja of Berar. He is not heard of again till 1790 when he entered De Boigne's first brigade as Lieutenant. In 1795 he commanded the 3rd brigade, in 1800 he raised the 4th brigade. After fighting against Thomas, he returned to Aligarh and was there when the British took it in 1803 (no. 64.) This is the last record we have of him, but it would appear from this tomb that he remained in India and was alive as late as 1807 at all events.]

158.—**1821**—THAGOUHI KHANUM. *Inscription* :—Thagouhi Khanum, wife of Mekertich, daughter of Shah Mirza, 62 years of age, 1821, July 1st. (Translation from Armenian.)

[Thagouhi=Queen.]

159.—**1826**—PARSICK, P. *Inscription* :—Petruse Parsick, died 2nd April 1826, aged 43 years.

[Petruse Parsick, more properly Petros Barsegh.]

160.—**1826**—DE SILVA J., DON. *Inscription* :—

دون جزے ڈیسلوا پرتکزدر سنه ۱۸۲۶ع یک هزار و هشت صد و بست
شش عیسوي تاریخ ——— ماه نومبر وفات یافت *

[The De Silva family, as I am informed by Mr. J. F. Fanthome, who knew many of the later members of it personally, are of good Portuguese descent, as the use of the prefix "Don" in this inscription testifies. Their ancestor, also a Don José, came up country from Goa at an early date and settled down in Jaipur. This Don José was, like many of his descendants, a physician. He had two sons of whom one stayed at Jaipur: the younger Don Ellis or Ellice (no. 160) settled down as a physician in Bhartpur. Of his three sons two migrated to Bhopal: one succeeded to his father's practice at Bhartpur, Augustin (no. 166). His only son was Joseph Augustin (no. 173), a man of a very strong personality, and a doctor of considerable merit, charitable to a fault in the exercise of his profession; a ripe Persian scholar, and the author of a monumental work (as yet, I believe, unpublished) in which he compares the Misrani or Vaid,

Greek or Yunani, and European methods of medicine. He died childless: and so ends a most interesting link between West and East—one of the many that exist, all but unknown, in such old world places as Agra, where from early days Anglo-Indians most did congregate.]

(Reference: *Communicated.*)

161.—**1829**—GRIGOR. Y., Captain. *Inscription*:—Captain Yohannas Grigor, of Constantinople, 1829, June 15th.—(Translation from Armenian).

162.—**1832**—BOURBON, S. A., Mrs.—*Inscription*:—

این روضه اهل خانه پیدرو بربون سمي بي بي آنا دختر حکیم عنایت
مسیح در سنه ۱۸۳۲ع مطابق سنه ۱۸۳۲ فصلي و مطابق بهادرن سدي
سمبت ۱۸۸۶ از جهان فني به عالم جاوداني

[This tomb and the next two appear to be those of descendants of John Philip Bourbon of Navarre. No. 162 is that of Simi Bibi Anna, daughter of Inayat Masih, wife of Pedro Bourbon. No. 163 is that of Pedro Bourbon *alias* Imdad Masih, son of captain Khairat Masih. Pedro Bourbon died at Bhopal.

The history of the Indian Bourbons is extremely curious. John Philip Bourbon was a relative of Henry IV of France, who slew a relative of rank in a duel, and fled to the East. He landed "*at Madras*" where one of his companions, a priest, remained. Bourbon sailed on to Bengal and so up country to Delhi, where Akbar give him a post at Court, and married him to Lady Juliana, sister of the Emperor's Christian wife, a lady doctor in charge of the health of the seraglio; he himself was put in charge of the women's apartments, a post which his family held till the sack of Delhi by Nadir Shah in 1737.

In that year Francis, great great grandson of John Philip, was head of the family. He collected all the members of the family in Sirghur Fort, in the state of Narwar—some 300 souls. In 1778 however the Narwar Raja massacred all the family; only Salvador, great grandson of this Francis, with his mother and a few children escaped. Among these was Pedro, his cousin. great great grandson of the said Francis. Salvador and Pedro took service in Bhopal, where his descendants still live. He and other members of his family served that state with great efficiency and they possess a considerable estate there.

Kincaid (*Asiatic Quarterly Review*) gives a genealogy of the family. But he admits that his materials were scanty, and his tree is probably incomplete. Pedro may or may not be the Pedro above mentioned; it is not impossible, but there is nothing to show it one way or another. The fact that there is an Indian as well as an European name has many parallels in the genealogy. Anthonia Bourbon, no. 155, is even more difficult to fit into the pedigree than Pedro Bourbon. If it be complete, the only place that seems to fit her in Mrs. Salvador Bourbon, in which case she was a Miss Thome.

Kincaid admits that his very interesting article is based on scanty materials. As a matter of fact, it raises some very difficult points. The words "at Madras" are italicized above because there was no "Madras" to land at till long after 1560; if it is not an error, it must mean merely the "neighbourhood of the present Madras." But more important still is the question of Akbar's Christian wife, whose sister Juliana John Philip married. C. A. Kincaid, in "*Tales of the Tulsi Plant*" refers to a Portuguese work called "Una dona Portugueza na corte do grande Mogal", by Ismael Gracias. He states that in the time of King John III there was at Lisbon a home for orphan girls who were shipped out to the colonies to make wives for the officials and settlers. Such an one was Maria Mascarenhas, who with her sister Juliana were captured by the Dutch, and sold at Surat. She became one of Akbar's Queens. It was this lady who is the Maria Makany whose room is shown at Fatehpur Sikri and it was her sister who married John Philip Bourbon.

This tale appears at variance with several facts. We are told that when the Moghul army attacked the Portuguese in Bassein and Damaun in 1581, they were repelled, but "the repulse would have been followed by an attack in force......had the Emperor not been stopped by.........the powers or tears of a Lusitanian lady." In other words, Maria Mascarenhas was married to Akbar before 1581. Yet the Dutch E. I. Co. was not even founded till 1594, so it is difficult to see how the Dutch sold her at Surat for a slave. Apart from this, the Jesuits never mention a Christian wife, which they would certainly have done if one existed. Moreover, Jerome Xavier was a Navarrois as Bourbon was: and he could hardly have failed to mention circumstances so interesting as the marriage of a descendant of Clovis to a sister of a Portuguese wife of Akbar. Father Desideri, S. J., in 1714, a traveller in the E. Indies, mentions a Lady Juliana Dias da Costa who was esteemed for her medical knowledge: and the Vicar Apostolic of Agra in 1832, says the Jesuits first gained Akbar's favour "per impegne di una certa Signora Giuliana di Goa che come dottoressa si trovava nel seraglio del suddito imperatore"; but this lady must not of course be confused with Akbar's alleged sister-in-law. Father Hosten holds that Akbar's Christian wife is a myth. But it is impossible to get away from the well attested fact that Bourbon *did* marry a Juliana at Akbar's court, and this tale of Garcia's at least explains how there came to be one at the court for him to marry.]

(References: *Calendar of Archdiocese Agra, 1907; Asiatic Quarterly Review, 1887; Tales of a Tulsi Plant.)*

163.—1833—BOURBON, P. *Inscription:—*

این روضه پیڈرو بربون عرف إمداد مسیح واد کپتان خیرات مسیح
صاحب است که در سال یک هزار شست صد و ...... عیسوے در شهر بوپال
إنتقال نموده ازین عالم فاني برجهان جاوداني .... سنه ۱۸۳۳ ع

[*Cf.* no. 162.]

164.—1845—DESILVA, E., Don. *Inscription:—*

دون الیش ڈیسلوا ... دون جزے ڈیسلوا بتاریخ بست و دوم ماه
دسمبر سنه ۱۸۴۵ عیسوي وفات یافت – سال عمر ۶۳ *

[*Cf.* no. 160; the name is Ellice.]

165.—1855—BOURBON, A. *Inscription:*—In memory, Anthonia Bourbon, who died on the 15th October 1855, aged 100 years.

[*Cf.* no. 162.]

166.—1856—DESILVA, A. *Inscription:*—In memory of Augustin DeSilva, physician, born January 1821, died 6th July 1856. R. I. P.

[Father of J. A. DeSilva, *cf.* nos. 160 and 173.]

167.—1857—CONNER, R. *Inscription:*—Sacred to the memory of Robert Conner of the Militia Cavalry who was killed in the battle of the 5th July 1857. This has been erected by one who greatly esteemed him. Amen.

[The battle of 5th July 1857 was that of Sacheta, for which see no. 256.]

168.—1859—DESILVA, Donna. *Inscription:—*

زوجه حکیم جزے ڈیسلوا تاریخ بستم ماه دسمبر سنه ۱۸۵۹ عیسوي
بعمر هشتاد و پنج سال مورث وفات یافت *

[Wife of Jose, great grandmother of J. A. DeSilva. *Cf.* nos. 160 and 173.]

169.—1865—DERRIDON, E., Mrs. *Inscription:*—Sacred to the memory of Mrs. Ellen Derridon who was born at Entree in the Gwalior district on the 23rd March 1777, and departed this life at Agra on the 25th September 1865 at 7 a.m., aged 88 years 6 months and 3 days.

[*Cf.* no. 250.]

170.—1887—DESILVA, E., Mrs. *Inscription:*—In memory of Mrs. Ellen DeSilva, died 13th March 1887, aged about 65 years R.I.P.

[She was mother of J. A. DeSilva, and wife of Augustin DeSilva. She came of a Sardhana family. *Cf.* nos. 160, 166, and 173.]

171.—**1893**—DESILVA, J., Mrs. *Inscription :*—Pray for the soul of Juliana, wife of Joseph DeSilva, Physician, of Bhurtpoor, born 29th April 1834, died 19th May 1893, aged 59 years 20 days.

Show Your mercy, Jesus dear.
On her soul who sleepeth here.—R. I. P.

[Also in Urdu. She was a Mrs. Pedron, and sister of Mrs. Louisa Derridon, no. 174. *Cf.* also no. 160.]

172.—**1905**—DERRIDON, G. S. W. *Inscription :*—Sacred to the memory of G S. W. Derridon who departed this on life (*sic*) 5th September 1905, aged 66 years and 6 days. Weep not for me, my loved ones, I rest in piece. (*sic*).

[*Cf.* no. 250.]

173.—**1909**—DESILVA, J. A. *Inscription :*—In memory of Joseph Augustin DeSilva, Physician, born 6th January 1838, died 9th June 1909. R. I. P.

[*Cf.* no. 160.]

174.—**1909**—DERRIDON, L. Mrs. *Inscription :*—Sacred to the memory of Louisa alias Lucy, relict of George Derridon, born 18th July 1838, died 20th June 1909. Perfect through suffering.

[Sister of Juliana DeSilva (no. 171), a Miss Pedron by birth. *Cf.* also no. 160. All the Derridon tombs in this cemetery are in the crypt of Hessing's tomb, no. 145.]

CATHEDRAL.

OLD ROMAN CATHOLIC GRAVEYARD.

175.—**1785**—TIEFFENTALLER, J., Padre. *Inscription :*—Pater J. Tieffentali obiit Lacnoi 5 June 1785.

[This tombstone is in the graveyard at the back of the old Roman Catholic Cathedral, now used, I am told for Indian Christians and close to the new Cathedral; I saw it myself. I lay stress on the point because many people are under the impression that the Agra slab was removed to Muttra. According to the Calendar, there are, or were, similar tombstones at Lucknow and Muttra. The one at Muttra is still there—in the house of the Roman Catholic Chaplain. Nobody seems to know anything about the Lucknow tomb. One can understand a tombstone at Lucknow where Tieffentaller died, and at Agra where he is buried; but it is difficult to see why there should be one at Muttra. He certainly went there in 1745; but he also went to many other places. It is just possible— either that the Muttra slab is a rejected stone (similar to the case mentioned in the introduction): or that somebody removed it to Muttra, perhaps at or after the mutiny, possibly for safety. Nor is there any doubt that Tieffentaller is the correct spelling of the name; it was the way he spelt it himself. Joseph Tieffentaller was a native of Bolzano (Botzen) in the Austrian Tyrol. (Botzen is the Pons Drusi of the Romans.) He left Germany in 1740 and stayed two years in Spain. In 1743 he sailed from Lisbon to Goa and thence went to Surat in the same year. He was probably destined, says Father Noti, for Jai Singh's observatory; but Jai Singh died in 1743, and Tieffentaller went to Agra as a teacher at the Jesuit College. He was a man of considerable linguistic attainments: he spoke German, Italian, Spanish and French, wrote good Latin, and acquired a good knowledge of Urdu, Persian Arabic and Sanskrit. He eventually composed a Sanskrit-Persian dictionary and wrote some treatises in Persian. He was also a mathematician and astronomer; in fact well-equipped for the geographical labours to which he devoted himself. He went first to Daman and returned to Surat, whence he proceeded by land to Broach, and thence via Udaipur and Jaipur to Dig and Agra, making many scientific observations on the way. He reached Agra at the end of 1744. He took the latitude of Agra and then (1745) went to the observatory of Jai Singh at Muttra, and also visited Brindaban. In 1746 we find him back in Agra and in 1747 with Strobl at Delhi. Thence he was sent to Narwar (C. I.); his new duties were to attend to the spiritual needs of a Christian community at that place. In 1750 he went to Goa, via Malwa and Bombay. He stayed there 6 months, and then went by Surat on a journey through Bombay and Gujarat to Marwar, Jodhpur and Ajmer; and in 1751 reached Narwar once more. He next travelled to Gwalior, Gohad and Agra and returned the same year to Marwar. He stayed here for some little time, with occasional excursions to Delhi, Brindaban, Agra and Kotah. He had good reasons to remain in Narwar: for in 1759 occurred the persecution of the Jesuits by King Joseph, and to leave the safety of Moghul dominions for Portuguese territory was to court imprisonment. The Order of Jesuits was abolished by Pope Clement XIV in 1773; and he had now no friends in India save F. X. Wendel. His Christian community at Narwar dwindled away, and he found himself, in 1765, penniless.

"Me trouvant embarrassé pour ma subsistance," as he writes, he determined to go to Bengal, relying on the charity of the "famous English nation so well known for their humanity, liberality and charity to the poor". He then travelled to Allahabad via Datia, Jhansi, Mahoba, Kalinjar, Chitrakot, Chatarpur, Panna and Ajaigarh. From Allahabad he went to Lucknow, Fyzabad, Jaunpur, Benares and thence by boat to Calcutta, landing at Patna, Monghyr, Rajmahal, Maqsudabad (now Murshidabad), Kasimbazar, Hooghly and Chandarnagore, and returning the same way, during which journeys he took observations and drew a map of the Ganges. Unfortunately he gives no details of his life in Calcutta, nor of how the English justified his trust in their liberality. Father Noti supposes that he was well treated, or he would have returned to Europe in an English ship by sea. We may hope so for the credit of our countrymen In 1766 he visited the English camp at Kora and then went to Lucknow, whence he traversed the whole of Oudh during the years 1766-1771. He had an assistant "versed in geography" whom he sent, *e.g.*, to the cataracts of the Ghagra. His other works he states to be (1) a Latin work on the religion, ceremonies and customs of the idolators, and the Gymnosophist philosophy; (2) a work on natural history; (3) a work on climatic and astronomical phenomena; (4) a little work on the sources of Indian rivers. The second and third works are said to have been lost. His editor, Bernoulli, does not regret that loss: for he says that the good father had not the requisite knowledge to do the subjects justice. But as has been shown, Tieffentaller was a man of wide learning, and his views were probably valuable.

His great work, "*Descriptio Indiae*", is, as one writer says, "curious and interesting." It is not, perhaps, of much value now, save for his chance references to people and facts that he observed. But that is not to depreciate it. The discoveries of each succeeding geographer annul those of his predecessors: but one does not despise Ross because of the discoveries of Scott and Shackleton. Tieffentaller had a very large share in the progress of the geographical knowledge of India, at a time when it was especially valuable. Unfortunately it is largely neutralized by the lack of maps, which, it would seem (J. A. S. B. 1872, an article by A. S. Allan) were destroyed with other of his records at Lucknow in the mutiny. But his value is considerable all the same, as gazetteer writers know. Father Noti says that Growse is the only Anglo-Indian writer who honours his memory by a laconic reference. But Anglo-Indian writers pay him the far greater honour of using him, as will appear from a cursory glance at any gazetteer, at all events of this province.]

(References: *Noti, East and West*: *Tieffentaller.*)

176.—**1791**—DA SYLVA, P., Don. *Inscription*:—Ca giaz o corpo da D. Pedro da Sylva morreo em Giapor aos 13 de 7bro 1791.

[Possibly one of the De Silvas, vide no. 160.]

177.—**1796**—FILOZE, M. *Inscription*:—Magdelena Filoze obiit Agra die Xbris 1796.

[This is no doubt a relative of the famous Filozes, but whether a sister of Jean Baptiste and Fidele, or a daughter of one of them, does not appear. The father, Michael Filoze, was a Neapolitan, born a muleteer. He enlisted in the French army and came from Madras to Delhi. After serving the Rana of Gohad, he joined De Boigne, but subsequently raised a force of his own, of 11 battalions. He finally had to fly owing to a piece of treachery that failed.

Fidele also was in Scindia's service and was imprisoned for treachery and committed suicide in prison. Baptiste fought against Thomas but was meantime corresponding with him: his troops were in part broken up at Assaye and he himself escaped to Rajputana where he rejoined Scindia and remained in his service till 1843, by which time he had become Scindia's Commander-in-Chief. After Punniar, Scindia's army was broken up and Filoze lost his employment. He died in 18..4. His grandson, Sir Michael Filoze, is still employed as an architect at Gwalior. An inscription in the Cathedral shows that he restored and enlarged it in 1835.]

(References: *Compton; Buckland.*)

178.—**1801**—DASYLVA, A. *Inscription:*—Ca giaz o corpo de Ana da Sylva morreo em Giapor aos 30 7bro 1801.

[*Cf.* no. 176.]

179.—**1803**—GARDNER, A. *Inscription:*—Sacred to the memory of Alida Gardner who died on the 10th January 1803, aged 5 years

[Alida "or Alaida" is a name common in the Gardner family. Colonel W. L. Gardner's mother was *née* Alaida Livingstone: and his grand-daughter, the daughter of James Valentine Gardner was also Alaida, *alias* the Morning Star. This however cannot be his grand-daughter. It is possibly a daughter of Colonel W. L. Gardner himself, whose name is not given in Fanny Parke's pedigree. *cf.* no. 395.]

(References: *Compton; Wanderings of a Pilgrim.*)

180.—**1803**—WENDEL, F. X., Padre. *Inscription:*—P. F. X. Wendel obiit Lacnoi die 29 Martii 1803.

[Francis Xavier Wendel was the last of the Jesuit missionaries. He came out to India in 1751 and was at Diu in 1756. He went to Agra in 1769 and restored the old church with the assistance of Sombre, as an inscription shows. In 1775 we find him petitioning the Emperor Shah Alam for the return of the cemetery, which had presumably been confiscated, and a parwana of the Emperor is extant confirming him in possession. He also did some geographical work.]

(Reference: *Hosten; Calendar, Agra Archdiocese*, 1907.)

181.—**1805**—MACE, J. *Inscription:*—Ca giaz o corpo de Joseph Mace morreo em Agra aos 12 de Junho 1805.

182.—**1824**—BENUCCI, Z., Revd., V. A. *Inscription:*—Ossa Revmi Dni Zenobi Benucci inventa 11 Februarii 1824.

[A Florentine, the first prefect apostolic of the Congo Mission, nominated in 1820. He was consecrated Bishop of Herma in Brazil, and then first Vicar Apostolic of Agra. He arrived in Chandarnagore in 1823 and died at Agra in 1824.]

(Reference: *Calendar, Agra Archdiocese*, 1907.)

183.—**185** —REGHELINI, J. B. *Inscription:*—Sacred to the memory of John Baptist Reghelini. Born Sirdhanah on 13th May 1837, died at Agra on the 6th March 1851. *Requiescat in pace.*

[From a letter of Dyce Sombre to Major Reghelini, who was formerly in the Begam Samru's service, dated 8th May 1851, this would appear to be a son of Pascal Reghelini, Major Reghelini's eldest son. The letter to which this is a reply was written by Major Reghelini on the 15th March, so that dates correspond.]

(Reference: *Dyce Sombre Depositions.*)

NEW ROMAN CATHOLIC CATHEDRAL.

184.—**1845**—FRANCIS, Father, O.C. *Inscription:*—Sacred to the memory of the Rev. Father Francis of St. Etienne, Apostolic Missionary of the Capuchin Order, who during the performance of his sacred duties towards the Catholic soldiers of the British Army, fell a victim by the sword of the enemy in the field of Moodki, on the 18th December 1845, aged 34 years. A martyr of charity whom no danger could deter from attending to his flock; a vigilant, a faithful shepherd. He attended the Kabul troops at Firozepore, was present with them at Maharajpore, administering to their spiritual wants when cholera was afflicting Agra in 1843, and raging in Meerut in 1845. He was seen day and night in the hospitals, venerated and beloved by Catholics, esteemed and admired by those of a different creed. Friend to all, and enemy to none, zealous for the honour and glory of God, unaffected in his piety and devotion, compassionate to the widow, orphan and poor. He sealed his glorious course with his blood for the sake of those whom Christ had redeemed. (B.O.).

[Beyond the fact that this Father came out to India in 1839, I have been able to discover nothing about him, nor the tablet itself.]

(Reference: *Calendar, Agra Archdiocese*, 1907.)

185.—1865—BEDENIK, A., Right Revd. Bishop. *Inscription:*—Depositus in pace die 2 Novembris an. 1865 Illmus ac Rnmus Dominus Bedenik a Capronza, O.M.S.F.C. Episcopus Leucensis et Vicar Ap. Agrae annos natus 58 monachus et episcopus vere angelicus.

Of your charity pray for the soul of the Right Revd. Fr. Angelicus Bedenik, O.M.S.F.C., Bishop of Leuca and Vicar Apostolic of Agra, who died on the 2nd November 1865 aged 58 years. R.I.P.

[Of Kopreinitz; born 3rd April 1808, nominated and consecrated Bishop of Leuca 1861.]

(Reference: *Calendar, Agra Archdiocese*, 1907.)

186.—1891—JACOPI, M. A., Most Revd. Archbishop. *Inscription:*—Hic in pace Christi quiescunt ossa et cineres Michaelis Angeli Jacopi, O.S.F.C. qui sui adventus in Indiam quinquagesimo jam revoluto anno, episcopatus tertio, et vigesimo quinto quoque ab Eccles: Hierarchia instituta primus Agrensis antistes Metropolita, solio pontifico proelatus assistens, pluribus perfunctus laboribus pro aucta religione catholica de Indis, optime meritus virtutibus cumulatus LXXIX aetatis Mussoorii pridie Idus Octobris MDCCCXCI piissime obiit. "*Quam speci osi pedes evangelizantium pacem, evangelizantium bona.*" Rom. X. 15. *R.I.P.*

[Of Saravezza. He came to India as Apostolic missionary in 1841. He was made Pro-Vicar Apostolic of the Punjab in 1855, and Vicar Apostolic of Agra in 1868. By the bull "*Humanae salutis auctor*" Pope Leo XIII constituted the Catholic Hierarchy of India and elevated the Vicariate Apostolic of Agra into a Metropolitan See with an Archbishop in 1886. Archbishop Jacopi was the first holder of the dignity.]

(Reference: *Calendar, Agra Archdiocese*, 1907.)

NEW CATHEDRAL GRAVEYARD.

187.—1849—LYNCH, J. F. *Inscription:*—A. . . Joannis Foley Lynch animi nobilitate religionis zelo, ingenii perspicuitate et conjugali affectu clarus, vix medio humanae vitae peracto cursu, videlicet anni 36 mens. 9 dier. 21 maligna febri laborans Delii 15 Decembris anni 1849 extremum exhalavit spiritum in sinum Dei, corpusque inter manus reliquit desolatae thoris Elisae piaeque Elizabeth Finnery quod pietate dilectationeque excitatae Agram tulere . . . . et hic . . . . (*rest illegible.*)

188.—**1856**—HARRINGTON, I, Captain. *Inscription* :—Sacred to the memory of Isaac Harrington, late a Captain in the Scindiah's service who departed this life on Monday the 10th November 1856, aged 70 years. *Requiescat in pace.*

BEHIND CIVIL COURT.

189.—**1818**—HALHED, Frances E. E. *Inscription* :—Sacred to the memory of Frances Elizabeth Ellen, the infant daughter of Nathaniel and Caroline Halhed, died 6th October 1818.

[This tomb is between "the present irrigation cutting which skirts the Munsarim's house and the S. W. end of the Halhedgar compound wall." Mr. Halhed was one of the earliest Collectors of Agra.]

PROTESTANT CEMETERY.

A.—*The English Factory at Agra.*—The tombs of Offley, Drake and Purchas are memorials of the old English Factory at Agra. They with Midnall's tomb (no. 105 in the Roman Catholic cemetery) are evidence of more than that. They are a proof, and the only proof in the United Provinces, of the antiquity of the British connection with India. As Sir W. Hunter points out, the Anglo Indian cyclical year dates back not only to Plassey and 1757, but to 1657, the year in which Cromwell granted his charter to the East India Company; and even to 1557. For British India is the result of a world-old struggle for Eastern trade and Eastern trade-routes: the English Muscovy Company, which tried to control Eastern trade by trans-continental routes, was a move in that struggle: and it was in 1557 that Anthony Jenkinson, a servant of that company, met the Indian merchants at Bokhara—the first Englishman to penetrate so far East. These old English merchants would indeed have been surprised, even shocked, to learn that they were pioneers of an Empire. But they were,—*si monumentum requiris, circumspice.*

The first adventure to India from England, made in 1589, the year after the Armada, was a failure. In 1600 the first charter for Eastern trade was granted to the Earl of Cumberland, and 215 knights, aldermen and merchants, trading under the name of "the Governor and Company of merchants of London trading into the East Indies." It is unnecessary here to tell the tale of all the various "joint stocks" and separate voyages; for our concern is only with Agra. In 1608, Hawkins landed at Surat and made his way to Agra with letters to the Great Moghul: but after a struggle of five years to obtain leave to trade, returned unsuccessful in 1612. In 1613 Paul Canning went to Agra to sue for a *farman* and died there: the same year his place was taken by the well-known Thomas Kerridge, and Withington; and in 1614, Edwards went there as resident factor with seven subordinates—Kerridge, Withington, Mitford, Browne, Younge, Ufflet, and Fettiplace. Sir Thomas Roe landed in 1615, and met the Emperor in 1616 though he was never in Agra; after much opposition from Shah Jahan, then Prince Khurram, he obtained farmans in 1618, and returned home in 1669, having proved a very "Joseph in the court of Pharaoh." Other factors of the time at Agra were Hughes, Salbanke (1617), Biddulph (1618), Parker (1619), Young (1620). Fettiplace died there in 1621.

But bad times were in store for the English at Agra. They were at open war with the Portuguese: they had quarrelled with the Moghul's officers at Surat: the Moghul's officers confused them with the Dutch and punished them for their rivals' aggressions. Worst of all, in 1619 English ships had captured a "frigate" belonging to natives, on the pretence that it was a Portuguese vessel. Retribution overtook them in 1621 when the true owners complained to Jahangir, and to Asaf Khan brother of Jahangir's wife Nur Jahan. The latter wearied by the complainants' inportunities, ceased to help his English protegés; Hughes and Parker were imprison d in Agra Fort, their goods sequestrated, and a sum of £10,200 recovered from them. In May 1621 the factory was broken up, to be reopened, with Offley, Willoughby, Goodwin and Bangham, in 1624. We find Offley at the head of the factors there from 1625 to 7: he was recalled and succeeded by Gregory Clement, afterwards a notorious regicide

So the factory went on. As a trade concern, for various reasons it was never over-prosperous; its importance lay in its presence at the headquarters of the Moghul Government. But when this shifted to Delhi, its reason for existing ceased. As early as 1655, orders are found from the company to recall the factors (Jesson was there at the time), sell the horses, plate, &c., but to keep the house. In 1656, Jesson was still there, though "long since sent for", according to a letter of the factors: and the company "presume" that the Agra and other up-country factors have been withdrawn. But in 1657 we read that Jesson was still there, as "his engagements" did not allow him to depart. In 1660, the company express a hope that the Agra factory has not been started again: and in 1661, the Surat factors writing to the company mention its dissolution by the latter, meaning apparently a second dissolution of the factory, if by any chance it had been resettled—the words are "you having dissolved the factorys of Agra and Ahmadabad, though in the former place we had settled none." Bernier writing in 1663 says the English had abandoned their factory which fixes a limit date: and though Manucci speaks of English factors at Agra taking part in events which other evidence shows should be referred to the year 1661, he is extremely inaccurate in his dates, and his chance mention of English factors, at this time, proves nothing. (For these events *cf.* no. 195.) At some time between 1657 and 1660, therefore, the factory came to an end altogether. Eight years laters Charles II handed over Bombay to the company, and for the first time, the British own d a portion of India.

(References: *Manucci; Foster, factories; Bernier; Hunter*)

B.—*The Dutch factory at Agra.*—The Dutch first settled at Surat in 1616, under the leadership of Van der Broecke. About 10 years before (according to Roe, but the date is uncertain), certain Dutch merchants at different times had tried to settle there but, for various reasons, without success. In 1616 Roe, who was struggling on behalf of his compatriots with Moghul intrigue, was not likely to relish added trouble in the shape of Dutch rivalry, and did his best to poison the ear of Asaf Khan and Khurram against them.—"more ingeniously than ingenuously" as Mr. Foster remarks. His efforts were only partially successful, for they were allowed to land some factors and merchandize. Next year the Dutch ships were wrecked near Surat, and Roe advised that all assistance should be refused them. But in 1618 Van Ravesteyn headed a Dutch embassy which obtained concessions from Jahangir "upon as good tearms almost as wee" as Roe writes. There was bitter rivalry, bitter dislike, and to a large extent, bitter misrepresentation, at work between the Dutch and English at this time. Roe accused them of covering piracy with the English flag, a fact probably untrue and certainly denied, but widely believed. Their proceedings were high-handed enough in all conscience: they captured French, Danish, Portuguese and native ships indifferently. Used to the petty princelings of the Spice Islands, they treated the Great Moghul to the same audacious proceedings, and it took them time to learn that there was a vast difference between Jahangir and the potentates of Java and Sumatra. They settled in Agra in 1621, though their factors had paid flying visits there before. Their first head was Wouter (or Walter) Heuten. He died in 1623, and was followed by Francis Pelsart, who at a later date was shipwrecked, according to Thevenot, off Australia. English and Dutch factors lived together on good terms, so long as the new-comers were weak: but when their competition became serious, they quickly fell out. Thevenot has a letter (dated 1627) from Pelsart to the Dutch East India Company, which contains a curious description of Agra, but is chiefly noticeable for its jealousy of English trade successes. In 1628 the English records show that the rivals were not on speaking terms, which was natural enough, in view of the massacre of Amboyna (1623) and its results. None the less, it is pleasing to note that the Dutch never carried resentment beyond the grave; and on at least two occasions offered their deceased rivals the last hospitality of sepulture. Both Offley and Drake were buried by them (nos. 190-191). Manucci mentions Jan Tack (no. 195); and a letter is extant, dated 1664, from the Dutch Company to their Government in which the Agra factory is mentioned. It is to be found in Thevenot. Bernier, writing in 1663, mentions the Dutch factory as having generally four or five factors: but their trade was not then very lucrative owing, he thinks, to Armenian competition, and the distance between Agra and Surat. But he considered it, at the time, unlikely that they would abandon the factory, as it was useful to have persons at court to look after their interests. But, even at this time Agra was beginning to give place to Delhi, and very possibly it was the removal of the court from Agra to Delhi which determined the Dutch to close their factory. When exactly the factory was closed is not known. Tieffentaller, writing presumably about 1750, says it had fallen into ruins; and probably it was closed soon after 1679, the date of the last tomb. Of the three factors, —de Boeck, assistant, Tack, leading merchant, and deLiem, accountant— we know nothing, save a solitary fact recorded by Manucci about Tack.

(References: *Foster, Factories; Bernier; Thevenot; Manucci; Roe; Tieffentaller*).

C.—*Site of the old tombs.*—All the old tombs nos. 190-196, with three others that bear no inscription, are on a large sandstone platform. They were found underground in 1854, when the foundations of St. Paul's Church, close by, were being dug; and were placed in the cemetery on a platform. In 1875 the Agra Archaeological Society's transactions mentions them as on a platform at the south side of the church; and about the same time it would appear from information received from Mr. Fanthome, that Mr. A. Thomson, principal of Agra college, for some reason or another had them put up on *another* (the present) platform.

From the story of Drake's death (no. 191), we find that these tombs—Drake's for certain and probably all the others—originally stood in the garden of the Dutch factory. It was the only piece of ground they owned in India; and the English themselves had no such garden in Agra, though they had elsewhere. As heretics, they could not be buried in the Roman Catholic cemetery; and it was natural that they should inter the members of their community who died in their garden. When the Dutch had to perform the last rites for their English rivals, they would naturally bury them there also. It would appear therefore that St. Paul's stands on the site of this old Dutch garden; so that the soil has remained purely European.

Of the nameless tombstones, one may be that of Wouter or Walter Heuten, chief of the Dutch factory, who died in 1623.

(Reference: *Bengal, Past and Present; communication from Mr. Foster, quoting Murray's hand book of Bengal, 1882; and other communications).*

190.—**1627**—OFLEY, J. *Inscription*:—Here lies the body of Justinian Ofley who was chief merchant in Agra for the English. He deceased the 18th April 1627.

[Justinian Ofley, or Offley was the son of Thomas Offley merchant, of London. He arrived in India in 1620. In March 1621 he was sent to Broach, and then on to Baroda, where he was very ill, a fact which he attributed to the "air and bad water." In 1622, he went with other factors to Burhanpur and was there till May or June, when the troubles with the Emperor Jahangir at Agra forced the settlement to be abandoned, as was that of Agra itself. Ofley in November was back at Broach and remained there till, at all events, October 1623. In that month he is found at Variao; in November it was decided to reopen the factory at Agra, and send Robert Young, Ofley and Goodwin there—"to obtayne the King's firman, to ratifie and confirme the contracts concluded on with Cosrooe the younge Prince" and to sell "sundrye goods and jewells." After a visit to Surat, he and Goodwin are found writing from Baroda on Christmas day 1623. There appears to be no further mention of him till December 1625, when he was at Agra; and in 1626, he is found there, with several others, as chief factor. In 1627, Ofley incurred the displeasure of his superiors at Surat—what the precise reason was is not clear, but it was apparently due to some friction with John Bangham, another factor who was in residence (chiefly) at the court, and had been ordered to go to Agra: at all events, we learn that the Surat Council were "mightily incensed against Bangham and still more against Ofley" in December 1626; whilst in February 1627 the same writer (Joseph Hopkinson at Ahmadabad writing to Bangham) says that Ofley's proceedings "were so hardly thought of that he will have need of a very sound and substantial apology for himself, on arrival." He was to be succeeded by the notorious Gregory Clement, later one of the Regicides, excluded from the Restoration amnesty and executed in 1660. But Ofley died in April, before Clement arrived there. "Whilst I was in Cambaia (writes Kerridge to the company) letters came unto me from Agra importing Justinian Offleyes decease, who departed this life after a lingering sicknes, the 18th of April last; and no other English being there" (they were all away with caravans) "was buryed by the Dutch"; and we then get a hint of the cause of the Council's anger against him: "his accounts are so imperfect that more than all we feare will not cleare them." His pay, it is stated in 1622, was R 104 pice 48 for the year.]

(Reference: *Foster English Factories.*)

191.—**1637**—DRAKE, J. *Inscription*:—Here lyes the body of John Drake............ [s] lane........ anno domini......1637. E. K. fecit. A......Domin......1647.

[John Drake's death occurred in a riot, between some villagers and a caravan of indigo of which he was in charge. He had been warned not to set out, because of the occurrence of the Holi festival which is described as "resembling the carnival". "At a village, called Paechuchra, four corse *(kos)* beyond Dholpur.. ......the gowars (ganwars) demanded rahdares, or, as we say, "toll" of the party." With John Drake, were Dhanji, the English broker at Agra, and his son-

Morar Das. Dhanji pointed out that their *farmans* exempted them from toll: and they let all the carts pass but two, which were guarded by four peons, which they stopped: and endeavoured, also, to disarm these men. This adds weight to the statement of some of those who wrote to the Surat factors on the subject, that the subsequent riot was caused by the abuse indulged in by the peons: it is just precisely what, in the circumstances, the peons might have been expected to do. The peons resisted the attempt to disarm them, whereupon, the villagers were reinforced by 300 others, variously armed, and a fight ensued. It is stated that "the gowars made a hoobub." The villagers carried off Dhanji to the village: John Drake and Morar Das were ahead and returned, but were surrounded by the villagers. Drake set spurs to his horse and broke through them: the fight began again and he was shot through with an arrow. This ended the fight: the peons were rifled, but not the carts; and when Drake was found to be seriously hurt, the villagers did all they could to assist. A surgeon was sent from Agra by Da Castro, the Jesuit rector; but his help was in vain. Drake desired to be moved to Agra, but died at Dholpur, on the 5th March.

The matter was reported to the Surat factors by, amongst others, Jeronimo Veronio (*vide* no. 110) and Father daCastro (no. 83.) The Dutch buried him as there was no other English factor in Agra. The map still shows a village called Pachokhra near the spot referred to above. By the irony of fate, on March 10th, within a day or two of Drake's burial, the company in London decided to raise his salary from £ 20 to £60 per annum, in recognition of his eight years of faithful service. E. K. is probably, Edward Knipe, a factor].

(Reference: *Bengal, Past and Present*).

192.—1647—DE BOECK, J. *Inscription*:—Hier leyt begraven Jan de Boeck van Amsterdam, in syn leven Adsisten. Obyt 19 September anno 1647, out 37 yaren.

193.—1649—TACK, E., Vrow. *Inscription*:—[Hi]er leyt begraven Elisabet in hear leven huisvrow van der op[e]r[c]oopman Johan Tack, obitten 19 October anno 1649, out 30 yare.

[Wife of Jan Tack No. 195.]

194.—1651—PURCHAS, G. *Inscription*:—(H)ere leyeth the body of George Purchas who deceased in Agra y(e) 14th May 1651 aetatis suae 24. (Me) mento (mori).

[Mr. Foster informs me that no account of Purchas' death has yet been found in the India office records. The only three mentions of him up to January 1652 are these:—(O. C. 2189) 19th December 1650. "List of factors at Surat and subordinate factories...... . George Purchas, Agra and Lucknow." In O. C. 2204 on the 31st January 1650—1, he is mentioned in a letter from the Surat General to the company, as follows. "Two more there are at Agra and Lucknow ....to wit Verity Roydon and George Purchas; the former came forth stewards mate on shipp Eagle, the other on your shipp Blessing, the same year, a very civill and industerous youth........and soe well deserveing that wee hope you will alsoe bee pleased to consider there past service by makeing them competent sallaryes from the tyme that these your last ships arrived"......In April of the same year (O. C. 2216), there is another letter which refers to the one already quoted and presses the company "that they may not escape your consideration." The Eagle arrived in Swally Road in September 1649; and as the Blessing arrived the same year, on the most liberal interpretation, Purchas had had no more than 2 years' service, and may have had as little as eighteen months.]

(Reference: *Bengal Past and Present*.)

195.—1663—TACK, J. *Inscription*:—Hier leyt begraven Joan Tack van Amboyna oudt 56 yaren in syn leven opercoopman obyt 11 Januari 1663.

Manucci mentions Tack as the factor, when all English and Dutch were called together, who was able to give Aurangzeb information of his brother Shah Shuja's death in Arakan in 1660.]

(Reference: *Manucci*.)

196.—**1679**—DELIEM, P. *Inscription :*—Hier leyt begraven Pieter de Liem van Randerhuysen, in syn leven Boeckhoder, obyt 29 Marci anno 1679, out 35 yaren.

197.—**1843**—LLOYD, W. K. *Inscription :*—Sacred to the remains of William Kirkman, infant son of T. K. Lloyd, B. C. S., and Annie his wife, who died on the 30th of March 1843, aged 4 months and 4 days.

[T. K. Loyd (or Lloyd—it is spelt both ways—but Loyd is the form in the Writer's Petition) was at Haileybury 1831—2. He joined the C. S. in 1833. He served in Hamirpur, Mirzapur, Etawah, Agra and Aligarh. He was joint magistrate at Agra at the time of this inscription. He was killed in the Mutiny at Hamirpur where he was magistrate, refusing to leave his post though he might have escaped to Banda. T. K. Loyd was born in London on the 15th October 1812. He was the son of William and Martha Loyd: his mother was the daughter of T. Kirkman. He was presented for nomination by the Director, J. Masterman.]

(References: *Prinsep C. L.*: *Haileybury*: *W.P.*)

198.—**1843**—HIGGINSON, H. A. *Inscription :*—In memory of H. A. Higginson, *obiit* 27th July 1843, aged 32 years.

199.—**1844**—(1) WHITE, S. (2) WHITE, S. C. *Inscription :*—Sacred to the memory of Samuel White, who departed this life on the 16th May 1844, aged 43 years and 5 days, leaving a widow and 5 children to deplore his loss. Also to the memory of Samuel Charles, his infant son, who died on the 27th June ensuing, aged 1 year and 4 months.

200.—**1845**—EDMONSTONE, G. F. *Inscription :*—Sacred to the memory of George Frederick, the infant son of George Frederick Edmonstone, Civil Service, and Ann Farley his wife, *obiit* 2nd Novr. 1845, *aetat* 6 months and 8 days.

[The child of Sir G. F. Edmonstone (1813-1864), K. C. B., Commissioner of the Cis-Sutlej States 1845-6, Foreign Secretary to Government of India 1855-9, and Lieutenant-Governor, N.-W. P., 1859-1863. He was 4th son of Neil Edmonstone, H. E. I.C.S., and grandson of Sir Archibald Edmonstone, the first Baronet, of an ancient Scotch family. His wife was the daughter of T. Turner.]

(References: *Buckland*: *Burke P.*)

201.—**1845**—DAVIDSON, J. W. *Inscription :*—In memory of James William, the infant son of James Davidson, Civil Service, and Mary his wife. Born August 25th, 1845, died September of the same year.

[James Davidson joined the H. E. I. C. S., in 1819 as writer, and arrived in India in 1820. He served in Bareilly, Pilibhit, Etawah, Mainpuri, Aligarh, Behar, Agra and Farrukhabad. In 1840, he was Commissioner of Rohilkhand and in 1842 Commissioner at Agra. He retired in 1846, as Judge of the Sadr Diwani Adalat and died in 1874.

James Davidson was the son of James Davidson, born in 1801, and educated (besides Haileybury) at Paris and Brighton.]

(References: *Haileybury*; *Prinsep C. L.*; *W. P.*)

202.—**1845**—SMITH, D. F. B. *Inscription :*—In memory of Donald Frederick Byland, the beloved son of Mr. David Smith and Mary his wife, who died on the 27th July 1845, aged 5 months. This tomb is erected in token of the affection of his parents.

203.—**1846**—ANDREWS. J. Y. *Inscription :*—Here rests the mortal remains of Joseph Yer Andrews, an Armenian of Julpha, died at Agra, 10th day of May 1846, aged 51 years, deeply regretted.

"Blessed are the pure in heart for they shall see God."

[Julpha or Julfa was a city on the banks of the Aras river. Shah Abbas the Great, King of Persia, visited it in 1605, and was so dazzled by the wealth of the Armenian inhabitants that he had it razed to the ground and transported the inhabitants wholesale to Ispahan. There they built the city of "New Julfa," close to Ispahan and it is their metropolis still.]

(Reference: *Seth*)

204.—**1847**—EDMONSTONE, E. L. *Inscription :*—Sacred to the memory of Eliza Louisa, the infant daughter of George Frederick Edmonstone and Ann Farley, his wife, *obiit* 23rd October 1847, *aetat* 1 year, 1 month and 15 days.

[*Cf.* no. 200.]

205.—**1847**—MARTIN, J. H. C. *Inscription :*—Sacred to the memory of J. H. C. Martin, infant son of Mr. Jas. Martin, *obīt* 25 July 1847, aged 7 months.

"Who can paint a mother's grief, who can tell her joy?
"'Twas hard to part, yet sweet relief, Her child's an Angel boy."

206.—**1847**—POWNES, E. A. *Inscription :*—Sacred to the memory of Evelyn Augustus, the infant son of William Frederick Pownes and Ellen, his wife, who died on the 30th April 1847, aged 1 year, 4 months and 20 days.

"Sweet flower, farewell, too fair for Earth;
Brief space to us thy charms were given;
He who bestowed thee, knew thy worth,
And took thee to Himself in Heaven."

207.—**1847**—MACLEOD, M., Mrs. *Inscription :*—Sacred to the memory of Mrs. Mary Macleod, relict of the late Mr. Condr Donald Macleod, who departed this life on the 20th May 1847, aged 65 years. This tomb is erected by her children as a tribute of affection. R. I. P.

208.—**1848**—MURRAY, J. H. *Inscription :*—In memory of John Harry, son of John Murray, Esq., M.D. Civil Surgeon, Agra, who died 25th August 1848, aged 1 year and 6 months.

209.—**1848**—(1) CLARKE, J. **1853**—(2) CLARKE, L. *Inscription :*—Here rest the remains of a father and daughter, James Clark, Sr., died 24th August 1848, aged 48 years. Louisa Clarke, died 6th October 1853, aged 15 years.

210.—**1848**—MACCUTCHAM, R. *Inscription :*—In memory of Robert, the infant son of Robert Arthur and Antoinette MacCutcham, died at Hatrass, 7th April 1848, aged 6 months and 20 days.

211.—**1848**—CONLAN, S. H. *Inscription :*—Sacred to the memory of Sophia Harriet Conlan, the beloved and only child of James Conlan and Eliza, his wife, who died on the 12th April 1848, aged 2 years, 3 months and 3 days. This tomb is erected in token of the affection of a father.

212.—**1848**—ELLIS, J. *Inscription :*—In memory of John Ellis, who departed this life on the 4th Decr. 1848, aged 28 years.

213.—**1848**—BURTON, T. *Inscription :*—In memory of Mr. Thomas Burton, who died on the 17th June 1848, aged 26 years. This tomb is erected in token of the affection of his disconsolate sister, Sarah Smith.

214.—**1849**—BLACKBURN, B. R. *Inscription* :—To the memory of Benjamin Ross Blackburn, born on the 13th August 1848, departed this life on the 16th April 1849.

> "His spirit mingled with the blest;
> His body with the clay.
> God grant that we may all unite
> On the last solemn day."

215.—**1849**—THOMPSON, G. P., B.C.S. *Inscription* :—To the memory of George Powney Thompson, Esq., Bengal Civil Service, Judge of the S. D. A., born February 7th, 1797 died November 11th, 1849. Erected by his children.

[The son of George Nesbitt Thompson, H. E. I. C. S. Private Secretary to Warren Hastings in 1783, and of Catherine Maria Powney, daughter of Thomas Powney, H. E. I. C. S. He was closely related to Sir A. R. Thompson, K. C. S. I. and Lieutenant-Governor of Bengal in 1882-7, the opponent of the Ilbert Bill. Sir G. Campbell who met G. P. Thompson at Allahabad in 1846 describes him as a civilian of the old school, the kind that joined in the last century and had never gone home, "the progenitor of a numerous race and equally distinguished for judicial acumen, knowledge of horse-flesh and piety." Three of his daughters married, respectively, Sir F. Currie (as his 3rd wife,) C. H. Lushington, B.C.S. and Arthur Malet, member of Council at Bombay.

G. P. Thompson joined the service in 1815. His early years were spent in Calcutta, 24 Parganas, Midnapore and Tipperah. In 1833 he was Judge of Gorakhpur and in 1839 became Judge of the Sadr Diwani Adalat.]

(References : *Campbell ; Buckland ; Burke L. G.; Foster, B ; Prinsep C. L.*]

216.—**1849**—MOORE, J. J., Reverend. *Inscription* :—In memory of the Reverend J. J. Moore, founder of the Secundra orphanage and late minister of St. Paul's Church who died at Agra on the 10th September, A. D. 1849, aged 38.

[The Secundra orphanage was founded by the C. M. S. in the famine of 1837-8.]

(Reference : *Gazetteer.*)

217.—**1850**—HOGAN, H., Mrs. *Inscription* :—In memory of Harriet Hogan, who died on the 1st of April 1850, *ae.* 32.

> "Tread gently, stranger, on this sacred spot,
> Where sleeps divinely one who's ne'er forgot;
> A wife, a mother, a Christian and a friend.
> Such as Heaven to earth doth but seldom lend;
> And for your own salvation's sake, forbear
> To disturb the ashes in deposit here."

218.—**1851**—LARKINS, E. L. *Inscription* :—Sacred to the memory of Emily Locke Larkins, who departed this life on the 1st March 1851, aged 24 years.

219.—**1851**—MURRAY, A. J. *Inscription* :—In memory of Agnes Jane, daughter of John Murray, Esq., M.D. Civil Surgeon, Agra who died Jany. 5th, 1851, aged 2 months.

220.—**1851**—MACCAY, J , Sergeant. *Inscription* :—In memory of John Maccay, Sergeant, H E. I. C. S., 1st E. Regt, Comg., Jail guard, who died at Agra on the 8th August 1851 A. D., aged 29 years.

221.—**1851**—CLAY, E. M. *Inscription* :—Sacred to the memory of Edward Musgrave Clay, Esq., 3rd son of Knightly Musgrave Clay, Esq., died 29th March 1851, aged 30 years.

222.—1852—STAFFORD, J. P. *Inscription* :—To the memory of Jacob Poole Stafford, who departed this life the 17th January 1852, aged 49 years and 8 days......

223.—1852—COLESTON, W. *Inscription* :—Sacred to the memory of William Coleston, the beloved and 2nd son of William Coleston, Garrison Key Sergeant of Allahabad and Mary, his wife, who in the prime of life after 5 months' severe illness departed this life on the 2nd June 1852, leaving his aged parents, three brothers, two sisters and a large circle of other relatives to bemoan their irreparable loss, aged 26 years 1 month and 8 days. This tomb has been erected by his affectionate brother...

224.—1853—LONGDEN, F. H. *Inscription* :—In memory of Florence Harcourt, daughter of Edward Harcourt Longden and Sophia Elizabeth, his wife, born 10th August, died 15th August 1853.

[There was a Mr. Longden at Agra during the Mutiny, probably the same.]

(Reference : *M. N.*)

225.—1853—BRETON, G. B. *Inscription* :—Sacred to the memory of George B. Breton, who departed this life on the 25th August 1853, aged 42 years, ten months and twelve days.

"Blessed are the dead who died in the Lord." The weary are at rest.

226.—1853—(1) CONLAN, J. (2) CONLAN. A. T. *Inscription* :—Sacred to the memory of James Conlan of the Sudder Court, N. W. P. Born 25th October 1812 : died 16th June 1853, deeply regretted. Also of Adonia Theresa, his only child, born 8th November 1849, died 17th June 1853.

"Thy Kingdom come." Erected as a mark of affection by John C.

227.—1853—WOLLASTON, A. H. *Inscription* :—Sacred to the memory of Arthur H. Wollaston, born at Calcutta, 11th March 1836, died at Agra of consumption, 10th June 1853.

[Possibly a relative of the Augustus Wollaston mentioned in No. 239 ; and if so probably of the Reverend M. W. Wollaston, No. 652 ; the connecting link being the uncommon name Lorenza which appears both in No. 239 and in No. 647—Augustus Wollaston's daughter and M. W. Wollaston's wife—and also the fact that the Reverend M. W. Wollaston originally belonged to Agra.]

228.—1854—CHAMBERS, W. J. *Inscription* :—In memory of William J. Chambers, died 3rd Decr. 1854, aged 46 years.

229.—1854—POEZOLD, J. W. *Inscription* :—In memory of John Wm. Poezold, died 21st April 1854, aged 34 years.

230.—1854—POEZOLD, M. V., Mrs. *Inscription* :—In memory of Mrs. Martha Viner Poezold, died 2nd April 1854, aged 30 years.

231.—1855—GLADWIN, A. Mrs. *Inscription* :—Sacred to the memory of Adelaide, the beloved wife of Thomas Gladwin, who departed this life on the 10th August 1855, aged 28 years. *Memento mori.*

232.—1855—LANE, C., B.C.S. *Inscription* :—Sacred to the memory of Charles Lane, Esq., Bengal Civil Service, son of H. S. Lane, Esq., late of the Bengal Civil Service, born 4th November 1835, died 25th June 1855. Deeply regretted by all who knew him.

(References : *Haileybury ; Prinsep C. L. ; W.P.*)

[C. Lane was at Haileybury in 1853—4 and died in his first year of service. H. Smith Lane, his father, joined the service in 1818 and retired in 1848, dying in 1865. H. S. Lane was son of H. Lane, banker of Hinckley, Lecestershire. C. Lane was born at Epsom in 1835.]

233.—**1855**—(1) ROWLEY, E. **1857**—(2) ROWLEY, J., Sergeant. *Inscription* :—In memory of Elizabeth, the beloved child of Sergeant John Rowley and Hannah, his wife, who departed this life on the 15th Septr. 1855, aged 11 months and 10 days.

"For there came One who loved the Flower,
And took it home to deck His bower;
Bore it away beyond the skies
To blossom in his Paradise."

Sacred to the memory of the late Ser. John Rowley, father of the above, who was cruelly murdered at Coorja by the rebels on the 20 May 1857.

"The Lord gave and the Lord hath taken away: blessed be the name of the Lord."

[This was apparently just before the outbreak of the mutiny in Bulandshahr. The 9th N. I. arrived at Khurja on the 21st, and it was doubtless then that Sergeant Rowley was murdered.]

(Reference: *M. N.*)

234.—**855**—MACKENZIE, A. F., C. E. *Inscription* :—Sacred to the memory of Alexander Fletcher Mackenzie, Civil Engineer, Agra, who departed this life on the 1st November 1855, aged 30 years and 9 months. This tomb is erected by his friends as a last token of respect to one who died deeply regretted by all who knew him.

235.—**1855**—CONSTANTINE, A. P. *Inscription* :—Sacred to the memory of Andrew Pythagoras Constantine, who died on the 12th August 1855, aged 22 years. R. I. P.

236.—**1855**—CONSTANTINE, A. *Inscription* :—Sacred to the memory of Andrew Constantine, born at Corinth, a Greek, who died on 29th July 1855, aged 77 years. R. I. P.

[*Cf.* nos. 216, 229 and 230.]

237.—**1856**—LOWE, H. L., Mrs. *Inscription* :—Sacred to the memory of Harriet Louisa, the beloved wife of W. H. Lowe, C. S., born 11th Septr. 1832, died 5th July 1856, aged 24.

[There was a Lowe, Joint Magistrate at Agra during the Mutiny, who did particularly well on several occasions. This is his wife. W. H. Lowe died in 1862 as Secretary to the Board of Revenue. He was the son of J. Lowe, of Messrs. Fergusson and Co., Calcutta, and was born there in 1831. He was educated at a school in Stepney and at Haileybury.]

(References: *Gazetteer; M. N.; W. P.; Haileybury.*)

238.—**1856**—DRUMMOND, F. *Inscription* :—Sacred to the memory of Frederick, eldest son of Hon'ble Robert and Anne Drummond. He was born December 22nd, 1855, and died at Agra, September 21st, 1856.

[R. Drummond was Magistrate at Agra during the Mutiny. His views were not approved by many of his superiors, but he was a strong man and rendered invaluable services in spite of mistakes. The ***Mutiny Narrative*** states "with all his admirable qualities, and all his energy and indefatigable activity, by administrative experience his views were regarded as wrong, and cordial co-operation being most essential at such a juncture in carrying out new arrangements it was perhaps better for the public service and more pleasant to him, that their execution should be entrusted to other hands." He retired in 1877 and died in 1887.

Robert Andrew John Drummond (1820—1887), was the 5th son of the 8th Viscount Strathallan, a title that had been in abeyance since Culloden, and is now merged in the Earldom of Perth. The history of the family is extremely complicated; it is of Hungarian origin and dates back to the time of Edgar Atheling and Margaret, his sister, wife of Malcolm III of Scotland. The Lordship of Drummond dates to 1487, the Earldom of Perth to 1605, the Earldom and Dukedom of Melfort (the latter honour is French) to 1686 and 1692, and the Viscounty of Strathallan also to 1686. The Strathallan branch of the Drummonds are descended from the 2nd son of the 2nd Lord Drummond. His wife Anna Maria was daughter of Compton Reade and died 1871. They had 9 sons and a daughter: the 2nd was born just before the Mutiny.]

(References: *Rice-Holmes; Raikes; J. R. Colvin (R. of I); M. N.; Haileybury; Gazetteer; Burke, P.*)

239.—**1856**—WOLLASTON, L. *Inscription*:—In memory of Lorenza Wollaston infant child of Augustus Wollaston, Vukeel of the Suder Court, born 11th Novr. 1855, died 7th Oct. 1856.

[*Cf.* nos. 225, 647, 652.]

240.—**1857**—(1) HUBBARD, F. C. (2) HUBBARD, A.R., Reverend. *Inscription*:—In memory of Frederick Cairns Hubbard, Esq., B.A., of Agra College, who was killed at Agra, July 5th, 1857, aged 28 years. Also of his brother, the Reverend A. R. Hubbard, Esq., B.A., of the Dehli Mission, who was killed at Delhi, May 11th, 1857, aged 33 years.

[Mr. F. C. Hubbard was Professor of Literature at Agra College. On his way from the Fort to the College he was fired on by the Police at the Kale Khan Darwaza Chauki, wounded, followed and killed. For his brother see no. 460.]

(Reference: *M. N.*)

241.—**1857**—NOWLAN, E., Mrs. *Inscription*:—In memory of Mrs. Elizabeth Nowlan, who was killed during the Mutiny on the 5th July 1857, aged 65 years.

[I have been able to find no record of this murder.]

242.—**1857**—SANDFORD, S. Mrs. *Inscription*:—Sacred to the memory of Sussanna, relict of the late E. M. Sandford, Esq., indigo planter of Maharajgunje, Behar, died at Agra, 3rd May 1857, aged 75 years.

243.—**1858**—COLESTON, L. B., Mrs. *Inscription*:—Sacred to the memory of Louisa Broughton the beloved wife of Samuel Coleston, who having survived the loss of 3 infant daughters and 1 son departed this life in humble dependance upon her Saviour Jesus Christ on the 14th January 1858, aged 23 years 5 months and 12 days. During the Mutiny and rebellion of 1857, she took ill in the Agra Fort whence she was removed to a place close by for recovery, but alas, after two months' ailment, died in the prime of life, leaving a dear infant daughter of nine months' old and a bereaved husband to bemoan a sad and heart-rending separation...

244.—**1858**—BURROWES, E. D., Miss. *Inscription*:—Sacred to the memory of Emma Dorothy, daughter of Charles James and Mary Burrowes who departed this life on the 4th February 1858 in her 22nd year.

"Blessed are the dead that die in the Lord."

245.—**1858**—DUDRENEC, W. P. *Inscription*:—Sacred to the memory of William Patrick Dudrenec, died in the Agra Fort, 10th May 1858, aged 32 years and 4 months.

[Yet another instance of a name celebrated among the military adventurers of the Maratha period. Agra alone contains tombs to men or the descendants of men as well known as Reinhardt, Perron, Filoze, Gardner, Pedron, Hessing, Derridon and Dudrenec; elsewhere we shall find Sutherland, Dyce, Hearsey and others. The name is in this case sufficiently uncommon to warrant the supposition that there is a connexion between the famous Chevalier Dudrenec and this tomb. Chevalier Dudrenec was a native of Brest, a Breton as his name shows, a gentleman of refinement and education, as is generally agreed. He had a most varied career, and served no less than seven masters, including the Begam Samru, Tukaji Holkar, Amir Khan, Hakwa Dada and Perron. He was a most unfortunate commander, and lost several important battles. His notions of loyalty were also not above question. Nevertheless encomiums have been passed on him, and for good as well as for evil there can be no smoke without fire. One thing is certain: he was a gentleman, and gentlemen were rare among the military adventurers. DeBoigne, Dudrenec, Skinner, Gardner and Hearsey were so, but it might be difficult to find another.]

(Reference : *Compton.*)

246.—**1859**—STURT, M., Mrs. *Inscription* :—Sacred to the memory of Madelaine, relict of the late Richard Roche Sturt, Esq., Bengal Civil Service, who departed this life at Agra on the 19th August 1859, deeply regretted, aged 51 years. This monument is erected by her children.

[This would appear to be Richard Roche Sturt, the seventh son of T. L. N. Sturt, H. E. I. C. S., and Puisne Judge, who joined the service in 1827 and died in 1854. He is said to have married Mary, the daughter of Colonel Whish, who died *sine prole*, so that this must have been a second wife, not recorded. His elder brother (Sir) Charles Sturt, K.C.M.G., was the Australian explorer. Several of the Sturts have served in India. The family is also connected with Lord Alington.]

(References : *Haileybury ; Burke, L. G., and P. ; Buckland.*)

247.—**1860**—CRAIGIE, J. A., B.C.S. *Inscription* :—Sacred to memory of John Adair Craigie, Bengal Civil Service, died 15th September 1860, aged 49 years.

[J. A. Craigie joined the service in 1831 and served in Allahabad, Saheswan, Budaun, Bijnor, Moradabad, Hamirpur, Azamgarh and Ghazipur. When he died he was judge of Saugor. He was the son of Lieutenant Colonel Craigie, H. E. I. C. S., and nephew of John Thornhill (father of R. B. Thornhill, No. 385), who nominated him. He was educated at Richmond and Haileybury.]

(References : *Prinsep C. L. ; Haileybury ; W. P.*)

248.—**1863**—PEDRON, M., Miss. *Inscription* :—Sacred to the memory of Miss Madelane Pedron, daughter of Colonel Pedron, Kilehdar of Allyghur, who died on the 4th August 1863 in the house of her adopted daughter, Georgiana Constantine, aged 68 years. R. I. P.

[*Cf.* no. 249.]

249.—**1865**—CONSTANTINE, G., Mrs. *Inscription* :—Sacred to the memory of Georgiana, the beloved wife of Archimedes Constantine, born 5th October 1832, died 6th August 1865, aged 32 years, 10 months, 1 day.

"Ah only to the ardent heart,
Where love and friendship dwell,
Is known how dreadful is to part,
How sad the last farewell.
Oh! Jesus kind, Thy mercy show,
Unto her soul who lies below."

[*Cf.* nos. 235, 236, 248.]

250.—**1877**—DERRIDON, J., Mrs. *Inscription* :—In memory of Jane, the beloved wife of William A. Derridon, who died on 30th March 1877, aged 48 years. R. I. P.

[These are undoubtedly descendants of Major Louis Derridon, a half-bred Frenchman, and related by marriage to both Perron and Hessing (cf. no. 132). He commanded one of Hessing's battalions and was wounded and taken prisoner at the battle of Ujjain. He was at Agra when the English took it in 1803. In

1838 he is mentioned as living at Koil by Lady Fanny Parkes. His grandson owned this property as late as 1871. In the Mutiny at Agra a Mr. and Mrs. Derridon and two children were killed, whilst Mr. Humphries, I.C.S., has told me that when he was at Aligarh (1900-1) a Derridon appeared in his court as witness in a case.]

(References : *Compton : Wanderings of a Pilgrim : M. N.*)

251.—**1877**—DERRIDON, A., Miss. *Inscription :*—In memory of Miss Anne Derridon who died on 9th April 1877, aged 79 years R. I. P.

[Possibly a daughter of Major Derridon.]

252.—**1878**—DERRIDON, W. A. *Inscription :*—In memory of William C. Derridon, who died on 25th July 1878, aged 56 years. R. I. P.

[*Cf.* no. 250.]

253.—**1878**—CURRIE, C., B.C.S. *Inscription :*—Charles Currie, B.C.S., Commissioner of the Agra division, fourth son of the late Sir Frederick Currie, Bart., born 1st July 1829, A.D., died 3rd September 1878, A.D.

[Fourth son of Sir Frederick Currie and Susannah, his second wife (cf. no. 813). He married Marian, third daughter of the Reverend T. T. Upwood of Sorells Hall, Norfolk, and had two sons and a daughter.]

(Reference : *Burke P.*)

254.—**1878**—FANTHOME, L., Miss. *Inscription :*—In memory of Miss Louisa Fanthome, born 25th July 1861, died 5th November 1878. "Blessed are the dead who die in the Lord."

[*Cf.* no. 401.]

255.—**1907**—FANTHOME, J. A. *Inscription :*—In loving memory of John Aitken Fanthome (Jack) born 28th November 1888, died 9th December 1907. I go to my Father. (Also 3 bars of music with word thrice repeated "Excelsior.")

[*Cf.* no. 401.]

FORT CEMETERY, AGRA.

256.—**1857**—LAMB, J. H., Lieutenant. *Inscription :*—In memory of John Henderson Lamb, Lieutenant of the Bengal Artillery, died on the 24th August 1857, of wounds received in action on the 5th July 1857.

"Death swallowed up in victory."

[The action of the 5th July 1857 was the battle of Sacheta or Shahganj, in which Brigadier Polwhele with 600 men attacked 5,000 rebels. The rebels were driven back but the ammunition ran short, and Polwhele was compelled to retreat, hotly pursued by the enemy's cavalry. It was a disastrous affair, and Polwhele was superseded shortly after.

Mr. Lamb was the son of D. Lamb, merchant, born at Liverpool in 1827. He was Lieutenant Pearson's subaltern. He was wounded by a grapeshot in his right thigh. "One of his guns was dismantled, but though exposed to a heavy fire and rushes of cavalry, he went to work to remount it as coolly as if it had been a practice with blank cartridge."]

(References : *Raikes : Rice-Holmes : Kaye : M. N. : C. P ; Forrest.*)

257.—**1857**—JOURDAN, J. C. *Inscription :*—In * memoire de Jean Charles Jourdan né le 10 Mars 1818 au Mans, France, mort sur le champ de bataille le 5 Juillet 1857 à Agra. In memory of Jean Charles Jourdan, born on 10th March 1818 at Mans, France, died at Agra on the field of battle on the 5th July 1857. R. I. P.

* Sic.

[The Agra Militia Cavalry, raised by Raikes and commanded by Major Prendergast, were the usual medley of officers without regiments, civilians, clerks, infantry privates who could ride, pensioners, planters, &c., &c. But to this list had to be added the equestrians of a wandering French circus. Of these M. Jourdan was the chief. He said he went out to fight *pour l' honneur de l' alliance;* and proved his sincerity by his death at Shahganj (Sacheta). Other foreigners fought for us at Lucknow and elsewhere—Geoffroi, Deprat, Barsotelli: and one and all proved allies above the average of bravery. This wandering circus master was not the least brave of them.]

[Reference: *Kaye.*]

258.—**1857**—JOURDAN, AMÉDÉ, C. *Inscription:*—"Ici repose Amédé Charles Jourdan né à Bangalore le 15 September 1851 décédé à Agra le 2 October 1857, âgé de 6 ans." Here lie the remains of Amédé Charles Jourdan born at Bangalore the 15 September 1851; died at Agra the 2 October 1857 aged 6 years. R. I. P."

[Doubtless son of the above.]

259.—**1857**—WATSON, W. C., B.C.S. *Inscription:*—Sacred to the memory of William Christian Watson of the Bengal Civil Service, second son of the late Colonel Thomas Colclough Watson, who died of cholera in the fort of Agra on the 12th of July 1857, aged 32 years and 6 months.

"They shall hunger no more: neither thirst any more: neither shall the sun light on them or any heat."

[Mr. Watson was Magistrate of Aligarh during the Mutiny. Assisted by a troop of volunteer horse raised by Mr. Saunders, an indigo planter, he held out till the 5th July. During this time he and his men kept up a regular patrol in disaffected villages and kept them in check. About the beginning of June the troop was recalled to Agra but 10 men held out at Mandrak, a planter's house 6 miles from Koil, whence they kept communications open and watched the Gwalior troops at Hathras. On the 2nd July whilst the twelve men (Watson, young Outram, Sir J. Outram's son, and their ten volunteers) were at dinner they were attacked by several hundred rabble. They left their meal and charged and defeated them, and went back to dinner. But as soon as the Gwalior troops rose they had to go, and rode in to Agra in time to fight at Shahganj on the 5th July. Watson, who was of weak physique, was killed by his exertions. His operations in Aligarh are peculiarly interesting, as showing the value of a small force of volunteers so long as they have only rabble to contend with.]

(Reference: *M. N.*).

260.—**1857**—SPAN, O. M., Lieutenant. *Inscription:*—Sacred to the memory of Lieutenant O. M. Span, 62 N. I., died 9th August 1857.

[Oliver McC. Span was at Addiscombe 1845-6. He was the son of Captain O. W. Span, H.C.S., born at Bareilly in 1827. It is not known how he died.]

(Reference: *Vibart; C. P.*)

261.—**1857**—BURLTON, F. M. H., Captain. *Inscription:*—Sacred to the memory of Francis Moria Hastings Burlton, Captain, 52nd Regiment, Bengal Native Infantry, and Commandant, 2nd Cavalry, Gwalior Contingent, son of Colonel William Burlton, C. B., Commissary-General, Bengal Army, died in the Agra Fort in the year of the Black Indian Mutiny 1857, from wounds received in action.

"Moria" should be "Moira." He was the son of Colonel Burlton, B. N. C., born in India in 1820. It is recorded that he was greatly beloved by his men, who escorted him from Gwalior to Agra and then left him. He was at Addiscombe 1835-6. He died of cholera on the 13th July.]

(References: *M. N.; Vibart; Coopland; C. P.*)

262.—**1857**—THOMAS, G. P., Major. *Inscription :*—Sacred to the memory of Major George Powell Thomas, 3rd Beng. Eur. Regiment, who died in the Fort of Agra on 4th August 1857, aged 48 years, from the effect of wounds received in action near Agra on 5th July 1858. This monument is erected by his brother officers.

[The date should be 1857, not 1858; it is the date of the battle of Sacheta. Major Thomas was the son of General L. Thomas and was born in India in 1808. He was assistant in the Thagi department in 1835 and in civil employ in the Central Provinces from 1835 to 1840. He was in command of the right wing, and was killed in the attack on the village by his regiment; his horse had just been shot under him. He had formerly been in the 6th N. I. and had distinguished himself in the Afghan War. Kaye, who knew him personally, writes that he was a man of consummate courage, a man of genius, an artist and a poet.]

(References : *Services B. A. list ; Coopland : Kaye.*)

CANTONMENT CEMETERY.

263.—**1806**—TURNER, W., Lieutenant. *Inscription :*—Lt. Willm. Turner, 2 Bn. 4th Regt., N. I., died on the 6th June 1806, Agra.

[Appointed cadet, 1796, lieutenant, 1800. He was the son of C. Turner of Durham, born 1778.]

(References : *D. and M. ; Services B. A. list.*)

264.—**1810**—INGLIS, E. *Inscription :*—Sacred to the memory of Edward Inglis, Esq., late Surgeon to the Horse Artillery, who departed this life on the [24th] Septr. 1810. Universally and justly regretted.

[Edward Inglis became assistant surgeon in 1789 and Surgeon in 1804. He died at Nohmallah; the day of the month is given by Dodwell and Miles.]

(Reference : *D. and M.*)

265.—**1811**—PATTON, J., H.E.I.C.C.S. *Inscription :*—Underneath lie the remains of James Patton, Esq., of the Hon'ble Company's Civil Service who died in consequence of a fall from his horse, the 25th Novbr. 1811. In his public duties he was an upright and honest man, in the near connexions of life equally revered as a husband, father, brother and friend. Under the affliction for his loss it is yet a consolation to reflect that his many virtues will not pass without their reward.

[J. Patton was appointed to the H.E.I.C.C.S. and arrived in India in 1798. He served in Murshidabad, Rajshahi, Shahabad, Allahabad, Farrukhabad, Aligarh, Saharanpur and Bareilly: in 1810 he was Judge and Magistrate of Agra. Both lists give the date of death as 24th November. He was the son of R. Patton, born in 1780 at Burntisland N. B.]

(References : *Prinsep C. L. ; D and M. ; W. P.*)

266.—**1812**—SHIPLEY, Lieutenant. *Inscription :*—This tomb is erected by his brother officers to the memory of Lieutenant Shipley, 2nd Bn. 23rd Regt., who died the 19th July 1812.

[John Shipley joined the service in 1803. The name is spelt Shepley by Dodwell and Miles, but his cadet papers are missing.]

(Reference : *D. and M.*)

267.—**1812**—SEARLE, W., Ensign. *Inscription :*—This monument was...several officers..... station of Agra to the memory of Ensign Wm. Searle., 2nd Battn, 14th Regt., N. I. who died at this place whither he had come for the recovery of his health, July 19th, 1812, aged 20 years.

[Appointed cadet in 1808, and ensign 1811. He had only 14 month's service when he died. He was son of F. Searle, born in 1792.]

(References : *D. and M ; Services B. A. List*).

268.—1813—MASSIE, F. L., Lieutenant. *Inscription* :—To the memory of Lieutenant F. L. Massie, 1st Bn., 22nd N. Regt. who departed this life on the 11th of June 1813, aged 25 years. This monument was erected by his brother officers as a mark of their esteem.

[For the 22nd N. I., cf no. 37. Frederick Lloyd Massie was appointed cadet in 1804 and lieutenant in 1807. He was the son of Charles Massie, a surgeon, and was born at Wrexham in 1789.]

(References : *D. and M.; C. P.*)

269.—1814—TAYLOR, A., Mrs. and INFANT. *Inscription* :—Sacred to the memory of Anna the beloved wife of Lt. J. Taylor of the Corps of Engineers and of their infant son who together with the mother departed this life the 11th day of July 1814 in the 23rd year of her age.

[*Cf.* no. 26.]

270.—1814—BOWIE, R., Colonel. *Inscription* :—To the memory of Colonel Robert Bowie of the Bengal Army this monument was erected by the officers, civil and military, Agra, 1814 *aetatis* LIV. Robertus Bowie, *ob.* 3rd Janry. A. D. MDCCCXIV.

[Robert Bowie became cadet 1778, lieutenant 1781, captain 1797, major 1803, Lieutenant-Colonel 1804, Colonel 1813. He commanded a force against Gohad in 1806.]

(References : *D. and M.; E. I. M. C.*)

271.—1816—GRAHAM, A., Captain. *Inscription* :—Sacred to the memory of Captain Allen Graham of the Ben. Art. as an affect. trib. to dep. worth this mon. was erect. by the hand of an attach. friend to com. equally pub. merit and priv. virt. *ob.* VII June A. D. MDCCCXVI *aet.* XXIX.

The "attached friend" obviously believed in brevity as the soul of an epitaph. Captain Graham joined the B. A. in 1803, and became captain-lieutenant in 1808. He fought with his corps in the reduction of Mauritius, 1810. He was the son of John Graham, born in 1786.]

(References : *Stubbs; Services B. A list; C. P.*)

272.—1818—CRAKE, J. *Inscription* :—Sacred to the memory of John Crake, Esqre., late Surgeon of H. M.'s 67th Regt. of Foot who departed this life in camp at Soonora Soonaree in the Jyepoor territory on the 12th day of Jany., 1818, in his thirty-ninth year. His death will ever be deplored by a large circle of sincere friends particularly his brother officers to whom he was endeared by his amiable qualities and as a last tribute to departed worth had his remains conveyed to this spot for interment.

[The 67th, now the 2nd battalion Hampshire Regiment, were in India 1805-26.]

273.—1818—BEEVOR, T. C., Lieutenant. *Inscription* :—Sacred to the memory of Lieut. T. C. Beevor, 1st Battn. 7th Regt., N. Infy., who departed this life on the 15th December 1818, aged 24 years. This monument erected by his brother officers will commemorate his worth and their regard.

(Appointed cadet 1808 (at the age of 14); ensign 1811; lieutenant 1814. He was the son of the Revd. G. Beevor, born in 1784 at Newton Flotman, Norfolk.)

(References : *D. and M.; C. P.*)

274.—1819—CAMPBELL, D., Lieutenant. *Inscription* :—Sacred to the memory of Lieutenant Duncan Campbell, Interpreter and quartermaster, 2nd Battn. 12th Regt. N. I., who departed this life at Agra, 20th July 1819, aged 30 years. As a testimony of their regard and esteem the officers of his corps erected the monument.

[Appointed cadet 1808, ensign 1810, lieutenant 1814. He was the son of G. Campbell of Invercholan, Argyle, born in 1788.)

(References: *D. and M.; C. P.*)

275.—**1823**—D'ACRE, C., Captain. *Inscription:*—Sacred to the memory of Capt. Charles D'Acre, 1st Bat., 12th Regt., N. I. Fort Adjutant, Agra, who departed this life on the 28 May 1823 This monument is erected by the officers and staff at Agra as a mark of their respect and regard for the deceased.

[Appointed cadet 1803, lieutenant 1804, captain 1815. He was the son of W. D'Acre and Elizabeth Wilkinson, his wife, of Kirklinton Hall, Cumberland, born in 1786.]

(References: *D and M.; C. P.*)

276.—**1826**—(1) CONDY, H. Lieutenant. (2) WANTLING, R. (3) VICKERS, G., privates. *Inscription:*—" This pillar is erected to the memory of Lieut. Henry Condy, Privates Richard Wantling and George Vickers of the Albion Society, Hon. Comp's., 1st Eurn. Regt. who gloriously fell at the assault and capture of the fortress of Bhurtpore, on the 1st January 1826. They fell honorably, so be their memories respected."

[The name is really Candy. He was ensign in 1823 and lieutenant in 1825, the son of R. Candy, born at E. Knoyle in 1803. A puzzling inscription. What the "Albion Society" was and what it had to do with the 1st European Regiment is a riddle. The date is wrong; it should be 18th January; for the capture of Bhurtpore cf. No. 17.]

(References: *E. I. R.; D. and M.*)

277.—**1826**—BULLER, W., Ensign. *Inscription:*—Sacred to the memory of Ensign William Buller, 58th Regiment, N. I., who departed this life on the 12th of June 1826.

[The name is really Buller, though Dodwell and Miles call him Butler. He was the son of the Revd. R. Buller, born at Colyton, Devonshire in 1803. He joined the service in 1824.]

(References: *D. and M.; C. P.*)

278.—**1827**—(1) CLIVE, J. R., Captain. **1864**—(2) CLIVE, J. C. *Inscription:*—Sacred to the memory of Capt. James Retchie Clive of the late 32nd Bengal N. I. *Obit* 2nd May 1827, aged 34 years 6 months. And John George Clive, son of above. *Obit* 22nd February 1864. Leaving a disconsolate mother and widow with a large circle of relatives to bemoan his inseparable loss.

Go home, dear wife, dry up thy tears,
I must lie here till Christ appears;
My debt is paid, my grave you see,
Prepare yourself to follow me.

[Untraceable in any Indian register about this date, or in Dodwell and Miles.]

279.—**1827**—JENKIN, C. C., Lieutenant. *Inscription:*—Sacred to the memory of Lieut. Charles C. Jenkin, late of the 18th Reg. N. I., who departed this life on the 26th July 1827, aged 20 years, greatly lamented by his brother officers.

[Appointed cadet 1823, ensign 1824, lieutenant 1826, the son of G. H. Jenkin, an East India broker, born in 1808.]

(References: *D. and M.; Services B. A., List.*)

280.—**1829**—BURROWE, R., Lieutenant. *Inscription:*—To the memory of Lieut. Robert Burrowe, B. H. A. Died 28th Dec. 1829, aged 27 years.

[The name is really Burrowes. He was appointed cadet in 1814, lieutenant-fireworker 1817, lieutenant 1818. He was at Addiscombe 1812-4. I could not find his cadet papers.]

(References: *Stubbs; B. A. List; Vibart.*)

281.—1830—CAMPBELL, A. F. M., Ensign. *Inscription:*—Sacred to the memory of Ensn. A. F. M. Campbell, 69th Regt. N. I., died on the 23rd Septr. 1830, aged 20 years. This monument is erected by his brother officers as a mark of their esteem.

[This inscription contains a curious error. I could not trace this officer till I found him by chance in the E. I. Register and Vibart. He died not in 1830, but in 1850; and either the sculptor cut a 3 for a 5 in the date, or omitted some words giving the date of birth which was in 1830. It is the tomb of Argyle Fincastle Murray Campbell son of Major C. H. Campbell, (cf. No. 377.) He was born in Calcutta in 1830.]

(References: *E. I. R; Vibart; C. P.*)

282.—1831—MACKAY, D. A., Lieutenant. *Inscription:*—Sacred to the memory of Donald Aeneas Mackay, Lieut., Bengal Artillery and Major of Brigade at Agra, whose earthly career closed Nov. 22, 1831 at the early age of 32 years. This tomb is erected by his brother officers at the station, a mark of esteem and regard for their departed friend.

[Appointed cadet 1816, lieutenant-fire worker 1817, lieutenant 1818. He was adjutant of the 1st Brigade, B. H. A., at the siege of Bhurtpore. He was at Addiscombe 1814-6, and was the son of Captain Mackay of the Madras army; born in 1796.]

(References: *Stubbs; Vibart; Services, B. A. List.*)

283.—1832—BUTTERFIELD, E., Captain. *Inscription:*—Sacred to the memory of Capt. Edward Butterfield, late in the Mahrattah service, who departed this life on the 12th Sept. 1832, aged 60 years, Agra.

[The son of an officer in the Company's service. Little is known of his early career, but before 1790, he was employed by the Raja of Karauli: he subsequently joined a Rajput chief, Durjan Lal by name, and then Scindia's service. In 1794 he was a Captain in De Boigne's 2nd Brigade and remained so several years. He distinguished himself at the battle of Chand Kori under Ambaji Inglia against the rebel Lakwa Dada, in command of 2 battalions; but most of Ambaji's irregular troops either proved cowards or traitors and Butterfield was forced to retreat. Nothing more is known of his career.]

(Reference: *Compton.*)

284.—1833—DUNCAN, B., Mrs. *Inscription:*—Sacred to the memory of Barbara Duncan, aged 31 years, the tenderly beloved wife of James Duncan, Civil Surgeon at Agra. She was snatched from life on the evening of Saturday the 23rd of February 1833 in a moment of genial enjoyment at the Taj. Having traversed hastily on the Eastern side, the marble quadrangle from which it springs, she sat down on the narrow parapet which environs this terrace, lost her hold and falling on the chequered pavement facing the garden instantly expired.

[James Duncan was the son of the Revd. A. Duncan, born at Dundee in 1781.]

(Reference: *S. P.*)

285.—1833—HALL, G. N. C., Ensign. *Inscription:*—To the memory of one respected and esteemed in life deeply and deservedly mourned in death, Ensign George Neville Clayton Hall, 28th Regt, Died 24th March 1833, aged 27 years. This monument is erected by his brother officers.

[Cadet 1825, ensign 1826. He was the son of T. Hall, solicitor, born at Saffron Walden in 1806.]

(Reference: *D. and M.; C. P.*)

286.—**1834**—OLDFIELD, F. B. R., Captain. *Inscription*:—Sacred to the memory of Frederick Bevan Rocke Oldfield, Captain 25th Regt., Bengal Native Infantry and Asst. Commissary-General at Agra, who departed this life on the 23rd August 1834, aged 27 years.

[Appointed cadet 1823, lieutenant 1824 and captain 1834. He was the son of C. Oldfield, born in India in 1807.]

(References: *D. and M.; C. P.*)

287.—**1835**—TAYLOR, J., Lieut.-Colonel. *Inscription*:—To the memory of Lieutenant-Colonel Joseph Taylor, Bengal Engineers, who departed this life, 20th April 1835, aged 45. The Taj and Akbar's tomb were repaired and restored to beauty by this officer. (B. O.)

[Lieutenant Taylor arrived in India in 1808 and was posted to Agra. He got his Captaincy in 1818. He was Assistant Garrison Engineer and Garrison Engineer there till 1826: then Executive Engineer at Dinapore, Garrison Engineer and Civil Architect at Fort William: and finally Superintending Engineer at Agra in 1830. He reduced many small forts belonging to refractory landholders near Agra: repaired the Taj at Agra in 1810 and Akbar's Tomb at Sikandra: he was a volunteer at the siege of Hathras in 1817 and was wounded at Bhartpur on the 18th January. He was endeavouring to blow open the sally port: a sentry was wounded, and Taylor closing with him fell. His soldiers then came up and bayoneted both by mistake. Taylor received 7 wounds, luckily none of them severe. He was made a Brevet Major then and Lieut.-Col. in 1831. B. O.]

(References: *Buckland; Pearse; B. O.; D. and M.*)

288.—**1835**—HALDANE, E., Mrs. *Inscription*:—Sacred to the memory of Eliza, the beloved wife of Lieut. R. Haldane, 45th Regiment, N. I., who died at Agra on the 25th of June 1835, aged 20 years.

[Radclyffe Haldane was the son of H. Haldane (H. M. service), born in 1808.]

(Reference: *C. P.*)

289.—**1836**—WRAY, O. *Inscription*:—Sacred to the memory of Octavius Wray, Surgeon of the Bengal European Regiment, who died at Agra on the 19th day of March 1836, aged 42 years. In testimony of their regard and to commemorate departed worth this monument is erected over his remains by the officers of the Regiment.

[Assistant surgeon 1816, surgeon 1827].

(Reference: *D. and M.*)

290.—**1836**—BECK, F. G., Lieutenant. *Inscription*:—Sacred to the memory of Lieut. F. G. Beck, 13th Regt., N. I. *Ob.* 2nd Aug. 1836 *aet.* 29; erected by the officers of the Regiment as a mark of their sincere regard and esteem for a friend and brother officer.

[The son of J. Beck, of Allesley Park, Coventry, born in 1806; he was appointed ensign in 1826, and lieutenant in 1828.]

(References: *E. I. R.; C. P.*)

291.—**1836**—PARKER, P., Mrs. *Inscription*:—Sacred to the memory of Phoebe, the beloved wife of William James Parker, Lieut, Hon. Company's European Regiment who departed this life at Agra on the 30th June 1836, aged 25 years 7 months.

[Lieutenant W. J. Parker was the elder brother of Sir G. Parker, Bart., who died of sunstroke at Cawnpore in 1857 (cf. no. 25). Mrs. Parker was the daughter of John Marshall, Surgeon, Dinapore: they were married in 1834. Lieutenant Parker predeceased his father: for the family see note mentioned above.]

(Reference: *Burke P.*)

292.—**1838**—TYTLER, M., Ensign. *Inscription:*—Sacred to the memory of Ensign Maurice Tytler who died 2nd January 1838, 23rd Regt., aged 22 years. This tomb is erected by his brother officers in testimony of their esteem.

[This appears to be Maurice William, 2nd son of James Tytler, writer to the signet, of Woodhouselee, Edinburgh, born in 1815 and appointed ensign in 1835. The family is traditionally said to be descended from a cadet of the house of Seton who in the time of James IV of Scotland slew a gentleman named Gray in a quarrel, fled to France and assumed the name Tytler. His two sons returned with Queen Mary and the present family is descended from the elder.]

(References: *Burke L. G.; C. P.*)

293.—**1838**—BOLTON, T., Major. *Inscription:*—Sacred to the memory of Major Theophilus Bolton, 47th Regt., Native Infantry, who died at Agra, March 2nd, 1838. Aged 47 years. This monument was erected by his brother officers.

[The 47th N. I. are the present 7th (Duke of Connaught's Own) Rajputs. This officer was appointed cadet in 1806, ensign in 1807, lieutenant in 1813, captain in 1824 and brevet-major in 1824. He was born at Benares in 1792 and was appointed in India.]

(References: *D. and M; C. P.*)

294.—**1838**—RABAN, H. T., Captain. *Inscription:*—Sacred to the memory of Capt. Henry T. Raban, [47th] Regt. Native Infantry, who died at Agra on the 16th April 1838, aged 37 years. This monument was erected by his brother officers.

[Appointed cadet in 1817, lieutenant 1818, brevet-captain 1833. He was the son of T. Raban, born in Calcutta in 1799. The number of his regiment comes from the E. I. Register.]

(References: *D. and M.; E. I. R.; C. P.*)

295.—**1838**—PATON. J. G. B., Lieutenant. *Inscription:*—Sacred to the memory of Lieut. J. G. B. Paton, 47th Regt., Native Infantry, who died at Kotah on the 18th April 1838, aged 26 years. This monument was erected by his brother officers.

[James George Brown Paton was appointed cadet in 1826, lieutenant in 1832. He was the son of P. Paton of Fraserburgh, a merchant, and born in 1809. He died at "Ungora in Harowtee, about 22 coss from Cota;" he was carrying a fowling-piece, which accidentally went off. He was on his way to see his brother in Nimach.)

(References: *D. and M.; Services, B. A. List.*)

296.—**1839**—OATELEY, J., Lieutenant. *Inscription:*—In memory of Lieutenant James Oateley, 39th Regiment, B. N. I., youngest son of the late Thomas Oateley, Esq. of Albrighton Hall, in the county of Salop, who died at Agra, 1st July 1839.

[Appointed cadet in 1828, ensign in 1829. I could not find his cadet papers.]

(Reference: *D. and M.*)

297.—**1841**—LECONTEUR, P., Captain. *Inscription:*—Sacred to the memory of Bt. Captain Philip Le Conteur, Lieut., H. M's. 31st Regiment, who died at Agra on the 29th of July 1841, aged 32 years. This tomb was erected by his brother officers.

[The 31st, now the 1st Battalion, E. Surreys, were in India from 1825-46.]

298.—**1841**—BACHHOUSE, P., Rev. *Inscription:*—Sacred to the memory of the Rev. Philip Bachhouse, Chaplain of Agra, deceased 30th March 1841, aged 32 years.

299.—**1842**—THOMPSON, W. F., B.C.S. *Inscription* :—Sacred to the memory of William Francis Thompson, Esqr., of the Bengal Civil Service, who died at Agra on the 28th December 1842 A.D., aged 32 years and 8 months. The wearied spirit rests and life's pilgrimage is over.

[W. F. Thompson, son of R. Thompson, was born in 1810. He was recommended to the Right Hon'ble G. Canning and nominated by Sir G. Robinson; he came out in 1828 and served at Bareilly, Banda, Delhi, Hissar, Ghazipur, Gorakhpur and Aligarh. In 1835 he was sent on medical certificate to New South Wales, and thence home. In 1842 he was joint magistrate at Agra. Prinsep gives the date of death as 20th December.]

(References: *Prinsep, C. L.; W. P.*)

300.—**1843**—HARRIS, E., Mrs. *Inscription* :—Sacred to the memory of Ellen, the beloved wife of Capt. P. Harris, 70th Regt. N.-I., eldest daughter of Thos. Blair, Esq. of Lucan near Dublin, who departed this life at Agra on 18th Nov. 1843, aged 27.

[P. Harris was the son of J. Harris, born at Clapham in 1805.]

(Reference: *C. P.*)

301.—**1843**—WALTON, C. J., Lieutenant. *Inscription* :—Sacred to the memory of Charles J. Walton, Lieutenant, Bengal Artillery, who died on the 4th September 1843, aged 21 years. This tomb has been erected by his brother officers.

[Charles Jacob Walton was at Addiscombe 1840-41, and appointed 2nd Lieutenant in the latter year. He was the son of Major Walton, 4th Dragoons, born in 1822.]

(References: *Vibart; Stubbs; Services B. A. List.*)

302.—**1843**—STRAKE, R., M.D. *Inscription* :—Sacred to the memory of Robert Strake, Esq., M.D., Surgeon of His Majesty's 39th Regiment who died at Agra on the 17th August 1843. This monument was erected by his brother officers.

[The 39th are now 1st Battalion, Dorsets, in India from 1832—47].

303.—**1844**—URQUHART, D., Lieutenant-Colonel. *Inscription* :—Sacred to the memory of Lieut.-Colonel Donald Urquhart, His Majesty's 39th Regiment, who died at Agra on the 26th of August 1844, aged 63 years and 11 months. Erected by his brother officers.

[*Cf.* no. 302.]

304.—**1844**—TOWGOOD, A. A., Mrs. *Inscription* :—Sacred to the memory of Amelia Augusta Wood Mason, the dearly loved wife of Captain J. Towgood, Adjt., 55th Lt. Infantry, who died at Agra, 28 June 1844. Aged 29 years and 9 months.

[J. Towgood was the son of J. M. Towgood, paper manufacturer at St. Neots, born 1810.]

(Reference: *C. P.*)

305.—**1844**—PRINGLE, A., M.D. *Inscription* :—Sacred to the memory of Anthony Pringle, Esq., M.D., of the 4th Reg. Light Cavalry, who died at Agra on the 3rd of Feby. 1844, aged 46 years.

306.—**1845**—RICHARDS, H., Lady. *Inscription* :—Sacred to the memory of Henrietta, wife of Major-General Sir William Richards, K.C.B., who departed this life at Agra Novr. 28th, 1845.

[Sir William Richards joined the army in 1794, and served at Seringapatam and in the Maratha, Nepalese and Arakan wars. He lived in India nearly 70 years without visiting England and died at Naini Tal in 1861.]

(Reference: *Buckland.*)

307.—**1845**—ALLEN, JESSIE, A. S. *Inscription :*—Sacred to the memory of Jessie Ann Susan, the beloved daughter of Charles Allen, Esq. C. S., and Mary his wife *obit* at Agra, 25th September 1845, aged 2 years 7 months.

[*Cf.* no. 309.]

308.—**1845**—ALLEN, JULIAN, B. *Inscription :*—Sacred to the memory of Julian Bird, the infant son of Charles Allen, Esq. C. S. and Mary his wife, *obit* at Agra, 20th July 1845, age 2 months 15 days.

[*Cf.* no. 309.]

309.—**1845**—ALLEN, MARGARET, K. *Inscription :*—Sacred to the memory of Margaret Katherine, the beloved daughter of Charles Allen, Esq., C.S., and Mary his wife, *obit* at Agra, 3rd October 1845, aged 1 year 5 months.

[The three children above are the children of Charles Allen, then Judge at Agra (1843-9). He held some high posts, including those of Foreign Secretary to the Government of India, Financial Secretary, and member of the Legislative Council (1854). After his retirement he was Mayor of Tenby and High Sheriff of Pembrokeshire (1876), and wrote the "Yellow Pamphlet" in support of Lord Dalhousie, in answer to Colonel G. B. Malleson's Red Pamphlet at the time of the Mutiny. He was the 5th son of the Revd. B. D. Allen: his wife was Mary, daughter of James Allen of Freestone Hale, Co. Pembroke, and he had (besides these three children) six other sons of whom three were in the Indian services. He belongs to a junior branch of the Allen family, which was founded by William Allen who served with Cromwell in Ireland. There are three branches in Pembrokeshire. The family is of Dutch extraction.]

(References : *Burke. L. G.*; *Buckland.*)

310.—**1845**—HAMILTON, E., Brevet-Captain. *Inscription :*—Sacred to the memory of Lieut. and Bv. Captain Edward Hamilton, H. M. 80th Regiment, who died at Agra on the 12th July 1845, aged 42 years 4 months and 10 days. This tablet was erected to his memory by his brother officers.

[The 80th are now the 2nd Battalion, South Staffordshire Regiment.]

311.—**1845**—MAINWARING, H., Lieutenant. *Inscription :*—Sacred to the memory of Lieut Henry Mainwaring Adjutant 2nd Regiment Grenadiers who died at Agra on the 3rd day of July 1845, aged 24 years and 11 months. Erected by his brother officers.

[The son of G. Mainwaring B. C. S., born in India in 1820. He was wounded in Afghanistan, and at Maharajpur.]

(Reference : *Services B. A. List.*)

312.—**1845**—LIMSDAINE, J. C., Captain. *Inscription :*—Sacred to the memory of John Charles Limsdaine Capt. 58th Regt. N. I. and Commandant 2nd Cavalry Regt. of Sindia's Contingent. Born 23rd July 1803. Died at Agra 6th Dec. 1845.

[The correct name is Lumsdaine. He was appointed cadet 1821, ensign 1822, lieutenant 1825, captain 1837. He was the son of Lieutenant J. Lumsdaine, H. C. S., killed at Bhurtpore (under Lord Lake) : he was born at Agra in 1805.]

(References : *D and M* ; *Services B. A. List.*)

313.—**1845**—LIGHTBODY, J., Captain. *Inscription :*—Sacred to the memory of Captain John Lightbody, H. M. 80th Regt. who departed this life at Agra on the 27th Augt. 1845, aged 28 years 9 months 23 days. This stone was erected by his brother officers as a token of their esteem.

314.—**1845**—MOORE, U., Lieutenant. *Inscription :*—Sacred to the memory of Lieutenant Urban Moore, Adjutant, 56 Regt. N. I., who died on the 29th of June 1845 aged 24 years. This tablet is erected by the officers of his regiment as a token of their esteem and regard.

[The son of the Revd. E. Moore, Rector of Gisleham, Suffolk, born in 1821. He became ensign in 1839, and lieutenant in 1842.]

(Reference : *Services B. A. List.*)

315.—**1845**—EYRE, G., Captain. *Inscription :*—Sacred to the memory of Captain Giles Eyre, H. M.'s 39th Regt. who died at Agra on the 4th of June 1845, aged 41 years and 11 months. Erected by his brother officers.

[*Cf.* no. 302.]

316.—**1846**—CARLISLE, S., Mrs. *Inscription :*—Sacred to the memory of Susannah Carlisle, the beloved wife of Charles H. Carlisle who died on the 24 Oct. 1846, aged 25 years, 10 months and 4 days. This tomb was erected by her affectionate husband.

317.—**1846**—SUTHERLAND, J., Lieutenant-Colonel. *Inscription :*— Beneath this stone lie the mortal remains of John Sutherland, late Lieutenant-Colonel, Bombay Cavalry and Agent to the Governor General in Rajputana. Sorrowing friends desire to inscribe on this humble tablet their tribute of affection to the man. A loftier and more durable monument will record the public worth of the departed soldier and statesman. He was born
He died 24th June 1846.

[This officer is mentioned by Lady Fanny Parkes who met him in 1838, with the Governor General, at Fatehgarh and Aligarh. He was then Resident of Gwalior. He joined the service in 1810.]

(References : *D. and M ; Wanderings of a Pilgrim.*)

318.—**1846**—PEDDIE, R. E., 2nd Lieutenant. *Inscription :*— Sacred to the memory of Robert Edward Peddie, 2nd Lieut., 21st Royal North British Fusiliers, who departed this life at Agra on the 20th September 1846, aged 19 years, 11 months and 18 days. This stone was erected by his brother officers as a mark of their esteem.

319.—**1847**—(1) BULL, E. S., Ensign. **1848**—(2) STAINFORTH, J., Lieutenant. *Inscription :*—Sacred to the memory of Ensign E. S. Bull, H. M. 24th Regiment who died at Agra on the 16th November 1847; also to the memory of Lieut John Stainforth of H. M. 24th Regiment, who died at Landour on the 6th April 1848. This stone is erected by their brother officers as a tribute of their esteem.

320.—**1847**—SMITH, E. P., B.C.S. *Inscription :*—Edward Peploe Smith, Bengal Civil Service, born 1st February 1803, died 6th April 1847. "Looking for the mercy of our Lord Jesus Christ unto Eternal Life."—*Jude* 21.

[Fifth son of George Smith, M. P. for Midhurst. He married first Henrietta, daughter of Charles Bailey, H. E. I. C. S., and secondly Harriet, daughter of George Chester. He had five daughters and one son murdered at Shahjahanpur in the Mutiny, cf. no. 410. He joined the service in 1820 and served almost entirely in Bengal, Shahabad, Birbhum, Nuddea and elsewhere; and in this province, mostly at Ghazipur. In 1839 he was Commissioner of Benares and was so when he died.]

(References : *Burke L. G. ; Prinsep, C. L.*)

321.—**1848**—GRAHAM, L., Mrs. *Inscription:*—Sacred to the memory of Letitia, the beloved wife of Major Joseph Graham, 50th Regt. N. I., who departed this life, 9th September 1848, aged 33 years. In your patience possess ye your souls.

322.—**1848**—LANE, F., Ensign. *Inscription:*—Sacred to the memory of Ensign Frederick Lane, 25th N. I., born 4th July A.D. 1830, died 24th April A.D. 1848, deeply regretted by all who knew him.

[Untraceable].

323.—**1848**—MACKECHNIE, M. A. P., Mrs. *Inscription:*—Sacred to the memory of Margaret Adelaide Playfair, the beloved wife of C. G. MacKechnie, Esq., H. M. 24th Reg. who died at Agra the 10th of January 1848, aged 25 years and 11 months.

324.—**1849**—ROBINSON, M. A., Miss. *Inscription:*—Sacred to the memory of Mary Ann, the beloved daughter of David and Mary Robinson who departed this life on the 18th December 1849, aged 18 years and 6 months.

"Jesus beheld her anguish,
Soft pity moved His breast,
Nor suffered her to languish,
But spake her soul to rest."

325.—**1849**—BUTLER, E. W., Lieut.-Colonel. *Inscription:*—Sacred to the memory of Lieut.-Col. E. W. Butler of the Bengal Artillery, who departed this life—August 1849, aged 49.

[There is a curious error in this inscription. The tomb appears to be that of Colonel E. W. Butler, who died in 1819, for there is no other E. W. Butler in the lists. Edward William Butler was an officer of some fame, who joined the service in 1783, became lieutenant-fireworker 1785, and passing through all the grades became Lieutenant-Colonel in 1818, and died 1st August 1819. He fought in the 2nd Mysore War, Lake's campaigns, Java, at Hathras and in the Pindari war. He was Brigade Major of the artillery under Lake, and fought at Aligarh, Delhi, Agra and Dig.]

(References: *Stubbs*: *B. A. List.*)

326.—**1850**—CLIFFORD, T. W., B.C.S. *Inscription:*—Sacred to the memory of Thomas William Clifford, Bengal Civil Service, who died at Agra 22nd day of December 1850, aged 22 years. This tomb was erected in token of affection and esteem by his brother Lieut. R. W. Clifford X Bl. Lt. Cavalry.

[T. W. Clifford was son of Captain R. Clifford in the E. I. C.'s merchant service, born at St. Omer in France in 1828. He was educated at Haileybury, 1846-8, and died as assistant to the Agra Commissioner after 2 years' service.]

(References: *Haileybury*: *W. P.*)

327.—**1851**—ELLIOT, G., Lieutenant. *Inscription:*—Sacred to the memory of 2nd Lieutenant George Elliot, 2nd Eurn. Benl. Fusiliers who died at Agra on the 27th day of September 1851, aged 21 years. This monument was erected by his brother officers as a mark of their esteem.

[Untraceable.]

328.—**1851**—BROWN, P., Lieut.-Colonel. *Inscription:*—Sacred to the memory of Lieutt.-Col. Peach Brown of the 6th Regiment N. I. who died at Agra on the 13th Octr. 1851, aged 48 years, universally regretted. "Blessed are the dead that die in the Lord."

[Appointed cadet 1818, captain 1831. He was the son of Mr. Brown of Northampton, where he was born in 1802.]

(References: *D. and M.; Services B. A. List.*)

329.—1851—ANDERSON, V. S., Mrs. *Inscription* :—Sacred to the memory of Veronica Scott, the beloved wife of James Anderson M. D. 2nd European Bengal Fusiliers, died 20th March 1851.

330.—1852—LITTLEFIELD, J. *Inscription* :—John Littlefield Senr. died at Agra 16th Janry, 1852 aged 71 years.

331.—1852—SMYTH, B. *Inscription* :—Sacred to the memory of Robert Smyth, 2nd E. B. Fusiliers, who died at Agra on the 12th of May 1852, aged 28 years. He was born near the town of Balleymena, County of Antrim, Ireland. This stone was erected in token of respect by his affectionate brother, Joseph Smyth, of the same corps.

332.—1853.—FORBES, S. A., Mrs. *Inscription* :—Sacred to the memory of Sophia Adams, the beloved wife of Captain Forbes, 27th Regt. N. I., who died at Agra on the 6th day of June 1853, age 23 years and 10 months.

[Sophia Adams, *née* Fell, was the first wife of Major-General William Forbes. She had an only son born in 1853. Her husband was the 2nd son of Alexander Forbes and grandson of Duncan Forbes-Mitchell, of Thainstone. A descendant succeeded to the Barony of Sempill, a family with which the Forbes are connected by marriage. The family is descended from Patrick Forbes armour-bearer of James III of Scotland, *circa* 1480. Many members of it have served in India.]

(Reference : *Burke P.*)

333.—1854—ANDREWS, N. E., Major. *Inscription* :—Sacred to the memory of Captn. and Bt. Major N. E. Andrews of the 73rd Regt. N. I., who departed this life on the 22nd May 1854, aged 45 years and 4 months. In token of their deep and sincere regret for his loss this monument is erected by his brother officers.

[This is most probably W. Eyre Andrews, who was appointed cadet in 1824, lieutenant 1826, captain 1840. There is no other Andrews who could be identified with this one. W. E. Andrews was the son of W. Andrews, a doctor at Richmond, and was born in 1808.]

(References : *D. and M.*; *Services B. A. List.*)

334.—1854—GRANT, B. D., Lieutenant. *Inscription* :—In this tomb erected by his sorrowing parents repose the mortal remains of Lieutenant Bethune D. Grant, Interpreter and Quartermaster of the 35th Regt. Bengal Lt. Infy., who died at Agra 30th November 1854 in the 28th year of his age.

"For the trumpet shall sound, and the dead shall be raised incorruptible, and he shall be changed."

[B. Donald Grant was the son of Surgeon J. Grant, H. C. S., born in 1827 at Calcutta and educated at Bath and Addiscombe.]

(Reference : *Vibart* ; *C. P.*)

335.—1855—HUDDLESTON, I. F., Mrs. *Inscription* :—Sacred to the memory of Isabella Frances the dearly beloved wife of G. E. Huddleston, Esq., 8th the Kings's Regt., who died at Agra on Sunday the 7th Octr. A. D. 1855, aged 24 years.

"I have finished my course ; I have kept the faith." *2 Tim. Chap. IV, Verse VII.*

336.—1855—L'ESTRANGE, F., Lieutenant. *Inscription* :—Sacred to the memory of Lieutenant F. L'Estrange, 30th Regt. N. I., who died at Agra on the 13th Sept. 1855. This tomb is erected by his brother officers as a token of esteem and regard.

[Son of Colonel L'Estrange, born in 1823, and educated at Addiscombe.]

(Reference : *Vibart* ; *C. P.*)

337.—1856—ARMSTRONG, H. *Inscription* :—Sacred to the memory of Henry Armstrong, Esquire, Surgeon, H. M.'s 85th Regiment, who was killed at Agra on the 2nd May 1856 by a fall from his horse, aged 31 years.

[The 85th, now the 2nd battalion King's Shropshire L. I., were in India 1853-6.]

338.—1856—TERRY, W. *Inscription* :—Sacred to the memory of William second son of the late Revd. Michael Terry, Rector of Dummer, Hunts, England, who departed this life July 19th 1856, aged 39 years. "There is joy in the presence of the angels of God over one sinner that repenteth."—[*Luke*] 15*th Chapter*, 10*th verse*.

339.—1856—ORCHARD, M. E., Mrs. *Inscription* :—Sacred to the memory of Maria Esperanza, widow of the late Col. J. W. Orchard, C. B. 1st European Bengal Fusiliers, who died at Agra June 24th 1856, aged 55 years. This monument is erected as a token of affection by her children.

[J. W. Orchard was a very well known officer. He was born in Newfoundland in 1790, and joined the service in 1804. He spent most of his service with the E. B. Fusiliers; he fought at Bhartpore and Ghazni where he was wounded, commanded the army of reserve in 1840 (as Brigadier) and the 7th brigade in the army of the Sutlej. He got his C. B. at the Queen's coronation, and the order of the Durani Empire from Shah Shuja after the Afghan war. He died in 1847 from a fall from his horse on parade.]

(References: *Services, B. A. List* : *P. R.*)

340.—1857—(1) HAILES, M. W. 1858—(2) HAILES, F. E. R., Mrs. *Inscription* :—Sacred to the memory of Fanny Elizabeth Ross who died 28th Jan. 1858, aged 23 years, and of Montague Wyllie, who died 16th May 1857, aged 8 months and 15 days, the beloved wife and son of Harris William Hailes, Esq., Lieut., 44th Regt. B. N. I.

341.—1857—HENDERSON, S., Mrs. *Inscription* :—Sacred to the memory of Susan the dearly beloved wife of Henry Henderson, Esqre., H. M.'s 10th Regt., who died at Agra on the 7th May 1857. "Believe in the Lord Jesus Christ and thou shalt be saved." *Acts*, *XVI*, 31.

[Lieutenant Henderson did good service in the early stages of the Mutiny with Saif-ulla Khan's force of matchlockmen, which had been raised by Mr. Drummond. In July, however, he returned his guns, as he did not think the matchlockmen capable to protect them. It is significant that the same night Saif-ulla Khan reported that his men were dubiously faithful. He himself remained so, however, and was rewarded after the Mutiny.]

(Reference: *M. N.*)

342.—1857—D'OYLY, E. A. C., Captain. *Inscription* :—The dying request of him who lies beneath this stone, Edward Armstrong Currie D'Oyly, Captain of Bengal Artillery, who was mortally wounded whilst commanding his battery in the action against the mutineers on the 5th of July 1857 and died in the fort of Agra on the following day, than whom no more gallant soldier or true-hearted man ever gloriously fell on the battle field, whose last words were—"Lay a stone over my grave and say I died fighting my guns"—is thus fulfilled.

[For the battle of Sacheta or Shahganj see no. 256. D'Oyly fought his guns so long as his ammunition lasted. The loss was most severe, for he was all that this epitaph says of him. He was "one whose dying moments Florence Nightingale herself might have been proud to soothe." His last spoken words were those recorded on the stone. He was at Addiscombe from 1840-41 and was

34 at his death. His brother T. D'Oyly was also in the Bengal artillery He was the son of Captain D'Oyly, Bengal artillery.]

(References: *Rice-Holmes; Raikes; M. N.; Vibart; Stubbs; C. P.*)

343.—**1857**—FRENCH, L. J., Captain. *Inscription:*—In memory of Captain Lucius John French, 9th Queen's Royal Lancers, who fell in action near this spot, October 10th 1857.

[The so-called battle of Agra was a discreditable affair. Greathed's column from Delhi arrived at Agra on the morning of the 10th. Colonel Cotton had withdrawn his vedettes and patrols; and civil authorities, who warned him that the enemy were closer than he thought were snubbed. Greathed accepted what he was told without question and himself posted no piquets, encamping his force on the parade-ground. The men lay down to sleep. They were suddenly attacked. But it was impossible to take soldiers like these by surprise. An officer galloped off for Greathed at the fort; independent fights were going on all over the parade-ground. "Here a couple of cavalry soldiers were charging each other. There the game of bayonet versus sword was being carried on in real earnest. Further on a party of the enemy's Cavalry were attacking one of Blunt's guns ...... Just in front, the 75th Foot (many of the men in their shirt sleeves) were forming square to receive a body of the rebel horse. A little to the left of the 75th Remington's troops of horse artillery and Bourchier's battery had opened fire from the park without waiting to put on their accoutrements .... still further to the left, the 9th Lancers and Gough's squadron of Hodson's Horse were rapidly saddling and falling in; on the right the 8th Foot and the 2nd and 4th Punjab Infantry were busy getting under arms, while beyond the three squadrons of Punjab Cavalry under Probyn and Younghusband were hurrying to get on the enemy's flank.

The enemy were gradually driven back, when Greathed appeared on the scene. The 9th Lancers made a series of brilliant charges, one troop recaptured Blunt's captured gun—the Captain (French) was there killed. He had already distinguished himself at Delhi.

The battle is remarkable, apart from its extraordinary nature—if ever a British force "muddled through" it was at Agra—for the number of officers of repute who were then young subalterns that took part in this hand-to-hand affairs. Sir Dighton Probyn, Lord Roberts, Sir John Watson, Sir Hugh Gough, all fought there; the former won his V. C. for capturing a standard, and Lord Roberts was nearly killed, being saved by a trooper of the 9th Lancers. Sir George Campbell also took part in the fight and captured several guns—an incident fully described in his memoirs.]

(References: *Roberts; M. N.; Rice-Holmes; Campbell.*)

344.—**1857**—(1) SHAPTER, W. (2) TUDGAY, F. **1858**—(3) WATTERS, W. *Inscription:*—To the memory of William Shapter, aged 19 years and Frederick Tudgay aged 31 years 1st Battalion H. M. 8th the King's Regt, who fell in action at Agra on the 10th of October 1857, also of William Watters, aged 32 years who died at Futtyghur Janry. 12th, 1858. Erected by the non-commissioned officers and privates of the Light Company.

[*Cf.* no. 343.]

345.—**1858**—SCARLETT, J. R. *Inscription:*—Sacred to the memory of James Robert Scarlett who died at Agra on the 8th of January 1858, aged 19 years and 11 months.

346.—**1858**—McCULLUM, W. *Inscription:*—Sacred to the memory of William McCullum who departed this life on the 30th October 1858, aged 41 years. This tomb was erected by his widow.

347.—**1858**—FAIRWEATHER, J., Lieutenant. *Inscription:*—Scared to the memory of John Fairweather, died 26th July 1858.

[J. Fairweather was a lieutenant in the Veteran establishment.]

(Reference: *E. I. R.*)

348.—**1859**—PHILLIPS, M., Mrs. *Inscription* :—Sacred to the memory of May the beloved wife of Alfred March Phillips, Esqr., B.C.S., who died at Agra on the 25th of March 1859, aged 20 years and 2 months. "As for me and my house we will serve the Lord." *Joshua, Chapter XXIV, V. 15.*

[Mr. A. M. Phillips was Joint Magistrate at Etah when the Mutiny broke out and was compelled to leave his district and go to Agra, where he succeeded Mr. Drummond. There he did good service and would have prevented the surprise of the 10th October if he had been listened to. A. Lisle March Phillips was the son of S. March Phillips, Under Secretary at the Home Office and was born in 1824. He retired in 1873 and died in 1887.]

(References : *Haileybury ; W. P.; Raikes.*)

AGRA FORT.

349.—**1857**—COLVIN, J. R., B.C.S. *Inscription* :—In memory of John Russel Colvin born May 29th 1807, died in this fort, September 9th 1857, Lieutenant-Governor of the North-Western Provinces, India.

[J. R. Colvin was of mixed Scotch and Irish descent. His grandfather was a Sterlingshire merchant, his grandmother, the daughter of a North Ireland clergyman. Their son, Alexander, founded a business (Colvin, Ainslie and Cowie) in India in 1778. He died in 1818, and a monument erected by his brother merchants to his memory is in St. John's, the Calcutta Parish Church. He is buried in the South Park Street Cemetery. His younger brother, James, joined his brother early in the eighties and married in 1802, Maria, daughter, of William Jackson, attorney to the Company and "Registrar" of the Supreme Court. Their fourth son was J. R. Colvin.

He was educated in private schools at St. Andrews and subsequently (1819) at St. Andrew's University; and in 1823 he entered Haileybury. In 1825 he sailed for India ; for a few months he was at the Fort William College and before the end of 1826 became an Assistant Registrar in the Chief Court of Appeal. He was subsequently Assistant at Cuttack and in Hyderabad. For four years (1831—35) he was in both judicial and revenue departments of the secretariat successively as Assistant and Deputy Secretary and Secretary. For the next six years he was Lord Auckland's Private Secretary and as such is said to have had considerable influence on his Afghan policy, which ended in the Kabul expedition of 1839. He was subsequently Resident in Nepal (1845) after three years furlough, Commissioner of Tenasserim in 1846, Judge of the Calcutta High Court and Lieutenant-Governor of the North-Western Provinces from 1853. His policy was mainly directed to reforms in the judiciary and police, and to the re-settlement of the land revenue.

The Mutiny broke out when Mr. Colvin was at Agra. The anxiety proved too much for his health, and he died in the fort, where he is buried. Controversy rages round two parts of his career : his connexion with the Afghan War, and his policy during the Mutiny. Sir Auckland Colvin has exhausted the subject in his life of his father, and those who wish to go deeper into the matter should consult it. This is no place for such a discussion. Whatever his errors, there can be no doubt that "he gave up his life for his country as much as if he had fallen on the battle-field." His death was due to his persistence in continuous mental labour when his health demanded complete repose. To his qualities—his gentleness, forbearance and energy, his administrative ability and devotion to duty—even his critics bear witness. Almost his last words were "*Nec patriam antiquam nunc est spes ulla videndi.*"

He married in 1827, Emma Sophia, daughter of the Reverend Wetenhall Sneyd in Calcutta. Of his sons, Sir Auckland Colvin was also Lieutenant-Governor of the North-Western Provinces and Oudh (1887—1892) and another son, Sir W. M. Colvin (died 1908) was a well-known barrister in practice at Allahabad.]

(References : *J. R. Colvin (R. of I.); Raikes ; Kaye : M. N.; Rice-Holmes ; Buckland ; Burke P.)*

350.—**1908**—STRACHEY, J., Sir. *Inscription* :—In grateful commemoration of services rendered to posterity by the Hon'ble

Sir John Strachey, G.C.S.I., to whom, not forgetting the enlightened sympathy and timely care of others, India is mainly indebted for the rescued and preserved beauty of the Taj Mahal and other famous monuments of the ancient art and history of these Provinces formerly administered by him. This tablet is placed by order of his friend, the Earl of Lytton, Viceroy and Governor-General of India, A. D. 1880.

[This tablet is not a memorial of Sir John Strachey, but in commemoration of his work. He died, however, in 1908 and this has been inserted here in consequence. Sir John Strachey, G.C.S.I., was born in 1823, the son of Edward Strachey, B.C.S. He was educated at Haileybury and went out to India in 1842. The chief posts he held were President of a Commission to inquire into the cholera epidemic of 1861: Judicial Commissioner of the Central Provinces in 1862: President of the Sanitary Commission in 1864: officiating Chief Commissioner of Oudh in 1866-67: Member of the Governor General's Supreme Council from 1868 to 1872: acting as Governor General during the interregnum after the death of Lord Mayo for a few days: Lieutenant-Governor of the North-Western Provinces from April 1874 to December 1876: Financial Member of the Supreme Council from 1876 to 1880: Member of the Council of India from 1885 to 1895. His works are "Hastings and the Rohilla War," 1892; "India, its Administration and Progress," 1903: and with Lieutenant-General Sir Richard Strachey, G.C.S.I., his elder brother, "the Finance and Public Works of India 1869—1881," in 1882. He was made K.C.S.I., in 1873, and G.C.S.I., in 1878. His son, Sir Arthur Strachey (died 1901) was Chief Justice, Allahabad, High Court, from 1899 to 1901.

The Strachey family is very ancient and has moreover been connected with India since the time of Clive. It traces its tree back as far as William Strachey of Saffron Walden born in 1493. The first baronet, Sir Henry (1737—1810) was Secretary to Lord Clive in 1764, and held other posts under Government, both at home and abroad. Edward Strachey, his second son, was in the B.C.S. His sons were Sir Edward, 3rd baronet, Henry (a Colonel in the Bengal Army), Sir Richard and Sir John (vide above) and George, formerly British Minister at the Saxon Court. Sir John Strachey married Katherine Jane, daughter of G. Batten, B.C.S. Besides Sir Arthur Strachey, mentioned above, another son was a Lieutenant-Colonel in the Indian Army; other members of the family have also served or been connected with India. The present (4th) baronet Sir Edward Strachey is M. P. for S. Somerset.]

(References: *Buckland; Burke P.*)

V.—CANTONMENT GARDENS, AGRA.

351.—**1837**—ADAMS, J. W., Major-General, Sir. *Inscription:*— Seringapatam, Rewah, Pindari War, Nagpur, Seonie, Entouri, Chandah. In honour of Major-General Sir John Adams, G.C.B., his European and Native friends and admirers of the Bengal Army erect this column. During a distinguished service of 56 years, his eminent military capacity and judgment, his just and generous feeling and his demeanour, ever courteous and kind, secured him the respect, love, and veneration of all classes, and more especially of the Bengal Sepoys.

[Sir John Withington (or Worthington) Adams (1764-1837) entered the Army in 1780. He fought against the Rohillas under Sir R. Abercromby at Bhitaura (1794): at Malavelly and Seringapatam 1799: and on the Sutlej (1809), when he commanded his regiment. In 1813 he commanded the field force in Rewah and captured the fort of Entauri. In 1815 he held command of a brigade on the Kali in Kumaun in the Gurkha war, becoming a C.B., and commander in Kumaun in the same year: held command in Nagpur in 1816: and in 1817 commanded the 5th division of the Southern Army at Hoshangabad on the Narbada against the Pindaris. He defeated the Peshwa at Seoni and took Chanda in 1818. He was also present at the capture of Bhurtpore in 1826. In 1828 he commanded the Sirhind Division. He became K.C.B. in 1830 and died at Subathu in 1837, where he is buried. The epitaph is as follows;

"Sacred to the memory of Major-General Sir John Withington Adams, G.C.B., who, after a distinguished career of 57 years in India in the service of the Honourable East India Company, departed this life on the 9th March 1837, in the 74th year of his age. This tomb is erected over his remains in commemoration of his private virtues. Agra contains the monument of his public services."]

(References: *Buckland; Hastings (R. of I.); Prinsep's Military Transactions; Grant Duff; B. O.*)

Muttra District

CANTONMENT CEMETERY.

352.—**1804**—FRAZER, H., Major-General. *Inscription:*—Sacred to the memory of Major-General Henry Frazer of His Majesty's 11th Regiment of Foot who commanded the British Army at the battle of Deig, on the 13th November 1804, and by his judgment and valour achieved an important and glorious victory. He died in consequence of a wound he received when leading on the troops and was interred here on the 25th of November 1804, in the 40th year of his age. The Army lament his loss with the deepest sorrow; his country regards his heroic conduct with grateful admiration. History will record his fame and perpetuate the glory of his illustrious deed.

[General Frazer's force consisted of the 76th, the Company's European Regiment and 6 battalions of sepoys. Holkar's troops were strongly posted but a succession of bayonet charges turned them out of their positions. "They charged one battery after another for 2 miles." Frazer's leg was shot off early in the engagement. He was removed to Muttra but died shortly after. "He was an able and brave soldier, and a worthy member of society: so that the whole army sincerely mourned his loss." Wellesley wrote to the Directors as follows: "The Governor General in Council laments with the deepest concern the irreparable loss of that gallant and distinguished officer Major-General Frazer, to whose eminent judgment and military skill and examplary valour is principally to be ascribed the signal success of the British arms on this memorable occasion." The 11th are the present Devonshire Regiment.]

(References: *Amir Khan: Grant Duff: Wellesley's Despatches: Thorn.*)

353.—**1804**—BOYD, W., Lieutenant. *Inscription:*—Sacred to the memory of Lieutenant William Boyd, of the 15th Regiment of Bengal Native Infantry, who was wounded at the battle of Deig on the 13th of November and departed this life on the 26th of the same month A. D. 1804.

Weep not for those that die in the Lord, for they rest from their labours.

[He belonged to the 2nd battalion of the 15th N. I, *cf.* nos. 352 and 40. He was appointed cadet in 1799, ensign in 1800 and lieutenant in 1803. He was born in 1785 at Londonderry, "of Protestant parents."]

(References: *D. and M; Services B. A. List.*)

354.—**1806**—SMITH, J., Major-General. *Inscription:*—Sacred to the memory of Major-General John Smith of His Majesty's Service, Commanding Officer in the Field, who departed this life 6th August 1806, age 41 years. In testimony of their high opinion of his public character and conduct and of their sincere respect and regard for his private virtues, this monument was erected by the unanimous subscription of the Hon'ble Company's officers and staff of the station of Muttra.

[This officer is that General Smith who pursued Amir Khan into Rohilkhand and defeated him at Afzalgarh (Bijnor) in 1805. He was for 25 years in the 15th Foot Guards and served with them in the Netherlands campaign of 1793-4.]

(References : *Thorn : Amir Khan : Gazetteer : Cardew : Grant Duff.*]

355.—**1808**—WOOD, R., Colonel. *Inscription :*—In memory of Colonel Robert Wood of His Majesty's 17th Infantry, who departed this life 18th July 1808.

[For the 17th cf. No. 14.]

356.—**1808**—DICKENS, R. M., Major-General. *Inscription :*—Sacred to the memory of Major-General Richard Mark Dickens, H. M.'s 34th Regiment of Foot, who departed this life on the 29th April 1808, aged 45 years.

[The only thing I have been able to discover about this officer is that he reduced Kamona and Ganauri. For an account of this *cf.* no. 59.]

(References : *Cardew : Gazetteer.*)

357.—**1809**—MOORE, A., Ensign. *Inscription :*—Sacred to the memory of En. A. Moore, 17th Regiment, Native Infantry, died 6th July 1809, aged 21 years.

[Augustus Moore was appointed cadet in 1805 and ensign in 1806. The list gives the date of death as August 5th.]

(Reference : *D. and M.*)

358.—**1814**—MORRIS, J., Lieutenant. *Inscription :*—To the memory of Lieutenant J. Morris, 1. B. 5 N. I. who died regretted by the whole corps, 12th August 1814.

[John Morris was appointed cadet in 1804 and lieutenant in 1807. He was born at Dunlan, co. Antrim, in 1784.]

(References : *D. and M ; Services, B. A. Lists.*)

359.—**1815**—ELLISON, F. C., Lieutenant. *Inscription :*—Sacred to the memory of Lieutenant F. C. Ellison, late of the VII Regiment, Native Cavalry, who departed this life November XXII, MDCCCXV, aged XXXII years.

[Frederick Crousdaile Ellison was appointed cadet in 1798 and cornet in 1801 and lieutenant in 1805. He was of Milford, Kilmaine, co. Mayo.)

(References : *D. and M. ; Services B. A. List.)*

360.—**1819**—FRITH, R., Brig.-General. *Inscription :*—In memory of Brigadier-General Richard Frith, 8th Regiment, Light Cavalry, and Commanding the Agra and Muttra Frontiers, who departed this life 26th July 1819, aged 63 years.

[He was appointed cadet in 1778 and cornet in 1779. After 19 years' service he became a captain and Lieutenant-Colonel 6 years later.]

(Reference : *D. and M.*)

361.—**1819**—KERR, W., Lieutenant. *Inscription :*—Sacred to the memory of Lieut. William Kerr of the 2nd Battalion, 12th Regt. Native Infantry, who died on the 18th November 1819, aged 26 years. In testimony of their regard and esteem for the deceased, the officers of his corps have erected this monument.

[He was appointed cadet in 1809, ensign 1812, lieutenant 1815. He was the son of Major-General Kerr (H. M. Service), born in 1794 at St. Vincent, and educated at Harrow.]

(References : *D. and M ; C. P.*)

362.—**1821**—RYDER, C., Major. *Inscription :*—Sacred to the memory of Major Charles Ryder of the 3rd Regiment, Light Cavalry, who departed this life on the 7th day of May in the year of Our Lord 1821. Deeply lamented by his brother officers and the men of the regiment.

[He was appointed cadet in 1797, lieutenant 1800, captain 1807, major 1818. He was the son of T. Ryder, born in 1781 at Hendon.]

(References: *D. and M; C. P.*)

363.—**1826**—DIBDIN, F., Lieutenant. *Inscription*:—Sacred to memory of Lieutenant Francis Dibdin, 5th Regiment, Light Cavalry, who departed this life at Muttra on the 16th of October 1826, aged 26 years. This monument was erected by his brother officers as a mark of their esteem for him while living and of their sorrow for his loss.

[He was appointed cadet in 1818, lieutenant in 1819. He was the son of the Revd. T. F. Dibdin, born in 1800 at Hampstead.]

(References: *D. and M; C P.*)

364.—**1827**—MANSFIELD, J., Lieutenant. *Inscription*:—Sacred to the memory of Lientenant James Mansfield, 1st Regiment, Native Infantry, who departed this life on the 24th of November 1827, much regretted by the whole corps, aged 32 years. This monument is erected by his brother officers.

[Appointed cadet in 1812, lieutenant in 1815. He was the son of J. Mansfield, born in 1795.]

(References: *D. and M; C. P.*)

365.—**1830**—DINGWALL, A. F., Captain. *Inscription*:—Sacred to the memory of Captain A. F. Dingwall, XIX Bengal Native Infantry, died 16th December 1830, aged 39 years.

[Arthur Fordyce Dingwall was appointed cadet in 1806, lieutenant in 1812, captain in 1824. He was the son of the Revd W. Dingwall born at Forgue, N. B., in 1789.]

(References: *D. and M; C. P.*)

366.—**1838**—CRAWFORD, D. H., B.C.S. *Inscription*:—Sacred to the memory of Douglas Hadow Crawford of the Bengal Civil Service, who was born on 5th April 1816 and died beloved by all who knew him on 2nd June 1838.

[D. H. Crawford was son of William Crawford, East India agent, of Dorking. He joined the service in 1834 and arrived in India the same year. He had served in Meerut and Muttra and was joint Magistrate when he died.]

(References:—*Prinsep C. L; W. P.*)

SUTHERLAND GARDENS.

367.—**1801**—(1) SUTHERLAND, C. P. **1804**—(2) SUTHERLAND, R., Colonel. *Inscription*:—In memory of Robert Sutherland, Colonel in Maharaja Daulat Rao Sindhia's Service, who departed this life on the 20th July 1804, aged 36 years. Also in remembrance of his son, C. P. Sutherland (a very promising youth), who died at Hindia, on the 14th of October 1801, aged 3 years.

[Originally an officer in the 73rd, from which he was cashiered, Col. Sutherland entered Sindhia's service in De Boigne's 1st Brigade in 1790. Soon after 1794 he obtained command of the 3rd and then of the 2nd Brigade. At De Boigne's retirement he was senior officer in Hindustan and hoped to succeed him: but Perron had Sindhia's ear and obtained the appointment for himself. He saw service in command in Bundelkhand in 1796: but shortly afterwards was dismissed for intriguing with rebellious chiefs. In 1799 he was restored through the influence of his father-in-law, John Hessing, and became commander of the 1st Brigade. In 1801 he won the important victory of Indore over Holkar's troops. In 1802 as the result of an unsuccessful intrigue against Perron, he resigned his commission. He was in Agra in a private capacity when Lake besieged it (not as Keene says in his "Handbook to Agra" as commandant): but the troops after imprisoning him and other Europeans sent him as an envoy to Lake to ask for terms. He passed over to the British and was given a pension of Rs. 800 a month. He had, so far as is known, two sons, of whom one is buried with him. His wife appears to have been Magdalene, daughter of John Hessing (cf. no. 145.)]

References : *Thorn : Compton : Keene's Handbook.*)

NEAR SADR BAZAR.

368.—**1857**—BURLTON, P. H. C., Lieutenant. *Inscription* :—Sacred to the memory of Lieutenant P. H. C. Burlton, 67th Native Infantry, who was shot by a detachment of his regiment and of the 41st Native Infantry near this spot on the 30th May 1857. This tomb is erected by his brother officers.

[Two companies—one of the 44th and one of the 67th N. I.—were sent from Agra to relieve a company of the 67th who were at Muttra. The relieved company was to escort the treasure to Agra. The treasure was packed in carts: and as soon as Mr. Burlton gave the order to march, the guard mutinied and shot him.

The *Mutiny Narrative*, Rice-Holmes and Raikes, give slightly different accounts of the incident, which leave it uncertain whether all three companies mutinied, or one or more of them, and if so which ; nor is it clear to which company Mr. Burlton belonged. Probably all three companies rose : and as Mr. Burlton was to march with the relieved company, in all probability he belonged to them.

[41st in the epitaph is a mistake for 44th. The 41st were at Sitapur, the 44th at Agra.]

(Reference : *M. N : Rice-Holmes ; Raikes.*)

SADABAD, NEAR TAHSIL.

369.—**1834**—WROUGHTON, B. F. *Inscription* :—To the memory of Bartholomew Francis, fifth son of Captain Robert Wroughton, 69th Regiment. N. I., Revenue Surveyor of the Agra Division, and Sophia, his wife. Born 17th January 1830, died 17th March, 1834, aged 4 years and 2 months.

[Captain Wroughton, son of G. Wroughton, attorney to the E. I. C., born in Calcutta in 1797, was afterwards Deputy Surveyor-General of India. Two of his daughters married brothers, one of whom was Captain G. W. W. Fulton, *cf.* no. 386.]

(References : *Burke L. G. I. ; Services B. A. List.*)

Farrukhabad District.

FORT CEMETERY.

370.—**1788**—SKARDON, S. *Inscription* :—To the memory of Mr. Samuel Skardon, who died October 30th, 1788 A.D., aged 57 years. This tomb was erected by his friend, Captain Richard Ramsay.

[The only Richard Ramsay I have been able to find is the one who deserted at Bhitaura, *cf.* no. 407.]

(Reference : *D. and M.*)

371.—**1794**—MACFIE, T., Lieut. *Inscription* :—Here lies the body of Lieutenant Thomas Macfie, who departed this life on the 6th July 1794, in the 35th year of his age. Deeply lamented by all to whom his amiable manner and many virtues were known.

[Dodwell and Miles gives the name as Macphee. He was appointed cadet and lieutenant in 1778.]

(Reference : *D. and M.*)

372.—**1797**—HODSON, F., Major. *Inscription:*—Sacred to the memory of Major Francis Hodson, who departed this life on April 27th, 1797.

[The name should be Hodgson: there is no F. Hodson in the list. He was appointed cadet in 1770, ensign in 1772, lieutenant in 1777, captain in 1781.]

(Reference: *D. and M*).

373.—**1799**—CLAYDON,* E., Captain. *Inscription:*—To the memory of Captain E. Claydon, 5th N. Regt., who departed this life the 16th of November 1799, aged 46 years.

[An English brigade was stationed at Fatehgarh from 1777 by the Treaty of Fyzabad (1775), and remained there continuously, though in Oudh territory, till the district was ceded to the British in 1801. It was this brigade that won the battle of Bhitaura in 1794. This no doubt explains the above entries. This name is Edward Clayton, not Claydon. He was appointed cadet in 1778 and captain in 1796.]

(References: *Gazetteer: Cardew; D. and M.*)

374.—**1806**—ROYLE, W. H., Captain. *Inscription:*—Herein was deposited the remains of William Henry Royle, late Captain in the H. C.'s Service which he served 23 years with fidelity, bravery and honor; he died October 29th, 1806, in his 40th year. This is erected to his memory by his afflicted wife, who, after nine years of uninterrupted felicity, now, with four children, is left to mourn his loss and tender goodness of heart and many amiable qualities. As it endeared so is he regretted by his family and friends with due submission to the will of Him who gave and has taken away.

[Appointed cadet 1781, lieutenant 1782, captain 1800. He belonged to the 1st Battalion, 10th N. I. and raised the 1st Battalion, 25th N. I., called, from him "Rayle-ki-paltan." He commanded a force against Khushal Rao, and beat him at Adalatnagar in 1805.]

(References: *D and M; Cardew.*)

375.—**1806**—SIMPSON, L., Lieutenant-Colonel. *Inscription:*—To the memory of Lieutenant-Colonel Leod. Simpson, 2nd Bn. 2nd Regt. who died on the 7th June 1806, in the 49th year of his age. As a commanding officer he was esteemed and respected, and in his death all the officers of his corps lament the loss of a most sincere friend.

[He was appointed cadet in 1776, ensign in 1777, lieutenant in 1777 and Lieutenant-Colonel in 1802.]

(Reference: *D. and M.*)

376.—**1812**—WARNER, G., Captain. *Inscription:*—To the memory of Captain Goodwin Warner, 2nd Batt., 22nd Regt. N. I., who departed this life on the 2nd of January Anno Dom 1812, aged 32 years.

[He was appointed cadet in 1794, ensign 1795, lieutenant 1797 and captain 1805. He is described as "of Carlow in the kingdom of Ireland."]

(References: *D. and M; Services B. A. List.*]

377.—**1832**—CAMPBELL, C. H., Major. *Inscription:*—(Destroyed.)

[Charles Hay Campbell was third son of the late William Campbell of Fairfield, N. B. He entered the Bengal Artillery in 1805. He served under Lord Lake, and in 1810 was Adjutant, and then quartermaster of his Corps. He also served on the staff in many posts, as Deputy Secretary in the Military Department (1819), in charge of the Cossipur Gun Factory (1821), and then of the similar factory at Fatehgarh. He wrote on professional subjects, specially on "Sieges in Bengal" in the *British Indian Military Repository*. He died at Fatehgarh on the 19th May 1832. The inscription was destroyed in the Mutiny.

The B. O., curiously enough, frequently omits to give the inscription when it gives a biography: and this is such a case. Major C. H. Campbell married (1824) Jane Wemyss, daughter of the Honourable L. Keith Murray, and granddaughter of the 4th Earl of Dunmore. By her he had 3 sons and 3 daughters: the eldest is still alive (or was in 1906) and is the head of the family. For another vide No. 286. All 3 sons were in the Indian Army, all 3 daughters married officers in it—two of them in the same regiment. Four of Major Campbell's brothers also served in India, as well as a grandson and a great grandson, also Charles Hay, now in the Guides. The family is a branch of the Campbells of Auchmannoch, co. Ayr, who have been landowners there for several centuries.]

(References: *Buckland; Burke L. G.; B. O.*)

378.—**1833**—GARRET, W. T., Lieutenant. *Inscription:*—Sacred to the memory of William Trigg Garret, Lieutenant in the H. C. Bengal Artillery, who departed this life on 25th July 1833, aged 29 years, deeply and sincerely regretted. (B. O.)

[The name is Trigge Garrett according to Dodwell and Miles, Tigg Garret according to B. O. He was appointed 2nd lieutenant 1819 and lieutenant 1822. He fought at the siege of Bhurtpore. He was the son of Captain H. Garrett, R. N. born in 1804.]

(References: *Stubbs: Services B. A. List.*)

379.—**1834**—TOMKYNS, J. W., Ensign. *Inscription:*—To the memory of Ensign John William Tomkyns, 1st Regiment, N. I., who departed this life on the 31st May 1834. Erected by his brother officers and friends at the station in testimony of their esteem and regard for his many amiable qualities. (B. O.)

[The name is spelt Tomkins by Dodwell and Miles. He joined the service in 1829.]

(Reference: *D. and M.*)

380.—**1835**—FISHER, J., Lieutenant. *Inscription:*—Sacred to the memory of Lieutenant James Fisher, Interpreter and Quartermaster 1st Regiment N. I., who departed this life at Fatehgarh on the 3rd January 1835. Erected by his brother officers and friends in testimony of their esteem and regard. (B. O.)

[He was the son of J. Fisher, born in 1803 and nominated in India. He became ensign in 1824 and lieutenant in 1825.]

(References: *Services B. A. List.*)

381.—**1836**—FULTON, R. B., Major. *Inscription:*—[Sacred to the memory of] Major [Robert Bell Fulton] of the Reg[iment of Bengal Artillery] who departe [d this life] on 11[th May 183]6, age[d 48 years.] He was an up[right, honourab] le man and a sincer[e Christ]ian, possessing high professional abilities and distinguished for those private virtues which endear men to society. This monument is erected by his brother officers and friends in testimony of their regard and esteem. (B. O.)

[The parts in brackets are now illegible and are reproduced from Führer's List and the B. O. R. B. Fulton (1788-1836) was the 2nd son of James Fulton of Lisburn, and father of Captain G. W. W. Fulton, (No. 886) and joined the Service in 1805. He married, at Gretna Green and afterwards at Hillsboro', Elizabeth Jane, daughter of G. Stephenson of Hillsboro', and had 6 sons and a daughter. The family is of Saxon origin and was settled in Ayrshire as early as 1296. It migrated to Ireland about 1614.]

(References: *Burke L. G. I.; D. and M.*)

382.—**1857**—(1) TUCKER, I. T., Lieutenant-Colonel. (2) JONES, J. M. (3) ABERN, J. *Inscription:*—Sacred to the memory of Lieutenant-Colonel I. Tudor Tucker of the late 8th Bengal Light Cavalry; John Moore Jones, Esq., of the uncovenanted service; and Sub-Conductor John Abern, Army Clothing Department, all of whom fell on the 28th and 29th of June 1857, whilst nobly defending the Fort at Fatehgarh against an overwhelming number of mutinous sepoys.

[Cf. No. 385. The first initial of Colonel Tucker is T., (Thomas) not I. He was appointed cadet in 1832. He was the son of Captain Tucker R. N. and nephew of H. St. G. Tucker, B.C.S. He was born in 1817, and became ensign in 1833. He was transferred to the cavalry as cornet in 1836, and became a lieutenant in 1839.]

(References: *D. and M.; Services B. A. List.*)

383.—**1858**—MACDOWELL, C. J. M., Lieutenant. *Inscription* :—To Lieutenant C. J. M. Macdowell, 2nd European Bengal Fusiliers, killed in action against the rebels at Shamshabad 27th January 1858, whilst second in command of Hodson's Horse. Erected by his brother officers as a slight token of their sincere esteem.

[After Sir Colin Campbell had relieved Windham at Cawnpore, he marched into Rohilkhand and seized Fatehgarh. Thence he sent out moveable columns in all directions. It was one of these under Adrian Hope that fought the battle of Shamsabad in which Lieutenant Macdowell was killed. Less than a month before Hodson and he had carried out a daring ride with despatches from Seaton at Mainpuri right through the enemy's outposts to Sir Colin at Miran-ki-Sarai, a distance of 67 miles, and back again.]

(References: *Raikes; Forrest.*)

384.—**1858**—O'DOWDA, H. C., Lieutenant. *Inscription* :—Sacred to the memory of H. C. O'Dowda, of the 48th B. N. I., Acting Adjutant of the 4th Punjab Rifles, who, having been preserved by God's mercy through the whole of the memorable siege of Lucknow in the year 1857, died at Fatehgarh on the 20th January 1858, at the early age of 18 years, 8 months and 17 days.

[This tablet is preserved in the cemetery wall. There is a tomb with a slightly different inscription in the graveyard, in which the regiment is given as the 43rd B. N. I: 48th is correct according to the Indian Register. He was ensign in 1855, lieutenant in 1857. Henry Cubitt O'Dowda was the son of R. O'Dowda, barrister at law, born at Calcutta in 1839, and educated at Brighton.]

(References: *E. I. R.; C. P.*)

FATEHGARH CHURCHYARD.

385.—**1857**—VICTIMS OF THE MUTINY. *Inscription* :—Erected by the Government, North-Western Provinces, to the memory of the Christian residents of Futtehghur in the year of Our Lord 1857, who perished in the troubles of that period. The bodies of some lie in the well beneath; of others the resting place is unknown; yet not one of them is forgotten before God. The Lamb which is in the midst of the throne shall feed them and shall lead them unto living waters, and God shall wipe away all tears from their eyes.

RIGHT SIDE—Colonel and Mrs. Goldie and three daughters; Mr. and Mrs. Thornhill, C.S., two children and Nancy Lang, servant; Revd. Mr. and Mrs. Fisher and child; Doctor and Mrs. Heathcote and two children; Lieutenant and Mrs. Monckton, B.E., and child, Miss Sturt. Merchants:—Mr. and Mrs. Sutherland, two daughters and one boy; Mr. and Mrs. Ives and daughter; Sergt. and Mrs. Roach and two children; Mr. and Mrs. Gibson and two children. Missionaries:—Mr. and Mrs. Campbell and two children; Mr. and Mrs. Johnston; Mr. and Mrs. Macmullen; Mr. and Mrs. Freeman. Mr. and Mrs. Palmer,

Deputy Magistrate, and nine children, Miss Finlay; Mr. and Mrs. Kew and family, Post-Master; Miss Kew; Mr. and Mrs. Sheils, Schoolmaster, and two children.

BACK—10th Native Infantry:—Col. and Mrs. Smith; Major Munro; Major Phillott; Captain Phillimore; Lieutenant Simpson; Lieutenant and Mrs. Fitzgerald and child; Lieutenant Swetenham; Lieut. Henderson; Ensign Eckford; Ensign Byrne; Mr. Wrixen (Senior); Mr. Wrixen (Junior); Sergeant Redman, wife and two children; Captain Vibart, 2nd Cavalry; Sergeant Best, wife and three children. Pensioners:—Mr. and Mrs. Bosco; Mr. Faulkner and family; Mr. Alexander; Mr. and Mrs. Cuise; Mr. and Mrs. Elliott and five children; two Misses Rays; Mr. and Mrs. Joyce and four children; Mr. and Mrs. R. Brierly and one child; Mr. and Mrs. I. Brierly and two children, Dhonkal Pershad and family.

LEFT SIDE.—Colonel and Mrs. Tucker and three children, Miss Tucker and Miss Humphreys; Mr. and Mrs. Lowis, C.S., and two children; Major and Mrs. Robertson, child and Miss Thompson; Doctor and Mrs. Maltby, Mr. E. James, Assistant Opium Agent. Indigo planters:—Mr. T. H. Churcher; Mr. and Mrs. J. M. Jones and child; Mr. and Mrs. Maclean. General Clothing Agency:—Mr. and Mrs. Jones, brother-in-law and four children; Conductor and Mrs. Ahern; Conductor and Mrs. Rohan and nine children; Mr. Anderson and mother; Mr. and Mrs. Madden and family; Mr. Finlay and family; Mr. and Mrs. Cawood and two children; Mr. and Mrs. Macklin, Head-Clerk, Collector's office, and eight children; Mrs. Shepherd and family; Mr. and Mrs. Catania, Inspector of Post offices; Mr. Macdonald and family; Mr. Bellington.

[The garrison at Fatehgarh consisted of the 10th N. I. The inhabitants were largely turbulent Muhammadans. The 10th were supposed to be faithful by their officers; their faithfulness extended so far that they said that whilst they themselves would not murder their officers, if another corps killed them, "it was not their fault." As the Lieutenant-Governor wrote "they were faithful in a peculiar way, and masters of the situation." When some mutineers (Oudh Irregulars) arrived, they received and made much of them. It was then that about 140 Europeans left in boats, who were joined later by four officers of the 10th N. I. They reported that on parade the sepoys had fired at their officers who had escaped to the fort: these four had been unable to do so.

These boats came under a heavy fire at Khoosumkhor. Shortly after some 40 went up to a fort of Hardeo Bakhsh's at Dharampur. The rest went on down the river. Meantime Mr. Probyn and two of the four officers returned to Fatehgarh. They found that the regiment had mutinied: they had fired on their officers and insisted on the treasure being taken from the fort to their lines. They had been pacified with two months' pay in advance and a promise of six month's *batta*; and they were then pronounced faithful and staunch. Mr. Probyn returned to Dharampur. Everybody there was dissatisfied with the place: and on a letter being received from Colonel Smith, all but Mr. Probyn and family and Mr. Edwards of Budaun, returned to the Fort. The Sitapur mutineers arrived two or three days later and on the 18th, the 10th mutinied. The Nawab was put on the *gaddi*; and the siege of the fort began. The fort was not defensible: there were only two guns, and a few model guns not mounted on the walls, the fort was out of repair and there was little ammunition. For nine days it was bravely defended, Colonel Tucker being among the slain. He was shot through a loop hole whilst looking out to see the effect of his last shot. On the 3rd July the fort was evacuated, and the party went off in boats, fired on most of the way. At Singirampur one boat grounded: a heavy fire was opened, and the passengers jumped overboard; they were all killed or taken prisoners except three. Others were also killed in another of the boats. They eventually reached Cawnpore only to be there murdered by the Nana.

Of those that left on the 4th June, those that did not branch off to Dharampur were made prisoners, taken to Cawnpore and there murdered.

The following list shows all the inhabitants of Fatehgarh and where and how they were murdered :—

Killed in the Fort :—Colonel Tucker, Mr. J. M. Jones, Conductor Ahern.

Killed at Singirampur :—One Miss Goldie ; Mr. Robertson and child ; Major Phillott ; Lieutenant Simpson ; Lieutenant and Mrs. Fitzgerald and child ; Miss Thompson ; Ensign Eckford ; Mr. T. H. Churcher ; Mr. Sutherland and one daughter, Mr. and Mrs. Jones and family ; Mrs. Fisher and child ; Conductor Rohan : Sergeant Redman and family : Mr. Anderson and mother.

Died of wounds at Khurar :—Major Robertson.

Killed near Bithur :—Major Munro.

Drowned near Bithur :—Mr. Lowis.

Taken prisoners and shot down with grape :—(Not as in *Mutiny Narrative* blown from guns—*cf.* a decision given by Mr. H. D. Robertson printed as an appendix to the Narrative). Mrs. J. M. Jones and child, Mrs. Sutherland, one daughter and son ; Dhonkal Prasad and family.

The rest were killed at Cawnpore. William Thornton Phillimore, son of W. Phillimore, barrister was born at Elstree in 1821. John James Eckford was the son of Col. J. Eckford H. C. S. born at Calcutta in 1825. Lieutenant John Rivaz Monckton (1833-1857) was 5th son of William Monckton, 8th son of the Hon'ble Edward Monckton, who was 5th son of the 1st Viscount Galway. Philip Monckton (*vide* No. 808) was an uncle of Lieutenant J. R. Monckton ; and an account of the family will be found there. His wife was Rose Catherine, daughter of Thomas Taylor.

Robert Nisbet Lowis was the son of J. Lowis, H. E. I. C. S., born in 1831 and educated at Bath and Haileybury (1849-51.) He came to India in 1851. At this time he was joint magistrate at Moradabad. *Cf.* nos. 424-5 but the list given there does not correspond with the above facts. Major Munro, Major Phillott, Conductor Rohan and Mr. Lowis are all given as killed at Cawnpore.) For personal details about other officers vide nos. 424—5.]

(References : *Rice-Holmes ; M. N. ; Burke P. ; Haileybury ; W P.; C. P.)*

COLLECTOR'S CUTCHERRY COMPOUND.

386.—**1788**—HAMILTON, T. *Inscription* :—Sacred to the memory of Thomas Hamilton, Esq., Head Surgeon, who died 12th August A.D. 1788, aged about 50 years. The monument is erected by Major S. Farmer, Executor.

[Thomas Hamilton joined the service in 1768 as assistant surgeon and became Surgeon in 1771. Major S. Farmer joined the H. E. I. C. S. in 1768 and died at Cawnpore in 1794].

. (Reference : *D. and M.)*

THATIA, TAHSIL TIRWA.

387.—**1803**—GUTHRIE, J., Lieut-Colonel. *Inscription* :—Sacred to the memory of Lieutenant-Colonel John Guthrie of Kilmarnock in Scotland, a Peer of the Mogul Empire. He was born the 6th of March 1749, and departed this life on the 18th October, in consequence of a wound received at the assault on the Fort of Tateeah 30th September 1803.

[In 1801, when Fatehgarh was ceded to the British, the change was resented by the Raja of Thatia, and in 1803 he rebelled. His fort was besieged and taken by a force under Colonel Guthrie. He was appointed cadet in 1771, ensign 1773 ; captain 1784 and Lieutenant-Colonel 1800. The date of birth is possibly wrong and a cadet was more likely to be appointed at 12 years old than at 22 in those days. He was the officer who gave his name to the present 3rd Brahmans (Guthrie ki paltan) whom he led into their first engagement at Thatia : at this time it was the 1st battalion 16th N. I.]

(References ; *D. and M ; Cardew ; Gazetteer.)*

Mainpuri District.

CEMETERY.

388.—**1844**—ALCOCK, W. Captain. *Inscription* :—Here repose the mortal remains of Captain Richard Ponsonby Alcock, 46th Native Infantry, and Assistant Quartermaster-General of the Army, who was murdered in this district on the 26th October 1844. This tomb has been erected to his memory by a few attached friends.

[R. P. Alcock was lieutenant in 1827, captain in 1840. He was murdered en route to Agra; and according to Führer was mistaken for the Collector. He was the son of G. Alcock, wine merchant at Bath, and was born in 1806. He fought at Maharajpur and was mentioned in despatches.]

(References: *D. and M.*; *E. I. R.*; *Services B. A. Lists.*)

ST. PAUL'S CHURCHYARD.

389.—**1857**—FAYRER, R. W. *Inscription* :—Sacred to the memory of Richard Wilkinson Fayrer, Esquire, who fell treacherously murdered by his own men when on duty commanding a detachment of Oude Irregular Cavalry near Mynpoory on the 1st June 1857. *Aetat* 23. This stone is placed here in affectionate remembrance of his brother by J. Fayrer, M.D., Surgeon, Bengal Army.

[Captain Fletcher Hayes, (*cf.* no. 391) Military Secretary to Sir H. Lawrence was sent to Cawnpore with 240 men of the Oudh Irregular Cavalry under Lieutenant Barbor (No. 390) in answer to a request for aid from Sir H. Wheeler, Mr. Fayrer (a brother of Sir Joseph Fayrer) went with the force as a volunteer. Finding all quiet at Cawnpore he suggested to Sir Henry that he should use his troops to keep the communications northwards open, along the Grand Trunk Road. He left his men 8 miles from Mainpuri and rode with Lieutenant Carey to consult the Magistrate. On their return, some native officers met them and urged them to fly. They did so but were pursued and Hayes, who was badly mounted, was cut down; Carey escaped. Fayrer had already been cut down from behind whilst drinking at a well, and Barbor was killed in trying to escape. Fayrer (born 1833, son of Commander Fayrer R. N. of Milnthope, Westmoreland,) had been a cadet in the Australian Mounted Police and was a young man of great promise. Hayes was an Oxford graduate, an oriental scholar of distinction, an able and skilful diplomatist, a man "of great ability, rare courage and unbounded ambition."]

(References: *M. N.*: *Forest*: *Rice-Holmes*: *Foster B.*: *Burke P.*)

390.—**1857**—BARBOR, G. D., Lieutenant. *Inscription* :—Sacred to the memory of Lieutenant George Douglas Barbor, Adjutant, 2nd Oude Irregular Cavalry, born 28th October 1829. He was killed by the men of his own Regiment while on detached command near Mynpoorie on the 1st of June 1857.

[*Cf.* no. 389. He was the son of Captain G. A. Barbor, 8th B. C., born at Nasirabad in 1830, and educated at Bath.]

(Reference: *C. P.*)

391.—**1857**—HAYES, F. F. C., Captain. *Inscription* :—Beneath this tomb rest the mortal remains of Fletcher F. C. Hayes, M.A., Captain in the 62nd Regiment and Military Secretary to Sir Henry Lawrence, K.C.B. He was an accomplished scholar and a distinguished soldier. At the commencement of the great Indian Mutiny he was treacherously slain near this station on this 1st June 1857, while in the discharge of an important duty for which he had volunteered. Born in Calcutta, January the 9th, 1818, he was the only son of Commodore Sir John Hayes and Catherine, his wife. This tomb is erected by his bereaved mother.

[*Cf.* no. 389. He was appointed ensign in 1835, and served as assistant to Sleeman in the Thagi Department. At Maharajpur he was A. D. C. to Sir H. Gough.]

(Reference: *Services, B. A. List.*)

Etawah District.

ETAWAH CHURCH.

392.—**1858**—DOYLE, C. J. *Inscription*:—Sacred to the memory of Charles James Doyle, who fell leading a small band against overwhelming numbers of savage foes at the battle of Harchandpore, December 8th, 1858. True-hearted, generous and gentle as he was brave. His companion in arms have erected this tablet in remembrance of their lost friend; thankful amid their grief that he died as became a Christian hero; fighting only in his country's cause, beloved and respected by all his comrades and at peace with God.

[The engagement of Harchandpur occurred about a month after the district was supposed to be pacified. A body of Oudh mutineers entered Etawah and plundered indiscriminately. They were severely defeated by the local levies: Mr. Doyle (he was a volunteer civilian, not a soldier) was in command of the cavalry, consisting of the Etawah Light Horse and the 13th troop of Police Cavalry. After killing two men he was dismounted and cut to pieces.]

(Reference: *M. N.*)

ETAWAH CEMETERY.

393.—**1858**—DOYLE, C. J. *Inscription*:—Sacred to the memory of Charles James Doyle, who was killed in action at Harchandpore in the Etawah district on the 8th December 1858, aged 29 years.

[*Cf.* no. 392.]

NEAR M. PHARHA, ON JUMNA.

394.—**1846**—FIREBRACE, W. J., Lieutenant. *Inscription*:—Sacred to the memory of William Jennings Firebrace, Lieutenant, Her Majesty's 21st Fusiliers, aged 23 years, who died on the 10th October 1846, on the left bank of the Jumna near the village and fort of Pharha on his way to Calcutta. This monument was erected by his brother officers as a mark of their esteem and regard.

Etah District.

CHHAONI, NEAR KASGANJ.

395.—**1828**—GARDNER, A. *Inscription*:—Alan Gardner died XXX January 1828.

[This is the only inscription in a very handsome marble mausoleum, containing however several other tombs of the Gardner family.

Alan Gardner was the son of Col. William Linnaeus Gardner (1770—1835), nephew of Alan, first Lord Gardner, a distinguished admiral. He was in the service of Jaswant Rao Holkar (1798), but left it because of an affront to his wife, who was a Muhammadan princess, daughter of the Beg of Cambay, by name Mahr

Manzul-un-nissa Begam. In 1804 he raised for the British Government the regiment known as Gardner's Horse. In 1815 he raised a force of irregulars and assisted in the reduction of Almora and Kumaun, where another relative, the Hon'ble E. Gardner was Resident. Until his death he resided on his estate at Chhaoni. Though there have been no distinguished members of this family in India except Col. W. L. Gardner, abovementioned, thanks to their marriages with various great houses, the family history is most distinctly interesting. The lineage is as follows :—William Gardner of Coleraine, Commander of a company during the siege of Derry, left a son, William, Lieutenant-Colonel of the 11th Dragoons. He had 5 sons and 7 daughters, of whom the 2nd, Valentine, was father of Col. W. L. Gardner by his wife Alida Livingstone; the 4th was Alan, 1st Baron Gardner.

Col. W. L. Gardner married Mahr Manzul-un-nissa Begam, Princess of Cambay. By her he had two sons, Alan and William James. Alan Gardner (whose inscription this is) married Bibi Sahiba Hinga, and left two daughters, Susan and Harmuzi. W. J. Gardner married first Bibi Sahiba Banu by whom he had a son, Hinga, and two daughters: and secondly, Mulka Humani Begam, daughter of Mirza Suleman Sheko, son of Shah Alam, and brother of Akbar Shah, Emperor of Delhi. Susan Gardner married Mirza Anjan Sheko, son of Mirza Suleman Sheko. Harmuzi married Stewart Gardner, son of Rear Admiral Francis Gardner, and grandson of Alan, 1st Lord Gardner, his cousin. Their son is Alan Legge Gardner, now in Government service. His son, Alan Hyde, married Jane, daughter of Anjan Sheko and Susan Gardner. There are also numerous ramifications, the descendants of Rear Admiral Francis Gardner and Stewart Gardner, his son.

Burke notes that since the death of the 3rd Baron (Alan Legge, son of Alan Hyde, 2nd Baron) the right to the barony has not been established though an heir obviously exists. A glance at the pages of Burke shows that the contention is sufficiently well founded: for the family is widespread to a degree. But for our purposes the most interesting point of the pedigree of this family is the remarkable relationship between an English baronial family, the house of Taimur, the Nawabs of Oudh and the Begs of Cambay.

The following members of the family are buried in this mausoleum, besides Alan Gardner :—

(1) Col. W. L. Gardner, 1778—1835.
(2) Mahr Manzul-un-nissa, his wife.
(3) W. James Gardner, died 1845.
(4) Mulka Humani Begam, his wife.]

(References: *Compton*: *Buckland*: *Wanderings of a Pilgrim*: *Burke P.*)

ROHILKHAND DIVISION.

Bareilly District.

CHRIST CHURCH.

396.—**1853**—THOMASON, J., B.C.S. *Inscription :*—Here lie the remains of James Thomason, late Lieutenant-Governor of the N.-W. Provinces. Died September 21st, A.D. 1853, aged 49 years. This grave was restored A.D. 1858.

"The souls of the righteous are in the hands of God : neither shall any grief hurt them."

[James Thomason was born in 1804 at Shelford, near Cambridge, the son of Revd. Thomas Thomason, a chaplain in Calcutta. In 1814 he went to England and was educated at Stansted and Haileybury. He returned to India in the B. C. S. in 1822. He became successively Assistant Registrar of the Sadr Court, Calcutta (1823) ; Deputy Secretary to Government (1830) ; and Collector of Azamgarh (1832), where he gained valuable settlement experience. In 1837 he became Secretary to Government, North-Western Provinces : extra Member of the Board of Revenue (1841) ; Foreign Secretary to the Government of India (1842), and Lieutenant-Governor of the North-Western Provinces in 1843 at the age of 39. His administration was directed to the improvement of settlement ("Land Revenue Administration prevalent in the North-Western Provinces" is his *magnum opus* on the subject) ; to the remodelling of the Public Works Department and to the execution of considerable public works, notably the Grand Trunk Road and the Ganges Canal. He founded the Thomason Engineering College at Roorkee in 1848, and opened the Benares College in 1853. He was responsible for causing many district statistical reports to be published and commenced the series of "Selections from the Records of Government". The spread of vernacular education by his system of tahsili schools was another feature of his policy. Conspicuous ability, devotion to the public service, conscientious discharge of every duty, surpassing administrative capacity, extensive knowledge of affairs, clear judgment, benevolence of character and suavity of demeanour are qualities attributed to him by the proclamation announcing his death. On the day he died he was appointed Governor of Madras.]

(References : *Muir ; Buckland.*)

397.—**1857**—RAIKES, G. D., B.C.S. *Inscription :*—Sacred to the memory of George Davy Raikes, Esq., of the Bengal Civil Service, who was killed at Bareilly by the rebels on the day of the outbreak, May 31st, 1857, aged 39 years. This tablet is erected to his memory by his bereaved widow, Margaret Julia Raikes.

"Be ye also ready ; for in such an hour as ye think not the Son of Man cometh."—*Matt.* xxiv, 44.

[Mr. Raikes was killed with Dr. Buch in the house of a Muhammadan, Aman Ali Khan, who had promised him assistance. G. D. Raikes was the son of G. Raikes, a Director of the East India Company, born in London on the 23rd July 1818. He was at Addiscombe first, and then at Haileybury (1833—5), and served in Allahabad, Mirzapur, Jaunpur, Hamirpur, Farrukhabad, Muttra, and Agra, as well as Bareilly.]

(References : *M. N. ; Haileybury ; Prinsep C. L. ; W. P.*)

398.—**1857**—HAY, J. M. *Inscription :*—John Macdowell Hay, May 31st, 1857, aged 38 years.

[He was killed by bad characters in the house of Hamid Hasan, the Munsif, with Messrs. Robertson and Orr. He was the son of J. Hay, Surgeon on the Madras establishment, born at Quilon in 1819.]

(References : *M. N.; S.P.*)

ST. STEPHEN'S CHURCH.

399.—**1857**—VICTIMS OF THE MUTINY. *Inscription* :—Sacred to the memory of D. Robertson, Esq., Judge of Bareilly; G. D. Raikes, Esq., Sessions Judge; Dr. J. M. Hay, Civil Surgeon; Dr. Hansbrow, Superintendent of the Central Jail; Dr. Buch, Principal of the College; G. Wyatt, Esq., Deputy Collector; R. Orr, Esq., Deputy Collector; Mr. J. Beale; Mr. Watts; Miss Watts; Brigadier H. Sibbald, C.B., Commanding in Rohilcand; Sergeant Staples, Artillery; Ensign R. G. Tucker, 68th Regiment, N. I.; Quartermaster Sergeant Henry, 68th Regiment, N. I.; Major H. C. Pearson, 18th Regiment, N. I.; Captain T. C. Richardson, 18th Regiment, N. I.; Captain H. B. Hathorn, 18th Regiment, N. I.; Lieutenant H. R. Steward, 18th Regiment, N. I.; Lieutenant J. C. Dyson, 18th Regiment, N. I.; Quartermaster Sergeant Cross and child, 18th Regiment, N. I.; Mr. A. Fenwick, Commissioner's Office; Mr. and Mrs. Alone and two children, Commissioner's Office; Mr. S. G. Nicholas, Commissioner's Office; Mr. and Mrs. Phellan and four children, Collector's Office; Mr. and Mrs. Davis and two children, Collector's Office; Sergeant Worrell, Jail Establishment; Mr. Cruiser, Jail Establishment; Mr. J. Bolst; Miss Bolst; Mr. Lawrence; Mr and Mrs. Aspinall and two children; Mrs. Aspinall, Senior; Mr. R. Richie; Mr. Jaques; Sub-Conductor Cameron, Engineering Department; Mrs. Cameron and two children.

"These are they which came out of great tribulation."—*Rev.* vii, 14.

"Blessed are ye when men shall revile you and persecu'e you and shall say all manner of evil aga nst you falsely for My sake."—*Matt.* v, 11.

"He that loseth his life for My sake shall find it."—*Matt.* x, 39.

This tablet and chancel windows were erected in memory of the above named persons, who were murdered at Bareilly in June 1857.—A.D. 1863.

[There had been rumours of approaching mutiny in Bareilly for two months before it actually broke out on the 31st May 1857. Consequently most of the ladies and children of the station had been sent in time to Naini Tal. The troops (18th and 68th Native infantry and 8th Irregular cavalry) rose on the 31st. Some officers who had taken refuge in the lines of the 18th, who were supposed to be loyal, found they were as mutinous as the rest, and also escaped to the hills. Others took refuge with natives of rank, but were hunted out and murdered, mostly by the orders of Khan Bahadur Khan, a descendant of the Rohilla chief Hafiz Rahmat Khan, who set up his government in the city and ruled there till the approach of the British troops under Sir Colin Campbell.

The following details of the deaths of certain of the persons mentioned in the tablet are given in the *Mutiny Narrative* :—

Messrs. *Robertson*, *Orr*, and *Hay* were killed in the house of Hamid Hasan, the Munsif, who had promised to protect them, by the Kotwal and other bad characters.

Messrs. *Buch* and *Raikes* were killed in the house of Aman Ali Khan by some Muhammadans, assisted by Aman Ali's nephew.

The *Aspinall* family took refuge with Zakir Ali, a *Karinda* of Mr. Aspinall's, who gave them up to be slaughtered to Khan Bahadur Khan.

The *Phellan* and *Davis* families, Mr. and Miss *Watts* and Mr. *Beale* were murdered by the mob near the Nil-ki-chauki.

The *Lawrence* family were murdered and robbed by Faiz-ullah, Saiyid, with whom they took refuge.

Mr. Bolst was murdered by the Jail guard; *Miss Bolst* in the streets. The *Camerons* were killed in a godown near their own bungalow; the *Alones* whilst escaping to Faridpur. Dr. *Hansbrow* hid in the Jail, but was discovered and murdered by Khan Bahadur Khan at the Kotwali, as were Messrs. *Nicholas* and *Jaques*. Major *Pearson*, Captains *Richardson* and *Hathorn*, Lieutenants *Dyson* and *Steward*, and Quartermaster Sergeant *Cross* and his child were killed by the villagers of Ram Patti whilst escaping along the Shahjahanpur road. Sergeant *Staples* was killed at Baheri on his way to Naini Tal, Messrs. *Fenwick* and *Richie* and Sergeant *Henry* in the City, and Sergeant *Worrell* and Mr. *Cruiser* disappeared.

As regards Lieutenant *Tucker*, Forbes Mitchell tells the following story: There were apparently some renegade Europeans among the ranks of the mutineers (both Rees and he give instances). One of these, as he was subsequently told by an ex-mutineer, had been Sergeant-Major in a Bareilly native regiment. He had advised the murder of all European officers, and himself shot his Adjutant Tucker. He quotes from "A Short Account" of the Bareilly mutiny, which stated:

"The European Sergeant-Major had remained in the lines and Adjutant Tucker perished while endeavouring to save the life of the Sergeant-Major."

This curious tale rests on a certainly circumstantial account of the ex-mutineer's, who gave details of this renegade's career, which in one point was checked by Forbes Mitchell's own experience. But it is to be noticed, firstly, that this does not agree with the *Mutiny Narrative* as regards Lieutenant Tucker's death: he is said there to have been killed by his sepoys whilst mounting his horse in the mess compound. And, secondly, that every sergeant in Bareilly is accounted for in the *Narrative*, except Sergeant Worrell, who belonged to the Jail Department: whilst of the two sergeants of the 68th one was killed and one escaped to Naini Tal. The story, therefore, though it may be true, certainly does not agree with the *Mutiny Narrative*.

David Robertson was the son of Major D. Robertson, Bengal Army, and born at Agra in 1811. He was educated at Edinburgh and Haileybury (1827—9): he served in Bareilly, Nuddea, Benares, Delhi, Mainpuri, Saharanpur, Bijnor, and Farrukhabad.

George Hansbrow was born at Preston in 1823; he was the son of J. Hansbrow, Governor of Lancaster Castle.

Richard Green Tucker was the son of Captain W. Tucker (H. E. I. C.'s Maritime service) and was born in London in 1837.

Henry Edward Pearson (so the birth certificate shows) was born in 1809, the son of the Revd. T. Pearson, Rector of Witley, Worcestershire.

Taylor Campbell Richardson was the son of a Bengal Civilian. He was born in Saugor Roads in 1812. He joined the service in 1831.

Hugh Vans Hathorn (so both E. I. Register and birth certificate show) was son of Vans Hathorn, Writer to the Signet, and born at Edinburgh in 1819.

Henry Ross Stewart (not Steward, an error of the inscription) was the son of R. Stewart, Merchant, born at Calcutta in 1831.

John Charles Dyson was the son of Captain J. Dyson of the Bengal Army, born at Simla in 1837.

For Raikes, Hay, and Sibbald, see Nos. 397—9 and 402.]

(References: *M. N.; Rice-Holmes; Forbes Mitchell; Haileybury; Prinsep, C. L.; Services B. A. List; W. P.; C. P.; S. P.*)

OLD CEMETERY, BAREILLY.

400.—1831—DICK, J. C. *Inscription:*—To the memory of James Charles Dick, Judge and Magistrate of Zillah Bareilly, 4th son of Dr. Dick of Tullymet, Perthshire, North Britain, born 23rd August 1792, died 17th November 1831. Deeply regretted by his friends and relations.

[Tomb not traceable. Inscription reproduced from Führer's List.]

James Chartres Dick is the correct name, according to the baptismal certificate. He was the son of W. Dick, Assistant Surgeon, H. E. I.C.S., and afterwards a Mayfair physician, born at Fort William in 1792. He was at Haileybury (1808-9), arrived in India 1810, and served in Aligarh, Farrukhabad, Meerut, Bulandshahr, Fatehpur and Bareilly. Prinsep shows him as Commissioner of Revenue and Circuit at Bareilly in 1829, but that must have been a temporary promotion, as all other authorities show him as Judge and Magistrate in 1831. There were at least nine Dick's in the C. S. before 1842.]

(References; *Prinsep C. L.; Haileybury; W. P.*)

401.—**1845**—FANTHOME, B., Captain. *Inscription* :—Sacred to the memory of Captain Bernard Fanthome, late of the H. E. I. Co.'s service, died at Bareilly November 25th, 1845, aged 74 years.

"The Lord is our defence."

—Pm. LXXXIX, 18.

[Bernard Fanthome was of French descent, and ran away from home probably about the time of the French Revolution. He served first under Raymond in Hyderabad and then migrated to Bhopal, where his brother Jean Baptiste commanded a brigade. He served under the Maharaja of Jaipur and fought at Madhogarh ; he then joined Sindhia's service, but left him with many other officers when war with the British broke out, and joined Lord Lake, being made a Captain in Colonel Gardner's Irregular Horse. He retired after the war and lived first at Patna and then at Bareilly, where a market called Faltunganj still commemorates his name. He had studied medicine in his youth and now began to practise it again. On one occasion he was summoned by Metcalfe to attend Shah Alam at Delhi, but the Emperor died before he could even see him. He became physician to the Nawab of Rampur and subsequently his chief minister for a time ; but disagreements followed and he returned to Bareilly, where he again practised medicine. He died somewhat suddenly in 1845.

He had several sons. Their father's circumstances had become embarrassed and they were compelled to earn a living. The second, John Bernard, became first tutor of the Maharaja of Bhartpur (Balwant Singh) and then head clerk of the Political Agent's office He was there in the Mutiny and rendered good service by transmitting intelligence to Agra. Of Captain Bernard Fanthome's two daughters, one married James Gardner, grandson of Colonel W. L. Gardner (No. 395), and the other, J. R. LeMaistre, a descendant of J. LeMaistre, Puisne Judge of Calcutta in Warren Hastings' time The family is still represented by Mr. E. C. LeMaistre, Deputy Magistrate in this province.

Mr. J. B. Fanthome's son is Mr. J. F. Fanthome, retired Deputy Magistrate, to whom I am indebted for the material for this and several other notes, chiefly relating to Agra. His grandson, J. A. Fanthome, lies buried in Agra (No. 255) ; he was a lad of the greatest promise and had a musical talent far above the ordinary His brother also died last year. Miss Louisa Fanthome (No. 252) was Mr. J. F. Fanthome's sister ; J. F., like his brother F. Fanthome, are both antiquarians of no small repute, whose speciality is Agra.

Captain B. Fanthome married a daughter of J. F. Fauvel, a Frenchman in the service of Rampur. The name is said to have been originally Fantome and the "h" was added to conceal it. But the two words would in French be pronounced exactly alike ; and considering the obvious meaning ("Fantôme, Phantôme" means "Phantom") it seems to me more probable that the whole name is a disguise.

This is a particularly good instance of the history of those Anglo-Indian families which came into existence at the end of last century, and provide many of our best officers at the present day.]

(Communicated)

NEW CEMETERY.

402. —**1857**—SIBBALD, H., Brigadier. *Inscription* :—In memory of Brigadier Hugh Sibbald, C.B , Commanding in Rohilcund and Kumaun ; murdered, after upwards of 51 years' service in the Bengal Army, by the mutineers of the Bareilly Brigade, on the 31st May 1857 in the 68th year of his age. This tomb is erected in token of affectionate remembrance by his widow and children.

[*Cf.* No. 399. He was "old and ill": he firmly believed in his troops and, like many other officers, fell a victim to his belief in their fidelity.

He was appointed ensign in 1805 and by 1837 was Brevet-Major, at which point the record stops. He fought in Java and at the siege of Bhartpore, and was the son of W. Sibbald, merchant of Leith, born in 1791.]

(References : *D. and M.* ; *Services B.A. List.*)

HIGHLAND CEMETERY.

403.—**1857—9**—42nd ROYAL HIGHLANDERS, SERGEANTS, *Inscription* :—Sacred to the memory of the Sergeants, 42nd

Royal Highlanders, who fell in the Campaigns of the Mutiny or died of disease in India during the years 1858-59, viz., George McCullock, died at Lucknow, 9th April 1858; James Fraser, killed at Rooyah, 15th April 1858; John Reed, died at Sandeelah, 19th April 1858; David Dalgleish, died at Shahjahanpur, 1st May 1858; Thomas Ridley, died at Fatehgarh, 3rd May 1858; Alexander Leitch, died at Allahabad, 21st May 1858; John McMillan, died at Bareilly, 22nd May 1858; John Hiddle, died at Bareilly, 31st May 1858; Robert Blackie, died at Moradabad, 14th June 1858; Thomas Adams, died at Bareilly, 1st July 1858; George Scott, died at Moradabad, 19th July 1858; Duncan Macpherson, died at Bareilly, 11th August 1858; Robert Thompson, died at Naini Tal, 21st September 1858; George Fraser, died at Bareilly, 6th October 1858; Andrew Landles, killed, Maylahghat, 15th January 1859; James Hunter, drowned in the Ganges, 21st July 1859; George Rankin, died at Naini Tal, 4th August 1859; Robert McNair, died at Bareilly, 1st September 1859. This stone is erected as a token of affectionate remembrance by their surviving comrades.

[The 42nd Royal Highlanders, better known as the "Black Watch", arrived in India about the beginning of November 1857, and joined Sir Colin Campbell at Cawnpore, just before the third battle of Cawnpore, in which they took part. Thence they went with Adrian Hope to Bithur (November and December 1857). They marched with Sir Colin to Fatehgarh, and thence were again detached with Adrian Hope and fought at Shamsabad (January 1858). They took part in the siege of Lucknow as part of the 4th Brigade, and took the Martinière (March 1858). They next went with Walpole in his advance into Rohilkhand, *via* Sandila, Rudhamau, Sandi and Allahganj, and fought at Ruiya, where Adrian Hope was killed, and on the Ramgunga. They were in the battle of Bareilly, where they were charged by "Ghazis", and did well. They remained in garrison there: one wing went to Moradabad. The 42nd are now the 1st Battalion, the Black Watch (Royal Highlanders). They were raised in 1729, and were in India from 1857 to 1868 and 1896 to 1902. Their Indian honour is "Lucknow". They also fought in Egypt, the Peninsula, at Waterloo, in the Crimea, Ashanti and Egypt (1882—6).]

(References: *Forrest; Rice-Holmes; Forbes Mitchell.*)

404.—**1857—8**—NON-COMMISSIONED OFFICERS and MEN, No. 2 Company, 42nd ROYAL HIGHLANDERS. *Inscription*:— Sacred to the memory of the undermentioned Non-Commissioned Officers and men of No. 2 Company, 42nd Royal Highlanders:— Private Alexander McDonald, died 28th November 1857; James McNair, died 30th November 1857; William McKane, died 3rd December 1857; John Dickson, died 7th December 1857; David Tennant, died 1st February 1858; Thomas Bell, died 18th April 1858, Sergeant John Reid, died 19th April 1858; Private Duncan McIntyre, died 23rd April 1858; Alexander Wilson, died 25th April 1858; Andrew Buchanan, died 5th May 1858; Corporal Donald McLardy, died 24th May 1858; Private Robert McKay, died 26th June 1858. This is erected by Captain G. Fraser, Commanding the Company, as a token of respect.

[*Cf.* no. 403.]

405.—**1857—1860**—NON-COMMISSIONED OFFICERS and MEN, No. 8 Company, 42nd ROYAL HIGHLANDERS. *Inscription*:— "No. 8 Company, XLII Royal Highlanders:—To the memory of the undermentioned non-commissioned officers and men of the above company and regiment, who died in the service of their Queen and country :—

Lce-Corp. Ar. Mackie, Private A. McKay, Ed. Spence, Josh. Bates, Jn. Hepburn — Killed or died of their wounds, received at Rooyah, 15th April 1858.

Hugh McKenzie, 12th April 1858 ... ...
James Baines, 2nd May 1858 ... ...
Alexander Burges, 12th June 1858... ...
Walter Swanson, 29th August 1858 ... — died at Lucknow.

James Wright, 22nd April, died at Allygunj.
John Todd, 7th July 1858, died at Naini Tal.
John March, 2nd Septemb r 1858, died at Naini Tal.

Sergeant John Hiddue, 31st May 1858 ...
Private Alexander Cormack, 20th June 1858 ...
Private John Cronan, 4th October 1858 ...
Corporal William Sheldon, 10th July 1859 ...
Private James Napier, 18th August 1859 ...
Alexander Shaw, 31st August 1859 ...
E. McPherson, 8th March 1860 ... ... — died at Bareilly.

[For Rooyah *cf.* No. 978. L. Corporal Spence assisted to recover Lieutenant Willoughby's body and would have had the V. C. had he lived.]

CANTONMENT CEMETERY.

406.—**1857—60**—OFFICER, NON-COMMISSIONED OFFICERS, and MEN, Light Company, 42nd ROYAL HIGHLANDERS. *Inscription* :—Sacred to the memory of the undermentioned officer, non-commissioned officers, and men of the Light Company, 42nd Royal Highlanders, who were killed or died in India in the service of their country, from November 1857 to August 1860 :—Lieutenant A. J. Brambly, killed 15th April 1858; Lance-Corporal R. Holmes, killed 11th March 1858; Private F Doyle, killed 11th March 1858; J. Monteith, killed 18th March 1858; A. Brodie, killed 15th April 1858; Private C. Fraser, killed 15th April 1858; J. Eadie, killed 15th April 1858; J. Dunns, killed 28th April 1858; D. Hennessey, killed 30th April 1858; D. McInnes, died 27th April 1858; T. Smith, died 8th May 1858; D. Lawson, died 25th August 1858; W. Haynes, died 2nd September 1858; R. Anderson, died 10th September 1858; C. Lavan, died 24th October 1858; G. Yates, died 28th October 1858; Sergeant W. Taylor, died 21st June 1860; Private D. Morrison, died 11th July 1860; Drummer A. Morrison, died 21st August 1860. Erected by the Company.

Sacred to the memory of Sergeant H. Lockhart, 42nd Royal Highlanders, who departed this life on the 17th March 1860, aged 38 years. This is erected by his beloved wife W. Lockhart.

"Blessed are they who die in the Lord."

[The last inscription is on the other side of the Tomb.—*Cf.* No. 403.]

BITUYA NEAR FATEHGANJ WEST.

407.—**1794**—OFFICERS, 13th Native Infantry. *Inscription* :—Here lie the bodies of Captain Norman Macleod, Lieutenant William Hinksman, Lieutenant William Odell, and Lieutenant Joseph Richardson, of the 13th Battalion, Native Infantry, killed near this place in the action of 26th October 1794.

درین جا لاش‌هاے کپتان نارمین میکلوڈ - لفٹننٹ ولیم هنکسمین - ولیم
اوڈل - جوزف رچارڈسن - سرداران در پلٹن سپاهیان سیزدهم که نزدیک
همین‌جا در جنگ بتاریخ بست و ششم ماه اکتوبر سنه ۱۷۹۴ع (یکهزار
هفت صد نود و چهار عیسوی) کشته شدند دفن اند *

[The battle of Bhitaura, or Fatehganj, was fought by Sir Ralph Abercromby against the Rohillas under Ghulam Muhammad—it was in a war with the State of Rampur, which had been handed over to the Rohilla chief Faiz Ullah Khan when Rohilkhand came under the Nawab Wazir of Oudh. Defeat was very narrowly averted. Captain Ramsay was ordered to charge with the Light Cavalry; but by an eror in judgment he presented his flank to the enemy, was charged, and his regiment was cut up. It was at this disastrous moment that Captain Mordaunt, Colonel Burrington, Major Bolton, Lieutenants Baker and Tilfer (see next entry), and all the officers of the 13th Native Infantry were killed. The rest of the line stood firm, however, and defeated the Rohillas after a fierce engagement in which we lost 14 officers and 600 men. Ghulam Muhammad was banished to Benares, and the State of Rampur, considerably reduced in extent, was given over to the infant son of Muhammad Ali, son of Faiz Ullah. Muhammad Ali had been defeated and killed by Ghulam Muhammad.

Captain Ramsay left the field and the country and is shown as "deserted" in official lists. It is said he entered the French service. He is probably the Captain Ramsay of No. 370.]

[References : *Strachey ; D. and M. ; Stubbs.*]

M. BHITAURA.

408.—**1794**—OFFICERS and MEN, killed at the battle of BHITAURA. *Inscription* :—Erected by order of the Governor-General in Council, in memory of Colonel George Burrington, Major Thomas Bolton, Captain Nor. Macleod, Captain John Maubey, Captain John Mordaunt, Lieutenant Andrew Cummings, Lieutenant Edmund Wells, Lieutenant William Hinksman, Lieutenant Joseph Richardson, Lieutenant John Plumer, Lieutenant J. Z. M. Birch, Lieutenant William Odell, Lieutenant Edward Baker, Lieutenant Firew. James Tilfer, and the European and Native non-commissioned officer and privates who fell near this spot in action against the Rohillas, October the 24th, A.D. 1794.

[*Vide* No. 407. Colonel Burrington commanded the reserve. He is first shown as captain 1768 and very possibly was transferred from H. M's Service. He became a colonel in 1793. Major Bolton commanded the 18th N. I. (cadet 1768, major 1784). Captain Maubey was cadet in 1771 and captain in 1781. Captain Mordaunt commanded a company of artillery: Baker and Tilfer were his subordinates. The first-named joined the service in 1772, the others in 1783. Lieutenant Cummings was appointed cadet in 1778 and lieutenant in 1781. Lieutenant Wells had joined the service in 1780, as had Lieutenants Odell and Plumer. Lieutenant Richardson was a cadet of 1781 and Birch of 1782.]

(Reference : *D. and M. ; Stubbs.*)

Moradabad District.

CEMETERY.

409.—**1829**—GROTE, R., B.C.S. *Inscription* :—Sacred to the memory of Robert Grote, Esquire, of the Civil Service, 7th son of George Grote, Esquire, of Badgemore in the County of Oxfordshire, who departed this life on the 23rd February 1829 at Jesspore near Moradabad, aged 20 years and 6 months (B. O.)

[Not now traceable. Robert Grote, son of George Grote, a banker, was born in 1808 at Beckenham, he was educated at Carshalton and Haileybury (1825-6), and came to India in 1827. He died after 2 years' service as Assistant Magistrate at Moradabad.]

(References : *Prinsep C. L.; Haileybury; W. P.*)

Shahjahanpur District.

ST. MARY'S CHURCH.

410.—**1857**—VICTIMS of SHAHJAHANPUR MASSACRE. *Inscription* :—I. H. S. This monument is erected by the friends and relatives of those honoured and beloved ones whose names are here inscribed, who yielded up their lives unto death, through the violence of a lawless and fanatical insurrection at this station on the 31st day of May A. D. 1857.

To the care of two poor natives, residents of this city, they owe a grave on this spot and in God their Saviour, we trust they have found a place.

"Lord Jesus receive my spirit."

"Lord lay not this sin to their charge."

Henry Hawkins Bowling, Surgeon, 28th Regiment, B. N. I., aged 43.

Captain Marshall James, 28th B. N. I., aged 37.

The Reverend John MacCallam, aged 45.

Mordaunt Ricketts, B. C. S., Magistrate and Collector of this district, aged 30.

Arthur Chester Smith, Esquire, B. C. S., aged 22, an only and beloved son of the late E. Peploe Smith, Esquire, B. C. S, and Harriet, his wife.

John Robert LeMaistre, clerk in the Magistrate's office, aged 42 years.

[The mutiny at Shahjahanpur broke out on the 31st May. The 28th Native infantry revolted, whilst most of the Europeans in the station were in church. In the midst of service "six or seven Sepoys, armed with tulwars and lathis, rushed in upon us. Ricketts received one tulwar wound as he stood by my side, when he ran through the vestry door, and must have been cut down by some mutineers who were waiting outside. Captain Lysaght (*cf.* No. 411) with some other officers and myself succeeded in closing the church doors against our murderous assailants . . ." The church was defended for about an hour. Captain James was shot on the parade ground and Mr. Bowling whilst driving to the church. The rest then made their way to Powayan. The Raja Baijnath Singh sheltered them a night, but then sent them off, saying he could no longer protect them. Mr. Smith was killed by the sepoys in a hut in the city, ; he was ill with fever and had not gone to the church. Mr. LeMaistre was killed in the church : Mr. MacCallam escaped out of the city but was murdered by some villagers in a melon field. A. C. Smith was son of E. P. Smith, B.C.S., by his 2nd wife Harriet Chester. E. P. Smith was the fifth son of George Smith, M P., for Midhurst. *Cf.* No. 320. He was at Haileybury 1852—4 and arrived in India 1855. Ricketts was the son of M. Ricketts, H.E.I.C.S., born at Lucknow (where his father was Resident, *cf.* no. 943) in 1826. He was at Haileybury 1843-5 and came to India in 1846. His body was recovered and carefully buried by Amjad Ali, the Tahsildar. The "two poor natives" were Nasir Khan and Amir Ali, who caused the bodies to be collected and buried near the church.

(References : *Burke L. G.; M. N; Haileybury; W. P.*)

411.—**1857**—OFFICERS and LADIES, 28th N. I., killed during the MUTINY. *Inscription* :— Sacred to the memory of the undermentioned officers of the 20th Regiment Native Infantry, who perished in the performance of their duty at the hands of the mutinous sepoys in 1857 :—

Captain M. James, killed at Shahjahanpur, 31st May 1857.

Captain I. H. Guise, killed at Benares, 4th June 1857.

Captain H. W. L Sneyd, killed
,, O. Lysaght, ,,
,, M. M. Salmon, ,,
Lieutenant A. Key, ,,
,, C. A. Robertson, ,,
,, C. F. Scott, ,,
,, W. W. Pitt, ,,
,, G. W. Rutherford, ,,
,, T. I. H. Spens, ,,
,, C. E. Scott, ,,
,, P. D Johnston, ,,
} at Aurangabad, 10th June 1857.

Surgeon H. H. Bowling, killed at Shahjahanpur, 31st May 1857.

Also

Mrs. Bowling, killed
,, Lysaght, ,,
,, Scott, ,,
,, Key, ,,
,, Scott, ,,
} at Aurangabad, 10th June 1857.

"The noble army of martyrs praise Thee."

[For the deaths of Captain James and Surgeon Bowling, see No. 388. I could not trace the papers of either officer. For Captain Guise, see No. 581. For the details of the Aurangabad massacre, see No. 976.

Henry Wilder Lambie Sneyd was the son of Captain Sneyd, B. N. I., born in India in 1823. He joined the service in 1840.

Cornelius Lysaght (*cf.* No. 976—"O." is an error in this inscription) was the son of J. Lysaght of Ennistymore, County Clare, and was born in 1819. He became an ensign in 1840.

Mordaunt Money Salmon was the son of Lieutenant-Colonel Salmon, B. N. I., born in India in 1823. He became an ensign in 1842.

Alexander Key was the son of J. Key, merchant, born in London in 1833, and educated at Chudleigh and Rugby.

Charles Frederick Scott was the son of Major T. H. Scott, 38th N. I., born in Calcutta in 1832. He was educated at Rurki.

William Wilberforce Pitt was the son of W. G. Pitt, banker, born at Cheltenham in 1883, and also educated there.

George William Rutherford was the son of Lieutenant-Colonel M. Rutherford, 28th N. I., born at Neemuch in 1837.

Thomas John Hope Spens was the son of Dr. T. Spens of the Bengal Establishment, born in Edinburgh in 1837.

I could not find the papers of Robertson, E. C. Scott, and Johnston.]

(References :—*C. P.; Services B. A. List.*)

SHAHJAHANPUR CEMETERY.

412.—1837.—BARWELL, H. M., Lieutenant. *Inscription* :—Sacred to the memory of Henry Montague Barwell, Lieutenant in the 69th B. N. I., second son of E. R. Barwell, Esquire, H. C.'s Service, who died 8th August of 1837, in the 26th year of his age. In every relation of life, whether as a Christian soldier, son, brother or friend, he commanded the love and esteem of all who knew him. This tablet is erected by his afflicted parents as a frail memorial of his worth and their affection. (B. O.)

[Not traceable in the cemetery. Reproduced from Führer's List. He was appointed cadet in 1827, ensign in 1828, and lieutenant in 1836. He was born in 1811 and was A.-D.-C. and Private Secretary to the Governor of Agra in 1835-1836.]

(References ; *D. and M.; Services B. A. List.*)

ALLAHABAD DIVISION.

Cawnpore District.

ALL SAINTS' MEMORIAL CHURCH.

THE church, erected on the site of General Wheeler's entrenchment, is itself a monument to the memory of the victims of the Cawnpore massacres. It is built of red brick faced with buff sandstone in the Lombardo-Gothic style: the nave and transept are paved with marble, the chancel with Minton tiles. On the walls are 14 memorial tablets, giving the names of those who died in Cawnpore in 1857.

The English troops in Cawnpore in 1857 consisted of a company of Artillery, 60 men of the 84th, 30 of the 32nd and 15 of the 1st Madras Fusiliers. The Native troops were the 2nd Light Cavalry and the 1st, 53rd and 54th N. I. They were all, with the possible exception of the 53rd, disaffected. With civilians, women and children, the Europeans numbered not less than 950.

At this time there was residing at Bithur Dundhu Pant, *alias* the Nana Sahib, the adopted son of Baji Rao and heir to all his possessions but his pension; "a man of no capacity and debauched tastes . . . strong passions, and no principles to guide them." Though he considered himself aggrieved by the lapse of Baji Rao's pension, he maintained civil, even friendly, relations with the European residents. He even offered them assistance: and such trust was put in him, that the Magistrate, Mr. Hillersdon, asked him to guard the Treasury when matters became threatening.

"No very serious view was taken of matters in general." If there was a General in India who knew the sepoy, it was Sir Henry Wheeler. It may be that he knew him too well: that he relied too greatly on the half century's fidelity of which he had experience. But it is certain that he watched the troops narrowly and formed the opinion that, if they did revolt, they would march at once to Delhi: consequ ently, he would only be called on to meet the city rabble. It was this that induced him to choose his miserably weak position in place of the strong magazine, to hold which Lawrence urged him: for to seize this would have meant removing the sepoy guard and precipitating the outbreak. At all events he decided to entrench a couple of buildings (barracks) with a low mud wall over which "an English subaltern could have ridden on a cast horse from the Company's stud." The women and children were sent into this place on the 21st May and it was victualled for 25 days. Of arms and ammunition there was plenty: but of guns only ten.

On the 4th June two native regiments, the cavalry and the 1st N. I., rose. Neither at the time did any harm; they merely broke and fled. The 56th N. I. yielded to the temptation the next day. The 53rd were, by some extraordinary error in judgment, fired into by Ashe at Sir H. Wheeler's orders "and were literally driven from us by nine-pounders." Even then the native officers and some 80 men remained faithful.

Sir H. Wheeler's view, that the regiments when they mutinied would at once march on Delhi, was so proved correct. But the Nana Sahib, on whom everybody had relied, changed the situation. Whether of his own motion, or prompted by Azim-ul-lah his agent, he decided to attack the Europeans at Cawnpore with the sepoys, whom he at once joined and induced to return, instead of marching to Delhi.

So the siege began on the 7th June. The entrenchments were as already stated of the weakest possible kind: they were also surrounded by cover. Matters, however, were slightly improved by two barracks close to the entrenchment which the besieged continued to occupy. It is unnecessary to dwell on the miseries of the next three weeks. The defence was so vigorous that the rebels themselves were—and admitted that they were—astounded. But one barrack was fired: the number of the defenders grew daily less. Every single artilleryman was slain at the guns; no water could be obtained save at the risk of almost certain death. Capitulation was the only alternative to annihilation: and when on the 26th June a missive was received which promised to spare and send to Allahabad "all soldiers and others unconnected with the acts of Lord Dalhousie," a capitulation was decided on, contrary to the advice of many officers who would have preferred even the other alternative.

On the 27th June boats were provided to convey the remains of the garrison to Allahabad. And now followed the most dastardly piece of treachery that has perhaps ever been perpetrated. The party took their seats in the boats at the Sati Chaura Ghat: but "at a signal from the shore, the native boatmen . . . . all jumped over and waded to the shore." Guns and musketry then opened on the boats: only one (Major Vibart's) could start, and they were reinforced by about a dozen swimmers. Of the passengers in the other boats, some were killed, some drowned, some taken prisoners. The slaughter went on till stopped by an order of Bala Rao, or the Nana. But only the women and children were spared. They were placed in the Savada Kothi.

The boat that escaped had 50 people on board and went down the river under a heavy fire. It grounded three times, the third time at Sheorajpur, thirty miles down the stream, on the morning, (it would seem) of the 29th. Here a party of fourteen—Mowbray Thomson, Dela Fosse, Sergeant Grady and eleven privates landed, to drive off their assailants. They actually drove them back without loss, but then, looking round, saw no signs of the boat. They retreated three miles and then seized a temple. Even here they drove the enemy back, and it was not till the mutineers brought up gunpowder and tried to blow up the place that they broke out and charged. Six fell: seven took to the water; of these three were killed. Mowbray Thomson, Dela Fosse, Murphy and Sullivan escaped and were saved by Raja Drigbijai Singh, of Murarmau, in the present district of Rae Bareli. The rest of the party in the boat were seized and brought back to Cawnpore, and the men were killed at once: the women and children were confined in the Savada Kothi. The first batch of Fatehgarh fugitives had been murdered as soon as they arrived (June 12th): the second batch now arrived; of them all the men but three were murdered, and the women and children with the Cawnpore prisoners were confined in the Bibigarh.

On the 15th July Havelock fought and won the battles of Aung and the Pandu Naddi. His army was within a day's march of the city. "Then ensued the last act of the tragedy of Cawnpore. It was pointed out to the Nana that the captives in the Bibigarh would supply damning evidence against all concerned in the massacres. First of all the five men were taken out and shot. Then a number of sepoys were selected and told to shoot down the women and children through the windows of the house. This was too much even for them : they fired at the ceiling instead. At the Nana's bidding four butchers, armed with knives, went in and hacked their victims to pieces Next morning a heap of corpses, a heap of wounded and a number of children were dragged out and thrown, the living and the dead together, into a well hard by."

Two days later Havelock entered Cawnpore "too late to save, but not too late to avenge." But comment is needless : "*sunt lacrimæ rerum.*" For the rest of the Cawnpore operations a skeleton is appended, which will assist to the understanding of the inscriptions.

7th July—Havelock leaves Allahabad.
12th „ —Battle of Fatehpur.
15th „ —Battles of Aung, and the Pandu Naddi (1st).
16th „ —Battle of Cawnpore (1st).
17th „ —Havelock enters Cawnpore.
18th „ —Havelock entrenches a position in the civil station of Nawabganj.
20th „ —Arrival of Neill.
29th „ —Battles of Unao and Bashiratganj (1st).
30th „ —Retreat to Mangalwar.
5th August—Battle of Bashiratganj (2nd), and second retreat to Mangalwar.
12th „ —Battle of Bashiratganj (3rd), and third retreat to Mangalwar.
16th „ —Battle of Bithur.
15th September—Arrival of Outram.
21st „ —Second advance towards Lucknow.
26th October—Arrival of Hope-Grant's Dehli Column.
1st November—Battle of Khujwa.
3rd „ —Arrival of Sir Colin Campbell.
9th „ —Sir Colin Campbell left to join column for relief of Lucknow. Windham left to defend Cawnpore from the Gwalior force.
17th „ —Windham encamps west of the town.
26th „ —Windham's battle of the Pandu Naddi (2nd).
27th „ —Windham's battle of Cawnpore (2nd).
28th „ —Action near Cawnpore (3rd).
6th December—Campbell's battle of Cawnpore (4th).
8th & 9th „ – Pursuit by Hope-Grant.

From this date there was no further fighting at Cawnpore.

(References : *Forrest* ; *Rice-Holmes* ; *M. N. (Sherer)* ; *Mowbray Thomson* ; *Kaye* ; *Roberts*.)

413.—**1857**—VICTIMS OF CAWNPORE MASSACRES. *Inscription :*—To the Glory of God and in memory of more than a thousand Christian people who met their deaths hard by between 6th June and 15th July 1857. These tablets are placed in this the Memorial Church, All Souls, Cawnpore, by the Government, N.-W. Provinces. STAFF : Major-General Sir H. Wheeler, K. C. B. ; Lady Wheeler and daughters ; Lieutenant G. R. Wheeler, 1st N. I., A.-D.-C.; Lieutenant-Colonel E. Wiggens, 52nd N. I., D. J. A. G.; Mrs. Wiggens;

Major W. Lindsay, A.A.G.; Mrs. Lindsay and daughters; Ensign C. and Mrs. Lindsay; Brigadier-General Jack, C. B.; Mr. Jack; Captain Sir G. Parker, 74th N. I., Cantonment Magistrate; Captain Williamson, 71st N. I., D.A.C.G., Mrs. Williamson and child.

[The memorial consists of 14 tablets. For the sake of convenience I give each tablet separately, so that the notes may not become unnecessarily confused. About many of the names not even so much as the manner of death is known: and where it is recorded, there are occasionally variations in the accounts given.

Sir Hugh Wheeler (1789-1857), son of Captain H. Wheeler, R. N., and Margaret, daughter of the 1st Lord Massy was educated at Richmond and Bath. He was appointed cadet in 1803 and joined the 24th N. I. and fought at Dehli in 1804 under Lake. He became Lieutenant-Colonel in 1835, and commanded the 48th N. I., at the storm of Ghazni. He was made C. B. for his services in the first Afghan war. In 1846 he became Brigadier; he commanded a brigade at Mudki and was wounded: but fought again at Aliwal. He commanded the Jalandhar Field force in 1848-49 and reduced the fortresses of Ranger Nagal, Kullawalha and Dulla. He became K. C. B. in 1850, and Major-General in 1854. He was doubtless killed in the boats.

Lieutenant G. R. Wheeler, his son and A. D. C., was killed by a round shot. He had just been wounded in the trenches and was resting on a sofa, when a round shot entered the door and killed him before all his family.

The Lindsays.—A slip of paper was found in the Bibigarh, as follows: "Mamma died July 12th; Alice died July 9th; George died June 27th...Uncle Willy died June 18th; Aunt Lilly died June 17th." Mowbray Thomson explains that this was in the handwriting of one of the Misses Lindsay: that "Mamma" was Mrs. George Lindsay; "George" was Ensign G. Lindsay: "Uncle Willy" and "Aunt Lilly" were Major and Mrs. W. Lindsay. In that case the three daughters (Alice, Frances and Caroline) would be daughters of Mrs. G. Lindsay, and either sisters or cousins of George Lindsay. The tablet is, therefore, misleading. C. Lindsay should be G. Lindsay: and the arrangement reads as if the first Mrs. Lindsay was Major Lindsay's wife, and mother of the three daughters: and the second, Ensign Lindsay's wife. To be clear the list should have read "Major and Mrs. W. Lindsay Mrs. G. Lindsay and daughters, Ensign G. Lindsay." Major Lindsay was blinded by splinters caused by a round shot. He lay for several days in extreme pain, but at last succumbed. (Dela Fosse says he died of fever.) Mrs. W. Lindsay died of grief, according to Mowbray Thomson. The other two Misses Lindsay were killed on the 15th July.

William Lindsay was the son of M. W. Lindsay, merchant, Dublin, born in 1810. He joined the service in 1826 and was a Major in 1854. G. Lindsay belonged to the 1st N. I. and joined the service in 1856: I could not find his papers.

Edwin Wiggins was the son of Lieut. Col. Wiggins of the Bengal Army and joined the service in 1835. He was born "abroad"—i. e. in India, but I could not trace the date. He was Deputy Judge Advocate General. His wife died on the 12th June.

Captain Williamson was the son of Lieut. Col. D. Williamson, born at Saugor in 1822. He joined the service in 1843.

For Jack and Parker, vide Nos. 429 and 425.]

(References:—*Mowbray Thomson; Buckland; M.N.; Forrest; Services B.A, List; C.P.)*

392.—**1857**—VICTIMS OF CAWNPORE MASSACRES. *Inscriptions:—Bengal Artillery.* Major C. Larkins, wife and children; Lieutenant C. Dempster, wife and children; Lieutenant B. Ashburner; Lieutenant J. Martin; Lieutenant St. G. Ashe; Lieutenant J. A. H. and Mrs. Eckford; 2nd Lieutenant G. M. W. Sotheby; 2nd Lieutenant F. W. Burney; Assistant Surgeon D. McAuley, M. D.; Hospital Steward W. Hefferan; Assistant Apothecary W. Slaney; 63 Non-Commissioned Officers and men, besides women and children. *Bengal Engineers:* Captain F. Whiting; Lieutenant S. C. Jervis. *32nd Light Infantry.* Captain J. Moore, wife and children; Lieutenant F., Mrs. and Miss Wainwright; Ensign E. C. and Mrs. Hill;

Assistant Apothecary I. Thompson; Hospital Apprentice W. A. Emmor and wife; 82 Non-Commissioned Officers and men, 41 women and 61 children. *84th Foot.* Lieutenant F. J. G. Saunders; 47 Non-Commissioned Officers and men. *1st K. M. Fusiliers:* 15 Non-Commissioned Officers and men; Lieutenant G. J. Glanville, 2nd E. B. F.

[Major George Larkins, son of J. P. Larkins (query John Pascal Larkins? of No. 313) was born in 1807 and joined the service in 1825. He was in general charge of the artillery, but could do little owing to ill-health. It is not known how he died.

Charles Dempster, son of Surgeon T. E. Dempster (Bengal establishment) was born at Buxar. He had fought at Chilianwala and Gujrat and commanded the west Battery. He was shot in the siege.

Burnett Ashburner, son of W. P. Ashburner of Westbury in Van Diemen's Land, was born at Longford in the same country in 1829. He was sent out on a reconnaissance on the 7th June, and never returned.

St. George Ashe, son of Major B. Ashe of the Bengal Army was born at Sitapur in 1830. He had seen service in Burma. He had brought his guns from Lucknow: he was killed whilst pushing off Vibart's boat.

John Alexander Haldane Eckford, son of Col. J. Eckford, 6th N. I., was born at Jaunpur in 1832. He commanded the S. E. battery, with Lieutenants Burney and Dela Fosse and was killed by a round short in the siege.

I could not trace Burney and Macaulay. The former was killed in Vibart's boat: the latter signalized himself by the most unremitting attentions to the wounded men in the out post. He was captured in Vibart's boat at Sheorajpur and murdered. For Martin and Sotheby, cf. Nos. 438 and 436.

"Slaney," should read "Slane," for which it is a nickname. My informant is a soldier in charge of the church who has private information on the subject.

F. Whiting, son of F. Whiting, merchant, was born in London in 1822, and joined the service in 1842. He was educated at Addiscombe. He had seen service in the Sutlej campaign and was killed in Vibart's boat.

Swynfen Charles Jervis, son of Capt. W. Jervis, B. N. I., was born at Neemuch in 1830. He "always scorned to run," and was shot whilst calmly walking across the open in the midst of a shower of bullets." For the officers of the 32nd, see No. 440. I could not trace Lieutenant Saunders. He was captured in Vibart's boat.

George Julius Glanville, son of F. Glanville, late Grenadier Guards, was born in 1831 at St. German's in Cornwall and was educated at Bedford Grammar school. He commanded a detachment in Barrack No. 2, and was killed in Vibart's boat.]

(References: *Mowbray Thomson; M. N.; Forrest; Services B. A. List; Vibart; C. P.)*

415.—**1857**—VICTIMS OF CAWNPORE MASSACRES. *Inscription:—2nd Light Cavalry.* Major E. Vibart, wife and children; Captain E. C. Vibart; Captain E. J. Seppings, wife and children; Captain R. U. and Mrs. Jenkins; Lieutenant R. O. Quin; Lieutenant C. W. Quin; Lieutenant J. H. Harrison; Lieutenant W. J. Manderson; Lieutenant F. S. M. Wren; Lieutenant M. G. Daniell; Lieutenant M. Balfour; Cornet W. A. Stirling; Surgeon W. R. and Mrs. Boyes; Veterinary-Surgeon E. G. Chalwin and wife; Ridingmaster D. Walsh, wife and children; Sergeant-Major H. Gladwell; Quartermaster-Sergeant F. and Mrs. Tress; Cornet C. Mainwaring, 6th L. C.; Lieutenant A. J. Boulton, 7th L. C. *1st Native Infantry:* Lieutenant-Colonel John Ewart, wife and child; Lieutenant J. H. C. Ewart, 12th N. I.; Captain A. Turner, wife and child; Captain E. J. Elms; Lieutenant H. S. Smith; Lieutenant R. M. Satchwell; Lieutenant F. Redman; Ensign J. C. Supple; Surgeon A. W. R. Newenham, wife and and children; Sergeant-Major G. Hilling, wife, and child; Quartermaster-Sergeant T. Andrews and family; 18 Musicians; 5 women and 9 children.

[Edward Vibart, son of Col. Vibart, H. M. service, was born in 1807 and joined the service in 1825. He had fought at Ghazni and Punniar, and commanded the Redan. He was the last man to leave the entrenchments. His was the only boat that escaped. For its capture see preliminary note. He was wounded on the 28th June, and probably died of his wounds.

Edmund Charles Vibart, son of T. Vibart, B. C. S., was born in 1825 and joined the service in 1842. He was at Fatehgarh (cf. No. 385.)

E. J. Seppings, son of J. M. Seppings, Surveyor to H. E. I. C. at Calcutta, was born there in 1826. He was wounded in the arm and his wife in the thigh in Vibart s boat ; he was murdered on the 30th June, she and her family on the 15th July.

Robert Urquhart Jenkins was the son of R. C. Jenkins, a Calcutta merchant, born in 1828. He had served at Multan and commanded the Railway Engineers' post in No. 4. He was shot through the jaw after a sortie by a wounded sepoy.

Richard Owen Quin, son of Lieut. T. Quin, 4th N. C., was born at Meerut in 1829. He died of fever during the siege.

Charles William Quin, son of W. C. Quin, barrister-at-law, of Stephen's Green, Dublin, was born in that town in 1830 and educated at Trinity College. He was wounded in Vibart's boat and captured.

John Hammond Harrison, son of B. Harrison, Madras C.S., was born at Barham, Kent, in 1832 and educated at King's College, London. He was killed in Vibart's boat on the 28th June.

William John Manderson, son of Captain J. R. Manderson (H. E. I. C's. Maritime service) was born in 1836 in London, and killed during the siege.

Francis Stoneham Montagu Wren, son of Major T. Wren, Madras N. I., was born at Northam, Devon, in 1836 and educated at Bedford Grammar school. His death is not mentioned.

Murray George Daniell, son of Captain E. M. Daniell (H. E. I. C's. Maritime service) was born at Carshalton in 1836.

Melville Balfour, son of C. Balfour, merchant, was born in London in 1838 and educated at Radley and Bradfield. Both these two officers were killed in Vibart's boat.

Walter Albert Stirling, son of Rear Admiral Sir J. Stirling, R. N., was born at Perth in West Australia in 1837. He did much execution during the siege as a sharpshooter.

I could not trace Dr. Boyes. He and his wife were both taken prisoners in Vibart's boat, and shot on the 30th June ; the wife refused to leave her husband, the sepoys could not separate them, and both were shot together—one of the most touching incidents in the Cawnpore story.

Charles Mainwaring, son of G. Mainwaring, B. C. S., was born at Calcutta in 1839 and educated at Cheltenham.

Arthur John Boulton was the only officer who escaped from the mutiny of the 7th N. C. (stationed at Lucknow) at Chaubepur. He was wounded then, but escaped to Cawnpore, riding his horse over the entrenchment wall. He was killed in Vibart's boat. He was the son of C. Boulton, of Brighton, born in 1834 and educated at Marlborough.

Lieutenant-Colonel Ewart, his wife and child were killed on their way to the boats near St. John's Church, by his own men, who mocked him with a sham parade. He was born 1803, the eldest son of Peter Ewart. The family is an old border family, dating back to 1370. Lieutenant-General J. F. Ewart, C. B., of Peninsula fame, was a cousin, and his son, the still more famous General, Sir J. A. Ewart, G. C. B., was the Colonel of the 93rd through the Crimea and Mutiny. Colonel Ewart's wife was *née* Emma Fooks.

James Henry Cruickshank Ewart was the son of J. S. Ewart, stockbroker, born in London in 1826.

Athill Turner was the son of C. Turner, of Liverpool, born in 1819. He joined the service in 1837. He was killed in Vibart's boat.

Edward John Elms was the son of the Revd. E. Elms, rector of Itchingfield, Sussex, born 1823. He joined the service in 1841.

Henry Sidney Smith was the son of Major-General J. N. Smith, Bengal Army. He was born in 1826 and joined the service in 1843. He was killed in the siege. Richard Murcott Satchwell, son of Major J. Satchwell, 29th N.I., was born at Bareilly in 1829. He was killed in Vibart's boat.

Frederick Redman, son of G. C. Redman, merchant, was born in London in 1831. He and Lieutenant Supple (whom I could not trace) were killed in the siege.

Arthur Wellesley Robert Newenham was the son of B. Newenham of the Excise Department, born in 1812 at Dublin. Mrs. Newenham was a sister of Mrs. Blair (No. 419). She, Mrs Turner, and their children died of fever during the siege.

(References : *M. N., Forrest ; Mowbray Thomson ; Burke L. G. ; M. C. Register ; Services B. A. List. ; C. P. ; S. P.*)

416.—**1857**—VICTIMS OF CAWNPORE MASSACRES. *Inscriptions :—53rd Native Infantry.* Major W. R. Hillersdon ; Captain J. H. Reynolds, wife and child ; Captain H., Mrs. and Miss Belson ; Lieutenant F. G. Jellicoe, wife and children ; Lieutenant H. H. Armstrong ; Lieutenant G. A. Master ; Lieutenant O. S. Bridges ; Lieutenant W. G. Prole ; Lieutenant F. H. Tomkinson ; Ensign A. Dawson ; Ensign T. W. Forman ; Surgeon N. Collyer ; Sergeant-Major T. McMahon, wife and children ; Quartermaster-Sergeant W. Gordon, wife and children ; 10 Musicians, women and children. *56th Native Infantry.* Colonel S. Williams, wife and daughters ; Major W. R. and Mrs. Prout ; Captain W. L. Halliday, wife and child ; Captain G. Kempland, wife and children ; Miss Kempland ; Lieutenant T. A. Raikes ; Lieutenant G. R. Goad ; Lieutenant W. A. Chalmers ; Lieutenant H. Fagan ; Lieutenant W. L. G. Morris ; Lieutenant H. J. G. Warde ; Lieutenant J. W. Henderson ; Lieutenant R. A. Steevens.

[W. R. Hillersdon was the son of J. Hillersdon, brother of C. G. Hillersdon, (No. 419) born in 1818. He joined the service in 1835 and had fought at Jellalabad.

John Hewetson Reynolds, son of Major Reynolds, H. C. S., was born at Banda in 1821 and joined the service in 1838. He was killed in the siege : his wife died of fever. H. Belson was born at Naples in 1825 and joined the service in 1843. Frederick Gilbert Jellicoe, son of G. Jellicoe, was born at Southampton in 1828.

Herbert Holmes Armstrong, was son of the Honourable A. S. Armstrong and Jane Munro his wife. He was born in Grenada in 1829 and educated at Elizabeth College, Guernsey.

Lieutenant Gilbert Augustus Master was the eldest son of Major-General R. A. Master, C. B., and grandson of G. C. Master, B. C. S. The family, an ancient one of Kentish origin dating back to John Master of Sandwich, *circa* 1520, has had many Anglo-Indian members, since the days of Sir Streynsham Master, Governor of Fort St. George from 1678—1681, including C. G. Master, C. S. I., member of Council at Madras 1884-9, and many others, mostly military men. It is not known when he died. His father was commanding the 7th N. I. at Lucknow at the time of the Mutiny.

William George Prole was son of Captain Prole, B. L., born in Bengal in 1835. He was killed during the siege.

A. Dowson (so the cadet papers) was son of the Revd. H. Dowson, born at Cambridge in 1836.

Thomas William Forman, son of R. Forman, of Merthy-Tydvil, Glamorgan, was born at Paris in 1837.

Stephen Williams, son of H. Williams, H. C. S., was born in 1805 and joined the service in 1821. He died of sunstroke in the siege on the 8th June. Mrs. Williams and her daughter Georgina were killed in the boats. May, another daughter, was killed in the siege on the 15th June, and the 3rd daughter, Fanny, on the 15th July.

Walter Robert Prout, son of Dr. Prout, was born in 1820 and joined the service in 1839. He also died of sunstroke. He had seen service at Maharajpur and commanded the main guard. Mrs Prout was killed on the 15th July.

Captain Halliday was shot whilst carrying some soup to his wife, who with her child died of small-pox. He was the third son of John Halliday of Chapel Cleeve, a family which claims connection with that to which Sir Leonard Halliday, Lord Mayor of London in 1605, belonged. His wife was Emma Lætitia, daughter of A. W. Wyndham of Blandford ; their child was a daughter, Edith Mabel by name.

Captain Kempland had served in the Punjab campaign and commanded the S. entrenchments. He was the son of Major G. A. Kempland, 8th L. C., born at Nasirabad in 1829. For G. A. Kempland, cf. No. 723.

H. T. A. Raikes (1831-1837) was the eldest son of H. T. Raikes, Judge in Calcutta. Of this family, too, very many members have served in India. It is a cadet branch of the Raikes of Bennington which dates back through Robert Raikes of Gloucester, the philanthropist and founder of Sunday schools, to Richard Raikes, a burgess of Hull (*circa* 1570). Another branch, the Raikes of Treberfydd, are also descended from him : to this Charles Raikes, C. S. I., Commissioner of Lahore, belongs (cf. No. 4).

Hornby Fagan was the son of W. T. Fagan, J. P., D. L., and at one time M. P. for Cork. The family is descended from Patrick O'Hagan, or Fagan, of Tullagh Og, co Limerick, and slain about 1233.

William Lucas Gordon Morris, son of G. Morris, R. N., was born at Lymington in 1838.

Henry John Gregory Warde, son of Vice Admiral C. Warde K. H. of Squerryes Court, Kent (a well known family) was born in 1837.

John Wright Henderson was the son of the Revd. R. Henderson of Stirling, born in 1838 at Stirling and educated at Glenalmond. Robert Willam Henderson (No. 418) was his brother (born 1836 and also educated at Glenalmond and at University College, Oxford) : the former was wounded whilst swimming to Vibart's boat, but reached it with Mowbray Thomson's help : the latter, who was with him, was drowned.

Robert Allen Stevens, son of Revd. H. Stevens, was born at Wilmington, Kent, in 1839 and educated at Marlborough.

I could not trace Bridges, Tomkinson, Collyer, Goad and Chalmers. Major Hillersdon, Lieutenants Jellicoe, Armstrong, Dowson, Forman, Bridges, Goad, Fagan, Warde and J. W. Henderson were all killed at the boats. Mrs. Belson, Mrs. Jellicoe and family, and Surgeon Collyer died of fever, and Lieutenant Chalmers was killed, during the siege.)

(References : *M. N.; Forrest ; Mowbray Thomson ; Gubbins ; Burke L. G., and L. G. I. ; Services B. A. List ; C. P.*)

417.—1857—VICTIMS OF CAWNPORE MASSACRES. *Inscription :*—Assistant Surgeon J. P. Bowling, wife and children ; Sergeant-Major T. Bell, wife and children ; Quartermaster-Sergeant T. and Mrs. Leak ; 14 Musicians, 5 women and 5 children. Captain A. M. Turnbull, 13 N. I ; Lieutenant, C. and Mrs. Battine, 14th N. I. ; Lieutenant F. G. Angelo, 16th N. I. ; Lieutenant G. J. Bax, 48th N. I. ; Lieutenant P. H. and Mrs. Jackson, 67th N. I. ; Lieutenant R. W. Henderson, 72nd N. I.; Surgeon C. Garbett : Assistant Surgeon H. P. Harris, wife and child ; Assistant Surgeon R. D. D. and Mrs. Allan ; Assistant Commissary N. Reilly and family ; Conductor W. Berrill, A. C. D., wife and family ; Officiating Sub-Conductor G. H. Manvilie and family ; Assistant Apothecary A. Peters and family ; Sergeant-Major Heron and family ; School-Master Gill, wife and children ; Sergeant Brooke, D. P. W., and wife ; Sergeant Kelly, D. P. W., wife and child ; Sergeant Maclanders, D. P. W., wife and infant ; Sergeant Wheelan, D. P. W., wife and children ; Sergeant Parker, Overseer ; Sergeant and Mrs. Carmody ; Bazar-Sergeant and Mrs. Reid.

[John Price Bowling, son of J. Bowling, Surgeon, was born at Hammersmith in 1825.

Adam Montague Turnbull, son of P. Turnbull, appraiser at Calcutta Custom House, was born at Calcutta in 1821 and joined the service in 1842. He commanded the main guard.

Charles Battine, son of Lieutenant-Colonel W. Battine, B. A., was born at Fort William in 1832.

Gilbert Ironside Bax was 3rd son of John Bax, Bo. C. S., by his wife Jane Ironside. The family is now Bax Ironside of Heronden House, Kent. He was shot in the siege.

Horatio Philip Harris, son of Assistant Surgeon Harris, H. E. I. C. S., was born at sea off Ceylon in 1823.

Robert Dallas Dove Allan, M. D., son of R. W. Allan, assistant to Gisborne and Company, Calcutta, was born there in 1819.

For Angelo and Jackson cf. Nos. 430—1, for Henderson cf No. 416. Surgeon Garbett died of fever during the siege, Mrs. and Miss Berrill, Mrs. Bell and Mrs. Gill and their families, and Mrs. and Miss Peters were killed on the 15th July.]

(References: *M. N.; Forrest; Mowbray Thomson; Burke L. G.; Services B. A. List,; C. P.; S. P.*)

418.—**1857**—VICTIMS OF CAWNPORE MASSACRES. *Inscription :*—Cattle-Sergeant Ryan and family; Sergeant Swan; Drum-Major Murray; Sergeant Warren, pensioner; Pensioner Green and family; Pensioner Nixon Reid; Pensioner Price; Pensioner Maloney; Mr. C. G. Hillersdon, Magistrate and Collector; Mrs. Hillersdon and children; Mr. J. Mackillop, C. S.; Revd. E. T. R. Moncrieff, wife and child; Revd. J. Rooney, Roman Catholic Chaplain; Mr. Maxwell; Mr. A. M. Miller, Resident Engineer, E. I. R.; Revd. Haycock, S. P. G., and mother; Revd. H. E. Cockey, S. P. G.; Mrs. Blair and daughters; Mr. and Miss Campbell; Miss Brightman; Miss Isabella White; the two Misses Glasgow; Lieutenant Harris' child; Mrs. F. L. Wade; Mrs. Fraser; Mrs. Evans and children; Mrs. Darby and infant; Miss Bissett; Mrs. Swinton and children.

[Mr. Hillersdon, the Magistrate, a brother of Major Hillersdon, was killed by a round shot during the siege, whilst talking to his wife, "a most accomplished lady...... universally a favourite in the station." She was killed by a fall of bricks soon after, as was Mrs. Evans. Charles George Hillersdon was the son of J. Hillersdon, of Barnes, Surrey and was born there in 1822. He was at Haileybury 1838-40 and came to India in the latter year. He had served, amongst other places, in Saugor, Allahabad and Meerut.

Mrs. Mary Darby (Foster B. gives the name as Darley) was the wife of a Surgeon, and daughter of John Jackson, brother of Sir Keith Jackson (cf. No. 908.) Mrs. Evans was the wife of Captain Evans, Deputy Commissioner of Purwa (Unao), who was in the Lucknow Residency, and gave his name to Evans's Battery.

The Revd. E Moncrieff "was held in high estimation by the whole garrison before the Mutiny on account of the zealous manner in which he discharged the duties of his high office, and his self-denial and constancy in the thickest of our perils made him yet more greatly loved of us all." He, his family, Mrs. Swinton, Mrs. Darby and their children were all killed in the boats.

Mrs. Wade, Miss Blair and Miss Brightman all died of fever during the siege.

Mrs. Blair and her other daughters, Mrs. Reid and Miss White, were killed on the 15th July.

The Revd. J. Rooney died of sunstroke, according to Mowbray Thomson, in the boats, according to the Mutiny Narrative.

For Messrs. Mackillop, Miller, Haycock, Cockey and Mrs. Fraser, see Nos. 428, 435, 460, and 432.]

(References: *M. N.; Forrest; Mowbray Thomson; Gubbins; Foster B.; Haileybury; Prinsep; C.; L.; W. P.*)

419.—**1857**—VICTIMS OF CAWNPORE MASSACRES. *Inscription :*—Miss S. E. Cripps; Captain Hollings; Mr. E. F. Greenway and family; Mr. T. Greenway and family; Mr. S. Greenway and family; Mr. W. H. Stacey, Deputy Collector; Mr. Cox; Mr. J. R. Collins, Inspector, P. O., and wife; Mr. R. B. Cook, Opium Department, wife and family; Mr. Alone, wife and children; Mr. J. G. Anderson, E. I. R., wife and child; Mr. J. C. Baines, E. I. R., and wife; Mr. Philip Baines; Mr. Barlow; Martha Batavia; Miss Eliza Bennett; Mrs. Beestal; Mrs. Bothwick; Mr. E. Brierley, Telegraph Department; Henry Brett; the two Misses Burn; Mr. Bunny; Mrs. Carroll; two boys Caley; Mr. and Mrs. Carter and infant; Miss Emma Chandler; Mary Cheeters.

[A party of mutineers went to capture the family of Mr. E. Greenway on the 8th June. Captain Hollings, an ex-officer, kept them at bay till his ammunition failed, when he was slain. The Greenway family was taken to the Savada Kothi and held to a two-lakh ransom. It was Mrs. Greenway who brought the missive from the Nana which resulted in the capitulation. Negotiations for the ransom came to nothing ; but it was not till the 15th July that Messrs. E. and T. Greenway were shot, and the rest massacred

Mr. Carter was toll-keeper of the Sheorajpur toll-bar. He and his wife were taken prisoners by the 7th N. C. Mr. Carter was sent to the Nana and shot on the 10th June; his wife was sent to Bithur where the widows of Baji Rao protected her. She was delivered of a child there, and only murdered after the arrival of Havelock's force on the 17th July. Mr. Cox, formerly of the 1st Bengal Fusiliers, lost both his legs by a shell which fell into a battery, killing or wounding seven soldiers' wives, and also killing Mr. Jacobi. (No. 422).

Miss Bennett, Henry Brett, two Misses Burn, Mrs. Carroll, the two Caley lads and Miss Cheeters were all killed on the 15th July. For Mr. Baines and Mr. Cook see nos. 435 and 431.]

(References: *M. N.*; *Forrest*; *Mowbray Thomson.*)

420.—1857—VICTIMS OF CAWNPORE MASSACRES. *Inscription:*—Mr. and Mrs. Christie; three Misses Christie; Miss Conway; James Cousins; Drummer Clooney; Miss Colgan; Mr. H. R. Cooper, E. I. R., wife and family; Mrs. Copeman; Master W. Copeland; Mrs. Crabb; Mr. Cummins, Surveyor, E. I. R.; Mrs. Dallas; Mrs. Darling and infant; Mrs Dachey and infant; Mrs. Daly; Mr. Davis and children; Mr. J. K. De Gama; Mr. John Duncan; Mr. David Duncan and children; Miss De Cruz; Mr. DeRussett, wife and children; Mrs. Dupton and sons; Master W. Dundas; Mr. Fagan, wife and children; Mr. Farmer, Telegraph Department; Mrs. Fairburn; Mrs Fenn; Mr. John Fitzgerald and family.

[Mr. Cummins was killed in the siege. Mr. Duncan was murdered at Janan by Ghansham Singh on the 13th June. Mrs. Copeman, Crabb, Dallas and Daly, Misses Conway and Colgan, Mrs. Dupton and Fitzgerald, and the families of the last two, were killed on the 15th July.]

(References: *M. N.*; *Forrest*; *Mowbray Thomson.*)

421.—1857—VICTIMS OF CAWNPORE MASSACRES. *Inscription:*—Mr. W. Forsyth, E. I. R.; Mr. Freeman; Mrs. Mary Frost; Mrs. Rebecca Frost; Miss Emelin Frost; Miss Sophia Fulton; Master W. Fulton; Mr. Garrett, Engineer, E I. R.; Mr. Galway, Telegraph Department; Mr. W. Gee and wife; Mrs. and Miss Gibson; Mr. Gilpin, wife and children; Mr Goodwin, Telegraph Department; Mrs. Grinsey; Mr. Gum, E. I. R; Mrs and Miss Guthrie; Mrs. Hagan; Mrs. Harkness and child; Mr Haycock and wife; Mr. J. D. Hay, wife and children; Mr. Hanna, Assistant Engineer, E. I. R; Miss Hampton; Mr. M. C. Herberden; Mr E. Henderson; Miss Elizabeth Holmes; Mr. W. James; Mr. F. Jacobi and wife; Mr. H. Jacobi and wife.

[Mr. H. Jacobi was killed in the siege (cf. No. 419).]

Mr. F. Jacobi did an act of great bravery during the siege, when he climbed up to the top of the magazine and flung over a "carcass," which he believed to be a live shell.

Mr. Henderson was drowned while trying to reach Vibart's boat.

Mrs. and Miss Guthrie, Miss Holmes and Mrs. H. Jacobi were killed on the 15th July.

For Messrs. Gee, Forsyth, Hanna and Heberden, cf. Nos. 462 and 435. They were all killed in the boats.]

(References : *M. N.* ; *Forrest* ; *Mowbray Thomson.*)

422.—**1857**—VICTIMS OF CAWNPORE MASSACRES. *Inscription :*—Mrs. Jackford ; Mr. Jones and wife ; Mr. A. R. Johnstone, E. I. R , wife and family ; Mrs. Keeler ; Mrs. Kinleside and children ; Mrs. Kight and children ; Mrs. Kirk, senior ; Mr. J. Kirk, wife and children ; Mr J. Kirkpatrick, wife and infant ; Mr. H. LaTouche, Assistant Engineer, E. I. R. ; Mr. J. Lawrence, E. I. R., wife and children ; Mr. Leary and sons ; Miss Leath ; James Lewis ; Mr. Little ; Miss Lucy Lyell ; Master McCullen ; Mrs. Mackinnon ; the two Misses Macmoran ; Miss N. Martindell ; Miss Ellen Mark ; Mrs. Jane Morfett ; Mr. Murphey, E. I. R.; Mr. C. Mackintosh and family ; Mr. G. W. Maling ; Mr. John Maling ; Mrs. W. Marshall ; Mr. Nelson.

[Mr. Murphey was killed on the 7th June. He and Mrs. Wade (No. 396) were the only two buried in the entrenchments. Mrs. Jones, Kinleside, Morfett, Miss Lyell, Mrs. Johnstone and Mrs. Knill and their families were killed on the 15th July.

For Mr. LaTouche, cf. Nos. 541 and 435 ; for the Mackintoshes, cf. No. 461.]

(References : *M. N.* ; *Forrest* ; *Mowbray Thomson.*)

423.—**1857**—VICTIMS OF CAWNPORE MASSACRES. *Inscription :*—Mr. W. North ; Mrs. Norris ; Mr. James O'Brien and wife ; Mrs. J. L. O'Brien and son ; Miss O'Connor ; Mr. M. Ogle, Canal Department, wife and family ; Mrs. Osborne ; Messrs. Fred. and Henry Palmer ; Mrs and Georgie Peel ; Mr. C. H. Peake, Telegraph Department ; Harriett Pistol ; Mrs. Pogson ; Mr. Purcell, wife and son ; Mr. Prebett, wife and children ; Mr. Ramsay, Telegraph Department ; Mr. Reilly ; Mr. George Reid, wife and children ; Mr. Ricketts, E. I. R. ; Mr. Roach, Postmaster ; Mr. Robinson, E. I. R. ; Mrs. Roberts ; Mrs. Russell ; Mrs. Eliza Russell ; Mr. Saunders and son ; Mr. Scott ; Mr. John Schorn ; Mr. Sherman.

[Mrs. J. L. O'Brien and son, Mrs. Peel and son, Miss O'Connor, Harriet Pistol, Mrs. Prebett, Mrs. Reid and their families, Mrs. Saunders and son, Mrs. and Miss Russell and Mrs. Scott were all killed on the 15th July.]

(References :—*M. N.*; *Forrest* : *Mowbray Thompson.*)

424.—**1857**—VICTIMS OF CAWNPORE MASSACRES. *Inscription :*—Mrs. Shore ; Mr. Sinclair, E. I. R., and wife ; Henry and William Simpson ; Mr. Shaw ; Mr. N. Sheriden, wife and children ; Daniel Shepherd ; Mrs. Ellen Shepherd and children ; Mr. Sliven ; Mr. Smith, E. I. R. ; Mr. Stanley ; Lucy and William Stoke ; Miss Margaret Stowell ; Mrs. Tibbets ; Mrs. Tomkins ; Mr. Todd ; Mrs. Tresham ; Mr. Tritton ; Mr. Vaughan ; Mr. J. Virgin, E. I. R., and wife ; Mr. Viscardo, E. I. R. ; Mrs. Wallett ; Mr. G. Warden, E. I. R. ; Mr. Walsh, E. I. R., wife and children ; Mr. A. Walker and son ; Mr. Wells, wife and children ; Mrs. Elizabeth West and children ; Thomas, Katharine and Jane Widlep ; Mrs. Willis and child ; Mr. Wilkinson, wife and child ; Mr. R. B. Wrixen, wife and child ; Miss Clara Wrixon : Mrs. Edward Williams ; Mrs. Yates.

[Mrs. Willis died on the 19th June ; Mrs. Sinclair, Mrs. Tibbetts, Mrs. Sheriden, Shepherd, West and their families were killed on the 15th July.]

(References : *M. N.* ; *Forrest* ; *Mowbray Thompson.*)

425.—**1857**—VICTIMS OF CAWNPORE MASSACRES (FATEHGARH VICTIMS). *Inscription :—Fatehgarh fugitives, 10th Native Infantry.* Colonel G. A. Smith, wife and child; Major R. Monro; Major J. Phillott; Lieutenant C. W. Swetenham; Lieutenant D. Henderson; Ensign R. S. Byrne; Surgeon T. G. and Mrs. Heathcote, Musician W. M. Wrixon; Colonel A. Goldie, wife and daughters; Lieutenant J. R. Monckton, Bengal Engineers, wife and child; Assistant Surgeon S. and Mrs. Maltby; Conductor M. Rohan, Ordnance Department and family; Schoolmaster Shiels and family; Sergeant Hammond, Gun Agency Department, and family; Pensioner Faulknór; Mr. M. B. Thornhill, Judge, wife and children; Mrs. Tucker and children; Mr. Alexander; Mr. J. Brierley, wife and children; Mr. R Brierley, wife and child; Miss E. and Miss F. Brierley; Mr. Billington; Revd. D E. Campbell, wife and children; Mr. Catania, wife and child; Mr. Cawood, wife and children; Mr. Elliott, wife and children; Revd. J. E. and Mrs. Freeman; Mr. Finlay, wife and children; Miss Finlay; Mr. and Mrs. Guise.

[George Acklom Smith was the son of the Revd. R. Smith, born at Sutton in 1797.

R. Munro was born at St. Thomas in Jamaica in 1806.

Johnson Phillott, son of J. Phillott, banker, was born at Bath in 1810 and joined the service in 1828.

Charles Worsley Swetenham, son of Captain J. Swetenham 10th N. I. was born at Cawnpore in 1832, and educated at Bedford Grammar School. It is worth noting how this young officer, born in the regiment at Cawnpore, was murdered, through the mutiny of the same regiment, at Cawnpore 25 years later.

David Henderson, son of Captain D. Henderson, was born at Oldfield in Caithness in 1833.

Thomas Godfrey Heathcote, son of O. Heathcote, was born at Mansfield, Notts, in 1818.

Andrew Goldie, son of the Revd. M. Goldie was born in 1793.

Samuel Maltby, son of the Revd. J. S. Maltby, rector of Shelton, Notts, was born in 1820.

For Monckton and Thornhill cf. Nos. 385 and 449. I could not trace Byrne. Colonels Smith and Goldie, Mr. Thornhill, Mrs. Tucker and their families, Mrs. Heathcote, and Mrs. Maltby were killed on the 15th July, the rest on the 12th June.]

(References: *M. N.*; *Forrest*; *Services B. A. List*; *C. P.*; *S. P.*)

426. –**1857**—VICTIMS OF CAWNPORE MASSACRES (FATEHGARH VICTIMS). *Inscription :*—Mr. J., Mrs. and Miss Ives; Revd. A. O. and Mrs. Johnson; Mr. J. Joyce, wifo and children; Mr. J. B. Kew, wife and children; Miss Kew; Miss Nancy Lang; Revd. J. and Mrs. MacMullen; Mr. and Miss Maclean; Mr. Macklin, wife and children; Mrs. Macdonald and children; Mr. J. R. Madden, wife and children; Miss E. and Miss A. Madden; Mr. J. Palmer, wife and children; Mr. R. and Miss E. Ray; Mr. and Mrs. Roach; Mrs. E. Shepherd and children; Miss Mary Shepherd; Mr. and Mrs. O'Hern, Head Tailor of Clothing Agency; Mrs. Robert Waresaw; Mrs. Woolcar and children; Mr. R. Nisbet Lowis, wife and two children.

Our bones are scattered at the graves' mouth as when one cutteth and cleaveth wood upon the earth, but mine eyes are unto thee O God, the Lord.

[Mr. Roach was killed on the 10th July; Mrs. Roach, Nancy Lang, Mrs. Woolcar and family on the 15th July; the rest on the 12th June.]

(References; *M. N.*; *Forrest.*)

427.—**1857**—2ND LIGHT CAVALRY. *Inscription :*—" Presented by the officers of the 2nd Light Cavalry in memory of their comrades who fell in the Mutiny, 1857."

[This refers to the Font ; for details of preliminary note.]

428.—**1857**—MACKILLOP, J. R., B. C. S. *Inscription :*—To the memory of John Robert Mackillop of the Bengal Civil Service, who was killed at Cawnpore, on or about the 25th June 1857, in his 31st year. He nobly lost his life when bringing water from the well for the distressed women and children. His death was deeply lamented.

[" He jocosely said that he was no fighting man but would make himself useful where he could, and, accordingly, he took this post (*i. e.*, of drawing water from the well, which was under fire.)......It was less than a week after he had undertaken this service when his numerous escapes were followed by a grape shot in the groin, and speedy death......His last words were an earnest entreaty that somebody would go and draw water for a lady to whom he had promised it." (Mowbray Thomson.) He was the son of G. Mackillop, agent, born at Calcutta in 1827. He was educated at Bishopwearmouth and Haileybury (1844-6). He came out to India in 1847. He was Joint Magistrate at Cawnpore in the mutiny. His brother C. W. Mackillop was also in the C. S.]

(References : *M. N.; Forrest ; Rice-Holmes ; Mowbray Thomson ; Haileybury ; W. P.*)

N. B.—Near the Memorial Church are 24 stone pillars marking the boundary of Wheeler's entrenchments, and inscribed B. P. W. E.—1857. There are also 12 brick pillars to mark the following spots of interest inside the entrenchment: (1) Main Gate, (2) Hospital, (3) Married Quarters, (4) House, (5) Eckford's Battery, (6) N.I. (7) Ashe's Battery, (8) Magazine, (9) Redan, (10) Dempster's Battery, (11) Sotheby's Battery, (12) Provision Godown.

429.—**1857**—(1) JACK, A. Colonel. (2) JACK, A. W. T. *Inscription :*—Sacred to the memory of Colonel Alexander Jack, C. B., Brigadier Commanding at Cawnpore; Andrew William Thomas Jack, sons of the late Very Revd. William Jack. D. D., Principal of King's College, Aberdeen, who were killed in the entrenchments of Cawnpore during the investment of that place by the mutineers in June 1857.

[Cf. No. 413. Mr. Jack was killed by a round shot. Colonel Jack died of fever. He was born in 1805, and was appointed cadet in 1823 ; he had seen service at Aliwal, Chillianwala and Gujrat,]

(References : *Services B. A. List.*)

430.—**1857**—ANGELO, F. C, Lieutenant. *Inscription :*—Sacred to the memory of Lieutenant Frederick Cortlandt Angelo, 16th Grenadiers, B. N. I., Superintendent of the 4th Division, Ganges Canal, who fell in the mutiny at Cawnpore on the 27th June 1857, in the 32nd year of his age.

"Jesus said—I am the resurrection and the life, he that believeth in me, though he were dead, yet shall he live."

[Cf. No. 417. He was killed in the boats. He was the son of Major F. Angelo, H. C. S., born at Karnal in 1826, and educated at Leytonstone and Addiscombe.]

(References : *Vibart ; O. P.*)

431.—**1857**—(1) JACKSON, P. H., Lieutenant. (2) JACKSON, J. A., Mrs. (3) COOKE, R. B. *Inscription :*—Sacred to the memory of Philip Hayes Jackson, Lieutenant, late 67th Native Infantry, who with Jane Amelia, his wife, and her brother, Mr. Ralph Blythe Cooke, were massacred by the rebels at Cawnpore on the 27th June 1857. This tablet has been erected as a tribute of affection to them by their sorrowing relatives.

" Vengeance is mine, I will repay, saith the Lord."

[P. H. Jackson was son of Major J. N. Jackson, H. C. S., born at Calcutta in 1828. All three were killed in the boats.]

(References: *M N; C. P.*)

432.—**1857**—FRASER, A. F., Mrs. *Inscription* :—In memory of Anne Fawcett, the beloved wife of Captain George William Fraser, 27th Bengal Native Infantry, who died at Cawnpore, July 1857, a victim of the great Indian Mutiny.

"Thy will be done."

[Cf. No. 417. She was the wife of an officer in the 27th Native Infantry who escaped from Delhi. She died "in captivity."]

433.—**1857**—MARTIN, J. N, Lieutenant. *Inscription* :—This tablet, in memory of an excellent son, is erected by his afflicted parents, Admiral and Mrs. Martin, to John Nickleson Martin, Lieutenant, Bengal Artillery, who, whilst gallantly fulfilling his duties, was treacherously killed by the mutineers in the boats at Cawnpore on the 27th of June 1857, in his 18th year, respected and beloved by all that knew him.

"The Lord gave and the Lord hath taken away, blessed be the name of the Lord."

[Cf. No. 414. Lieutenant Martin assisted Lieutenant Dempster in the W. Battery, and was wounded in the siege. It is not known when he died.]

434.—**1857**—(1) CHALWIN, E G. (2) CHALWIN L., Mrs. *Inscription* :—Sacred to the memory of E. G. Chalwin, 2nd Light Cavalry, and his wife, Louisa, who both perished during the siege of Cawnpore in July 1857.

"These are they which came out of great tribulation."

[Cf. No. 415. Mr. Chalwin was killed in the trenches, Mrs. Chalwin on the 15th July.]

435.—**1857**—ENGINEERS OF THE EAST INDIAN RAILWAY. *Inscription* :—To the memory of Engineers in the service of the East Indian Railway Company, who died and were killed in the great insurrection of 1857. John Hodson, Locomotive Superintendent, died at Allahabad, June 21st. R. N. M. Mantell, District Engineer, died at Allahabad, June 30th. A. M. M. Miller, Resident Engineer, killed at Cawnpore, June 27th. A.C. Heberden, Resident Engineer killed at Cawnpore, June 27th. W. Digges LaTouche, Assistant Engineer, killed at Cawnpore, June 27th. Robert Hanna, Assistant Engineer, killed at Cawnpore, June 27th. J. C. Baynes, Assistant Engineer, killed at Cawnpore, June 27th. Thomas Byrne, Assistant Engineer, died at Calcutta, July—. J. W. Allen, Assistant Engineer, died at Mirzapur, August 12th. John Mackerness, Assistant Engineer, died at Agra, August—. W. Forsyth, Assistant Engineer, killed at Cawnpore, June 27th. F. Cussen, Junior Engineer, died on board steamer. C. B. Taylor, Junior Engineer, killed near Delhi, May 17th. A. Spencer, Junior Engineer, died at Agra, August—. F. L. Mudge, Resident Engineer, died at Sitapahar, October—. W. F. Thompson, Assistant Engineer, died near Buxar, July 19th; and to the following Foremen and Inspectors:—George Richardson, Foreman, died at Allahabad, August 11th; W. S. Benn, Articled Inspector, killed near Delhi, May 17th; J. Holmes, Articled Inspector, killed at Cawnpore, June 27th. This monument is erected in affectionate remembrance by their brother Engineers in the North-Western Provinces, India.

[Of these Engineers those who were killed are to be found on the tablets. Mowbray Thomson says of them: "I remember particularly Messrs. Heberden,

LaTouche and Miller as prominent for their eminently good services. They held Barrack No. 4 for three days with no military aid whatever; they were then put under Captain Jenkins. Their trained sharpness of vision and correct judgment of distances, acquired in surveying, made them invaluable as marksmen." Mr. Heberden was killed by a round shot. Messrs. Miller and LaTouche in the boats.]

(References: *Forrest; M. N.; Mowbray Thomson.*)

436.—**1857**—BEATSON, S., Captain. *Inscription:*—In memory of Stuart Beatson, Captain, 1st Regiment, Bengal Light Cavalry, who died at Cawnpore on the 19th of July 1857, in the discharge of his duty, as Assistant Adjutant-General with the force under the late Sir H. Havelock, aged 32 years.

[W. S. Beatson, son of Col. W. S. Beatson, Bengal Army, was born at Calcutta in 1825 and educated at Edinburgh and Haileybury. He was Deputy Assistant Adjutant-General not Assistant Adjutant-General, (as in inscription,) of Havelock's force. He did good work at the battles of Fatehpur and at Cawnpore, and was twice mentioned in despatches. He died of cholera. The story goes that though he was so ill that he could not ride, he had himself carried into action on a tumbril. His son was Major-General Sir Stuart Beatson, K. C. S. I., C. B., late Inspector-General of Imperial Service Troops.]

(References: *Forrest; Rice-Holmes; C.P.; Burke, P.*)

437.—**1857**—HARDY, W. N., Captain. *Inscription:*—To the memory of Whaley Nicol Hardy, Captain, Royal Artillery, who was killed in battle at Lucknow, 17th November 1857, aged 30 years.

[In command of some heavy guns at the attack on the Sikandrabagh, on the 16th November in Campbell's relief of Lucknow. "One of Travers's guns and a howitzer, which with considerable difficulty had been dragged up the bank opened fire on the point selected by Sir Colin for the breach—the south east corner of the wall surrounding the Sikandrabagh. Instantly Hardy (the Captain of the battery) was killed." The date 17th is a mistake. It should be 16th.]

(References: *Roberts; Forrest.*)

438.—**1857**—(1) GORDON, J., Captain. (2) HENSLEY, A. P. Lieutenant. (3) THOMPSON, W. T., Ensign. *Inscription:*—Sacred to the memory of Captain John Gordon, Lieutenant Arthur Platt Hensley, H. M.'s 82nd Regiment, who fell in the defence of Cawnpore in November 1857. Also of Ensign William Temple Thompson, H. M.'s 82nd Regiment, who was killed at the second relief of Lucknow on the 18th November 1857. This tablet is erected by their brother officers.

[Captain Gordon was killed in Windham's defence of Cawnpore on the 28th November.

Lieutenant Hensley was killed in Windham's defence of Cawnpore on the 29th November.

Ensign Thompson was killed in Campbell's relief of Lucknow. The fighting on the 18th November was street-fighting round the Residency. The 82nd were formerly the Prince of Wales Volunteers, and are now known as the 2nd Battalion the Prince of Wales South Lancashire Regiment. They were raised in two Battalions in 1793: the 2nd Battalion was disbanded in 1795, raised again in 1803 and disbanded in 1815. The first Battalion was in India from 1856 to 1869 and from 1895. They have the honour "Lucknow." They also fought in the Peninsula, Canada (1815) and the Crimea.]

(Reference: *Forrest.*)

439.—**1857**—OFFICERS and men, 34th Regiment. *Inscription:*—Sacred to the memory of Lieutenant Edward Jordan, Ensign Theophilus G. B. Applegate, died of wounds, Ensign Lyndon J. Grier, Colour-Sergeant Charles Feddon, Sergeant Patrick Jones, Corporal James Stock, Corporal William Clarke, one drummer, and twenty-four privates, all of Her Majesty's 34th or Cumberland

Regiment, who were killed in action or died of wounds received at Cawnpore on the 28th November 1857. This tablet is erected by the officers of the regiment to' mark their esteem and regard for their late youthful and gallant brother officers, and to record the sincere sorrow expressed by all ranks at their early deaths; also as a tribute of respect and admiration to the bravery and devotion of their late comrades, the Non-Commissioned Officers, drummers and private soldiers who fell upon the same occasion.

[The 34th are now the 1st Battalion, the Border Regiment. They fought in the Peninsula: their only Indian honour is Lucknow. The operations in which these soldiers fell were those under Carthew in the action near Cawnpore (3rd.) For the vexed question of his retreat, see references given below. Edward Jordan born 1836 was the son of the Revd. G. W. Jordan of Wheatley Oxon. He was educated at Marlborough.]

(References: *Holmes: M. C. Register: Forrest.*)

440.—**1857**—OFFICERS and men, 32nd Light Infantry. *Inscription:*—In memory of the following officers of the Thirty-Second Cornwall Regiment, Light Infantry, who with four hundred and forty-eight Non-Commissioned Officers and private soldiers were killed, or died in the discharge of their duty during the defence of Lucknow and Cawnpore and the subsequent compaign against the mutineers in the year of Our Lord 1857:—Colonel C. A. F. H. Berkeley, C. B.; Lieutenant-Colonel W. Case; Captains C. Steevens, J. Moore, J. W, Mansfield, W. Power, B. M. Cabe; Lieutenants E. DeL. Joly, J. D. Thompson, F. Wainwright, P. C. Webb, J Brackenbury, E. C. Hill, W. H. Study, J W Charlton. Also in memory of Mrs. Moore, Mrs Wainwright, Miss Wainwright, Mrs. Hill; forty-three soldiers' wives and fifty-five children of the same Regiment, murdered at Cawnpore in June of the same fatal year. This monument is erected by friends and comrades in token of affection and sorrow.

"The sufferings of this present time are not worthy to be compared with the glory which shall be revealed in us."

[The 32nd Cornwall Light Infantry, now the 1st Battalion Duke of Cornwall's Light Infantry, have the Indian honours of "Punjab," "Multan," "Gujrat" and "Lucknow." They were in all the Lucknow operations and bore the brunt of the heavy fighting in the trenches both there and at Cawnpore. They also were at Dettingen, in the Peninsula, at Waterloo, and in S. Africa. Of the officers mentioned:—

Colonel Berkeley—(1818-1858).—He was the second son of General Sir G. Berkeley, and great grandson of the fourth Earl of Berkeley, a very ancient family dating back to Robert Fitzharding, *circa* no. 1160. He was formerly in the Scots Fusilier Guards and died on the "Simla" off Socotra. He was Deputy Adjutant-General and Military Secretary to Sir J. Outram; "he displayed remarkable activity and intelligence," and did good service all through the Lucknow operations. He was severely wounded in a charge of Hodson's Horse at the Alumbagh on the 25th February. He was reported for honourable mention.

Colonel Case—Was killed at Chinhat. It appears that he protested against immediate attack on the ground that the men were not ready, *i.e.*, had not rested or had their breakfasts. When the retreat began Captain Bassano, of the 32nd, wanted to bring him away, but Case refused; and when he persisted, "issued his last command—'Leave me, Sir, and rejoin your company.'"

Captain Steevens.—Took command when Colonel Case was killed and also lost his life at Chinhat.

Captain Moore.—Was the life and soul of the Cawnpore defence. A tall genial Irishman, he was wounded early in the siege, but he went about with his arm in a sling, doing his duty. He carried out one daring and successful sally. "He was cheerful and animated to the last and inspired all around him with a share of his wonderful endurance and vivacity." He was killed in Vibart's boat on the 27th June. Mrs. Moore "sometimes came across with him to our barrack and we fitted up a little hut for her, made of bamboo, and covered over with canvas; there she would sit for hours, bravely bearing the absence of her husband while he was gone on some perilous enterprise."

Mrs. Moore, Lieutenants Wainwright and Hill and their families were also killed at Cawnpore.

Captain Mansfield was A. D. C. to General W. R. Mansfield (afterwards Lord Sandhurst), Sir Colin's Chief-of the Staff. He was severely wounded at the taking of the Subadar's tank in the 4th battle of Cawnpore on the 6th December. (It does not however seem clear whether this officer or another Captain Mansfield is meant. The only Captain J. W. Mansfield given in Forrest is the above: but his regiment is not mentioned. There is another Captain Mansfield of the 32nd whose initials are not given, who died of cholera at Lucknow on the 13th September.)

Captain W. Power was shot in the front verandah of the Residency on the 2nd July and died of his wounds on the 10th August. He was son of George Power, a member of His Majesty's Council, St. Vincent, who was a younger son of Sir John Power of Tullamaine, Co. Tipperary.

Captain McCabe did excellent service all through the defence of the Residency. He had won his commission at Multan where hé was the first man to plant the British flag. He led a sally on the 20th August against Johannes' House and another soon after Havelock's arrival. He was killed in a sortie on the 29th September, his fourth sortie according to Rees, who places him second only to Fulton among the defenders of the Residency (cf. No. 958).

Lieutenant Joly had been absent on leave from his regiment and had joined the 78th Highlanders. He was wounded at the storming of the Alumbagh and died soon after in the Residency.

Lieutenants Thomson and Brackenbury were both killed at Chinhat. Lieutenant Webb did his best to stop the retreat at that battle—"his face black with gunpowder and the peak of his cap shot off, he made himself hoarse with shouting to the men to halt." He was killed by an 18 pounder in Gubbins' compound on the 28th August. Ensign Studdy was wounded in the arm by a round shot in the Residency; he suffered amputation "which, as usual, proved fatal:" he died on the 9th August. Lieutenant Charlton was shot through the head at the Residency on the 13th July, but Gubbins says he was not killed. The musket ball hit him in the back of the head and lodged in the brain: and nine months later it showed itself at the aperture and was removed in England. Whether the inscription or Gubbins is in error, or Lieutenant Charlton died after the operation, is not clear].

References: *Forrest: Rees: Harris: Burke, P: Gubbins).*

441.—**1857—1870**—OFFICERS, 88th Regiment. *Inscription:*—

In memory of the undermentioned Officers of the 88th Connaught Rangers:—Captain H. H. Day, killed in action at Pandoo Nuddee, 26th November 1857, aged 20 years; Ensign F. M. Mitchell, died at Cawnpore, 7th December 1857, of wounds received in action at Pandoo Nuddee, 26th November 1857, aged 36 years; Ensign W. King, died at Cawnpore, 20th June 1858, aged 24 years; Ensign J. R. Perrin, died at Lucknow, 11th October 1858, aged 23 years; Lieutenant R. Miller, died at Dehra Ghat, 5th November 1860, aged 23 years; Quartermaster M. Evans, died at Cawnpore, 20th June 1864, aged 23 years; Lieutenant F. M. M. Mapleton, died at Cawnpore, 17th August 1865, aged 21 years. Captain L. S. Watson, died at Galle, 12th September 1865, aged 33 years; Captain L. C. Scott, died at Jullunder, 1st April 1870, aged 31 years. Erected by their brother officers

[The 88th, now the 1st Battalion of the Connaught Rangers, were in Windhams' operations at Cawnpore, and it was in his battle of the Pandu Naddi (2nd) that Captain Day "a very promising young officer" and Ensign Mitchell were killed. These were the only operations in Upper India in which the 88th took part; presumably they were subsequently sent to join Rose or Whitlock, as they have the honour "Central India." They were raised in 1793, and were in India from 1799-1801, 1857-1870, 1879-1891. Their only other Indian honour is "Seringapatam" with the elephant. They also fought through the Peninsular war, in the Crimea, S. Africa (1877-9) and the Boer war.

(Reference: *Forrest.*)

442.—**1858**—LITTLE, J., Lieutenant. *Inscription:*—In memory of Lieutenant John Little, H. M.'s 20th Regiment, third son of John Little, Esq., of Stewartstown, Ireland, who died at the Field Hospital, Cawnpore, 9th April 1858, aged 22 years. This tablet is erected by his parents and family as a memorial of one deeply lamented.

"The dead shall be raised incorruptible."

[John Little, (1835-58) was the 3rd son of John Little, descended from the family of Little's, of Legacurry, Co. Tyrone. He served in the Crimea: a younger brother is Canon Knox-Little The 20th are now the Lancashire Fusiliers.]

(Reference: *Burke, L. G. I.*).

443.—**1888**—LYNCH, W. W., Major-General. *Inscription:*—In loving memory of Major-Gen. William Wiltshire Lynch, C. B., of Pareora Stoke, near Guilford, Surrey, born 1st April 1831, died 4th August 1888. He began his military life at Cawnpore with the 70th Regt. He led the volunteers of Havelock's column in the advance on Cawnpore. He was severely wounded when serving under that heroic leader before Lucknow, and was promoted to a company in the 2nd Queen's Royals for his services in the Mutiny. He died of cholera at Allahabad while in command of the district. This tablet is inscribed by his wife.

[One of Barrow's volunteer cavalry, who did so well with Havelock. Their charge at the battle of Cawnpore elicited from Havelock the remark "Well done gentlemen volunteers. I am proud to command you." Twenty strong when they left Allahabad, they lost 3 killed and 11 wounded by the time they reached Lucknow. Lieutenant Lynch was wounded in the arm at Lucknow].

(References: *Forrest*; *Rees.*)

ALL SOUL'S CHURCHYARD.

444—**1857**—WHEELER'S GARRISON. *Inscription:*—The garrison of the entrenchment consisted of about 950 souls, thus—

63 artillery men.	55 women.
16 women	40 children.
20 children.	100 non-military.
15 Madras Fusiliers.	80 women.
84 32nd Regiment.	100 children.
45 women.	45 musicians, &c.
60 children.	29 women.
48 84th Regiment.	100 children.
100 officers.	

445.—**1857**—FIRST VICTIMS OF THE SIEGE. *Inscription:*—This stone marks a spot which lay within Wheeler's Entrenchment; it covers the remains, and is sacred to the memory, of those who were the first to meet their deaths when beleaguered by the mutineers and rebels in June 1857.

["The first casualty occurred at the West battery, M'Guire, a gunner, being killed by a round shot; the poor fellow was covered with a blanket and left in the trench till nightfall. Several of us saw the bullet bounding towards us and he also suddenly saw it, but . . . . seemed fascinated to the spot." (Mowbray Thomson). But these are probably the tombs of Messrs. Wade and Murphy of the East Indian Railway, who were the only persons buried inside the entrenchments, according to Mowbray Thomson].

(Reference. *Mowbray Thomson.*)

446.—**1857**—VICTIMS OF SHEORAJPUR. *Inscription* :—In three graves within this enclosure lie the remains of Major Edward Vibart, 2nd Bengal Light Cavalry, and about seventy officers and soldiers who, after escaping from the massacre at Cawnpore on the 27th June 1857, were captured by the rebels at Sheorajpoor and murdered on the 1st July. These remains were originally deposited within the compound of Savada House and were removed to this place in April 1861. This memorial was erected by the Government, North-Western Provinces, in the month of October 1867.

In memoriam.

"In the world ye shall have tribulation, but be of good cheer, I have overcome the world."

[Cf. preliminary note.]

KURSAWAN MUHAMMADAN CEMETERY.

447.—**1857**—REED, J., Private. *Inscription* :—In memory of No. 740, Private John Reed, 2nd Battalion, Rifle Brigade, who was killed at Cawnpore on the 7th December 1857.

[The official return shows only one man killed during these operations. On the 7th December the Brigade were fighting an action under General Mansfield, at the Subadar's Tank and through the old cantonments, on the north of the city.]

(Reference: *Forrest.*)

MEMORIAL GARDENS.

448.—**1857**—VICTIMS OF THE BIBIGARH MASSACRE (Memorial Well). *Inscription* :—Sacred to the perpetual memory of a great company of Christian people, chiefly women and children, who, near this spot, were cruelly massacred by the followers of the rebel, Nana Dhoondo Punt of Bithoor, and cast, the dying with the dead, into the well below, on the 15th day of July MDCCCLVII.

[The monument consists of a marble statue of a palm-bearing angel (by Marochetti), standing on a stone base at the foot of a cross. The well is surrounded by a light Gothic screen of sandstone designed by Colonel H. Yule, Bengal Engineers. On the portal is inscribed; "These are they which came out of great tribulation." It was erected by Government in 1863.]

MEMORIAL GARDENS CEMETERY.

449.—**1857**—(1) THORNHILL, R. B., B.C.S. (2) THORNHILL, M., Mrs., and two children. *Inscription* :—In memory of Robert Bensley Thornhill, Judge of Fatehgarh, Mary his wife, and their two children, killed July 15th, 1857.

"Though he slay me yet will I trust in Him."

[Cf. No. 385-425. R. B. Thornhill was the son of J. Thornhill, B.C.S., and a Director of the E.I.C. He was born at Great Stanmore in 1818, educated at Addiscombe (he was originally intended for the army) and Haileybury (1853-6) and arrived in India in the latter year. He served in Jessore, Allahabad, Agra, Budaun, Meerut, Farrukhabad, Cawnpore, Muzaffarnagar, Mainpuri and Banda.

He was one of the Thornhill's, eight of whom were "Bensley Thornhill," who served in the C S. R.B. Thornhill's grandfather was a Cudbert Thornhill, in all probability the Cudbert Thornhill who was known as the 18th century Sindbad; he had lived in Calcutta long before 1756, and escaped the Black Hole by fleeing to Fulta. From 1785 to 1808 he was master attendant at Calcutta. His son John Thornhill was born there in 1778; this was R. B. Thornhill's father. Other Bensley Thornhill's were John, first in the China service of the E.I.C. and then in the B.C.S. (born 1808); his mother's name was Henrietta Sarah Thornhill; Cudbert (born 1820), Secretary to Government at Agra in the Mutiny; Mark, (born 1826), Magistrate of Muttra in the mutiny; Henry, (born 1826), Deputy Commissioner of Sitapur, where he was killed in the mutiny. These three, with R B. Thornhill, were also sons of John Thornhill and Henriette Philippine, his second wife. J. B. Thornhill No. 883 and E. B. Thornhill (born 1834) were sons of J. B. Thornhill above mentioned. They also served in the mutiny; so that six Bensley Thornhill's—four brothers and two nephews of theirs—were all serving in the mutiny in this province together. Besides them, a "relative" of John Thornhill's named George, son of Thomas Thornhill, was also in the C. S. Mr. A. H. Bensley has informed me that the origin of the name Bensley was this. Robert Bensley the actor on retiring from the stage made his home with the Thornhill's, and as his cousin Sir W. Bensley was a Director of the E.I.C., their careers were naturally turned India-wards. As a matter of fact this was only an additional cause: for the family was always Anglo-Indian, and their father himself was in the B.C.S. However it was Sir W. Bensley who nominated John Thornhill the father; though all his sons as well as G. Thornhill were nominated by himself (save in one case where the son was nominated by his father's executor.) Of the younger generation, J. B. Thornhill was nominated by H. St. G. Tucker and E. B. Thornhill by J. C. Whiteman.]

(Reference: *Haileybury; Prinsep, C.L.; Communicated; W.P.*)

450.—**1857**—WOMEN AND CHILDREN, 32nd L. I. *Inscription:*—In memory of the women and children of H. M.'s 32nd Regiment who were slaughtered near this spot, 16th July A.D. 1857. This memorial was raised by 20 men of the same Regiment who were passing through Cawnpore, November 21st, 1857.

"I believe in the resurrection of the body."

[The date is wrong. It should be 15th July.]

451.—**1857**—BIBIGARH MASSACRE. *Inscription:—In memoriam.* On this spot stood the House of Massacre July 15th, 1857.

[Site of the Bibigarh.]

452.—**1857**—WOMEN AND CHILDREN, 1st Company, 6th Battalion, BENGAL ARTILLERY. *Inscription:*—In memory of the women and children of the late ill-fated 1st Company, 6th Battalion, Bengal Artillery, who were slaughtered near this spot by mutineers on the 18th July 1857. This monument is erected by a non-commissioned officer who formerly belonged to the 1st Company 6th Battalion.

"Spare Thy people, O Lord, and give not thine heritage to reproach, that the heathen should rule over them; wherefore should they say among the people, where is their God? Fear not, O Lord, be glad and rejoice, for the Lord will do great things."

[The date given is wrong. It should be the 15th July. The text (Joel ii, 17 and 21) is wrong; it should read "Fear not O *Land*."]

435.—**1857**—YOUNG, J. Captain. *Inscription:*—Captain James Young, 4th Bengal Native Infantry, born at Edinburgh, 27th November 1822, died at Cawnpore 11th August 1857, of cholera, while serving under General Neill in the suppression of the great mutiny.

454.—**1857**—CAMPBELL, H. D., Captain. *Inscription:*—Sacred to the memory of Howard Douglas Campbell, Captain in the 78th Highlanders, who died at Cawnpore of cholera on the 16th August 1857, deeply regretted by his brother officers who have erected this tablet.

[Howard Douglas Campbell (1821—1857), 4th son of Rear Admiral Donald Campbell of Achanduin, was recommended for the V. C. before his death. The family is a cadet branch of the Campbells of Lochiel, who are descended from the 2nd son of the 3rd Earl of Argyle. Captain H. D. Campbell was married to Anne Jane, daughter of T. Davidson, and had two sons and two daughters.]

(Reference: *Burke, L. G.*)

455.—**1857**—WOODFORD, C. J., Lieutenant-Colonel. *Inscription* :—Sacred to the memory of Lieutenant-Colonel C. J. Woodford, 2nd Battalion, Rifle Brigade, killed in action before Cawnpore, November 28th, 1857. This stone was erected to his memory by his brother officers.

[Killed in the 3rd day's fighting in defence of Cawnpore by Windham. Windham reported that the victory of that day was due to Colonels Woodford, Walpole and Watson.]

(Reference : *Forrest.*)

456.—**1857**—N.-C. O.'s and MEN, 64th Regiment. *Inscription* :—In memory of Sergeants J. Kelly, H. Donaughey; Corporal J. Lankham, W. Smith : Private J. Gee of the Band, H. M.'s 64th Regiment, who died at Cawnpore between the months of September and November 1857, deeply regretted by their comrades, who have erected this stone. Also of B. Fitzpatrick and D. Muir, who fell at the action of Cawnpore on 28th November 1857.

[The 64th were first with Havelock and fought at Fatehpur, Pandu Naddi, Aung, Cawnpore, Unao, in three actions at Bashiratganj, two actions at Bithur, in the first relief of Lucknow, at Khajuha, at the second relief of Lucknow, and in Windham's and Campbell's operations at Cawnpore. This was the regiment Sir H. Havelock-Allan obtained the V. C. for leading at Cawnpore. They did magnificent service all through the mutiny. They are now the 1st Battalion, The Prince of Wales' (North Staffordshire) Regiment. They were raised in and were in India from 1849 to 1861, and 1897 to 1908. They also fought in 1758, at St. Lucia, Surinam, in Persia, and the Dongola Expedition of 1896.]

(References : *Forrest : Rice-Holmes.*)

MIRPUR CEMETERY.

457.—**1858**—PEEL, W., Sir, Captain, R. N. *Inscription* :—To the memory of William Peel. His name will ever be dear to the British inhabitants of India, to whose succour he came in the hour of need and for whom he risked and gave his life. He was one of England's most devoted sons, and with all the talent of a brave and skilful sailor, he combined the virtues of a humble and sincere Christian. This stone is erected over his remains by his military friends in India and several of the inhabitants of Calcutta. Captain Sir William Peel, R. N., K.C.B., was born in Stanhope-street, Mayfair, on the 2nd November 1824, and died at Cawnpore on the 27th April 1858.

William Peel was 3rd son of Sir Robert Peel (1824-1858). He entered the Navy in 1838 and saw service in the Mediterranean, China, the Pacific, N. America and W. Indies. He became Post-Captain in 1849. He was the author of "A Ride through the Nubian Desert" (1852). He won his V. C and the C. B. at Sebastopol with the Naval Brigade. When in command of H. M S. *Shannon* he took a Naval Brigade up country, with ten 8-inch guns. He was at the battle of Khujwa where on the death of Col. Powell, he assumed command : at the 2nd relief of Lucknow, at the assaults on the Martiniere, Shah Najaf and Kaisarbagh, where he " behaved very much as if he had been laying the *Shannon* alongside an enemy's frigate," bringing his guns up to a few yards of the building. He was also at the 4th battle of Cawnpore and at the siege of Lucknow, where he was wounded, but not dangerously, in the thigh. A carriage was prepared for him but he preferred to use a doolie "like one of his bluejackets." This had apparently been used by a small-pox patient; he caught the disease and died on the 27th April at Cawnpore. "The loss of his daring but thoughtful nature joined with eminent abilities is a very heavy one to his country : but it is not to be more deplored than the loss of that influence which his earnest character, admirable temper, and gentle, kindly bearing exercised on all within his reach." So ran the proclamation issued after his death : these sonorous phrases state no more than the simple fact that he was a fine specimen of a British sailor.

The Peel family is of considerable antiquity. It dates back to Robert Peel of Hole House, who died in 1608. The first baronet was Sir Robert Peel (1750-1830) and M. P. for Tamworth from 1790-1818. His son the Right Honourable Sir Robert Peel, father of Sir William (1788-1850) was the celebrated orator and statesman. Of his five sons four attained considerable distinction, viz., Sir Robert Peel, P.C. G.C.B., M.P., Chief Secretary for Ireland (1861-65): Sir Frederick Peel, P.C. K.C.M.G., M.P., Sir William Peel, and Arthur Wellesley first Viscount Peel, Speaker from 1884 to 1895. The present baronet is also Sir Robert.]

(References : *Roberts ; Forrest ; Kaye ; Rice-Holmes ; Buckland ; Burke, P.*)

CHRIST CHURCH, CIVIL LINES.

458.—**1857**—SOTHEBY, G. M. W., Lieutenant. *Inscription :*—In memory of George M. W. Sotheby, Lieutenant, Bengal Artillery, only son of G. H. Sotheby, Captain, 34th Regiment, Madras Infantry, who in the 19th year of his age met his untimely death amongst the victims of the massacre of Cawnpore, in June 1857. His orphan sister erects this memorial in token of her sorrow and devoted affection.

"And God shall wipe away all tears from their eyes."

[Cf. No. 414. He assisted Lieutenant Ashe in his Battery ; it is not known how he died.]

459.—**1857**—OFFICERS AND MEN, 64th Regiment. *Inscription :*—In memory of Major Stirling, Captain Morphy, Captain McCrae, Lieutenant Mackinnon, Lieutenant Gibbon, 52nd Regiment attached, and twelve Non-Commissioned officers and men of the 64th Regiment, killed in action at Cawnpore, 27th November 1857.

[These officers fell in Windham's action of the 28th (not 27th) in the much criticized operations of Brigadier Carthew. The 64th moved up a ravine commanded in front and on both flanks by the enemy. There were four guns on the ridge in front of them. They rushed the ridge led by Brig. Wilson (their own colonel), and charged the guns, which they took. Major Stirling, Captain Morphy and Captain McCrae were all killed here: the two Lieutenants are returned as "missing." Major Stirling at Havelock's battle of Cawnpore had been slightly wounded just at the time when Lieutenant Havelock took his place at the head of the regiment, and had gone to the rear.]

(References : *Forrest ; Rice-Holmes.*)

460.—**1857**—MISSIONARIES of the S. P. G. *Inscription :*—To the Glory of God. In memory of W. H. Haycock, Priest, and Henry Edwin Cockey, Deacon, of the S. P. G. Mission to Cawnpore ; also of M. J. Jennings, Priest, Chaplain, founder of the S. P. G. Mission to Delhi; also of Alfred Roots Hubbard, Priest, and Daniel Corrie Sandys, Catechist, and Louis Koch, Catechist, of the S. P. G. Mission to Delhi. The Society for the Propagation of the Gospel in Foreign Parts dedicates this memorial of its brethren who glorified God by their deaths in the Mutiny of 1857.

"Here is the Patience and the Faith of the Saints." (*Also in Urdu.*)

[The S. P. G. Mission in Delhi was founded by the Revd. Midgely John Jennings, a chaplain of the E. I. C., in 1850. A Fellow of Christ's College, Cambridge, he had accepted an Indian chaplaincy in 1832. He had long dreamed of a mission in Delhi, but it was not till 1851 that he was stationed there. Next year occurred the conversion of Ram Chandra, a Kayasth professor of the Delhi College, and a leading Hindu of Delhi ; and also of Chimman Lal, Assistant Surgeon in the Delhi Hospital. Mr. Jennings now felt justified in pressing for help from England. The S. P. G. at once agreed, and sent out the Revd. S. Jackson and the Revd. A. R. Hubbard. By 1856 the mission had made considerable progress and was contemplating an extension to Rurki. But in 1857 the Mutiny burst. Mr. Jennings and his daughter were murdered in the palace whilst attending to the wounds of Mr. Hutchinson, the Collector, and Captain Douglas, Commandant of the Palace Guards. Miss Clifford, Mr. Hubbard, Mr. Sandys and Mr. Koch were also all murdered that day, as were Chimman Lal and Wilayat Masih, the chief convert of the Baptist Mission. The Delhi Mission had been completely swept away. But only for a time; special efforts were made at home to restore it. In October 1857 the Revd. T. Skelton, Fellow of Queen's College Cambridge, offered his services for the purpose; he was succeeded in 1860 by the Revd. R. R. Winter. In 1877 was started the Cambridge Mission, which was amalgamated with it.

It is now one of the most successful and largest missions in India. Its work is many-sided. It has many small "bastis" or settlements of Indian Christians in and around Delhi. It has branches at Rohtak, Karnal, Riwari and Gurgaon. St. Stephen's College and St. Stephen's High School both belong to it: it has long possessed a fully equipped hospital (also St. Stephen's) and a new one is now being built. St. Mary's Home and the Victoria Boarding School for girls are some of its institutions for women. It has two churches in Delhi besides others elsewhere. Among its famous names are those of Mr. Skelton, Prebendary of Lincoln, Mr. Whitley, later Bishop of Chota Nagpur, Mr. Bickersteth, afterwards Bishop of Japan, Mr. G. A. Lefroy, Bishop of Lahore. The mission founded by Jennings and "baptized in his blood" has grown and flourished.

The S. P. G. Mission at Cawnpore is considerably older than the sister Mission at Delhi, and was a well-established institution at the time of the Mutiny. In 1853 Mr. Haycock was one of the Revd. H. Sells' assistants, but in 1857 Mr. Sells went home ill, and Mr., (by then the Revd.) W. H. Haycock was in charge, with Messrs. Willis and Cockey, both students of Bishop's College, to assist him. Mr. Willis had to go to Calcutta to be ordained and so it fell out that only Messrs. Haycock and Cockey were left to go into the entrenchments. Of Mr. Haycock little appears to be recorded. I found a tomb at Agra in the Protestant cemetery to a child of a W. H. Haycock, which makes it possible that at one time, previous to his ordination, he was in Agra. At the time of the Mutiny his wife had died, and his children were at school in the Himalayas: they were afterwards supported and educated in England by the S. P. G. How he died is uncertain. One account is that he was killed on the 7th June by one of the first shots as he was entering the entrenchments. But Mowbray Thomson says: "He (the Revd. Mr. Haycock) had been accustomed to bring out his aged mother every evening into the verandah for a short relief from the fetid atmosphere within the barrack walls: the old lady was at length severely wounded, and her acute sufferings overcame the son's reason, and he died." It is a good instance of the uncertainty which hangs over the fates of so many of the Cawnpore victims—in one case a quick and merciful death: in the other as horrible a death as could be devised—and authority for both views. Of Mr. Cockey, Mowbray Thomson says that he remembered his being in the entrenchment, but did not know how he met his death; the only statement on the point I have been able to find is that of Mrs. Bradshaw, the wife of a musician, who said she saw Mr. Moncrieff and two other clergymen, one of whom was the R. C. Padre, the Revd. J. Rooney, at the boats on the 27th June. "We saw the clergyman take out a book; we did not see him read it, for a sowar rode into the water and cut him down....He then killed the Padre and the other, who was a missionary." The S. P. G. account states, however, that some witnesses attribute this reading to Mr. Cockey. The book was a prayer book: the part of it read the Burial Service. At all events, it seems clear that Mr. Cockey was killed with Messrs. Moncrieff and Rooney by a sowar of the 2nd B. C. at the boats.

As at Delhi so at Cawnpore, the mission grew stronger after the Mutiny than it ever was before. In 1858 the Revd. W. Willis returned, to find the mission in ruins. But in 1860 Christ Church was restored and handed over to the S. P. G., as a mission church: the first incumbent was the Revd. S. B. Burrell. In 1860 Mr. Willis left and the mission was joined by the Revd. J. R. Hill (now at Banda and to whom I am indebted for the material for this note). Christ Church College, with four schools, St. Martin's Home, the Orphanage of the Epiphany for girls, the Deaconess' Home, the Women's Missionary Association Hospital the Poorhouse, are some of the institutions belonging to the mission. Fatehgarh,

Orai and Hamirpur are the out-stations. To both these missions an old saying is peculiarly applicable—"The blood of martyrs is the seed of the Church."]

(References: *Story of the Delhi Mission*: *Story of the Cawnpore Mission*; *Forrest*; *M. N.*; *Mowbray Thomson.*)

461.—**1857**—(1) MACKINTOSH, C. (2) MACKINTOSH, D. C., Mrs. (3) MACKINTOSH, J. A. (4) WALKER, A., Mrs. *Inscription*:—To record the melancholy fate of their parents and brother, and as a tribute of affection and esteem, this tablet is erected by Edwin and Isaac Mackintosh, to the memory of Mr. Charles Mackintosh, Mrs. Dorothy Charlotte Mackintosh, their son Joshua Alfred Mackintosh, and her mother, Mrs. Amelia Walker, Senior, who were for many years members of this Church and fell victims to the Mutiny at Cawnpore in June and July 1857.

"I call upon thy name, O Lord, out of the low dungeon. Thou drewest near in the day that I called upon Thee. Thou saidst, Fear not, I will ransom them from the power of the grave. I will redeem them from death."

[These persons were found secreted under a bridge disguised in native clothes and killed by the insurgents on the 7th June on the road leading to the Customs ghat.]

(Reference: *M. N.*)

462.—**1857**—GEE, W. *Inscription*:—Sacred to the memory of William Gee, who was killed in Sir Hugh Wheeler's entrenchment during the Mutiny in 1857, aged 75 years. Erected by his children as a token of affection and respect.

[Cf. tablet 421. It is not known how he died.]

CHRIST CHURCHYARD.

463.—**1857**—MITCHELL, F. M. Ensign. *Inscription*:—Sacred to the memory of Fitzgerald Massey Mitchell, 88th Connaught Rangers, who died in the Field Hospital at Cawnpore, 7th December, of wounds received in action on the 26th November 1857. This memorial is erected by his brother officers as a token of their esteem and regard.

[Cf. No. 445.]

NEAR BILHAUR RAILWAY STATION.

464.—(Uncertain)—SMITH, Lieutenant. *Inscription*:—Sacred to the memory of Lieutenant Smith of the Bengal European Regiment, who was killed in action on the Frontiers.

[This tomb is said to be over a hundred years old. I have looked through Dodwell and Miles and other lists, but have failed to identify this Lieutenant Smith. "Lieutenant Smith" without initials or date of death, would seem as elusive as the proverbial needle in a haystack: but I have discovered the following facts. Working on the supposition that the tomb belongs to the latter end of the 18th century, we find that the B. E. Regiment was stationed at Cawnpore from 1796 onwards; and was concerned in two small expeditions from that station in 1797 and 1798. The former was directed to putting Saadat Ali on the throne of Oudh, the latter against Zeman Shah. In a list of the officers of the B. E. Regiment of 1796, there is no Smith given; so that this officer, if he died in either of these expeditions, must have been killed almost as soon as he joined the Regiment. If the tomb is rather older than 1796, Dodwell and Miles offers two possibilities, one Thomas Smith died 1783, one John Smith died 1789: but there was no fighting round Cawnpore at the time, so far as is known to me, and there is nothing to show that either was in the B. E. Regiment. On the other hand, if the tomb is rather later than 1796, we find two Lieutenants named Smith in the B. E. Regiment in 1804—James and John R. Smith, who joined it in 1798 and 1800; and of course at this time there was plenty of fighting of all sorts, from

Lake and his important campaigns to petty actions in the "Mud war," of which Kachaura was an example.]

(References : *D. and M.; P. R. Innes.)*

GOVERNMENT HARNESS FACTORY.

465.—**1857**—WILSON, N., Brigadier. *Inscription :*—Sacred to the memory of Colonel N. Wilson, K. H., H. M.'s 64th Regiment, Brigadier Commanding at Cawnpore, who fell mortally wounded while nobly leading his regiment to repel an attack made by the Gwalior rebels on Cawnpore, November 28th, 1857.

[Brigadier Wilson was killed whilst charging 4 guns with his own regiment, which he had asked to be allowed to lead in support of Brigadier Carthew. The regiment was driven back. Several other officers were killed in this unfortunate affair.]

(Reference : *Forrest.*)

466.—**1857**—OFFICERS, 34th Regiment. *Inscription :*—In memory of Lieutenant Edward Jordan, Ens. Thomas G. B. Applegate, Ens. Lyndon J. Grier, H. M.'s 34th Regiment, who fell at Cawnpore on the 28th November 1857. This stone was erected by their brother officers.

[Cf. No. 439.]

SATI CHAURA GHAT.

467.—**1857**—SATI CHAURA MASSACRE. *Inscription :*—"*In memoriam* 27th June 1857."

[Cf. preliminary note.]

GOVERNMENT EXPERIMENTAL FARM.

468.—**1857**—CURRIE, E., Captain. *Inscription :*—Sacred to the memory of Captain Eugene Currie, 84th Regiment, who was mortally wounded at the action of Cawnpore, and died on the 19th July 1857, in the 32nd year of his age.

[Wounded in Havelock's battle of Cawnpore by a round shot, which carried away nearly the whole of his back, and died of his wounds.]

[Reference : *Forrest.*)

469.—**1857**—BEATSON, S., Captain. *Inscription :*—"Stuart Beatson."

[The tomb is ¼ mile east of the farm. Cf. No. 436.]

NEAR MAGAZINE OF EUROPEAN TROOPS.

470.—**1857**—CHISHOLM, T. A., Lieutenant. *Inscription :*—In memory of Lieutenant T. A. Chisholm of the Madras Fusiliers, who died at Cawnpore on the 19th August 1857. *R.I.P.*

[Cf. No. 898.]

NEAR EUROPEAN BARRACKS No. 4.

471.—**1857**—WELL, in which were buried those who died during SIEGE of WHEELER'S ENTRENCHMENT. *Inscription :*—In a well under this cross were laid by ye hands of their fellows in suffering, ye bodies of men, women, and children, who died hard by during ye heroic defence of Wheeler's Entrenchment when beleaguered by ye rebel Nana, June 6th to 27th, A.D. MDCCCLVII.

"Our bones are scattered at ye grave's mouth as one cutteth and cleaneth wood upon ye earth. But our eyes are unto Thee, O God the Lord."

At the four corners of the iron railing are stone crosses inscribed as under :—"In memory of Lieutenant Glanville, 2nd Battalion,

Fusiliers, and Sergeant J. Magrath and 15 privates of No. 9 Company of the Madras Fusiliers, who formed part of Sir H. Wheeler's Garrison and were killed during its investment by the Bengal Mutineers in June 1857. This stone is erected by the Madras Fusiliers in remembrance of the above brave men."

"In memory of Captain Robert Urquhart Jenkins of the 2nd Light Cavalry, who died from wounds received shortly before the surrender of the Garrison of Cawnpore and was buried in this well with many others."

"Though he slay me, yet will I trust in him."

"In memory of Captain Sir George Parker, Bart., 74th Regiment, Native Infantry, Cantonment Magistrate of this place. Died in Wheeler's Entrenchment, July 1857."

"In the memory of Lieutenant E. Saunders, Sergeants Mulvehill, Gildea and Grady; 3 Corporals and 45 privates of G. Company. H. M.'s 84th Regiment, who while serving in General Wheeler's Garrison fell fighting against the Nana and his followers; of this company one man, Private Murphy, escaped."

[The well was outside the Entrenchments and used as a burial place for those who were killed or died during the siege. It was about 200 yards away and the dead were buried there at night. Lieutenant Glanville and his Madras Fusiliers were all killed in Barrack No. 2, which was the key of the position to keep down the fire from Barrack No. 1.]

(References: *Forrest: Mowbray Thomson.*)

KACHAHRI CEMETERY.

472.—**1781**—STAINFORTH, J., Lieutenant-Colonel. *Inscription:*—To the memory of Lieutenant-Colonel John Stainforth, who lived universally beloved and died equally lamented on October 27th, 1781.........*(rest illegible.)*

[Captain 1765, major 1774, Lieutenant-Colonel 1780. As he appears first as a Captain, he was very possibly transferred from a King's regiment.]

(Reference: *D. and M.*)

473.—**1817**—HORSFORD, J., Major-General Sir. *Inscription:*—Sacred to the memory of Sir John Horsford, Knight Commander of H. M.'s Most Honourable Order of the Bath, a Major-General on the Staff and Colonel Commandant of Artillery on the H. C.'s Establishment, who after a long career of meritorious service distinguished by the most perfect integrity and honour, departed this life on the 20th of April, A. D. 1817, aged 66; an exemplary victim to that spirited ardour and high sense of duty which led him but a few weeks before under great bodily sufferings and in very severe weather, to manifest his professional skill and fortitude at thesiege and capture of Hathras.

[John Horsford (1757-1817), son of John Horsford, educated at Merchant Taylor's and St. John's, Oxford (fellow 1768-71) was destined for the church, but enlisted in the E. I. C.'s Artillery under the name of John Rover to escape that career (1772). His identity was discovered by Colonel T. D. Pearse in 1778 and he was given a commission. He served in Mysore, (1790-1) at Bangalore, Arikera and Seringapatam, and at a later date under Lake, commanding the artillery at Aligarh, Dehli, Agra, Dig and Bhurtpore, always with great distinction. He became captain in 1786, major in 1801, Lieutenant-Colonel in 1804 (Brevet-Major 1795, Brevet-Lieutenant-Colonel 1800), Lieutenant-Colonel Commandant 1805, Colonel Commandant 1810, Major-General 1813. He received his K. C. B. in 1817. His last active service was at the siege of Hathras, the stronghold of Daya Ram, a rebellious zamindar; he died a few days after the reduction, of ossification of the heart. He never had a day's leave in 45 years' service, and is a fine example of the older race of Anglo-Indian worthies.]

[References; *Thorn; Buckland; Stubbs; Wellesley's Despatches; B.O.*]

474.—**1827**—FOLEY, R. *Inscription :*—Sacred to the memory of Richard Foley, who departed this life on the 3rd August 1827, aged 45 years and 11 months. He was gifted with an excellence of heart, an urbanity of manners and a benevolence of disposition which seldom come to the lot of one man, and his virtues had so truly endeared him to his friends, that it is only when memory shall fail to record them, that they can cease to regret his loss ; this monument is erected by his affectionate wife, in testimony of respect and esteem for the many eminent and excellent qualities he possessed as a husband, a father and a friend. (B. O.)

[A merchant at Cawnpore.] (Reference : *E.I.R.*)

475.—**1828**—NATION, Lieutenant-Colonel. *Inscription :*—Sacred to the memory of Lieutenant-Colonel Commandant Nation, C. B. This monument is erected as a tribute of respect, affection and regret by the European and Native Commissioned and Non-Commissioned officers of the 9th Regiment, Native Infantry, in which he rose from the rank of an Ensign to that of a Lieutenant-Colonel Commandant and to which during a period of almost 31 years' service he had actually been attached 28 years. When proceeding to the charge of Brigadier's command at Dehli he died at Cawnpore on the 2nd August 1828, *ætat.* 49. (B. O.)

[Stephen Nation, son of M. Nation, born at Somerset in 1780, was appointed cadet in 1796, Ensign in 1797, and would have had 31 years' service on the 27th September 1828. He became Lieutenant in 1798, Captain in 1804, Major in 1814, and Lieutenant-Colonel in 1823. He fought at Sasni (1802) and in Lake's campaigns at Dig and Bhurtpore ; in the Nepalese War at Magwampar, and in the Pindari War. From 1821—3 he commanded at Kaitha.]

(References : *D. and M. ; C.P. ; E.I.M.C.*)

476.—**1829**—McMURDO, E. A., Lieutenant. *Inscription :*—The sorrow, esteem and love of his brother officers are feebly displayed by this monument raised to the memory of Edward Aston McMurdo, Lieutenant, 33rd Regiment, Native Infantry, in whose amiable character the rarest and most endearing qualities were combined ; manly ! intelligent ! and generous ! the integrity of his conduct, the gentleness of his manners, his noble spirit and feeling heart caused him to be valued and beloved in life, in death most deeply lamented ! He was born in Edinburgh, and died at Cawnpore 25th January 1829, aged 25 years. (B. O.)

[E. A. McMurdo, son of Col. C. McMurdo, was born at Edinburgh in 1804 and educated at the Edinburgh High School. He joined the service in 1821 and became lieutenant in 1823.]

(References ; *D. and M. ; C. P.*]

477.—**1830**—STARK, H. Lieutenant-Colonel. *Inscription :*—Sacred to the memory of Lieutenant-Colonel Harry Stark, of the Bengal Horse Artillery, who departed this life on the 26th September 1830, aged 55 years. He lived universally respected as an honest man and gallant soldier. (B.O.)

[He joined the Bengal Artillery as lieutenant fireworker in 1794. In 1795 he was present at the conquest of the Dutch settlements in Ceylon. From 1799 to 1802 he was in Egypt with a detachment of artillery (Wellesley's Red Sea Expedition); from 1803 (December) he was with Lord Lake and present at the sieges of Dig and Bhurtpore. He subsequently went with Major-General John Smith's detachment into Rohilkhand and was present at the battle of Afzalgarh and afterwards of Fatehgarh under Lord Lake. He was also present at the sieges of Kamona and Gunnauri (Aligarh) where he was wounded. He served in 1813-14 under Colonels Martindell and Adams in Bundelkhand and Rewah commanding the artillery as Major at the siege of Entauri. He also served in the Pindari War of 1817-18 and at the capture of Bhurtpore in 1826.]

(References: *Stubbs*; *B. O.*)

478.—**1833**—PEACH, H. E., Major. *Inscription*:—Underneath rest the remains of Major Henry Edmund Peach, of the 16th Regiment, Native Infantry, and Deputy Commissary General of the Bengal Army, *obiit*, May 3rd, 1833. His brother officers and friends have erected this monument as a last tribute of respect to his memory and in testimony of their esteem, affection and regret. (B. O.)

[H. E. Peach, son of the Revd. H. Peach, was born in 1786, and joined the service in 1806. He became Captain in 1823 and Major in 1829. He served with the Rewah Field Force in 1813 and in the Nepalese war and almost all his time was spent in the Commissary General's Department.]

(References: *D. and M.*; *Services B. A. List.*)

479.—**1833**—CROFTON, G., Lieutenant. *Inscription*:—Sacred to the memory of George Crofton, Esquire, Lieutenant, Her Majesty's 16th Lancers, youngest son of the late A. B. Crofton, Esquire, of Roebuck Castle, County of Dublin. *Obiit* 24th August 1833, *ætat.* 26 years (B. O.)

[Not now traceable.]

480.—**1833**—WHITE, P. T. R., Lieutenant. *Inscription*:—Sacred to the memory of P. T. R. White, Esquire, Lieutenant H. M.'s 31st Regiment of Infantry, second son of W. R. White, Esquire, Surgeon H. M.'s 16th Lancers. *Obiit* 1st September 1833, *ætat* 26 years. (B. O.)

[Not now traceable.]

481.—**1833**—DAVIS, W. W., Lieutenant-Colonel. *Inscription*:—Sacred to the memory of the late Lieutenant-Colonel William Worsly Davis, Bengal Army, who departed this life on the 15th September 1833, aged 49 years. (B. O.)

[Son of W. Davis of Trenthide, Dorset, born in 1784, he joined the service in 1801, became Captain in 1815, Major in 1824 and Lieutenant-Colonel in 1827. He died on leave.]

(References: *D. and M.*; *Services B. A. List.*)

482.—**1833**—HOME-MURRAY, G., Brigadier. *Inscription*:—This monument is erected by the officers of Her Majesty's 16th Lancers as a token of respect and regard to the memory of Brigadier George Home-Murray, C. B., Lieutenant-Colonel of Her Majesty's 16th Lancers, in which corps he served with the utmost gallantry and distinction for a period of nearly forty years. Died in command of the Cawnpore station on the 15th December 1833, aged 59 years (B. O.)

[G. H. Murray was Brigadier of the 1st Cavalry brigade at the siege of Bhurtpore in 1825.]

(Reference: *Stubbs.*)

Fatehpur District.

FATEHPUR CEMETERY.

483.—**1833**—SMYTH, E., B.; C. S. *Inscription*:—Sacred to the memory of Edward Smyth, Esquire, of the Civil Service, eldest son of Edward Smyth, Esquire, of the Fence, near Macclesfield, Cheshire. Born 22nd July 1808, and died 14th September 1833. This tomb is erected by his affectionate brother W. M. S. (B. O.)

[E. Smyth was born at Prestbury in Cheshire in 1808. His father was a banker. He was educated at Haileybury and came to India in 1827. He served at Allahabad, Mirzapur, Fatehpur and Etawah, and died when officiating as Collector of Fatehpur.]

(References: *Prinsep C. L.; Haileybury; W. P.*)

484.—**1835**—GROTE, A., Mrs. *Inscription:*—Sacred to the memory of Arabella Grote, the beloved wife of Andrew Grote, Esquire, of the Civil Service, and daughter of Captain Macdonald of the—Reg., who departed this life on the 5th September 1835, aged 30 years.

[A. Grote, son of George Grote and brother of G. Grote (No. 397), was born at Beckenham in 1806 and was educated at Charterhouse. He had just come out after three years' furlough and was Judge at Fatehpur when his wife died. He died there six weeks later, on the 17th October 1835.]

(References: *Haileybury; Prinsep C. L.; W. P.*)

485.—**1840**—TIMINS, D. T., B. C. S. *Inscription:*—Sacred to the memory of Douglas Thomson Timins, of the Bengal Civil Service, third son of John F. Timins, of Hilfield in the county of Herts. Born October 13, 1811, died October 25, 1840.

"For as in Adam all die, so in Christ shall all be made alive."

[D. T. Timins, son of Captain J. Timins (H. E. I. C.'s maritime service) was born at Aldenham, Herts. He was at Haileybury 1829 and came to India in 1830. His service was spent in Agra, Bareilly, Pilibhit, Benares, Gorakhpur and Fatehpur, and he was officiating Collector of the last district when he died.]

(References: *Prinsep C. L.; Haileybury; W. P.*)

486.—**1857**—O'BRIEN, C., Lieutenant-Colonel. *Inscription:*—Sacred to the memory of Charles O'Brien, Lt.-Col., Bengal Infantry, who died at Fatehpur, 21st October 1857, aged 50 years.

[He was son of Dr. M. M. O'Brien, born at Ennis in 1807; and is apparently the officer who was in command at Allahabad after the departure of Neill. He is last heard of as escorting money to Cawnpore and being ordered back to Fatehpur (17th October.)]

(Reference: *C. P.; Forrest.*)

487.—**1857**—TUCKER, R. T., B. C. S. *Inscription:*—R. T. Tucker fell at the post of duty 1857, looking unto Jesus.

[Robert Tudor Tucker, cousin of Colonel Tudor Tucker, killed at Fatehgarh (No. 385,) was the son of H. St. G. Tucker, B. C. S., born at Edinburgh in 1817. He was educated at Addiscombe and Haileybury and came to India in 1836. He had served at Patna, Etawah, Agra, Azamgarh, Ghazipur, Benares and Aligarh. He was at this time Judge at Fatehpur, and was the life of the Fatehpur defence. When the rest abandoned a certainly untenable position and made their way to Banda he remained at his post, and kept the rebels at bay from the top of the cutcherry. It was not till he had killed some 14 of his assailants that he was slain. He was a devout Christian, whose epitaph sums up both his life and his death. "It is impossible not to admire, how far it may be regretted, the heroic devotion of the late Mr. Tucker: nor is it much a matter of wonder that his conduct and his personal prowess actually succeeded in preserving, for a few hours longer, some show of order. Mr. Tucker by his earnest and open profession of religion, and by his unbounded pecuniary liberality had commanded the respect, if not the affection, of a large number of the inhabitants of the city, and when the excited mob returned in triumphant procession from his slaughter, two Hindus of the town stood out before them and reviled them as the murderers of a just and holy man; it is scarcely necessary to add that they immediately shared his fate."]

(References: *M. N.; Rice-Holmes; Haileybury; W. P.; Prinsep C. L.: Gazetteer.*)

M. KARANPURA, TAHSIL KORA.

488.—**1857**—POWELL, T. S., Colonel. *Inscription:*—"Sacred to the memory of Thomas Sidney Powell, Colonel, 53 Regiment, who fell gloriously in the moment of victory, commanding H. M.'s forces at the action of Khujooa, near Fatehpore, 1 Nov. 1857. Erected by the officers of the Regiment."

[Colonel Powell was in command of a small force which defeated a strong force of mutineers at Khajuha. Powell was shot through the head at the outset but Peel who, with the Naval Brigade, was charging in flank cut the rebels in two and seized two guns. The English losses were severe.

Nailed to a tree trunk is an inverted tin plate on which the following words have been scratched—"To the memory of Private Thomas Richards, Her Majesty's 5th Fusiliers died 5th July 1858." It is not clear when the 5th were here—probably in passing through after the mutiny was over.]

(References: *Forrest; Rice-Holmes; Gazetteer.*)

Banda District.

ST. GEORGE'S CHURCH.

489.—**1857**—COCKERELL, H. E., B. C. S. *Inscription:*—In memory of Henry Edmund Cockerell of the Bengal Civil Service, who perished in the insurrection in the town of Banda on the 15th June 1857, in the twenty-seventh year of his age.

[Mr. Cockerell was stationed as Joint Magistrate at Karwi. He maintained his post there single-handed, saving the tahsili of Tarauhan (now Karwi). Meantime at Banda the troops mutinied and the inhabitants fled. Mr. Cockerell had, however, refused to come into Banda till actually ordered to do so. When he did arrive he found that everybody had gone, and he was murdered at the Nawab of Banda's gate. The Nawab, if he did not actually instigate the murder, took no steps to stop it as he could easily have done. He was the son of the Reverend H. Cockerell of Northweald, Epping, and was born in 1831. He was educated at Marlborough and Haileybury and came to India in 1853.]

(References: *M. N.; Cadell; M. C. Register; Haileybury; Gazetteer.*)

PORCH OF ST. GEORGE'S CHURCH.

490.—**1809**—JAMIESON, W., Lieutenant. *Inscription:*—Sacred to the memory of Lieutenant W. Jamieson, 1st Battalion, 19th N. B. V., who was mortally wounded at the assault of the heights of Ragauli, Janry. 22nd, and died February 2nd 1809, aged 24 years. This monument was erected by the officers of the corps as a mark of respect and esteem for his exemplary valor and virtues.

[The tomb is at Ragauli in Tahsil Girwan. In December 1878 the inscription was lost but the zamindars afterwards recovered it. It was removed to the Church; those that follow come from the old cemetery.

When the officers of Shamsher Bahadur surrendered their fortresses Ajaigarh should have been amongst them; but Lachman Dowa, a zamindar seized it and it was necessary to send a column against him under Lieutenant-Colonel Martindell. He found the enemy posted on the heights of Ragauli in a very strong position, from which they were only driven at the cost of one officer and 28 men killed and two officers and 115 men wounded. Ajaigarh was captured on the 13th February. Of Lieutenant Jamieson Pogson writes that he was shot through both thighs. "Honorable, upright and accomplished, he possessed the esteem of all who knew him," writes Pogson, and quotes the "Vicar of Wakefield:" "Go and if you fall, though distant, exposed, and unwept by those that love you—the most precious tears are those with which heaven bedews the tomb of a soldier."]

William Jamison (so Dodwell and Miles) was the son of J. Jamison, merchant at Glasgow, and was born in 1784. He joined the service in 1803.]

(References: *Cadell; Pogson; D. and M.; C. P.*)

491.—**1825**—FANE, JULIA C. *Inscription:*—Sacred to the memory of Julia Charlotte, sixth daughter of William and Louisa

Fane. She died on the 21st of August 1825, aged 5 months and 16 days.

[This is an instance where children who die in infancy are omitted by Burke, but there is no doubt that this is a child of William Fane, H. E. I. C. S., fifth son of the Hon. H. Fane, younger son of the 8th Earl of Westmoreland, who married Louisa Hay, daughter of Thomas Dashwood and sister of T. J. Dashwood (No. 64,1) and aunt of the two Lieutenants Dashwood killed at Lucknow in 1857 (Nos. 868 and 924). William Fane had eight other children, six daughters, including another Julia Charlotte, and two sons one of whom was in the C. S. He was ancestor of the present Fane's of Fulbeck Hall, county Lincoln, an estate purchased from the Rutland family by the first Earl of Westmoreland in 1622 for his younger son, Sir Francis Fane. The family is of Welsh extraction, going back to Howell ap Vane of Monmouthshire; and with more certainty to Henry Vane, *circa* 1450.

The Fane's, Dashwood's and Alexander's are much interconnected; Julia Charlotte Fane (this child's sister and namesake) married R. Alexander, whose father, James, was married to Charlotte Dashwood, sister of Mrs. Louisa Fane. To this family belongs E. B. Alexander, B. C. S.—a name well-known to district officials in the U. P. as that of the author of a certain "scheme." W. Fane joined the service in 1808 and was one of the first Haileybury students. In 1832 he was member of the Board of Revenue; he died at the Cape in 1832.]

(References: *Burke L. G., L. G. I, and P.; Prinsep, C. L.; Haileybury*)

492.—**1833**—COLE, W., Lieutenant. *Inscription*:—Sacred to the memory of W. Cole, late a Lieutenant in the 6th Regt., Nat. Infantry, who died at Banda, on the 22nd September 1833, aged 29 years and 3 months. This monument is erected by his brother officers (as) a mark of their esteem and regard.

[Son of W. Cole, born 1804, he joined the service in 1824 and became a lieutenant in 1827.]

(References: *D. and M.; Services B. A. List.*)

493.—**1833**—MERCER, L. A. *Inscription*:—Sacred to the memory of Leslie Alexander, son of Lt. and Bt. Captn. A. Mercer, 70th Regt., N. I., and Mary his wife, who departed this life at Banda on the 4th June 1833, aged 5 months and 28 days.

494.—**1833**—(1) MERCER, MRS. (2) MERCER, A. *Inscription*:—"Sacred to the memory of Mary, the beloved wife of Bt. Captn. A. Mercer, who departed this life on the 20th August 1833, aged 30 years. Also of Alexander, his eldest son who died on the 24th August 1833, aged 6 years.

[Probably relatives of Alexander Mercer who joined the service in 1818 and became captain in 1836 (brevet not mentioned). He was son of W. Mercer, born in 1800.]

(References: *D. and M.; Services B. A. List.*)

495.—**1838**—KILLIEN, J. G. *Inscription*:—Sacred to the memory of John Gill Killien, (son of Sub-Condr. Rich. Killien, Orde. Department), died 6th June 1838, aged 4 years, 3 months and 26 days.

496.—**1839**—HORNE, J. *Inscription*:—Sacred to the memory of James Horne. He was 42 years as a Fife-Major in the 29th Regt., N. I., died at Banda August 14th, 1839. Erected by his beloved wife.

497.—**1840**—REID, F., Mrs. *Inscription*:—Sacred to the memory of Frances Reid, relict of the late P. Reid, Esquire, who departed this life on the 8th October 1840, aged 44 years, 3 months and 24 days.

[P. Reid was a tent maker at Fatehgarh, *circa* 1832.]

(Reference; *E. I. R.*)

498.—**1845**—BLACKALL, T. *Inscription:*—Sacred to the memory of Thomas Blackall, Esquire, Deputy Collector and Deputy Magistrate, who departed this life on the 9th August 1845, aged 28 years.

499.—**1847**—IRWIN, (infant daughter). *Inscription:*—Sacred to the memory of the infant daughter of Harriet and Harry Irwin, who died at Banda, on the 29th of June 1847, aged 1 month and 23 days.

"All flesh is grass, the grass withereth the flower fadeth; but the word of our God shall stand for ever. (B. O.)

[Henry Irwin of Mount Irwin (1816-1883), married in 1846, Harriet Josephine, daughter of G. O. L. Jacob, H. E. I.C.S. He had two sons, H. C. Irwin, late B. C. S., now of Mount Irwin, and G. R. Irwin, C.S.I., I.C.S., Superintendent of Thagi and Dacoity. The family dates back to W. J. Irwin of Carnagh, co. Armagh, *circa* 1680.]

(Reference: *Burke L. G. I.*)

500.—**1851**—GODFREY, G. J. *Inscription:*—Sacred to the memory of George James Godfrey, the beloved son of Isabella and George Godfrey, Drum-Major, 60th Regt., N. I., who departed this life on the 5th day of Dec. 1851, aged 2 years, 4 months and 20 days."

Though in the paths of death I tread
With gloomy horrors overspread,
My steadfast heart shall fear no ill,
For Thou, O Lord! art with me still." *XXIII Psalm, 1 verse.*

501.—**1857**—VICTIMS OF THE MUTINY. *Inscription:*—Sacred to the memory of Horace Edmund Cockerell, Joint Magistrate of Banda, (also) of George Gwynne Benjamine, C. Benjamine, his wife, Henry Augustus Bruce, Chte. Anne Bruce and his mother John Lloyd (*sic*), the lamented victims of the Mutiny in the Bengal Army who were massacred at this place on the 15th and 16th June 1857, and whose remains were collected after the defeat of the insurgents by Major-General Whitlock's field division and intered in this spot on the 9th May 1858.

[The Mutiny in Banda began with an insurrection in certain villages of the district, in Parganas Baberu, Mau and Darsenḍa (now Kamasin). This was in early June; but Banda remained quiet after the district had gone. In Banda was a detachment of the 1st N. I. The Fatehpur fugitives reached Banda on the 8th June; and on the same day the English took refuge with the Nawab of Banda, Ali Bahadur. About the 14th the sepoys showed signs of disaffection, as did the jail guard and *najibs*. An attempt was made to suppress them with the assistance of the Nawab's forces, but it failed: for the Nawab's forces were even more rebellious than the sepoys. They joined the sepoys and all broke into open mutiny. The English managed to escape to Nagode. On the 15th June Mr. Cockerell, who had refused to leave Karwi and had preserved the tahsili and treasure, rode into Banda with the latter and was killed at the Nawab's gateway (cf. No. 489). On the 16th Mr. Bruce, in charge of the Nawab's villages, his mother, Captain Benjamine, commanding the Nawab's guards, his wife and her brother, Mr. Lloyd (all Eurasians) were discovered in the house of an old Arab named Maghribi Sahib. They were murdered by the retainers of the Nawab: their bodies were flung into a field.]

(References: *M. N.; Gazetteer; Cadell.*)

ST. GEORGE'S CHURCH YARD.

502.—**1858**—READHEAD, T. H., Lieutenant. *Inscription:*—In memory of Lieutenant T. H. Readhead, Royal Artillery, died at Banda, 20th May 1858, aged 21 years.

503.—**1858**—HANCOCKE, J., Lieutenant. *Inscription :*—In memory of Lieutenant J. Hancocke, XII Royal Lancers, died at Banda, 8th May 1858.

[The 12th Royal Lancers (now the 12th Prince of Wales' Royal Lancers) were with the Saugor and Nerbudda field force, i.e., Whitlock's column. They were present at the actions of Jaiganj, Kabrai and Lowherra (*sic*), the battle of Goera Mughali, where they did very well, the reduction of Karwi and many minor affairs. They were in India 1854-55, 1857-1860 and 1877-1887. They were in the Crimea in 1855-56, marching across Egypt: and went home between the end of the Crimean War and their return to India in 1857.]

(Reference: *Private Papers.*)

ON BANDA-FATEHPUR ROAD, NEAR ST. GEORGE'S CHURCH.

504.—**1858-59**—OFFICERS AND MEN, WHITLOCK'S FORCE. *Inscription :*—In memory of the British officers and men of the Madras Column, commanded by Major-General Whitlock, who fell in action or died during the campaign of 1858 and 1859, against the rebels and mutineers of the Bengal Army in Bundelkhand.

[Whitlock's Madras Column left Jubbulpore on the 17th February 1858, marched through Rewah to Saugor, and thence to Banda. He reached Kabrai on the 17th April 1858, fought a small action there and another sharply contested action at Goera Mughali and then occupied Banda. Among his troops were the 12th Lancers, the 3rd Madras Europeans, the 2nd Hydrabad Contingent Cavalry, and guns of the R. A. and Madras Artillery. He sent detachments to punish the rebels and pacify the country, and occupied Karwi. A garrison was left there and at Banda and the column left the district in September.]

(References: *Rice-Holmes; Cadell; M. N.*)

OLD CANTONMENT CEMETERY.

505.—**1836**—HUNTER, J., Lieutenant-Colonel. *Inscription :*—Sacred to the memory of John Hunter, born at Virginia on the 1st day of May 1781, and died at Banda on the 17th day of Sept. 1836. A Lieutenant-Colonel in the E. I. C. S.

[James Hunter, Provost of Ayr in 1698, had four sons: the youngest settled in Virginia (born 1746). His youngest son, of four, was this John Hunter. The family dates back to James Hunter, who acquired the lands of Abbotshill in the parish of Ayr from Alan Stewart, Abbot of Crossraguel in 1569. The family subsequently succeeded (*circa* 1750) to the estate of Thurston, in Co. Haddington.

John Hunter was born in 1781, joined the service in 1801, and became Lieutenant-Colonel in 1830. He fought at the siege of Bhurtpore, was wounded, mentioned in despatches and obtained his majority after the siege.]

(References: *Burke L. G.; D. and M.; Services B. A. List.*)

506.—**1848**—EDGEWORTH, C. F. E. *Inscription :*—To the memory of Christina Frances Edith, only child of Mr. M. P. Edgeworth, C.S. and Christina his wife, born January 10th, died December 5th, MDCCCXLVIII.

"Of such is the Kingdom of Heaven."

[Michael Pakenham Edgeworth, son of R. P. Edgeworth, the well known educational writer, and half brother of Maria Edgeworth, the authoress, married, in 1846, Christina, daughter of Dr. Hugh Macpherson of Aberdeen, and had two daughters. The Edgeworth's, originally a family from Edgeware in Middlesex, settled in Ireland at Edgeworth's town, Co. Longford, in 1573. M. P. Edgeworth retired as Commissioner of Multan in 1859, and died in 1882.]

(References: *Burke L. G. I.; Haileybury.*)

507.—**1848**—CHAMBERS, C. *Inscription :*—To the memory of Charlie, son of Captain Joseph Chambers and Maria his wife, born April 5th, 1848 and died July 17th, 1848.

"Of such is the Kingdom of Heaven."

[Joseph Chambers, son of C. W. Chambers, born 1814, belonged to the 21st N. I.]

(Reference : *Services B. A. List.*)

CEMETERY NEAR KANDHAR DAS' TANK.

508.—**1814**—SPENCER, N., Mrs. *Inscription :*—Sacred to the memory of Nancy Spencer, aged 23 years and 2 months, who died on the 4th of Decr. 1814. Her loss has been most dearly lamented by her affectionate husband and two children.

509.—**1857**—BARBER, J. H., Lieutenant. *Inscription :*—Sacred to the memory of Lieutenant J. H. Barber, XII Regt., B. N. I., flying to save his life from the mutinous sepoys of his own corps at Nowgong in the month of June 1857, and ruthlessly pursued from village to village by the inhabitants of the country thirsting for his blood. He was struck down by the sun, and died alone and untended in the field of M. A. Pundu Perch Banda (*sic*) ; eighteen months afterwards his remains were collected and interred on this spot."

Blessed are they which are persecuted for righteousness sake.

[Nowgong was garrisoned by detachments of the Jhansi regiments. They broke on the 10th June. The officers could only retreat ; those of them who did not perish on the road—in various villages of Sihonda (now Girwan) and Badausa—ultimately reached Banda. Some of them were taken prisoners by the zamindars of Goera Mughali, who brought them to the Nawab. He, however, treated them kindly, and sent them to Nagode. "They (the fugitives) had had to leave some of their friends, struck down by the sun," such as Lieutenant Barber.

"M. A. Pundu Perch Banda" is possibly Ma (Mauza) Pandui (a village on the border of parganas Banda and Girwan,) Perg. (pargana) Banda.]

(Reference : *Rice-Holmes ; M. N.*)

510.—**1858**—TRANTHAM, J. *Inscription :*—Sacred to the memory of Trumpeter John Trantham, H. M. XII R. L., died 14th May 1858, aged 19 years.

511.—**1859**—GALVIN, W., Drum-Major. *Inscription :*—Sacred to the memory of Dm.-Major Wk. Galvin, H. M.'s 97 Regt., who died at Banda 21st November 1859, aged 33 years. Erected by his three sorrowing brothers serving in the same Regt. R. I. P.

[The 97th, now the 2nd Battalion Queen's Own (Royal West Kent) Regiment, were with General Franks in his march through Oudh and the Lucknow operations in March 1858. It is extremely improbable, therefore, that they were also with Whitlock. They were doubtless sent to garrison Banda later. They were raised in 1824 and fought at Sebastopol and in the Boer War. They were in India 1857 66.]

(Reference : *Forrest.*)

512.—**1859**—McKAY, C., Lieutenant. *Inscription :*—Sacred to the memory of Lieutenant C. McKay, H. M. 97th Regt. He died at Banda Feby. 13th, 1859. This monument was erected by his brother officers as a mark of respect and esteem.

CEMETERY NEAR KALI KUAN.

513.—**1859**—SERGEANTS, 97th Regiment. *Inscription :*—Sacred to the memory of the undermentioned non-comd. officers of H. M.'s 97th Regt. who died at Banda.

Sergt. R. Jeffery, Feby. the 20th, 1859, aged 22 years.
P. M. C. Sergt. J. Hickey, March the 5th, 1859, aged 23 years.
S. M. P. Wattine, May the 24th, 1859, aged 26 years.
P. M. C. Sergt. T. Cooper, June the 5th, 1859, aged 22 years.

Sergt. G. Begby, June the 10th, 1859, aged 41 years.
Erected by their brother non-comd. officers as a mark of esteem and respect: and also Cr. Sergt. A. White, 8th Septr. 1859, aged 31 years and 7 months.

514.—1859—(1) LEGH, E. C., Lieutenant-Colonel—**1902.**—(2) LEGH, N. E. C., Lieutenant. *Inscription* :—In loving memory of Edmund Cornwall Legh. This cross is erected by his wife and children.

'Blessed are the merciful.'

And Neville Edward Cornwall, son of E. C. Legh, Lieut., who died at Sydney, N. S. W., June 21st, 1902, aged 48.

'There is mercy with Thee.'

Sacred to the memory of Lieut.-Col. E. C. Legh, C. B., H. M. 97th Regt. He died at Banda, June 3rd, 1859. This monument was erected by his brother officers as a mark of their respect and esteem.

[There are here three inscriptions: two to Lieutenant-Colonel Legh, one by his wife and one by his brother officers, and one to his son. Edmund Cornwall Legh (1821-1859) was 6th son of G. J. Legh, of High Legh. He married Julia, daughter of Neville Parker of New Brunswick, and left a son, Neville Edmund Cornwall, (not Edward as in inscription), born 1854, and a daughter. The family traces its descent to Oswald de Lega of East Hall, Cheshire; the date is not given but it was 11 generations before 1451, so that the family must be extremely old. The succession of High Legh has been unbroken since at least the 7th generation.]

(Reference: *Burke, L. G.*)

MANIPUR, NEAR KALINJAR.

515.—1812—MACMANUS, J. *Inscription* :—To the memory of James MacManus, late of H. M.'s 8th or K. R. I. L. Drgs., who died 12th Febry. 1812, aged 29 years.

[This tomb is in a cemetery in Manipur, an "island" village of native state territory about 2 miles north of Kalinjar. It contains twenty one tombs of which two are rather larger than the rest: one of the nineteen has the above inscription. It is undoubtedly the cemetery of those that fell in the siege of Kalinjar in 1812.

Kalinjar is a famous old fort at the south-east extremity of the Bundelkhand plain on a hill 1,230 feet above sea level, with steep and in the upper part almost perpendicular sides. It is mentioned as a famous place in the *Mahabharata* and its authentic history dates back to the early Chandels who made it their capital and the "King of Kalinjar" is mentioned as early as 978 A. D. It was attacked successively by Muhammad Ghori (1202 A. D.), Humayun (1530 A. D.), Sher Shah (1554 A. D.) and others. It was held first by Musalmans and then by Baghels and finally gave name to a *sirkar* in the time of Akbar. It was subsequently taken by the Bundelas and passed first to Hardeo Sah of Panna, and then to the Chaubes, of whom one was Kiledar (Kaimji). At the time of the British occupation it was still held by his descendants. One of them was confirmed in his possession of Kalinjar. He, however, ignored the British rule: Kalinjar became a mere resort of outlaws and plunderers; in 1812 it was decided to capture it. The force assembled under Colonel Martindell consisted of a squadron of the 8th Light Dragoons (now 8th K. R. I. Hussars), five companies of the 53rd (now Shropshire L. I.), six battalions of Native Infantry and four squadrons of Native Cavalry Guns were pulled up a hill 780 feet high (a tremendous feat on a Bundelkhand hill) and the investment was commenced on the 18th January. It was bombarded: and on the 1st February the breach was reported practicable. But the wall which had been breached was on an abrupt cliff which had to be scaled; and this was found impossible. The losses were heavy, Captain Fraser and Lieutenant Nice of the 53rd were killed: the regiment also lost 16 men killed, and 10 officers and 114 men wounded; the total loss was about 200. Next day, however, the Chaubes offered to surrender and evacuated the fort on the 13th February.

The larger tombs are doubtless those of the two officers.]

(References: *Gazetteer; Pogson; Cadell.*)

MANIKPUR, TAHSIL KARWI.

516.—**1859**—(1) EVANS, W. (2) LIMUEL, C. *Inscription* :—In memory of William Evans, Chief Engineer, and Charles Limuel, Resident Engineer, who were murdered by rebels at Entowah near the 80th milestone from Allahabad on the 26th February 1859.

[From enquiries made in the neighbourhood, the following facts were discovered. No such place as "Entowah" is known. There is however a village called Itwan which would be about 80 miles from Allahabad; and this is undoubtedly the place meant, as an old map, which spells the word in this way, proves. An old man in Manikpur stated that one Ranwant Singh, a Baghel Thakur of Rewah, remained in arms for a considerable period, and murdered some Englishmen both at Itwan and Kasauli (in Rewah state). He also stated that he could remember the body of an Englishman being brought from Itwan and buried in Manikpur, but does not remember his name. As Itwan is close to the railway line (East Indian Railway) it is possible that these gentlemen were railway Engineers.]

(References: *Private inquiry.*)

KALINJAR, TAHSIL GIRWAN.

517.—**1818**—WAUCHOPE, J. *Inscripiton* :—Sacred to the memory of John Wanchope,[1] Esquire, of Niddrie,[2] near Edinburgh, Collector of Bundelkhand 1809 and 1810 A.D., and Judge of Bundelkhand in 1818 A. D. He successfully exerted himself to gain affections,[3] and promote the happiness of those over whom he was placed, and supported by his personal conduct and character the honour and interests of Government by whom his valuable services have been frequently and most honourably acknowledged. Mr. Wanchope[1] was of the ancient family of Neddery[2] near Edinburgh, and he departed this life at Kalingar[4] on the 12th August 1818, in the 36th year of his age.

[The tomb of John Wauchope is situated within the Fort at Kalinjar. (For some account of the fort *vide* no. 493). The present inscription is a restoration, and not a very intelligent one, as the obvious errors prove. The original inscription was considerably longer and was defaced when a Sikh regiment was stationed at Kalinjar. Führer reproduces its remains: it will be seen that the major part of the present epitaph (from "he successfully" to the end) was only the final part of the old epitaph.

"Age ....
In Bu..
Alike Emin...
In his private and.....................................
He was beloved of his kin..............................
Amiable and affectionate...............................
Exclusive benevolence and..............................
And as his...
Was devoted to the exercise............................
His public conduct was.................................
By the zealous and cons................................
Of the important duties with which.....................
With distinguished ability and.........................
And noble integrity and disinterest....................
He successfully exerted himself," &c., &c. (as in present inscription, inserting a "the" before "affections," reading "respectfully" for "frequently" and spelling "Wauchope," "Niddrie" and "Kalinjar" correctly.)

Conjecture as to the exact phraseology is immaterial: sufficient remains to show that the epitaph was of the long and stately kind common at the period.

John Wauchope is celebrated firstly for his settlement of the Bundelkhand revenue: and secondly for his political achievements.

---

(1), (2), (3), (4)—*sic.*

As regards the first he was given instructions of a nature that were bound to result in, and actually produced, an enhancement of not less than 29 per cent. Good seasons made it possible to collect it, and Mr. Wauchope obtained, of course, great credit for his settlement. He was collector of Bundelkhand from 1808 to 1810, and after two years at Allahabad, returned as judge and magistrate of Bundelkhand with political powers (1812). In 1813 he became Superintendent of Political affairs and Agent to the Governor General in Bundelkhand and in June 1818, Agent to the Governor General in Rohilkhand and Saugor. During this interval, he made engagements with Gobind Rao of Jalaun (1817), Rao Ram Chand of Jhansi (1817), and the Rajas of Datia (1818), Sampthar (1817), and Orcha (1812): and finally with the Rani of Saugor. The sole treaty chiefs in Bundelkhand at the present day are Datia, Sampthar and Orcha; the rest hold under sanads and ikrarnamas. It is curious that this epitaph should wrongly assert that Wauchope was Judge of Bundelkhand in 1818, and omit all references to his political posts. It was probably mentioned in the old inscription, if from the fragments of the first two lines preserved by Führer, we may conjecture "Age(nt for political affairs) in Bu(ndelkhand.)"

John Wauchope was the son of Andrew Wauchope of Niddrie, and Alice Baird, his wife, born in 1781 at Herdmanston and arrived in India in 1800. To this family belongs Major-General Andrew Wauchope, killed at Magersfontein in 1899. The family, now extinct in the male line after a life of over 5 centuries, dates back to 1380; the Wauchope's were hereditary Bailies to the Keiths, Marischals of Scotland, afterwards Earl Marischals. From them they obtained the lands of Niddrie Marischal. (Cadell sneers at the reliance placed by the Board on Mr. Wauchope's "local knowledge" of Bundelkhand, which he supposes had been acquired "in a few months." He was apparently unaware that Mr. Wauchope had already served in lower grades for two years in Bundelkhand (1805—7) and doubtless possessed his fair share of "local knowledge.")]

(References: *Cadell; Führer; Aitchison; Prinsep; Prinsep C. L.; Grant Duff; Burke L. G.; W. P.*)

NEAR UNCHADIH, TAHSIL KARWI.

518.—**1865**—BUYERS, W., Revd. *Inscription:*—Sacred to the memory of the Revd. W. Buyers, for 30 years missionary in India, who died near this place on the 4th October 1865, aged 63 years.

"I have waited for thy salvation, O Lord

"Grata quies patria sed et omnis terra sepulcrum."

[William Buyers (1804-1866) was born at Dundee. He studied at the Missionary College, Hoxton, and was appointed to Benares. He was ordained in 1831 at Woolwich. He arrived in Calcutta in October 1831 and at Benares in January 1832. In 1833 he married Eliza Anne Walker, of Aberdeen. In 1840 he took sick leave to England where he arrived in 1841. He returned to India in June and arrived in Benares in September 1843. At the end of 1845 he was again compelled to go home on account of ill-health. It was not thought advisable to send him out again: but he returned at his own expense to Benares, leaving Mrs. Buyers at home. In 1850 he was re-engaged by the L. M. S. and Mrs. Buyers and her family rejoined him. Mrs. Buyers died at Benares in 1857; there is a tablet to her in the L. M. S. Church there. In 1859 Mr. Buyers went to Almorá, remaining there from 1859 to 1861, when he returned to Benares. In 1863 he resigned his connection with the Society and died at Unchadih in 1868. Unchadih is a jungle village near the line of rail. At one time it was a railway settlement and possessed a station, marks of which, and of various bungalows, still remain. The tomb, which is actually inside the railway fencing, close to the metals and also to the old station, was erected by the Rev. W. Buyers' son, who was a railway Engineer.]

(*Communicated.*)

519.—**1869**—BATES, W. *Inscription:*—Sacred to the memory of No. 2994, Pt. W. Bates, H. M.'s 5?th Regiment, died at Oonchadeeh, the 13th day of August 1869, aged 39 years.

[This tomb is in a cemetery containing several graves, but no other inscription, in the jungle close to the East Indian Railway line, and less than a mile from Unchadih. The wire fencing has now disappeared, but the stone in which it was fixed remains. Legend has it that some troops once came here from

Jubbulpore in cholera camp. One could hardly imagine a less suitable place for a cholera camp in the rains than Unchadih, but possibly it was less obviously objectionable at that time, when it was a railway settlement, than it is now.]

SITE UNCERTAIN.

520.—**1833**—SINCLAIR, P. C., Captain the Hon. *Inscription :*—This stone is sacred to the memory of the Honorable Patrick Campbell Sinclair, Brevet Captain in the 70th Regiment, N. I., who died at this place on the 13th March 1834, in the 34th year of his age. Erected in grateful affection by his afflicted widow. (B. O.)

[This tomb is not now traceable so far as I have been able to discover, and the inscription is taken from Führer. As he only gives the cemetery as "Banda cemetery" and there are several cemeteries at Banda the task of discovery is made none the easier. This officer is undoubtedly the 4th son of Sir James Sinclair, 7th baronet of Mey and 12th Earl of Caithness: he married Isabella, a daughter of Major-General M'Gregor. He was appointed cadet in 1817, ensign in 1818 and lieutenant in 1825. The family is exceedingly ancient. Sir James was descended from George Sinclair of Mey, Chancellor of the Diocese of Caithness, and third son of the 4th Earl of Caithness. The first Earl of Caithness in this family was William Sinclair, Earl of Orkney and Chancellor of Scotland, who exchanged the Earldom of Orkney and the Lordship of Nithsdale for the Earldom of Caithness and the lands and castle of Ravenscraig in Fife. Before this the Earldom of Caithness was held, as far back as the 11th century, by the Norse Earls of Orkney, who held Orkney from the King of Norway and Caithness from the King of Scotland: it subsequently passed to the Earls of Angus and of Strathern respectively; then to the Crown, the Stewarts, the Crichtons and the Sinclairs in succession. The Sinclair Earls of Caithness are descended from the Sinclair's of Rosslyn, one of whom (great-grandfather of the first Earl) married Isabella, daughter of Malise, Earl of Strathern, Caithness and Orkney. It is a far cry from the Scottish and Norse Earls of the 11th century and from Caithness and Orkney to this forgotten tomb of the 19th century in Banda. When it is added that the present Earl's residence is given as North Dakota, U. S. A., the "ship under sail *or*, for Caithness," which appears in the family's arms seems peculiarly appropriate.]

(Reference : *Burke, P.*)

Hamirpur District.

KAITHA CEMETERY (TAHSIL RATH).

521.—**1810**—CAR, S. *Inscription :*—Sacred to the memory of Sarah Car, infant of H. Car, U.M.S. 1st Battallion, 17th Regiment. Born December 10th, A.D. 1809, and died June 8th, 1810.

[One result of British policy as regards the Bundelkhandi chiefs was the establishment of several cantonments in different places—Kaitha, Supa, Kalpi, Tarauhan, Kartal, Kunch and Banda. The relations between the British Government and the treaty states—Rewah, Orchha, Datiya and Samthar—were based on friendship and protection against the Marathas: of the other, or sanad, chiefs many held lands included in the assignment of 36 lakhs of revenue ceded by the Peshwa under the Treaty of Bassein. It was a fundamental principle of British politics to confirm such chiefs in the possession of such possession of such part of their territories as they held under Ali Bahadur's government, on condition of their fidelity to the British power. Some merely marauding chiefs were also so confirmed, with a view to pacifying the country. This explains the large number of states and small jagirs in this part of India. There are some 28 such states besides others that have lapsed, the best known being (besides the four already mentioned) Panna, Charkari and Ajaigarh. Obviously to keep the peace amongst all these states, many of them used to a state of continual warfare, troops and cantonments were necessary: such cantonments have already been met with at Banda and will be found subsequently at Kalpi and Kunch. Kaitha was a cantonment from 1812 to 1828, which explains the majority of these tombs.]

(References ; *Gazetteer : Aitchison's Treaties.*)

522.—**1815**—BYERS, J. L., Lieutenant. *Inscription* :—Sacred to the memory of Lieutenant John Lawson Byers, Adjutant of the 6th Regiment, Native Cavalry, who departed this life on 27th August 1815, aged 28 years. He was esteemed by all that knew him and died sincerely lamented.

[Sir J. B. Hearsey in his autobiography mentions a Lieutenant Rogers, Adjutant of the 6th B. C., who died "during the rainy season" of 1815. "He was seized with fever and died raving mad in three days;" he was also a great tiger-slayer. This may be Lieutenant Byers and the name given by Sir J. Hearsey be due to a slip of the pen, especially as he was succeeded as Adjutant by Hearsey himself, so that there was no time for another Adjutant to intervene.

J. L. Byers, son of J. Byers, Customs officer, was born in 1785 at Bowness, Cumberland. He joined the service in 1805.]

(References : *Pearse ; D. and M. ; C. P.*)

523.—**1817**—TOD, A., Captain. *Inscription* :—Here lie the mortal remains of Captain Alexander Tod, of the 26th Regiment of Native Infantry, whose soul left this world on the 31st January 1817. A memorial of friendship and esteem to departed worth.

[A. Tod, son of R. Tod of Belay (?) in Banff, was born in 1779. He joined the service in 1799 and became captain in 1809.]

(References : *D. and M. ; C. P.*)

524.—**1817**—BARNARD, P. D'A. *Inscription* :—Sacred to the memory of Philip D'Auvergne Barnard. Born 14th March 1816, died, 17th April 1817.

525.—**1820**—STERLING, M. A., Mrs. *Inscription* :—Sacred to the memory of Mrs. Mary Anne Sterling, wife of Major R. G. Sterling, 7th Light Cavalry, who departed this life on the 18th day of March 1820.

526.—**1820**—HARDING, J., Mrs. *Inscription* :—Sacred to the memory of Jane, the wife of Mr. G. Harding, Ridingmaster, 3rd Regiment, Light Cavalry, who departed this life on 20th November, A.D. 1820. Aged 37 years. Most deeply regretted by her affectionate husband, parents and friends.

527.—**1822**—PAGE, J., Cornet. *Inscription* :—Sacred to the memory of Cornet John Page, of the second Regiment of Light Cavalry, who departed this life on the 11th of September 1822. Aged 19 years.

[The son of W. Page, Member of the Bombay Council, born in 1803 at Bennington, Herts, and educated at Charterhouse.]

(Reference : *C. P.*)

528.—**1824**—HAWKINS, M., Mrs., *Inscription* :—Sacred to the memory of Mary, the wife of Lieutenant Hawkins, Adjutant 38th Regiment, Bengal Native Infantry, who departed this life on July 15th, 1824. Aged 17 years. Most deeply mourned by her afflicted husband, parents and friends.

529.—**1825**—LOWRIE, E. T. *Inscription* :—Sacred to the memory of Edward Thomas Lowrie, late a writer in the Department of Public Works, who departed this life on March 20th, 1825.

530.—**1826**—URQUHART, C. L., Mrs. *Inscription* :—Sacred to the memory of Catherine Long, wife of G. T. Urquhart, Esq., M. D., who departed this life on the 20th January 1826, in the 22nd year of her age. This monument was erected by a disconsolate husband to record the virtues of an amiable and loving wife, a fond and tender mother and a most generous and warm friend.

[G. T. Urquhart was son of J. Urquhart, merchant, born at Kirkwall in 1791.]

(Reference: *S. P.*)

531.—**1823**— ELLIOT, J. T., Sergeant-Major. *Inscription* :—James Tanfield Elliot, Sergeant-Major of the 32nd Regiment, Native Infantry, departed this life the 14th December A. D. 1826. Aged 36 years, 4 months and 13 days.

532.—**1827**—ERSKINE, C., Lieutenant. *Inscription* :— Sacred to the memory of Lieutenant Charles Erskine, 2nd Regiment, Native Infantry, who was unfortunately killed by a fall from his horse on the 29th September 1827, aged 19 years, 5 months and 5 days. This monument was erected by his brother officers as a tribute of respect to his memory. He lived beloved and died deeply regretted.

[Third son of David Erskine, of Cardross, Ceylon C.S., he joined the service in 1824. Of Anglo-Indian members of the family there are several, mostly nephews and grand nephews of this Charles Erskine, as also an uncle. The family is decended from Colonel H. J. Erskine, a 3rd son of the 2nd Lord Cardross, a title now borne by the Earls of Buchan. Colonel Erskine went to Holland and served under the Prince of Orange, returning to England at the Revolution in 1688. The Cardross Erskines are a cadet branch of the baronial family of Cardross descended from John Earl of March (1604); whilst the Buchan family are another branch of the same family.]

(Reference: *D. and M.*; *Burke, L. G. and P.*)

533.—**1828**—LODER, J. W. S. *Inscription* :—Sacred to the memory of Joseph William Sandly, only son of Major Joseph William and Harriet Mary Loder, who departed this life on 10th January 1828. Aged 2 years, 1 month and 26 days.

534.—**1828**—MACKENZIE, J. H. *Inscription* :—Sacred to the memory of James Hector Mackenzie, Surgeon to the 3rd Native Cavalry, H. C. S., who departed this life on the 23rd May 1828, aged 40 years and 5 months, in the full hope of the promise made to all who believe in our Saviour Jesus Christ. He was a dutiful son, an affectionate husband and brother; this small tribute is erected to his memory by his disconsolate widow.

[Appointed in 1804, though over age.]

(Reference: *S. P.*)

535.—**1828**—POOLE, A. J. B. *Inscription* :—Sacred to the memory of Andrew James Brockless Poole, son of Quarter-Master Sergeant Poole, 3rd Light Cavalry, and Sarah, his wife, who died on 26th June 1828, aged 3 months and 20 days.

536.—**1829**—MILLER, J. S. *Inscription* :—Sacred to the memory of John Stuart, infant son of Sergeant J. W. Miller and Louisa, his wife, who departed this life on 26th April 1829, aged 4 months and 25 days.

537.—**1829**—MACLEOD, A. F. E., Captain. *Inscription* :—Sacred to the memory of Captain A. F. E. Macleod, of the 22nd Regiment, Bengal Native Infantry, who departed this life on 4th June 1829, aged 43 years. This small token of esteem is erected by a well-wisher.

[Alexander Fraser Peter Macleod (the initial "E." is a mistake,) joined the service in 1807 and got his captaincy in 1824.]

(Reference: *D. and M.*)

538.—**1829**—JORDAN, P. *Inscription* :—Sacred to the memory of Patience, infant daughter of Riding-Master M. Jordan, 7th

Light Cavalry, and Annie, his wife, who departed this life on 7th June 1829, aged 11 months and 9 days.

539.—**1829**—STEDMAN, J. F. *Inscription :*—Sacred to the memory of John Frederick, eldest son of Captain R. A. and Anne Stedman, born 5th September 1822, died 10th August 1829.

Of such is the Kingdom of Heaven.

540.—**1831**—SMITH, S., Q.-M. Sergeant. *Inscription :*—Sacred to the memory of Quarter-master-Sergeant S. Smith, late of the 7th Light Cavalry, who departed this life on 19th . . . . . 1831, aged 42 years. Erected by his sincere friend S. Smith, Sergeant, XI Light Dragoons.

541.—**1831**—(1) LATOUCHE, F., Mrs.—(2) LATOUCHE, C. *Inscription :*—Sacred to the memory of Frances, the beloved wife of Captain LaTouche, Major of Brigade in Bundelkhand, who departed this life upon the 22nd July A. D. 1831, aged 20 years 11 months and 20 days. Most deeply deplored by her disconsolate husband and relatives. Sacred to the memory of Cecil, the son of Captain LaTouche, who departed this life upon the 2nd July A. D. 1831, aged 1 year, 6 months and 18 days. Most deeply lamented.

[Sir J. J. Digges LaTouche has kindly given me the following information about the members of the LaTouche family. "All these LaTouches," he writes, "are descended from a Huguenot who left France on the revocation of the Edict of Nantes, fought at the Battle of the Boyne as a lieutenant under King William III and settled in Dublin. He was called David Digues de LaTouche and had two sons; the eldest dropped the 'Digues,' the younger son, James, anglicized the name into Digges LaTouche. Cornwallis LaTouche (cf. No. 792) was the brother of William LaTouche of Bellevue, Co. Wicklow, whose widow is still alive. He and Peter LaTouche (who lies buried in the Almora cemetery, No. 847) and also Captain LaTouche belong to the elder branch.

William Digges LaTouche (No. 435) who was killed in the massacre at Cawnpore was first cousin of my father and a brother of Henry D. LaTouche who in 1868 came out as a railway Engineer and built the bridge over the Chambal. He then went to south India and retired, and died at Ross in Herfordshire some years ago. William was not married. The name of the man killed at Cawnpore is, I think, correctly given on the windows of the Memorial Church at Cawnpore as William Digges LaTouche. (Also in No. 435; it is incorrectly given in the tablet No. 422). There were also a number of LaTouches (not Digges) on the Bombay side.........."

It is clear from Burke that this Captain LaTouche is the Peter LaTouche buried at Almora; the dates in Dodwell and Miles also support this view. Burke mentions the death of Mrs. Frances LaTouche and her son Cecil, giving the dates, and stating that they died at Kaitha. She was daughter of Brigadier-General W. G. Maxwell, C. B., of Dalswinton, Dumfries, and married Peter LaTouche in 1829. His second wife was Fraulein Ellen Bestandig, of Gottingen.]

(References: ***Burke L. G. I.; communicated.***)

HAMIRPUR CEMETRY.

542.—**1825**—GALL, F. H. *Inscription :*—Sacred to the memory of Fortnam Herbert, eighth son of Lieutenant-Colonel Geo. Herbert Gall, B.L.C., died 15th December 1825, aged 2 months and 11 days.

Ere sin could blight or sorrow fade,
Death came with friendly care,
The opening bud to heaven conveyed,
And bade it blossom there.

[Cf. No. 724.]

543.—**1833**—URQUHART. R., *Inscription :*—Sacred to the memory of Robert Urquhart, Conductor of Ordnance, who died on the 25th September 1833. Aged 44 years, 8 months.

Sleep kindred dust till that last day,
When earth and heaven shall flee away;
Then shalt thou join thy soul above,
And sing the chimes of heavenly love.

544.—**1838**—McGREGOR, A., Q.-M.-Sergeant. *Inscription :*—Sacred to the memory of Adam McGregor, Quartermaster-Sergeant, 5th Native Infantry, who departed this life on the 17th April 1838. Aged 32 years.

545.—**1848**—MUIR, M. F., B.C.S. *Inscription :*—Sacred to the memory of Mungo Fairlie Muir, Bengal Civil Service, died 30th May 1841, aged 26 years.

[M. F. Muir (1815-1841) was third son of William Muir, and brother of John James and William Muir, all in the Civil Service. John Muir, the eldest, is most famous as a Sanskrit scholar; his great work is "original Sanskrit Texts on the Origin and History of the People of India." Sir William Muir, the youngest, held many important posts both in the North-Western Provinces and the Government of India and was Lieutenant-Governor of the North-Western Provinces from 1868-1874, Finance member from 1874-76, member of the Indian Council 1876-1885, Principal and Vice-Chancellor of Edinburgh University 1885-1902, and author of many books, mostly on Islam. Four of his sons also served in India—the eldest: William, in the Artillery and in the Political service retiring as a Colonel; the second, John Fairlie, in the Bombay C. S.; the third, Archibald Mungo, was first in the Native Cavalry, and then in the Political service, dying as resident at Khatmandu: whilst the last Charles Wemyss, served in the Afghan, Soudan and Burmese wars. M. F. Muir was at Haileybury in 1835; at the time of his death he was Assistant Magistrate at Hamirpur.

By the similarity of the crest, and the identity of the motto, Sir J. F. Muir of the firm of Findlay Muir and Co. would appear to be of the same family; but the family, which comes from north Ayrshire, has many branches. Mr. G. B. F. Muir, C S., son of J. F. Muir and grandson of Sir William, is the present representative of the family in these provinces, and to him I am indebted for the family details in this note.]

(Buckland: *Haileybury; Prinsep C. L.; Communicated.*)

Allahabad District.

HOLY TRINITY CHURCH.

546.—**1843-44**—OFFICERS, 3rd Regiment. *Inscription :*—To the memory of the Officers of Her Majesty's 3rd or Buffs Regiment, who were killed in action, or who died when on service in the State of Gwalior in 1843-44. Captain Donald Stewart, killed in action at Punniar, on the 29th December 1843, aged 45; Captain Richard Nicholson Magrath, died of his wounds in camp at Gwalior on the 14th January 1844, aged 33; Surgeon Alexander Macqueen, M. D., died in camp at Gwalior on the 24th January 1844, aged 50, Captain Thomas Chatterton, died in camp at Seundah on the 27th January 1844, aged 45. This table is inscribed by their brother officers.

[These officers and the men mentioned in the next inscription lost their lives in a war which sprang out of a palace intrigue. On the death of Jankoji Scindia of Gwalior in 1843 his widow, a girl of 12, adopted a boy of 8. Lord Ellenborough and the girl-queen had rival nominees for regent. Lord Ellenborough's was appointed, but the queen dismissed him and handed over the Government to her own nominee. The Governor General insisted on his dismissal and ordered the resident to leave Gwalior, but the regent had won over the overgrown Gwalior army of 40,000 men, and disturbances arose which had to be put down by force. Sir Hugh Gough fought two battles in one day of which the second was Punniar, and that was the end of the war. One of its results was the raising of the Gwalior contingent. The 3rd are now the Buffs (East Kent) Regiment.

It was their 1st battalion who fought at Punniar. They have the four "Marlborough" honours, Dettingen, all the Peninsular honours from the Douro to Toulouse, Punniar, Sebastopol, Taku Forts, South Africa 1879, and Chitral. The old 3rd Fort was raised in 1604 as the Duke of York and Albany's Maritime regiment of Foot. In 1689, or shortly after, it was incorporated in the 2nd Foot Guards, and the old 4th (Prince George of Denmark's Regiment) became the 3rd. It was first called the Buffs in 1708.]

[References: *Wheeler; "On Service" (Groves).*]

547.—**843**—N.C.Os. and Men, 3rd Regiment. *Inscription:*—This tablet is erected by the officers to the memory of the Non-Commissioned Officers and men of Her Majesty's 3rd Regiment or Buffs, who were killed or mortally wounded in action at Punniar on the 29th December 1843. Colour-Sergeants Jacob Wheeler, John Devory, Henry Eborall; Sergeant Michael Mannion; Privates Thomas Allen, Francis Purton, James Thorne, Thomas Clarke, William Petworth, Andrew Travers, Joseph Britton, Thomas Baily, Thomas Watkins Wood, James Greig, Benjamin Lockwood, Edward Simmons.

[Cf. No. 546.]

548.—**1857**—VICTIMS of the MUTINY. *Inscription:*—"In memory of John Plunket, Captain; Robert Stewart, Lieutenant and Adjutant; George H. Hawes, Lieutenant and Quartermaster; Thomas L. Bailiff, Ensign; Philip S. Codd, Ensign; Marshall D. Smith, Ensign; Arthur M. H. Cheek, Ensign; George L. Munro, Ensign; George S. Pringle, Ensign; Thomas Foley, Sergeant-Major; George Watkins, Quarter-master-Sergeant; Charles G. Way, Ensign; Edward E. Beaumont, Ensign; Arthur J. Scott, Ensign; Edward M. Smith, Ensign.

DOING DUTY with 6th REGIMENT, N. I.—Thomas C. H. Birch, Captain, 31st Regiment, N. I., Fort Adjutant; Charles D. Innes, Lieutenant, Engineers, Executive Engineer, 6th Division; Augustus H. Alexander, Lieutenant, 68th Regiment, N. I., second-in-command, 3rd Oudh Irregular Cavalry.

Geoffry Coleman, Conductor Ordnance Department, Anthony Fernando, pensioned Drummer, Julien Boilard, merchant, Henry Archer, merchant, Joseph Fulow, merchant, George D. Castro, pensioned clerk, David Thomas, Inspector, E. I. R., William Lancaster, assistant contractor, E. I. R., Robert George, platelayer, E. I. R., James Barrett, toll collector.

Julia L., wife of Major Ryves, retired list, Madras Army, Mary, wife of Sergeant Collins, Frederica, daughter of Mr. John Jones, W. R. R., Mary Thomas, widow, Susan Benson, widow, Ann, George and Catherine, wife, son and daughter of Drummer Diddea;—

Who were killed in the station and district of Allahabad, between the 6th and 10th days of June 1857, by sepoys of the 6th Regiment, Native Infantry, and other mutineers and rebels. This monument is erected by the surviving residents of Allahabad."

[The troops at Allahabad consisted of the 6th Native Infantry, of whom one company was in the Fort: a wing of the Ferozepore Regiment of Sikhs under Lieutenant Brasier, also in the Fort: two troops of the 3rd Oude Irregulars under Lieutenant Alexander, divided up into jail and treasury guards and night patrols. There were also 60 European invalid artillerymen.

On the 5th June a company of the 6th Native Infantry with two 9 pounders (under Lieutenants Hicks and Harward) were sent to Daraganj to meet the 13th Irregulars, supposed to be marching from Benares on Allahabad. This step was against the views of many: and it was at Daraganj that the mutiny first broke out. The sepoys seized the guns: Lieutenant Harward galloped off to Lieutenant Alexander who had some of his cavalry at Alopibagh. He led his men after the guns and charged them, but was shot through the breast in the volley that met the charge: only 3 of his men followed him, the rest joined the mutineers. Harward sent a note to Brasier in the Fort which explained matters: but it did not reach the others. In the 6th Mess House 17 officers, including 8 unposted cadets, were assembled, a bugle call sounded in the lines, and the officers hurried there. As they came up they were shot: 7 officers and 8 cadets were killed. That night 31 Europeans were murdered by the prisoners released from the jail and the city *badmashes*. Brasier with his Sikhs and the Europeans disarmed the company of the 6th Native Infantry. On the 7th Neill arrived, and at once set about restoring order.

Of the names here mentioned the officers, ensigns and sergeants mentioned as doing duty with the 6th were killed, except Cheek, in the lines after the treacherous bugle call. Cheek was wounded and taken prisoner: during his captivity he adjured a fellow prisoner (a Native Christian) not to recant when pressed to do so. He died in the Fort after Neill's troops had rescued the prisoners. Captain Birch and Lieutenant Innes were two of those who refused to enter the Fort. The death of Lieutenant Alexander has already been related. The last four men mentioned were killed in the district, Mr. Thomas and Mr. Lancaster while trying to escape to Barwari. Mrs. Ryves was with a party of railway officers who were besieged for two days on the top of a tank at Barwari by a mob till relieved by a party of a 3rd Oude Irregulars. Mrs. Ryves died immediately on being removed from the tank. The details regarding the deaths of the rest are unknown. In the words of the Mutiny Narrative: "It may be as well that the details of but few of so many murders are known with certainty."

John Plunkett (so the services B. A. List) was son of W. Plunkett, Excise Officer, born in 1816. He joined the army in 1835.

Robert Stewart was son of R. Stewart, a Calcutta merchant, born in India in 1823. He joined the service in 1843.

George Harry Hawes, son of W. Hawes, was born at Colgong in Bengal in 1831.

Philip Shirley Codd, son of Captain Codd, His Majesty's Service, was born at Karnal in 1839.

Marshall Deverell Smith, son of E. Smith, merchant, was born at Calcutta in 1838.

Arthur Marcus Hill Cheek, son of O. Cheek, solicitor, was born at Evesham in 1840, and educated at Cheltenham Grammar School.

George Stewart Pringle was 4th son of W. A. Pringle, B. C. S. His grandfather, father, three uncles, three brothers and a cousin all served in India, the most distinguished of them being his uncle R. K. Pringle, who was Commissioner of Scinde. This branch of the Pringles (a name which is supposed to be a corruption of "Pelerin") dates back to Robert Hop-Pringle, Esquire to James Earl of Douglas at the battle of Otterburn in 1388.

C. G. Way was son of the Revd. C. J. Way of Spaynes Hall, Essex, born in 1838. He was educated at Marlborough. The family is a junior branch of the Ways of Denham, who date back to the Tudors.

Edward Ernest Beaumont, son of E. Beaumont, and ward of Sir H. Lytton Bulwer, was born at Southwell, Essex in 1838.

Edward Morris Smith, son of N. T. Smith, was born at Eltham, Kent in 1839.

T. C. Birch, son of the Revd. H. B. Birch, was born in Bengal in 1814, and joined the service in 1832.

Charles Daubuz Innes, son of R. H. Innes, of Leyton, Essex was born in 1821.

I could not trace Bailiff, Munro, and Scott. For Alexander see No. 567.]

(References: *Forrest; Rice-Holmes; Burke L. G.; M. N.; M. C. Register; Services B. A. List*; *C. P.*]

549.—**1857**—RYVES, J. L., Mrs. *Inscription* :—Sacred to the memory of Julia Louisa, wife of Major Thomas James Ryves, retired list, Madras Army, who departed this life on the 9th June 1857, from exposure to the sun at Barwarie during the Mutiny. Aged 45 years and 17 days.

[Cf. No. 548.]

550.—**1857**—ARCHER, H., *Inscription* :—Sacred to the memory of Henry Archer, who was killed by the mutineers at Allahabad on the 7th June 1857, aged 52 years.

"What though in lonely grief I sigh;
For husband loved, no longer nigh;
Submissive still, I would reply :—
"Thy will be done."

This tablet is erected by his widow.

[Cf. No. 548. Mr. Archer was an agent of Rees, the author of a book on the siege of Lucknow, at which he was present.]

(Reference : *Rees*.)

KYDGANJ CEMETETRY.

551.—**1798**—HEARSEY, A. W., Lieutenant-Colonel. *Inscription* :—To the memory of Lieutenant-Colonel A. W. Hearsey, who departed this life on 10th July 1798, aged 46 years. This monument is erected in token of regard by his affectionate widow Charlotte Hearsey.

[This tomb is reported to be untraceable now and the inscription is taken from Führer's list.

The Hearsey family is very ancient. A member of the family, a Cumberland Squire, was "out in" 1745 for the Pretender at Colloden. One of his sons was a London merchant; his second son Andrew had two sons, the younger of whom, also Andrew, was in command of an East Indiaman. He died in 1778; his son was Andrew Wilson Hearsey. Born in 1752, he entered the service of the H. E. I. C. in 1765. He fought in 1768 in the raid from Bengal on the Northen Circars, which resulted in their cession to the Company. In 1780 he went with Captain Popham's force which marched to Colonel Goddard's support, and on the way took the forts of Lahar and Gwalior, the latter supposed impregnable. After Gwalior Hearsey was recalled and sent with Colonel Pearse's force down the coast line to Madras to assist in its defence against Haidar Ali. Hearsey was the column's baggage master. Pearse joined Eyre Coote at Pulicat after Porto Novo, and Hearsey was present at the indecisive action of Pollilore and the victory of Sholingar. Hearsey was now baggage master of both armies with over 40,000 camp followers under him. At Pollilore he repulsed three cavalry attacks on the baggage. He was at Vellore and the fighting round Cuddalore. In 1780 he went to England to support a claim of his against the Company for certain perquisites, but in vain. He married Miss Crane in England in 1787. He returned to India, and in 1790 again went with a Bengal column into Madras. He was present at the captures of Coimbatore, Dindigul and Palaghat: at the battle of Calicut: at the sieges of Bangalore and Seringapatam and the battle of Arikera. He became a Major in 1794—after 29 years' service, most of it in the field!—and Lieutenant-Colonel and first commandant of the Allahabad Fort in 1797. He had one son, Lieutenant-General Sir John Bennet Hearsey, of Mutiny fame, and three daughters who married officers in the army.

The Hearseys have long been connected with India. Captain Andrew Hearsey commanded an East Indiaman: his son was Colonel A. W. Hearsey. By his marriage with Miss Charlotte Crane (1787) Colonel Hearsey had one son, the famous Sir J. B. Hearsey, K. C. B., and Lieutenant-General, of Mutiny fame: and three daughters:

(1) Mrs. Charlotte Bradshaw, wife of Colonel Paris Bradshaw who did good service on the Nepal frontier and died in 1821 when on his way to take up the post of Resident at Lucknow. His son died a General and a K. H.

(2) Mrs. Marion Salmon, wife of General W. B. Salmon;
(3) Mrs. Sophia Hall, wife of Colonel F. Hall, killed in Chili. His son Colonel J. F. W. D. Hall served in India and was a famous tiger-slayer.

Sir J. B. Hearsey had a long glorious career, into which I need not now enter. He married his kinswoman Harriet (daughter of Major H. Y. Hearsey) in 1832; and by her had a family of four sons and three daughters.

(1) John (1833-1863), A. D. C. to his father and with him when he captured the first mutineer, Mangal Panday: he had a son, John Hampton who died young (Captain, 2nd V. B. S. Wales Borderers).
(2) Andrew (1839-1896), also A. D. C. to his father in 1857, who served as a volunteer with Havelock. He married Harriet, daughter of Captain W. M. Hearsey.
(3) and (4) two other sons who died young (one at Sandhurst; the other was in the 19th Hussars.)
(5) Mrs. Harriet Carew, wife of Captain G. O. B. Carew, C. I. E., of the late Indian Navy: her daughter married Mr. W. L. Wyllie, A. R. A.
(6) Mrs. Amelia Hearsey, wife of Mr. L. D. Hearsey of Lakhimpur.

Sir J. B. Hearsey's second wife was Miss Emma Rumball and by her he had two sons: Captain C. J. R. Hearsey, 9th Lancers, killed in the Afghan war; and C. C. Hearsey of the Indian Marine.

There is also the other branch of Hearseys connected with this branch; viz.

Major Hyder Young Hearsey, son of Captain H. P. Hearsey, who fought under both Perron and Thomas: with Lord Lake at Agra, Delhi and Deig, in the Gurkha war and at Bhurtpore, and explored Chinese Tartary. He married a Princess of Cambay, sister of Colonel W. L. Gardner's wife. His sons were Captain W. M. Hearsey, Captain J. B. Hearsey and Hyder Hearsey. All three were in the Oudh service, and the first two served in the Mutiny, the first at Lucknow, the second at Sitapur, whence he managed to escape, and both, later, in the Intelligence Department. The third died before the Mutiny. Captain W. M. Hearsey was the father of Mr. L. D. Hearsey of Lakhimpur, Kheri.]

(Reference: *Pearse.*)

552.—**1798**—SILCHAIR, H. *Inscription:*—Here lies the body of Hobson Silchair, late of His Majesty's 78th Regiment, from Lincolnshire, who departed this life the 16th April 1798, aged 26 years.

[Rank unknown.]

553.—**1798**—BRANNAN, J. *Inscription:*—Here lieth the body of John Brannan of the L Company, 78th Regiment, who departed this life October 8th, 1798. Born in the Parish of Boyle, Co. Roscommon, Ireland, aged 24 years. This stone is erected by Andrew Brannan, cousin-german to the deceased.

[Rank unknown.]

554.—**1804**—RALPH, R., Lieutenant-Colonel. *Inscription:*—Lieutenant-Colonel Richard Ralph, died on November 18th, 1804, aged 55 years.

[R. Ralph joined the service in 1778. He became lieutenant in 1779, captain in 1796, major in 1802. It is not clear when he became Lieutenant-Colonel.]

(Reference: *D. and M.*)

555.—**1806**—HUMPHRAY, R., Lieutenant-Colonel. *Inscription:*—Lieut.-Colonel Richard Humphray, Commandant of Allahabad, died April 4, 1806. Aged 49.

[The name appears to be Humfrays. He was an ensign in 1778 and a captain in 1806, but held the "rank in the army" of Lieutenant-Colonel. Dodwell and Miles by a slip give his date of death 1805: the E. I. Register has it correctly.]

(References: *D. and M.; E. I. R.*)

556.—**1813**—BROWNING, C., Lieutenant. *Inscription:*—Sacred to the memory of Lieutenant Charles Browning of the 1st Battalion,

14th Regiment, N. I., who died at Allahabad on the 6th of April 1813, aged 28 years. Erected by the officers of his corps as a sincere mark of their esteem.

[Untraceable in all lists. Probably there is some mistake in the name.]

557.—**1815**—TURNER, R. *Inscription* :—Sacred to the memory of Richard Turner, Esq., late Judge and Magistrate of the zillah of Agra, died 21st September 1815.

[Son of R. Turner, born at Yarmouth in 1784 He arrived in India in 1799. He served entirely in Lower Bengal (Rajshahi), Behar, Midnapur, Bhagalpur, Jessore, Shahabad and Murshidabad), till his last appointment at Agra which he was holding when he died.]

(References : *Prinsep C. L.; W. P.)*

558.—**1820**—BANONGARDT, A. A., Mrs. *Inscription* :—Sacred to the memory of Anna Aloria, wife of Captain J. G. Banongardt, 8th Light Dragoons, who departed this life on the 19th September 1820, in her twenty-eighth year.

559.—**1828**—BULL, E., Mrs. *Inscription* :—Sacred to the memory of Elizabeth, wife of Mr. Michael Bull, merchant of this station, who departed this life on the 23rd May 1828, aged 27 years and 7 months.

To-day and to-morrow.

To-day, man's dressed in gold and silver bright ;
Wrapp'd in a shroud before to-morrow night.
To-day he's fed on delicious food ;
To-morrow dead, unable to do good.
To-day he's nice, and scorns to feed on crumbs ;
To-morrow he's himself a dish for worms.
To-day he's honoured and in vast esteem ;
To-morrow, not a beggar envies him.
To-day he rises from the velvet bed ;
To-morrow, lies in one that's made of lead.
To-day. his house though large he thinks too small ;
To-morrow, can command no house at all.
To-day, has forty servants at his gate ;
To-morrow, scorned, not one of them will wait.
To-day, perfumed as sweet as any rose ;
To-morrow, stinks in every body's nose ;
To-day, is grand, majestic, all delight ;
Ghastly and pale, before to-morrow night.
True, as the scripture says, man's life's a span ;
The present moment is the life of man.

Elizabeth Bull, January 31st, 1826.

This tomb is erected by a tender, kind and indulgent husband, as a mark of his esteem and regret."

560.—**1844**—SCOTT, W. *Inscription* :—Sacred to the memory of Walter Scott, Esquire, Assistant Surgeon, E. I. Company's Service, second son of Walter Scott, Esquire, of Wauchope, Roxburgshire, N. B., who died at Allahabad, 17th August 1844, aged 27 years. (B. O.)

[Walter Scott, M. D. (1817-1844), was the third (second surviving) son of Walter Scott of Wauchope. The family, now Macmillan-Scott, is descended through a long series of Walters from a son of Walter Scott, laird of Buccleuch, and great-great-grandfather of the 1st Earl of Buccleuch.]

(Reference : *Burke, L. G.)*

561.—**1853**—BIRELL, J. R., Major. *Inscription* :—" Sacred to the memory of James Ramsay Birell, Major, 11th Regiment, Native Infantry, who died of cholera at this station on the 26th July 1853, aged 50 years and 3 months. This tablet is erected as a mark of respect by the officers of the regiment."

[The son of G. Birrell (so spelt in all lists) of Edinburgh, born in 1803, he became cadet in 1818 and captain in 1832. The date of his majority is not given.]

(References: *D. and M.; Services B. A. List.*)

562.—**1847**—BOILEAU, E. J., Lieutenant. *Inscription:*—Sacred to the memory of Edward John Boileau, Lieutenant and Adjutant of the 8th Regiment of Bengal Light Infantry who died at Jahanabad while removing from Allahabad to Barrikpore on 8th November 1847. He departed in Christian faith and hope, being an affectionate husband, a kind father and a gallant soldier. This tablet was erected by his most attached widow in A. D. 1848.

[E. J. Boileau was son of J. T. Boileau of Dublin, and was born in 1820. He joined the service in 1837, fought at Jellalabad, and was mentioned in despatches for the attack on Jagdalak. Many of this family have served in India. It dates back to Nicholas Boileau, Lord of Castelnan and St. Croix in Languedoc (*circa* 1598) and traditionally to Etienne Boileau, grand provost of Paris in 1255. The grandson of Nicholas Boileau fled to Holland at the revocation of the Edict of Nantes and thence to England.]

(References: *Services B. A. List; Foster B.*)

563.—**1847**—GRIFFITH, H. C., Lieutenant. *Inscription:*—Sacred to the memory of Henry Charles Griffith, Esquire, Lieutenant and Adjutant of the 3rd Regiment, Native Infantry, who died at Allahabad, April the 1st A. D. 1847, aged 26 years, having survived only three days an accident from his charger suddenly falling lifeless under him. This tablet is erected by his brother officers of the 3rd Regiment, N. I., to whom virtues and qualities of higher than ordinary character had eminently endeared him, in testimony of their sincere attachment and of their deep and heartfelt sorrow at his loss.

[The son of Capt. C. Griffiths, 37 N. I., born in India in 1820, he joined the service in 1839.]

(Reference: *Services B. A. List.*)

564.—**1847**—(1) MUMFORD, W.—**1864**.—(2) MUMFORD, C., Mrs. *Inscription:*—In memory of Mr. William Mumford, late of the Ordnance Comt. Dept., who died on the 20th Nov. 1847, aged 76 years, and of his widow Mrs. Catherine Mumford, who died 2nd November 1864, aged 65 years, 10 months and 15 days. They rest from their labours. This tablet has been erected by their surviving sons Edward and George Mumford.

565.—**1857**—OFFICERS, 6th N. I. *Inscription:*—Beneath this stone were laid, June 18th, 1857, the remains of seven officers of the 6th Regiment, N. I. who were murdered by their own men at the mutiny of that regiment on the night of June 6th. Eight other officers of the same, or doing duty with it, were murdered at the same time, but their bodies were not recovered.

[Cf. no. 548.]

ALFRED PARK.

566.—**1857**—WATKINS, G. R., Q. M.-Sergeant. *Inscription:*—Sacred to the memory of George Richard Watkins, Quartermaster-Sergeant of the 6th Regiment, who was killed on the 6th June 1857. Aged 30 years 1 month and 21 days.

[Cf. no. 548.]

ALLAHABAD FORT.

567.—**1857**—ALEXANDER, A. H. Lieutenant. *Inscription :*—In memory of Lieutenant A. H. Alexander, 68th N. I., 3rd Oudh Irregular Cavalry, killed by the mutineers at Allahabad on 6th June 1857.

[Cf. no. 548. Augustus Hay Alexander was son of Major W. Alexander, 5th B. C., born at Neemuch in 1827.]

(Reference : *C. P.*)

M. PAHARPUR, TAHSIL PHULPUR.

568.—**1857**—BARRETT, J. P. *Inscription :*—Sacred to the memory of James Philip Barrett, Collector of this toll-bar, Bairagi-ka-nala. Born November 1808, killed during the Mutiny on the 7th June 1857. This tablet is erected by his son Mr. P. Barrett.

I am killed here, leaving my beloved children and friends behind committed to the protection and guardianship of my Redeemer to battle in the pilgrimage of this dark world. Farewell children, and brethren, the ransom of my sins has been paid. Shed no tears, but leave me here until my Redeemer Christ appears. The Grace of our Lord be with you all. (*Rest illegible.*)

[Cf. no. 548. Five lines mutilated and illegible.]

M. USMANPUR, TAHSIL HANDIA.

569.—**1849**—GRIFFIN, W. *Inscription :*—"Sacred to the memory of William Griffin, for many years an assistant at Doomdoomah Indigo Factory, where he departed this life on the 13th April 1849, under a lingering attack of small-pox, aged about 43 years and 9 months. This tablet is erected as a testimony of affectionate remembrance by his brother Thomas Griffin of Buxar."

Jhansi District.

SAGAR GATE, JHANSI CITY.

570.—**1857**—VICTIMS of the MUTINY. *Inscription :*—Erected by the British Government in memory of the persons who were murdered at Jhansi in June 1857, and whose names are recorded within. A.D. 1862. Captain Alexander Skene, Superintendent; Mrs. Skene, and two children; Mrs. Browne, wife of Captain Browne, Native Infantry, Deputy Commissioner, Jalaun; Miss Browne, his sister; Captain F. D. Gordon, 10th Madras N. I., Deputy Commissioner, Jhansi; Lieutenant Burgess, Revenue Surveyor, Bundelkhand; Lieutenant Turnbull, Assistant Revenue Surveyor, Bundelkhand; Lieutenant Powis, Irrigation; Mrs. Powis; Mrs. Powis' child; Dr. McEgan; Mrs. McEgan; Mr. T. Andrews, Principal Sadr Amin, Jhansi; Mr. Robert Andrews, Deputy Collector and Magistrate; Mrs. Andrews and four children; Mr. W. S. Carshore, Collector of Customs; Mrs. Carshore and four children; Mr. D. C. Wilton, Patrol; Mrs. Wilton and one child, and two sisters of Mrs. Wilton; Mr. D. D. Blyth, Asst. Revenue Surveyor; Mrs. Blyth, her mother and four children; Sergeant Millard, Sub-Asst. Surveyor; Mrs. Millard and three children; Mr. Bennett, Sub-Assistant Revenue Surveyor; Mr. J. Young, Sub-Assistant Revenue Surveyor; Mrs. Young;

Mr. G. Young, Apprentice; Mr. Palfreyman, Apprentice; Mr. Munrow, Sub-Assistant Revenue Surveyor; Mr. A. Scott, Head Clerk, Deputy Commissioner's office; Mr. G. Parcell, Head Clerk, Superintendent's office; Mr. J. Parcell, Clerk, Deputy Commissioner's office; Mr. Mutlow, Clerk, Superintendent's office; Mr. Mutlow, unemployed; Mr. D. G. Elliott, Clerk, Deputy Commissioner's office; Mr. Elliott, father of above; Mrs. Elliott, mother of D. G. Elliott; Mr. Flemming, unemployed; Mr. Crafurd, unemployed; Captain Dunlop, 12th Bengal Native Infantry, Commanding at Jhansi; Lieutenant Taylor, 12th Bengal Native Infantry; Lieutenant Campbell, Commanding Detachment of Irregular Cavalry; Quarter-Master-Sergeant Newton; Mrs. Newton and two children.

[Jhansi was taken over by the doctrine of "lapse" in 1854, on the death of Ganga Dhar Rao, the Raja. His widow the Rani, Lachmi Bai by name, was given a pension of Rs. 5,000 a month and 10 lakhs' worth of her husband's property, but she was aggrieved by the refusal of Government to allow her to adopt an heir to her husband and in vain pleaded her cause in England. She had also many other minor causes of irritation, most of them trivial, and in some of them at all events she was undoubtedly in the wrong. She was consequently in a state of mind to welcome any chance of revenge and possessed of a masculine spirit well fitted to carry it out.

As soon as the Mutiny broke out she began to intrigue with the garrison; and also actually misled Captain Skene, the Superintendent, into allowing her to raise troops for her own defence. On the 6th the 12th N. I. mutinied: by this time most of the Europeans had however taken refuge in the Fort. The regiment shot Captain Dunlop, Lieutenants Campbell and Turnbull and Q.-M. Sergeant Newton and his family. The rest of the day was spent in releasing the prisoners, incendiarism and pillage. On the 7th Mr. Scott and the Messrs. Parcell were sent by Captain Skene to the Rani to request her protection when the party left the Fort. They were seized by her troops and sent by the Rani to the mutineers' lines where they were murdered. Mr. Andrews also left the Fort and was murdered by the Rani's own servants. The Fort was attacked on the 8th without success: but Lieutenant Powis was killed by some natives inside who tried to open the gates to the mutineers, and Captain Gordon shot in the assault. He had been "the life and soul of the garrison" and his loss was severely felt.

Captain Skene then offered to treat: and the mutineers swore by the most sacred oaths that they should be allowed to depart in safety. The terms were accepted, and the besieged were taken to the Jokhan Bagh outside the city walls. There on an order from the Risaldar of the mutineers, they were massacred. Captain Skene was cut down by the Jail darogha. Their bodies were left exposed for three days and then thrown, the men into one and the women and children into another gravel-pit, and covered over.

A. Skene was the son of Dr. C. Skene, born at 1817 in Aberdeen. He joined the service in 1837.

Francis Jaques Burgess was the son of F. Burgess, barrister-at-law and Chief Commissioner of Police for Birmingham, born in 1822. He joined the service in 1842.

Francis David Gordon (1821-1857) was eldest son of Mr. M. F. Gordon of Abergeldie, of a family descended from Sir Alexander Gordon, second son of the the 1st Earl of Huntley. This particular branch of the Gordons dates back to Sir Adam Gordon, circa 1305.

Owing to the absence of initials, I was unable to trace the other officers.]

(References: *M. N.; Rice Holmes; Burke, L. G.; Services B.A. List.*)

OLD ENGLISH CEMETERY.

574.—**1857—59**—N. C. O.'S. & MEN, 3RD BOMBAY EUROPEAN REGIMENT. *Inscription:*—Erected by the Non-Commissioned Officers and Privates of the 3rd Bombay European Regiment to the memory of gallant comrades, who fell during the campaign of Central India under Major-General Sir Hugh Rose, K.C.B., 1857-59.

SERGEANTS.

Martin Hart.
William Sharp.
Thomas Cummings.
John Anderson.
James Wood.
Robert Stephens.
Patrick O'Grady.

CORPORALS.

Michael Hennessy.
Alexander Anderson.
Luke O'Brien.
Joseph Davis.
William Tooth.
William Taylor.
James Evans.
John Christie.
George Nichol.

PRIVATES.

Thomas Clinch.
Cornelius McCormack.
Thomas Robinson.
James Finlay.
William Smith.
John Smith.
Thomas Jackson.
Frederick Perry.
Thomas Canavan.
Saunders Palmer.
Charles Miller.
John Osborne.
Patrick Daly.
Daniel Donovan.
Hugh Cameron.
Henry Eggington.
John Hitchcock.
Thomas Panton.
James Madden.
Peter Brown.
Patrick Doyle.
George West.
John Hastings.
John Reynolds.
William Wilkinson.
Robart Howard.
Michael Cosgrove.
John Paul.
William Percy.
James Harris.
Thomas Craig.
James Byrne.
James Duane.
William Cannon.
John Nye.
Charles Dunn.
John Brennan.
Bernard Dempsey.
William Amos.
James Watson.
John Harrison.
James McLaren.
Jahn Crady.
Thomas Burnam.
John McKenna.
Miles Brien.
Patrick Maher.
Willam Wheeler.
William Cox.
Charles Eaton.
George Baker.
Patrick Meehan.
Thomas Laird.
George Town.
Stephen Darcy.
Samuel Ford.
James Sullivan.
James Evans.
Patrick Bryan.
David Young.
Richard Allen.
Joseph Fitten.
William Healy.
Charles Hudson.
William Moore.
Hugh Kennalty.
James Bleak.
John Carty.
John Flinn.
John Hayes.
George Booth.
James Shields.
Thomas Farrell.
John Dunn.

William Sturgess. | Ambrose Parfrey.
John Boyle. | Adam Falkner.

[The 3rd Europeans after fighting their way to Jhansi with Sir H. Rose were left in garrison there, and had a great deal of work to do, mostly in small detachments, in pacifying Jhansi and other Bundelkhand districts. Their record in Central India included the siege and capture of Rathgarh, the relief of Saugor, the capture of Garhakota, the siege and storm of Jhansi, the battles of Barodia, Madanpur, the Betwa, Kunch, Golauti and Kalpi, and the battle and storm of Gwalior. They were raised in 1853, and are now the 2nd Battalion, the Prince of Wales' Leinster Regiment (Royal Canadians).]

(Reference: *Rice-Holmes; M. N.; Communicated.*)

572.—**1857-58**—MEN, 1st Troop, BOMBAY HORSE ARTILLERY. *Inscription:*—In memory of the men, 1st Troop, Bombay Horse Artillery, killed and died from wounds received in action and otherwise during the Central India Campaign, A.D. 1857-58. R. Hiles; R. Barkley; J. Connors; E. Johnson; J. Saunders; T. Dalton; F. Hurst; D. Burns; W. Bright; T. Paulding; M. Hennessy; J. Cathcart; D. Wardrop; W. Quinlan; G. Darley; J. May. Raised by their officers and comrades as a memorial of their past worth and service.

[Also with Sir H. Rose. Cf. no. 571.]

573.—**1858**—PARK, A. A., Lieutenant. *Inscription:*—Sacred to the memory of Lieutenant A. A. Park, 24th Regiment, Bombay Native Infantry, who fell while gallantly leading on his men at an attack on some rebels in a neighbouring hill, on 3rd April 1858, the day of the assault on Jhansi. This monument is erected by his brother officers as a mark of esteem and regard.

[Atherton Allan Park, son of A. A. Park, Barrister, was born at Wimbledon in 1834 and educated at Harrow. The 24th Bo. N. I. are now the 124th Duchess of Connaught's own Baluchistan Infantry.]

(Reference: *C. P.*)

574.—**1858**—SINCLAIR, J., Captain. *Inscription:*—Sacred to the memory of John Sinclair, younger, of Barrock, Captain, 39th Regiment, Madras Army and commanding a wing of the 3rd Infantry, Hydrabad Contingent, killed in action at Jansie on the 5th of April 1858, aged 36 years.

[I thought at first that "younger" was part of the name. A chance discovery in Burke, however, coupled with the fact that no "Younger" could be traced in the 39th Madras N. I. or any where else in the East India register of the date, showed me that it merely was a (now somewhat antiquated) synonym for "junior." Burke mentions John Sinclair, "39th Madras N. I., born 2nd May 1822, killed while gallantly commanding the left wing, 3rd regiment, Hydrabad contingent at the capture of Jhansi, 5th April 1858;" so there can be no doubt of the identification. He was the son of Sir John Sinclair, Bart., and grandson of John Sinclair, of Barrock. The family is descended from George Sinclair of Mey, 3rd son of the 4th Earl of Caithness for which family vide No. 520.]

(References: *E.I.R; Burke P.*)

575.—**1859**—AITCHISON, A., Sergeant. *Inscription:*—Sacred to the memory of Sergeant Adam Aitchison, 92nd Highlanders, who departed this life on 21st September 1859, at the age of 31 years. Erected by his brother George Aitchison, 92nd Highlanders.

"Stranger or friend, as you draw nigh,
As you are now, so once was I;
But as i *(sic)* am, so shall you be;
Prepare yourself to follow me."

[The 92nd, now the 2nd battalion Gordon Highlanders, were in India from 1858 to 1863.]

576. —**1862**— PINKNEY, F. W. Major. *Inscription :*— In memory of Major F. W. Pinkney, C.B., Commissioner of Jhansi, died 30th July 1862.

[Major Pinkney was sent with orders to take charge of Chanderi district on the 20th June 1857, but if Captain Skene had been killed to take his place as officiating Superintendent. He was however sent on other duty and did not return till February 1858, when he did a great deal to restore order.]

(Reference : *M. N.)*

577.—**1863**—MEADE, R. G. W. *Inscription :*— Sacred to the memory of Richard George Wright, the beloved infant son of Major R. J. Meade, Agent to Governor General for Central India, who died in the camp of Duttia, on 24th January 1863, aged 1 year 2 months 21 days.

"Is it well with the child ?" and she answered, "It is well."

[Major, afterwards Colonel Sir R. J. Meade, K.C.S.I., C.I.E., was Political Agent at Gwalior (1860), A. G. G., Central India (1861), and later, Chief Commissioner of Mysore and Coorg, and Resident at Hyderabad. He was son of Captain J. Meade, R. N., and married in 1853, Emily Salter, daughter of Lieutenant General Malcolm, Bo. Army.]

(Reference : *Foster B.)*

ON BRIGADE PARADE GROUND.

578.—**1858**— (1) MEN, 86TH ROYAL REGIMENT.—(2) STACK, Doctor. *Inscription :*—Sacred to the memory of the soldiers of Her Majesty's 86th Royal Regiment, who fell gloriously at the battle of the Betwa and the storming of Jhansi on the 1st and 3rd of April 1858. Erected to their memory by their comrades-in-arms.

Requiescant in pace.

Sacred to the memory of Dr. Stack, Her Majesty's 86th Regiment, who was shot at the storming of Jhansi on the 3rd of April 1858, whilst attending on a wounded soldier. Aged 39 years. Erected by his brother officers in testimony of their esteem.

[The 86th (Royal County Down) Regiment are now the 2nd Battalion, Royal Irish Rifles. They were raised in 1793, were in India from 1799 to 1819, and again from 1842 to 1859 and 1894 to 1899. They were with Sir Hugh Rose all through and did particularly well at the capture of Gwalior.]

(Reference: *Rice-Holmes.)*

LALITPUR CEMETERY.

579.—**1862**—CARY, S., Lieutenant. *Inscription :*— Sacred to the memory of Lieutenant Stanhope Cary, Assistant Commissioner of Lalitpore, 2nd son of W. H. Cary, Esq., Woodford, Essex, died 2nd September 1862, aged 29.

[This officer belonged to the 37th N. I. and joined the service in 1854.]

(Reference : *E. I. R.)*

580.—**1866**—HOOPER, J., Surgeon. *Inscription :*—Sacred to the memory of John Hooper, Esq., Surgeon, H. M.'s 35th Regiment, died August 5th, 1866, aged 41 years. Erected by his brother officers.

[The 35th are now the 1st Battalion, Royal Sussex Regiment, in India from 1853 to 1868.]

581.—**1865**—TYLER, W. G. B., Captain. *Inscription :*—In memory of Captain William George Bygrove Tyler, Deputy Commissioner of Lullutpore, who died on the 20th August 1866.

M. RANGAON, PARGANA MANDAURA, TAHSIL MAHRONI.

582.—**1859**—BIRKILL, J., Gunner. *Inscription* :—Sacred to the memory of Gunner J. Birkill, 8th Field Battery, Royal Artillery, who departed this life on 8th April A. D. 1859, aged 29 years.

[This tomb is North-east of Rangaon village. There is also an inscription in a script which Mr. Thomas, Librarian of the India office (to whom I showed it), told me was Tamil of a kind. It was not entirely decipherable and apparently quite untranslateable. How it came to be on this gunner's tomb, is an insoluble mystery. So far as it was possible to make anything of it, it appeared to reproduce the English inscription.]

M. SINDWAHA, PARGANA BANPUR, TAHSIL MAHRONI.

583.—**1810**—ALEXANDER, Mrs. *Inscription* :—(Destroyed).

[Mr. Silberrad reports that in 1900 the words "Catholica Romana" "26th December 1810" and "Dien te sauve" were legible but even these have now disappeared. It is however known to be the tomb of the wife of Major Joseph Alexander, in the service of Gwalior. This officer only appears in history once when Colonel Stephen Nation (no. 475) marched from Kaitha to protect the Raja of Tehri against aggressions by Gwalior troops under Alexander's command (1822). His wife died at Khajuria, 3 miles away: his descendants still own a *jagir* at Jaria, 2 miles away. There is also a tomb without inscription to his (Major Alexander's) son, Napoleon, and (at Jaria) is the tomb of an unknown French captain, one of Alexander's subordinates. The Sindwaha tombs are in a garden near the village.

(Reference : *E. I. M. Calendar* ; *Communicated.*)

Jalaun District.

KALPI CEMETERY.

584.—**1824**—MOODIE, T. *Inscription* :—To the memory of Thomas Moodie, Esquire, officiating Political Agent in Bundelkhand, who departed this life on April 27th, 1824, aged 33 years (B. O.).

[This officer was in the army, which he joined in 1810. He became a lieutenant in 1823.]

(Reference : *D. and M.*)

ORAI CEMETERY.

585.—**1851**—THORNTON, H. M., Mrs. *Inscription* :—Sacred to the memory of Harriet Maria, the beloved wife of Samuel Thornton, Assistant Superintendent of Jalaun, who departed this life at Garotha in Bundelkhand on the 28th June 1851, aged 24 years 8 months 13 days.

In the midst of life we are in death.

KUNCH CEMETERY.

586.—**1804**—OFFICERS AND MEN, killed near KUNCH. *Inscription* :—Sacred to the memory of Captain Feade, Lieutenant Morris, Artillery; Lieutenant Gillespie, 1st Battalion, 18th Regiment; Assistant Surgeon Hooper, and other brave men, who fell in action with Mir Khan, Pindari, near Kunch, 22nd May 1804.

[In 1804 Colonel Fawcett, commanding in Bundelkhand, sent 7 companies to reduce the fort of Omanta Malaya, 5 miles from Kunch. The Kiladar sent for help to Amir Khan who was plundering Mau and Irichh. He marched in person and sent his Pindaris to plunder the camp, and attacked the British in their trenches with three bodies of men. The British formed square, but were attacked in front and rear and defeated, with the loss of 5 guns, 2 companies of N. I. and about 50 European artillerymen. The British then retreated.

Some reinforcements from Kalpi were also attacked and overpowered. Amir Khan plundered Kalpi and a month later he was severely defeated by Colonel Shepherd. Captain W. Feade joined the service in 1785 and became a Captain in 1802. He had fought in the 2nd Mysore War and at the siege of Gwalior. Lieutenant Robert Morris, son of Mrs. Mary Morris, born at Dublin 1777 (father's name not given), joined the service in 1794 and had fought at Aligarh, Delhi, Agra and Gwalior.]

(References: *Amir Khan; Gazetteer; Grant Duff; Stubbs; C. P.; D. and M.*)

587.—**1857**—PASSANAH, R., Mrs. *Inscription:*—Here lies the remains of Rita Passanah, widow of Urban Passanah, cruelly murdered by mutineers at Orai on the 15th of June 1857, aged 70 years.

She sleeps in Jesus.

[Mother of G. Passanah, Deputy Collector of Jalaun, who had many adventures during the mutiny, being taken prisoner two or three times and released as often. He at last escaped to Cawnpore. Mrs. Passanah was unable to bear the fatigue of travel, and was left concealed at Orai: but her servants brought her back to her own house, and she was murdered by some Jhansi mutineers.]

(References: *M. N.; Gazetteer.*)

588.—**1859**—PRIVATES, 48th Regiment. *Inscription:*—H. M. 48th Regiment—Edward Taffingham, aged 29 years; Matthew Beaumont, aged 30 years; Henry Clarke, aged 30 years; Samuel Montgomery, aged 27 years; died at Kalpi, on 2nd May, 3rd June and 5th July 1859.

589.—**1859**—RUSSEL, L. *Inscription:*—"10th Company, 48th Regiment—Lawrence Russel, aged 33 years, died on 14th August 1859."

590.—**1859**—(1) KEARNEY, J.—(2) GLYM, J. *Inscription:*—H. M. 48th Regiment—John Kearney, aged 33 years; James Glym, aged 26 years, died on 9th October 1859.

591.—**1859**—LUGGETT, R. *Inscription:*—H. M. 48th Regiment—Robert Luggett, aged 34 years, died on 13th June 1859.

592.—**1859**—RIVETT, J. *Inscription:*—"Sacred to the memory of Joseph Rivett, Tahsildar of Daboh, who departed this life, 10th November 1859, aged 44 years and 2 days, leaving a wife and six children to deplore severe loss. "May his soul rest in peace."

M. MARGAYAN, TAHSIL KALPI.

593.—**1778**(?)—CRAWFORD, J., CAPTAIN. *Inscription:*—

برائے یادگاریست کہ بتاریخ سوم ماہ جون سنہ ...۱۷ع کپتان جیمس

گرانرڈ صاحب بہ سنہ بست و نہ سال در اینجا وفات یافت *

[This tomb is a large masonry structure, East of Margayan (Margawan or Margaon.) Führer read the date 1790; the Collector of Jalaun informed me that M. Matin-uz-zaman Khan, Deputy Collector, thought it was 1758. I am of opinion that the true date is 1778. According to the Deputy Collector's report, there can be no doubt of the 8; the third figure is badly damaged, but from what he says, it might as well be a 7 as anything else, and Führer who saw it thirteen years before M. Matin-uz-zaman, and was a professed antiquarian, read it as a 7. Apart from these arguments, we have firstly the negative fact that an Englishman would hardly be in the neighbourhood of Kalpi in 1758, the year after Plassey, and the positive fact, that a Captain James Crawford did die near this spot about the 3rd June 1778.

In 1778 occurred Warren Hastings' trans-continental expedition from Bengal to the assistance of Bombay against the Marathas. In the course of that expedition Colonel Leslie seized Kalpi. Philip Francis who had been opposed to the expedition all along, never lost a chance of criticizing it adversely, and Hastings through it. On the 22nd June Colonel Leslie sent to Calcutta some despatches from Bombay, urging him to hasten west. Incidentally, they mentioned the news just received, of General Burgoyne's surrender in the American War. Francis commented that in one breath they told one English army to proceed across one continent, and stated that another English army, which had attempted a passage across another continent, had been forced to capitulate. He pointed out that this was an evil omen, and pressed for the recall of the troops. He also quoted a private letter from Leslie's camp describing the privations that the troops had suffered, and stating that Crawford had died on the first march out of Kalpi, raving mad for want of a simple drink of water, and more than hinted that Leslie or Hastings had suppressed the news of his death. Hastings replied that the death had been unofficially reported in a letter received at the same time as a public despatch from Colonel Leslie, and in a moment of confusion he had supposed the death was mentioned in the despatch and so had not produced the letter. He then did so, giving an extract as follows: "I have had the misfortune to lose Captain James Crawford, who commanded the 4th Battalion of Sepoys, by a most violent fever which carried him off in less than two hours." The letter was dated 5th June: and we find an official despatch dated 15th June, from Leslie from "Meergawa"—of course Margawan or Margayan. It seems therefore quite clear that the Captain James Crawford of this tomb must be the unfortunate officer whose death Leslie reported. But for this absurd attack of Francis on Hastings, the letter would never have emerged from the obscurity of Hasting's waste paper basket into the glare of the proceedings of the Secret Select Committee; and the tomb would have remained a puzzle. *Parturient montes.*"

Nothing else is definitely known of James Crawford. He appears to be the officer mentioned by Dodwell and Miles, who became an ensign in 1764 (at the age of 15), a lieutenant in 1765, was dismissed the service on 16th February and restored on 7th July 1767; and then Dodwell and Miles know no more of his fate. We find a Lieutenant James Crawford giving evidence in the trial of Sir R. Fletcher for mutiny in 1766; if this is the same, it would explain the dismissal, whilst the subsequent restoration was more or less universal (even Sir R. Fletcher was reinstated). But it is not certain, for there are two James Crawfords mentioned about this time, and distinguished as senior and junior. It is pretty clear however that this was the James Crawford who was appointed to command the 1st Battalion of the 4th Sepoys in 1768, and gave his name to them—Crawford ki paltan; in which case he was the senior of the two.]

(References: *Forrest 1772—1785; Cardew; Broome: D. and M.; Führer; communicated.*)

BENARES DIVISION.

Benares District.

OLD CIVIL CEMETERY.

594.—**1799**—(1) CHERRY, G. F. (2) CANWAY, Captain. (3) GRAHAM, R. (4) EVANS, R. *Inscription* :—This obelisk was erected in memory of George Frederick Cherry, Esq., Governor General's Agent, Captain Canway, Robert Graham, Esq., Richard Evans, Esq., who were murdered by Wazir Ali, 14th January 1799.

[Wazir Ali succeeded his reputed father Asaf-ud-daula as Nawab of Oudh in 1797. Doubts were however thrown on his legitimacy: though put on the throne by the intervention of the company, he nevertheless proved faithless: and Sir John Shore after personal inquiry deposed him, and placed Saadat Ali on the throne in his place (1798). Wazir Ali was conveyed to Benares and took up his residence in Madho Das' garden.

Mr. Cherry was A. G. G., and Mr. Davis, judge and magistrate at this time. Mr. Davis warned Mr. Cherry that Wazir Ali entertained sinister designs: Mr. Cherry refused to credit them, but the Calcutta authorities realizing the error of keeping him at Benares decided to remove him to Calcutta. This led to the climax for it upset all Wazir Ali's plans. On the 14th January, by his own desire, Wazir Ali paid a visit to Mr. Cherry. In the course of conversation Wazir Ali stabbed at Mr. Cherry and he was cut down by his followers whilst trying to escape. Mr. Evans, a young Private Secretary, was killed in a neighbouring field and Captain Canway was killed as he rode up to the house. Mr. Graham, a young civilian, was murdered by the party as they marched to attack Mr. Davis. This gentleman defended himself at the top of a narrow staircase leading to the roof with a hog spear till relieved by General Erskine and his troops. Wazir Ali managed to escape: a reward of Rs. 20,000 was put on his head; but he was ultimately surrendered to Colonel Collins by the Raja of Jaipur, with whom he had taken refuge. He was imprisoned in a bomb proof building in Fort William for several years and subsequently transferred to Vellore, where he died (1817.)

G. F. Cherry (1761-1799) entered the B. C. S in 1778, was Lord Cornwallis' Persian Secretary and went with him to Madras, and on a mission to Seringapatam, when he painted Tippu Sultan's portrait, now at the India Office. Of his two brothers one was Member of Council, Bombay (J. H. Cherry died 1803) and the other in the Madras C. S. (Peter Cherry died 1823). Two sons, a grandson, and a great-grandson of J. H. Cherry were in the Madras services. Robert Graham was the eldest son of the 12th laird of Fintry and was born in 1775. The family is very ancient and of considerable note. It goes back legendarily to William Graham of Abercorn and Dalkeith *circa* 1120. The line is traced unbroken to Sir William Graham of Kincardine (1400). From him, by his first marriage, are descended the Dukes of Montrose: by his second marriage he is ancestor of the Grahams of Fintry and Knockdollian, and the Graemes of Garrock. Graham of Claverhouse, Viscount Dundee, was a member of the Fintry family. Robert Graham's brother was that Colonel John Graham who gave his name to Grahamstown (S. Africa.) Another famous member of the family in the Garrock branch was Thomas Graham, the victor of Barrosa. This extremely ancient family has made its full share of history in its time. Captain E. S. Canway (so Dodwell and Miles) was appointed lieutenant in 1778 and captain in 1796.]

(References; *Davis; Buckland; Burke, L. G.; Cotton; D. and M.*)

595.—**1822**—WILFORD, F., Lieutenant-Colonel. *Inscription :*—Sacred to the memory of Francis Wilford, Lieutenant-Colonel in the Engineer Service of the East India Company, aged 71 years, deceased on the 4th of September 1822. Encouraged by the liberality of the Government of British India, he fixed his residence at Benares in the year 1788; and whilst yet, in the vigour of his days, devoted his life to retirement and study, eminently qualified by previous education, extensive erudition, a true intellect and indefatigable zeal. He made himself master of the classical language and literature of the Hindus, and applied his knowledge to the eradiation of the dark periods of antiquity, with a success that perpetuates his own reputation and the honour of the British name in the East. In the social relations of life, his merits were proportioned to his talents, and the abilities of the scholar were reflected by the virtues of the man.

[Colonel Wilford was an Oriental and Sanskrit scholar of considerable repute, a devoted supporter of the Asiatic Society of Bengal, and a voluminous contributor to the pages of the Asiatick Researches. Many of his dissertations on the chronology, history and antiquities of India show great learning, labour and ingenuity: but the extravagance of their conjectures at once makes the reader dubious of their real value. The very titles of these articles are almost enough to throw doubt on them; e.g. one finds essays "on Egypt and other countries adjacent to the Nile, from the ancient books of the Hindus;" "on Semiramis, the origin of Mecca, &c. from the Hindu Sacred Books;" "on the names of the Cabirian Deities and on some words used in the mysteries of Eleusis;" "on Mount Caucasus;" "on the sacred Isles of the West," &c., &c. It is not therefore surprising to come across the discovery, stated by Wilford himself in a later essay, that he had been imposed upon by his pandits, who with an oriental's characteristic desire to say that which would prove acceptable to the hearer, did not hesitate to forge the names of such places as "Egypt" or "Mount Meru" in old manuscripts, by substituting them for the names of other places, and in one case at least even went so far as to write themselves a whole book of several thousand lines to prove something Wilford wanted to prove. But in the wild conjectures of which Wilford was guilty he was by no means alone; and it is not perhaps surprising that in an age when the orator still quoted Virgil in the House of Commons or over the wine, classical scholars brought face to face with an ancient literature should allow their fancy to run riot in analogies and comparisons between what they knew and what they were striving to learn. Certainly Wilford, when he discovered how he had been cheated, published with the most complete candour a recantation of his former opinions; with the result that his later works (e.g. his essays on the Geography of India) are of great value.

He was well fitted for the direction of Jonathan Duncan's new Sanskrit College at Benares. The College had been opened in 1791: but things did not go well: disputes and abuses occurred: and Government appointed (1798) a committee consisting of Messrs. Cherry and Davis and Captain Wilford to inquire into these. It was in 1799 that Wilford reported and obtained the dismissal of the Pandit who had deceived him, Vidyanand by name, and a professor in the College. In 1800 Captain Wilford became Secretary to the Committee which took over the management of the College; and for some years he practically ruled the institution. It is not quite clear when he severed his connection with it. Of the man himself, all that is discoverable is that he was of Swiss extraction; but his name is remembered as that of a scholar. He joined the service in 1781, became lieutenant-colonel in 1814 and was subsequently invalided. Otherwise he appears to have no history. As was said of a greater philosopher, philosophers seldom have any history: "it is a compensation."]

(References: *J. A. S. B. Cent. Rev. Nichols; Arch. Sur. Rep.*)

596.—**1825**—SNODGRASS, G., Captain. *Inscription :*—Sacred to the memory of Captain George Snodgrass, 23rd Regiment, N. I., Deputy Paymaster, Benares, who departed this life on the 11th January 1825, sincerely regretted by his friends, aged 43 years.

[Captain G. Snodgrass joined the service in 1805, became a lieutenant in 1808, and brevet captain in 1821.]

(Reference: *D. and M.*)

597.—1833—LOWTHER, W. *Inscription*:—Sacred to the memory of William Lowther, Esq., Judge of the Court of Appeal at Benares, who died on the 2nd March 1833, in the 50th year of his age.

[The son of Colonel J. Lowther, he was born in 1782 at Tottenham. He joined the service in 1803 and served in Ramgarh, Patna, Jaunpur, Bundelkhand, Mirzapur, Rangpur, Saran, Chittagong, and Benares from 1826 to 1833.]

(References: *Prinsep C. L; W. P.*)

598.—1833—BROOKE, W. A. *Inscription*:—Sacred to the memory of William Augustus Brooke, Senior Judge of the Court of Appeal, and Agent to the Governor General at Benares, who died on the 10th July 1833, in the eighty-first year of his age. His amiable character endeared him alike to the Hindu, the Musalman and the Christian inhabitants of this city.

[Mr. W. A. Brooke was at Benares for at least some 20 years. In 1813 he is found as President of the Sanskrit College Committee, an institution in which he took a very great deal of interest all through his residence at Benares. In 1824 he was visited by Bishop Heber who stayed with him in his house at Secrole on his journey through Upper India. The Bishop writes of him "Mr. Brooke has been 56 years in India, being the oldest of the Company's resident servants. He is a very fine healthy old man, his manners singularly courteous and benevolent." As he was born in 1752 and came out to India about 1768 (according to these dates) it is probable that he came out as a very junior writer.]

(Reference: *Heber: Nichols.*)

599.—1838—BROWN, C., Major-General. *Inscription*:—Sacred to the memory of Clements Brown, Companion of the Most Honourable Military Order of the Bath, Colonel in the regiment of Bengal Artillery, and Major-General on the staff of the army. A soldier from his youth, he delighted in his profession, and after an uninterrupted career of more than half a century of gallant and honourable service, and while still in the active and zealous discharge of his duties, departed this life 25th April 1838, aged 72 years.

[The name, according to Stubbs, is Clement Brown; but most authorities give it as "Clements", whilst the "Services B. A. List" have the variant "Clements Browne." This officer is one of the most famous of half-forgotten Anglo-Indian worthies. He came of an Irish family and arrived in Bengal as an infantry ensign in 1785, but was transferred to the artillery in 1789. He fought in the Mysore war of 1790-2, and at Bhitaura (1794), and in 1800 was selected as first commander of an experimental troop, which developed into the famous Bengal Horse Artillery. He fought with Baird in Egypt in 1802, and in some of Lake's later actions, in the pursuits of Holkar and Amir Khan, and also at Bhurtpore (1804). From 1810 to 1812, he was home on leave; in 1814 he became gun carriage agent, first at Allahabad and then at Fatehgarh. In 1824 he became Lieutenant-Colonel Commandant, and 1825 was present at the second and successful siege of Bhurtpore, in command of the B. H. A. In 1831 he succeeded to the command of the Regiment, became a Brigadier in 1836 and Major-General in 1837. He was given his C. B. in 1826. He was warm-hearted and impulsive, extremely liberal, subscribing for instance £100 for the racquet court in the artillery lines at Meerut—one of the gallantest members of one of the gallantest corps known to history.]

(References: *Stubbs; E. I. M. Calendar; Services B. A. List.*)

600.—1850—SMALL, G. B., Mrs. *Inscription*:—" Georgina Beck, fifth daughter of the late Robert Cat. H. Cart, Esq., of Drum, country of Midlothian, N. B., born 31st December 1804. Became the wife and fellow labourer of the Reverend George Small, Baptist

Missionary to India, July 17th, 1840. On the night of May 1st, 1850, her brief but luminous career on earth was suddenly terminated by a violent and instantaneous death occasioned by the explosion of a large magazine fleet at Rajghat."

[The explosion referred to occurred as follows: A fleet of 34 boats laden with gunpowder and military stores was moored near Rajghat. It consisted of 3,000 barrels of gunpowder and 6,000 shells besides other stores. The thatch covering of one of the boats was set on fire, and the gunpowder in two of the boats exploded: the rest of the fleet and some thirty other boats laden with merchandise were sunk by the shock. The houses of Messrs. Gordon, Tattle, Charles, Small and the Shahzada Mirza Muhammad Shujah, an ex-prince of Delhi, were destroyed and their inmates perished in the ruins. 818 persons are said to have been killed and 71 wounded. "Cat. H. Cart" is obviously a ludicrous sculptor's error for Cathcart.]

(Reference: *communicated.*)

ST. MARY'S CHURCHYARD.

601.—1781—(1) STALKER, J., Lieutenant. (2) SCOTT, A., Lieutenant. (3) SYMES, J., Lieutenant. *Inscription*:—This monument to the memory of Lieutenants John Stalker, Archibald Scott, and Jeremiah Symes, who were massacred at Shivala on the 16th day of August 1781, though erected by the hand of friendship, shall offer no praise which themselves might blush to read, yet be it remembered that the determined courage they showed was not an act of desperation, but a part of their characters as British officers that they fell not wholly useless to their country's cause in the sentiments, awe and respect they impressed on their enemies, in the tears of regret and emulation they drew from their fellow-soldiers.

Removed from the old burial ground 1829.

[Raja Chait Singh of Benares, a feudatory of the Government, was called on by Warren Hastings to pay a yearly subsidy of 5 lakhs. He did so for two years, after much delay and reluctance. Hastings then demanded 2,000 horse: though the demand was reduced to 1,000, none were sent. There was no doubt that he was also generally disaffected. Hastings, determined to punish him, went himself to Benares. On the 15th August, he sent the Raja a formal statement of the charges against him with a demand for a full and categorical reply. The reply was both unsatisfactory and offensively worded. Hastings then sent Mr. Markham, the Resident, to place him under arrest. This he did next day, and the Raja was made a prisoner in his own palace at Shivala Ghat with a sepoy guard of two companies under Lieutenant Stalker, Scott and Symes. The Raja's armed retainers then came over from Ramnagar on the other side of the river and set upon the guard, which by a fatal mistake, had taken no ammunition with them; the bodies of the Lieutenants were found lying close together and shockingly mangled. "These officers were the first victims to the fury of the tumultuous assembly", writes Warren Hastings: but not until they had by astonishing efforts of bravery, and undismayed amidst the imminent dangers which surrounded them, involved a much superior number of their enemies in their fate..........I yield to my own feelings in bestowing this just but unavailable tribute to these unhappy gentlemen." Lieutenant Archibald Scott is probably the 4th son of John Scott of Maluny by his wife Susan, grand-daughter of the 2nd Marquis of Tweeddale. (Burke merely records him as "H. E. I. C. S., killed in action," without dates: but the general facts correspond). Two of his brothers died, and another also served in India. The Scotts of Maluny are of the same stock as the house of Buccleuch. Stalker joined the service in 1771, Scott in 1776 and Symes in 1778.]

(References: *Wheeler; Warren Hastings; D. and M.; Burke, L. G.; Forrest*, 1772-1785.)

602.—1829—BODIES removed from another burial-ground. *Inscription*:—Erected over the remains of XII bodies removed from the old city burial-ground to this spot, 10th January 1829, by James Prinsep.

OLD ARTILLERY LINES.

603.—1857—GUISE, H. J., Captain. *Inscription* :—To the beloved memory of my husband, Captain Henry John Guise, 2nd son of General Sir J. W. Guise, Baronet, of Gloucestershire, who fell when in command of the 13th Irregular Cavalry, and in the gallant discharge of his duty, by the hands of the mutineers, 4th June 1857.

[Benares was by its geographical position, its wealth, and the fact that it was a divisional capital, a most important post, and at the same time one peculiarly exposed to danger. The force consisted of a mere handful of British Artillerymen and three native regiments: the 37th Native Infantry, the 13th Irregular Cavalry and the Ludhiana Sikhs. Luckily F. Gubbins, the Judge, and Tucker, the Commissioner, were both strong men, especially Gubbins. Brigadier Ponsonby was of a somewhat vacillating nature however, and moreover not in good health. On the 30th June, Neill arrived with a detachment of his regiment. The next day the news of the Azamgarh mutiny arrived : and it was decided to disarm the troops. Neill persuaded Ponsonby to do it at once. The troop turned out, Olpherts with his guns and the Madras Fusiliers facing the 37th. The 37th were ordered to pile arms and had begun to obey when the advance of the British troops frightened them : they seized their muskets and fired a volley. Olpherts at once opened on them with grape. The Sikhs advancing to support the English, were startled by firing in their rear : one of the Irregulars had fired at an officer : and the Sikhs, some of whom were positively disloyal and the rest confused and fearful of treachery, attacked the artillery. Olpherts turned his guns on them. The Sikhs also broke and fled.

It has been held that this was a mismanaged affair ; that the Sikhs were driven into rebellion with grape. That it was mismanaged is certain : but there is very good evidence that a proportion of the Sikhs (who were by no means *all* Sikhs) were disloyal. Accounts vary : but there seems a possibility that some of the Sikhs would at all events have stood firm, as they did at Mirzapur and Allahabad.

Captain Guise was killed by the 37th, Ensign Hayter by the Sikhs. Ensigns Chapman and Tweedie were also wounded. Captain Guise (1817-1857) was 2nd son of General Sir J. W. Guise, G. C. B., 3rd Baronet, Colonel of the 85th. He married Frederica, daughter of Sir W. Verner, Bart., M. P., and left two sons. Sir J. W. Guise distinguished himself in the French wars, in Egypt, and the Peninsula. The family is a very old one, dating back to Nicholas deGyse, A. D. 1262, who married a relative of John deBurgh, son of Hubert, Earl of Kent.]

(References : *M. N.* ; *Rice-Holmes* ; *Kaye* ; *Forrest* ; *Burke P.*)

604.—1857—HAYTER, J. Y., Ensign. *Inscription* :—Sacred to the memory of Julian York Hayter, 25th Bengal Native Infantry, who fell mortally wounded in the mutiny at Benares, June 4th, and died June 16th, 1857, leaving a bright example of truly Christian fortitude and resignation under his sufferings.

[Cf., no. 603. He was the son of J. Hayter, artist, born in 1836 in London.]
(Reference : *W. P.*)

RAJGHAT CEMETERY.

605.—1858—BINER, B. *Inscription* :—In memory of Benjamin Biner, Gunner of 8th Co., 2nd Battalion, Royal Artillery. Died May 23rd, 1858, aged 27 years. This stone was erected by his comrades.

[The Rajghat Fort, now disused, was built in the mutiny by order of the Government].

606.—1858—TAYLOR, W. *Inscription* :—In memory of William Taylor, Gunner of 8th Company, 2nd Battalion, Royal Artillery. Died May 23rd, 1858, aged 26 years. This stone was erected by his comrades.

607.—**1858**—EXCELL, J. *Inscription* :—In memory of John Excell, Bombadier of 8th Company, 2nd Battalion, Royal Artillery. Died May 23rd, 1858, aged 27 years. This stone was erected by his comrades.

608.—**1858**—THORNTON, J. *Inscription* :—Sacred to the memory of Pt. John Thornton, H. M. 20th Regiment, who departed this life on the 8th of January 1858. Aged 38 years.

609.—**1859**—FLANAGAN, H. *Inscription* :—Sacred to the memory of Henry Flanagan, of no. 2 Battery, 14th Brigade, Royal Artillery, who departed this life on the 27th day of May 1859. Aged 39 years. This stone is erected by the N.-C. officers of the company as a mark of respect.

610.—**1859**—CALLAGHAN, H., Sergeant. *Inscription* :—In memory of the late Sergeant Henry Callaghan. H.M.'s 77th Regiment, who departed this life 14th October 1859, aged 34 years, leaving his beloved wife and child to lament his loss.

Jesus receive me now as Thine ;
In life and death O, be Thou mine,
And when before Thy bar I stand,
O, welcome me to Thy right hand.

[The 77th, now the 2nd Battalion Duke of Cambridge's Own (Middlesex) Regiment, were in India 1858-70.]

611.—**1860**—(1) CHAMBERLAYNE, C. H. (2) CHAMBERLAYNE, M. *Inscription* :—Sacred to the memory of Charles Henry Chamberlayne, Bandman, H. M.'s 77th Regiment, who departed this life on the 6th July 1860, aged 28. Also to his daughter Mary, who died on the 20th July 1860, aged 4 hours.

While I am on a pilgrimage here,
Let Thy love my spirit cheer,
As my guide, my guard, my friend,
Lead me to my journey's end.

This stone is erected by his comrades of the Band.

M. SITAPUR.

612.—**1848**—HASTED, G. H. *Inscription* :—Sacred to the memory of George Henry Hasted, the only son of G. Hasted, born on the 3rd February 1828, died on the 29th September 1848, leaving an unconsolable father to lament his untimely loss.

"Oh my son, Absalom, my son, my son Absalom, would to God I had died for thee, O Absalom, my son, my son!"

Samuel II. chapter XVIII, verse 33rd.

613.—**1850**—HASTED, G. H. *Inscription* :—Sacred to the memory of George Hasted, Esq., of the Dooleypur Indigo concern, who departed this life on the 6th day of October 1850, born A. D. 1798, aged 51 years 9 months and 16 days.

In this cold grave this frame must rest,
And worms shall feed on this poor breast;
These hands shall there be useless grown,
And alas! no more be known.
Then, my Lord, do then be nigh,
And bear and bring me to the sky.

This is erected by his sincere friend M. B. T. William, Esquire.

QUEEN'S COLLEGE, BENARES.

614.—**1811**—DUNCAN, J. *Inscription* :—In memory of Jonathan Duncan who founded the Sanskrit College at Benares in 1791.

[This tablet, and the next, were set up in 1905 by order of the Lieutenant-Governor, Sir J. J. D LaTouche, in memory of the founder of the Sanskrit College and the Architect of the Queen's College, its present home. They are placed in the south-east corridor on each side of the main door of the College. Though not actually epitaphs, they have been included, as Sir J. Strachey's tablet at Agra has been included, as the memorials, possibly the only memorials in the province, of two of its great men.

Jonathan Duncan (1756—1811) son of Alexander Duncan, arrived in Calcutta in the E. I. C. Service in 1772. At the early age of 32 (in 1788) he became Resident and Superintendent at Benares, where his administration was marked by a vigorous suppression of administrative scandals and of infanticide. At the even more remarkable early age of 41 (1795) he became Governor of Bombay—a post he retained for so long a period as 26 years, till his death in 1811. He was at Bombay in the stirring times of Wellesley's rule: and the latter's despatches have frequent reference to the Honourable the Governor of Bombay. During the 2nd war against Tippu, the Maratha wars of Lake, Baird's expedition to the Red Sea, and the operations in Gujrat and Kathiawar, he played a not inconsiderable part, seconding Lord Wellesley's efforts in a way which the latter readily and frequently acknowledges.

He was a man of some literary ability. He contributed three papers to the "Asiatick Researches," all published in the 5th volume (1794). They were "Historical remarks on the coast of Malabar," "an account of two Fakeers," and "an account of the discovery of two urns in the vicinity of Benares." These urns were the subsequently celebrated urns of Sarnath, to which Cunningham refers in his Archaeological report. His interest in Sanskrit literature was shown in a practical way by his foundation of the Sanskrit College. In 1791 he urged Lord Cornwallis to set apart 20,000 sicca rupees from the revenue of the Benares *zamindari* "for the support of a Hindu College or academy, for the preservation and cultivation of the Sanskrit literature and religion of that nation, at this the centre of their faith and the common resort of their tribes." Lord Cornwallis sanctioned his proposal: and on the 28th October 1791 a number of "professors in the principal Hindu Sciences" met for the first time in a house hired for their reception. Such was the origin of the present Queen's College and more particularly of its Sanskrit department, whose pandits, as was said by Sir James LaTouche in 1904, "are household names among scholars in India and Europe." And if Jonathan Duncan had never played a part in making history his name would still have been famous wherever Orientalists are gathered together.]

(References: *Buckland; J. A. S., Cent. Rev.; Wellesley's despatches; Nichols*).

615.—1853—KITTOE, M., Major. *Inscription*:—In memory of Major Markham Kittoe who designed and built this college at Benares 1848—1852.

Markham Kittoe was the son of R. Kittoe, R.N., born in 1808, and joined the service in 1825. In 1836 he met James Prinsep. He was then preparing his work "Illustrations of Indian Architecture." His antiquarian zeal and architectural knowledge commended him to Prinsep, who described him as an "invaluable antiquarian traveller." In 1837 Kittoe was removed from the army for bringing indiscreet charges of oppression against his commanding officer. Prinsep's influence secured him the post of Secretary of the Coal Committee which led to a long tour in Orissa, and articles in the Journal of the A. S. B. He was reinstated in the army in 1838, by order of the Court of Directors. In 1841 he went on leave to Europe, and on his return was given the charge of one of the divisions of the High Road from Calcutta to Bombay. It was not till 1846 that he had a chance of returning to archaeology when he travelled over Bihar and Shahabad "catering for James Prinsep." "He added much to archaeological knowledge but spent (or according to Cunningham, in view of photography, "wasted") much time in a collection of drawings of sculpture. These drawings are, or were, in the library of the East India Museum. He was then appointed by Mr. Thomason, "Archaeological Engineer" to Government. One of his duties was the preparation of a design for the Benares College. This work lasted the rest of his career, though he also undertook some extensive excavations at Sarnath. At the beginning of 1853 he went home to recoup, but he was so ill that "he went straight to his home and died."

The Journal of the A. S. B. for several years was full of his papers. There are no less than 27 such papers (Vols. VII, VIII, XVII, XVI, XVIII, XIX, XXI.) He was not a man of great knowledge "a self-educated man and no classic or Sanskrit scholar," as he said of himself: but he was an accurate draughtsman and an enthusiastic explorer. He provided the material for others' discoveries and notably for Prinsep's.

The Queen's College, which he built, is in a severe style of perpendicular Gothic consisting of a nave and transepts with a tall central tower; both nave and transepts are adorned with dark carved woodwork. This "Academe of the Indian Athens" reminds the spectator forcibly of Oxford and Cambridge Colleges and shows that Kittoe was no mean architect.]

(Reference: *Arch. Sur. Rep.; J. A. S. B. Cent. Rev.; Nichols.*)

MUHALLA SHIVALA, BENARES CITY.

616.—**1781**—(1) STALKER, J. (2) SCOTT, A. (3) SYMES, J. Lieutenants. *Inscription* :—This tablet has been erected by the Government, North-Western Provinces, to preserve the last earthly resting place of Lieutenants A. Scott, 1st Battalion, Sepoys; Jeremiah Symes, 2nd Battalion, Sepoys; J. Stalker, Resident's Bodyguard; who were killed 17th August 1781, near this spot, doing their duty.

[Cf., no. 601.]

CANTONMENTS, BENARES, NEAR RAILWAY.

617.—**1843**—POGSON, W. R., Lieutenant-Colonel. *Inscription* :— Sacred to the memory of Lieutenant-Colonel Wredenhall Roberts Pogson, of the XLVII Regiment, Native Infantry. Born on the 1st July 1787, and died at Benares on the 6th of August 1843, aged 56 years 11 months and 6 days. This monument is erected by the officers of the 47th and his friends and family as a token of respect to his memory.

[This is the tomb of Captain W. R. Pogson, author of the "History of the Bundelas." There can be no doubt of the identification; there is only one W. R. Pogson in Dodwell and Miles; he joined the service in 1803, became a captain in 1819 and a major in 1833, so that in 1828 (when the book was published) he was a captain; we find him transmitting several books for the acceptance of the Court of Directors in 1832; and he is described in the Services B. A. List as "a man of learning and author of some rather eccentric writings." Those who read his history will notice both the learning and the eccentricity. He was the son of B. Pogson, of Sutton; he fought at Bhurtpore and was mentioned in despatches. "He was buried by a roadside, according to a direction in his will," says the Services B. A. List. Tradition in Benares avers that he wished to be buried within sound of his bugles (the tomb is on the far side of the Native Infantry parade ground, and the N. I. lines.) It was doubtless unconscious irony which sent young buglers to learn their art (in 1904-5 at all events) in the grove in which his tomb stands, and prompted the bandmaster to choose that place as a fit spot for bugle practice generally.]

(References: *Pogson; D. and M.; Services B.A. List.*)

CHAITGANJ, BENARES CITY.

618.—**1781**—VICTIMS OF INSURRECTION OF CHAIT SINGH. *Inscription* :—The enclosed ground was the burial place of brave men who died in the performance of their duty on the 16th August 1781 A.D. This wall has been built to protect the spot from desecration, A.D. 1862.

[Cf., no. 601.]

Mirzapur District.

ST. JOHN'S CHURCH.

619.—**1847**—CURRIE, A.P., B.C.S. *Inscription* :—To the memory of Alfred Peter Currie, Civil and Sessions Judge of Mirzapur, one of the founders of this sacred edifice, who died on the 3rd day of February 1847. This tablet is dedicated by his friends as a testimonial of their esteem and regret.

Take ye heed, watch and pray, for ye know not when the time is.

[Alfred Peter Currie (1806-1847) was a younger brother of Sir Frederick Currie, Bart. For some account of the Currie family in India, vide no. 813.

A. P. Currie arrived in India in 1826: he was at Haileybury from 1823 to 1825. He served in Burdwan, Gorakhpur, Benares, Hamirpur, Ghazipur, Etawah, Farrukhabad and Mirzapur. His wife was Jane Latham, daughter of G. Mainwaring, B.C.S.]

(References : *Prinsep C.L.* ; *Burke P.* ; *Haileybury*.)

620.—**1857**—MOORE, W. R., B.C.S. *Inscription* :—This tablet is erected to the memory of William Richard Moore, of the Bengal Civil Service, Joint Magistrate and Deputy Collector of Mirzapur, whose mortal remains rest in the burial-ground of this station He was the second son of Major J. A. Moore and Sophia Stewart, his wife, and was among the early victims of the fearful mutiny which desolated India in 1857, having been barbarously and treacherously murdered while in the energetic performance of his duty on the 4th July in that year. The remembrance of his high qualities as a public servant, of his excellence in all the relations of life, of his unsullied purity and honour as a man, and of his warm and unaffected piety as a Christian, furnishes to surviving relatives and friends consolation under a loss of which, alas! it also tells the greatness. He was born on the 28th October 1832, and died on the 4th July 1857, in the 25th year of his age.

He being made perfect in a short time, fulfilled a long time. *Wisdom*, chapter IV, verse 13.

[W. R. Moore was at Haileybury 1850-1 and arrived in India in 1852. The mutiny in Mirzapur was not of a very serious nature, and the authorities were able to make head against the rebels all through. It was at first garrisoned by half a Sikh corps, and when those were sent to Allahabad and replaced by the 47th Native Infantry, they too remained faithful, though suspected. On a false alarm the majority of the European residents fled to Chunar: but the only serious events were those connected with Bhadohi and the murder of Mr. Moore. Bhadohi belonged to the Raja of Benares, but the former Rajput owners had never been wholly uprooted, and now one of them, Udwant Singh, assumed his ancestral title and commenced to raise forces and plunder his weaker neighbours. He was, however, delivered up by his own Diwan to Lieutenant Palliser and his sowars, and hanged. They vowed vengeance on Moore, the Joint Magistrate and official Superintendent of the Raja's Domains, who they supposed was the chief cause of the execution. On the 4th July he made a raid from Gopiganj and arrested some prisoners whom he brought to an indigo factory at Pali. He was at once surrounded by Jhuria Singh and a large body of men and he and the two managers of the factory, E. S. Jones and C. M. Kemp, were murdered. Kemp was only 15 years old (*vide* nos. 759-60). His head was taken to the widow of Udwant Singh: she had offered Rs. 300 for it. The bodies were recovered by a party of the 64th Regiment. The rebels were attacked but the real murderers escaped.]

(References : *Gazetteer* ; *Haileybury M. N.*)

MIRZAPUR CEMETERY.

621.—**1801**—WHITE, C.S. *Inscription* :—Sacred to the memory of Catharine Sarah White, daughter of Captain Samuel White, who departed this life, February the 19th, 1801, aged one year nine months and ten days.

[S. White joined the service in 1781 and died at Fort William in 1806.]

(References: *D. and M.*)

622.—**1801**—WARD, V. L., Lieutenant. *Inscription:*—Here lies interred the body of Lieutenant Vere Lumby Ward, His Majesty's 27th Regiment, L. D., who departed this life, 26th July 1801, aged 33 years.

623.—**1805**—BARBER, J., Lieutenant. *Inscription:*—Sacred to the memory of James Barber, late a Lieutenant in the 1st Battalion, 19th Regiment, N. I., who departed this life on the 5th May 1805, aged 25 years. To perpetuate the remembrance of an officer they esteemed and a friend they loved, this monument is erected by the officers of the 1st Battalion, 19th Regiment.

[James Barber, son of J. Barber, of Otley, was born in 1780. He joined the service in 1798. Dodwell and Miles give these dates of his death as 15th August 1805.]

(References: *D. and M.*; *C. P.*)

624.—**1807**—O'SHEA, A., Captain. *Inscription:*—Sacred to the memory of Capt. Andrew O'Shea. He was born at Cork in Ireland on the 21st March 1787, and he died at this place on the 18th November 1817. He was an honour to his friends, to his profession and to society, and his loss will ever be deeply felt and lamented by his afflicted relations.

[He joined the service in 1803, and became a captain in 1816.]

(Reference: *D. and M.*)

625.—**1812**—CHAPMAN, R. *Inscription:*—"Sacred to the memory of Robert Chapman, Esq., who died July 21st, 1812."

626.—**1816**—BARTON, C., Captain. *Inscription:*—Sacred to the memory of Capt. Chawil Barton, 8th Regiment, N. I., a tender and beloved husband and father, who departed his life on the 30th of October 1816. This tomb is erected with affection and tributary tears by the bereaved wife.

[Dodwell and Miles mention a C.W. Burton who died at Tarra Mirzapore, on 30th October 1816. He was appointed cadet in 1800, ensign in 1801, lieutenant in 1803, captain in 1814. This explains the extraordinary name Chawil. It stands, clearly, for Cha. Wil. (Charles William); Barton is also an error for Burton.]

(References: *D. and M.*)

627.—**1817**—GREENHILL, J., Lieutenant. *Inscription:*—Sacred to the memory of Lieutenant James Greenhill, of H. M.'s 17th Regiment of Foot who departed this life near Mirzapur, 27th June 1817, aged 26 years. This monument is erected by his brother-officers as a testimony of the highest regard for a sincere friend and an honourable man.

[The 17th were in India 1810-1831].

628.—**1822**—HOPE, H., B. C. S. *Inscription:*—Sacred to the memory of Hugh Hope, Esq., late of the Bengal Civil Service, second son by his second marriage of the late Sir Archibald Hope, Bart. of Craighall. Born A. D. 1783, died A. D. 1822, *ætat* 39.

[Hugh Hope was fourth son of the ninth Baronet. He joined the service in 1803; one of his first posts was "second assistant to the export warehouse-keeper and deputy appraiser of piece goods at the Calcutta Customs," a title which shows how varied were the duties of our predecessors in the Civil Service. He was employed in Java, Patna, Jessore and Mirzapur, where he was "officiating import warehouse-keeper and naval store-keeper." The Hope's of Craighall are an old family of French extraction, dating back to John de Hope who came to Scotland in the train of Magdalene. Queen of James V. The first baronet was Sir Thomas Hope, an eminent lawyer, and Law Advocate (1626). Among other famous members of the family are Genl. Sir James Hope, G.C.B., who served in the French wars; Genl. Sir William Hope, K. C. B., who served in the Crimea; and Sir Theodore Hope, K.C.S.I., C.I.E., of the Bombay C. S. Hugh Hope was married to Isabella, daughter of Æneas Mackay of Scotston, and left a son.]

(References: *Prinsep C. L.; Burke, P.*)

629.—**1826**—CAMPBELL, J., Lieutenant. *Inscription:*—Sacred to the memory of Lieutenant John Campbell, 4th Extra Regiment, who died 25th June 1826, much regretted by his brother officer, by whom this monument is erected as a memorial of his intrinsic worth. *ob. ætat.* 20.

[The son of the Revd. A. Campbell, born at Portree, N. B., in 1805, and educated at Musselburgh, he joined the service in 1821.]

(References: *D. and M.; C. P.*)

630.—**1827**—MACDONALD, A., Lieutenant-Colonel Sir. *Inscription:*—Sacred to the memory of Lieutenant-Colonel Archibald MacDonald, K.C.B., late Adjutant-General of H. M.'s Forces in India, who died on the 15th November 1827.

[Untraceable. The only Archibald Macdonald I could find in the Knightage was K. H. not K. C. B.]

631.—**1827**—PIERCY, J. R., Ensign. *Inscription:*—Sacred to the memory of Ensign J. R. Piercy, 6th Extra Regiment, N. I., who departed this life on the 17th November 1827, aged 17 years. This monument is erected by his brother officers as a mark of their esteem. (D. O.)

[Jeffery Rand Piercy, son of Capt. J. Piercy, H. M. 53rd Regt. was born at Fort William in 1809. He joined the service in 1826, and died at Jubbulpore.]

(References: *D. and M.; C. P.*)

632.—**1827**—DOUGLAS, C.S., Mrs. *Inscription:*—Sacred to the memory of Charlotte Sarah, wife of Lieutenant J. F. Douglas, who departed this life at Mirzapore on the 20th of April 1827, aged 25 years.

[James F. Douglas, son of A. Douglas of Leith, born in 1798, joined the service in 1819.]

(References: *D. and M.; C. P.*)

633.—**1828**—SKENE, E. E. N., Mrs. *Inscription:*—Sacred to the memory of Emma Eliza Neville Skene, wife of Major W. Skene, 5th Extra Regiment, N.I., who departed this life on the morning of the 8th September 1828, aged 37 years and 10 months; this monument is erected by her disconsolate husband as a tribute of affection and regard for one who had for nearly 22 years fulfilled her duties as an affectionate wife with true Christian piety and virtue.

The Lord gave and the Lord hath taken away, blessed be the name of the Lord. (B. O.)

[William Skene, son of Professor G. Skene of the Marischal College at Aberdeen, joined the service in 1800 and retired in 1832. It will be noticed that he married his wife at a remarkably early age.]

(References: *D. and M.; C. P.*)

634.—**1828**—MONIN, L. *Inscription:*—Léon Monin décédé le 18 Septembre 1828.

635.—**1829**—BURROWES, C., Lieutenant. *Inscription:*—To the memory of Lieutenant Cosby Burrowes, 45th Regiment, N. I., who died December 9th, 1829. (B. O.)

Cosby Burrowes, son of T. Burrrowes of Stradone House, co. Cavan, joined the serv.ce in 1817 and died according to Dodwell and Miles in the Mauritius. The Burrowes' settled in Cavan under James I, at the settlement of Ulster.]

(References: *Burk, L. G. I.; D. and M.*)

636.—1830—PLATT, W., Lieutenant. *Inscription:*—Sacred to the memory of Lieutenant W. Platt, of the 18th Regiment, Native Infantry, who was drowned near Mirzapur on the 1st July 1830. This tomb was erected by his brother officers as a token of their esteem.

[W. Platt joined the service in 1824. I could not trace his papers.]

(Reference: *D. and M.*)

637.—1832—LIND, A. F., B.C.S. *Inscription:*—Sacred to the memory of Alexander Francis Lind, C.S., born January 8th, 1798, died February 8th, 1832.

[A. F. Lind, son of Dr. J. Lind of Windsor, was born in 1797 not 1798, according to his birth certificate. He was recommended for a nomination by Lord Ailesbury at the desire of Her Majesty Queen Charlotte in 1811, was at Haileybury 1812-13 and arrived in India in 1814. He served in Benares, Rangpur, the Sunderbunds, Murshidabad, Birbhum, Calcutta, Rajshahi, Fatehpur and Mirzapur. He was Judge and Magistrate of Mirzapur when he died.]

(References: *Haileybury; Prinsep C. L.; W. P.*)

638.—1833—VINCENT, M. *Inscription:*—"Mathieu Vincent décédé le 27 Juilect, 1833."

639.—1833—LINDSAY, M., Mrs. *Inscription:*—Sacred to the memory of Margaret, the beloved wife of C. Lindsay, Esq., C.S., who departed this life in childbed, aged 20 years, on the 7th October 1833.

[This was Margaret Browne, the second wife of Colin Lindsay, C.S., married in 1832. Colin Lindsay, B.C.S., was at one time judge of Delhi. He died in 1864. He was the 4th son of Lieutenant-General James Lindsay (died 1793), grandson of the 5th Earl of Balcarres (1691—1768); one of his brothers was Robert James Loyd Lindsay, first and only Lord Wantage. This very ancient family has possessed and still possesses no less than three Earldoms. It dates back to Sir William de Lindessi, of the 12th century. The 8th in succession, Sir David de Lindesay (Ambassador to England in 1349 51) first signed himself as Lord of Crawford: and his youngest son Sir William—one of Froissart's "Enfants de Lindsay"—was ancestor of the Earls of Lindsay. The 4th Lord of Crawford was made Earl of Crawford. The 2nd son of Lord Menmuir (a lord of session) who was 2nd son of the 9th Earl, became the 1st Lord Balcarres: and his son was made 1st Earl of Balcarres. The 16th Earl of Crawford died without heirs and Charles I regranted his Earldom to the Earl of Lindsay, but with remainder to the Crawford line. Accordingly in 1808 the Earldom of Crawford passed back to the 6th Earl of Balcarres who became also 23rd Earl of Crawford.]

(Reference: *Burke, P.*)

640.—1834—VENABLES, G. H. Ensign. *Inscription:*—Ensign G. H. Venables, 29th Regiment, deceased 9th September 1834.

[The son of Reverend G. Venables, and rector of Machynlleth, Montgomeryshire, born in 1809. He joined the service in 1828.]

(Reference: *Services B.A. List.*)

641.—1836—DASHWOOD, T. J., B.C.S. *Inscription:*—Sacred to the memory of Thomas John Dashwood, Esq., Civil and Sessions Judge of zillah Tirhoot, who died suddenly near Mirzapur on the 17th of June 1836, aged 44. (B.O.)

[Son of Thomas Dashwood, E. I. C. S. and Charlotte, daughter of J. Auriol and described as "senior merchant on the Bengal Establishment and Judge of Tirhoot." Thomas Dashwood in 1783 was appointed an "Examiner" in the office of the Secret Department, when it was divided off from the Public Department, and "J. Auriol," is probably J. P. Auriol, the last secretary of both departments before their separation. Thomas Dashwood married Miss Auriol in 1782. T. J. Dashwood married Susan, daughter of Thomas Wodehouse. T. Dashwood was 2nd son of Sir James Dashwood, 2nd Baronet, LL. D., M.P., for Oxford. A. J. Dashwood and C. K. Dashwood, both killed at Lucknow in the mutiny (nos. 868 and 924), were nephews of T. J. Dashwood. The family goes back to an Alderman George Dashwood, Commissioner of Excise and Hearthtax (1617—1682.) T. J. Dashwood joined the service in 1810 and served in the 24-Parganas, Patna and Tirhut. He was on leave for 5 years (1818—1823). He died on a river steamer after a few hours' illness. He was at Haileybury 1808-9.]

References : *Forrest* 1772-85 ; *Burke P ; Prinsep C. L.*)

642.—**1837**—HINDE, H., Major. *Inscription* :—To the memory of Henry Hinde, Major, Brazilian Service, died 14th March 1831, aged 45 years.

643.—**1840**—TAYLOR, E. E. *Inscription* :—Sacred to the memory of Emily Eliza, the beloved child of R. J. Taylor, C.S., and Eliza, his wife, born on the 12th of May 1839, died on the 12th of August 1840. *Dolce nella memoria.*

[R. J. Tayler, (so birth certificate and other lists) was son of G. Taylor, merchant, born in 1794. He came to India in 1813, and in 1839-40 was Sessions Judge of Mirzapur. He retired in 1857 and died in 1860.]

(References : *Prinsep C. L. ; W. P.*)

644.—**1842**—NOBLE, G., Ensign. *Inscription* :—Sacred to the memory of Ensign George Noble, 13th Native Infantry, who died here, November 10th, 1842, aged 18.

[Son of Lieutenant G. Noble, R. N., born in 1824. He arrived in India in July 1842 and died on his way to join his regiment at Banda.]

(References : *Services B.A. List.*)

645.—**1843**—SALMON, W. B , Lieutenant-Colonel. *Inscription* :—To the memory of W. B. Salmon, Lieut -Col., 58th Regiment, B. N. I., who departed this life on the 5th February 1843, aged 56 years, after a service of 39 years. This monument is erected by his brother officers as a tribute of their sincere esteem and respect.

[There is only one W. B. Salmon in Dodwell and Miles, so that it would seem that this must be William Broome Salmon, Sir J. B. Hearsey's brother-in-law. (Cf. nos. 551 and 850). Pearse says he died, a General, in England. This seems certainly an error, in so far as his rank was concerned, though this may, of course be a cenotaph. All the facts given in the Services B. A. List about W. B. Salmon correspond with those given by Pearse, whilst the date of death is mentioned by the former. W. B. Salmon is stated to have been a captain in 1825, in command of the Resident's Bodyguard at Lucknow 1823—5, and even as going on leave to the hills in 1827—all facts mentioned of Hearsey's brother-in-law by Pearse ; so there can be little doubt of the identification. He was the son of G. Salmon born in 1787 and joined the service in 1803.]

(References : *Pearse ; D. and M. ; Services B.A. List.*)

646.—**1844**—MALING, N., Mr. *Inscription* :—Nona, the beloved wife of Captain C. S. Maling, 68th Native Infantry, died at Mirzapur, 28th March 1844. *Aetat* 36 years.

When from the dust of death I rise,
To claim my mansion in the skies ;
E'en then shall this be all my plea,
Jesus hath lived and died for me.

[Cf. no. 654.]

647.—**1846**—(1) WOLLASTON, L. H., Mrs. (2) WOLLASTON, L. *Inscription* :—"Sacred to the memory of Lorenza Hilaria, the beloved wife of M. W. Wollaston, missionary, who died 27th July 1846, aged 36 years. Also of Lorenza, their infant daughter, who died 30th July 1846, aged one year and one month."

[Cf. no. 652.]

648.—**1847**—ROSE, H., B.C.S. *Inscription* :—To the memory of Hugh Rose, of Kilravock in Scotland, a Civil Servant of the H. E. I. Company, who died at this place on the 29th January 1847, and is here interred.

[Hugh Rose, eldest son of Hugh Rose, of Kilravock, to Nairn, according to Burke, "went to India where he became highly distinguished in the C. S. in Bengal." Prinsep gives his most important post as that of settlement officer at Cawnpore (1839-41) : and he was magistrate of Banda when he died. This Hugh was apparently the first of the family to go to India, but of his brothers three served in India, all during the mutiny and two were killed, one at Gwalior and one at Kaira in Bombay. Sir Hugh Rose, (Lord Strathnairn) was a kinsman. Two sisters also married Anglo-Indians. The family is ancient, dating back to the time of Alexander III ; and settled at Kilravock in the time of King John Balliol, since when the estate has descended unbroken to the present owner. The eldest son has apparently been a Hugh without any exception since the time of John Balliol. The Rose Innes family of Netherdale and the Roses of Holme Rose are junior branches of the same family.]

(Reference : *Prinsep C. L.* ; *Burke L. G.*)

649.—**1847**—TODD, F. B., Captain. *Inscription* :—Beneath this stone is interred all that was mortal of Fryer Bowes Todd, Captain in the Hon'ble Company's Military Service. He was born on the 25th November 1800 and his spirit ascended to his God and Saviour on the 7th October 1847.

Blessed are the dead which die in the Lord.
Revelation, Chapter XIV, verse 13.

Erected as a last token of affection by his afflicted widow.

[Son of F. Todd, a volunteer in the pilot service, born in 1800. He joined the service in 1819.]

(Reference : *Services B. A. List.*)

650.—**1847**—CURRIE, A. P., B.C.S. *Inscription* :—Sacred to the memory of A. P. Currie, Esq., Judge of Mirzapur, who departed this life on the 3rd day of February 1847, *ætat* 41.

What I do thou knowest now, but thou shalt know hereafter.
St. John, Chapter XIII, verse 7th.

Erected as a last token of love by his afflicted widow.

[Cf. no. 619.]

651.—**1850**—PITTS-FORSTER, H., Lieutenant. *Inscription* :—Lieutenant Henry Pitts-Forster, Adjt., Shekhowattee Battalion, departed this life, 26th May 1850, aged 27 years.

[The Shekhowattee Battalion are the present 13th Rajputs.]

652.—**1851**—(1) WOLLASTON, M. W., Revd. (2) WOLLASTON, E. W. *Inscription* :—Sacred to the memory of M. W. Wollaston, Missionary of L. M. S. at Mirzapur. He was born August 24th, 1802, joined the Mirzapur Mission, March 30th, 1844, and died June 10th, 1851. Also interred in the same tomb, Edward Budden Wollaston, son of the abovenamed, and Emma, his wife. Born June 22nd, 1850, died June 13th, 1851.

Them also which sleep in Jesus will God bring with Him.
I *Thessalonians*, Chapter IV, verse 14.

This monument is erected as a last token of love on the part of his afflicted widow.

[Mr. Wollaston, previous to joining the L. M. S., was engaged in education at Agra where he published a "practical grammar of the Sanskrit language" and some other books. He joined the mission in 1804 and was ordained in November of the same year. He again gave his time to educational work, but in later years took to bazar preaching in which he greatly delighted.]

(Reference : *Communicated.*)

653.—**1857**—MOORE, W. R., B.C.S. *Inscription* :—Sacred to the memory of William Richard Moore, Bengal Civil Service, Joint Magistrate and Deputy Collector of Mirzapur, who was murdered on duty at the Parlee Factory in that district during the rebellion in India on 4th July 1857, in the 25th year of his age.

Blessed are they who die in the Lord.

[Cf. no. 620.]

654.—**1858**—(1) MALING, A. E. C. **1860**—(2) MALING, C. S., Colonel. *Inscription* :—For ever with the Lord. I Thessalonians, Chapter IV, verse 7. Most sacred to the much loved memory of Colonel C. S. Maling, late Commandant of the 68th regiment, B. N. I., who departed this life at Mirzapur, March the 18th, 1860, in perfect faith in his redeemer. Most deeply deplored and lamented by his afflicted widow, family and friends, and sincerely regretted by his brother officers. "The name of the Lord is a strong tower, the righteous runneth into it and is safe." (Prov. Chapter 18, verse 10.) Also to the sweet memory of Anna Eliza Constance, the much loved infant child of the above and Eliza Caroline, his beloved wife, born in England 19th October 1856, and entered into Heaven 31st December 1858, aged 2 months and 12 days. He shall gather the lambs in his arms and carry them in his bosom. (Isaiah XL, verse 11th.) This sad monument is erected to the most fondly and most deeply-beloved memory of her beloved and very attached husband, by his bereaved and most deeply mourning widow, in the sure and certain hope of being most gloriously re-united to him in heaven for ever.

Not lost, but gone before.

[This was erected by Colonel Maling's second wife. His first died in 1844 cf. no. 646. C. Simpson Maling, son of Captain C. Maling, 9th N. I., was born in India in 1808, and entered the service in 1823. He was captain in 1834, and commanded the Jodhpur legion 1839-41.]

(Reference : *Services B. A. List.*)

655.—**1860**—HANDSIDE, C. E., Lieutenant. *Inscription* :—In memory of Lieutenant Charles E. Handside, 5th Bengal Europeans, son of H. Handside, W. S., Edinburgh, died 2nd September 1860. Erected by his sorrowing parents.

656.—**1862**—FAIRLIE, E., B. C. S. *Inscription* :—Sacred to the memory of Edward Fairlie, Esq., Bengal Civil Service, the fifth son of James Fairlie, Esq., who died here on the 30th September 1862, in the 28th year of his age, much regretted by all who knew him.

Fear not, for I have redeemed thee ; I have called thee by thy name ; thou art Mine.

[The 5th son of James Fairlie of Holms, co. Ayr, he was at Haileybury 1854-6 and came to India 1857. Two of his brothers were also in the Indian Army. The family is descended from Robert de Ros, of Trabet, who obtained the Fairlie lands from Robert Bruce, and changed his name. This branch is descended from a cadet of the family who lived *circa* 1661. The Fairlies are connected with the Muirs by marriage (cf. no. 545); whether it is this branch I am however uncertain. A Jean Fairlie married a John Muir of Netheraith, and died in 1829, but I cannot identify the latter. At all events Fairlie appears in the names of a brother, son and grandson of Sir William Muir ; whilst Mungo, another "Muir" name is also common amongst the Fairlies : it was the name of a brother of the

Jean mentioned and also of a brother of Edward Fairlie, amongst others. The probability is, therefore, that this Fairlie is a distant connection of the many Muirs in this province.]

(Reference: *Haileybury ; Burke L. G.*)

657.—**1862**—HOGG, E. H., Mrs. *Inscription* :—To the memory of Elizabeth Helen, wife of Fergusson Floyer Hogg, who died at Mirzapur, 4th December 1862, aged 24 years.

Blessed are the pure in heart, for they shall see God.

[Cf. no. 658.]

658.—**1862**—HOGG, F. F., B.C.S. *Inscription* :—Sacred to the memory of Fergusson Floyer Hogg, Bengal Civil Service, who died at Chunar, 19th December, 1862, aged 35 years.

He rests in the Lord Jesus.

[F. F. Hogg, (1829-1862) was 3rd son of the Right Hon. Sir James Weir Hogg, P. C., Registrar of the Supreme Court of Calcutta, 1822—33, Director and Chairman of E. I. C. and practically (as M. P. for Honiton) their representative in Parliament, and one of the first members of the Indian Council in 1888. He refused the Governorship of Bombay in 1853. Amongst other well-known Anglo-Indian members of this family are C. S. Hogg, Administrator-General of Bengal (1824—1870), Sir S. S. Hogg, B.C.S., Commissioner of Police and Chairman of the municipality, Calcutta, who also served in the North-West Provinces and the Punjab (born 1833); Sir F. R. Hogg, K.C.I.E., C.S.I., I.C.S., D.G. of the Post Office in India (born 1836), all brothers of F. F. Hogg ; whilst a son of Sir F. R. Hogg is now in the Indian Postal Department.

Sir J. W. Hogg's eldest son became the first Lord Magheramorne. The family is a Scotch one that emigrated to Ireland at the end of the 17th century. By intermarriage with the McGarel family (the name is now McGarel Hogg) they came into possession of Magheramorne, a place of considerable antiquity. The name means "the settlement of the Mornes," a famous ancient Irish tribe ; as early as 511 A. D. it is mentioned as the birthplace of St. Comgale. It is on the borders of Lough Larne.

F. F. Hogg was educated at Haileybury and came to India in 1849. He was Joint Magistrate of Mirzapur when he died. He married in 1861 Elizabeth Helen, eldest daughter of the Hon. L. Parsons, 3rd son of the 2nd Earl of Rosse. (Cf no. 657). (According to Burke the date of the birth of F. F. Hogg is 1829: according to the inscription it would be 1827.)]

(Reference: *Haileybury ; Burke P.*)

659.—**1863**—ROSS, J., C.E. *Inscription* :—Sacred to the much-cherished memory of James Ross, Esq., Civil Engineer and Architect, born at Inverness, who departed this life on the 25th December 1863 at Mirzapur. This is erected by his much-pitied but sorrowing son, Duncan Ross.

660.—**1864**—DEMINE, J. *Inscription* :—Sacred to the memory of John Demine, Commander of the Ganges Company Flat *Alpha*, who died of cholera at Mirzapur, June 3rd, 1864, aged 32 years. "Verily, every man at his best state is altogether vanity."

Psalm XXXIV, verse 5.

661.—**1864**—KIRKPATRICK, T., Captain. *Inscription* :—"Sacred to the memory of Captain Thomas Kirkpatrick, Madras Staff Corps, who died June 12th, 1864, aged 31 years. This monument is erected by his attached brother, J. Kirkpatrick, M. D."

[Son of R. Kirkpatrick, born at Troqueer, Kirkcudbright, in 1827.]

(Reference: *C.P.*)

CHUNAR (SARAIYAN—SIKANDARPUR) OLD CEMETERY.

662.—**1783**—HUMPHREYS, E., Major. *Inscription* :—Sacred to the memory of Major Edward Humphreys, who died 6th May

1783, aged 46 years. This monument is erected by Captain Patrick McDougal, November 1783.

[The Chunar fort was handed over to the British after the battle of Buxar in 1764. It was an advanced post on the British frontier, a cantonment for many years and then the residence of European invalids up to the 60's at least. This of course explains the numerous cemeteries found here. In 1824 Bishop Heber visited it and describes it as follows: There were "some very good European habitations and a tale Gothic Tower"—that of the Mission Church. The whole scene is entirely English.. ....the Castle with its union flag is such as would be greatly admired but not at all out of place in any ancient English seaport. The congregation was more numerous than I have seen out of Calcutta: there were about 200 European invalids besides officers, civil and military, and their families. Some of the Europeans are very old: there is one (1824) who fought with Clive."

Edward Humphries (so Dodwell and Miles) joined the service in 1767, became captain in 1777 and major in 1781.]

(Reference: *D. and M.*; *Heber*; *Gazetteer*.)

663.—**1798**—CLARK, G. *Inscription*:—"In memory G. Clark, private, 78th Regt., deceased 21st June 1791, aged 27 years."

CHUNAR (NEAR INVALID BARRACKS), OLD CEMETERY.

664.—**1791**—MCDONALD, J., Ensign. *Inscription*:—"In memory of Ensign John McDonald, departed this life the 24th December 1791, aged 55 years."

[There are one or two very curious tombs at Chunar; of these this and no. 685 are the strangest. In this case, the officer was born in 1736 and was an ensign, presumably, about 1752—five years before Plassey: in the other we have an officer born about 1702 and presumably an ensign about 1720. Yet there was no Bengal Army at these dates. From a very early date the Calcutta factors were allowed to keep an ensign and thirty men as a guard of honour: and one can only suppose that these were survivals of those early days unless indeed they were Madras officers who found their way up to Chunar at a later date.]

CHUNAR (NAGPUR), OLD CEMETERY.

665.—**1785**—ASHURN, G., Sergeant-Major. *Inscription*:—"Here lyeth the body of Geo. Ashurn, Sergeant-Major, who departed this life the 31st of December 1785, aged 49 years.

CHUNAR (NEAR DARGAH), OLD CEMETERY.

666.—**1784**—PENNYNG, T., Major. *Inscription*:—To the memory of Major Thomas Pennyng, who died on the 22nd of July 1784, aged 54 years.

[Appointed cadet in 1764, lieutenant in 1766, captain in 1769, major in 1781.]

(Reference: *D. and M.*)

667.—**1785**—DAWSON, E., Captain. *Inscription*:—"Sacred to the memory of Edward Dawson, Esquire, Captain in the Hon'ble Company's Service, who died the 23rd of March 1785, aged 54 years."

[Appointed cadet in 1780. The age must certainly be wrong. Probably 24 is right.]

(Reference: *D. and M.*)

668.—**1783**—KUNDSON, C., Colonel. *Inscription*:—Sacred to the memory of Christian Kundson, Colonel in the Hon'ble Company's Service, who died in command of this station on the 31st of August 1793, aged 48 years.

[The name is spelt both Kundson and Knudson. Christian Kundson came into the service from H. M.'s 84th in 1764 as an ensign, becoming a lieutenant in the Bengal European Regiment. There was a Christopher Kundson in the army as well.]

(Reference : *P. R. Innes.*)

CHUNAR (BHAURALI), OLD CEMETERY.

669.—**1791**—ARMSTRONG, A., Lieutenant. *Inscription :*—A tribute of friendship to the memory of Lieutenant Archibald Armstrong, who departed this life on the 29th of August A.D. 1791, age 27 years.

[Archibald Armstrong, born in 1763, was the eldest son of Andrew Armstrong of Garry Castle, King's Co., an officer in the 14th Regiment who was severely wounded at Louisberg. He joined the service in 1780.]

(Reference : *Burke, L.G.I. ; D. and M.*)

CHUNAR (SHAMSPUR), OLD CEMETERY.

670.—**1789**—MONTEATH, C., Lieutenant. *Inscription :*—Sacred to the memory of L. Col. Monteath, who died January 24th, 1789, aged 38 years.

[" L.-Col. " does not stand, as one might suppose, for Lieutenant-Colonel but for Lieutenant Colin. He joined the service in 1776 and became a lieutenant in 1778.]

(Reference : *D. and M.*)

671.—**1792**—WILKINS, D. *Inscription :*—A tribute of friendship to the memory of Mr. D. Wilkins, Assistant Surgeon, who departed this life on the 27th March, A. D. 1792, aged 37 years.

672.—**1793**—CLAYTON, E. M., Mrs. *Inscription :*—Sacred to the memory of Mrs. Emma Maria Clayton, who departed this life, June the 1st, 1793, aged 24 years. This humble tribute is erected in memory of her many exemplary virtues by her affectionate and disconsolate husband, Captain Thomas Clayton.

[T. W. Clayton joined the service in 1771 and died at Barrackpore as a Lieutenant-Colonel in 1804.]

(Reference : *D. and M.*)

673.—**1794**—CHEAP, J., Lieutenant. *Inscription :*—To the memory of Lieutenant James Cheap, of the 27th Battalion, who departed this life, September the IX, 1794, aged 33 years.

[Cadet 1778, ensign 1779, lieutenant 1781.]

(Reference : *D. and M.*)

674.—**1794**—BLACK, A., Lieutenant. *Inscription :*—To the memory of Lieutenant Andrew Black, of the 5th Battalion, who departed this life, October the 6th, 1794, aged 33 years.

[Appointed cadet in 1781, lieutenant in 1782.]

(Reference : *D. and M.*)

675.—**1794**—PARRY, R., Lieutenant. *Inscription:*—This monument is erected to the memory of Lieutenant Reparry, of the 5th Battalion of Sepoys, who departed this life the 11th of October 1794, aged 33 years, by his disconsolate friend and school-fellow, Elliot Vayle.

[There is no such name as " Reparry " in the lists. This is probably the tomb of Richard Parry. " Re " is doubtless a contraction of " Richard " probably misspelt. "Elliot Vayle" similarly should be Elliot Voyle, a distinguished officer, who saw much service and was invalided in 1816. He was a contemporary of R. Parry, who joined the service in 1782. Dodwell and Miles gives the date of death of R. Parry as 10th October 1794 at Chunar.]

(References : *E. I. M. Calendar ; D. and M.*)

676.—**1796**—WHINYATES, C. C. *Inscription :*—To the memory of Caroline Chatte Whinyates, who departed this life October the 29th, 1796, aged 22 months.

677.—**1797**—PUGH, J., Captain. *Inscription:*—Sacred to the memory of Captain James Pugh, Adjutant of the 2nd Battalion, 8th Regiment, Native Infantry, who departed this life the 16th day of April 1797, aged 56 years.

[Captain Pugh joined the service in 1779 and became a lieutenant in 1781.]
(Reference : *D. and M.*)

678.—**1797**—LLOYD, A., Mrs. *Inscription :*—Sacred to the memory of Mrs. Ann Lloyd, who departed this life, August 3rd, 1797, aged 24 years. This monument is erected by her affectionate husband Captain Edwin Lloyd.

[Edwin Lloyd joined the service in 1779 and died as a major at Cuttack in 1804.]
(Reference : *D. and M.*)

679.—**1797**—MACDOUGAL, P., Colonel. *Inscription :*—Sacred to the memory of Colonel Patrick MacDougal, who died 9th September 1797, aged 46 years.

[Joined the service in 1770 and became a major in 1794. According to Dodwell and Miles, he died in 1798.]
(Reference :—*D. and M.*)

680.—**1798**—WHITE, M., Captain. *Inscription :*—Sacred to the memory of Captain Mark White, who died 9th August 1798.

[Mark White joined the service in 1777 and became captain in 1796. Dodwell and Miles gives the date of death as 8th August.]
(Reference : *D. and M.*)

681.—**1800**—BRUMSTENPH, M., Mrs. *Inscription :*—Sacred to the memory of Mary Brumstenph, who departed this life the 10th of June 1800, aged 20 years.

How loved, how valued, now avails thee not ;
To whom related or by whom begot.
A heap of dust alone remains of thee ;
'Tis all thou art and all the proud shall be.

This monument was erected by her affectionate husband J. Brumstenph, Master of 12th Native Regiment Band.

CHUNAR, NEAR RAILWAY BRIDGE (SHAMSPUR) OLD CEMETERY.

682.—**1794**—CHAWNER, T., Lieutenant. *Inscription :*—Sacred to the memory of Lieutenant Thomas Chawner, *obiit* October 10th, 1794, aged 20 years. Erected June 1795 by the officers of the 3rd Battalion, Sepoys.

[The name, according to Dodwell and Miles, is Chawne. He joined the service in 1780, and died according to Dodwell and Miles on the 19th, not the 10th.]
(Reference : *D. and M.*)

CHUNAR, LOWER LINES, OLD CEMETERY.

683.—**1789**—WALSH, J. E., Ensign. *Inscription :*—Sacred to the memory of John Elisha Walsh, Ensign in the Honourable Company's Service, who departed this life July 25th, 1789, aged 38 years.

684.—**1799**—CUSSON, C. *Inscription :*—To the memory of Charles Cusson, infant son of Lieutenant Thomas Cusson, who departed this life, * * October 1799, aged seven months.

Ere sense of sorrow, grief or care,
Therein from this rude world hastily I flew,
Almighty God thro' his an * *
Removed me hence to * *

CHUNAR, BELOW FORT, OLD CEMETERY.

685.—**1782**—CAMERON, H. S., Ensign. *Inscription:*—Here lyes the body of Ensign Hugh Stranack Cameron, of Forbalness, county of Ross in North Britain, who departed this life the 21st of October 1782, aged about eighty.

686.—**1791**—MILNE, G. *Inscription:*—Sacred to the memory of Mr. George Milne, Assistant Surgeon, who died at Chunar, 18th November 1791, aged 33 years.

687.—**1792**—CAMERON, J., Mrs. *Inscription:*—To the memory of Mrs. Judith Cameron, August 10th, MDCCXCII.

688.—**1795**—WHITE, J., Colonel. *Inscription:*—Sacred to the memory of Colonel John White, who departed this life on the 6th day of October, MDCCXCIV, aged 64. To all acquainted with him he was known to be a kind and tender husband, an affectionate father, a zealous officer during the 38 years which he served in the country, and a sincere friend. This monument is erected by his affectionate and disconsolate widow.

[This officer joined the service in 1759, become captain in 1763, major in 1773, Lieutenant-Colonel in 1781 and Colonel in 1786.]

(Reference: *D and M.*)

689.—**1794**—DINIGAN, J. *Inscription:*—In memory of Mr. John Dinigan, late apothecary at the Chunar General Hospital. He was born in the Cemety (County ?) of Longford of Ireland and died on the 24th December A.D., 1794, A.M. 5794, aged 46 years. This monument and tablet was thoroughly repaired by his affectionate Annis after 59 years.

[A. M.—Presumably *anno mundi;* which particular theory makes the pre-Christian era exactly 4,000 years long, I cannot say.]

690.—**1794**—(1) FORBES, R., Mrs. **1813**—(2) FORBES, R., Colonel. Date not clear. (3) FORBES, E. (4) FORBES, H. (5) FORBES, A. Sacred to the memory of Richard Forbes, late a Lieutenant-Colonel in the Hon'ble East Indian Company's service on the Bengal establishment who departed this life on the 17th February 1813, aged 55 years. This monument is erected by his children as the last mark of respect and gratitude they can pay to the ashes of an affectionate and beloved parent and sincere friend.

The memory of the just is blessed. Bor. (?) Ch. 10, V. 7.

In memory of Rebecca Forbes, wife of Lieutenant-Colonel R. Forbes, who died 1794, also of Edward Forbes, Henry Forbes, Alice Forbes, children of above and Lieutenant-Colonel R. Forbes.

[R. Forbes joined the service in 1776. He became Lieutenant-Colonel in 1801 and was invalided in 1804.]

(Reference: *D. and M.*)

691.—**1795**—TURNBULL. *Inscription:*—The remains . . Turnbull, Esq., who departed this life the 5th November 1795, aged 44 years. A most affectionate husband . . . . an indulgent father . . . . . .

692.—**1797**—MARLEY, H. *Inscription:*—In memory of Harriott Marley, infant daughter of Major B. Marley, who died 18th April 1797.

[Bennet Marley, afterwards Lieutenant-General, joined the service in 1771. He became major in 1797 and Lieutenant-General in 1891. He commanded a column in the Nepalese War.]

(Reference: *D. and M.; Stubbs.*)

693.—1797—HARTLE, Lieutenant-Colonel. *Inscription* :—Sacred to the memory of Lieutenant-Colonel Hartle, who died 24th October 1797.

[Anthony Hartle joined the service in 1768 and became Lieutenant-Colonel in 1794.]

(Reference: *D. and M.*)

694.—1798—BUTLER, W., Captain. *Inscription* :—To the memory of Captain W. Butler, Fort Adjutant and Barrack-Master, who departed this life August the 2nd, 1798.

695.—1798—McGOWAN, S., Ensign. *Inscription* :—To the memory of Ensign S. McGowan, of Engineers, who departed this life, May the 27th, 1798.

[This officer was born in 1775, and joined the Army in 1793. His Christian name was Suetonius.]

(Reference: *D. and M.*)

696.—1803—PLUMER, S., Mrs. *Inscription* :—Sacred to the memory of Mrs. Sophia Plumer, who departed this life on the 31st of October A.D., 1803, in the 34th year of her age.

697.—1807—GRANT, W. H. *Inscription* :—Sacred to the memory of William Henry, the adopted son of Lieutenant-Colonel Lewis Grant, who departed this life the 2nd of August 1807, aged 4 years and 1 month.

698.—1808—LEWELLYN, J. L., Lieutenant. *Inscription* :—This monument, sacred to the memory of Lieutenant John L. Lewellyn, who died October 16th, 1808, aged 54 years, was erected by his faithful friend Flora.

699.—1808—GALE, C., Captain. *Inscription* :—Sacred to the memory of Captain Christopher Gale, Commissary of Ordnance, who departed this life on the [16th] December 1806, aged * * years.

[He joined the service in 1785, and became captain in 1804. The date of death is filled in from Dodwell and Miles.]

(Reference: *D. and M.*)

700.—1809—MITCHELL, A. *Inscription* :—Sacred to the memory of Adam Mitchell, Esq., Surgeon, who died at Chunar, January 23rd, 1809.

701.—1809—EDWARDS, C., Sergeant-Major. *Inscription* :—Sacred to the memory of Charles Edwards, Sergeant-Major of the 2nd Battalion, Native Invalids, who departed this life at Chunar on the 9th of February 1809, aged 56 years. He was a man useful to his country and an old servant. He served with credit on the Coromandel Coast in the war with Tippo Sultan and a number of years first writer in the Adjutant-General's office with the Army against that tyrant. Erected by his disconsolate housekeeper Rezia do Rozia, who lived with him for many years.

702.—1809—BERKELLY, H. L., Lieutenant. *Inscription* :—Sacred to the memory of Lieutenant H. Lionel Berkelly, a sincere Christian.

How loved, how valued, now avails thee not;
To whom related or by whom begot.
A heap of dust alone remains of thee;
'Tis all thou art and all the proud shall be.

He departed this life on the 25th October 1809, aged 52 years 10 months and 13 days.

[Probably this is H. N. L. Barkley who joined the service in 1779 and was invalided in 1787.]

(Reference : *D. and M.*)

703.—**1810**—GRANT, C. E. *Inscription* :—Sacred to the memory of Charlotte Jane, the daughter of Lieutenant-Colonel and Mrs. Grant, who departed this life on the 1st of February 1810, aged 6 months and 12 days.

704.—**1810**—(1) REDISH, C., Captain. (2) REDISH, C. C. *Inscription* :—Sacred to the memory of Captain Charles Redish of this establishment who departed this life at the station on the 8th of June 1810. Likewise to the memory of his infant son, Charles Canning Redish, born on the 3rd August 1807, and died on the 23rd June 1810. This monument was erected by their afflicted wife and mother.

[C. Reddishe (so all lists) son of S. Reddishe, born in London in 1779, was appointed cadet in 1797 and became a captain in 1807.]

(References : *D. and M.* ; *C. P.*)

705.—**1810**—GRANT, M. *Inscription* :—Sacred to the memory of Mary, the daughter of Lieutenant-Colonel and Mrs. Grant, who died at Chunar, the 15th August 1810, aged 7 months and 20 days.

706.—**1813**—TUDOR, T., Ensign. *Inscription* :—Sacred to the memory of Ensign Thomas Tudor, late of the European Infantry invalids, who departed this life 23rd January 1813, aged 24 years. This stone is erected by Ramjohn Mistry.

[Ensign Tudor became a lieutenant in 1811 and was invalided immediately after.]

(Reference : *D. and M.*)

707.—**1814**—PASCHOUD, J. F., Lieutenant-Colonel. *Inscription* :—Sacred to the memory of John Francis Paschoud, late a Lieut.-Col. in the Bengal Artillery, who departed this life on the 18th January 1814, aged 47 years. This monument is erected by his sons J. and C. Paschoud as a lasting testimony to the ashes of an affectionate and beloved parent. (B. O.)

[Paschoud is spelt Paschaud by all authorities. He joined the service in 1782, became a lieutenant-colonel in 1880, and was invalided soon after.]

(Reference : *D. and M.*)

708.—**1816**—VIGNE, E., Lieutenant. *Inscription* :—Sacred to the memory of Lieutenant Edward Vigne who departed this life on the 21st of July 1816, aged 33 years.

....Sore long time,....
All phisic was in v,....
....u death gave ease
....God did please."

[This officer was appointed lieutenant in 1805 and was pensioned in 1809. He was the son of J. Vigne, born at Dublin in 1784.)

(Reference : *C. P.*; *D. and M.*)

709.—**1819**—NUGENT, G., Captain. *Inscription* :—Sacred to the memory of Captain George Nugent, late Fort Adjutant & Barrack-Master, who departed this life on the 14th of June 1819, aged 39 years. He was a man of most honourable and upright principles, a tender, kind and indulgent husband, a fond and affectionate father, a warm and sincere friend, possessing an elegant mind and energy and wit blended with the most affable manner; he was a charming companion and an excellent member of society.

[This officer was appointed cadet in 1799, lieutenant in 1803, and captain in 1814.]

(Reference; *D. and M.*)

710.—**1820**—GREENE, W. H., Major. *Inscription* :—Sacred to the memory of W. Horatio Greene, Major, Artillery Invd., who departed this life August 30th, 1820.

[Green is the spelling in all lists. He was transferred from the infantry: he became an ensign in 1783, fire worker in 1789, lieutenant in 1795, captain in 1806 and major in 1810. He was invalided soon after. He fought in the Mysore war under Lord Cornwallis.]

(Reference: *B. A. List; Stubbs.*)

711.—**1821**—WILSON, W. T., Captain. *Inscription* :—Sacred to the memory of Captain W. T. Wilson, of the Corps of European Invalids, who departed this life 2nd July 1821, aged 36 years.

[William Freullateau Wilson (T. is an error for F.,) was appointed cadet in 1803, and captain in 1819. He was invalided in 1820. He belonged to the 5th Native Infantry.]

(Reference: *D. and M.*)

712.—**1822**—CATES, J., Ensign. *Inscription* :—Sacred to the memory of Ensign J. Cates, 2nd Battalion, 19th Regiment, N. I. who died 13th September 1822, aged 20 years.

[He was appointed in 1821 and died on his budgerow near Chunar.]

(Reference: *D. and M.*)

713.—**1822**—GRANT, L., Lieutenant-Colonel. *Inscription* :—Sacred to the memory of Lieutenant-Colonel Lewis Grant, who died 10th November, A.D. 1822, aged 70 years.

[He was appointed cadet in 1771 and Lieutenant-Colonel in 1800. He was invalided in 1803.]

(Reference: *D. and M.*)

714—**1822**—CAMPBELL, D., Ensign. *Inscription* :—Sacred to the memory of Ensign Dave Campbell of the 19th Regiment, Native Infantry, who died at Chunar on the 28th of November 1822, in the 19th year of his age: erected by the officers of his corps, the old XIX Volunteers, in testimony of their extreme regret

[I cannot trace "Dave" Campbell. There was a Daniel Campbell who was appointed in 1820. Dave may be an error for Danl.]

(Reference: *D. and M.*)

715.—**1824**—BATEMAN, M.A., Mrs. *Inscription* :—To the memory of Mrs. Mary Ann Bateman, wife of William Bateman, H. M. 87th Regiment. She departed this life on the 7th January 1824, aged 23 years.

716.—**1824**—(1) MOTHERALL, R. (2) MOTHERALL, W. *Inscription* :—Sacred to the memory of Robert Motherall, Esq., Deputy Commissary of Ordnance, who departed this life on the 7th October 1324, aged 41 years 11 months and 7 days. Sacred also to the memory of William, the infant son of R. Motherall, Esq.

717.—**1824**—GORE, G. W. M., Lieutenant. *Inscription* :—Sacred to the memory of Geo. William Mollencana Gore, Lieutenant of the 52 Regiment, B. N. I., who departed this life on the 26th of October 1824, aged 22 years 11 months and 26 days.

[G. W. Molyneux Gore (Mollencana is of course an error) was the son of Major W. Gore, 33rd Regiment, born at Brislington, Somerset, in 1801. He joined the service in 1819.]
(References: *C. P.*; *D. and M.*)

718.—**1825**—LAWRENCE, J. *Inscription:*—Sacred to the memory of Mr. John Lawrence, Assistant Commissary of Ordnance, who departed this life on the 10th February A. D., 1828, aged 52 years. This tomb is erected by his afflicted widow. (B. O.)

719.—**1831**—BALL, J. *Inscription:*—Sacred to the memory of Mr. James Ball, trader, late of Ghazipur, who departed this life in the garrison on the 21st of May 1831, aged 38 years.

720.—**1834**—TAYLOR, D. W. *Inscription:*—Sacred to the memory of Daniel William Taylor, late Assistant Apothecary, H. C. Service, who departed this life on 30th August 1834, aged 29 years and 22 days.

That blameless virtue, which adorned thy bloom,
Lamenting Sarah, now weeps o'er thy tomb,
What neither wealth could buy, nor power decree,
Regard and pity waits sincere on thee,
While soft remembrance drops a willing tear.
And thy dear Sarah sits chief mourner here.

This tomb was erected by his truly affectionate widow, Sarah Taylor.

721.—**1838**—LAW, G. U., Ensign. *Inscription:*—This tomb has been erected by the officers of the 50th Regiment, Native Infantry, to the memory of the late Ensign George Udny Law of the same corps as a mark of their regard and esteem for the deceased brother officer who departed this life at Chunar on the 10th of August 1838, aged 23 years and 23 days.

[His cadet papers do not give the name of his father, as he was nominated in India. It is stated that he was living in Calcutta with W. Palmer, B.C.S.]
(Reference: *C.P.*)

722.—**1839**—SHINKS, H. *Inscription:*—Sacred to the memory of Henry Shinks, Apothecary, General Hospital, Chunar, born 25th July 1809, died 10th July 1839.

Thy wife, dear Henry, o'er thy mouldering earth,
Erects this tribute to departed worth.
Thy faith and virtue, gifts of Grace Divine,
Mark'd thee for bliss, then why should I repine?
But yet, thy love, to my remembrance dear,
Exacts the rising sigh, the gushing tear.
O may thy wife and babes, life's wandering o'er,
Meet thy loved shade in heaven to part no more. (B. O.)

Chunar (Sultanpur).

OLD CEMETERY.

723.—**1816**—(1) KEMPLAND, L. G. **1817**—(2) A CHILD. *Inscription:*—Sacred to the memory of a beloved child, Lucius George, son of Lieutenant G. A. Kempland, 8th Native Cavalry, who departed this life on the 27th of August 1816, aged 15 months and 10 days; also of a second beloved child, who departed this life on the 27th of April 1817, aged 11 months.

[G. A. Kempland, son of A. Kempland, joined the service in 1806 and retired in 1836 as a Major. He served in Java. His son, G. Kempland, was killed at Cawnpore in 1857.]

(References: *D. and M.; Services B. A. List.*)

724.—**1823**—GALL, W. H. *Inscription:*—To the memory of Walter Herbert, sixth son of Major G. H. Gall, 8th Light Cavalry, who departed this life 5th of October 1823, aged 20 months and 9 days.

Ere sin could blight or sorrow fade,
Death came with friendly care;
The opening bud to heaven conveyed,
And bade it blossom there.

[George Herbert Gall, born at Farrukhabad in 1779, joined the service in 1795. In 1799 he went from Fatehgarh to Jaipur with Colonel Collins to obtain Wazir Ali's surrender (cf. no. 593). He saw active service at the captures of Bijaigarh and Kachaura under Lord Lake (1803.) He also fought in Java. He commanded the Viceroy's Body Guard for sometime, and died in 1826 as a Lieutenant-Colonel, cf. no. 542.]

(Refereuces: *E. I. M. Calendar; D. and M.; Services B. A. List.*)

725.—**1825**—O'BRIEN, L. R., Lieutenant-Colonel. *Inscription:*—Lieutenant-Colonel Lucius R. O'Brien, C.B., Colonel Commandant, 8th Regiment, Bengal Light Cavalry, *obiit* July 10th, 1825, aged 51 years.

[Lucius Robert O'Brien, son of Sir L. O'Brien, Bart., was born in 1775. He joined the service in 1795 and seems to have spent most of his early service in raising and drilling new regiments. He was on furlough when Lake's campaigns began. Being ordered out, he found himself in a naval engagement off Mauritius, between Sir T. Trowbridge and Admiral Linois. He served in Java, and the Nepalese and Pindari wars. He was made a C. B. in 1823. He died at Benares.]

(References: *E. I. M. Calendar; D. and M.; C. P.*)

726.—**1830**—WHALLEY, F. E., Cornet. *Inscription:*—Sacred to the memory of Cornet Frederic Elidor Whalley, 6th Regiment, Light Cavalry, who died on the 11th of October 1830, aged 19 years.

[The son of C. Whalley, attorney, born at Calcutta in 1810, joined the service in 1828.]

(References: *C. P.; D and M.*)

727.—**1830**—THOMSON, M. G., Miss. *Inscription:*—Sacred to the memory of Mary Glen Thomson, eldest daughter of Colonel Harry Thomson, died 11th September 1830, aged 17 years and 3 months.

728.—**1832**—KEY, A. M., Captain. *Inscription:*—Sacred to the memory of Captain Alexander Maxwell Key, late of the 9th Regiment Light Cavalry, who departed this life on the 4th December 1832. This tomb is erected by his brother officers as a mark of their respect and esteem.

[A. M. Key, son of A. Key, merchant, was born in London, and joined the service in 1822. He served at Bhurtpore in 1825.]

(References: *Services B. A. List; D. and M.*)

729.—**1833**—STUART, E., Lieutenant. *Inscription:*—Sacred to the memory of Edmund Stuart, Lieutenant, His Majesty's 44th Regiment, who died near this spot, July 4th, 1833, in the 24th year of his age. This tomb is raised by his brother, Robert Stuart Lieuteuant, His Majesty's 44th Regiment, February 1838.

730.—**1836**—SPILLER, F. J., Major. *Inscription:*—To the memory of Francis John Spiller, Major, 8th Light Cavalry, *obiit* 5th October 1836, *ætat* 54 years. This monument is erected to his memory by the officers of the corps.

[The son of G. Spiller, Commissary-General, H. M's. Land Forces, born in 1785, he was first an ensign in the York Fusiliers, and joined the service in 1805. He fought in Nepal and at Bhurtpore.]

(References: *D. and M.; C. P.*)

731.—**1841**—KNOX, R. T., Captain. *Inscription:*—Sacred to the memory of Robert Trotter Knox, Lieutenant and Brevet Captain, 6th Regiment, Light Cavalry, who departed this life on the 20th November 1841, aged 33 years.

[The son of Major Knox, R. A., born in 1807, he joined the service in 1826.]

(References: *C. P.; D. and M.*)

CHUNAR, LOWER LINES, NEW CEMETERY.

732.—**1829**—MAXWELL, H., Major. *Inscription:*—Sacred to the memory of Major Hamilton Maxwell who died 17th June 1829, aged 42 years.

[H. Maxwell, 41st N.I., son of Captain W. H. Maxwell, 3rd Guards, was born in Canada in 1787, joined the service in 1805 and was invalided in January 1829, two years after attaining his majority.]

(References: *Services B. A. List; D. and M.*)

733.—**1833**—AURIOL, J., Lieutenant-Colonel. *Inscription:*—Sacred to the memory of Lieutenant-Colonel James Auriol, Commanding the European Invalids and Garrison of Chunar, died 13th September 1833. (B. O.).

[Son of J. P. Auriol, born in 1785 in London, he joined the service in 1800 and spent most of his service with the Bengal European Regiment. He was invalided in 1828.]

(References: *D. and M.; C. P.*)

734.—**1849**—LLOYD, C. H., Lieutenant-Colonel. *Inscription:*—To the memory of Charles Heath Lloyd, Lieutenant-Colonel, Commandant of the Garrison, Chunar, who died on the 20th August 1849, aged 65 years.

[The son of the Revd. W. Lloyd, of Frogmore, Hertford, born in 1785, he joined the service in 1803 and was invalided in 1827.]

(References: *D. and M.; C. P.*)

735.—**1855**—RICHARD, R., Revd. *Inscription:*—Sacred to the memory of the Revd. Robert Richard, an old servant of the Church Missionary Society, who departed this life on the 17th February 1855, aged 66 years.

736.—**1856**—RAVENSCROFT, E. W., Lieutenant. *Inscription:*—Sacred to the memory of Lieutenant E. W. Ravenscroft of the 72nd Bengal Native Infantry, who departed this life on the 22nd December 1856, aged 48 years. This tablet is raised by his affectionate widow.

Many are the afflictions of the righteous, but the Lord delivereth him out of all.

[Edward William, son of W. Ravenscroft, born in 1809, joined the service in 1827 and was invalided in 1835.]

(References: *C. P.; D. and M.*)

CHUNAR, NEW CEMETERY, NORTH OF R. C. CHURCH.

737.—**1816**—WILLIAMS, J., Major-General. *Inscription:*—Sacred to the memory of Major-General J. Williams who departed this life, July 31st A.D., 1816, aged 62.

[John Williams joined the service in 1780, and became Colonel in 1812. He was invalided in 1813.]

(Reference: *D. and M.*)

738.—**1820**—FRIEND, C., Revd. *Inscription :*—Sacred to the memory of the Revd. Charles Friend who died June 12th, 1820. He was both an indefatigable minister and a genuine missionary of the Church of England.

739.—**1825**—WILLIAMS, J. D., Sergeant. *Inscription :*—Sacred to the memory of James David Williams, late Pension Sergeant, who departed this life the 5th June 1825, aged 101 years and one day.

"Life is the time to serve the Lord,
The time to win the great reward;
And while the lamp holds out to burn
The last sinner may return.
There are no acts of pardon grant (?)
In the cold grave to which he haste;
But darkness, death and long despair
Reign in eternal silence there."

[The first of three centenarians buried in this cemetery, and a contemporary of all four Georges.]

740. **1829**—MALTBY, B., Captain. *Inscription :*—Sacred to the memory of Captain B. Maltby, Bengal Army, who died on the 2nd November 1829, aged 37 years (B. O.)

[Brough Maltby joined the service in 1807, became captain in 1825 and was invalided the same year.]

(Reference : *D. and M.*)

741.—**1831**—DALLAS, P., Mrs. *Inscription :*—Sacred to the memory of Penelope, wife of Captain C. Dallas Aortu *(sic)* died 17th August 1831, aged 26 years.

742.—**1833**—ETESON, S. M., Mrs. *Inscription :*—Here lieth the remains of Sarah Martha, wife of Ralph Eteson, minister of the place. She died on the 16th October 1833 in the 30th year of her age.

"Hic labor illic omnes" (?)

743.—**1836**—MENZIE, R., Captain. *Inscription :*—Sacred to the memory of Captain R. Menzie of the Invalid establishment, died 22nd August 1836.

[Robert, son of Captain J. Menzies (so cadet papers) was born in 1805 at Fort ngale, N. B. He joined the service in 1821 and was invalided in 1834.]

(References : *D. and M. ; C. P.*)

744.—**1836**—FAITHFUL, W. R. L., Captain. *Inscription :*—Sacred to the memory of Captain W. R. L. Faithful, of the Bengal Army, who died on the 78th November 1836. (B. O.)

[William Richard Lee, son of Revd. J. Faithful, was born in 1792 at Warfield, Berks. He joined the service in 1809 and was invalided in 1830.]

(References : *C. P. ; D. and M.*)

745.—**1839**—WALKER, W. B., Lieutenant-Colonel. *Inscription :*—Sacred to the memory of L.-Col. William Bensley Walker, Commanding the European Invalids, who died 19th September 2839, aged 58 years and 9 months. (B. O.)

[W. B. Walker, born at Patna in 1781, joined the service in 1797, became Lieutenant-Colonel in 1823 and was invalided in 1825.]

(References : *C. P. ; D. and M.*)

746.—**1841**—WILLIAMS, R. *Inscription :*—Sacred to the memory of Roza Williams, who departed this life on the 21st of May 1841, aged about 90 years. She was a consistent Christian and died in the happy prospect of being with the Lord. A short time before her death when in good health she made over to the mission for the propagation of the gospel the sum of Rs. 2,100. Thus in life and death she showed her choice of the one thing needful.

747.—**1843**—BOWLEY, W., Reverend. *Inscription* :—Sacred to the memory of the Reverend William Bowley, who departed this life 10th October 1843, aged 58 years. He was for 30 years an active, zealous and successful missionary of the Church Mission Society, by whom his loss is deeply lamented.

They that be wise shall shine as the brightness of the firmament: and they that turn many to righteousness as the stars for ever and ever (B. O.)

[This is probably the missionary mentioned by Bishop Heber as having worked several years at Chunar in 1824, where he made many converts. A most interesting detail mentioned by the Bishop is that Mr. Bowley had first received Lutheran ordination in this country, in which he was born. Desiring however to obtain a more apostolic commission, he was re-ordained by Bishop Heber, who ordained him priest as well as deacon at once, with only a month's interval between ceremonies, a fact which he reported to the Archbishop of Canterbury. He was resident for many years at Chunar and collected the funds to build the Church.]

(Reference: *Heber*).

748.—**1843**—POOLE, C., Colonel. *Inscription* :—In the memory of Col. Charles Poole, of the Invalid Establishment, Commanding the Garrison, who died 14th Nov. 1843. This monument is erected as a tribute of affection and regret for the best and kindest of brothers by his two surviving sisters, M. J. and L. Poole (B. O.)

[C. Poole, son of the Revd. H. Poole, rector of Whitchurch, Middlesex, was born in 1777. He joined the service in 1797, became Lieutenant-Colonel in 1823 and was invalided in 1828.]

(References: *C. P.*; *D. and M.*)

749.—**1855**—BAIRD, T. C. E. *Inscription* :—I. M. Thomas Baird, C.E., East Indian Railway Company, who died December 15th, 1855, aged 23 years. This monument was erected by his brother Engineers.

750.—**1869**—MINGLE, C., Mrs. *Inscription* :—Sacred to the memory of Mrs. Catharine Mingle, b. 16th March 1760, died 22nd November 1869. May she rest in peace.

751.—**1885**—McDONALD, M. Mrs. *Inscription* :—Sacred to the memory of Mrs. Mary McDonald, d. 12th May 1885, aged 110 years.

HOLY TRINITY CHURCH, CHUNAR.

752.—**1843**—BOWLY, W., Reverend. *Inscription* :—Sacred to the memory of the Reverend William Bowley, who died October 10th, 1843, aged 58 years. He was for thirty years an active, zealous, and successful missionary of the Church Missionary Society. To the erring Natives of India he was the unwearied evangelist, ever proclaiming: "Behold the Lamb of God!" To the converts (and God gave him many), and every Christian within the sphere of his ministrations, he was the faithful and tender shepherd, feeding them with food "convenient for them."

They that be wise shall shine as the brightness of the firmament; and they that turn many to righteousness as the stars for ever and ever.

Daniel, XII, 3.

[*cf.* no. 747.]

753.—**1850**—STEWART, W. M., Major. *Inscription* :—Sacred to the memory of William Murray Stewart, Major in the 22nd Regiment of Native Infantry, Agent to the Governor General, &c. formerly for nearly twenty years resident in this station. In commemoration not of his virtues and good deeds, for those do follow him and will outlast this cenotaph, but of the respect and gratitude they inspired, this tablet is erected by a few of the inhabitants of Chunar, and the soldiers of the Invalid Battalion, MDCCCLIV.

[William Murray Stewart (1804—1850) was second son of William Stewart of Ardvorlich, co. Perth. He married Charlotte, daughter of John Athanas, a Calcutta merchant and had seven sons and a daughter. Of the sons six served in India. The eldest, William, was killed at Gwalior in the Indian Mutiny: he was in the Bengal Artillery. The second, Robert, was Commissioner of Assam: the third, Colonel John Stewart, C.I.E., is the present head of the family; the fourth and sixth were in the Indian Army, and the youngest in the Bombay Civil Service. No less than four of his grandsons were also in the Indian Army; whilst his daughter and five grand-daughters are married to Anglo-Indians.

The family dates back to the Stewart Dukes of Albany, and therefore to Robert II of Scotland; in other words they are of the blood of the royal Stewarts.]

(Reference : *Burke, L. G.*)

CHUNAR, OLD TAHSIL (NOW A GODOWN).

754.—**1789**—FRAZER, W., Sergeant. *Inscription* :—In memory of Sergeant William Frazer, Steward to General Hope, who died 10th August 1789.

755.—**1793**—STONEY, A. *Inscription* :—Here lies the body of Ann Stoney who deceased 16th December 1793, aged 7 months.

756.—**1799**—STONEY, J. *Inscription* :—In memory of Mr. James Stoney, late Sergeant of Artillery, apothecary to the Chunar General Hospital, deceased the 5th August 1799, aged 39 years. In his situation as a soldier he was an ornament to the profession. His liberal, tender, and humane treatment to the sick while he held the situation both as Steward and apothecary at the Station Hospital will ever cause his memory to be honoured and his loss sincerely regretted.

757.—**1860**—BLAKE, G., Lieutenant-Colonel. *Inscription* :—In memory of Lieutenant-Colonel Geo. Blake, of the European Invalid Battalion, Commanding at Chunar, who died near Ghazipur on his way to Darjeeling, on the 6th day of November 1860, after a lingering illness borne with Christian meekness and resignation, aged 67 years 10 months and 6 days. This tablet is erected as a last token of affection and regard by his disconsolate relatives and friends.

[The son of W. Blake, born in 1791, he joined the service in 1809, became Lieutenant-Colonel in 1844 and was invalided in 1847. He served in Nepal and at Bhurtpore: he was in the artillery.]

(References : *Stubbs ; B A. List ; C. P.*)

HALIA, PARGANA KANTIT.

758.—**1811**—MEN killed at Bhopari. *Inscription* :—Under the auspices of Lord Minto, Governor General of India, and General Hewett, Comdr.-in-Chief and Vice-President, a passage was made through the Kirahe Pass of vast height, two miles in extent, into Burdee for 18-pounders, &c. by Lt.-Col. J. Tetley, Comdg. the

2nd Battln., 21st Regt. Native Infantry, aided by the great exertions of his gallant and willing corps, the following of whom fell courageously assaulting Boparrah Ghurry in Burdee, April A. D. 1811, which is now destroyed and levelled with the ground. Golaub Sing, Naick, Sepoys Cassie Deen, Pheroo Singh, Jysook Deenah, Boodie, Incha, Byjenant, Goorange Singh, Phoorun Bahader Cauri; Golundauze Punchoo, Gun Laskar, Soane Head Bullockman. Tilleock Singh, Sepoy of the same corps, killed at Bissore Gaut.

Feby. 14th 1811 Jem 2 Havel IIIII 2 Naik IIIIII 30 sepoys defending the post against 300 bandits beating them off.

[This tomb stands opposite the police station at Halia. It commemorates a little expedition undertaken at the intance of one Lalla Naik, a Mirzapur merchant, to punish the Rewah highwaymen who plundered the convoys of merchandise. These men fell in attacking the fort of Bhopari on the 18th April 1811. The inscription is roughly cut on a large flat slab about 7 feet 8 high by 4 feet broad. The last sentence is distinctly curious in its lettering, matter and manner.]

(References: *Gazetteer; Führer.*)

M. GOPIGANJ, PARGANA BHADOHI.

759.—**1857**—JONES, E. S. *Inscription:*—In memory of Edmund Short Jones, killed at Pallee, July 4th 1857, aged 27 years.

[For this murder cf. no. 620. These two tombs stand in a small enclosure near the junction of the Gopiganj-Mirzapur and Grand Trunk Roads.]

760.—**1857**—KEMP, C. M. *Inscription:*—In memory of Clinton Melville Kemp, killed at Pallee, July 4th 1857, aged 15 years.

[cf. no. 602.]

UJH, PARGANA BHADOHI.

761.—**1828**—ANDREWS, C. *Inscription:*—To the memory of Charlotte, daughter of Captain Chas. Andrews. She departed this life the 6th November 1828, aged 13 months and 20 days.

[Close to mile 467 of Grand Trunk Road, not far from the thana.]

M. BIKHNA.

762.—**1809**—ELLIOT, E., Mrs. *Inscription:*—In memory of Mrs. Elizabeth Elliot, wife of Sergeant-Major Thos. Elliot, 1st Battalion, 1st Regiment, Native Infantry, who died on the 17th day of March 1809, in the 37th year of her age. The unaffected simplicity of her heart joined to a life of virtue must ever make her husband and her children feel and friends lament her loss.

[This and the next tomb are in a masonry enclosure south of the Tanda Road].

763.—**1813**—TURNER, W. D., Captain. *Inscription:*—Sacred to the memory of William D. Turner, late a Captain-Lieutenant in the 1st Battalion, 15th Regiment, Native Infantry, who departed this life on the 24th June A.D. 1813. This monument was erected by his brother-officers, in token of the high respect they entertained for his conduct as a soldier, and affection as a friend.

[William Donaldson Turner joined the service in 1802 and became brevet captain in 1812.]

(Reference: *D. and M.*)

MIRZAPUR, GARDEN OF GURGURI KOTHI.

764.—**1805**—MOWVIOBU, J. E. V. *Inscription:*—Ci gît Joseph Vandeoil Mowviobu, né à Rennes le 15th Aout 1749, mort le 10th November 1805.

[The sculptor has certainly succeeded in disguising the correct name. It is dubious whether such a conglomeration of letters would be possible or pronounceable in French.]

MAUZA TILIYANI, THANA BINDHACHAL.

765.—**1833**—DODD, E. Mrs. *Inscription :*—Sacred to the memory of Eliza Dodd, who departed this life on the 2nd November 1833. This monument was erected by the affection of a disconsolato husband.

Jaunpur District.

KAKURGAHNA CEMETERY, JAUNPUR.

766.—**1796**—COOK, V. *Inscription :*—To the memory of Valentine Cook, Esq., who departed this life the 20th of April 1796, aged 32 years.

767.—**1803**—WATT, J. *Inscription :*—Sacred to the memory of James Watt, born in London the 8th October 1768, died at Baksha on the 18th day of August 1803.

768.—**1811**—LOWTHER, C. O. *Inscription :*—Sacred to the memory of Catherine Olivia Lowther, who departed this life the 6th of August 1811, aged 9 months and 29 days, youngest daughter of William Lowther, Esq., of Jaunpur.

The parent's heart that nestled fond in thee,
That heart now sunk a prey to grief and care,
So deck'd the woodbine sweet yon aged tree;
So from it ravish'd leaves it bleak and bare. (B. O.)

[Cf. no. 597. W. Lowther was Assistant Magistrate at Jaunpur in 1811.]

769.—**1812—3**—WYNNE, infant sons. *Inscription :*—To the memory of the infant son of Richard Owen and Sarah Wynne, died September 28th 1812. Infant son of Richard Owen and Sarah Wynne, born the 24th August 1813, died the 6th October 1813. (B. O.)

["Richard Owen Wynne, 3rd son of William Wynne of Wern, married Sarah Pearce by whom he had an only daughter who died young. He died 1821." So Burke. The infants here mentioned are children of this Richard Owen Wynne, who was Magistrate of Jaunpur 1809-16. He died at Dacca in 1821.

It is an instance of the curious connection of extremely ancient British families with out-of-the-way places in India. The family dates back to Osborn the Wyddel (or Irishman) a Fitzgerald of the great sept of the Irish Geraldines, who came to Wales and obtained "by grant or marriage or both" large possessions in Merioneth, about 1293. The family then descends through a long series of Welsh chieftains from Cymric ap Osborn, Osborn's son, to Robert Wynne ap John, died 1589. His grandson (died 1658) was the first to droop the "ap". Apparently, R. O. Wynne was the only one that ever came to India.]

(Reference: *Prinsep C.L.; Burke, L. G.*)

770.—**1814**—HAMILTON, J., Lieutenant. *Inscription :*—Sacred to the memory of Lieutenant James Hamilton, 2nd Battalion, 12th Native Infantry Regiment, native of Galway in Ireland, who died near this place on the 9th November 1814 A.D., *æt* 33. The officers of his Battalion, deeply lamenting the untimely fall of their friend, have erected this monument in testimony of their respect for his professional character and love for his private virtues. (B. O.)

[J. Hamilton, of Heathlawn, was born at Killimor, co. Galway in 1783. He joined the service in 1804.]

(References : *C. P.; D. and M.*)

771.—1890—DAVIES, R.G. *Inscription* :—Sacred to the memory of Robert Glass, son of Robert and Sarah Davies, died on the 2nd July 1819, aged 7 years 11 months and 10 days.

[A merchant at Jaunpur.]

(Reference : *E. I. R.*)

772.—1824—INGLE, H., Lieutenant. *Inscription* :—Sacred to the memory of Henry Ingle, late Lieutenant, 31st Regiment, N. I., who departed this life 15th September 1824, aged 32 years.

Grant, Lord, when he from death shall wake,
He may of endless joys partake.

This monument is erected by his disconsolate widow, Helen Ingle. (B. O.)

[This tomb has disappeared. He was the son of the Revd. S. Ingle, born in 1793 at Bury St. Edmund's. He joined the service in 1809.]

(References : *C. P.; D. and M.*)

773.—1825—CUPOLA, L. *Inscription* :—To the memory of Lewis Cupola, who departed this life the 28th April 1825, aged 28 years and four months.

This monument a hapless widow rears
To prove her love, and to record her tears.
'Tis hers on lasting marble to attest
How good her husband was, herself how blest.
Yet for these virtues mercy will be shown,
What caused her happiness, will cause his own.

Erected by his disconsolate widow, Catherine Cupola. (B. O.)

[This tomb has disappeared.]

774.—1826—SHOWERS, H., Mrs. *Inscription* :—Sacred to the memory of Harriet Showers, wife of Major H. D. Showers of the Hon'ble Company's Service, who departed this life on the 17th October in the year of our Lord one thousand eight hundred twenty-six, aged 37 years. (B. O.)

[Howe Daniel Showers, son of J. H. Showers, born at Fatehgarh in 1786, joined the service in 1801, became a major in 1825, and died in London in 1829.]

(References : *C. P.; D. and M.*)

775.—1828—NORTHAM, S. *Inscription* :—Sacred to the memory of Samuel Northam, who departed this life on the 2nd June 1828, aged 33 years and 7 months, leaving a wife and three helpless children to bemoan his loss.

"The Lord gave and the Lord hath taken away. Blessed be his name."

CEMETERY NEAR POLICE LINES.

776.—1829—SMITH, E., Mrs. *Inscription* :—Sacred to the memory of Elizabeth Smith, widow of the late Fife-Major James Smith. 16th Regiment, Native Infantry, who departed this life on the 22nd February 1829, aged 14 years 9 months and 21 days. This tomb is erected in memory of esteem by her affectionate father.

777.—1832—CRACKLOW, G., Captain. *Inscription* :—This monument was erected by the officers of the 6th Regiment, Native Infantry, to the memory of their brother-officer Captain George Cracklow, who departed this life 5th October 1832. (B. O.)

[Son of H. Cracklow, born in 1789, joined the service in 1811.]

(Reference : *C. P.; D. and M.*)

778.—**1834**—TURNBULL, I. J., Mrs. *Inscription :*—Sacred to the memory of Isabella Jane, the beloved wife of Gavin Turnbull, Esq, Civil Surgeon, died 11th September 1834, aged 32 years. (B. O.)

[G. Turnbull was the son of A. Turnbull, of Hassendean, born 1800, joined the service in 1821.]

(Reference : *S. P.*)

779.—**1835**—BURNEY, G. J. D. *Inscription :*—Sacred to the memory of George John Doveton, beloved son of Captain George Burney, born at Barrackpore, 13th April 1833, died at Jaunpur 11th May 1835 (B. O.)

[G. Burney was son of Revd. R. C. Burney, born at Calcutta in 1803. He died at Burdwan in 1833.]

(References : *C. P.; D. and M.*)

780.—**1840**—THREIPLAND, M. A., Mrs. *Inscription :*—Sacred to the memory of Mary Anne, beloved wife of Thomas Threipland, Esq., Deputy Collector of Jaunpur, who departed this life on the 4th August 1840, aged 29 years 9 months. Also of Maria, their only daughter, who died on the 7th *idem*, six days old. (B. O.)

781.—**1844**—BARWISE, J. S. *Inscription :*—Sacred to the memory of James South Barwise, Esq., late of Faridabad in the zillah of Jaunpur, *obiit* December 15th, 1844, *ætat* 54 years. (B. O.)

[Mr. J. S. Barwise was born in the Isle of Thanet, Kent, and became an indigo planter. He was bred to a maritime life but settled in 1827 at Faridabad and obtained a considerable property in land and factories. Owing to the enmity caused by a long course of successful litigation with a zamindar called Mahesh Narayan Singh for the possession of an ancestral estate of the latter's he was murdered at night in his house at Faridabad; Mahesh Narayan was generally supposed to have instigated the crime and was tried for it but acquitted. He founded a school at Faridabad in connection with the C. M. S.]

(Reference : *B. O.*)

782.—**1850**—TAYLOR, R. *Inscription :*—Sacred to the memory of Robert Taylor, Esq., who departed this life on the 3rd May 1850, aged 37 years.

Spes mea Christus.

783.—**1858**—HAVELOCK, C. W., Lieutenant. *Inscription :*—Sacred to the memory of Charles Wemys Havelock, Lieutenant, 66th Goorkhas, and Second in Command, 12th Irregular Cavalry, the beloved and only son of Lieutenant-Colonel Charles Frederick Havelock, H.M.'s Service, and of Mary, his wife, aged 24 years. He was killed in action at Tighra with Sir E. Lugard's force, whilst gallantly leading his men of the 12th Irregular Cavalry in a charge against the rebels. Born February 16th, 1834, died 11th April 1858.

[This young officer, nephew of Sir Henry Havelock, did good service in Benares, Jaunpur and Mirzapur against the rebels: he then became first Extra Aide-de-camp to Sir Colin Campbell, and then orderly officer to Hope Grant and distinguished himself in the capture of Lucknow. He was then attached to Sir E. Lugard's column and perished in a small affair against Ghulam Husain and Mehdi Hasan in Jaunpur. For the Havelocks *vide* no. 918].

(References, *Forest ; M. N ; Rice Holmes*).

JAUNPUR FREE SCHOOL.

784.—**1807**—HOWE, L., Miss. *Inscription :*—Sacred to the memory of Lucy Howe, who departed this transitory life on Friday, the 13th of November in the year of our Lord MDCCCVII, in the 28th year of her age (B.O.)

BHATURALI INDIGO FACTORY.

785.—**1809**—MURRAY, infant. *Inscription :*—The infant son of Mr. and Mrs. Murray, who departed this life on the 18th June 1809, aged nine months and 22 days. (B.O.)

Jacob Murray was an indigo planter.]
(Reference : *E.I.R.*)

786.—**1825**—MATTHEWS, infant. *Inscription :*—Sacred to the memory of the infant daughter of William Matthews, Esq., who departed this life on the 28th January 1825, aged six months and five days. (*B. O.*)

(This factory is seven miles north of Jaunpur. W. Mathew (so E. I. Register) was an indigo planter].
(Reference : *E.I.R.*)

KALINJRA INDIGO FACTORY.

787.—**1811**—MAGUIRE, T. *Inscription :*—Sacred to the memory of Terence Maguire, who departed this life on the 5th day of June in the year of our Lord one thousand eight hundred and eleven, aged 30 years. (*B. O.*)

[T. Maguire was an indigo manufacturer at Benares.]
(Reference : *E.I.R.*)

788.—**1827**—FERRIER, J. *Inscription :*— Sacred to the memory of James Ferrier, Esquire, who died on the 19th June 1827, aged 40 years, deeply lamented by his surviving brothers, who have erected this tomb.

What I say unto you, I say unto all, watch.—*St. Mark, XIII, 37,* (B.O.)—
[This factory is 10 miles from Jaunpur. The B.O. states that this inscription is also to be found in Ghazipur. J. Ferrier, with David Ferrier, were indigo planters.]
(Reference : *E.I.R.*)

Ghazipur District.

CANTONMENTS.

789.—**1805**—CORNWALLIS, C., Marquess. *Inscription :*—Sacred to the memory of Charles, Marquess Cornwallis, Knight of the Most Noble Order of the Garter, General in His Majesty's Army, Governor General and Commander-in-Chief in India, &c., &c.

His first administration, commencing in September 1786, and terminating in October 1793, was not less distinguished by the successful operations of war, and by the forbearance and moderation with which he dictated the terms of peace, than by the just and liberal principles which marked his internal Government. He regulated the remuneration of the servants of the State on a scale calculated to ensure the purity of their conduct. He laid the foundation of a system of revenue which, while it limited and defined the claims of Government, was intended to confirm hereditary rights to the proprietors, and to give security to the cultivators of the soil. He framed a system of judicature which restrained within strict bounds the power of public functionaries, and extended to the population of India the effective protection of laws adapted to usages and promulgated in their own languages. Invited in December 1804 to resume the same important station, he did not hesitate, though in advanced age, to obey the call of his country. During the short term of his last administration he was occupied in forming a plan for the pacification of India which, having the sanction of his high authority, was carried into effect by his successor. He died near this spot, where his remains are deposited, on the 5th day of October 1805, in the 67th year of his age. This monument, erected by the British inhabitants of Calcutta, attests their sense of those virtues which will live in the remembrance of grateful millions long after it shall have mouldered in the dust.

[Charles, 1st Marquess and 2nd Earl Cornwallis, Viscount Browne (1738—1805) was son of the fifth Baron and 1st Earl Cornwallis, Chief Justice of Eyre south of Trent, and Constable of the Tower. He was educated at Eton and at the Military Academy of Turin. He entered the army and served at Minden, Labina, and other minor actions. In 1760 he was member for Eye, but in 1762 succeeded to the Earldom. In 1768 he married Jemima, daughter of Colonel Jones of the Foot Guards. In 1776, he commanded a division in the American War of Independence though, politically, he had opposed the war and the actions that led to it. He won the battles of Rugeley Mills and Guildford, but was compelled to surrender at York Yown. In 1784 and 1785 he was twice offered and twice declined the Governor Generalship; but against his own desires accepted it in 1786. He reformed both the civil and military services. In 1790 he took command (as Commander-in-Chief) of the Army against Tipu, captured Bangalore (1791), defeated Tipu at Seringapatam and took Nandidrug, Savandrug and besieged Seringapatam in 1792, when Tipu submitted, and ceded territory and paid a large indemnity. For those services he was made a Marquess. He carried out the permanent settlement of Bengal in 1793 against the advice of Sir John Shore. He forbade trading by civil servants and restricted the practice of commission. He also defined a collector's powers, which are very much those of a modern collector as regards revenue, court of wards, *khas* (or Government) estates, partition and excise. He also reformed the judiciary and magistracy: all of these reforms are embodied in the Cornwallis Code. He reduced Pondicherry in 1793 and then returned home. On his return he was sent on a mission to Flanders in connection with the allied armies. In 1795 he became Master of the Ordnance and commander of the troops in Essex and Hertfordshire, then an important post. In 1797 he was selected to go out to India to settle certain grievances of the officers of the Bengal Army, but his services were required in Ireland as Viceroy and Commander-in-Chief, where he crushed the rebellion of 1798, defeated the French under General Humbert, and supported the Act of Union, but resigned in 1801, over the question of Catholic Emancipation. In 1802 he was sent to conclude the peace of Amiens. At the age of 67 he was sent out to India once more as Governor General with the avowed object of replacing Lord Wellesley's expansive policy by a more pacific regime. He at once prepared for a visit to the Upper Provinces, but his duties were now too severe a tax on his age and health and he died at Ghazipur.

Cornwallis's character has not always been fairly drawn. "The highest order of commonplace" is perhaps the unkindest form of the general verdict. But he was certainly nothing of the kind. In many points, especially in his transformation of the Company's servants from merchants and clerks to administrators, he was far ahead of his time. He was essentially a "safe" statesman, one on whom a ministry could rely. The purifier and reconstitutor of the civil administration of India, the founder of modern Indian law, the statesman who carried out the Union of Ireland, the diplomat who brought about the Peace of Amiens, has done a good deal to counterbalance the censure which rightly belongs to his reversal of Lord Wellesley's policy. He was not in the same flight as Dalhousie, Wellesley or Warren Hastings: but his place in the list of Governor Generals is high.

His life was one of uninterrupted devotion to duty. He fought in three continents and ruled in two. "*Bonum virum facile crederes: magnum libenter.*" And lastly, he died in harness; *finis vitae ejus nobis luctuosus, amicis tristis, extraneis etiam ignotisque non sine cura fuit*" was an apt Tacitean quotation that appeared in the Gazette of Calcutta at the time of his death.

The family of Cornwallis was of some importance in Ireland before it became famous in England. Thomas Cornwallis was Sheriff of London in 1378,

The first Baron Cornwallis was a loyal supporter of the two Charles' (baron 1661) The fifth baron was Marquess Cornwallis' father. The family is now extinct in the male line. Cornwallis's son died in 1823. At his death the earldom passed to the Bishop of Lichfield and then to his son, and the title became extinct in 1852. On the distaff side however, descendants are to be found in the families of Lord Braybrooke (who is the great-great-great grandson of the Governor General) and Earl St. Germans.

Cornwallis' monument is a domed quasi-Grecian building with a cenotaph by Flaxman. Heber has some hard things to say of it. He says it is an imitation of the Sybil's Temple, of large proportions, and solid masonry, raised on a lofty basement. But its pillars are of "the meanest Doric," "too slender for their height," and he notices various other architectural defects. But at his time and from his description it would appear to have been unfinished. There is a statue by Bacon in the Town Hall, and a full length portrait in the Council Chamber at the India Office. The statue does not appear to be a happy effort, as Cornwallis is in the garb of an ancient Roman, with two female figures of justice and truth, of no particular age or country, and a cornucopia pouring forth all sorts of Indian fruits and vegetables from lichis and custard apples to Indian corn. There is a similar statue over one of the staircases at the India Office.]

[References: *Cornwallis (R. of I.)*; *Buckland*; *Heber.*]

GHAZIPUR CEMETERY (OPEN.)

790.—**1827**—WHARTON, M.E.M.F., Mrs. *Inscription:*—Beneath this column are deposited the mortal remains of Madelina Elizabeth Maria Frances Wharton, eldest daughter of the late J. J. LeMarchand, Esq., of Muddiford House, Christ's Church, in the county of Hants, wife of Thos. Ramsay Wharton, Esq., late of the 8th or K. R. I. Hussars, who departed this life on the 2nd December A. D. 1827, aged 36 years. (B. O.)

791.—**1831**—FRITH, W., Lieutenant-Colonel. *Inscription:*—To the memory of William Frith, Esq., Companion of the Most Honorable Military Order of the Bath, Lieutenant-Colonel, H. M. 38th Regiment, born July 1780, died 27th May 1831. This column has been raised as a tribute of their sincere esteem and respect by the Officers, Non-Commissioned Officers and Privates of the Corps.

[The 38th, now the 1st Battalion, S. Staffordshire Regiment, were in India 1822—36. As a Major, Colonel Frith fought with distinction in the Burmese war.]

(Reference: *Stubbs.*)

792.—**1837**—LATOUCHE, C., B C.S. *Inscription:*—Sacred to the memory of Cornwallis LaTouche, Esq., Bengal Civil Service, who died 17th April 1837, aged 29 years. The tribute of attached friends.

[Cf. no. 541 C. LaTouche was son of Peter LaTouche, and brother of W. LaTouche of Bellevue. He was educated at Haileybury. His service was entirely in the present Benares division: he was transferred to Azamgarh by an order dated three days after he died.]

(References: *Haileybury*; *Burke, L. G. I.*; *Prinsep, C. L.*)

793.—**1849**—SWIFT, M., Mrs. *Inscription:*—Sacred to the memory of Mary, the beloved wife of Dr. Benjamin Swift, H. M., 98th Regiment, who died suddenly of fever on the Ganges off Ghazipur on the 29th May 1849, aged 29 years, after having been rescued on the 9th May 1849, when her only child Benjamin Pratt Swift, aged 5 months, was drowned in consequence of the boat sinking in the Ganges near Fatwa.

"Boast not thy self of to-morrow for thou knowest not what a day may bring forth.—Proverbs, Chapter 27, v-1.

["Nevertheless, not my will, but thine be done."—Luke, Chapter 22, v. 42. The 98th are now the 2nd Battalion, N. Staffordshire Regiment and in India from 1846 to 1855.]

794.—**1857**—LEWIS, E.D.F., Lieutenant. *Inscription* :—"In memory of Edward Dacre Fraser Lewis, Lieutenant of Bengal Native Infantry, Adjutant, 2nd Oudh Infantry, son of the late R. F. Lewis, Esq., of Madras, who died 1st September 1857, from a wound received in action at Azamgarh, 19th July 1857. This tablet was erected by his affectionate widowed mother, and uncle, E. F. Tyler, Esq., late B. C. S."

[The action at Azamgarh on the 19th July is probably some severe street and house fighting carried out by Mr. Venables on the 18th, according to the Mutiny Narrative. E. F. Tyler retired in 1855 and died in 1880.]

(Reference : *M. N.*)

795.—**1857**—POMEROY, R. H., B.C.S. *Inscription* :—Sacred to the memory of Robert Henry Pomeroy, B.C.S., Assistant Magistrate of Ghazipur, late scholar of Trinity College, Cambridge, only son of the late Hon'ble Henry Pomeroy. Born May 18th, 1832, died at Ghazipur, August 1st, 1857. The many fine gifts with which God had graciously endowed him, he early consecrated to the service of their Giver. Prompted by a stern sense of duty he voluntarily assumed office in the hour of the State's most imminent peril. In his short but toilsome term of service, his vital powers were exhausted, and he fell asleep in Jesus, leaving a noble example of Christian self-denial forcibly illustrating his own words "It is of more importance how I live, than how long I live."

[As stated in the inscription, only son of the Hon'ble Henry Pomeroy, fifth son of the 4th Viscount Harberton. Sir George Pomeroy-Colley, killed in South Africa, was his first cousin.]

(Reference : *Burke, P.*)

GHAZIPUR CEMETERY (CLOSED).

796.—**1800**—PIGOTT, T., Lieutenant-Colonel. *Inscription* :—"To the memory of Lieutenant-Colonel T. Pigott, of the 6th Regiment of Native Cavalry, who died at this station on 12th November 1800, aged 46 years. By his affectionate friend Thomas Alcock."

[The correct name is undoubtedly J. P. Pigot : Dodwell and Miles, who mention place and date of death, make this clear. He joined the service in 1778, raised the 6th N. C. and became its Colonel in 1800.]

(References : *D. and M.* ; *Cardew.*)

797.—**1801**—THRESHER, J. *Inscription* :—"John Thresher, overseer in the department of Quarter Master General who died at this station on the 13th January 1801, aged 59 years. Erected by his affectionate daughter Harriet."

798.—**1801**—MERCER, W., Captain. *Inscription* :—"Here lies the remains of Captain William Mercer of the Hon'ble Company's 5th Regiment Native Cavalry, deceased, 5th August 1801, aged 47 years."

[He joined the service in 1781 and became captain in 1800.]

Reference : *D. and M.*)

799.—**1809**—RIDER, J. *Inscription* :—"In memory of John Rider Esquire, who died regretted on the 25th day of August 1809, aged 63 years."

800.—**1810**—ROBERTSON, J., Captain *Inscription* :—"To the memory of Captain James Robertson of Engineers. This monument was erected by his affectionate and grateful wife, Sarah Anne Catherine Robertson, 1906. 4th November 1810, aged 35."

801.—**1815**—GOWANS, J., Mrs. *Inscription* :—"To the memory of Jane Gowans, wife of William Gowans, His Majesty's 17th Regiment, who departed this life in October 1815, aged 45 years. This stone is erected by her disconsolate husband, a mark of sincere esteem."

" Dear husband adue (*sic*)
For you and I must part:
Prepare yourself for death.
For all must feel the smart.
The sting of death is......
To joy that is above.
I recommend my soul to God, and to you I leave my love."

802.—**1816**—BUCHANAN, R., Captain. *Inscription* :—"Sacred to the memory of Captain R. Buchanan, 2nd Battalion, 24th Regiment, Native Infantry, who departed this life on the 10th May 1816, aged 32 years. Erected as a mark of esteem and regard by the officers of his corps."

[Robert Hamilton, son of R. Buchanan, born 1785, joined the service in 1800.]

(References: *Services, B. A. List.; D. and M.*)

803.—**18'8**—ROWTHORN, L. *Inscription* :—" To the memory of Louisa, daughter of Elizabeth Rowthorn (of His Majesty's 17th Foot)* who departed this life 21st May 1818, aged 7 months 7 days and 1 hour.

" Good attendance was applied,
Physicians proved in vain,
For God thought fit to call her hence
And ease her of her pain."

" In the morning it was green and growing up, in the evening it was cut down and withered like a flower."

(* *Sic.*)

CHRIST CHURCH.

804.—**1829**—(1) DE L'ETANG, E., Lieutenant—**1840**—(2) DE L'ETANG, A., Chevalier. *Inscription* :—Lieutenant Eugene de L'Etang, 1st European Regiment, born 5th May 1803, died 15th November 1829.

Chevalier Antoine de L'Etang, Knight of St. Louis, born 20th July 1757, died 1840.

Requiescat in pace.

[These are doubtless father and son. Chevalier A. de L'Etang, K. S. L., was an assistant at the Company's stud at Pusa; Eugene de L'Etang joined the service in 1827 and died at Buxar.]

(References: *D. and M.; E. I. R.*)

805.—**1871**—PRATT, J. H., Ven'ble. *Inscription* :—In affectionate remembrance of the Venerable John Henry Pratt, Archdeacon of Calcutta, who died of cholera at Ghazipur, December 28th, 1871, in his 63rd year, having just entered on his final visitation after a residence in India of 33 years.

A good soldier of Jesus Christ. Be thou faithful unto death and I will give thee a crown of life."

[John Henry Pratt, (1809-1871) was educated at Caius College, Cambridge, where he took his degree (3rd wrangler) in 1833. In 1838 he was appointed a Chaplain on the East India Company's establishment, and became Archdeacon in 1850. A gifted mathematician, it is said that he corrected the trigonometry of the Survey of India in its early stages. He wrote "Mathematical Principles of Mechanical Philosophy," and "Scripture and Science not at variance." He is described as a 'quiet, earnest worker, solitary in his habits, incessant in his labours, a wise counsellor in times of difficulty, and..........an ardent though undemonstrative controversialist."]

(Reference: *Buckland*)

GORAKHPUR DIVISION.

Gorakhpur District.

GORAKHPUR CEMETERY.

806.—**1815**—GRANT, J. W. *Inscription* :—Sacred to the memory of J. W. Grant, Esq., late Collector of Gorakhpur, who departed this life on the 1st November 1815, aged 34 years (B. O.)

[Son of R. Grant of Drominner, born in 1778. He joined the service in 1795 and came out in 1798: he served in Jaunpur, Mirzapur, Benares, Rajshahi, Cawnpore and Gorakhpur, in the last four places as Collector. The age as given in the inscription is three years wrong: it should be 37.]

(References: *Prinsep C. L., D. and M., W.P.*)

807.—**1817**—ROWLAND, A. M., Captain. *Inscription* :—To the memory of Captain A. M. Rowland, 17th N. I., died 9th August 1817, aged 34 years. (B. O.)

[Alexander Mall Rowland, son of J. Rowland, born at Berwick on Tweed in 1774, joined the service in 1797 and became a captain in 1804. 34 in the inscription should be 43—another instance of gross carelessness on the part of the sculptor.]

(References: *D. and M., C.P.*)

808.—**1820**—MONCKTON, P. *Inscription* :—Sacred to the memory of Philip Monckton, Judge and Magistrate of Gorakhpur, died on 6th January, A. D. 1820, aged 33 years. (B. O.)

[Philip Monckton (1787-1820) was 5th son of the Hon'ble Edward Monckton, who was 5th son of the 1st Viscount Galway. He arrived in India in 1803 and served in Aligarh, 24-Parganas, Jessore, Calcutta, Rangpur, Purnea, Rajshahi, Tirhut, Shahabad, Mymensingh, and Gorakhpur. The first Lord Galway (1695-1751) was an M. P. and held a post in Ireland. This, and his creation as a peer of Ireland, presumably accounts for the title, for the family is a Yorkshire one, dating back to the 14th century. Sir Philip Monckton was a devoted adherent of the Stuarts and suffered at the hands of the Parliamentarians in consequence. His son Robert Monckton was an active promoter of the Revolution of 1688; another famous member of the family was Lieutenant-General R. Monckton, Wolfe's second-in-command at Quebec, and an uncle of Philip Monckton. A large number of the members of the family have served in India: a great grandson of Philip Monckton lives at Champaran at the present time. Philip Monckton married Henrietta, daughter of Michael Carter, and had 3 sons and 2 daughters of whom two served in India. He was uncle of Lieutenant J. R. Monckton, cf. No. 385.]

(References: *Burke, P., Prinsep, C. L.*)

809.—**1821**—BIRD, J. G., Mrs. *Inscription* :—Here reposeth all that is perishable of Jane Grant, daughter of the Rev. D. Brown, and wife of Robert M. Bird, Esq., C.S., who fell asleep in Christ on the 6th September 1821. *Nata* 22nd August 1792; *Nupta* 21st September 1810.

[Robert Merttins Bird, C.S., was an officer of considerable note in Gorakhpur, where he was Commissioner of Revenue in 1829. In 1832 he was made member of the new Board of Revenue, North-Western Provinces, and from 1833 to 1841 was in charge of the settlement of the Land Revenue of that Province, a work which "established his reputation for all time as a Revenue officer." He retired in 1842 and gave much time and attention to the C. M. S. His sister Miss Mary Bird was a celebrated missionary lady at Gorakhpur and in Calcutta. The tomb is that of his wife: his son (No. 821) and one of his daughters (No. 818) are also buried in this cemetery.]

(Reference; *Buckland.*)

810.—**1826**—CLARK, A., Miss. *Inscription :*—This table is erected in memory of Agabel Clark, sister to the Civil Surgeon of Gorakhpur, who closed her short and exemplary life in humble dependence on the blood and righteousness of the Redeemer for acceptance before God, July 25th, 1826, aged 19 years 5 months.

In the Lord put I my trust, for we which have believed do enter into rest.
Happy the souls who love the Lord.
And make His grace their only trust. (B. O.)

811.—**1827**—CROMMELIN, C. B. *Inscription :*—Sacred to the memory of Charles Barker Crommelin, born 13th December 1790, died 27th February 1827.

He was a dutiful son, an affectionate husband and brother, a tender parent and a sincere friend; his conduct was marked by integrity, disinterestedness and liberality in all his transactions. He was the benefactor of the poor and the cheerful contributor to every charitable purpose during a residence of fourteen years at Gorakhpur, where his numerous acts of kindness and benevolence ensured to him, while living, the affection of his friends, and to his memory the regret of his survivors. (B. O.)

[There used also to be a replica of this inscriptoin at Lucknow, according to the B. O. I found a C. B. Crommelin mentioned (casually) as a civilian: but could not trace him in any list. In 1825 there was a C. C. M. Crommelin, a merchant, at Gorakhpur, who is probably a relative.]

(Reference: *E. I. R.*)

812.—**1829**—ARMSTRONG, G. C. *Inscription :*—Sacred to the memory of George Clermont, infant son of James Armstrong, C. S., and Susan his wife, who departed this life on the 15th day of November 1829, aged 9 months and 8 days.

Jesus said :—Suffer little children to come unto me and forbid them not, for of such is the Kingdom of Heaven. (B. O.)

[Cf. No. 816.]

813.—**1832**—CURRIE, S., Mrs. *Inscription :*—This table is inscribed in memory of Susannah, eldest daughter of J. P. Larkins, C. S., wife of Fred. Currie, Judge of Gorakhpur, born 10th November 1802, married 7th August 1820, who departed this life on the 14th January 1832. In sure faith in the atonement of Jesus and humble dependence for pardon and acceptance on His merits, resigned her spirit into the hands of God her father.

Them which sleep in Jesus will God bring with him. (B. O.)

[This and tomb No. 818 are those of the 1st and 2nd wives of Sir Frederick Currie. Sir Frederick Currie (1799-1875) had a very distinguished career. Educated at Charterhouse and Haileybury, he reached India in 1820. In 1840 he became Judge of the Sadr Adalat of the North-Western Provinces and, in 1842, Foreign Secretary to the Government of India, in which capacity he attended Lord Hardinge throughout the 1st Sikh War and after Sobraon drew up, with Sir H. Lawrence, the treaty with the Sikhs. He became a Baronet in 1847 and succeeded Sir H. Lawrence as Resident at Lahore the next year, meantime officiating as Member of the Supreme Council. He resumed his seat as Member in 1849, retired in 1853, was made Director of the East Indian Company in 1854 and Chairman in 1857; Member of the Council of India from 1858: D. C. L. Oxford in 1866 and died in 1875.

The Currie family has sent many representatives to India. It is a branch of the old Scotch family of Currie, and can trace its records back to William Currie of Dunse in 1609. Through a succession of Williams and Marks the line passes to Mark Currie (1759) of Hayes in Middlesex, father of Sir Frederick, Edward and Alfred Peter, all H. E. I. C. S. (for A. P. Currie see No. 619). Sir Frederick married—1st in 1820, Susannah eldest daughter of John Pascal

Larkins, H. E. I. C. S. (whose tomb this is), and by her had four sons of whom one was in the C. S. (Charles Currie. died 1878, cf. No. 253). He married 2nd, Lucy Elizabeth, daughter of R. M. Bird, C. S. (in 1834 cf. No. 818) and by her had one son, Robert George (also C. S.) He married 3rd, Katharine Maria, daughter of George Powney Thomson, B. C. S.: by her he had three sons and four daughters, of whom the eldest was Major-General Fendal Currie, late a Commissioner in Oudh. Several of Sir Frederick's grandsons also were or are still in India in various services, whilst three of his granddaughters are also married to officers in India. Two of Frederick Currie's infant children are also buried in the Gorakhpur cemetery, according to the B. O.)

(References: *Buckland; Hardinge (R. of I): Cunningham; Burke P.; B. O.*)

814.—**1832**—NUNN, J., Lieutenant. *Inscription:*—Sacred to the memory of Lieutenant J. Nunn, 7th N. I., died 8th October 1832, aged 29 years. (B. O.)

[James Nunn, son of R. Nunn, born in 1803 joined the service in 1824. He served at Bhurtpore and became a lieutenant in 1826.]

(References: *Services B. A. List; D. and M.*)

815.—**1833**—SYM, G. *Inscription:*—This tablet is erected to the memory of George Sym, Esq., sixth son of James Sym, Esq., of Glasgow, whose uprightness, gentleness and meekness gained him the respect and affection of his friends and associates, while his even and kind temper and high principles conciliated the regard of the natives; his early and sudden death was deeply regretted by all who knew him. He died at Gorakhpur on the 10th December 1833 in the 21st year of his age.

All flesh is as grass, and the goodliness thereof is as the flower of the field; but the mercy of the Lord is from everlasting to everlasting upon them that fear him—*Psalm* CIII. 17. (B. O.)

816.—**1835**—ARMSTRONG, J. B., C.S. *Inscription:*—To the memory of James Armstrong, Magistrate and Collector of Gorakhpur, who departed this life on the 10th September 1835, aged 37 years. This tablet is erected by the residents of the station in token of their esteem for the many virtues which adorned his character (B. O.)

[All available lists agree in stating the year of death as 1834, but they are probably all wrong, especially as the last two are doubtless based on the first. He was the son of Col. Armstrong (A. D. C. to the Duke of York) of Lisgoole Abbey, Enniskillen, and born at Clunish, co. Fermanagh in 1798. He was nominated by the Earl of Buckinghamshire at the instance of Lady Grantham, was educated at Haileybury and came to India in 1819. He served at Sirdah, Cawnpore, Tirhut, Rajshahi, Hugli, Burdwan and Gorakhpur—at Rajshahi, Burdwan and Gorakhpur as Collector.]

(References: *Haileybury; Prinsep C. L.; D. and M.; W. P.*)

817.—**1835**—STAINFORTH, E., Mrs. *Inscription:*—This tablet is placed here in sorrowful and affectionate remembrance of Eliza, wife of Frederick Stainforth, Esq., C.S., and daughter of John Thornton, Esq., who, after a residence of 3 years at this place, died at Allahabad on the 30th December 1835, in the 27th year of her age. The following words are inscribed in willing compliance with her dying request:—

Them which sleep in Jesus will God bring near him. (B. O.)

[F. Stainforth, son of R. Stainforth of Clapham, born in 1810, joined the service in 1828 and was at Gorakhpur as Joint Magistrate from 1832 to 1836. There was a John Thornton, C. S. at Gorakhpur in 1833, but as he was of the same service as Stainforth could not have been his wife's father. More probably he was her brother.]

(References: *Prinsep C. L.; W. P.*)

818.—**1835**—CURRIE, L. E., Mrs. *Inscription* :—In memory of Lucy Elizabeth, daughter of R. M. Bird, Esq., C.S., and Jane Grant, his wife, and wife of F. Currie, Esq., C.S., born 19th September 1811, died 25th July 1835.

She walked with God and God took her. (B. O.)

[Cf. No. 813.]

819.—**1840**—WYBROW, F, Revd. *Inscription* :—Sacred to the memory of the Revd. Frederick Wybrow, of the C. M. S., who died after 10 days of severe suffering on the 19th of December 1840, aged 36 years. This tablet is erected by his sorrowing widow in remembrance of the most affectionate of husbands and most faithful of ministers. (B. O.)

[The Revd. F. Wybrow was Secretary to the C. M. S. at Calcutta and came to Gorakhpur in 1839. He was head of an agricultural settlement at Basharatpur, a jungle clearing of 2,000 bighas; he lived in a house close to a tank and caught malaria of which he died.]

(*Communicated.*)

820.—**1858**—AUGUSTIN, J. *Inscription* :—In memory of Joshua Augustin, who fell a victim during the Mutiny on 21st April 1858.

821.—**1867**—BIRD. F. M., B.C.S. *Inscription* :—Sacred to the memory of Frederick Martins Bird, B.C.S., son of Robert Martins Bird, Esq., late of the Bengal Civil Service, who departed this life on the 7th September 1867, aged 41 years.

[Cf. No. 809. He did good service in the Mutiny when he remained after everybody else had left in the hope of saving the district, but he was finally compelled to flee. He was at Gorakhpur first as Joint Magistrate and then as Collector. He joined the service in 1849 and was educated at Haileybury.]

(References : *M. N.* ; *Haileybury Gazetteer.*)

ST. THOMAS'S CHURCH.

822.—**1889**—PEPPE, W. *Inscription* :—In memory of William Peppe, son of George Peppe, died 19th July 1889. He rendered valuable services during the troubled times of the Indian Mutiny, which Government rewarded by a grant of land in this district.

[Deputy Collector during the Mutiny. The Mutiny narrative only mentions him as burning a Muhammadan village (Mahua Dabar) whose inhabitants had murdered six officers, refugees from Fyzabad. He also rescued some other refugees. He was in fact the sole representative of Government, and had great difficulty in preserving his own life. His grant of land is in Basti district, round Birdpur. He was first manager and then owner of a large European estate there, which is still held by his successors, his sons Messrs. W. C. and G. T. Peppe and Mrs. Larpent, his daughter. Annie Jane Peppe married Lieut.-Col. L. H. P. Larpent, H. C. S.]

(References : *Gazetteer* ; *Foster B.*, *M. N.*)

Basti District.

GROVE BETWEEN CIVIL STATION AND OLD BASTI.

823.—**1853**—THOMPSON, W. A. F., Captain. *Inscription* :—Sacred to the memory of Captain W. A. F. Thompson, 5th Native Infantry, died at Basti, 1858.

[In a mango grove on the north side of Mr. Churcher's house. I could not trace this officer.]

M. MALI MANIBA, NEAR DOMARIAGANJ.

824.—**1858**—(1) GIFFORD, A., Captain, (2) CURRAN, A. *Inscription* :—(5) Sacred to the memory of Captain Arthur Gifford,

Bombay Army, Second in Command, B.Y.C., and Trooper Adrian Curran, B.Y.C., who were killed in action with the mutineers near Domariaganj, 27th November 1858.

[This tomb is in a grove near the Domariaganj road bungalow. The action was fought by Colonel Rowcroft's column with the mutineers concentrating in Gonda. The officer appears to be A. Giffard, 16th Ben. N. I.; I cannot find any interpretation for "B. Y. C."]

(References: *E. I. R.; Gazetteer.*)

M. JADIPUR, PARGANA AMORHA, TAHSIL HARAIYA.

825.—**1858**—TROUP, H. B., Lieutenant. *Inscription:*—To the memory of Hugh Bedford Troup, Lieutenant, Bengal Army, son of Colonel R. Troup, who died of wounds received in action with the rebels on the 17th April 1858. Born 5th February 1836.

[This officer was born at Sultanpur in 1836 (probably Sultanpur near Chunar). The tomb is near the 4th furlong of mile 65, Gorakhpur-Basti-Fyzabad road. Colonel Rowcroft was left in charge of Gorakhpur with 2 regiments of Gurkhas, the Behar Light Horse, and Captain Sotheby R. N., and his "Pearl" naval brigade. In March he started against a strong body of rebels, some 14,000 in number, who were encamped near Amorha, and defeated them on the 5th March and again on the 17th and 25th April, but they practically blockaded him at Amorha and he was compelled to retire.]

(References: *C. P.; Gazetteer.*)

Azamgarh District.

OLD CEMETERY.

826.—**1821**—CLARKE, J., Miss. *Inscription:*—Sacred to the memory of Jane, eldest daughter of J. H. Clarke, Esq., who departed this life the 13th May 1831, in her 31st year. (B. O.)

[J. H. Clarke was an indigo merchant at Lucknow.]

(Reference: *E. I. R.*)

827.—**1829**—SMITH, A., Captain. *Inscription:*—Sacred to the memory of Captain Adoniah Smith, late 50th Regiment N. I., who departed this life on the 10th January 1829, aged 38 years. This tomb is erected by the brother officers of the deceased as a small token of their high esteem and regard which, during his life, he so deservedly merited. (B. O.)

[Adonijah Smith, son of the Revd. W. Smith, was born at St. Budeaux, Devon, in 1792. He joined the service in 1807.]

(References: *D. and M.; C. P.*)

828.—**1830**—LEIGH, G. *Inscription:*—Sacred to the memory of Gerras Leigh, Esq., who departed this life on the 24th March 1838, aged 40 years. (B. O.)

829.—**1841**—GORDON, A. *Inscription:*—In remembrance of Alexander Gordon, who died at Azamgarh on the 5th December 1841, aged 22 years. Erected by a small circle of friends, amongst whom he was most sincerely esteemed, and his early death deeply regretted.

Better is the memory engraved on warm hearts,
Than what the steel can plough on cold earth. (B. O.)

830.—**1858**—VENABLES, E. F. *Inscription:*—Sacred to the memory of Edward Fredrick Venables, Esq., of Deoriaghat, near Azamgarh, who though not in the service of Government, upheld its authority in this district during a time of trial and difficulty, with equal valour, ability and prudence, and after attaining the highest personal distinction, fell in the gallant discharge of his duty, leaving a name dear both to his own countrymen and to the loyal portion of the native community, by whose joint subscriptions this monument is erected.

[The Mutiny at Azamgarh began on the 3rd June 1857, and most of the Europeans fled to Ghazipur. On the 18th June, however, Mr. Venables, an indigo planter of Ghazipur, marched into Azamgarh with a few sowars and three non-official Europeans. He was given full magisterial powers. He attacked the Palwars at Koelsa without success. On the 18th July he was reinforced and attacked the Palwars again: and though he was driven back, the enemy suffered severely and disappeared. On the 28th July Azamgarh was once more evacuated: but Mr. Venables joined the approaching Gurkha force, and the enemy, compelled to retreat, were defeated at Mandoni by Captain Boileau and Mr. Venables on the 20th September. Mr. Venables went on to Lucknow with General Franks, but returned to Azamgarh when it was threatened by Kunwar Singh and in the pursuit of that chief by Sir E. Lugard received the wound of which he died. Mr. E. F. Venables was born in 1815 and was the son of Lazarus Venables, Barrister-at-law. The family originally belonged to Bolington, co. Chester, and then to Woodhill, co. Salop. Mr. Venables married Eliza Power, daughter of R. H. Kinchant of Oswestry, but had no children. The family is now extinct in the male line: its present representative is Mrs. Dillwyn-Venables-Llewelyn of Llysdinam Hall, co. Brecon.]

(References :—*Buckland, M. N.; Burke, L. G.*)

TRINITY CHURCH.

831.—1858—VENABLES, E. F. *Inscription* :—Sacred to the memory of Edward Frederick Venables, Esq., of Deoriaghat near Azamgarh, who, though not in the service of Government, upheld its authority in this district during a time of trial and difficulty, with equal valour, ability and prudence, and after attaining the highest personal distinction, fell in the gallant discharge of his duty, leaving a name dear both to his own countrymen and to the loyal portion of the native community, by whose joint subscriptions this monument is erected.

[Cf. No. 830.]

GROVE NEAR OLD CANTONMENTS.

832.—1820—AMMAUN, S., Mrs., and son. *Inscription* :—Sacred to the memory of Mrs. Sarah Ammaun and her still-born son who departed this life on the 29th June 1820.

Just fifteen years she was a maid.
And scarce eleven months a wife;
Four days and nights in labour laid,
Brought forth, and then gave up her life.
Ah! loveliest of beauties!
Whither art thou flown?
Thy soul which knew no guile,
Is sure to heaven gone,
Leaving thy friends and thy kindred,
Thy sad exit to mourn. (B. O.)

[This tomb is now not to be found. The inscription, which possesses some curious verses, is reproduced from Führer's list.]

PUBLIC GARDENS, AZAMGARH.

833.—1824—BURY, E., B. C.S. *Inscription* :—Sacred to the memory of Edward Bury, Esq., of the Bengal Civil Establishment, born at Nazing in Essex, and died at Azamgarh on the 11th November 1824, aged 27 years. (B. O.)

[This and the next three tombs stand in an enclosure at the south-east corner of the Public Gardens. Edmund (not Edward) Bury, son of J. Bury, stockbroker, of Nazing, was born in 1797. He arrived in India in 1817, served as Assistant Registrar of the Sadar Diwani Adalat, and Assistant Superintendent of Stamps, and then at Rajshahi and Tirhut. He died at Nattore on the 15th November 1824 according to all authorities save Burke who puts the death in 1821. There can be no doubt of the identification: apart from the fact that there is no other Bury in the lists, the occurrence of Nazing in the birth certificate proves it.]

(References:—*Haileybury; Prinsep C. L.; D. and M.; W. P; Burke L. G.*)

834.—**1858**—OFFICER and MEN, 13th L. I. *Inscription:*—In memory of Captain Wilson, H. Jones and Privates William Brown, William Claybyn, Thomas Collins, Patrick Connell, George Staywell, John Stewart, Thomas Wilson, Edward Crawford, Robert Smith, John Sutton, George Amos, 1st Battalion, 13th Light Infantry. All were killed or died of wounds received in action at the relief of Azamgarh on the 6th April 1858.

[Azamgarh was besieged by Kunwar Singh in March and April 1858. Colonel Lord Mark Kerr was then at Allahabad with part of the 13th L. I., and was ordered to march at once to the relief of Azamgarh. At Benares he was joined by a troop of the Bays and four guns. At night on the 5th April he was within eight miles of Azamgarh and fought and defeated the enemy on the 6th and in a few hours entered Azamgarh.

The 13th L. I. now the 1st Battalion, The Prince Albert's (Somersetshire Light Infantry) were raised in 1685, were in India from 1824 to 1847, 1857 to 1864 and from 1893. Their Indian honours are Afghanistan, Ghaznee, Jallalabad and Cabool 1842.]

(References: *Rice-Holmes; M. N.; Gazetteer.*)

835.—**1858**—JONES, W. H., Captain. *Inscription:*—Sacred to the memory of Wilson Henry Jones, Captain, H.M.'s 13 Light Infantry, third son of Wilson Jones, Esq., of Hartsheath, Flintshire, North Wales. Killed in action at Azamgarh, the 6th April 1858, age 27 years.

[Cf. No. 834.]

836.—**1858**—NEWAL, T. *Inscription:*—To the memory of Thomas Newal, Royal Artillery, died April 21st, 1858, aged 23 years.

KUMAUN DIVISION.

Naini Tal District.

ST. JOHN'S IN THE WILDERNESS.

837.—1880—VICTIMS OF THE LANDSLIP. *Inscription :*—To the glory of God and those who perished in the great landslip, 18th September 1880. They died according to the word of the Lord and he buried them in this valley. Lester, Lance-Corporal, 1st Battalion, 25th Regiment; McEwan, Sergeant-Instructor, 92nd Regiment and Naini Tal Volunteer Corps; C. Morgan, Clerk, Government Secretariat, North-Western Provinces and Oudh; E. Morgan, Municipal Board Overseer, late 88th Regiment; Martin Murphy, Major, 40th Regiment, Isabell Murphy, wife of last-named; E. Moss, Assistant to W. Bell; G. H. Carden Noad, Esq., North-Western Provinces and Oudh Police; Revd. A. Robinson, M.A., Senior Chaplain, Bengal Establishment; R. S. P. Robinson, Second-Lieutenant, 23rd Regiment; R. I. Rogers, Sergeant-Major, 1st Battalion, 25th Regiment; A. Shiels; C. Shiels; I. W. Shiels, Plate-layer, East Indian Railway; T. W. Shiels; J. E. H. Sullivan, Lieutenant, 73rd Regiment; F. S. Taylor, Brevet Colonel, Royal Engineers; Leonard Taylor, Esq., Bengal Civil Service; W. F. Tucker, Clerk, Government Secretariat, North-Western Provinces and Oudh; Sarah Kate, wife of H. F. Turnbull, Captain, 40th Regiment; Turner, Private, 73rd Regiment; Archibald Balderston, Captain, 34th Regiment; W. Bell, Merchant, and Captain, Naini Tal Volunteer Rifle Corps; Brown, Private, 73rd Regiment; J. B. H. Carmichael, Second-Lieutenant, 33rd Regiment; Chisholme, Private, 73rd Regiment; James Drew, Assistant to W. Bell; Farrance, Private, 13th Hussars; Infant son of Mr. Francis; Flood, Sergeant, 33rd Regiment; Talbot Goodridge, Captain, Bengal Staff Corps; W. S. Gray, Assistant to W. Bell; Grover, Sergeant, 33rd Regiment; C. I. L. Halket, Second-Lieutenant, 73rd Regiment; J. B. Hannah, M.B., Surgeon-Major, Army Medical Department; Hayes, Private, 33rd Regiment; H. S. F. Haynes, Captain, Royal Engineers; Helmuth, Private, 2nd Battalion, 6th Regiment; Kennedy, Private, 73rd Regiment; G. A. Knight, Assistant to W. Bell; Infant daughter of G. A. Knight.

[The great landslip of 1880 was due to an unprecedented fall of rain. It rained without cessation from the 16th to the 19th September and about 25 inches fell in the last 40 hours. The soil was saturated wherever the loose *debris* of shale allowed the water to penetrate. The first slip occurred about 10 a.m., on the 18th, carrying away part of the outhouses and the western wing of the Victoria Hotel and burying in the ruins an English child and its nurse and some native servants. Mr. L. Taylor, Mr. Morgan and some officers and soldiers from the depôt were soon at work digging out the victims. Meantime the hotel residents removed to safer quarters, except Col. Taylor, R.E., who retired to a small room below the hotel. About half past one the second slip took place. The whole hill side was a semi-fluid mass and a shock of earthquake set it in motion. A large part of the hill disunited, completely buried the hotel and dashed the orderly room, a shop (Mr. Bell's) and the Assembly Rooms into an unrecognizable heap, part of the last being hurled into the lake. The whole catastrophy only lasted a few seconds and escape was impossible. The dead and missing numbered 151, including 43 Europeans and Eurasians. Of the names here given Mr. Noad was assistant to the Inspector-General of Police: the Revd. A. Robinson (M.A., Trinity College, Dublin) was Chaplain at Bareilly, and at Naini Tal on leave; Col. F. S. Taylor was Consulting Engineer for Railways to the Government of India and Mr. L. Taylor was a young assistant commissioner of five years' service.

Lieutenant James Barre Hood Carmichael (1860-1880) was son of Col. J. D. Carmichael, C.B., of the family of Carmichael of Balmedie. Many of the members of this family have served in India. Mr. Carmichael's grandfather (D. S. Carmichael) was Judge of the Calcutta Supreme Court early in the century: his uncle, C. P. Carmichael, C.S.I., was Commissioner of Benares; another uncle, D. F. Carmichael, was a member of the Madras Council, whilst there have also been representatives in the North-Western Provinces Police and the Indian Army. Mr. J. B. H. Carmichael's brother, the present head of the family, is in Madras (C. D. J. Carmichael). The family is a very old one; in 1386 an ancestor held the barony of Carmichael from the Earl of Douglas and Mar. His descendant William was created Baron Carmichael in 1647; and the latter's grandson, John, was made Earl of Hyndford in 1701. These titles became dormant in 1817, but are claimed by the present head of the family. John Ernest Holt Sullivan, born 1856 was the 3rd son of J. J. Sullivan, J. P., of Curramore, Co., Limerick. He is descended through his grandmother (also a Sullivan) from Oliol Ollum, King of Munster, A. D. 125, and legendarily from Heber Fionn, son of Milesius. Historically, the family goes back to Daniel O'Sullivan, died 1682.]

The regiments represented are now:—

25th, 1st Battalion, the King's Own Scottish Borderers.
92nd, 2nd Battalion, the Gordon Highlanders.
88th, 1st Battalion, the Connaught Rangers.
40th, 1st Battalion, the Prince of Wales's Volunteers (S. Lancashire Regiment).
33rd, 1st Battalion, the Duke of Wellington's (West Riding Regiment).
73rd, 2nd Battalion, the Black Watch (Royal Highlanders).
34th, 1st Battalion, the Border Regiment.
6th, 2nd Battalion, the Royal Warwickshire Regiment.]

(Reference: *Gazetteer: Burke, L. G. and L. G. I.*)

838.—**1880**—OFFICER AND MEN, N. T. R. V. C. *Inscription:*—In memory of Captain W. Bell; Sergeant G. A. Knight; Volunteer G. H. C. Noad; Volunteer J. Drew; Volunteer E. T. Moss; Volunteer C. Morgan; Volunteer A. Shiels; Volunteer T. Shiels; Volunteer C. Shiels; Sergeant-Instructor A. McEwan of the Naini Tal Volunteer Rifle Corps, who were killed by the landslip on the 18th September 1880. This is erected by their comrades.

[Cf. No. 837.]

839.—**1880**—HANNAH, J. B. *Inscription:*—Sacred to the memory of John Barlow Hannah, A. M. D., Staff Surgeon, Allahabad, who was killed in the great landslip at Naini Tal, while nobly endeavouring to save life, 18th September 1880. This tablet is erected as a token of love and respect by his widow.

[Cf. No. 837.]

840.—**1880**—(1) FRANCIS, E. M., (2) MARTHA. *Inscription:*—In loving remembrance of Edward Maiston Francis, the dearly loved son of Thomas Maiston and Maria Eyre Francis, killed by a landslip at Naini Tal on the 18th September 1880. Aged 1 year and 11 months. Also in memory of Martha, a faithful Native Christian servant, who perished with the child in her arms.

[Cf. No. 837. Doubtless the victims of the first slip.]

841.—**1880**—TAYLOR, F. S., Colonel. *Inscription :*—In memory of Frederick Sherwood Taylor, Colonel, R. E., Consulting Engineer for Railways to the Government of India. Born, November 10th, 1828, overwhelmed by the landslip in this place, September 18th, 1880.

[Cf. No. 837.]

Almora District.

CANTONMENT CEMETERY, ALMORA.

842.—**1821**—WHISH, M. T., B.C.S. *Inscription :*—Sacred to the memory of Martin Thomas Whish, Esq. of the Bengal Civil Service, who departed this life at Almora, May 19th, 1821, aged 30 years and 6 months.

[M. T. Whish, son of M. Whish, born 1790, was one of the original Haileybury students, being 5th on a list in which R. M. Bird was 2nd. He went to India in 1809 and served in Benares, Bareilly, Shahjahanpur and Shahabad; in 1821 he was officiating judge and magistrate of Bareilly.]

(References : *Haileybury ; W. P. ; Prinsep C. L.*)

843.—**1832**—STILES, J. W., Captain. *Inscription :*—Sacred to the memory of Captain John William Stiles, 30th Regiment N. I., who departed this life 4th October 1832, aged 35 years 9 months and 4 days. This monument is erected as a tribute of respect by the officers of his Corps.

[J. W. Stiles was born in the West Indies in 1800 (so birth certificate). He was a cousin of Lord Gambier. He joined the service in 1817.]

(References : *D. and M. ; C. P.*)

844.—**1832**—LEACOCK, H., Captain. *Inscription :*—Sacred to the memory of Captain Henry Leacock, 30th Regiment, N. I., who departed this life 24th April 1832, aged 26 years 10 months and 24 days. This monument is erected as a tribute of respect by the officers of his Corps.

[William H. Leacock (so birth certificate) was son of J. Leacock, born at Madeira in 1805. He joined the service in 1820 and on a return from leave was wrecked on the *Lady Holland* in 1830. According to Dodwell and Miles he died at Karnal.]

(References : *D. and M.: Services B. A. List : C. P.*)

845.—**1839**—LUSHINGTON, M., Mrs. *Inscription :*—Sacred to the memory of Marianne, the beloved wife of George Lushington, B.C.S., who departed this life on the 16th day of February 1839, after giving birth to a son stillborn, aged 30 years.

He that loveth not knoweth not God, for God is love.
Blessed are the dead which die in the Lord. (B. O.)

[The wife of Mr. G. T. Lushington, vide No. 848.]

846.—**1840**—RAMSAY, A., Lieutenant. *Inscription :*—Sacred to the memory of Lieutenant Andrew Ramsay, fourth son of Major-General the Hon'ble Ramsay, who departed this life at Almora on the 1st July 1840, aged 30 years and 9 months.

[The district authorities conjecture that Andrew Ramsay was a brother of Sir Henry Ramsay, and are doubtless correct. Andrew Ramsay's "Services" in the Services B. A. List show him to be the son of the Hon'ble Colonel Ramsay H. M.'s Service, born in 1809. Sir Henry's father was Lieutenant-General the Hon'ble John Ramsay : Burke does not mention Andrew Ramsay above his sons, but he occasionally has omissions : and there is nothing against fitting Andrew Ramsay into the pedigree for John Ramsay's other sons were born in 1804, 1806,

1808, 1811 and 1816; so that Andrew Ramsay (born in 1809) would be the 4th son. Further we find him in 1834 A. D. C. to Major-General the Hon'ble J. Ramsay, Commanding at Meerut; and in 1837 Assistant Commissioner in Kumaun—an appointment objected to by the Court of Directors on the ground of his lack of experience. In 1839-40 John Ramsay was still a Major-General; he died in 1842, a Lieutenant-General. In short, all facts point to the correctness of the view of the district authorities; there can be no doubt that Andrew Ramsay belonged to the same family, at all events, as Sir Henry, for there is no other family of Ramsays who are entitled to the prefix of Honourable. John Ramsay was 4th son of the 8th Earl of Dalhousie, and Sir Henry himself was "raised to the rank of an Earl's son" (i.e. obtained the prefix of Honourable) in 1874, when his brother succeeded to the title.

(References: *Burke P.; Services B. A. List: D and M.*)

847.—**1849**—LATOUCHE, P., Major. *Inscription:*—Sacred to the memory of Major Peter LaTouche, 7th Regiment N. I., who died at Almorah on the 17th May 1849, aged 49 years.

[Cf. No. 541. Peter LaTouche is the Captain LaTouche of that inscription. He was son of David LaTouche, born in 1799. He joined the service in 1817 and served as Brigade Major at Bhurtpore.]

(References: *Services B. A. List; Burke, L. G. I.*)

848.—**1848**—LUSHINGTON, G. T., B.C.S. *Inscription:*—Sacred to the memory of George Thomas Lushington, C.S., Commissioner of Kumaun, born May 29th, 1806, died at Naini Tal October 25th, 1849.

[Mr. G. T. Lushington was educated at Haileybury and came to India in 1825. In 1826 he was Assistant Persian Secretary to the Governor General, and served in various secretariat posts till 1830. He then was in the political branch at Delhi and Bhurtpore (Agent 1832) and went on medical leave 1835-7. On his return he served as Collector of Bareilly and Etawah and then as Commissioner of Kumaun from 1839 to his death. He was one of the first founders of Naini Tal, which was discovered in 1839 by Mr. J. H. Batten and his brother-in-law, Mr. P. Barron. In 1842 the latter began to build, and Mr. Lushington also built a house; and also allotted sites for a bazar and public buildings, mostly at Talli Tal. Mr. Lushington was 3rd son of the Right Honourable S. R. Lushington, P. C., Governor of Madras (1827-35), and an M. P. Many of his relatives have served in India, mostly in Madras: *i.e.*, Sir. J. L. Lushington, G.C.B., his uncle (Director of the E. I. C.); C. M. Lushington, another uncle, a Circuit Judge in Madras, two of whose sons became Accountants General (Madras and Bombay): and a nephew, T. D. Lushington, also Madras C. S. The family belonged originally to Sittingbourne. Mr. Lushington's wife was *née* Gordon: there were no children.]

(References: *Burke, L. G.; Haileybury; Prinsep C. L.*)

ON SITOLI HILL.

849.—**1815**—(1) KIRK, Lieutenant. (2) TAPLEY, Lieutenant. *Inscription:*—Sacred to the memory of Lieutenants Kirk and Tapley, both of the 2nd Bn., 27th Regt. N. I. This cenotaph is erected by their brother officers as a testimony of their regret and esteem. The latter was killed on the evening of the 26th April 1815 on duty at an advanced post in the town of Almora. The former died on the 16th of May following, a victim to zealous and continued exertion in the final operations of the campaign.

[Even in 1814 Lord Hastings had determined on annexing Kumaun. The Hon'ble E. Gardner was sent to try negotiations with Ram Sah, supposed to be disaffected to the Gurkha Government. Negotiations however failed, and it was decided to use force. Colonel W. L. Gardner and Captain H. T. Hearsey (cf. nos. 395 and 551) were employed to raise Rohilla levies; and in February 1815 Colonel Gardner entered the hills by the valley of the Kosi, whilst Captain Hearsey entered them from Pilibhit up the Kali by the Timla pass. All went well with the first force which by mixed fighting and manœuvring, drove the Gurkhas back on Almora and reached Katarmal, seven miles thence.

Meantime Captain Hearsey, at first successful, was defeated at Khilpati and taken prisoner. On the 6th April Lieutenant-Colonel Gardner was reinforced by a force of 2,025 regulars under Colonel (afterwards Sir Jasper) Nicolls, who superseded him. On the 23rd April the Gurkhas were attacked and defeated at Gananath : and on the 25th the heights of Sitoli were taken, two miles west of Almora. A counter-attack was delivered the same night ; the sortie from Almora on the advanced post was very determined, and it was during this attack that Lieutenant Tapley was killed. On the 26th the fort of Almora was bombarded, and the Gurkhas surrendered. Kumaun was delivered up to the British the next day by a convention.

David Kirk was appointed cadet in 1804 and lieutenant in 1805 : he was the son of J. Kirk, merchant, born at Perth in 1785. Richard Tapley, son of R. Tapley of Great Torrington, Devon, was born in 1791, joined the service in 1807 and became a lieutenant in 1814.]

(References : *Pearse : Gazetteer ; D. and M. ; C. P.*)

HAWALBAGH NEAR ALMORA.

850.—**1827**—SALMON, E., Miss. *Inscription* :—Sacred in the memory of Elizabeth [daughter of] William [and Ma]rian Salmon, w[ho was killed through the break]ing of an Alpine bridge whil[e] she [was c]rossing it on the 20th September 1827 at the age of 16 years and 14 days. The monument is erected as the last tribute of their affection by her afflicted and disconsolate parents.

[This tomb, in spite of the partially defaced inscription can be identified as that of Miss Salmon, daughter of General W. B. and Mrs. Salmon, who was killed in the following circumstances. She, her parents and her uncle, Sir J. B. Hearsey (as he became later—cf. No. 551) were on a tour in the Garhwal hills. On their return in crossing the Nundakwe river the log bridge broke in two. The girl and her uncle were dashed into a boiling snow torrent from a considerable height. Captain Hearsey did his best to save her, but was nearly drowned himself. The body was found 14 miles lower down the stream caught in the fork of a tree. It was taken to Hawalbagh, five days' journey away, and buried in Mrs. Traill's garden.

Captain Salmon, as he was then, was commandant of the Resident's guard at Lucknow.]

[Reference : *Almoriana : Pearse.*]

851.—**1834**—TRAILL, W. *Inscription* :—To William Traill, died the 26th of February 1834, aged two and a-half years.

[Probably a son of Mr. G. W. Traill, assistant to the first Commissioner of Kumaun from 1815, and appointed his successor shortly afterwards. He ruled Kumaun for 20 years. His history from 1815 to 1835 is that of Kumaun, and it is unnecessary here to give further details of it.]

[Reference : *Gazetteer.*]

LUCKNOW DIVISION.

Lucknow District.

Note.—Almost all the Lucknow tombs belong to the Mutiny period. The operations in and around Lucknow are necessarily complicated. Fighting went on almost without cessation from June 1857 to the end of March 1858, and during that time six scenes of the great drama were played out all on the same stage, viz. (1) Lawrence's and Inglis's defence of the Residency, (2) Havelock and Outram's so-called relief (really no more than a reinforcement), (3) Havelock and Outram's second defence of an extended position, (4) Sir Colin Campbell's second relief, (5) Outram's operations at the Alambagh, (6) Sir Colin Campbell's capture of Lucknow. If the tombs are to be presented in some intelligible form and not as a mere jumble, passing from one to another of these scenes in the most confusing way, it is necessary that a sort of key, in the shape of a chronological skeleton of the operations should be given. This seems to be the easiest method of attaining lucidity without sacrificing the ordinary arrangements of the tombs by localities.

26th May 1857.—The English residents were housed in the Residency.

30th May—Mutiny of the 13th and 71st N. I. and destruction of the cantonments by fire.

31st May—Mutiny of the rest of the troops (48th N. I., Oudh force and cavalry); pursuit by British troops and faithful native troops.

1st June—Sir Henry Lawrence took up his quarters in the Residency.

30th June—Battle of Chinhat, and commencement of the siege of the Residency.

1st July—Destruction of the Machi Bhawan by its garrison.

2nd ,, —Sir Henry Lawrence mortally wounded.

4th ,, —Death of Sir Henry Lawrence. Succeeded by Brigadier Inglis in military command, and Major Banks as Chief Commissioner.

7th July—Sortie against Johannes' House.

20th ,, —First assault. Mining operations commenced and went on regularly to the end of the defence. (There were 37 mines, of which only one was successful, between this date and the 25th September).

10th August—Second assault.

12th ,, —A vigorous cannonade rendered the Cawnpore Battery untenable. Two sorties under General Inglis and Lieutenant Hutchinson.

17th August—Destruction of Johannes' House.

18th ,, —Successful mine, and 3rd assault on Sikh Square.

5th September—Fourth assault.

6th ,, —Fulton's sortie.

23rd ,, —Havelock and Outram's battle of the Alambagh.

25th September—First Relief.—A running fight began at the Alambagh, which ended at the seizure of the Char Bridge, which was held by the 78th Highlanders. The route was then along the canal as far as the Dilkusha Road, thence to the Sikandra Bagh and then to the Moti Mahal. The 78th lost their route and came down the Hazratganj. The rest of the column had meantime reached the Chattar Manzil. The 78th and the rest then forced their way through the lanes and Sher Darwaza, or Neill's Gate, through the Khas Bazar to the Baily Guard.

26th September—2nd Defence.—A party was sent out under Major Simmons to extricate Col. Campbell, left in the Moti Mahal passage with the wounded and baggage. This party was also surrounded and rescued by another party under Col. Napier.

27th September—Capture of a garden near the Chattár Manzil and the Ruri Kothi and Farhat Bakhsh Palace. Massacre of the Dooley Square; sortie against the Garden Battery.

28th September—Capture of the buildings round the Khas Bazar. Sorties from Sikh Square against houses, etc., towards the iron bridges; from Left Square, Brigade Mess, against the Cawnpore Road Batteries, and from Innes's post.

2nd October—Capture of Phillips' House and Garden Battery.

10th November—Arrival of Kavanagh from Residency in Sir C. Campbell's camp at Banthra.

12th November—2nd Relief operations.— Fight near Jalalabad.

14th ,, —Advance from Alambagh, eastwards. Fighting at Dilkusha and Martiniere, which are occupied.

16th November—Storm of the Sikandra Bagh, Shah Najaf. Kadam Rasul; storm of the Hiran Khana by the defenders.

17th November—Capture of the Rest House and Moti Mahal. Meeting of Outram, Havelock and Campbell. Capture of Banks' House.

18th November—Operations in support of force holding Banks' House.

19th November—Withdrawal of women and children.

27th ,, —Outram's operations at the Alambagh.—Outram is left here with 4,400 men.

22nd December—Affair at Gaili.

12th January 1858—Second attack on Outram.

16th ,, —Third attack.

15th February—Fourth attack.

21st ,, —Fifth attack.

25th ,, —Sixth attack.

2nd March—Capture of Lucknow.—The army advanced on Lucknow; capture of Dilkusha.

6th March—Outram's column crosses the Gumti. Skirmish near the Fyzabad Road.

7th March—Attack on Outram near Ishmailganj.

9th ,, —Capture of Chukkur Kothi and Badshah Bagh by Outram. Capture of Martiniere by Campbell.

10th March—Capture of Banks' House by Campbell. Capture of Dilaram Kothi, and street fighting by Outram.

11th March—Storm of Begam Kothi by Campbell. Occupation of Shah Najaf. Seizure of suburbs and iron bridge by Outram.

14th March—Capture of the Little Imambara by Campbell. Seizure of Kaisar Bagh and other buildings (Mess House, Tara Kothi, Moti Mahal and Chattar Manzil).

16th March—Seizure of Residency, Machi Bhawan and Great Imambara.

17th March—Explosion at the Jama Masjid.
19th ,, —Capture of Musa Bagh and route of enemy.
(References : *Forrest* ; *Macleod Innes.*)

THE RESIDENCY.

852—**1857**—DEFENDERS OF THE RESIDENCY. *Inscription:*—In memory of Major-General Sir Henry Lawrence, K.C.B., and the brave men who fell in the defence of the Residency, A.D. 1857.

[This memorial cross stands on a high mound between the Residency and Banqueting Hall.

The troops at Lucknow consisted of the 13th, 48th and 71st Native Infantry, the 4th and 7th Oudh Irregulars, the 3rd Native Police, the 7th Light Cavalry, the 2nd Oudh Irregular Cavalry, 1½ regiment of mounted police and 2 batteries of artillery. Of English troops there were only the 32nd and one weak company of artillery. As early as the 4th May the 7th Oudh Irregulars showed signs of disaffection. The position was also very unfavourable : the native troops were scattered about in the city and as far out as Mariaon and Mudkipur on the far side of the river : the English troops were a mile to the east of the Residency. Sir H. Lawrence proceeded to fortify the Machi Bhawan and the Residency. On the 30th May the outbreak of the sepoys occurred. About 200 men of the 13th and a few of the 71st stood firm. The rest mutinied. Sir H. Lawrence then moved to the Residency. The rising had been quelled and the mutineers driven off with grape and some faithful cavalry. Lucknow was quiet for a time : and the defences were pressed on.

On the 29th of June a large body of mutineers, encouraged by the fall of Cawnpore, marched on Lucknow. On the 30th was fought the disastrous action of Chinhat : and the siege commenced. The Machi Bhawan was blown up, and all the defenders collected in the Residency.

It is extremely difficult to understand the Residency entrenchments from what remains of them at the present day. Many buildings have been swept away, and without a plan or model the task is nearly impossible. The present account is taken from Macleod Innes's "Lucknow and Oudh in the Mutiny" which contains a series of excellent plates.

The entrenchments were in shape nearly a square with sides about 440 yards long, and enclosing an area of between 32 and 36 acres. There were four fronts, which may be called the river (North) Front, the Baily Guard (East) Front, the Cawnpore (South) Front, and City (West) Front. It was on the edge of a bank, sloping down to the river. On the North Front was the only clear space the enemy had for attack ; on the other three intervening buildings prevented the lower defences from being reached by artillery fire.

Along the Northern Front the posts were Innes' (north-west corner), the Redan and the Hospital, with the Baily Guard and Aitken's post in advance, at the north-east corner. The line of defence along this edge had been scarped down, and on the line itself, along the crest of the high bank, was a stout seven foot parapet, "reveted with gabions and fascines, topped with sandbags, and finished with a banquette for musketry."

Along the Eastern Front, which was in two tiers, the posts were, on the higher tier, the Hospital (north-east corner), Fayrer's, the Post Office, Germon's, and Anderson's (south-east corner) ; on the lower tier, the Baily Guard, Saunders' and Sago's. The line of defence was the boundary wall of the Residency and other buildings, which in its northern half was lined and strengthened inside with a musketry parapet but merely loopholed elsewhere : beyond were the verandahs, with archways bricked up and loopholed ; and further back still the supporting posts, parapeted and loopholed. At the south-east corner it was specially strengthened.

The South Front had at the south-east corner Anderson's, at the south-west corner Gubbins' posts : with the Cawnpore Battery, Deprat's, the Martiniere, the Brigade Mess and the Sikh Squares. This was the most dangerous front, with the Cawnpore Battery commanded by Johannes' House, and no protection from distant artillery fire. The defences were the buildings themselves, which were loopholed.

The West Front lay between Gubbin's and Innes' Posts, and consisted of three ranges of outhouses, with the Church and Cemetery and Evans's Battery on high ground behind it. These outhouses were loopholed and parapeted.

The Redan, Cawnpore Battery and Slaughter-house Posts were held by English soldiers only: the Hospital, Baily Guard, Germon's and the Sikh Square by sepoys: and all other posts by a mixture of English soldiers, sepoys and volunteers.

There were also inner buildings—the Residency, Ommaney's House, the Begam Kothi—and in these and the lower storeys of Fayrer's, the Post Office, the Martiniere, the Brigade Mess and Gubbins' were housed the English families.

The Commandants were Lieutenant Loughnan at Innes' Post, Colonel Palmer, (North Curtain), Captain Lawrence (Redan), Lieutenant Langmore (Hospital), Lieutenant Aitken (Baily Guard), Captain Weston (Fayrer's), Captain Saunders (Saunders'), Lieutenant Clery (Sago's), Captain Germon (Germon's), Captain McCabe (Post Office), Lieutenant Anderson (Anderson's), Mr. Schilling (Martinière), Colonel Masters (Brigade Mess), Lieutenant Hardinge (Sikh Square), Captain Forbes (Gubbin's), Captain Boileau (outhouses), Captain Evans (Evan's Battery), with a relief of Captains at the Cawnpore Battery and Deprat's. Of the siege nothing need be said. The sufferings of the garrison are so well known as to need no fresh description. They are written in the pages of Rees and Polehampton, Fulton, and of Lady Inglis and Mrs. Harris. From every point of view they are described—that of the British grumbler who grumbled as he fought and slew, in Rees; that of the jovial English officer who saw the humour of any situation, however dangerous, in Fulton; that of the brave and gentle Mrs. Harris, a Sister of Mercy in every sense but the professional one. The post that Sir H. Lawrence thought could be held for a fortnight, was held for 87 days. "There does not stand recorded in the annals of war an achievement more truly heroic than the defence of the Residency at Lucknow."]

(References: *Macleod Innes; Forrest; Rice-Holmes; Kaye.*)

853.—**1857.**—PALMER S. Miss. *Inscription:*—Susanna Palmer, killed in this room by a cannon ball on the 1st July 1857, in her ninteenth year.

[This tablet is on the east verandah wall of the Women's Quarters.

Miss Palmer was daughter of Colonel Palmer and had just come out to India. She was shot in the leg, which had to be amputated. She survived the operation only a few days.]

(References: *Forrest; Rees; Harris.*)

854.—**1857.**—*Inscription:*—The Right Hon'ble the Earl of Canning, G.C.B., G.C.S.I., Viceroy and Governor-General of India, expressed his admiration of the defence of the Residency of Lucknow in the following words:—"There does not stand recorded in the annals of war an achievement more truly heroic than the defence of the Residency at Lucknow." On 30th June 1857 A.D., the day after the battle of Chinhut, the siege began. On the 2nd July, Sir Henry Lawrence was mortally wounded by a shell which burst within the Residency building. The command then devolved on Brigadier J. E. W. Inglis, Her Majesty's 32nd Regiment. The force within the defences then consisted of 130 officers, British and native, 740 British and 700 native troops, and 150 civilian volunteers. There were 237 women, 260 children, 50 boys of La Martiniere College, 27 non-combatant Europeans and 700 non-combatant natives, being a total of 2,994 souls.

[This tablet is on the south wall of the Women's Quarters.—Vide no. 852.]

855.—**1857.**—HER MAJESTY'S 32ND FOOT. *Inscription:*—To commemorate the gallant part taken by Her Majesty's 32nd Foot in the heroic defence of this Residency during the Indian Mutiny, 1857. Also to the memory of the officers, non-commissioned officers, men, women and children of the Regiment who perished during the Mutiny here and at Cawnpore. This monument of granite from the Bosahan quarry, Cornwall, was erected by the officers, warrant officers, non-commissioned officers and men past and present of the 32nd Light Infantry, now the 1st Battalion Duke of Cornwall's Light Infantry, while the battalion was quartered at Lucknow.

[Cf. no. 440. It is unnecessary to add to what has already been said. The very names of the officers afford sufficient proof of what the regiment did. The 32nd is perhaps the regiment *par excellence* of the Mutiny.]

856.—**1857**.—NATIVE OFFICERS AND SEPOYS, 13TH BENGAL NATIVE INFANTRY. *Inscription* :—Erected in memory of the devoted gallantry and fidelity of the Native Officers and Sepoys of the Hon'ble Company's 13th Bengal Native Infantry (*Garud-ka-Pultan*), who fell during the defence of Lucknow. This monument is erected by the surviving European officers of the Regiment in the Baillie Guard Post, which was held by the regiment throughout the defence. Subadar Doondayal Pandey, Subadar Ram Pershad and Subadar Sheo Charan Singh, Jamadar Bhawani Bux Chowbe, Kalka Tewari, 9 Havildars, 8 Naiks, 5 Drummers, 24 Sepoys.

[This tablet is inside the Baily Guard. The 13th Native Infantry, about 200 men, stood firm. They did excellent service at the Baily Guard all through the siege. On the 1st July 1857 there were 12 native officers, 28 non-commissioned officers, 13 drummers and 136 rank and file. At Chinhat some of the sepoys were seen saving wounded European soldiers and abandoning their own wounded; whilst in the battle itself they behaved most bravely. They helped willingly with the spade as well as the rifle. They made a battery for an 18 pounder and worked it themselves. When Havelock's force entered the Baily Guard, three of the sepoys were bayoneted by mistake. "Never mind," said one of them, "it was fated: "victory to the Baily Guard" ("*Kuchh parwa nahin, kismat hai—Baily Guard ki jai.*") They did splendid work also all through the second siege. They were so close to the enemy that conversation was possible: but threats and promises were alike of no avail to seduce them from their allegiance. "Their courageous constancy under the severest trials is worthy of all honour," wrote Lord Canning. As a reward every member of the three faithful regiments (13th, 48th and 71st) were formed into a new regiment—the present 16th Rajputs (the Lucknow Regiment). In the end 1 Subadar Major received the 1st class, 11 Subadars the 2nd class of the Order of Merit: 16 Havildars were promoted to Jamadars of whom 2 also got the 2nd Class of the Order: 23 Naiks were promoted to Havildars, and 55 sepoys to Naiks; drummers and other followers received three months' pay. One Naik was promoted to Subadar with the 2nd Class of the Order, and 3 Naiks and 3 Sepoys to Jamadars in the Cawnpore Levy.]

(References: *Forrest*; *Macleod Innes*; *Rees*; *Rice-Holmes*; *Kaye*.)

857.—**1857**—NATIVE OFFICERS AND SEPOYS. *Inscription*:—To the memory of the Native Officers and Sepoys of the 13th Native Infantry, 41st Native Infantry, 48th Native Infantry, 71st Native Infantry, the Oudh Irregular Force, Native Pensioners, New Native Levies, Artillery, and Lucknow Magazine, who died near this spot, nobly performing their duty, this column is erected by Lord Northbrook, Viceroy and Governor-General of India, 1875.

[This monument stands north of the Baily Guard Gate.—

What applies to the 13th Native Infantry applies also to the rest of our Indian soldiers. The figures on the 1st July 1857 were as follows:—

41st Native Infantry.—16 Drummers.

48th Native Infantry.—5 Native Officers, 18 Havildars, 24 Drummers, 26 rank and file.

71st Native Infantry.—12 Native Officers, 14 Havildars, 11 Drummers, 71 rank and file.

Oudh Irregular Force.—7 Native Officers, 17 Havildars, 72 rank and file.

Native pensioners.—6 Native Officers, 3 Drummers, 109 rank and file.

New Native Levies.—3 Native Officers, 1 Havildar, 44 rank and file.

Artillery.—5 Native Officers, 18 Havildars, 6 Drummers, 146 rank and file.
Lucknow Magazine.—4 Havildars, 10 rank and file.
7th Light Cavalry.—4 Native Officers, 2 Havildars, 4 rank and file.
Total, with the 13th Native Infantry.—54 Native Officers, 102 Havildars, 73 Drummers, 618 rank and file;

or 847 out of a total force of 1,698.
(Reference: *Forrest.*)

858.—**1857-58**—OFFICERS AND MEN, 78th HIGHLANDERS. *Inscription*:—Sacred to the memory of the officers, non-commissioned officers and private soldiers of the 78th Highland Regiment, who fell in the suppression of the Mutiny of the Native Army in India in the years 1857 and 1858. This monument is erected as a tribute of respect by their surviving brother officers and comrades, and by many officers who formerly belonged to the regiment, A.D. 1883.

[This memorial stands in the Residency enclosure south of the cemetery.—The 78th Highland Regiment, now the 2nd Battalion Seaforth Highlanders (Ross-shire Buffs, the Duke of Albany's) were Havelock's famous Highlanders. They were with him in his advance and in all the subsequent Lucknow operations up to the final reduction by Sir Colin Campbell. This battalion was raised in 1793. The 1st Battalion was raised in 1778, and was also numbered 78th up to 1786, when the number was changed to 72nd. The two battalions between them have a long Indian honour roll. The 1st Battalion were in India from 1781-1798, and 1857-1865 and 1871-1882; the 2nd from 1797-1811; 1842-59; 1880-1897. The honours won in India are "Carnatic" and "Mysore," "Hindostan," "Assaye," "Lucknow," "Central India," "Peiwar Kotal," "Charasiah," "Kabul 1879," "Kandahar 1880," "Afghanistan 1878 80," Chitral." Carnatic, Mysore, Central India and all the Afghan honours belong to the 72nd and the rest to the 78th.

(Reference: *Forrest.*)

859.—**1862**—INGLIS, J. E. W., Major-General, Sir. *Inscription*:—Sacred to the memory of Major-General Sir John Inglis, K.C.B., Colonel, Her Majesty's 32nd Regiment, who with a handful of devoted men defended the Residency of Lucknow for 87 days, from 3rd July 1857 to 27th September 1857, against an overwhelming force of the enemy. Born November 15th, 1814, died at Homberg, Germany, September 27th, 1862, from illness contracted during the siege. This memorial is erected by his surviving comrades and friends, A. D. 1894.

(This memorial stands to the south-east of the residency building.)

[Sir John Eardly Wilmot Inglis (1814-1862), son of the very Reverend John Inglis, D.D., Bishop of Nova Scotia, joined the 32nd Regiment in 1833. In 1837 he was in Canada, and present at the actions of St. Denis and St. Eustace. He was at both sieges of Multan and commanded the 32nd at Surajkund; he was also present at Cheniole and Gujrat (1846-49.) He succeeded to the command of the garrison on Sir H. Lawrence's death until the relief by Havelock; and as the general order said, the British Government owed him a heavy debt of gratitude. After the final relief of Lucknow he fought against Tantia Topi in December 1857; commanded the troops in the Ionian Islands in 1860, and died at Homberg in 1862. He was made Major-General and K.C.B. "for his enduring fortitude and persevering gallantry in the defence of the Residency of Lucknow for 87 days against an overwhelming force of the enemy." "An honourable Christian gentleman......a staunch friend, a lover of all that was high and noble, a soldier of unsurpassable gallantry."]

(References: *Rees; Buckland; Rice-Holmes; Forrest; Hutchinson.*)

860.—**1887**—AITKEN, R. H. M., Colonel. *Inscription*:—This monument is erected to the memory of Colonel Robert Hope Moncrieff Aitken, V.C., Bengal Staff Corps, and formerly of the 13th Regiment, Bengal Infantry, by some of his surviving comrades and other friends in token of their appreciation of his sterling worth as a man, and of the splendid gallantry and chivalrous devotion which he displayed as a soldier in command of this post, which he held with the faithful and loyal remnant of the regiment to which he belonged throughout the defence of the Residency of Lucknow. Born 8th February 1828, died 18th September 1887.

[This memorial stands close to the Baily Guard Gate. Robert Hope Moncrieff Aitken (1828-1887) belonged to the 13th Native Infantry and had served in the Punjab campaign of 1848-49. In the defence of the Residency he was in command of the Baily Guard though another post, the Treasury Post close by the Baily Guard, was also called by his name. He and his faithful sepoys did excellent service on the 20th July in the assault of that date. He commanded them "with signal courage and success." He and his men also constructed a battery for an 18-pounder and worked it themselves. After the first relief he did good work in the capture of the Ruri Kothi, and at a sortie on the 29th September. He also fought in the operations before Cawnpore and in the Oudh Campaign of 1858, and gained the V.C. for various acts of gallantry at Lucknow. He became Inspector-General of Police in Oudh, and Colonel in 1876. Lord Roberts, on seeing the Baily Guard, marvelled that it could have been held for five months, as it was, by Aitken and Loughnan.]

(References: ***Buckland*** ; ***Forest*** : ***Roberts***.)

861.—**1904**.—INGLIS, J., Lady. *Inscription* :—This tablet is erected as a memorial of the heroic and self sacrificing devotion to duty displayed by Julia, wife of Major-General Sir John Inglis, K C B., during the defence of the Residency, June to November 1857.

[This tablet is on the top of the steps leading down to the Residency tyekhana. The Hon'ble Julia Selina, Lady Inglis (1833-1904), was fourth daughter of the first Lord Chelmsford (Sir Frederic Thesiger, Lord High Chancellor 1858-59 and 1866-68). She published "The Siege of Lucknow, a diary" in 1892. She was shipwrecked on her way home and died in 1904.

Of her self-devotion one instance will suffice. Rees relates that the ladies from the Residency after the 2nd relief had to walk about 6 miles. For Lady Inglis a doolie was prepared ; but she "unhesitatingly refused it, saying that she was well able to walk while so many wounded men and sick women were so much in need of a conveyance." This incident will not be found in her own diary.]

(References: ***Forest*** : ***Rees*** ; ***Buckland*** ; ***Burke, P.***)

RESIDENCY CEMETERY.

862.—**1857**—(1) POLEHAMPTON, H. A. (2) POLEHAMPTON, H. S., Revd. *Inscription* :—In memory of Henry Stedman Polehampton, Chaplain of this station, born February 1st, 1824, died July 20th, 1857. Also of Henry Allnutt, his only child, born December 30th, 1856, died January 3rd, 1857. Enter thou into the joy of thy Lord.—*Matthew*, xxv, 21.

[Henry Stedman Polehampton (1824-1857), son of the Revd. Edward Polehampton, was educated at Eton and Pembroke College, Oxford (Fellow in 1848). In the same year he was ordained and became Rector of St. Aldate's, Oxford. In 1855 he become a Chaplain in the E.I.C.S. service, and in 1856 landed in Calcutta and was made Chaplain at Lucknow. Like the Anglo-Indian Padres all over the province—Moncrieff at Cawnpore, Jennings at Delhi, Campbell at Fatehgarh—he did his duties as bravely as the soldiers whom he attended. Severely wounded "whilst shaving" at the beginning of the siege, his enfeebled constitution succumbed to an attack of cholera. "The death of Mr. Polehampton was a serious loss: for that reverend gentleman had been unremitting in his kindness to the sick and wounded in hospital. From morning to night Mr. Polehampton was constantly by the bedside of some poor sufferer, inspiring him with confidence in Providence and hope in his recovery : or if hope was at an end, with the prospect of salvation in a better world. He never swerved from this self-imposed duty and only left the hospital to go to his meals." His services were gratefully acknowledged in the various orders passed by the military authorities and the Governor General.]

(References: *Forrest; Buckland; Harris; Rees.*)

863.—**1857**—(1) HALE, H. G. F. (2) HALE, F. E., Mrs. (3) HALE, K. C. S. *Inscription:*—Sacred to the memory of Frances Ellen Hale, the beloved wife of George Herbert Hale, Lieutenant-Adjutant, 2nd Oudh Light Infantry, who died in Lucknow Garrison on the morning of the Battle of Chinhut, 1857, aged 20 years. Sacred also to the memory of Kate Caroline Sophia, eldest child of the above, who died in Lucknow Garrison on the 23rd of September 1857. Sacred also to the memory of Henrietta Georgiana Frances, her infant child, who died at Secrora, Oudh, on the 18th of April 1857.

The Lord is good, a stronghold in the day of trouble: and he knoweth them that trust in him.—*Nahum*, 1, 7.

[Lieutenant Hale had been stationed at Secrora and came to Lucknow when his regiment (2nd O. I. Infantry) revolted.]

(Reference: *Gubbins.*)

864.—**1857**—GRANT, A. P., Lieutenant. *Inscription:*—To the memory of Aldourie Patrick Grant, 71st Native Infantry, killed on duty at Muriaon in the Mutiny of 1857.

[Son of Field Marshal Sir Patrick Grant, then Commander-in-Chief, Madras Army, and temporarily Commander-in-Chief in India after the death of General Anson, by his wife Jane, daughter of W. Fraser-Tytler of Balnain and Aldourie (whence presumably comes the son's unusual Christian name.) He was murdered by his own men when on duty at the Centre Picket in the midst of cantonments on the 30th May.]

(References: *Kaye; Forrest; Hutchinson; Harris.*)

865.—**1857**—CLANCEY, T. J. *Inscription:*—Near this spot are interred the remains of Thomas John Clancey of the Chief Commissioner's office, Lucknow, who was killed during the siege of Lucknow on the 1st of July 1857, aged 28 years and 5 months.

"I shall go to him, but he will never return to me."

This tomb has been erected by his beloved wife, Elizabeth Clancey, and subsequently renewed by his sons John, Charles and Dominic James. "*Requiescat in pace.*"

866.—**1857**—LAWRENCE, H. M., Sir. *Inscription:*—Here lies Henry Lawrence who tried to do his duty. May the Lord have mercy on his soul. Born, 20th June 1806, died 4th July 1857.

[Henry Montgomery Lawrence (1806-1857), 4th son of Colonel Alexander Lawrence, was born in Ceylon. He was educated at Foyle College, Derry, Bristol and Addiscombe. He joined the Bengal Artillery in 1823. He served in Burma (1826) and was invalided home: on his return to India he joined the Revenue Survey of the North-Western Provinces (1833-38). He was Assistant to the Agent Governor-General on the North-West Frontier at Firozpur in 1840, during the first Afghan War. He went with Pollock to Kabul in 1842, getting his brevet-majority. In 1843-06 he was Resident in Nepal. He was Agent Governor-General for the Punjab during the 1st Sikh War and present at Sobraon. He was Resident at Lahore in 1847 and compelled the surrender of Kashmir to Gulab Singh. In 1848 he was made K. C. B. In 1849 he was present at Multan and Chilianwala. He then became President of the Board of Administration of the Punjab and Agent Governor-General, in April 1849. When the Board broke up in 1853 he was transferred to Rajputana as Agent Governor-General. In 1854 he was made Aide-de-Camp to the Queen and Chief Commissioner of Oudh in 1857.

His great work began in the Punjab. He was strongly opposed to annexation: yet, when it occurred, he carried it out loyally, and there ensued a "rule unsurpassed for efficiency." But differences arose between Henry and John

Lawrence: and Lord Dalhousie appointed the latter "as trained Civil Cffcer" to the Chief Commissionership of the Punjab. In the Mutiny he prepared with great skill and foresight for the defence of Lucknow (vide no. 852). The battle of Chinhat was a disaster, and Sir Henry himself admitted that he was the cause of it: it may be true, as one of his critics says, "that history has dealt very tenderly with Henry Lawrence in this matter, because he was Henry Lawrence," but it would take a great deal more than a single disaster to overshadow Henry Lawrence's fame. He was wounded almost as soon as the siege began. A shell had already burst in his room and Couper (his Private Secretary) and other friends implored him to change it. He said he was tired: he would do so next day: he jested on the subject, saying that sailors always considered the safest place in a ship was the hole made by the last shot. But another shell burst in the room, whilst he was lying down, and nearly took off his thigh. He was taken to Dr. (Sir Joseph) Fayrer's house where he died two days later. An extract frcm Major Banks' diary given by Hutchinson shows that even on his deathbed he thought of everybody and everything to the smallest detail. Besides military directions, he directed that "every servant should be enrolled as a beldar or carrier of earth;" that every horse save enough for four guns and one other (his own) should be turned out of the entrenchment: that natives who were working were to be paid "liberally, double, quadruple;" that his servants should be given a year's wages. When he died a few soldiers were summoned to carry his corpse to burial. Before they lifted the couch on which it lay, one of them raised the coverlet and, stooping down, kissed the forehead of his dead general: and all the rest did the same.

It is unnecessary to ransack the dictionary with the historians for adjectives to describe him. The epitaph he chose for himself and this story show what manner of man he was. "A god-fearing, upright man, resolute and brave, powerful in mind, noble and generous-hearted," the "noblest hero of the old Bengal Artillery."

He was charitable to a fault as the history of the Lawrence Asylums for the children of British soldiers, which he founded, will prove. He was moreover a writer of considerable literary merit. After his death a provisional order appeared appointing him Governor General "on the death, resignation or coming away of Lord Canning." His son was made a baronet in honour of his father's services.

Sir Henry was the 4th son of Colonel Alexander Lawrence, who served at Seringapatam. His eldest surviving brother was Major-General Alexander William Lawrence of the Madras Cavalry (died 1868); and his other brothers, Lieutenant-General G. St. P. Lawrence, K.C.S.I., C.B., John, Lord Lawrence, and Major-General R. C. Lawrence, C.B., are all well known names in India. He married Honoria, daughter of the Reverend G. Marshall of Carndonagh, Co. Donegal (died 1854) and had two sons, Sir Alexander Hutchinson Lawrence, 1st baronet, who was in the I.C.S. and was accidentally killed in 1864 on the Hindustan-Tibet Road, and Sir Henry Waldemar Lawrence, 3rd and present baronet. Of two daughters one died an infant, the other, Honoria Letitia, married H. G. Hart, late headmaster of Sedbergh School.]

[Reference: *Sir H. Lawrence (R. of I.); Rice-Holmes; Hutchinson; Forrest; Rees; Harris; Buckland; Burke, P.)*

867.—**1857**—OMMANEY, M. C., B S.C. *Inscription*:—Sacred to the memory of Manaton Collingwood Ommaney, Esq., for 26 years in the Bengal Civil Service, the sixth son of Sir F. M. Ommaney, Kt., and Georgiana Frances, his wife. He was born March 19th, 1813 and died July 8th, 1857, from the effects of a round shot during the memorable defence of Lucknow in the Province of Oudh, of which he was Judicial Commissioner, leaving a widow and six children to sorrow, not without hope, for the one thus suddenly cut off in his career of Christian integrity, benevolence and usefulness, beloved by themselves and esteemed by all who knew him.

The righteous are taken away from the evil to come—*Isaiah* LVII—1.

[M. C. Ommaney was at Haileybury 1828-1831, came to India in 1832, and served in Saugor and elsewhere in the C. P. and in Jhansi. He had also settled in Jaunpur. With Mr. Gubbins, Major Banks, General Inglis and Major

Anderson he formed a provisional council during Sir Henry Lawrence's illness. He was wounded on the 3rd and died on the 8th July.]

(References: *Haileybury; Gubbins; Hutchinson.*)

868.—1857—(1) DASHWOOD, A. J., Lieutenant, (2) DASHWOOD, H. J. G. *Inscription:*—In memory of Alexander John Dashwood, Lieutenant, 48th Regiment, Bengal Native Infantry, who died at Lucknow, July 9th, 1857, aged 27 years. Also of his second son, Herbert John Garrett, who died at Lucknow, August 19th, 1857, aged one year.

[Wounded during the defence of Lucknow and died of cholera. The child died of fever. Mrs. Dashwood, another child and one born during the siege survived. Lieutenant Dashwood was son of Lieutenant-Colonel A. W. Dashwood of the 19th Lancers and 71st Highlanders and nephew of T. J. Dashwood (vide no. 641). He married Emma Blanche, daughter of Captain J. B. Garrett R.N. (died 1907). His brother, C. K. Dashwood, was also killed at Lucknow. Cf. no. 924.]

(References: *Forrest; Harris; Burke, P.)*

869.—1857—(1) MARSHALL, W. (2) SANSON, A., Mrs. *Inscription:*— Sacred to the memory of William Marshall, who died 13th July 1857, of a wound received while defending Sago's Garrison. Also of mother-in-law, Anna Sanson, who died within the Residency entrenchment on the 24th October 1857.

Enter thou into the joy of the Lord.

This monument is erected by his disconsolate widow and daughter.

[A member of the Uncovenanted Service. For Sago's House vide no. 852.]

(Reference: *Forrest.*)

870.—1857—THOMAS, C. E., Mrs. *Inscription:*—Sacred to the memory of Cordelia Ellen, the beloved wife of Captain Lancelot F. C. Thomas, Madras Artillery, who died during the siege of Lucknow, 16th July 1857, aged 22 years.

Those that seek Me early shall find Me.

Proverbs, viii, 17.

[Francis Charles, son of Major R. A. Thomas, Bengal Army, was born at Slough in 1828. He was the officer who blew up the Machi Bhawan.]

(Reference: *Gubbins; C. P.; Harris.*)

871.—1857—STRANGWAYS, M. H. D. *Inscription:*—Sacred to the memory of Mary Hamilton Dunbar, the beloved child of Captain and Mrs. George Strangways, who died in the Residency during the siege of Lucknow on the 17th July 1857, aged two years and two months.

Of such is the Kingdom of Heaven.

[Died of cholera.]

(Reference: *Harris.*)

872.—1857—MORGAN, C. R. J. *Inscription:*—Sacred to the memory of Charles Robert John, the beloved son of Mr. J. J. Morgan, Barrack-Master, Cawnpore, who died at Lucknow during the siege on the 19th July 1857, aged 13 months and 17 days.

Of Such is the Kingdom of Heaven.

873.—1857—ARTHUR, L. A., Lieutenant. *Inscription:*—In memory of Leonard Augustus Arthur, Lieutenant, 7th Bengal Light Cavalry, who fell while commanding the Cawnpore Battery, 19th July MDCCCLVII.

[L. A. Arthur (1832-1857) was the 7th son of Lieutenant-General the Right Honorable Sir George Arthur, Bart., K.C.H., P.C., D.C.L., Governor of Bombay

(1842-46) and appointed provisionally Governor General in 1846, and the brother of Lady Bartle Frere. He was shot through the eye whilst aiming at one of the enemy in the Cawnpore Battery.]

(References : *Forrest ; Hutchinson ; Rees ; Burke, P.*)

874.—**1857**—BANKS, J. S., Major. *Inscription* :—Near this spot are interred the remains of John Sherbrooke Banks, Major of the 33rd Regiment Native Infantry, who fell at Lucknow on the 21st July 1857.

I shall go to him ; but he will not return to me.

[John Sherbrooke Banks (1811-1857), son of Surgeon S. Banks, H. M.'s service, born at Burton on Trent, joined the Indian Army in 1829. Most of his service he was employed on civil duties : but in 1842 served in Pollock's Kabul Force. He was on Lord Dalhousie's personal staff and went with him to Burma. He was Commissioner of Lucknow at the time of the Mutiny and succeeded Sir Henry Lawrence as Chief Commissioner. His diary shows how heavy were his duties during this time, (it is given in full by Hutchinson). He was shot through the head whilst looking over the top of Gubbins' House in examining an outpost (21st July). "He was a leader in whom we had every confidence, far seeing, careful and brave." He was also an excellent Hindi scholar and much valued in the Military Secretary's department at Calcutta.]

(References : *Gubbins ; C. P.; Buckland ; Forrest ; Rice-Holmes ; Hutchinson*)

875.—**1857**—ERETH, T. W. *Inscription* :—Sacred to the memory of T. W. Ereth, who died on the 2nd July 1857 from wounds received during the siege, aged 32 years, 3 months and 13 days.

[The date is wrong and should clearly be 22nd July. He was a corporal of the volunteers and distinguished himself in an attack on the Residency on the 20th July, at Innes' Post ; he was shot in attempting to reinforce the guards there by a bullet in the neck. In hospital he asked a visitor, whilst he was dying, whether all was right at his garrison (Innes' Post). He had only been married 3 months. He was a railway contractor.]

(Reference : *Gubbins ; Rees.*)

876—**1857**—SHEPHERD, J. S. Captain. *Inscription* :—Sacred to the memory of Captain James S. Shepherd, 7th Bengal Light Cavalry, who was killed during the defence of the Lucknow Residency on 26th July 1857.

[Official returns state that he was "Lieutenant" and of the 2nd Oudh Irregular Cavalry. He was killed "at his post" by his own men whilst making a reconnaissance at night. J. Stevens Shepherd, son of Capt, J. Shepherd, was born in 1823.]

(References : *Forrest ; C. P., Rees.*)

877.—**1857**—(1) LEWIN, E. P., Lieutenant. (2) LEWIN, E. S. *Inscription* :—In memory of Lieutenant Edward Powney Lewin, Bengal Artillery, who was killed at his post, the Cawnpore Battery, in the defence of this position, on the 26th of July 1857, aged 24 years, 11 months. Also of his daughter, Edith Scot, who died within the Residency entrenchment on the 20th of August 1857, aged one year, seven months.

Father, I will that they also, whom Thou hast given me, be with me—*St. John*, xvii, 24.

[Cf. no. 895. He was the son of Lieut . W. C. J. Lewin, Bengal Army, born at Calcutta in 1832.]

(Reference : *C.P.*)

878.—**1857**—HALFORD, W. H., Colonel. *Inscription* :—In memory of William Hamilton Halford, Colonel, Commanding 71st Regiment, Bengal Native Infantry, who died at Lucknow, 27th July 1857, from the effects of the siege. This monument is erected by his bereaved widow.

[Died of disease : he was ill all through the siege. Mrs. Harris states the date as 29th July. He was the son of J. Halford, of Windsor, born in 1797.]

(References : *Harris, Gubbins ; C. P.*)

879. **1857**—(1) FULLERTON, E. (2) FULLERTON, J., Lieutenant. *Inscription* :—In memory of James Fullerton, born in Argyleshire, August 30th, 1833, died in the Residency at Lucknow during the defence, September 15th, 1857, and of his child, Elphinstone Fullerton, born November 28th, 1856, died August 7th, 1857.

Looking for that blessed hope, and the glorious appearing of the Great God and our Saviour Jesus Christ—*Titus*, II, 13.

Erected by his widow and mother.

[This was Lieutenant Fullerton, 44th N. I. He walked out of a window on an upper story in his sleep. The Hon'ble James Fullerton was son of Lord Fullerton (senator of the College of Justice in Scotland) born in 1830 at Glenfinnart, Argyle. He had been Assistant Commissioner at Dariabad.]

(References : *Forest ; Gubbins ; C. P.; Harris.*)

880.—**1857**—HUXHAM, E. F. *Inscription* :—Sacred to the memory of Ellen Frances, the beloved child of Lieutenant and Mrs. G. C. Huxham, 48th Native Infantry, who died on the 9th August 1857, aged 11½ months, in the Residency during the siege of Lucknow.

Of such is the Kingdom of Heaven.

[George Corham, son of J. Huxham, was born at E. Teignmouth, Devon.]

(Reference : *C. P.*)

881.—**1857**—(1) ALLNUTT, A., MRS. (2) ALLNUTT, L. E. *Inscription* :—In memory of Ann, wife of Mr. C. D. Allnutt, late Accountant, Delhi Bank, Lucknow, who died during the siege on the 17th August 1857, aged 37 years and 8 months. Also of their infant daughter, Louisa Ellen, died 28th August 1857, aged one month.

882.—**1857**—FITZGERALD, J. F. *Inscription* :—Sacred to the memory of Justitia Florence, the beloved child of Mr. and Mrs. W. Fitzgerald, died at Lucknow during the siege on the 18th of August 1857, aged 18 months.

Of such is the Kingdom of God.

883.—**1857**—(1) THORNHILL, M. C. B., (2) THORNHILL, J. B., B.C.S. *Inscription* :—Sacred to the memory of John Bensley Thornhill, Bengal Civil Service, born May 7th, 1832, died from wounds received during the siege of Lucknow, October 12th, 1857. Also of Mary Charlotte Bensley Thornhill, infant daughter of John Bensley and Mary Thornhill, died September 1st, 1857, aged six days.

The Lord gave and the Lord hath taken away ; blessed be the name of the Lord.

[Mr. Thornhill was Assistant Commissioner before the siege, and did good work all through. On the 12th June he took part in the pursuit of a mutinous Oudh police regiment, and was wounded. He was again wounded during the siege. He got his death-wound as follows. He had volunteered to go out and fetch in the wounded after Havelock's arrival, and being well acquainted with Lucknow his offer was accepted. On his return he missed his way, and guided the bearers of the doolies into the square where Neill fell, now called "Doolie Square." They were met with a murderous fire. As soon as he found out his mistake, he rushed out to turn the rear doolies back. He was struck in the arm and the eye, and died on the 12th October.

He was the son of John Bensley Thornhill (first in the H. E. I. C.'s China, then Bengal, C.S.) Born at Macao in 1832, and educated at Harrow and

Haileybury. For the family cf. no. 449. Mrs. Thornhill was daughter of Col. C. F. Havelock, sister of C. W. Havelock, no. 783.]

(References :—*Hutchinson ; Forrest ; Gubbins ; Harris ; Foster B.; W. P.; Haileybury.)*

884.—**1857**—(1) GRAHAM, F. J., (2) GRAHAM, J., Lieutenant., (3) GRAHAM, G. M. L. *Inscription* :—Sacred to the dear and beloved memory of Lieutenant James Graham, 4th Battalion Light Cavalry, who departed this life during the siege of Lucknow on the 5th September 1857. Also of his two children, Fanny Jane, who died on the 2nd September 1857, aged one year and seven months, and Georgina Mary Louisa, who died on the 27th September 1857, aged one month and four days.

And they shall be mine, saith the Lord of hosts, in that day when I make up my jewels.—*Malachi*, III, 17.

This monument is erected by his widow.

[Lieutenant Graham died in a fit of temporary insanity during the defence of the Residency.]

(Reference : *Kaye.*)

885. **1857**—BOILEAU, G. E. *Inscription* :—Sacred to the memory of Georgina Emma, child of Major and Mrs. G. W. Boileau, who died on the 13th September 1857 in the Garrison of Lucknow, aged two years and six days.

[The child of George Wilson Boileau, son of G. W. Boileau, of Dublin, and Fanny Elizabeth, his wife, daughter of General W. Knyvett. Major Boileau had commanded the 2nd O. I. infantry at Secrora. Cf. no. 562.]

(References : *Gubbins ; Foster B.)*

886.—**1857**—FULTON, G. W. W., Captain. *Inscription* :—Sacred to the memory of Captain G. W. W. Fulton, Bengal Engineers, who was killed in the Residency during the siege of Lucknow on the 14th September 1857, aged 32 years.

[Captain Fulton did magnificent work during the defence of the Residency. It was he who constructed the Redan Battery. He collected a few ex-Cornish miners from the 32nd and was responsible for all the counter-mining. He would descend into a countermine and wait for the enemy's approach, revolver in hand. Somebody once asked a Sergeant, his right-hand man, if he were in the mine. "Yes Sir," was the reply : "there he has been the last two hours like a terrier at a rat-hole, and not likely to leave it all day." He says in his own diary that, on one occasion, "I found.........the rascals were at work in the road ....It seemed a bore to begin to counter, so I just put my head over the wall and called out in Hindustani a trifle of abuse............when such a scuffle and bolt took place, I could not leave for laughing. They dropped it for good, that's the best of the joke." On another occasion he and a few sepoys captured a house : "I put two barrels of powder in it and retired, and to my disgust found some of the people who had gone with me loitering. The consequence was I was delayed, and the powder going off half buried me in ruins. A sepoy by my side was buried up to his waist and I got a very severe contusion..... " True ; but by no means the whole truth. He found the sepoys had loitered : he had fired the train and the danger was imminent. He made them mount the ladder *first* ; but the explosion took place before the last man could even start. His escape was marvellous ; and the act he so modestly relates was one of extraordinary generosity. But, as was said of another officer, Fulton deserved to be covered with Victoria Crosses from head to foot. On the 14th September he was struck dead by a round shot. He had won for himself the title his comrades gave him—" The defender of Lucknow." George William Wright Fulton, born 1825, son of Major R. B. Fulton (no. 381), married in 1840 Isabella Sophia, daughter of Major R. Wroughton (no. 369) and had five sons and a daughter, one of whom commanded the 1st Gurkha Rifles. The Indian branch of the family goes back to John Fulton, a Calcutta merchant, born 1716.]

(References ; *Forrest ; Burke L. G. I.; Hutchinson ; Rice-Holmes.)*

887.—**1857**—(1) OUSELEY, R., (2) OUSELEY, G., (3) OUSELEY, E. A., Mrs. *Inscription:*—Sacred to the memory of Elizabeth Anne, the beloved wife of Ralph Ouseley, Esq. She died at Lucknow on the 14th of November 1857, aged 24 years and 6 months; and of their two children Ralph and Gore, who left them on the 20th September 1857.

The Lord gave and the Lord hath taken away; blessed be the name of the Lord.

[Lieutenant Ouseley, son of Major J. W. J. Ouseley, 23rd No. I, was born in Calcutta in 1829. He was Quartermaster of the 48th N. I. The children died, according to Mrs. Harris, on the 1st October. Mrs. Ouseley was sister of Miss Palmer, vide no. 858.]

(References: *Forrest; C. P.; Harris.*)

888.—**1857**—NAZARETH, E. C., Mrs. *Inscription:*—Sacred to the memory of Elvia Carina, beloved wife of M. V. Nazareth, who died during the siege of the Residency, on the 21st September 1857, aged 36 years, 2 months, 8 days.

"Thou hast protected us from the assembly of the malignant and from the multitude of the workers of iniquity."—*Ps.* lxiii. v. 3.

[The wife of a member of the Uncovenanted Service.]

(Reference: *Forrest.*)

889.—**1857**—CUNLIFFE, F. J., Lieutenant. *Inscription:*—Sacred to the memory of Foster John Cunliffe, 2nd Lieutenant in the Bengal Artillery. Born October 14th, 1834, died September 22nd, 1857.

[F. J. Cunliffe (1834-1857), sixth son of General Sir Robert Cunliffe, Bart., C.B., of the Bengal Army, was educated at Addiscombe. His brother, C. W. Cunliffe, B.C.S., was murdered by the mutineers at Bairamghat in 1857. The Cunliffes are a very old family, dating back to Adam de Conlive (*temp.* Edward I). Cf. no. 895.]

(References: *Vibart; Burke, P.*)

890.—**1857**—RADCLIFFE, C. W., Captain. *Inscription:*—Sacred to the memory of Captain Charles Wilbraham Radcliffe, 7th Light Cavalry, who died from the effects of his wounds on the 25th September 1857, aged 35 years.

Erected by his only son, Captain A. W. T. Radcliffe, 14th Sikhs.

[C. W. Radcliffe, son of the Revd. E. S. Radcliffe, Rector of Walton le Dale, was born in 1820 and joined the service in 1839. He commanded the Volunteer Cavalry at Chinhat, and routed 400 Cavalry and 2 guns with 35 sabres. He was killed in the defence of the Residency.]

(References: *Forrest; Rice-Holmes; Services B. A. list; Kaye.*)

891.—**1857**—LUCAS, F. D. *Inscription:*—In memory of Fitzherbert Dacre Lucas, formerly Captain in the Tipperary Militia Artillery, third son of the Right Hon'ble Edward Lucas of Castle Sha[n]e, Monaghan, born in August 1823. Travelling in India when the Mutiny broke out, his services were accepted of as a volunteer by Sir Henry Lawrence. He fell mortally wounded in the last sortie of the Garrison of Lucknow on the 29th September 1857.

[Mr. Lucas, son of the Right Hon'ble E. Lucas, M.P. for Monaghan, Under Secretary for Ireland (1841 to 1846) and P. C. (1845), married Laura Adelaide, heiress of Lieutenant-Colonel J. F. Scudamore. The family is now Lucas-Scudamore. F. D. Lucas was a traveller and speculator who had come to India more for pleasure than business. He served as a volunteer all through the siege of Lucknow. He earned himself a reputation for coolness and gallantry, was mentioned in despatches, and was mortally wounded in a sortie from the 3rd Sikh Square on the 29th September.]

(References: *Burke, L. G. I.; Forrest; Rees.*)

892.—**1857**—ARNOW, R. E., Mrs. *Inscription* :—Sacred to the memory of Mrs. Rebecca Elizabeth Arnow, who departed this life on the 7th of October A.D. 1857, burnt with a shell ball during the siege, aged 37 years.

My great Physician, Thy will be done.
Sorrow not, even as others which have no hope.

I. Thess IV, 13.

[Not traceable, unless "Miss Arno" of the official list published on the 30th December 1857 is the same.]

893.—**1857**—CONNELL, J. *Inscription* :—Sacred to the memory of John Connell, the beloved child of Overseer Andrew Connell and his wife, Mary. He died at Lucknow during the siege on the 4th November 1857, aged 13 months.

God himself will come and will save you.

Isaiah xxxv, 4.

894.—**1857**—OFFICERS, 13th N. L. I. *Inscription* :—Sacred to the memory of Major C. F. Bruére, Captain R. B. Francis, Lieutenant G. W. Green, Ensign R. L. Inglis of the Hon'ble East India Company's 13th Regiment Native Infantry, who fell whilst serving with their Regiment in the defence of Lucknow in 1857. Also of Captain A. M. Turnbull, who died in the Cawnpore entrenchment, and Lieutenant E. W. Barwell, killed at Hissar. This monument is erected by their brother-officers as a testimony of the respect and affection with which they cherish their memory.

[Major Bruére was slightly wounded at Chinhat. During the defence he was shot on top of the Brigade Mess in picking off a rebel rifleman. He was himself a splendid shot and greatly loved by his men. His Brâhman sepoys insisted on carrying his corpse to burial in spite of the loss of caste it involved. Charles Fleming, son of Captain J. Bruére, was born at Bedford in 1812 and joined the service in 1829. Robert Bransby Francis, son of R. B. Francis, Surgeon H. C. S. (Bengal), was born in 1824 and joined the service in 1842. He commanded the Brigade Mess and lost both his legs by a round shot. "Not a murmur escaped him : his only anxiety being that the authorities would bear testimony that he had performed his duty." George Willaume, son of John Green of Woburn, Beds, was born in 1835 and educated at Marlborough. He distinguished himself in the sortie against Johannes' House on the 7th July : he died of dysentery on the 8th October. Robert Loveday, son of Lieutenant J. Innes, was born at Simla in 1839. He was wounded in the defence : it is not known when he died. The 13th, 48th and 71st are now the 16th Rajputs (the Lucknow Regiment.]

(References : *Forrest* ; *M. C. Register* ; *Services B.A. List* ; *C.P.*)

895—**1857**—OFFICERS, B. A. *Inscription* :—To the memory of Captain A. P. Simons, Lieutenant D. C. Alexander, Lieutenant E. P. Lewin, Lieutenant J. H. Bryce, Lieutenant F. J. Cunliffe, Officers of the Bengal Artillery, who died of wounds, disease and exposure while defending the Residency, Lucknow, during the memorable months of July, August and September 1857. Erected by their brother officers who survived the siege.

[Captain Simons was in command of the Residency Artillery. He was wounded at Chinhat and died on the 8th September. He was the son of W. Simons, E. I. House, born in 1824 : he joined the service in 1841. Daniel Clare Alexander, son of the Reverend D. Alexander, was born at Lambeth in 1827 and was educated at Tiverton. He commanded the O. I. Light Horse Battery, did good service at Chinhat, was severely wounded in the first and killed during the second defence. John Henry Bryce was son of Dr. J. Bryce, Chaplain, H.C.S. (Bengal), born at Edinburgh and educated at the Edinburgh University. He had saved a gun at Chinhat, was wounded and when nearly recovered, died of cholera on the 8th August. For personal details about Cunliffe and Lewin see nos. 867 and 855. The former was wounded at Chinhat and died of fever. Of

8 officers of the Bengal Artillery and one of the Madras Artillery, five were killed and three wounded: only one escaped. The 8 officers had eleven wounds between them. No wonder that Rees remarks that the B.A. suffered severely.]

(References : *Forrest ; Harris ; Rees ; Gubbins ; C. P.; Services B.A. List.*)

896.—**1857**—BECHER, A., Captain. *Inscription :*—In memory of Andrew Becher, Captain, 40th Native Infantry, who died in the Residency of wounds received in Havelock's advance whilst serving with Her Majesty's 90th Regiment.

[A. A.-G., with Havelock's and Outram's force; was killed in the affair of the Doolie Square in the first relief. A. Alameth Becher, son of Col. G. Becher N. C., was born in 1823.]

(References : *Forrest ; Gubbins ; C.P.*)

897.—**1857**—(1) MARTIN, J. R. B., (2) MARTIN. H. B. *Inscription :*—Sacred to the beloved memory of James Ronald Burnard and Henry Burnard, the children of Simon and Mary Martin, who died during the siege of Lucknow, August 1858.

Of such is the Kingdom of Heaven.

[Children of the Deputy Commissioner of Lucknow, Simon Nicolson Martin. His brother was Martin of the 7th Cavalry (who was murdered by his men). They were sons of "the celebrated Indian physician," probably Sir J. R. Martin, President of the India Office Medical Board in 1858. 1858 should be 1857.]

(References : *Buckland ; Harris.*)

898.—**1857-58**—OFFICERS AND MEN 1st MADRAS FUSILIERS. *Inscription :*—Sacred to the memory of Brigadier-General J. G. S. Neill, C.B., and A.-D.-C. to the Queen.

Lieutenant-Colonel J. L. Stephenson, C.B., and Major G. C. S. Renaud.

Lieutenant W. J. Groom.
,, W. D. Arnold.
,, J. A. Richardson.
,, W. Hargood.
,, J. A. Chisholm.
,, F. Dobbs.

352 non-commissioned officers, drummers and rank and file of the First Madras Fusiliers who fell during the suppression of the Rebellion in Bengal, 1857-58.

This monument is erected over the remains of the late Brigadier-General Neill by the surviving officers of the regiment, as a mark of esteem for their late comrades, and in remembrance of their noble example and glorious deeds.

[James George Smith Neill (1810-1857) was the son of Col. Neill. The family dates back to the middle of the 16th century and belongs to Burnwell, Co. Ayr. He had six sons, all in the army, and three daughters: his wife was Isabella, daughter of Col. William Warde, of Squerryes Court, of the 5th B. N. C., and great-grandniece of Lord Cornwallis. Educated at Ayr and Glasgow University, he joined the E. I. C.'s 1st European Regiment (Madras), in 1827. He was D.-A.-A.-G. in 1841 and served in the Burmese War; and as second in command of the Turkish contingent in the Crimean war, showed that Bashi Bazouks could be turned into good soldiers. He was sent to Calcutta with his regiment in 1857. As Adjutant and Colonel, he had turned it into a fine fighting machine. He was responsible for the disarming of the troops at Benares, and went on to Allahabad, where he restored order. Second-in-command to Havelock, he punished the mutineers at Cawnpore with great severity. He was left at Cawnpore till Outram arrived when he went on with him as Brigadier and was killed by a bullet through the head near the present Neill's Gateway in the First Relief. At this spot there stands an inscription as follows:—"*Dulce et decorum est pro patria mori.* This tablet marks the spot where towards the evening of the 28th September 1857, General Neill fell mortally wounded by a shot fired from the adjacent gateway." His monument at Ayr describes him as "a brave, resolute, self-reliant soldier, universally acknowledged as the first who stemmed the torrent of rebellion in Bengal."

Lt. Col. Stephenson (then Major) did good work in Havelock's battles of Cawnpore and Unao. He "showed throughout the day (at Unao) how the calmest forethought can be united with the utmost daring" He commanded a sortie, after the First Relief, to capture the Garden Battery, and was killed in demolishing houses round the Residency a little later.

Major Renaud left Allahabad on the 30th June with a force of 900 men for Cawnpore. He marched nearly to Fatehpur, pacifying the country and punishing rebels, and was then overtaken by Havelock's column. He distinguished himself at the battle of Fatehpur and also at Aung, where he was mortally wounded. Sydenham George Charles, son of C. Renaud, Merchant, was born in London in 1810.

Lieutenant Groom did good service at the capture of Phillips' House on the 2nd October 1857. It is not clear where he died. William Tate Groom, son of R. Groom, solicitor to the India Board, was born in 1831 and educated at Rugby.

Lieutenant Arnold distinguished himself with his skirmishers at the crossing of the Char Bridge in the First Relief: he was in the massacre at the Doolie Square, lying wounded in a doolie, and died a few days later (vide no. 883). Privates Ryan and McManus tried to save him; both got the V. C. He appears to be William Delafield Arnold, son of Dr. Arnold, the famous headmaster of Rugby, and was born in 1828. But if so he was only attached to the 1st M. F. There was an N. H. Arnold in that regiment, but apparently he was not killed. W. M. Hargood was son of Capt. W. Hargood, R. N., born at Seaford in 1833. I could trace none of the other officers.

Lieutenant Dobbs was killed at the storming of the Shah Najaf in the Second Relief.

The 1st Madras Fusiliers, now represented by the 1st Battalion, Royal Dublin Fusiliers, has a long and distinguished history. It existed in detached companies belonging to the H. E. I. C. as early as 1645, and is therefore of earlier date than even the premier regiment on the old Company roll—the 1st Bombay Europeans—raised by Charles II in 1661. It was consolidated into a battalion by Stringer Lawrence in 1748. It served under Clive at Arcot and Plassey; and all through the Lucknow Mutiny operations up to the capture. It has been successively known as the "Madras European Regiment" (1799), "1st Madras European Regiment," (1839), 1st Madras Fusiliers" (1843), and, on becoming a Queen's Regiment, 102nd Royal Madras Fusiliers (1862).]

(References: *Roberts; Rice-Holmes; Campbell; Buckland; Forrest; Burke L. G.; Rees; C. P.*)

899.—1857-58—OFFICERS AND MEN, 90TH L. I. *Inscription:*—This monument is erected by the officers of Her Majesty's 90th Light Infantry in memory of their comrades who fell during the Indian Rebellion of 1857 and 1858, and as a tribute to their gallantry:—Colonel Robert P. Campbell, C.B., died of his wounds at Lucknow, 12th November 1857; Major Roger Barnston, died of his wounds at Cawnpore, 23rd December 1857; Brevet-Major James Perrin, died of his wounds at Alum Bagh, 30th September 1857; Captain Harry Denison, died of his wounds at Lucknow, 29th October 1857; Lieutenant Nicol Graham, killed in action at Alum Bagh, 23rd September 1857; Lieutenant John Joshua Nunn, killed in action at Alum Bagh, 24th September 1857; Lieutenant Arthur Moultrie, killed in action at Lucknow, 26th September 1857; Lieutenant W. H. L. Carleton, died of small-pox at Lucknow, 19th April 1858; Lieutenant R. D. Synge, died of consumption at Lucknow, 8th September 1858; Lieutenant N. Preston, died of his wounds at Alum Bagh, 27th September 1857; Ensign Arthur Chute, died of dysentery at Calcutta, 23rd February 1858; Ensign Hugh Gordon, died of *coup de soleil* at Lucknow, 26th May 1858; Assistant Surgeon R. Nelson, died of fever, 18th August 1857. Also to the memory of 271 non-commissioned officers and privates of the regiment, who fell in the gallant performance of their duty at the Relief, the Defence and the Capture of Lucknow, and during the subsequent campaign in Oudh.

[Colonel Robert P. Campbell, C. B., had won his C. B. in the Crimea. On the 25th September in the First Relief he did excellent service at the Char Bridge. He was left with about 100 men and all the wounded, heavy guns, &c., in a passage near the Moti Manzil Palace that night. Next day he was reinforced but had to stay there all day, and got out at night. He was shot in the knee, and died after amputation.

Major Barnston (1826-1857) was first left in command at Fatehpur and then sent up to his regiment at the Alum Bagh. He was dangerously wounded by the premature bursting of one of our shells at the taking of the Shah Najaf and died at Cawnpore. He was the eldest son of R. H. Barnston, of a family (Barnston of Crewe Hill) which dates back to Hugh de Bernstone of Edward I's time.

Lieutenant Robert Daly Synge was 10th son of John Synge of Glanmore, Co. Wicklow. The family dates back to one Millington "*Cognominatus Sing, quia canonicus fuit,*" and his grandson, Richard Synge, of Bridgnorth, Co. Salop, *circa* 1623.

Ensign Arthur Rowland Chute, born in 1838, was son of R. Chute J. P., D. L., of Chute Hall, Co. Kerry. The Chutes, said to be a branch of the Kentish Chutes, went to Ireland during the Desmond Rebellion, and obtained their present estates in 1630.

Major Perrin, Captain Denison (who was struck by two bullets in the arm and succumbed to amputation) and Lieutenants Nunn, Graham, Moultrie and Preston were all killed or severely wounded during the First Relief. Lieutenant Hugh Gordon was the eldest son of James Gordon of Manor, Co. Aberdeen, an estate purchased by his ancestor Hugh Gordon of the H.E. I.C.S. (1767-1834).

The 90th, now the 2nd Battalion, the Cameronians (Scottish Rifles) were with Havelock and Outram in the advance to the First Relief and in all the subsequent Lucknow operations.]

(References : ***Forrest ; Rice-Holmes ; Roberts ; Burke, L. G. and L. G. I.; Foster B. ; Gubbins.***)

900—1857-8.—OFFICERS AND MEN, 84TH REGIMENT. *Inscription :*—To the memory of Lieutenant-Colonel C. Seymour, Captain E. Currie, Captain R. Pakenham, Lieutenant B. Sandwith, Lieutenant F. Saunders, Lieutenant H. Ayton, Lieutenant P. Chute, Lieutenant A. Gibaut, Lieutenant W. Poole, Lieutenant R. Maybury, Ensign H. Kenny, Paymaster G. Eddy, Quartermaster H. Donelan, and 360 non-commissioned officers and privates of the 84th York and Lancaster Regiment, who were killed, died of their wounds or of disease during the Indian Mutiny Campaign, nobly performing their duty. To record the devotion, gallantry and true discipline displayed by the above at all times and upon all occasions, this monument is erected by the officers of the regiment.

[Lieutenant-Colonel Seymour was a Captain at the siege of Lucknow and officiated as Q.-M.-G. It is not known where he died.

Captain Currie was killed at Havelock's battle of Cawnpore (16th July 1857).

Captain Pakenham, "an able officer and devoted soldier," fell whilst entering the city in the First Relief (25th September 1857). He was the 4th son of Sir Hercules Pakenham, K.C.B., who distinguished himself in the Peninsular War, and grandson of the 2nd Lord Longford. Lieutenants Gibaut and Poole were also killed during that relief.

Lieutenant Sandwith, acting Field Engineer, did good service at the Alum Bagh during the First Relief and was killed during the second.

Lieutenant Ayton was mentioned in despatches after the battle of Fatehpur : it is not known where he died. Lieutenant Chute was wounded in Outram's 4th action at the Alam Bagh on the 25th February 1858.

Lieutenant Saunders was killed in the defence of Cawnpore. It is not known where the rest died.

Henry Kenny and his brother Edward (also in the 84th) were sons of Colonel E. Kenny, 89th Regiment, of Ballyornan, Co. Wicklow The family is of French Huguenot extraction and settled in Ireland about 1660

The 84th had detachments at both the defences of Lucknow and Cawnpore. Other detachments were in Havelock's column, and in action at Fatehpur, Unao, Bashiratganj, Bithur and the First Relief. They stayed in garrison in Lucknow till the Second Relief. They were raised in 1758, and were in India from 1753-1758, 1763, 1842-1859, 1897-1902. Their Indian honours are "India" (with Royal Tiger) and "Lucknow;" they are now the 2nd Battalion of the York and Lancaster Regiment. They also fought at the Nile and in Egypt 1882.]

(References : *Forrest : Burke, L. and L. G. I.*)

901.—**1857-58**—OFFICERS AND MEN, 5TH FUSILIERS. *Inscription :*—Sacred to the memory of Major J. E. Simmons, Captain J. W. L'Estrange, Captain A. E. Johnson, Captain W. M. Carter, Lieutenant E. J. Haig, Lieutenant J. C. Brown, 5 Sergeants, 2 Corporals and 77 Privates of Her Majesty's 5th Fusiliers, who lost their lives in the advance upon Lucknow under General Havelock, during the defence of the Residency, under Sir J. Outram, G.C.B., during the subsequent operations at the Alum Bagh and at the final capture of Lucknow. This monument is erected by the officers of the regiment, now in India, December 1st, 1858.

[Major Simmons was in the Moti Manzil with Colonel Campbell, 90th Light Infantry (*vide* no. 899) whom he reinforced. He was killed during the Second Defence (Outram's) in a sortie from the left square Brigade Mess on the 29th September 1857. Captain L'Estrange was the officer who lent his men without orders to assist Vincent Eyre to relieve Arrah House when besieged by Kunwar Singh.

Captain Johnson did good service at Kundan Patti under Major Eyre and at Lucknow: he and Captain L'Estrange were both wounded severely in the First Relief. Lieutenant Haig and Captain Carter were both killed in the First Relief. Captain Carter (William Marcon, 1827-1857) was the second and eldest surviving son of John Langham Carter of Worthwold, a family dating back to 1692. Lieutenant Brown did good service at the seizure of the Phillip's Garden Battery where he captured two 9-pounders in the Second (Outram's) Defence. It is not known where he was killed. For Lieutenant Haig, cf. no. 917.

The 5th Fusiliers, now the Northumberland Fusiliers or "Fighting Fifth," were with Outram's force in the Second Relief, Outram's Defence of the Alum Bagh, and with Windham at Cawnpore. Their Indian honours are "Lucknow" and "Afghanistan 1878-80." They also fought in the Peninsula and at Khartoum.]

(References : *Forrest ; Rice-Holmes ; Burke, L. G.*)

902.—**1858**—MOORSOM, W. R., Lieutenant. *Inscription :*—In memory of Lieutenant W. R. Moorsom, Her Majesty's 52nd, Quarter-Master-General, 1st Division, killed in action near the Iron Bridge, March 11th, 1858.

Fervent in spirit serving the Lord.

[Acting Deputy Assistant Quartermaster-General with the Oudh Field Force. He was mentioned in despatches after the Pandu Naddi, Fatehpur, Cawnpore, Relief of Lucknow and the Alum Bagh, and was shot down while guiding Outram's column in the reduction of Lucknow. "I deplore sincerely," wrote Outram "the loss of this most gallant and promising young officer." In 1856 he had carried out a survey of Lucknow on which all military plans were based.]

(References ; *Gubbins ; Forrest.*)

903.—**1858.**—KIRWAN, H. Revd. *Inscription :*—In Christ. Revd. Hyacinth Kirwan, Chaplain of the 2nd Division of the Besieging Army, who died at Lucknow, 3rd April 1858. This stone is erected by his friend, Revd. H. Smith, D.D., Chaplain of the Field Hospital.

[Hyacinth Kirwan (1820 1858) was the 4th and youngest son of Patrick Kirwan of Cregg, Co. Galway. He was educated at Eton and King's College, Cambridge (Fellow). He was given an Indian Chaplaincy in 1848. He founded a fund in the Calcutta diocese, called the 'Kirwan and Kay fund." This originated in a bequest by the Rev. H. Kirwan, when a Chaplain in Bengal, which was increased by a donation from Revd. Dr. Kay, formerly Principal of Bishop's College. The interest of the fund is employed for maintaining a native reader or clergyman in the neighbourhood of Bishop's College." He was learned in Eastern languages and from his earliest days was devoted to reading and study. When the Bishop of Lincoln founded the "Voluntary Theological Examination" early in the forties, he and one other were the only two that passed—possibly the only two that appeared at the examination. It is dubious whether he is actually buried at this spot as he died of small-pox in one of the field hospitals at the final siege of Lucknow. The family settled in Galway in 1488.]

(References : *Burke L.G.I.; Communicated.*)

904.—1858—COSSERAT, J. F., Captain. *Inscription* :—Here lie the remains of Captain J. F. Cosserat, 34th Madras Light Infantry who died of his wounds, 10th April 1858, aged 32.

A tribute of affection from the officers of his regiment to the memory of a brave and beloved comrade.

[Wounded severely on the 23rd March 1858 at the action of Kursi under Hope Grant Captain Cosserat was then in command of a squadron of the 1st Punjab Cavalry.]

(References : *Forrest; Roberts.*)

905.—1858—SPRINGATE, R., Colour-Sergeant. *Inscription* :—"Sacred to the memory of Colour-Sergeant Richard Springate of Her Majesty's, XCth Light Infantry, who departed this life on the 19th of April 1858, aged 36 years and 5 months. Deeply regretted by all who knew him."

906.—1858—FAIRHURST, P. Revd. *Inscription* :—Pray for the soul of the Rev. Patrick Fairhurst, who, to assist his Catholic Brethren amid the perils of the great Indian Rebellion, left his home and fell a martyr to charity, a victim to hardship and privations on the 16th of June A. D. 1858. The Catholic soldiers of Her Majesty's 53rd Regiment here testify their admiration and gratitude.

ENCLOSURE OF TOMB OF SA'ADAT ALI KHAN.

907.—1858—OFFICERS, R. E., AND B. E., AND MEN, R. E. *Inscription* :—To the memory of Captain J. Clerke, Royal Engineers, Lieutenant E. P. Brownlow, Bengal Engineers; Corporal Frederick Morgan; Lance-Corporal James Davis; Sapper James Bunting; Sapper George Beer; Sapper Michael Daily; Sapper John Ford; Sapper Andrew Fairservice; Sapper David Northwood; Sapper William Outerson; Sapper William Robinson; Sapper James Slade; Sapper Alfred Smith; Sapper Charles Tucker; Sapper John Yeo, of the 23rd Company of the Royal Engineers, who were killed by the explosion of a quantity of gunpowder abandoned by the mutineers in their retreat from Lucknow on the 17th March 1851.

[During the final reduction of Lucknow a quantity of powder in tin cases and leather bags was found in a yard behind the Jama Masjid. Outram directed it to be destroyed by the Engineers. It was taken to a large and deep well as rapidly as possible. When one of them was being thrown down it struck the side of the well and exploded. A flame of fire flashed up, ignited case after case, caught the powder in the carts and blew it up, killing or severely wounding 2 officers and 14 men.

Captain Clerke had done excellent work at Khujwa, and both he and Lieutenant Brownlow had been honourably mentioned by the Chief Engineer, Brigadier Napier. Clerke was the Adjutant of the R. E.]

(Reference : *Forrest.*)

ON NEILL'S ROAD.

908.—1857—VICTIMS FROM SITAPUR. *Inscription :—On south face.*—Sacred to the memory of (1) Sir Mountstuart Jackson, Bart ; (2) Captain Patrick Orr ; (3) Lieutenant G. J. H. Burnes, 1st Bombay European Fusiliers ; (4) Sergeant-Major Mortan.—Victims of 1857.—*On north face.*—Sacred to the memory of (1) G. P. Carew, Esq.; (2) Mrs. Greene ; (3) Miss Jackson and others, European and Native, faithful servants of Government. Victims of 1857.

[Captain Orr was First Assistant Commissioner at Muhamdi in Kheri, a district corresponding to a part of the modern district. On the arrival of the Shahjahanpur fugitives, a body of troops was sent from Sitapur to escort them to that place : and Orr went with them. On the road, however, occurred the massacre of Aurangabad (vide no. 976). Orr was spared by the intervention of some troops which he had himself raised and escaped to Mitauli, where he had already sent his wife and child. Here he was joined a few days later by those who had escaped from Sitapur, Sir M. Jackson (Assistant Commissioner) and his sister, Lieutenant Burnes, Sergeant-Major Mortan and Sophy Christian, a child of Mr. Christian, the Commissioner. They were protected by Raja Loni Singh till the 6th August, though in constant fear of treachery on his part. On that date he turned them out of his fort, a piece of deliberate treachery, for, though he would not give up the fugitives, he turned them adrift and told the sepoys where they were. They remained, however, in the jungles in safety till the 20th October, when they were arrested by 300 men of the Raja's, under a scoundrel named Zahur-ul-Husain, whom Captain Orr had actually befriended. The men were heavily fettered and taken to Lucknow, and imprisoned in the Kaisarbagh in a miserable room in an out-house. They were shown some kindness however, by Wajid Ali, a steward of one of the ex-king's wives, and Raja Man Singh ; and their fetters were removed. Here they remained until the arrival of Sir Colin Campbell with the second Relieving Force. On the 16th November, the men were taken away by some of the 71st Regiment and shot. The ladies were spared : little Sophy Christian died on the 24th November, but the rest were rescued by Wajid Ali and handed over to Sir J. Outram on the 20th March.

As regards the rest, their story is as follows. Captain J. B. Hearsey was saved by some of his men of the Military Police as well as Miss Jackson (another sister of Sir M. Jackson), Mrs. Greene, wife of Lieutenant Greene of the 9th Oudh Irregulars, and Sergeant-Major Rogers, his wife and step-son named Sullivan. They were allowed to go and travelled first to Oel and thence, on hearing from Mr. Gonne, to Mallanpur. With Mr. Gonne were Messrs. Carew and Brand of the Rosa Factory in Shahjahanpur. They started down the river in boats but news of mutineers at Bairamghat compelled them to return to Mathiara, a village of the Raja of Dhaurahra. Here they remained two months, the party consisting of Miss Jackson and Mrs. Greene, Captains Hearsey and Hastings, Messrs. Gonne, Brand and Carew, Sergeant-Major Rogers and his wife, Mr. Brown, a writer, and Mr. Sullivan. The Rani of Dhaurahra (the Raja was a minor) was as treacherous as the Raja of Mitauli, and the band agreed to be taken to Lucknow ; but suspecting treachery on the road, they fled to Khairigarh. They were pursued, but night came on and they managed to escape. Here the party was separated ; Mr. Carew and Mrs. Rogers and her son were on an elephant, and got ahead. We need not follow the adventures of the rest except to say that all but Captain Hearsey perished. Mr. Brown was seized by an alligator in swimming a river, Mr. Gonne died of jungle fever, Captain Hastings also died of fever, while Brand and Rogers also died somewhat later.

The ladies and Mr. Carew eventually fell into the hands of the Rani of Dhaurahra and were sent into Lucknow. They were at first well treated and placed in the Kaisarbagh, but "after an unsuccessful attack on the Alum Bagh" (which was either, probably, in Havelock and Outram's advance or during

Macintyre's occupation of it—i.e., either in the last week of September or first week of October 1857), they were dragged out and murdered in a nullah near the Tara Kothi (present Bank of Bengal), with 22 others of whom 17 were Europeans or Eurasians. Of the "others" not named one was Sullivan, Roger's step-son: another was possibly Mrs. Rogers unless she had already perished, for she was not named in a memorandum provided by Wajid Ali, and he also names Mr. Coldayra, a writer, as belonging to the party.

The form of this memorial was apparently that suggested by Capt. Hutchinson; merely the names with the addition "victims of 1857." Sir Mountstuart Goodriche Jackson (1836-1857) 3rd Baronet was educated at Eton and Haileybury and entered the C. S. in 1856. He was the eldest son of Sir Keith Jackson, 2nd Baronet, A.-D.-C. to Mountstuart Elphinstone, and then to Sir John Macdonald in Persia. The family is an old Cumberland family. The sister who was murdered was Miss Amelia Georgina Jackson; the one who escaped, Anna Madeline, married her cousin Elphinstone Jackson, Judge of the Calcutta High Court (d. 1873). George James Holmes, son of J. Burnes, Residency Surgeon at Bhooj in Cutch, was born in 1830 and educated at Edinburgh Academy.]

(References: *C.P.; Haileybury; Hutchinson; Rice-Holmes; Burke, P.*)

WILAYATI BAGH.

909.—**1858**—GARVEY, H. P., MATE, R. N. *Inscription:*—Here lies Mr. Henry P. Garvey, Acting Mate, Her Majesty's Ship "Shannon," killed before Lucknow, March XIth, MDCCCLVIII.

Blessed are the dead which die in the Lord.

[This officer was probably killed during the attack on the Begum Kothi.]

(Reference: *Forrest.*)

910.—**185**—HUTCHINSON, W. H., Captain. *Inscription:*—Sacred to the memory of Captain W. Heley Hutchinson, 9th Royal Lancers. Born 5th March 1833, mortally wounded in an attack on the rebels near the Moosa Bagh, 9th March 1858, died 22nd March 1858. This monument is erected by his brother officers.

[During the operations at the Moosa Bagh on the 9th March the 9th Lancers repeatedly charged the flying enemy, following them up for about four miles. A small body of them reached a deep ravine through which they could not ride; and it was here that Hutchinson was mortally wounded. He died on the 22nd and was buried in "the beautiful walled garden at the riverside below the Dilkusha."]

(Reference: *Forrest.*)

911.—**1858**—NEWMAN, S. Sergeant. *Inscription:*—In memory of Sergeant S. Newman, 9th Queen's Royal Lancers, who fell mortally wounded in pursuit of the rebels near the Moosa Bagh, 19th March 1858.

[Wounded in the same affair as that mentioned above. In Forrest he is given as a corporal.]

(Reference: *Forrest.*)

LA MARTINIERE PARK.

912.—**1857**—MAYNE, A. O. Lieutenant. *Inscription:*—Here lies the body of Lieutenant Augustus Otway Mayne, Bengal Artillery, killed in action at the relief of Lucknow on the 14th of November 1857, in the 28th year of his age.

Waiting the coming of the Lord Jesus Christ.

[Deputy Assistant Quartermaster-General, assisting Lord Roberts. During Sir Colin Campbell's relief heavy firing was heard unexpectedly from Banks' House. Roberts and Mayne galloped off to find out the cause; but became separated. Mayne was then seen to fall, shot through the breast. Roberts looked that evening for his body in vain: next morning he found it in a dooli at the Martiniere. He buried him at once with the aid of some gunners and some other officers "just as he was, in his blue frock coat and long boots, his eyeglass in his eye as he always carried it." His sword Roberts took away and made over to his family. On a tree over the grave he cut the initials "A. O. M." "not very deep for there was little time." But they remained long enough for the present stone to be erected. The spot is south of the metalled road passing through the Park.]

(Reference : *Roberts.*)

913.—**1858**—HODSON, W. S. R. Major. *Inscription* :—Here lieth all that could die of William Stephen Raikes Hodson, Captain and Brevet-Major, 1st E. B. Fusiliers, and Commandant of Hodson's Horse, son of the Ven'ble George Hodson, Archdeacon of Stafford. Born March 19th, 1821, fell in the final assault at Lucknow, March 11th, 1858.

A little while. II *Cor.* IV, 12.

[This tomb lies north of the road leading to the College near the College Hospital. William Stephen Raikes Hodson (1821-1858), son of the Revd. George Hodson, was educated at Rugby and Trinity College, Cambridge, where he took his B. A. in 1844. In 1845 he joined the army and fought at Mudki, Firozshahr and Sobraon. In 1847 he became 2nd in command of the Guides and Assistant to the Resident at Lahore. In the 2nd Sikh war he was engaged with the Guides in partizan warfare, and was also at Gujrat on Sir H. Gough's staff. He then became Assistant Commissioner in the Punjab. In 1852 he married Susan, daughter of Capt. Henry R.N., and widow of John Mitford, of Exbury ; and the same year succeeded Lumsden in command of the Guides and also held civil charge of Yuzafzai. He built the fort at Mardan and saw much frontier fighting. In 1855 he was reverted to his regiment (the 1st E. B. F.) on account of certain inaccuracies in the regimental accounts and other grounds. When the Mutiny broke out General Anson made him head of the Intelligence Department, and ordered him to raise a regiment of irregular horse. At this time occurred his famous ride of 152 miles from Karnal to Meerut and back again, with despatches. He took a prominent share in the Delhi operations, and wound up his services by the capture of Bahadur Shah, the Emperor, and his three sons, whom he killed with his own hand. He then took part in minor operations in Rewari, and the Meerut and Agra divisions, during which occurred his second famous ride—Mainpuri to Miran Ki Sarai and back to Bewar, 94 miles in all. He was wounded at Shamsabad and was in all Sir Colin Campbell's operations up to the reduction of Lucknow. He was mortally wounded in the assault on the Begam's Kothi, whilst leading some Highlanders to attack a strongly fortified room. He died on the 12th March.

His life was a continual series of adventures. Men used to wonder why he never got the V. C.; one explanation was that he won it every day of his life. Controversy rages round certain incidents of his career ; whatever the truth may be about these matters, it is certain that he was loved and respected by great men such as Seaton, Campbell, Norman, Lord Napier, Lawrence, Currie and Montgomery and idolized by soldiers, whether his old guides, who sat about his house merely "to look at the sahib," or the Highlanders who fetched each other to "come and see Hodson." He was the perfection of a cavalry soldier, a born partizan leader, a man who not only could lead the rawest of raw recruits (as they said themselves) into hell but out again on the other side. When he raised Hodson's Horse, enough men flocked to his standard to raise three regiments, though only one was required. Two regiments, the 9th and 10th Lancers, still exist to keep the memory of Hodson and his Horse green. If some critics must insist that his name points a moral, none venture to deny that it adorns many a tale.]

(References :—*Trotter ; Roberts ; P. R. Innes ; Rice-Holmes ; Kaye ; Forrest ; Buckland ; Forbes-Mitchell.*)

914.—**1858.**—DACOSTA, L., Captain. *Inscription* :—Sacred to the memory of Captain L. DaCosta, 56th N. I., attached to Ferozpur Regiment of Sikhs, who fell in the final assault on the Kaisar Bagh, the 13th March 1151, aged 32 years.

[Lionel Gomez DaCosta, son of Mr. DaCosta, a merchant, was born in 1824 and joined the service in 1841. The Ferozpur Sikhs are now the 14th Prince of Wales's own Ferozpur Sikhs (raised 1846.)]

(Reference ; *Services B. A. List.*)

LA MARTINIERE COLLEGE.

915.—1800—MARTIN, C., Major-General. *Inscription* :—Here lies Claude Martin, born at Lyons, the 5th day of January 1735. Arrived in India as a common soldier and died at Lucknow, the 13th September 1800, a Major-General. Pray for his soul.

[Claude Martin (1735-1800) was son of a French silk manufacturer of Lyons. He was intended for the same calling, but preferred a more adventurous profession and enlisted in the French Army. In 1757 Lally, when appointed Governor of Pondicherry, applied for volunteers for his bodyguard and Martin offered himself and was accepted. He arrived in India in 1758. Lally's discipline was extremely severe and his behaviour tyrannical; his conduct may have been necessary for many of his bodyguard were military criminals and deserters; but it only made them more insubordinate; and when Coote laid siege to Pondicherry the bodyguard deserted to the English *en masse*. Martin volunteered to raise a corps of French *chasseurs* for the Company from among the prisoners of war. The proposal was accepted, and he was made its commander with the rank of Ensign. On one occasion he and his corps were shipwrecked on their way to Bengal; and it was with the greatest difficulty that he saved them in the boats. He became Captain in due course: but his men mutinied in 1764, and the corps was broken up. Martin did his best to keep them faithful: and as a reward he was given an appointment in the N.-E. districts of Bengal, which, being an able draftsman, he was sent to survey. Later he obtained a similar position in Oudh. At Lucknow he spent his leisure in mechanics, and amongst other things manufactured "the first balloons that ever floated in the air of Asia." This brought him to the Nawab's notice, who came to think so highly of him, and especially of his skill in gunnery, that he obtained permission for Martin's services to be transferred to him; and on his request being granted made him superintendent of his park of artillery and arsenal.

Martin soon ingratiated himself with the Nawab, and became his confidential adviser. He contrived to remain always on the right side and made himself indispensable in negotiations between the Nawab and the Company. Wisely preferring the substance of power to its shadow, he remained in the background; but he had more real influence on politics than the ministers.

Martin of course drew large pay and enjoyed extensive sources of emolument. He was the recognized channel for petitions, and made large sums in this way. He taught the Nawab to appreciate European articles, and then acted as go-between in obtaining them. He had profitable transactions with the native bankers. Finally his position was so secure that in troublous times it was with him that valuables were deposited for security on a commission. He acquired consequently an immense fortune.

During his life he was hospitable in an unostentatious way: his chief vanity was military rank—a fact to which his epitaph bears witness. He had retained his commission in the Company's service, though relinquishing his pay and allowances, and he rose in the ordinary course. His Colonelcy he obtained in 1790 by presenting the Company with sufficient fine horses to mount a troop: and when, in 1796, the Company's officers were granted brevet rank by the King, he was made a Major-General to his infinite delight.

His house, "Constantia," was a castellated edifice designed for defence if necessary and constructed on strictly hygenic principles. It had a series of rooms adapted to the various temperatures of different seasons. One room was designed as vault for his tomb. He built this because the Nawab refused to pay him the price he asked for the house: and in a fit of pique he declared that his tomb should be handsomer than any palace in Oudh. It was called "*Constantia*," from the motto "*Labor et constantia*" carved on its front.

His will, which he drew up himself, was an extraordinary production. It began by a confession that self-interest had guided him through life. His fortune of 33 lakhs of rupees was almost entirely bequeathed to charity. There were legacies to the poor of Calcutta, Chandranagore, Lucknow and Lyons, the interest of which was to be doled out daily at certain fixed places marked by tablets notifying that the alms were the gift of General Martin and were to be so distributed in perpetuity. He left a large sum in trust to the Government of Bengal to establish and endow a school to be called *La Martiniere* in Calcutta, which still exists. Other legacies were to his relatives and the town of Lyons, and also two sums, to Lyons and Calcutta, to be devoted to releasing poor debtors from jail on the anniversary of his death. His house "Constantia" was never to be sold but to serve as a mausoleum for his remains, and as a college for educating children in the English religion and language. He also gave elaborate instructions for his own burial and epitaph. Fanny Parkes mentions that, in 1831, a bust of the General adorned the vault and lights were constantly burned before the tomb. The figures of four sipahis large as life, with their arms reversed, stood in niches at the sides of the tomb. Mrs. Harris states that the tomb was broken to fragments in the Mutiny and "his old bones scattered to the winds"; but if so it has since been restored. "Dynasties have died out, thrones have tottered and fallen, kingdoms have crumbled into dust and been forgotten since this private soldier sought to perpetuate his name, and it is not an unpleasing thought that.... his testamentary charity still keeps alive the pious memory of the founder of *La Martiniere;*" a memory which generations of Anglo-Indian parents and children have had cause to bless.]

(References: *Compton; Buckland: Wandering of a Pilgrim; Harris: B.O.*)

ALUM BAGH CEMETERY.

916.—1857—(1) PERRIN, J., Major., (2) GRAHAME, V., Lieutenant., (3) NUNN, J. J. Lieutenant., (4) PRESTON, M. Lieutenant. *Inscription:*—Sacred to the memory of Major J. Perrin, Lieutenants V. Grahame, J. J. Nunn and M. Preston, 90th Light Infantry, who were killed in action near this spot, 24th September 1857. Erected by their comrades.

[Cf. no. 899.]

917.—1857 HAIG, E, Lieutenant. *Inscription:*—"In memory of Edwin Haig, Lieutenant and Adjutant of the 5th Fusiliers, who was killed by a round shot at the attack on the city of Lucknow on the 25th September 1857, aged about 20 years. This stone is erected by the officers, non-commissioned officers and privates of the 5th Fusiliers."

[Cf. no. 901. Edwin Fell Haig was born in 1834, and therefore was 23 not "about" 20 when he died. He was the 5th son of Robert Haig of Dundalk. Many of this family (Haig of Bemersyde) have served in India from the time of this officer's uncle, who was a Madras Judge, *circa* 1810, and married the daughter of the Magistrate of Pondicherry. A cousin, J. F. Haig, was serving in the 90th Light Infantry all through the Mutiny; and two brothers were in the Indian Army. There are representatives of the family (though in another branch—the Haigs of Pen-Ithon) serving in India at the present moment, and one in this province. The family is extremely ancient and traces its ancestry back to Peter de Haga of Bemersyde, *circa* 1150. A century later Thomas the Rhymer prophesied of them: "Tyde what may betyde Haig shall be Haig of Bemersyde." The 17th laird of Bemersyde disposed of Bemersyde to his brother William. William was identified as the author of the "Supplication" in 1633, fled to Holland and left Bemersyde to his nephew, David. From him after six generations the succession reverted to the present owner, younger brother of E. F. Haig, in 1866; he is a descendant of the 17th laird already mentioned, through his second son. The Haigs of Blair-Hill, Pen-Ithon and Ramon.o are also all lineal descendants of this 17th laird. The earliest Haig who came to India was the 10th son of this same laird, the 17th: he is said to have gone there in 1639.]

(Reference: *Burke, L. G.*)

ALUM BAGH CEMETERY.

918.—1857—HAVELOCK, H., Major-General Sir. *Inscription:*—Here rest the mortal remains of Henry Havelock, Bart Major-General in the British Army, Knight Commander of the Bath, who died at Dilkusha, Lucknow, of dysentery produced by the hardships of a campaign, in which he achieved immortal fame, on the 24th November 1857. He was born on the 5th April 1795, at Bishop Wearmouth, County Durham, England. Entered the

Army 1815, came to India 1823, and served there with little interruption till his death. He bore an honourable part in the wars of Burmah, Afghanistan, the Maharatta Campaign of 1843 and the Sutlej of 1845-46. Retained by adverse circumstances during many years in a subordinate position, it was the aim of his life to prove that the profession of a Christian is consistent with the fullest discharge of the duties of a soldier. He commanded a Division in the Persian Expedition of 1857. In the terrible convulsion of that year his genius and character were at length fully developed and known to the world. Saved from shipwreck on the Ceylon coast by that Providence which designed him for yet greater things, he was nominated to the command of the column destined to relieve the brave garrison of Lucknow. This object, after almost superhuman exertions, he, by the blessing of God, accomplished. But he was not spared to receive on earth the reward so dearly earned. The Divine Master whom he served saw fit to remove him from the sphere of his labours in the moment of his greatest triumph. He departed to his rest in humble but confident expectation of greater rewards than those which a grateful country was anxious to bestow. In him the skill of a commander, the courage and devotion of a soldier, the learning of a scholar, the grace of a high bred gentlemen, and all the social and domestic virtues of a husband, father and friend, were blended together and strengthened, harmonized and adorned by the spirit of a true Christian: the result of the influence of the Holy Spirit on his heart and a humble reliance on the merits of a crucified Saviour.

I have fought a good fight; I have finished my course; I have kept the faith: henceforth there is laid up for me a crown of righteousness which the Lord, the Righteous Judge, shall give me that day, and not to me only, but to all those that love his appearance.

His ashes in a peaceful urn shall rest,
His name a greaten sample stands to show,
How strangely high endeavours may be blest,
Where piety and valour jointly go.

This monument is erected by his sorrowing widow and family.

[Henry Havelock (1795-1857), son of William Havelock of Ingress Park, Kent, and Jane, daughter of John Carter of Yarm, Yorkshire, was born at Bishop Wearmouth and educated at Swanscombe and the Charterhouse. He was at first entered at the Middle Temple, but in 1815 joined the 95th (Rifle Brigade). He studied his profession with diligence both practically and theoretically. In 1823 he exchanged into the 13th Light Infantry and then came out to India. In 1824 he served with credit as D. A. A. G. of the Burma expedition, and in 1828 published his "Campaigns in Ava," whilst Adjutant of the depot of King's troops at Chinsura. The work was scholarly, and showed clear mastery of detail: but his severe strictures made him many enemies. In 1829 he married Hannah Shepherd daughter of Dr. Marshman, the celebrated Baptist Missionary at Serampur, which community he joined. In 1838 he became a captain, and joined the staff of Sir W. Cotton in the Kabul expedition. He played a not obscure part both in the storming of Ghazni and the defence of Jalalabad. He wrote a memoir of the war which attracted no attention, though it deserved a better fate. In 1841 he returned to Kabul as Persian interpreter on the staff of General Elphinstone. He was with Sir R. Sale on his march to Jalalabad and was present in the siege and at the defeat of Akbar Khan in 1842. He next became D. A. A. G. of the Infantry Division. For his services in Afghanistan he was made C.B.

In 1843 he became Major. He was appointed to Sir H. Gough's staff and did conspicuous service at Maharajpur, being made Brevet Lieutenant-Colonel. In the 1st Sikh War he was at Mudki, Firozshahr and Sobraon. He then became D.A.G. of the Queen's troops in Bombay. In 1849 he took furlough and on his return took up his old post. In 1854 be became Q. M.-G. of the Queen's troops in India, Lieutenant-Colonel and Brevet Colonel. In 1855 he became A.-G.; and in 1856-57 commanded a division in the Persian War. When peace was signed, he returned to Bombay and there heard the news of the Mutiny. He sailed for Calcutta, but was wrecked off Ceylon. In Calcutta he was made Brigadier-General and on the 25th June, set off up country, to commence the marvellous march which saved Lucknow. He fought action after action: six between the 12th and 29th July: three between the 4th and 16th August: and finally left Cawnpore with Outram on the 21st September, fought two actions, and by the 25th had relieved Lucknow. There he stayed till Sir Colin Campbell again relieved it; and on the 17th November Outram, Havelock and Campbell met on the ground sloping down to the Mess House. "Havelock, the hero of a hundred fights," says Lord Roberts, "looked ill, worn and depressed, but brightened up a little when Norman told him he had been made a K. C. B." On the 24th November he died and was buried in the Alum Bagh. So ended Havelock's five months of glorious history.

In character he was simple and austere; a man of the strongest religious convictions, yet no bigot: reserved, yet liked by many wild young officers who had little in common with him. A true Christian, who expounded the Bible to his men in spite of the ridicule of his brother officers, who called his company "Havelock's Saints"—yet he never forgot his military instincts: if he taught his men to be good men he taught them also to be good soldiers, and if "Havelock's Saints" were never drunk, they were always ready for service. All his life his ambition had been to command a British Army in the field: and all his life he had studied to that end. "He was familiar with every axiom of Vauban and Jomini: he could describe from memory every evolution of Marlborough and Wellington, Frederick and Napoleon." He could apply them too, as he applied the strategy of "old Frederick at Luethen," in his battle of Cawnpore. In the words of his epitaph: "It was the aim of his life to prove that the profession of a Christian is consistent with the fullest discharge of the duties of a soldier."

Years before Lord Hardinge had said of him: "If India is ever in danger the Government have only to put Havelock in command of an army, and it will be saved." Yet in 1857 nobody out of India had ever heard of Havelock: even in India they sneered at him as "an old fossil, dug up and only fit to be turned into pipe-clay." He left Calcutta on the 25th June little better than a nobody; when he died, on the 24th November, his name was known all over the English-speaking world, so that the flags were hung at half-mast in New York when he died.

His son (*vide* no. 921) was given the baronetcy and pension destined for his father. Of his three brothers two, Lieutenant-Colonel W. Havelock, K. H., killed at Ramnagar in the Sikh War 1848, and Thomas, died of fever in the Peninsular War, lost their lives on active service. The third, Lieutenant-Colonel C. F. Havelock, fought at Bhurtpore, in the first Afghan War and in the first Sikh War, and commanded the Irregular Osmanli Cavalry. His son, Lieutenant C. W. Havelock, was killed in the Mutiny (*vide* no.783). Lieutenant-Colonel W. Havelock's son, Sir Arthur E. Havelock, G.C.M.G., G.C.S.I., G.C.I.E., was Governor of Ceylon (1890-5), Madras (1895-1900) and Tasmania (1901-4).]

(References; *Kaye*; *Rice-Holmes*; *Forrest*; *Buckland*; *Roberts*; *Burke, P.*)

919.—**1857**—AYTON, H. Lieutenant. *Inscription*:—*Resurgam*.—In memory of Henry Ayton, H. M.'s 84th Regiment, who died on the 28th November 1857 of wounds received at Lucknow on the 16th November 1857, aged 28 years.

[Cf. no. 900.]

920.—**1858**—GORDON, D. W., Lieutenant. *Inscription*:—Sacred to the memory of Dundas W. Gordon, Lieutenant, Bengal Artillery, killed at his post during General Outram's defence of this garden on the 8th January 1858, aged 24 years."

[Lieutenant Gordon was with Major Eyre and did good service at the battles of Mangalwar and in the Alam Bagh and in General Outram's operations there. He was killed by a round shot. He was the son of A. Gordon, born in Kent in 1883].

(Reference; *C. P.*; *Forrest*).

921.—1897—HAVELOCK-ALLAN, H. M. Sir. *Inscription :*— In memory of Lieutenant-General Sir Henry Marshman Havelock-Allan, Baronet, V.C., G.C.B., M.P., son of Major-General Sir Henry Havelock of Lucknow, K.C.B., born the 6th August 1830, killed by Afridis in the Khyber Pass the 30th of December 1895, whilst watching the military operations. Fought in Persia, the Indian Mutiny and New Zealand. A true soldier, fearless, heroic and devoted to his country's service, buried at Rawalpindi by brave soldiers in a soldier's grave.

"My times are in Thine hand."

[H. M. Havelock, elder son of Sir H. Havelock, born at Chinsura, and educated at St. John's Wood, London. He joined the 39th Regiment in 1846 and went out to India in 1848. He fought in the Persian War at Mahamera (1857) and was his father's A.D.C. on his march to Lucknow. He won the V. C. at Cawnpore for leading the 64th to attack a gun. He was then made D.A.A.G., first to Outram and then to General Franks, in the siege of Lucknow. He fought all through the Oudh campaign, and became Brevet-Major and Lieutenant-Colonel. He fought in the Maori War (1863-64) and was made C.B. in 1866. He was A.Q.M.-G. in Canada from 1867-69 and M.P. for Sunderland (1874-81), and S. E. Durham (1885-1892, and in 1895). He became a Lieutenant-General in 1881, and a G. C. B. in 1897, (so both Burke and Buckland) and was killed in that year.

In 1880 he assumed the name Allan by royal license. He married Lady Alice Moreton, 2nd daughter of the Earl of Ducie, and had two sons and two daughters.

The tablet has been placed on his father's monument (vide above, no. 918.)]

(References : *Forrest ; Burke P ; Buckland.*)

NEAR THE SIKANDRA BAGH GATE.

922.—1857—OFFICER AND MEN, 1st MADRAS FUSILIERS. *Inscription :*—Sacred to the memory of Lieutenant Francis Dobbs, who was killed in action at the storm of Shah Najaf on the 16th November 1857, and buried here ; also of Privates Edward Donaghey, Hugh Gray, Alexander Comb, Patrick Collins, Thomas Kenny, all of the 1st Madras Fusiliers, who were killed in action on the same day and interred in the same grave.

[Cf. no. 838.]

NEAR DILKUSHA.

922.—1857—PAUL, W., Lieutenant. *Inscription :*—Here lie the remains of Lieutenant W. Paul, of the 4th Punjab Rifles, who was killed in the attack upon Sikandra Bagh with the relieving force under Major-General Sir Colin Campbell, K.C.B., on the 16th of November 1857. Erected by the officers of the 4th Punjab Rifles.

[This tomb is in the Dilkusha Gardens, near the south-east corner of the main building. W. Paul, son of Dr. J. Paul of Elgin, was born in 1828 and educated at Aberdeen University.

The 93rd Highlanders (2nd Battalion Prince Louise's Argyle and Sutherland Highlanders) and the 4th Punjab Rifles, with the 53rd (Shropshire Light Infantry) and a battalion of detachments stormed the Sikandra Bagh. The 4th were led by Paul and lost three English officers out of four, and sixty-nine native officers and men. The 4th P. I. are now the 57th Wilde's Rifles (Frontier Force).]

(References ; *C. P.; Roberts ; Forrest.*)

924.—1857—DASHWOOD, C. K., Lieutenant. *Inscription :*— In memory of Charles Keith Dashwood, Lieutenant, 18th Regiment, B. N. I., third son of Lieutenant-Colonel A. W. Dashwood.

He died at Dilkusha, Lucknow, November 22nd, 1857, aged 19 years.

[This tomb is in the gardens near the south-east corner of the main building. Lieutenant Dashwood had both legs shot off whilst sketching in the Residency compound on the 4th November. *Cf.* no. 641.]

(Reference : *Harris.*)

925.—**1858**—McDONALD, C. W., Captain. *Inscription* :—Sacred to the memory of Captain Charles William McDonald, 93rd Highlanders, who was killed in the assault on the Begam's Palace on the 10th day of March 1858, in the 23rd year of his age. This simple inscription is erected by his sorrowing relations in memory of his simple virtues as a Christian and his noble conduct as a soldier.

[This and the next tomb are in a small enclosure west of the road leading to the race-course. Captain McDonald was killed in the assault on the Begam's Kothi. "Although he had been a captain for some years, he was still almost a boy." He was wounded early in the day by a splinter of a shell in his right arm but remained with his company, led it through the breach, and was shot down inside, through the throat. He was third son of General Sir John McDonald, K.C.B., of Dalchosnie, Perthshire. This family, one of soldiers ever since Culloden, descends from John, Lord of the Isles and his wife, the daughter of Robert II of Scotland. There is not a male member of the family who was not in the Army from Alexander McDonald, who fell at Culloden, to Lieutenant-General Alastair McDonald, the present head of the family, who fought in the Crimea.].

(References : *Forrest ; Burke, L. G. ; Forbes-Mitchell.*)

926.—**1858**—SERGISON, C. W., Lieutenant. *Inscription* :—Sacred to the memory of Charles Warden Sergison, Lieutenant in Her Majesty's 93rd Regiment (Highlanders), who fell in the attack on the Begam's Palace, Lucknow, on the 10th March 1858, in the 24th year of his age. This simple monument has been erected by his heart broken surviving parent as a testimony of his deep regard and admiration of his son as a brave and noble soldier.

[Also killed in the assault on the Begam's Kothi, whilst breaking in the door of a room. He was the eldest son of the Revd. W. T. Sergison of the family of Sergison of Cuckfield, Sussex, which dates back to Charles Sergison, M.P., born 1654.]

(References : *Forrest ; Burke, L, G. ; Forbes-Mitchell.*)

927.—**1858**—COOPER, L. E., Lieutenant. *Inscription* :—Sacred to the memory of Lieutenant Lovick Emilius Cooper, 2nd Battalion, Rifle Brigade, who died on the 18th March 1858 of wounds received before Lucknow, aged 20 years.

[Wounded on 11th March 1858 in the final attack on Lucknow. He was the eldest son of the Revd. J. L. Cooper, of Mablethorpe, Lincoln, and a relative of Sir Astley Cooper, the eminent surgeon (1768-1841).]

(References ; *Forrest : Burke, P.*)

928.—**1858**—PELLEW, B. R., Major the Hon'ble. *Inscription* :—Sacred to the memory of Major the Hon'ble Barrington R. Pellew, 2nd Battalion, Rifle Brigade, who died at Lucknow on the 6th of December 1858. This stone is erected by his brother officers.

[The tomb is south of the main Dilkusha building as is the next tomb. He was fifth son of the 2nd Lord Exmouth (1833 1858). He had been A.-D.-C. to General van Straubenzee, and served with distinction in the Kaffir war, at Sebastopol, at the storming of Canton and at Lucknow.]

(Reference ; *Burke, P.*)

LUCKNOW-SULTANPUR ROAD.

929.—**1858**—SMYTH, P. C., Lieutenant. *Inscription* :—Sacred to the memory of Lieutenant Percy C. Smyth of Her Majesty's 97th Regiment, who died on the 4th of March 1858 of a wound received at the attack on the Fort of Dhowrara, on the morning of that day.

[This is near the sixth mile of the road. The 97th, now the 2nd Battalion, The Queen's Own Royal West Kent Regiment, were with Franks. This attack occurred on Franks' march through Oudh to join Sir Colin Campbell at Lucknow.]

(Reference : *Forrest.*)

LUCKNOW-FYZABAD ROAD.

930.—**1858**—SANDFORD, C., Captain. *Inscription* :—Beneath this monument rest the mortal remains of Charles Sandford, late Captain of the 3rd Bengal Light Cavalry, who, when gallantly leading a body of dismounted Punjab Cavalry in an assault on a fortified place near Lucknow, 10th March 1858, met a soldier's death. Strangers, respect the lonely resting-place of the brave. Re-erected 1877.

[Captain Sandford did some brave deeds during the Mutiny. When Hodson was carrying out his famous ride from Karnal to Meerut he met Sandford, who was riding from Meerut to Karnal. Hodson's ride has become historic : by an irony of fate Sandford's is recorded merely in the mention of his arrival in a despatch and in a footnote. He commanded the Guides Cavalry at Delhi and was twice mentioned in despatches. He later took Younghusband's place in command of his squadron of the 5th Punjab Cavalry and was killed in clearing a village during Outram's operations at the capture of Lucknow. C. Ayshford Sanford (so birth certificate), was the son of E. A. Sanford, Nynehead Court, Somerset, born in 1828.]

(References : *C. P.; Roberts ; Forest.*)

931.—**1858**—THYNNE, W. F., Captain. *Inscription* :—Sacred to the memory of Captain William Frederick Thynne, 2nd Battalion, Rifle Brigade, killed in action before Lucknow on the 11th of March 1858, aged 23 years.

Sacred to the memory of Captain W. F. Thynne, 2nd Battalion, Rifle Brigade, who was killed at the siege of Lucknow, 11th March 1858. This stone was erected by his brother officers.

[The Rifle Brigade were with Outram's column during the final operations round Lucknow. Captain Thynne was killed during some severe street fighting in the suburbs near the Iron Bridge on the far side of the Gumti. He was resting on a cot in a house captured by his company, when he was killed by a round-shot. Captain W. F. Thynne was 4th son of the Hon'ble and Revd. J. Thynne, and grandson of the 2nd Marquis of Bath. The tomb is at the 3rd mile of the road and has two inscriptions as shown above.]

(References ; *Fo rest : Burke, P.*)

932.—**1858**—SMITH, J. P. Major. *Inscription* :—Sacred to the memory of Major John Percy Smith, 2nd Dragoon Guards (Queen's Bays), who was killed in action near the Kokrail Bridge on the 15th March 1858. This tablet is erected by his brother officers.

[This tomb is at the 5th mile near Ghazipur village. On the 6th March (not the 15th as in the epitaph) Outram crossed the Gumti with his division to commence his turning movement. He met the enemy in some force and his cavalry—Bays, 9th Lancers and 2nd Punjab Cavalry—charged them. The Bays were young soldiers, and "intoxicated with blood," rode into the infantry posts, where their commander, Percy Smith, was shot. Cornet Sneyd and Corporal

Goad made a gallant attempt to rescue his body but failed. It was found next day and the remains buried in a grove.]

(References : *Forrest ; Roberts.*)

LOTAN BAGH.

933.—**1858**—PRICE, J. G., Major. *Inscription :*— Sacred to the memory of Major John Griffith Price, 2nd Dragoon Guards (Queen's Bays), who died of fever at the Musa Bagh, on the 12th of May 1858. This tablet is erected by his brother officers.

[At Lotan Bagh, north of the Malihabad road.]

MUSA BAGH.

934.—**1858**—WALE, F., Captain. *Inscription :*—Sacred to the memory of Captain F. Wale, who raised and commanded the 1st Sikh Irregular Cavalry, killed in action at Lucknow on the 21st March 1858. This monument is erected by Captain L. B. Jones, Acting-Commandant, 1st Sikh Irregular Cavalry, as a token of regard for his officer, whom he admired both as a friend and a soldier. Captain Wale lived and died a Christian soldier.

[This occurred during the pursuit of the enemy after Lucknow had been reduced. Brigadier Campbell by some misconception did not send his cavalry in pursuit till too late, and after a s'ern chase of several miles Wale gave the order to halt. "Then from the far side of a ravine, a solitary figure fired his musket at a group of officers" and killed Wale, shooting him in the throat and mouth. In a few minutes "to the deep grief of his officers and men, by whom he was loved as few commanding officers are ever loved, poor Wale breathed his last." Frederick Wale (1822—1858) was the 8th son of General Sir C. Wale, K.C.B., of H. M.'s 33rd Regiment, out of a family of 16. The family belongs to Shelford and traces its descent to Richard Fitz Wale of Eydon, *temp.* Henry II.]

(References : *Forrest ; Roberts : Burke L. G.*)

NEAR VILLAGE OF BARGAWAN.

935.—**1857-58**—OFFICERS AND MEN, 5TH FUSILIERS. *Inscription :*—This column is erected by the officers, non-commissioned officers and privates of the 5th Fusiliers, to their undermentioned comrades who fell during the occupation of the Alam Bagh Camp under Sir J. Outram, K.C.B., 1857-58: Lieutenant J. Brown; Armour-Sergeant H. Whitnorth; Sergeant W. Walters; Private W. Anderson; Private W. Baldry; Private T. Hill; Private D. McEvoy; Private H. Wright; Private I. Baker; Private L. Martin; Private W. Chamberlain; Private I. Cleray; Private J. Kelly; Private T. Mora; Private I. Monaghan; Private W. Connolly; Private D. Donnolly; Private R. Preston; Private I. Doughty; Private W. Pottle; Private W. Moran; Private W. Messenger. Sacred to the memory of James Samuel Swinton, Lieutenant, Bengal Infantry, who died here on the 29th October 1858, aged 19, in consequence of severe fatigue and exposure at Cawnpore and Lucknow.

He fought the good fight and trusted in his Redeemer.

[Sufficient justice has seldom been done to Outram's defence of the Alam Bagh between the 2nd relief and the capture of Lucknow. His position extended from the Alam Bagh to Ram Bagh and thence across to Jalalabad on one side and also east, a circuit of about 11 miles. He was to keep the rebels at Lucknow in check, and had some 4,000 men to do it with: whilst of rebels there were about 120,000. He was attacked in force six times, and succesfully repulsed all attacks. The 5th Fusiliers was one of his regiments and did good service (Cf. also nos. 901 and 937.) The village of Bargawan was included in his lines and the 5th Fusiliers were posted close to it.]

(Reference ; *Forrest.*)

PROTESTANT AND R. C. CEMETERY.

936.—**1857**—LAWRENCE, H. T. W. *Inscription* :—In memory of Herbert Thomas William Lawrence. Born at Hooshyearpore, Punjab, 2nd July 1851. Died of cholera on the 15th August 1857, within the besieged position of the British Residency at Lucknow. His remains were exhumed on the 13th August 1858 and placed under this stone.

[The son of an unconvenanted civilian.]

(Reference : *Rees.*)

937.—**1858**—SWINTON, J. S., Lieutenant. *Inscription* :—Sacred to the memory of James Samuel Swinton, Lieutenant, Bengal Infantry, who died here on the 29th October 1858, aged 19, in consequence of severe fatigue and exposure at Cawnpore and Lucknow.

He fought the good fight of faith and trusted in his Redeemer.

[Cf. 935. James Samuel Swinton born in 1839 at Edinburgh was 5th son of George Swinton, Chief Secretary to the Governor-General, and of a very old family which in the last century has had some sixteen representatives in the Indian services. The family is of Saxon origin, and dates back to Liuff of Swinton, Sheriff of the Northumbrians at the time of the conquest. He was educated at Loretto.]

(References : *C. F.*; *Burke, L. G.*)

938.—**1859**—LYNCH, W. E. *Inscription* :—W. E. Lynch, Esq., Assistant Surgeon, 7th Hussars, died at Lucknow, 24th January 1859.

[The 7th (the Queen's Own) Hussars were in the Lucknow operations.]

939.—**1859**—MELLIAR, R. F., Lieutenant. *Inscription* :—Sacred to the memory of Lieutenant R. Foster Melliar, H.M.'s 20th Regiment, who died at Lucknow on the 15th of April 1859, aged 19 years and 10 months. The original tomb having fallen into disrepair this cross was erected by his brothers and sisters in 1896.

"Them which sleep in Jesus shall God bring with Him." 1 Thess., IV, 4. Erected by his brother officers.

[Robert Foster Melliar was second son of Andrew Foster Melliar of North Aston Hall, Co. Oxford.]

(Reference : *Burke, L. G.*)

OLD CANTONMENT CEMETERY, MARIAON.

940.—**1858**—MACDONNELL, F. J., Lieutenant. *Inscription* :—Sacred to the memory of Lieutenant F. J. MacDonnell, Adjutant, 2nd Punjab Cavalry, who was killed in action at Courci, near Lucknow, March 1858, ætat 23, while gallantly charging at the head of his men. Beloved and respected by all who knew him. Erected by his brother officers.

[Hope Grant was sent to Kursi in pursuit of the enemy and came on them when in retreat. The cavalry (a squadron of 1st Punjab Cavalry under Captain Cosserat—vide no. 904—and the 2nd Punjab Cavalry under Captain Samuel Browne, a well known name,) were sent after them and charged through them three times : but they never wavered, and killed MacDonnell and Cosserat.]

(References : *Forrest* ; *Roberts.*)

941.—**1858**—RICHARDS, H. E., Lieutenant. *Inscription* :—Sacred to the memory of Lieutenant H. E. Richards, 3rd Battalion, Rifle Brigade, who was mortally wounded in the attack on the fort of Birwah on the 21st October 1858. He died at the Old Cantonment, Lucknow, on the 8th December 1858.

[The attack on the fort of Birwa was carried out by the column under Brigadier Barker during the pacification of Oudh. Birwa is in Hardoi.]
(Reference: *Gazetteer.*)

OLD PROTESTANT CEMETERY, NEAR AMINABAD.

942.—1807—COLLINS, J., Colonel. *Inscription:*—In memory of Colonel John Collins, Resident at the Court of Lucknow, 1806-07, died 18th June 1807.

[*N.B.*—All the succeeding tombs, save this, have lost their inscriptions, which are reproduced from Führer's List.]

John Collins (?—1907) joined the E. I. C.'s Bengal infantry in 1770, and became Major in 1794. He was Resident at the Court of Daulat Rao Sindhia from 1795-1803. He possessed great influence over him: but failed to dissuade him from fighting the British Government. When Sindhia was secretly mediating as the result of the Treaty of Bassein he succeeded in obtaining the truth, and it was largely as a result of his discoveries that war was declared. In 1799 he went on a mission to Jaipur and there Wazir Ali, the murderer of Mr. Cherry (vide no. 594,) surrendered to him. He was subsequently Resident at Lucknow. He is described as "cold, imperious and over-bearing," and was nicknamed "King Collins."]
(References: *Buckland; Wellesley's Despatches; Thorn; Davis.*)

943.—1827—RICKETTS, F. F. *Inscription:*—Frederick Fitz-gerald, son of Mordaunt and Charlotte Ricketts, born 10th October 1827, died 8th March 1828.

I shall go to him, but he shall not return to me. (B. O.)

[Son of the Mordaunt Ricketts, Resident at Lucknow, whose marriage was celebrated by Bishop Heber in 1824. M. Ricketts was son of G. Poyntz Ricketts, B.C.S., born in 1786, and joined the service in 1802. He was at Lucknow in 1822-9 and retired in 1830. His son, Mordaunt, was killed in the Mutiny at Shahjahanpur, cf. no. 410.]
(References: *Prinsep C. L.; W. P.; Heber.*)

944.—1828—WYLDE, C. V., Lieutenant. *Inscription:*—Sacred to the memory of Charles Vincent Wylde, Lieutenant and Adjutant, 14th Regiment Bengal Native Infantry, born 14th February 1798, died 19th October 1828. This tomb was erected by the officers of his regiment to commemorate their esteem for him whilst alive, and their regret at his early death. (B. O.)

[Son of the Revd S. T. Wylde, born in 1799 at Burrington, Somerset.]
(Reference: *C. P.*)

945.—1831—PATTON, S., Mrs. *Inscription:*—Sacred to the memory of Mrs. Sophia Patton, who departed this life on the 3rd of November 1831, deeply regretted. (B. O.)

[J B. Hearsey writing from before Bhurtpore in 1825 to his brother-in-law, Salmon, at Lucknow, sends a message to Mrs. Patton that her husband was well. This is possibly that lady, and if so, her husband must have been in the army.]
(Reference: *Pearse.*)

946.—1835—MOORE, S., Mrs. *Inscription:*—Sacred to the memory of Sarah, the beloved wife of Lieutenant-Colonel George Moore, 59th Regiment, Native Infantry, who departed this life the 23rd December 1835, aged 31 years.

[Sarah Cattell, second wife of Col. G. Moore, afterwards Brigadier-General in command of the Rajputana Field Force (1789-1848). She had four sons and a daughter. The family is descended from Lord Chancellor Moore.]
(Reference: *Burke L. G.*)

947.—1837—MONTEITH, L. F., Mrs. *Inscription:*—Sacred to the memory of Lucinda Florence, the lady of Lieutenant-Colonel Monteith, 35th Regiment, who died at Lucknow on the 2nd of September 1837.

948.—**1845**—MERCER, M. C., Mrs. *Inscription :*—To the memory of Maria Caroline, the beloved wife of F. W. Mercer, Esq., 46th Regiment, Bengal Native Infantry. She was born on the 7th November 1826, married 7th November 1844, and departed this life 7th November 1845, aged 19 years.

To Thee, dear Lord, my flesh and soul I joyfully resign ;
Blessed Jesus, take me for Thine own, for I am doubly Thine.

"For our light affliction, which is but for a moment, worketh for us a far more exceeding and eternal weight of glory." (B. O.)

949.—**1847**—WILCOX, J., Colonel. *Inscription :*—(Destroyed.)

[Nothing appears to be known of this officer except that he was a pensioner in Oudh, and built the Tarawala Kothi for an observatory.]

CHRIST CHURCH.

950.—**1856**—(1) MAGNESS, R. J. H., Captain. **1857**—(2) MAGNESS, M. A., Mrs. *Inscription :*—Sacred to the memory of Captain R. J. H. Magness, Oudh Service, who departed this life at Lucknow, 18th December 1856, and of his widow, Mary Anne Magness, who was killed at Lucknow by rebels in June 1857.

951.—**1857**- (1) POLEHAMPTON, H. A., (2) POLEHAMTON, H. S., Revd. *Inscription :*—In memory of Henry Stedman Polehampton, Chaplain of this station, born February 1st, 1824, died July 20th, 1857 ; also of Henry Allnut, his only child, born December 30th, 1857 ; died January 3rd, 1857.

Enter thou into the joy of the Lord.—*Mat.* XXV, 21.

[Cf. no. 862.]

952.—**1857**—HANDSCOMB, J. H., Brigadier. *Inscription :*—Sacred to the memory of Colonel Isaac Henley Handscomb, Brigadier-General, Commanding the Oudh Field Force, who was shot by Lucknow mutineers when in the firm execution of his duty on the night of the 30th May 1857. Aged 52 years. A brave soldier, a loving kinsman, and a sincere friend ; he lived and died honoured and beloved by all who knew him. This tablet is erected as a tribute of affection by his nephew, Captain H. T. Bartlett, Bengal Army.

[In command of the Oudh Forces at Lucknow. He was shot dead by a stray bullet as he took his place by the 32nd on parade. He was the son of J. Handscomb, merchant of Newport Pagnell, born in 1805. He fought in the Afghan war.]

(References : *Services, B. A. List ; Forrest.*)

953.—**1857**—THOMASON, J. G., B.C.S. *Inscription :*—To the memory of James Grant Thomason, B. C. S., Deputy Commissioner of Mohumdi, murdered by the mutineers at Aurangabad in Oudh, 5th June 1857. This tablet is erected by George E. L. Cotton, D.D., Bishop of Calcutta, formerly his tutor in Rugby School, in thankful recollection of his character in boyhood and in sure confidence that he is now with Christ.

[For the massacre at Aurangabad, vide no. 976. Mr. Thomason was the son of Mr. J. Thomason, no. 396, born at Calcutta in 1830. He was educated at Rugby, Addiscombe and Haileybury and came to India in 1851.]

(References : *Haileybury ; W. P.*)

954.—**1857**—MACLEAN, W. G. M., Captain. *Inscription :*—To the memory of Wellwood George Mowbray Maclean, Captain, 7th Regiment, N. I., who fell while gallantly serving with the small body of the Oudh Volunteer Cavalry in the attack against the mutineers at Chinhut on the 30th June 1857. Aged 41. This tablet is erected by Nawab Mohsin-ud-Dowlah, Bahadur, of this city, as a token of his friendship and regard.

[For this charge see no. 890. His horse was killed by a round shot and he was wounded twice before he was killed. He was the son of Captain Maclean H. M. Service, born in 1819: he joined the service in 1840.]

(References: *Services B. A. List; Rees.*)

955.—**1857**—LAWRENCE, H. M., Sir. *Inscription*:—Sacred to the memory of Sir Henry Lawrence, K.C.B., the statesman who administered in succession the great provinces of India; the soldier who died in defending the garrison entrusted to his charge; the Christian who in his last hour humbly trusted that he had tried to do his duty, and committed his soul, in full assurance of faith, to the mercy of his Lord. Born 28th June 1806. Died 4th July 1857. His body rests in the burial-ground of the Residency.

[Cf. no. 866.]

956.—**1857**—BRYSON, A. *Inscription*:—To the memory of Alexander Bryson, a Volunteer, who was killed on the 9th July 1857, within the Residency defences, while singly building, under a deadly fire, a barricade for the safety of his post, a duty he volunteered to perform. He was honourably mentioned in the official report of that memorable defence. Aged 37 years.

(Formerly Sergeant-Major of the 16th Lancers. He was appointed Sergeant of Ratcliffe's Volunteers. With four others, a Lieutenant of Bengal N. I., an ex-private of the 32nd and two native officers of the 7th N. C—of such heterogeneous material were those volunteers composed—he charged 18 rebel troopers in the reconnaissance before the battle of Chinhat. Whilst retreating from Chinhat he remained "at least 20 yards in the rear, and coming on at a gentle trot only. He was shot through the head whilst endeavouring to strengthen the Brigade Mess. That morning he had jestingly told his wife that the bullet had not yet been moulded that was to hit him. His body was rescued by a party of volunteers under heavy fire. He was a noble and gallant fellow, an excellent husband, a fond father, and a staunch friend; a practical philosopher, always gay and smiling."]

(References: *Forrest; Rees.*)

957.—**1857**—(1) SIMONS, L. A. C., (2) SIMONS, A. P., Captain. *Inscription*:—In memory of Alfred Parmenter Simons, Captain, Bengal Regiment of Artillery, who died from the effects of his wounds during the siege of Lucknow, September 8th, 1857, aged 33 years. Also of Lucy Amelia Collingwood, elder child of the above. She died at Naini Tal, August 20th, in the same year, aged nearly three years.

Jesus said, I am the resurrection and the life.

St. John, II 25.

[Cf. no. 895.]

958.—**1857**—McCABE, B., Captain. *Inscription*:—To the glory of God and in memory of Captain Bernard McCabe, H. M.'s 32nd Regt. who served with conspicuous gallantry in the defence of the Residency of Lucknow. He was mortally wounded when leading his fourth sortie, and died on the 1st October 1857. He obtained his commission when serving with H. M.'s 31st Regt. at the battle of Sobraon for distinguished bravery in planting the Regimental Colours on the enemies' works under a heavy fire.

[Cf. no. 440.]

959.—**1857**—SWANSON, J., Lieutenant. *Inscription*:—In memory of Lieutenant John Swanson, H. M.'s 78th Highlanders, who died in the Residency of Lucknow, 2nd October 1857, of wounds received on the 25th and 26th September 1857. Aged 22 years.

[Wounded during Havelock's Relief of Lucknow.]

(Reference : *Forrest.*]

960.—**1857**—BENSON, G. S., B.C.S. *Inscription* :—Sacred to the memory of George Sackville Benson, B.C.S., mortally wounded in action at Secundra Bagh, Lucknow, 16th November 1857. Died 18th November 1857, *ætat* 29 years.

A time of war and a time of peace.

Ecc. LIII. 8.

[Georg Sackville Benson (1828—1857), eldest son of Rev. Ralph Lewin Benson, of the family of the Bensons of Ludwyche Hall, Co. Salop. The family is a yeoman family of Lancashire. He was educated at Marlborough and Haileybury and joined the C.S. in 1849. In 1857 he was Deputy Commissioner of Dariabad. He was with Havelock's force, and died of wounds received on entering Lucknow.]

(References : *M. C. Register ; Haileybury ; Gubbins ; Burke, L. G.*)

961.—**1857**.—(1) CLARK, E., MRS., (2) CLARK, M. E., (3) CLARK, E. *Inscription* :—In affectionate memory of Elizabeth Clark, his wife, aged 26 years, Matthew Edgar, aged 1 year and 9 months, Elizabeth, aged 10 days, his children, all of whom died during the siege of the Lucknow Residency in that year of sorrow 1857.

This tablet is erected by Captain Edgar Clark, Bengal Staff Corps.

The Lord gave and the Lord hath taken away.

Job 1. 21.

[Mrs. Clark died of small-pox. Her husband was Assistant Commissioner at Gonda.]

(Reference : *Gubbins.*)

962.—**1857**—FRANKLAND, T., Lieutenant. *Inscription* :—Sacred to the memory of Thomas Frankland, Esq., Lieutenant, 48th Madras Native Infantry, and second in command of 2nd Panjab Infantry, who fell at the head of his regiment at the storming of the Alam Bagh during the relief of Lucknow, the eldest surviving son of Sir Frederick Frankland, eighth Baronet of Thirkely, County York.

I can do all things through Christ who strengtheneth me.
The Lord is my strength and my shield.

[There is a curious mis-statement in this inscription. Lieut. Frankland was killed whilst leading a company of the 2nd Panjab infantry to the assault of a tower in the Sikandra Bagh (according to Burke) during the Second Relief of Lucknow. The Alum Bagh had been in our hands ever since the First Relief. Lieut. Frankland was twice wounded at Delhi. The Franklands are an ancient Yorkshire family dating back to Edward III. Sir. F. Frankland served all through the Peninsular and Waterloo campaigns.

N.B.—Burke says Lieut. Frankland was killed on the 17th November. This date must be wrong if he was killed at the Sikandra Bagh, which was taken on the 15th. The Mess House and Moti Mahal were taken on the 17th, and the Punjab Infantry were in both assaults.]

(References : *Forrest ; Roberts ; Burke, P.)*

963.—**1857-58**—OFFICERS AND MEN, 93rd HIGHLANDERS. *Inscription* :—Erected by the officers, non-commissioned officers and soldiers of the 93rd Sutherland Highlanders, in memory of their comrades who fell in action, or died of wounds or of disease caused by fatigue and exposure during the suppression of the Mutiny in India in 1857-58. Killed in action :—Officers 5 ; non-commissioned officers and soldiers 45. Died of wounds :—Officer 1 ;

non-commissioned officers and soldiers 36. Died of disease :—Officer 1 ; non-commissioned officers and soldiers 83.

[This very famous regiment, now the 2nd Battalion, Princess Louise's Argyle and Sutherland Highlanders, was raised in 1800. They were in India from 1857 to 1870 and again from 1891. Their only Indian honour, however, is "Lucknow." They were Sir C. Campbell's Highlanders : he had been with them in the Crimea and they looked on him as one of their clan. They were at the battle of Khujwa, at the Lucknow relief operations where they were prominent, at the capture of the Sikandrabagh, the Shah Najif and the Begam Kothi. They fought again at Cawnpore and again at the reduction of Lucknow ; and everywhere they did magnificently. Of the officers killed (6), Captain Dalzell, Captain Macdonald, Lieutenant Sergison and Lieutenant Sterling, with Brigadier Hope, make 5. The 6th is possibly Captain Lumsden, attached.]

(References : *Forrest ; Forbes-Mitchell.*)

964.—**1857**—(1) LUMSDEN J. T. Captain, **1858**—(2) CAPE, J., Lieutenant. *Inscription* :—Sacred to the memory of Captain J. T. Lumsden and Lieutenant John Cape, both of the late 30th Regiment. B. N. I., who were killed at Lucknow in the campaigns of 1857-1858. This tablet is dedicated by their brother officers.

[John Tower Lumsden, son of H. Lumsden, advocate, Aberdeen, was born in 1823. He was attached as interpreter to the 93rd Highlanders and was one of the first to enter the Sikandrabagh—according to Lord Roberts, the fifth, being preceded by a Highlander, a Punjabi, Lieutenant Cooper and Colonel Ewart. He was shot dead inside. Colonel Ewart said that he would have tried to get him the V. C. had he lived. Jonathan (not John) Cape, was son of T. Cape of Cheltenham, born at Ashby La Touche in 1838, and nephew of the Revd. Jonathan Cape, for over 30 years senior professor of Addiscombe. Lieutenant Cape was Assistant Baggage Master to the Engineer Brigade and was killed on the 20th March 1858.]

(References : *Vibart ; C. P.; Roberts ; Forest.*)

965.—**1858**—HARDINGE, G. N., Captain. *Inscription* :—In memory of Captain George Nicholas Hardinge, late 45th B. N. I. and Commandant, 3rd Oude Irregular Cavalry. He served in the Sutlej and Punjab campaigns ; he commanded the Sikh Cavalry and acted as Deputy Assistant Quartermaster-General throughout the defence of Lucknow. From the wounds and privations endured in that memorable siege, he died at the Sandheads, March 16th, 1858. Aged 29 years.

[Captain Hardinge did excellent service all through the defence of Lucknow. When the Mutiny broke out he patrolled the lines with a few cavalry in spite of a wound, and also pursued the mutineers with a few faithful troopers. He covered the retreat from Chinhat and was mentioned in despatches for it. He commanded the Sikh Square and Cavalry in the defence, and also acted as Deputy Assistant Quartermaster-General. He also distinguished himself in several sorties during both defences. George Nicholas Hardinge (1828-1858) was son of General R. Hardinge, K.H., and nephew of the first Viscount Hardinge.]

(References : *Forrest ; Hutchinson : Burke, P.*)

966.—**1858**—PELLEW, B. R., Major the Hon'ble. *Inscription* :—Sacred to the memory of Major the Hon'ble Barrington Reynolds Pellew (2nd Battalion, Rifle Brigade), grandson of Admiral Viscount Exmouth, who died of dysentery at Lucknow, on the 6th December 1858, in the 26th year of his age, and rests in the burying-ground of the Dilkusha. This tablet is erected by his bereaved and widowed mother to a son greatly beloved and deeply mourned by his sorrowing family and friends.

[Cf. no. 928.]

967.—**1857-59**—OFFICERS AND MEN, 2ND D.G.S. *Inscription* :—In memory of Brigadier-General William Campbell, C.B., Major

John Percy Smith, Major John Griffith Price, Captain Orlando Frederick Cavendish Bridgeman, Captain Robert Blair, V.C., Cornet William Agnew, Riding Master Israel Kirk; one Regimental Sergeant-Major; one Trumpet-Major; two Troop Sergeant-Majors; eight Sergeants; seven Corporals; one Farrier; ninety Privates of the 2nd Dragoon Guards (Queen's Bays), who were either killed in action, died of their wounds or of disease or exposure during the campaigns of 1857, 1858 and 1859 in India; this tablet is erected by the officers of the regiment.

[Brigadier W. Campbell was for some time in command at Allahabad and had some fighting there. His career is a trifle dubious, but it would appear that he joined Outram at the Alum Bagh and assisted in its defence; and subsequently commanded at the operations round the Musa Bagh. I have not been able to discover where he died.

For Majors Smith and Price, vide nos. 932 and 933. Captain Blair won the V.C. "for conspicuous gallantry when attacked by superior numbers" on the 28th September 1857. I have not been able to trace the other officers. They no doubt lost their lives in the small pacificatory expeditions that went on over Oudh and elsewhere till 1859.

The 2nd D. G.s were engaged only in Sir. C. Campbell's reduction of Lucknow and subsequent operations.]

(References: *Forrest; Roberts; Muddock; Rice-Holmes.*)

968.—**1863**—OUTRAM, J., Lieut.-General Sir. *Inscription:*— In grateful memory of Lieut.-General Sir James Outram, Bart., G.C.B. This tablet is erected in this city of Lucknow to recall his valour and generosity in the memorable relief and siege and his far-seeing wisdom which reconciled this province to British rule; in this Christian Church, because by thoughtful kindness he gained the title of the Soldier's Friend and because in simplicity and sincerity he had his conversation in the world. Born 29th January 1803, died 12th March 1863. His body rests in Westminster Abbey."

[James Outram, second son of Benjamin Outram of Butterley Hall, Derbyshire, and his wife Margaret, daughter of Dr. James Anderson of Mounie, Co. Aberdeen, was educated at the Marischal College, Aberdeen, and entered the Indian Army in 1819 as an Ensign in the 23rd N. I. A keen sportsman, of whom it is said that he took 74 "first spears" out of 123 in a single year, and during a period of nine years was at the deaths of 191 tigers. From 1825 to 1838 he was employed in subjugating and civilizing the Bhils, the aboriginal tribes of Khandesh. He first attacked them and then enlisted his captives as soldiers; and for 12 years was turning these savages into peaceful and faithful citizens. He was Political Agent in Mahi Kanta, when the first Afghan war broke out, and joined Sir John Keane's staff, when he took the Bombay Army through Kandahar and Ghazni to Kabul. He was sent in pursuit of Dost Muhammad across the Hindu Kush in 1839 and took a prominent part in pacifying southern Afghanistan. He then became Political Agent in Lower Sind (1839) and in 1841 in Upper Sind. In 1842 his post was abolished on Sir Charles Napier's investiture with full diplomatic and military power in Sind; and it was on his departure that Sir Charles Napier, in proposing his health, called him "the Bayard of India, *sans peur et sans reproche*"—an epithet which will always remain linked to his name.

In 1843 he returned as Commissioner to carry out a treaty with the Amirs. The Amirs disliked the treaty as much as Outram did; the Residency at Haidarabad was attacked, but Outram defended it resolutely. Shortly after was fought the battle of Miani which gave us Sind. Outram was bitterly opposed to annexation, and even distributed his prize-money to charitable institutions on that ground. He was made a Brevet Lieutenant-Colonel and a C.B.

In 1844 he took leave; in 1845 he became Resident at Satara and in 1847 at Baroda. Here he exposed corruption in high places in a report which caused offence and the Bombay Government removed him; but in 1854 Lord Dalhousie sent him back to Baroda, thence to Aden and thence to Oudh as Resident. It fell to his lot to prepare a report on the existing state of the country. Even the defender of the Sind Amirs could not resist the clear evidence of misrule, and he supported annexation, which was carried out in 1856. In 1856-57 he was in command in Persia, but was summoned back to India and lost no time in reaching Calcutta (31st July 1857). He was made Commander of the Dinapore and Cawnpore divisions, and at once went up to take over the command. There was not, as is often stated, any supersession of Havelock who was merely a Brigadier-General in command of a field force. On the 15th September he arrived at Cawnpore and then joined Havelock, and published that famous order which proved his title to the name of "Bayard." In it he waived his rank, so as not to deprive Havelock of his command, and accompanied him as a military volunteer, and in his civil capacity as Chief Commissioner of Oudh. This order Sir Colin Campbell confirmed in terms as honorable to himself as to Outram and Havelock. It was a material as well as a sentimental sacrifice. Outram, already a G.C.B., could get no further reward than a permanent title and a pension; and this he believed he was, if not surrendering, at all events jeopardizing. He was also surrendering the General's substantial share of prize-money for that of a civilian volunteer. It was a magnificent act of self-sacrifice which has probably no parallel in history.

From this time till the relief Outram was a volunteer, riding in the charges of Barrow's volunteer cavalry and "whacking the fugitives" with a "Penang Lawyer." Even between two such men as Outram and Havelock the position was bound to have its difficulties: but they were overcome. Outram, after the relief, resumed his proper position and was in command at Lucknow during the Second Defence; and subsequently, after Sir Colin's relief, held the Alam Bagh with 4,000 men until the final capture in 1858 (a magnificent feat of arms, for which vide no. 935.) He was Military Member of the Supreme Council from 1858 to 1860, when he retired. He was made K.C.S.I., in 1861 and D.C.L., and a Baronet after the Mutiny (1858). His exploits and his great character have made him one of the most conspicuous heroes of Indian history. His character has been described as an embodiment of the old idea of the true and perfect knight, untainted by the influences which sapped mediæval chivalry. "It is impossible to conceive of any consideration that could have tempted Outram to stoop to a dirty action..................though there have been greater men in Anglo-Indian history there has never been one more loveable." As for his military qualities "a fox is a fool and a lion a coward by the side of Sir J. Outram" was the saying on the Bombay side in 1857.

Sir J. Outram married (1835) Margaret, daughter of James Anderson, J.P., of Brechin and had one son, Sir F. B. Outram, B.C.S., Under Secretary to the Government of the North-Western Provinces, 1858-1860, and wounded in the Mutiny; he is the present baronet.]

(References; *Roberts; Rice-Holmes; Forrest; Buckland; Buker, P.*)

969.—**1883**—KAVANAGH, T. H., V.C. *Inscription*:—In honour of one whose name should never be forgotten, Thomas Henry Kavanagh, V.C., who, on the night of the 9th November 1587, with the devotion of an ancient Roman taking his life in his hand, went forth from the beleaguered Residency and, passing through a city thronged with merciless enemies, successfully guided Sir Colin Campbell and his army to the relief of the garrison.

[The son of a British soldier and a clerk in one of the Civil officers in Lucknow, his physical strength and iron nerve made him fitter for the sword than the pen. In the defence of Lucknow he did good service as Assistant Field Engineer in several sorties. The deed for which he won the V. C. was this. He offered his services to Colonel Napier to go out in disguise, and guide Sir Colin Campbell in his advance. Colonel Napier demurred: but Sir J. Outram, after refusing on the score of the danger, at last consented. He disguised himself as a badmash or swashbuckler with sword and shield, native made shoes, tight trousers, a silk *kurta*, a tight fitting muslin shirt, turban and *kumarband*; he also disguised his face with lamp-black. Outram himself daubed him once more, and he and Napier shaking his hand bade him God speed. He went out with the scout, Kanauji Lal, and reached the Gumti. They crossed it, and were stopped by a rebel officer. They satisfied him and proceeded on their way. They lost their way in the Dilkusha Park. They were put on the right track by two women in a village and later by a picquet of sepoys. They were questioned by them and by another picquet. They waded through a swamp, and passed unseen between two more picquets. Shortly after they were challenged by a British cavalry outpost. A Sikh officer in charge sent two troopers to guide Kavanagh to Sir Colin—"As I approached the door, an elderly gentleman with a stern face came out, and going up to him, I asked for Sir Colin Campbell. 'I am Sir Colin Campbell' was the sharp reply 'and who are you?' I pulled off my turban and opening the folds took out a short note of introduction from Sir James Outram.'' Kavanagh subsequently led the Army in its advance.

It was a splendid act of gallantry, and of the most invaluable service. Kavanagh received the V.C., being the first non-military man who ever obtained it (the next being Fraser McDonnell and Ross Mangles of the B.C.S.), a donation of Rs. 20,000, and the post of Assistant Commissioner. He rose to be a Deputy Commissioner. He wrote an account of his deed, entitled "How I won the Victoria Cross."]

(Reference: *Buckland; Forest; Roberts; Rice-Holmes.*)

970.—**1891**—QUINTON, J. W., B.C.S. *Inscription:*—In sacred and loving memory of James Wallace Quinton, Bengal Civil Service, who was murdered at Manipur, on the 24th March 1891.

"Enter into the joy of thy Lord.

Matt. xxv, 21.

[J. W. Quinton, C.S.I., born 1834, was educated at Trinity College, Dublin, and joined the I. C. S. in the North-Western Provinces in 1856. He served as a junior officer chiefly in Ghazipur and Meerut; but most of his service in this province was in Oudh (1865-75), and chiefly in Lucknow as Deputy Commissioner. Form 1875-77 he was Judicial Commissioner in Burma. In 1878 he was Commissioner of Jhansi: and in 1883 fourth Member of the Legislative Council, Member of the Board of Revenue, North-Western Provinces (1885) and Public Service Commissioner (1886). In 1889 he became Chief Commissioner of Assam and in 1891 was sent to Manipur, a petty state on the confines of Assam, to put down the rebellion. The Residency was attacked, and when Mr. Quinton visited the fort to negotiate with them he and four other officers were treacherously murdered. Two columns were sent who speedily avenged the murder.]

(References: *Roberts; Buckland; N. W. P., C. L.* 1879.)

971.—**1893**—JOHNSON, W. T., Major. *Inscription:*—In loving memory of William Thomas Johnson, Major, H. M.'s Indian Army. He volunteered for service in the Crimea and was attached to H. M.'s XXth Foot. Took part in the battles of Alma, Balaclava, and Inkerman, and in the trenches before Sebastapol. Served with the 1st Scinde Horse through the Persian Campaign, and commanded a squadron of the XIIth Irregulars, the only Native Cavalry at the first relief of Lucknow. At the action of the Alam Bagh he gallantly charged and took one of the enemy's guns; and went out with led horses from the Residency to bring in the wounded. He died at Seaford, Sussex, May 31, 1893, aged 66."

[Major W. T. Johnson is one of the forgotten heroes of the Mutiny. He was with the detachment under Major Vincent Eyre and took part in the action of Kundun Patti, and joined Eyre just before the action, having been 24 hours in the saddle. In the battle of the Alum Bagh one gun persisted in "bowling nine-pounders" down the road, after the rebels had been driven back. Captain Johnson charged it with 25 troopers and sabred the gunners. He was forced to abandon it, as he was under fire: but the enemy did not dare to serve it again. During the night after the relief Johnson and Dr. Greenhow and half a troop of his cavalry went out in search of the wounded. They found a number who were brought in on the horses led by Johnson's troopers.]

(Reference: *Forrest.*)

972.—**1902**—CAPPER, W. C., B.C.S. *Inscription:*—To the glory of God and in memory of William Copeland Capper, Bengal

Civil Service, second son of Samuel James Capper, of Snaresbrook, in the county of Essex. As one of Anderson's Garrison he served through the defence of the Residency, and, after filling many posts in the Government of this Province, retired therefrom as Judicial Commissioner. Died at Eastbourne, Sussex, July 8th, 1902, aged 70.

[W. C. Capper was educated at Haileybury, and joined the B.C.S., in 1852 and was attached to the Punjab. In 1856 he was transferred to the Oudh Commission and was the first Deputy Commissioner of Mallawan (Hardoi). He was there when the Mutiny broke out and remained there till the 8th June by which time the troops had shown unmistakable signs of mutiny. He rode into Lucknow and served throughout the defence, in which he was wounded. After the relief he was made a Special Commissioner in Farrukhabad and then took leave. On his return in 1859 he served as Deputy Commissioner at Rae Bareli, Dariabad, Lucknow (1861) and with brief periods of officiating as Commissioner and of leave, remained there till 1868. He then became Commissioner of the Rae Bareli Division (1868-1870) and then, after leave, Commissioner of Fyzabad (1873) and Judicial Commissioner from 1877 and retired in 1882.]

(References : *Forrest ; N. W. P. C. L.* 1879 ; *Haileybury ; Gazetteer.*)

CANTONMENT CHURCH.

973.—**1858**—MACDONNELL, F. J., Lieutenant. *Inscription :*—Sacred to the memory of Lieutenant F. J. MacDonnell, Adjutant of 2nd Punjab Cavalry, who was killed in action at Courci, near Lucknow, on 23rd March 1858, *aet* 23, while gallantly charging at the head of his men ; beloved and respected by all who knew him. This stone has been erected over his mortal remains by the officers and men of his regiment to mark their grief for his early death and to record their lasting sense of his many good qualities as a soldier and a man.

[Cf. no. 940.]

974.—**1857-58**—MEN OF THE 3rd COMPANY, 8TH BATTALION, R.A. *Inscription :*—In memory of the soldiers of no. 3 Company 8th Battalion, Royal Artillery, who were killed or died in India during the campaigns of 1857-58. They are 48 in number.

Dulce et decorum est pro patria mori.

[It is very difficult to distinguish one company or battalion of R.A. from another in the records. This particular company however was with Havelock in his advance and at all his battles ; and subsequently also in the capture of Lucknow. With Havelock it was commanded by Maude, one of the four most famous artillery officers of the Mutiny, the other three being Tombs, Blunt and Olpherts. If it remained continuously under Maude, it was also in Outram's Alum Bagh operations.]

(Reference : *Forrest.*)

975.—**1880**—OFFICERS AND MEN, 73RD REGIMENT. *Inscription :*—In memory of Lieutenant J. E. H. Sullivan, 2nd Lieutenant Colin J. L. Halkett, Privates H. Brown, T. Chisholm, T. Kennedy, W. Turner, of the 73rd Perthshire Regiment, who were killed by a landslip at Naini Tal on the 18th September 1880, while employed with a working party endeavouring to rescue some of their fellow-creatures. This tablet is erected by the officers of the regiment as as a tribute to their heroism and devotion to duty.

[Cf. no. 837.]

Kheri District.

AURANGABAD, TAHSIL MUHAMDI.

976.—**1857**—VICTIMS OF AURANGABAD MASSACRE. *Inscription :*—To the Glory of God and in memory of those honoured ones who fell on this spot, the 5th of June, in the year of Our Lord 1857. James Grant Thomason; Charles John Jenkins; Henry Wilder Lambie Sneyd; Cornelius Lysaght; Mrs. Lysaght; Mordaunt Money Salmon; Alexander Key; Mary Key; Colin Alexander Robertson; Charles Frederick Scott; Mrs. Scott; Miss Scott; William Wilberforce Pitt; George William Rutherford; Thomas John Hope Spens; Ensign Johnson; Ensign E. C. Scott; Quartermaster-Sergeant Grant; Mrs. Bowling and child; Mrs. Grant; Lieutenant Sheils; Mrs. Sheils; Mr. Pereira and four children; Mr. Hurst; Mr. Smith; Drummer-boy August Schlottauer.

[It has already been described (no. 410) how Mr. Jenkins and a party of the Shahjahanpur fugitives escaped to Pawayan. Thence they made their way to Muhamdi, then headquarters of a district corresponding to Kheri. Mr. Thomason, a son of Mr. James Thomason, was Deputy Commissioner, and Captain P. Orr (no. 908), his assistant. Trouble there had been anticipated since May 1857 on the arrival of the Shahjahanpur fugitives: but the troops showed symptoms of mutiny and it was decided to retire to Sitapur. An escort was sent thence for them. This belonged to the 41st. They showed undoubted signs of mutiny, but Mr. Thomason made them swear on Lachman, a jamadar, doubtless a Brahman, to be faithful. The party left Muhamdi on the 5th for Aurangabad: but close to that place the massacre began. Lieutenant Sheil, a pensioner, was first shot down by a sepoy. They then shot down the whole party. The poor ladies all joined in prayer, coolly and undauntedly awaiting their fate. Lysaght was killed as he knelt down in the open: the wounded and the children were "butchered in the most cruel way." Captain Orr was spared because of the intervention of the Muhamdi troops—the 9th Oudh Irregulars—a regiment which he had raised and commanded.

Of these victims all but Mr. Thomason, Mr. and Mrs. Smith and Mrs. Hurst belonged to Shahjahanpur. Mr. Smith and Hurst were clerks of Mr. Thomason's. All the officers belonged to the 28th N. I. The tomb is looked after by S. Tasadduq Husain, Honorary Magistrate of Aurangabad. For Mr. Thomason see no. 953. C. J. Jenkins was at Haileybury and came to India in 1851.]

(References : *Hutchinson ; Haileybury ; Gazetteer.*)

Sitapur District.

SITAPUR CEMETERY.

979.—**1854**—NICHOLETTS, W. H., Major. *Inscription :*—Sacred to the memory of W. H. Nicholetts, Major, 28th Native Infantry Commandant, 1st Regiment, Oudh Light Infantry, who departed this life on 19th October 1854, aged 45 years. This monument is erected by the officers of the 1st Regiment Oudh Light Infantry, and Major Bunbury, as a mark of their friendship and regard.

[William Hamilton, son of Captain Nicholetts, H. C. S., was born in India in 1808 and joined the service in 1824.]

(References : *D. and M. ; C. P.*)

Hardoi District.

MADHOGANJ, TAHSIL BILGRAM.

978.—**1858**—HOPE, A., Brigadier, the Hon'ble. *Inscription :*—Brigadier the Hon'ble Adrian Hope, C.B., Lieutenant-Colonel,

93rd Royal Highlanders. Born 3rd March 1821. Killed at Ruiya, 15th April 1858.

[Adrian Hope (1821-1858) was the ninth son of General Sir John Hope, the famous Peninsular veteran, who was created first Lord Niddry, and subsequently succeeded to the Earldom of Hopetoun as fourth Earl. He was of a family that goes back to Sir James Hope (1641) the great Scotch mineralogist, and to the Hopes of Craig Hall (a still older family, cf no. 628). To this family Sir Theodore Cracroft Hope, K.C.S.I., C.I.E., and many famous soldiers and sailors have belonged, whilst the first Marquis of Linlithgow, who was Governor General of the Australian Commonwealth, was the 7th Earl. Adrian Hope was Colonel of the 93rd Highlanders, and as Brigadier did excellent service in the Second Relief of Lucknow, at Cawnpore and again at the siege of Lucknow. One of the best loved officers in the army, idolized by his men, he was sacrificed to a blunder. After the siege of Lucknow, Walpole (much to everybody's surprise—nobody thought Sir Colin would entrust his favourite Highlanders *to* him) was given a column to advance into Rohilkhand. Ruiya, the jungle fort of Nirpat Singh, was held in force and it was decided to attack it. The place was *not* reconnoitred and was found to be much stronger than was expected: and the assailants were driven back with heavy loss, including Lieutenants Douglas and Bramley of the 42nd (spelt Brambly on the memorial at Bareilly, no. 406), and Lieutenant Willoughby. Hope was shot dead from a high tree inside the fort, as it was supposed, by a European renegade (cf. no. 399). According to Forbes-Mitchell this would be the same man who murdered Lieutenant Tucker. "A true soldier, a kind, courteous, noble gentleman, in word and deed, devoted to his profession, beloved by his men, adored by his friends" is W. H. Russell's description of Adrian Hope.]

(References: *Forrest; Rice-Holmes; Forbes-Mitchell; Gazetteer; Burke, P.*)

979.—**1858**—(1) HOPE, A., Brigadier the Hon'ble., (2) DOUGLAS, C., (3) WILLOUGHBY, H., (4) HARINGTON, Lieutenants. *Inscription:*—Sacred to the memory of Brigadier the Hon'ble Adrian Hope, Lieutenant Charles Douglas, 42nd Royal Highlanders, Lieutenant H. Willoughby, 4th Punjab Infantry, Lieutenant Harington, Royal Artillery. Who fell at Fort Ruiya on the 15th April 1858.

[For the facts leading to the death of these officer see no. 978. H. Willoughby is an error: it should be Edward Cotgrave Parr Willoughby. He was the son of Major-General M. W. Willoughby, Bombay Artillery, and Louisa Frances, his wife, daughter of Robert Anderson, born at Poona in 1834. A brother of his, Lieutenant-General M. W. Willougby, C.S.I., served in Persia and Abyssinia, and was Military Secretary to the Bombay Government. All these officers, with their men, were buried in the same grave, in a tope of trees at Rudamau, close to Madhoganj, and 3 miles from Ruiya Fort. There seems a probability, therefore that General Hope's tomb is a cenotaph. There are two other graves, which belong to Wazir Singh, a Christian zamindar of Rudamau, and his wife. Wazir Singh was Mr. Edwards' orderly and remained with him whilst he was at Khasaura. Cf. no. 980. The name of Lieutenant Bramley is not, as it should be, on this inscription.]

(References: *Forbes-Mitchell; Gazetteer; Burke, P.; Communicated.*)

KHASAURA, TAHSIL BILGRAM.

980.—**1857**—(1) PROBYN, E. M., (2) PROBYN, L. D. *Inscription:*—Sacred to the memory of Elliot Markillof, born 25th March 1857, died 25 July 1357; and of Letitia Domina, born 7th February 1856, died 12th August 1857, the beloved children of William George Probyn, Esq., C.S.

Suffer little children to come unto me and forbid them not; for of such is the Kingdom of God.

Luke XVIII, 16.

[William George Probyn came to India in 1847 and retired as Judge of Saharanpur in 1877. He died in 1911. During the Mutiny, he was Collector of Fatehgarh (cf. no. 385) and entrusted himself and his family to Hardeo Bakhsh of Katiari when he left Fatehgarh. Hardeo Bakhsh and Keshri Singh protected them, as well as Mr. R. M. Edwards, Collector of Budaun, from June to September at Khasaura and Rampura (which Mr. Edwards calls Ranjpura). Their troubles and sufferings were terrible and are fully described in Mr. Edwards' account. They were moved from Khasaura to Rampura and then back again. The boy was taken ill at Rampura, and died on arriving at Khasaura, according to Edwards, on the night of the 26th-27th July. He was buried under some trees, the only dry spot that could be found. The girl was also taken ill at Rampura and died on the 21st August, according to Edwards. She was buried by her brother. The rest escaped at length to Cawnpore.

Hardeo Bakhsh was given the title of Raja and the K.C.S.I. The Probyns were sheltered in a farmyard belonging to Thakur Keshri Singh, his uncle.]

(References : *Edwards ; Haileybury ; Gazetteer.)*

BARAMAU, TAHSIL BILGRAM.

981.—**1857**—ROBERTSON, A., Major. *Inscription :*—The grave of Alexander Robertson, Brevet-Major of the Bengal Artillery, and Gun Carriage Agent, Fatehgarh, who died of wounds inflicted by the insurgent mutineers on the 17th September 1857. His memory lives in the hearts of his brother officers and friends, a few of whom have erected this tomb.

[For the Fatehgarh massacre, *vide* no. 385. Major Robertson was in one of the three boats that escaped : it grounded at Singirampur, and could not be got off again. What followed was the Cawnpore massacre on a smaller scale. Only three people escaped, Major Robertson, Mr. Jones and Mr. Churcher, the first two badly wounded. Major Robertson, assisted by Mr. Churcher, escaped ashore and the two were sheltered in Kulhaur by some herdsmen. Thence he might have escaped with Edwards and the Probyns (see above entry) who were in communication with him : but he was either unable or dissuaded from doing so, and died, watched over by Mr. Churcher, who might have escaped, to the last. Mr. Churcher in the end escaped to Cawnpore. A. Robertson was the son of G. Robertson, of Edinburgh, born in 1820.]

(References : *M. N. ; Services B.A. List ; Rice-Holmes ; Edwards ; Kaye.)*

FYZABAD DIVISION.

FYZABAD DISTRICT.

NEAR TANDA.

982.—**1837**—ORR, J. *Inscription :*—Sacred to the memory of James Orr, Esquire, who departed this life, the 15th September 1832, aged 80 years.

[On the road between Tanda and Mubarakpur, about 1¼ miles from Tanda. Mr. Orr was a Paymaster in the British Service and introduced great reforms in the manufacture of cotton fabrics at Tanda. From the latter end of the 18th century Europeans had had factories for cotton bleaching at Tanda. Mr. Orr was one of these, and imported English patterns, improving the art of printing and introducing beautiful designs. He built a large house at Tanda.]

(Reference : *Gazetteer.)*

BAHRAICH DISTRICT.

M. BHABARPUR.

983.—**1837**—RAVENSCROFT, G. *Inscription :*—In memory of George Ravenscroft, B.C.S., who was brutally attacked by a gang of robbers on the night of the 6th and died on the 7th May 1837. Restored by the Raja of Bhinga, June 1837.

[Mr. G. Ravenscoft born in 1777 and educated at Christ Church, Oxford, came to India in 1797 and served almost entirely in Bengal. He was Collector of Cawnpore for 5 years (1813—1816 and 1818 to 1820). He rendered himself notorious by entering largely into rash speculations and when it became necessary to fulfil obligations, he did not hesitate to appropriate large sums, amounting to nearly 2¾ lakhs out of the Government Treasury for the purpose.

He fled into Oudh when the defalcations were discovered and lived for 9 months near Fyzabad. When discovered, he fled to the Raja of Bhinga, who concealed his presence. He gave him land to cultivate and a house. When Mr. Ravenscroft began to plant indigo, the Raja's eldest son became alarmed and hired some dacoits to kill him. An Ensign Platt, from Secrora, was staying with him at the time. In the night the dacoits, some 60 in number, attacked the house with spears : they wounded Ravenscroft, who died next day (7th May 1823). Platt though himself wounded, managed to save Mrs. Ravenscroft and the child.

There is extant a letter by him written to the Board of Commissioners on the 1st January 1810. (Selections from the Revenue Records of the N. W. P. 1818—1820, p. 264.) The date on the tomb is wrong. It should be the night of the 6th-7th May 1823. It is probably a mere sculptor's error, induced by the following date.]

(References : *Sleeman ; S.R. Cawnpore ; Revenue Records ; Shore ; W.P.*)

APPENDIX.

Agra District.

NEAR PUIYA GHAT ROAD.

984.—**1736**.—D'ESSA, BIBI ANNA.—*Inscription* :—Aqui jaso Bibi Anna D'Essa bizneta de Mirza Gulcaren faleceo em Dilli aos 2 de Marco de 1736.

[This and the next three tombs, with two others that have no inscriptions, are those referred to in Note E on page 31 as first discovered by Dr. Christison. They are still in existence.

Father Hosten suggests that this is the great-granddaughter (bizneta) of Mirza Zu'l Qarnin, referred to at the bottom of page 28 and elsewhere. The name D'Essa is also written Dessa, De Sa and D'Esa. Bibiana is a "very Portuguese" name, but the words can also be read as Bibi Anna, with an obvious meaning.]

985.—**1736**.—DE SAIA (?), D. C.—*Inscription* :—Aqui jais Domingos Cardozo De Saia [fa] leceo em Agra a 22 de Julho de 173 [6?].

[De Saia is probably also D'Essa in another form.]

986.—**1761**.—CARDOZO, S.—*Inscription* :— — — — — sioao Cardoz [o] [o]*biit* em Bhart [p]ur por nome Urtucuer Knan (?) 2 de [D]ezembro 1761.

[This inscription is much mutilated. M. Ismael Garcias of Goa, whom Father Hosten got to read this and the other inscriptions for me, conjectures that the first five letters represent Sebastiao, or a part of it. "Por nome" is "by name" or "*alias*"; and "Urtucuer Knan" he conjectures to represent some Muhammadan name or title—"Knan" being "Khan." Such double names are common.]

987.—**1761**.—DA CRUZ, R.—*Inscription* :—Aqui falecco Rita (?)em Bharatpur filha de Alde(c)dre da Cruz aos 10 de Dezembro de 1761 annos... .

[Alde[c]dre probably is Aldecandre or Alexander.

Father Hosten conjectures that possibly D'Essa's, Cardozo's, and Da Cruz's were all connected, and that this was a family cemetery.]

Cawnpore District.

988.—**1857**.—SAVADA KOTHI.—*Inscription* :—*In memoriam* Savada Koti, 1857.

[Cf. the preliminary note on Cawnpore.]

989.—**1857**.—WELL IN WHEELER'S ENTRENCHMENT.—*Inscription* :—This well supplied the only water available during the siege.

[This is the well associated with John Mackillop's name.

My attention was drawn to these inscriptions by the late Mr. C. E. Crawford, C. S. He made a remark on that occasion which is worthy of reproduction. He pointed out that in all the public inscriptions which commemorate the events of the Cawnpore massacre there are only two words too many. Their keynote is extreme simplicity—a mere description of what occurred with no redundant panegyric and no unnecessary adjectives, a mark of the highest taste: for as Mr. Crawford said "the facts speak for themselves and supply the adjectives." This acute criticism was characteristic of Mr. Crawford's own high taste.

INDEX.

Note.—(1) Figures in italics are the numbers of the pages.
(2) Figures in ordinary type are the numbers of the entries.

A.

B.

C.

D.

G.

H.

I.

J.

L.

P.

Q.

R.

S.